story matters

Contemporary Short Story Writers
Share the Creative Process

MARGARET-LOVE DENMAN
University of New Hampshire

BARBARA SHOUP
Indiana University–Purdue University at Indianapolis
and
The Writers' Center of Indiana

HOUGHTON MIFFLIN COMPANY
Boston New York

Publisher: Patricia Coryell
Editor in chief: Suzanne Phelps Weir
Assistant Editor: Jane Acheson
Senior Project Editor: Christina Horn
Editorial Assistant: Michelle O'Berg
Senior Art and Design Coordinator: Jill Haber
Senior Photo Editor: Jennifer Meyer Dare
Associate Photo Editor: Stacey Dong
Composition Buyer: Chuck Dutton
Senior Manufacturing Coordinator: Renée Ostrowski
Senior Marketing Manager: Cindy Graff Cohen

Acknowledgments appear on pages 489–490, which constitute an extension of the copyright page.

Cover photograph © Rebecca Floyd/Graphistock.

Printed in the U.S.A.

Library of Congress Control Number: 2005927255

ISBN: 0-618-47027-1

3 4 5 6 7 8 9-QUF-10 09 08 07 06

contents

Part Two

Stories and Conversations 61

preface

Stories matter. We hear them all around us from the moment we're born, tell them as soon as we are able to speak, write them down in letters and e-mails to our families and friends. The stories we tell each other, the way we tell them, define who we are. They connect us to those we know and love and, sometimes in spite of ourselves, to those who trouble us, those we once thought we'd never want to know.

The stories we tell evolve over time. The fish we caught get bigger, the muggers meaner, the lost loves more beautiful and pure. If someone stops us midstory with a question we don't know how to answer, more often than not, we embroider. We invent. Grace Paley observes, "I always like to say that the first time you tell a story, you tell a story. The second time you tell it, it's fiction."

But how do you learn to *write* a story? Writers' processes vary so much that one cannot write a simple how-to manual; instead, learning about writing requires discovery and experimentation, advice and ideas. At the heart of *Story Matters* are discussions with twenty-one of America's best short story writers, talking about their craft. These in-person conversations, a selection of wonderful stories, an introduction to the elements of fiction, and writing prompts provide the college creative writing class, the contemporary short story class, the writing workshop, or the closet writer with useful and inspiring insights into the way stories are made. Students beginning the journey to become writers themselves will, by reading short stories and by listening to writers talk about the nuts and bolts of fiction writing and the joys, frustrations, and mysteries of the creative process, come to understand the type of hard work required to write well. And yet there's real encouragement, too. A story is a made thing, students learn—something they are capable of creating themselves with discipline, determination, and the ability to dream.

Part One: Writing Matters

Beginning with the observation that good writers are good readers, the first five chapters introduce the student to the basic elements of fiction, explain what is required of a good story, and give the beginning writer the language necessary to talk about stories-in-process and finished works of fiction. Writing exercises throughout the book also invite the reader to exercise and expand his or her writing muscles. Simple checklists of questions to consider offer students the opportunity to reflect on their work, thinking it through to completion.

Part Two: Stories and Conversations

Conversations with writers, paired with those writers' short stories, offer readers a wide range of the voices being heard today. These writers talk in depth about the craft of writing stories and also, specifically, about several of their own stories— one included in *Story Matters*, and others that are often anthologized and easily available to interested readers. These writers talk about where their stories came from, how they evolved, what problems they faced, and how they went about solving those problems.

Short stories come in so many wonderful types. The stories anthologized in this book exhibit various styles and techniques, from Pam Houston's second-person "How to Talk to a Hunter" to Dave Eggers's dog's-eye view in "After I Was Thrown into the River and Before I Drowned." The settings—postwar Vietnam, New York City in the 1960s, contemporary life in the projects, the world of the Ku Klux Klan in the Midwest—show students that story can happen anywhere. And they can be told by anyone: a college friend, a surgeon, a translator for immigrants, even a dog.

Supplements: Beyond the Book

A website for *Story Matters* offers students and teachers more resources, including further writing prompts and discussion ideas, and information about publishing in the short story market. Each exercise and writing prompt in Parts One and Two is reproduced on the website for your convenience. Visit the website at **http://college.hmco.com/english.**

Acknowledgments

Many thanks to the writers who offered their time and insight in the Conversations in Part Two of this book. They are Dorothy Allison, Russell Banks, Charles Baxter, Dan Chaon, Stuart Dybek, Dave Eggers, Carolyn Ferrell, Amy Hempel, Pam Houston, Ha Jin, Jamaica Kincaid, Jhumpa Lahiri, Michael Martone, Jill McCorkle, Susan Neville, Grace Paley, Joan Silber, Elizabeth Tallent, Luis Alberto Urrea, Daly Walker, and Tobias Wolff.

For those who spent time and effort to review the various drafts of this text, we are extremely grateful: A. Papatya Bucak, Florida Atlantic University; Zee Edgell, Kent State University; Richard C. Hay, University of Wisconsin–Milwaukee; Susan Hubbard, University of Central Florida; Marie Iglesias-Cardinale, Genesee Community College; Jim Manis, Pennsylvania State University; Alyce Miller, Indiana University; Stephanie Mood, Grossmont College; Tom Williams, Arkansas State University. Their careful reading and cogent suggestions were most helpful in crafting, this, the latest draft.

We have begged, borrowed, and stolen—with permission—exercises from the following sources: Herb Budden, the Gotham Writers' Workshop, Margaret McMullan, Alyce Miller, Steve Moss, Rebecca Rule, Scott Russell Sanders, Sue Wheeler, and Patti White. Many thanks to all of them for their willingness to share their teaching tools.

Margaret-Love Denman
Barbara Shoup

part one

Writing Matters

One way or another, the stories you write will come from the ones you live and the ones being lived all around you. They're grounded in your real life. A short story may begin in your mind with a memory, an image, an object, a place, a painting, a musical composition, a family story, a conversation overheard in a checkout line at the grocery, a story on the evening news. What you make of this material may be almost completely autobiographical, an actual experience tweaked just a bit to give it shape, a collage of real things arranged, "glued" together with fabrication to give them meaning. It may be something almost completely new, grown from some small detail, watered with "What if?"

The leap from the spoken story to a made-up story on the page is not as great as you might think. Tobias Wolff's "Say Yes" grew directly from an argument he had with his wife; Amy Hempel's "Going" came from an accident her brother had while driving her car. Daly Walker, a surgeon, observes, "Eventually I started writing about medicine and my own life. . . . I think my best stories hit close to home." Pam Houston laughingly admits that she once wrote so closely to her personal experience that her friends said, "'Pam writes eleven days behind her life.'"

Regardless of how stories begin, writers go through five—not necessarily chronological—phases in the process of creating a finished story: thinking of an idea, getting the first draft down, focusing the idea, fine-tuning it, and polishing the prose. While most writers find that each story they write goes through this process somewhat differently, most would agree that once an idea comes, it's best to write the first draft of the story as well as you can, assuming that there will be considerable work to do on it once you are through.

There are no rules for getting it down; there's no formula. You don't have to know exactly what's going to happen in the story to begin it. You don't have to begin on page one and work through the story chronologically, either—though many writers do work that way. Write the end and work your way backwards to the beginning, if that's what seems possible to you. Or write a scene or series of scenes, experimenting with order to discover the connections among them. Try the same thing with dialogues. If you're lucky enough to have a character enter your head, full-blown, set him in motion in a scene and let him lead you through the story. Whatever works!

Both in reading and writing, the best stories surprise us—not necessarily with a trick ending, but in moments along the way to the end that allow us to view the ordinary world in a new way or bring new perspectives to the human condition. It may be news both to readers and beginning writers that the surprises that delight them in a story may have surprised the writer in process as well, but it's one of the few things all good writers would agree is true. "A surprise is what identifies a short story for me as a really worthwhile endeavor," Pam Houston says. "If I do manage to write a story that doesn't surprise me at all, I hope I have the sense to throw it away or put it away until one day when it might."

So, when reading, pay attention to those moments of surprise in a story and expand your understanding of it by considering how it works and what it reveals. When writing, expect your story to surprise you. In fact, sometimes a story in process will take a turn and become something completely different from what you thought it was going to be. Expect to be frustrated, full of doubt—even despairing at times along the way. Describing what writing fiction feels like, Virginia Woolf wrote, "The creative power which bubbles so pleasantly in beginning . . . quiets down after a time, and one goes on more steadily. Doubts creep in. Then one becomes resigned. Determination not to give in, and the sense of an impending shape keep one at it more than anything."

Perhaps you are thinking, but all this sounds so—depressing! It's not, really. It's just what you have to do to earn those moments in which your imagination takes flight, when the words come magically, in a rush, and you live for a while inside your own story. The better you understand what creative process is, the more you devote yourself to learning the craft of fiction and how stories work, the better you'll be able to trigger those moments and make good use of them. Part One, "Writing Matters," will help you make those moments happen and direct you in your efforts to get the best story you can write on the page. Working through the no-fail writing exercises here will bring insight to readers and writers alike, enriching their understanding of short fiction and enlivening their conversations about literature.

....

........chapter 1

Rules of the Game

First, Read

One simple, absolutely nonnegotiable rule: To write well, you must read. The best writers read widely, constantly, even obsessively. Tobias Wolff says, "One of the things that I love about fiction, both reading it and what I hope to do writing it, is the way it forces you to enter deeply into the spirit of others. You break out of the shelter you're in most of the time, you are forced to enter other ways of seeing, other ways of living, other ways of being, the particular realities that other people inhabit. One of the banes of this world is how easily we reduce others to Them. The minute you get one of Them up close, suddenly your ideas don't hold up."

You've *got* to read this—or that, or something else—is something that writers and serious readers are always saying to one another. But that is not to say that there is some magic list of books that every serious writer or reader must read. Perhaps the smartest, most useful advice on this issue came from poet William Stafford, who, after listening to fellow panel members' vehement assertions about what any self-respecting writer absolutely *must* read, said quietly, but very firmly, "Read what you love and it will take you to what you need."

Maybe, like Luis Urrea, you fell in love with Charles Dickens as a child because your mother read Dickens aloud to you. Maybe your early influences were the Bible and *Paradise Lost*, like Jamaica Kincaid. Maybe you were conversant about the great poets, as Grace Paley was, by the time you were in high school. Great! It's not a moral issue, though. If you want to understand and embrace literature fully, eventually you will have to read beyond the classics to the good and great literature of your own time. If Dickens and Milton and Shakespeare don't do a thing for you, that's fine, too. But as you proceed as a writer or serious reader, the time is likely to come when you'll need to take a look at the classics to get a better general understanding of literature and the particular writers you love.

You'll read to fill your well of understanding about life and to bring depth and insight to your material. "You'll get lost, you'll get completely stuck if you stop reading," Susan Neville says. "You will go over the same ground, over and over again, because you have these sort of hard-wired obsessions. But you have to find ways of getting outside the box of yourself."

Jamaica Kincaid says, "When people say, 'I'm having a writer's block,' I say, 'Read.' If you're reading, you're writing. Read anything. It's just essential that you never stop reading."

Whether you are reading what you love or what you need, it is important to learn how to read well and how to discuss a story intelligently. All too many writing and literature students come to class having read a story just one time. Such students are limited to discussing what happened on the surface of the story and how what happened made them feel, usually relating those feelings to their own personal experiences.

Talking about how a story makes you feel is fine; a big part of why we love stories is *because* they seem connected to our own lives and bring forth strong emotion. It's true that the memories and experiences you bring to a story, your own worldview, add a dimension to the story that greatly enriches your reading experience. The way a character brings to mind a real person you love or loathe, the way the issues a story turns on mirror issues in your own life, the way setting dredges up times and places you remember are fascinating to consider, but probably won't bring much understanding to the story itself and how it works. Neither "This is a good story because I liked it" nor "This is a bad story because I didn't like it" is likely to generate useful conversation about literature.

The stronger your personal feelings about a story, whether they are positive or negative, the more important it is to separate them from the feelings the writer crafted into it—and, for the most part, leave them out of any academic consideration of the story. When you can do this, you'll be better able to make observations and formulate questions as you study a story and to speak about it not in terms of what you like and don't like, but in terms of how it *works.*

Obviously, reading a story one time won't bring you to this point. The best you can hope for is a basic understanding of what happened, which is just one aspect of any work of fiction. A good story reveals itself over time, bringing new insights and understanding, eventually revealing its "bones," so that readers begin to intuit how it works. *Like detectives, good readers study the evidence a story presents, returning to the text again and again as they formulate ideas about craft and effect. Unless you are willing to read this way, it will impossible to develop useful, intelligent opinions about a story or engage in the kind of discussion that will deepen both your emotional and intellectual understanding of it.*

exercise

Choose a story from the anthology (or any good story) and read it six times. You may read it six times in a row or six times over a period of several days. In either case, freewrite a one-page response *immediately* after each reading.

Note the word *freewrite*. This means that you do not have to worry about organization, grammar, word choice, punctuation, or quality of content. You simply write (or type) whatever is on your mind. It is sometimes freeing to pretend you are writing about the story in a letter to a friend.

A first reading is all about stepping into a fictional world, fully experiencing it, so your first response will probably be a general one. Write your first impressions of the story, what you liked and didn't like about it, what the story made you think or feel, what surprised you, what about the story you didn't understand.

Go deeper in your next five responses, focusing on various aspects of the story. For example, one time through you might pay attention to character and focus your response on that. Other aspects to consider are setting, theme, plot, scene, description, exposition, transitions, time, dialogue, voice, or tension.

It may help you to mark up your copy of the story as you read. If you notice something, jot it down in the margin. Use highlighters to isolate what you've decided to look at.

As you read the story again and again, you will have to look more closely and open your mind more widely if you are going to find something new to say. Don't think that there's anything too insignificant to consider. Specific things that characters say, the clothes they wear, the objects that surround them are all worthy subject matter. You may write about what you *don't* know about the story—what confuses or intrigues you. You may imagine things about the characters' lives that the story doesn't include. You may write about something in the story that makes you mad, considering *how* the author accomplished that.

You may consider the story's weaknesses as well as its strengths. Are there gaffes of detail that make you cringe, dialogue that hits a false note? Are there things in the story that the writer didn't quite make you believe? What felt wrong, inauthentic—and why?

After several times through, pay special attention to how your feelings about the story may be changing.

- ✓ Do you feel differently about the characters' behavior toward one another?
- ✓ Do you begin to feel sympathy toward a character you didn't like earlier? Do you begin to feel less sympathy toward one you first liked?
- ✓ Do you feel differently about the setting of the story?
- ✓ Do you have a different feeling about what the story is meant to be about?
- ✓ Do you notice anything about the story that you didn't notice before?
- ✓ Does anything in the story (an object, an incident, a person) seem to take on a larger—perhaps even a symbolic—meaning as you read?
- ✓ Does the story have anything to do with your own life or help you to understand anything about life in general?
- ✓ Does the story teach you anything about your own writing generally? Does it teach you anything specific about a story you are writing now?

After your sixth reading and writing, do a last freewrite about the story. In two to three pages, consider what you know about the story and how it revealed itself to you over subsequent readings.

You'll be amazed by what you discover—about the story, about how fiction works, and about yourself. Good writers *read.* It is their best training, after all, their best hope for writing stories that bring their hearts and minds fully to the page.

What Is a Story, Anyway?

The traditional short story is character driven, its plot, structure, length, voice, and point of view dependent on a turning point in the main character's life. Moving toward a moment when the character will change or not change as a result of the action of the story, it fulfills Edgar Allan Poe's maxim: "A short story should be written for the sake of its last line."

But there are also language-driven stories that work as extended metaphors. There are stories that feel like riffs or meditations, stories created in list form, stories made solely of dialogue, stories constructed to mirror musical compositions or the working of the human mind. A fully formed story may be as short as a sentence, like Amy Hempel's "Housewife," or as long as William Faulkner's "The Bear."

There are about as many ways of saying what a story is as there are writers writing them.

Charles Baxter says, "When people reach a crisis point, and their lives threaten to shatter, you have a story on your hands." Susan Neville defines the traditional short story in geometrical terms. "Any single character's life can go on infinitely in one direction or another—a line," she says. "With a novel you pick an inch or two inches on the line. . . . But a story . . . is more a point . . . a moment." Amy Hempel's sense of what a story is comes from her teacher, Gordon Lish, who believes, "A story happens when two equally appealing forces, or characters, or ideas try to occupy the same place at the same time, and they're both right." Once asked what she thought were the requirements of short fiction, Grace Paley replied, "I hate the word *fiction*. In the *Times* there was a discussion of Israeli writers and someone said, 'We don't have a word for fiction. We just have the word *story*.' It's just the way I feel. I write what I am. I am a storyteller."

Clearly, there's no one definition that all writers would agree on. But most will agree that character, visual imagery, tension of some kind, movement, and clarity of language must be present to make a work of short fiction compelling.

To get a feel for story in its most fundamental form, consider the following *New Times* "55 Fiction Contest" winners. Each fulfills the contest requirements to tell a story that has setting, character, conflict, and resolution in only fifty-five words.

> **Getting to Know You**
> "I'm going to help block the clinic tomorrow," Judy told Tammy excitedly. Her best friend looked surprised. "I'm going to the clinic tomorrow, too." "Great! I'll pick you up!" "No," said Tammy. "No . . . I don't—I really don't think that's such a good idea." Her eyes filling with tears, she turned away from her friend.

> **Perspective**
> "I think it's easy to see, my students, that by careful examination of these former inhabitants, of their behavior patterns, their simple, pointless lifestyles, the things they held of import, and of the complete and utter corruption of their selves and their environment, that Earth deserved no better than Galactic extermination. Thus, us. Any questions?"

> **Fate**
> This was the only way, such a blur of rage and bliss and hurled toasters as our time together had become. Appeal to fate: heads, we'd marry, tails, we'd separate

forever. The coin flipped, thudded, skipped and lay still, an eagle showing. We stared as it sank in. Then, together, "Best two out of three?"

Consider what makes each one a story and how it works.

exercise

Now write your own story of fifty-five words, using the following guidelines partly borrowed, partly adapted from the *New Times'* rules.

Setting: All stories have to be happening someplace, which means they have to have a setting of some kind, even if it's the other side of the universe, the inner reaches of someone's mind, or just the house next door. Ground readers in that place.

Characters: Characters can have infinite variations. People, animals, clouds, microbes. Anything. Make them come alive in readers' minds. What they do, think, and/or say must be believable in the context of the situation you put them in.

Conflict: In the course of the story, something must happen to create tension and make readers curious about how the story will play out.

Resolution: This is simply the outcome of the story. It doesn't necessarily mean that there's a moral, or even that the conflict itself is resolved. But it *does* mean that, somehow, something shifts, and readers experience some kind of revelation that brings with it a sense of satisfaction and an understanding about the characters and their situation.

If you find this exercise difficult, even maddening—and you almost certainly will—good! The frustration that comes from wrestling with words and form is part of every writer's process for writing every story. As a reader, you'll begin to understand and appreciate a story's "cost" to its writer. If you're an aspiring writer, a taste of frustration here will help prepare you for the rigors to come as you discover your own story and bring it to the page.

A Word About Talent

It would be an excellent idea to print out Gustave Flaubert's definition of talent and tack it near where you work. Better yet, memorize it so you'll have it with you wherever you go. "Talent is a long patience, and originality an effort of will and intense observation."

To look at talent another way, this metaphor works nicely. Consider a person who seems to have been born to ride a bicycle—six-time Tour de France winner Lance Armstrong, for example. Who knows where this talent or gift comes from, or why? It's just there, part of who he is. A person with that kind of gift may or may not love—or even like—to ride a bicycle. He may or may not choose to use the gift he's been given in a competitive environment. But when he does use it, adding discipline and intense training to the mix, as Armstrong does, he will be virtually unbeatable.

Another person, ordinary in his abilities, who loves to ride a bicycle, loves to compete, and disciplines himself to do whatever training is necessary to make him the best bike rider he can possibly be, can achieve a lot. He'll never beat a "gifted" cyclist at his best, but his hard work, good technique, and sheer drive may allow him to beat a gifted cyclist who's undisciplined or having an off day.

So maybe you have a gift for writing as Lance Armstrong has a gift for cycling. Maybe not. It really doesn't matter. Talent won't *write* your stories. You have to do that yourself, and doing it a whole variety of talents come into play. A large heart, for example. A complicated mind. The ability to step outside your own experience, to think from inside someone else's head. Curiosity, sheer stubbornness, drive.

A real writer writes because she loves and needs to write, because the joys and frustrations she experiences while writing make her feel fully alive. Substitute *short story writer* for *novelist* and John Gardner's advice to aspiring novelists works for those who want to write stories, too. "Nothing is harder than being a true novelist, unless that is all one wants to be, in which case though becoming a real novelist is hard, everything else is harder."

Face it. Whether you're talented or not, writing stories is going to be hard. So let go of the idea that your success as a writer will hinge on how talented you are or the even worse, absolutely deadly idea that because you're talented (or think you are) the writing world owes you fame and fortune. Humbly, passionately begin the work you need to do to become the best writer you can be.

chapter 2

The Story in the Mind

What If?

Imagination is no more than your ability to ask, "What if?" and your willingness to ask it in endless variations throughout the process of discovering and bringing a story to the page. While it is impossible to predict the specific ways this question will present itself, two basic variations are useful to consider both in working through any particular story and in understanding the way your own mind generates ideas for stories.

Some writers are first experimenters. Their inspiration comes from external impulses. They love "What if?" and are happy looping and branching, considering the question in every possible way. What if I did a riff on this word? What if I combined these details? What if I put this kind of person in that kind of setting? Curious, suggestible, playful, they see possibilities for stories everywhere they look. They create from bits and pieces of the world that present themselves. Experimenters are often prolific, the act of creating essential to their equilibrium. Their work may be uneven, however, because the multitude of ideas in their heads and the joyful energy they bring to beginning ideas may make them reluctant revisers.

Other writers work mainly from inner vision. This kind of writer sees something specific in his mind's eye, senses its shape, feels its emotional content profoundly. He's driven by an internal impulse to recreate this vision in words. It's the only thing he's interested in creating, and he often feels frustrated and even desperate in his efforts to bring words to the page, particularly in the early stages. Writers who work this way usually are not as prolific as those whose work is generated through experiment. They tend toward writer's block; they may be obsessive revisers. The writer who works this way asks "What if?" in the service of his vision. What if I try this, or maybe that, to create exactly the effect I want on the page?

Having perhaps recognized yourself as a writer who first asks "What if" as an experimenter or one who asks it in the service of an inner vision, it is important to know that the question will almost certainly flip for you in the long process of creating a finished work of fiction. The constant rush of ideas, the ease and pleasure with which the experimenter brings a first draft to the page usually results in many pieces of writing, most of which will need revision to become finished, polished stories. At some point, an experimenter must stop generating new material, look at what she's brought to the page, and decide on something to develop. Having made a choice, she must decide on a focus. With focus comes a vision for the finished piece. Revising, she works from that inner vision, critically considering the difference between what she wants the piece to be and what is there, on the page.

The writer who begins with an inner vision often works slowly to bring the first draft to the page. When he comes to a wall, which he invariably does, he must think playfully, as an experimenter thinks, opening his mind to the most absurd possibilities as he searches to pin down his vision.

Where Stories Come From

Whether a story is born of experimentation or an inner vision, it does not come zinging into the writer's mind out of the blue. Nor is it, as some theorists believe, primarily a document reflecting the world from which it was made, channeled somehow through the "who" of an author. A story indeed may serve as such a document, may perfectly reflect a place, time, philosophy, or idea, but it is first a product of what Albert Camus called a "long journey through the detours of art to the two or three simple and great images which first gained access to [a writer's] heart." Stories are crafted from a writer's particular experiences, her dreams, all she knows and will never know about life, all she longs for. This is her material, the "stuff" that gives her both the impulse to write and the questions she will try to answer by writing, all her life.

For Amy Hempel the questions are, "How do you survive now? . . . How do you understand what happened to you? How do you continue?" For Joan Silber, they stem from a sense of wonderment about what life brings. Charles Baxter writes "to make the seemingly 'ordinary' . . . new." Writing about her poor, working class family, Dorothy Allison wants to "put them on the table" of literature, where they have never had a place before. Carolyn Ferrell observes, "When I was a child, it was hard to come to terms with the racial climate . . . those bad feelings, those kinds of hatreds, were inexplicable to me . . . . How to articulate my confusion? When I was nine years old I turned to fiction."

Talking about what happens to a writer when he fully engages with the questions that compel him, Russell Banks says, "Under the strictures and restrictions and rigors of fiction, the writer, when writing, is always more honest and more intelligent than at any other time. The requirements of art create a possibility of greater honesty and greater intelligence and greater insights, a greater access to one's unconscious, greater access to the world around us than at any other time in one's life. As a result, when engaged in storytelling, one is able to say things that are not available consciously to him at the time and to conduct a kind of relationship with strangers that is much more intimate than is possible any other time."

Everyone has material. Artists are just people who use their material as the raw material to create in whatever art form compels them—symphonies, sculptures, stories. Finding and facing your material is absolutely necessary if you want to write stories that are compelling to you throughout the process of creating them and compelling to readers once you've gotten them to the page. Finding and facing your material will make you a better reader, too. You'll understand why some stories move you more or less than others do, and this will help you more easily separate your personal and intellectual responses to them.

Warning: This can be painful. Even frightening. In her memoir *Two or Three Things I Know for Sure* Dorothy Allison says, "The best fiction comes from the place where the terror hides, the edge of our worst stuff. I believe, absolutely, that if you do not break out in that sweat of fear when you write, then you have not gone far enough."

"Wait!" you might be thinking. "My life hasn't been that bad. I had a perfect childhood; I have a fabulous life now. What could I possibly have to write about?" Well, think about the fact that your idyllic childhood is over forever and how writing stories might take you back to it, for a little while allowing you to be that joyous child again. Or dig around in it and see if you find it wasn't quite as perfect as you remember. As for your fabulous life now, what might threaten your happiness? What if you'd never gotten to that life at all, having taken a different turn somewhere along the way?

You have material. Flannery O'Connor, who was right about virtually everything, once said, "Anyone who has survived his childhood has enough information about life to last him the rest of his days." To discover your material, spend some time freewriting answers to the following questions. Let your memory range back to the defining moments in your life. Look intensely at now. Pay attention to what floats up again and again, the way seemingly disparate experiences combine themselves. Look for patterns. Notice single moments, crystal clear in your memory, resonating through time.

- ✓ What broke your heart?
- ✓ What broke or nearly broke your spirit?
- ✓ What scares you to death?
- ✓ What hurts you more than anything?
- ✓ What makes you so happy you can hardly bear it?
- ✓ What are your secrets?
- ✓ Was there some ideal time in your life to which you long to return?
- ✓ What is still so painful that you cannot let it go?
- ✓ What and/or whom do you wish you could eliminate from your life?
- ✓ What enrages you?
- ✓ What do you wish never happened to you or someone you love?
- ✓ What deeply offends your sense of justice?
- ✓ What about your own life do you feel that you will never understand?

How Stories Gather

Talking about the way writers gather the bits and pieces of the real world that stories are made of, Russell Banks says, "You feel like you're walking through life as a blue serge suit, picking up lint. You can't predict what's going to stick and what's not going to stick—or why."

Susan Neville recognizes a detail as something she can use the way she knows "I'm going to buy that vase!" Elizabeth Tallent knows "the way you know you're interested in a person. It is almost a body intuition." For Pam Houston, "Whether it's a dog, three lines of dialogue, a boat, or the way a mother is treating her child," certain things in the world "glimmer."

exercise

To feel what a writer feels as details gather and begin to shape themselves into a story, think of an object that is or was once important to you. In a notebook, jot down a brief description of the object and then write, also briefly, a memory in which the object comes into play.

Now, notebook in hand, take a walk around your neighborhood or through a flea market or yard sale—anyplace where you might discover something that someone threw out, gave away, lost, or abandoned. The important thing is to keep your eyes open for an object that appeals to you. When you've found it, look closely at it and jot down details, clues. What is it? Was it made or bought? What might its function be? Is the object old or new? Was it well taken care of, well loved? Or was it carelessly treated, even purposely ruined in some way? How do you know? Is it dirty, torn, crumpled up? Polished, set carefully in a case? Cracked, scratched, shiny from use? Is it from this or another time? What kind of person might have owned it—a child, an elderly person, a dad, a hippie, a businesswoman—and why?

After looking at the object, sit a moment and let a memory from your own life float up. It may be directly connected to the object or have no apparent connection at all. Briefly, write down that memory.

Now imagine a simple scenario for the object: Who owned it, and how did end up where you found it? Use the observations you made looking closely at the object to help you construct this little story.

When you've done that, imagine a second scenario for the same object, something completely different and equally believable based on what you know.

Into the mix, throw the first memory you wrote down. Do you think the object you chose has anything at all in common with what you remembered? Consider the memory that floated up after you looked at the object. Does it make a better, more interesting connection to the object you chose? Are the two memories connected somehow? Spend a few moments freewriting about the object and your memories. Let your thoughts flow; let your brain make its own connections and go wherever it wants to go.

Notebook in hand, continue your walk until another object catches your eye. Stop, look at it, and imagine how this new object might be incorporated into one of the scenarios you created for the first object. Or create a whole new scenario that incorporates both objects. Or abandon the first object all together and create a scenario for the new object you found.

Consider the various scenarios you have created so far and decide which one you like best. Or think of something totally different again, perhaps something that uses one or both of your memories in a new way. Maybe a new memory floats up and seems significant, as well.

If by now you are feeling both exhilarated and confused by the infinite possibilities that have begun to present themselves, you know how a writer feels in the gathering phase of a story. Add to the mix something random that presents itself—an object someone hands you or that appears out of the blue. And something you saw or someone said to you that you just can't forget. A friend's memory that touches you in some way. A snippet of dialogue you overheard.

Jot down ideas for a story you might make using the ideas triggered by way of these objects and memories. Who are the characters? Where are they? What are they doing and saying? What do they want from each other?

The gathering you do for a story may be purposeful, as in the above exercise; more likely, it happens subconsciously, over time. Dan Chaon keeps a folder for an emerging story idea, placing bits and pieces of things it. "I feel that they are connected," he explains, "but I'm not sure how they are connected." Grace Paley keeps folders, too. In hers "are the beginnings of many stories. Or the middles or whatever. Paragraphs written."

It is common, especially for writers who are mainly short story writers, for a series of stories to gather simultaneously. Ideas come in clusters for Susan Neville when she's in the storywriting mode. "I can't wait to get done with one so that I can go on to the next one," she says.

Sometimes ideas gather around an idea or theme, though the central focus of the collection may not be evident to the writer at the outset. Joan Silber wrote "My Shape" and then decided to give the villain of the piece his own story. Once she'd done that, she began to think of other links and eventually created the collection, *Ideas of Heaven: A Ring of Stories,* in which each story is linked to the one before it—the last story in the collection coming full circle to the first. In keeping with its theme of animal behaviors reflected in humankind, Jill McCorkle thinks of her collection *Creatures of Habit* as a "litter" of stories—though the theme was not evident to her until she began to revise the stories.

Russell Banks's *Trailerpark* was "consciously structured, . . . concept-driven . . . . I really wanted to write a story cycle that participated in the tradition of story cycles like *Winesberg, Ohio*, and *Dubliners*—going all the way back to *The Canterbury Tales*—just for the dramatic possibilities." All of the stories in Jamaica Kincaid's collection *At the Bottom of the River* are connected in that each was "written out of an impulse to break some mold."

When to Start Writing

Regardless of how a story gathers in your mind, eventually there is a moment of combustion in which a set of details emerge from the chaos of details floating around in your head and gather like filings to a magnet, giving you what Virginia Woolf called the "impending shape of a story."

Once that happens, when do you begin to write the story—and how? There's no hard, fast rule for this, but it helps to know the variety of ways successful writers face the task. Grace Paley goes through her folders every few weeks, adding a few sentences to one thing, taking sentences out of another. At some point, a story " begins to have body," she says. "It becomes peopled in some way. Once I have that, I begin working on it."

Dan Chaon says that, finally, some of the pieces he's collected in folders and in his mind move to a center of gravity, triggering a first line or a series of actions that give him a "tunnel" through the story. For Susan Neville, it is just the feeling she associates with a word or a place. "If I feel it strongly—[that] makes me know it's time to start a story. Right away!"

There are three crucial things to know about when to begin writing the story that's taking shape in your head.

1. You don't have to have the story all worked out in your mind before you start. Making an outline of the story you want to write is not required—in fact, an outline is likely to get in the way of discovering what you'll need to know to tell the story most effectively. You can make one if it seems helpful to do so, but you must be willing to adapt it or even trash it if new and better ways of telling your story present themselves.
2. You don't have to write the story perfectly the first time through.
3. It's good to separate the *act* of beginning from what your sense of the *actual* beginning of the story should be. Beginning, putting the first words on the page, is a gateway to your story. No more.

So before writing the first word, give yourself permission to be confused during the process of bringing the story to the page and to write badly in the service of writing well.

Eighteen Writing Exercises

1. **Take a long walk and pick up whatever appeals to you as you walk along.** Find a place to sit, spread things out, look at them for a while, and then freewrite to find the story they belong in.
2. **Spend one day assuming every single thing you see carries a message.** Throughout the day, jot down your thoughts. Then write.
3. **Put your notebook and a pen next to your bed.** Set the alarm for twenty minutes earlier than usual and, as soon as it goes off, sit up and start writing. Anything.
4. **Appropriate a first line from someone else's story.** Use it to write the beginning of a story of your own.
5. **Cut out words and phrases from magazines and newspapers.** Play with them, arranging and rearranging, until they suggest a story. Then write it.
6. **Write a childhood memory, beginning with "I remember."** Write in the past tense, as the person you are now, looking back. Then retell the story. Eliminate "I remember." Write in the present tense. Actually become that child again, recording the event and how you feel about it as though it were happening to you now.
7. **Remember a story you heard from a person of an older generation.** Write in this person's words, just as it was told to you.

8. **Think about your name.** Freewrite answers to these questions and any others that come to mind: My real name is . . . My name once was . . . My mother thinks my name is . . .
9. **Imagine a box, any kind of box.** When you see it clearly in your mind's eye, reach in and begin to remove what's inside. It can be anything. Some items may be larger than the box you imagine. That's okay. Make a list as you go. When you've got ten to twelve items, stop and consider them. What do they have in common? Which are imaginary? Which are real? Do some or all reflect a particular time or interest? Is there any item that doesn't seem to belong in the group? Why? Write about what the list says about you and your life.
10. **Look for a photograph that *feels* like somewhere you've been.** It could be anywhere: a café in Paris, a lake cottage, a war memorial, an old farmhouse with a wraparound porch. Write whatever the photograph brings to mind.
11. **Gather an assortment of objects from your house.** Put them all in a bag. Reach in and pull out the first four you touch. Look at them. Write.
12. **Choose one object in your house.** Write its story.
13. **Think of something you'd like to forget.** Write every single thing you know about it.
14. **Make a list of all the things you've lost in your life—tangible and intangible.** Write about them.
15. **Suddenly you're invisible!** Write about what that's like. What would you do? Where would you go? What would you see that you normally couldn't see?
16. **Spend five minutes writing the story of your life.** Then read it and write for five minutes more about what you were surprised you left out of it. Write for another five minutes about what you were glad you left out.
17. **Imagine that it is a summer night and you are in the backyard of your summer home.** Close your eyes; *be there.* Then, in your imagination, walk into the house and through all the rooms to an attic room where there is a shelf of all the toys you loved in your childhood. Pick one. Write about it.
18. **Tell the story of your parents in love.** Make sure readers know where these people are (in time and place); what they're wearing, eating, saying; what's going on in the news; where they're working or how they spend the time they're not together. You may make yourself a part of the story, or not. You may take the ending as far as you wish—ending in a birth, a divorce, or happily ever after. If you don't know all the facts, look them up or make them up—just make them believable.

chapter 3

The Story on the Page

Remember what it was like when you learned to ride a bicycle. You'd concentrate on balance and forget to look where you were going. You'd pick up speed and get so excited you'd drift sideways and glance off the shrubbery. Or be so careful *not* to go fast you'd take a slow fall onto the concrete. You'd look down to make sure your feet were working right on the pedals and run into a tree. "Steer!" someone would holler and you'd steer so hard you'd lose your balance. Righting a wobble, you'd bounce off the curb into the street.

You just kept riding—up the street and back again, a trusty parent or sibling running along behind you, hand on the fender—until you learned well enough not to have to think about what you were doing and it was safe to let you go.

Writing is like that. Learning how a story works, you identify such elements of fiction as character, plot, scene, and structure and concentrate on them in isolation to achieve mastery. But when it's time to write a story, you just write. You trust the image in your head and let it take you where it wants to go.

So feed your head with the random but useful ideas, explanations, techniques, and tricks that follow. But remember the bike thing. If you think too much about technical matters in the drafting stage, your analytical brain will kick in and you'll fall out of the story. When it's time to write, trust that what you know will channel its way onto the page.

Elements of Fiction

Character, dialogue, voice, point of view, scene, plot, time, structure, world: These are the tools a writer has at hand with which to construct her stories. In the first draft, she uses them intuitively. If dialogue comes easily, she does that first. If she likes description, she starts there. Maybe she starts by getting the basic structure of the story on the page. Then she goes back again and again, layering in the other elements, fine-tuning to deepen the effect. It's not unlike the way a painter begins with broad shapes and then slowly layers in color to bring up the picture, eventually washing the canvas with dozens of translucent glazes.

Character

Remember the very first time you encountered someone you love. Maybe you thought, "Wow! This is a person I want to know better." Or perhaps you thought exactly the opposite. "Ugh, I don't like her at all." In either case, why did you come to that conclusion? Did she do something, say (or not say) something that got your attention? Was she wearing something that made you think of her in a certain way? Was she in a place or with a person that made you assume something about her?

Maybe she made no impression at all, and it was the second or third or tenth time you met that you connected. Was it an accumulation of small moments that paved the way for the connection, or something she did that surprised you and brought her suddenly into focus? If "ugh" was your first response, what was it that changed your mind? Jot down the defining moments in your relationship to help you remember how your sense of your loved one grew clearer over time—rather like holding a Polaroid photo in your hand and watching the image emerge. Eventually, you came to know her almost as well as you know yourself. But still, she is capable of surprising you.

Writers come to know their fictional characters much the same way. As with the real people in their lives, the first encounter, the first spark of connection, may happen in a variety of ways. Dorothy Allison's characters appear "doing something and . . . talking as they are doing." Pam Houston's emerge as a part of a "chunk" of the physical world that interests her, say, a cruise boat. Michael Martone's characters form around an idea or a question. The dance master who is the main character in Joan Silber's "The High Road" appeared first as the villain in "My Shape." She decided she wanted him to have his own story, too. Jhumpa Lahiri's Mr. Pirzada grew from her curiosity about a scholar from Bangladesh who visited her parents frequently during her childhood. Speaking about the main character in "The Cures for Love," Charles Baxter says, "First I fell in love with her." Amy Hempel finds characters "just following certain people around with a notebook."

Regardless of how you first meet your characters, they will evolve in process, coalescing, taking on the particularity of real people as you go. If you're writing well, they will surprise you. Your idea of who they are will shift—sometimes slightly, sometimes enormously—as they come alive and move through the story to its resolution. One thing is absolutely sure: Creating living, breathing characters that readers will care about is your most important task. Without strong characters, there *is* no story.

exercise

If it seems possible, take a character that's beginning to form in your mind to a party or a family dinner or the mall—anywhere. Sit for a moment, eyes closed, imagining the details of the scene. Then set it in motion and, freewriting, see what your character does and says. See what he notices, who he encounters while he's there, who he avoids or who avoids him. See where the tensions lie. Do what most writers do: Just *go*, trusting that the characters will begin to tell you what you need to know.

If that seems overwhelming, try this—or try it after you've written the scene to expand your understanding of your character. In fact, you can do this exercise, or whichever parts of it seem appropriate, at any time during the process of writing your story. Jot down everything you know about your character. *Everything.* Make no judgments. Then let him answer any or all of the following questions about himself. Freewrite in first person, tricking your mind to believe that the character really is speaking to you in his own voice. Feel free to bypass questions that don't seem to apply as the character develops or to ask and answer questions that float up in process. If he feels cranky, weepy, or recalcitrant about some answers, let that show. Let him explain why he feels that way. Write his memories, if they apply. Remember, no judgments! Let him ramble. The questions are triggers, that's all. Let them take you wherever your character wants to go.

✓ What do you look like? Height, weight, hair color? What do you like or dislike about how you look?
✓ How old are you? How do you feel about being the age you are now?
✓ How do you spend most of your days? If you work, what kind of work do you do? How do you feel about it? If you are in school, what is school like for you?
✓ What do you do for fun?
✓ What do people who know you think about you? What do people who don't know you think about you?
✓ What are (were) your parents like? What do you like or dislike most about each one?
✓ Do you have siblings? What is your relationship with them?
✓ Who is your best friend? What is your history together?
✓ What makes you ecstatically happy? What makes you unbearably sad?
✓ What or whom do you hate most in the world? Why?
✓ What happened in your childhood that made you the way you are today?
✓ What is your favorite possession? Your favorite piece of clothing?
✓ What makes you angry?
✓ What do you long for?
✓ What are you afraid of?
✓ What do you most regret?
✓ What are your secrets?
✓ What do you wish you could forget?

exercise

For this exercise, you'll freewrite again, this time in author mode. What do you know about your character that you didn't know before you started the exercise? Was there anything he said that surprised you? Did your sense of who he is change or evolve in any way?

Go through your pages of freewriting and highlight anything you might make use of in the story. For example:

- Scene possibilities
- Beginnings/endings
- Conflicts
- Conversations

- Relationships
- Settings
- Objects

If new things float up as you write, include them. Now—

✓ Consider the contradictions in your character's life. If he's meticulous and fussy, what is the one way he behaves that is reckless in some way or out of control? If he is rotten and mean, what one person is he a sucker for? If your character is a nice, decent person, what is the one thing he does or knows that he is ashamed of or embarrassed by? If he's not a good person, consider what kindness he might (secretly?) render. What might make him cry?

✓ Consider the tiniest details of his existence. What is his favorite color or favorite music? What kind of furniture is in his bedroom? What is his cat's name? If he went to the post office to buy a stamp, which design would he choose? What kind of underwear does he buy?

✓ Consider his fears. Are they emotional? Physical? How do they affect his behavior?

✓ Consider his dreams. What does he want more than anything? Does he believe there is any possibility at all that he will get it? Does he try?

✓ Imagine a series of photographs from your character's childhood. Describe each image in detail; then move beyond the frame of the photograph to imagine what was happening just outside it. Imagine, too, the moment before each photo was taken; then imagine the moment after. Play with language, like, "It wasn't long after this photo was taken that . . ." to imagine the character progressing through time.

✓ What does he remember from his childhood? What *doesn't* he remember?

✓ Play around. Add *but* to some things you know about him and see what pops into your mind. He has blond surfer-hair, but ________. He loves to travel, but ________. He grew up in a nice suburban neighborhood, but ________.

✓ Write as if describing your character to someone who will be meeting him at the airport and will need to recognize him.

✓ Think of a photograph of your character that typifies him and describe it completely.

✓ Make a list of all the people in your character's world who might end up in the story and jot down what you know about them; why they matter; what conflict, tension, or understanding they might bring to illuminate your character's situation.

Read what you have written and, again, highlight possibilities for scene, conflicts, relationships, objects, settings. Do lines or paragraphs emerge that might be used as they are or expanded? By now, you've got a wealth of information about the character. Some of it will end up in your story; most of it won't. But everything you know and will come to know during the process of writing your story will direct your character on the page and, if used effectively, will deepen your readers' understanding of him.

The following practical and philosophical considerations should help you decide whether the path you and your characters are on is likely to result in a good story.

Good writers are curious about human nature. They live in a constant state of observation, noting the behavior of people they know intimately and those they see only in passing. They wonder why people do what they do and why those around them respond to their actions as they do, considering this scenario or that in an attempt to understand them. They eavesdrop. They sit in cafés or on park benches, notebooks at the ready.

For such observation to be useful for fiction, writers must cultivate a kind of detachment that allows them to observe objectively. For some, this is inborn. They are the children who stood outside the circle, watching the others play, or the adults who gravitate to the edge of a cocktail party or sit quietly at the family dinner table fascinated by the little dramas playing out all around them.

Characters may be born directly from observation. They may be fictional versions of you or people you know. Most often they are cobbled together combining bits and pieces of people you encounter with a dash of imagination. You'll create them from a variety of impulses, depending on the kind of story you want to write.

Be careful, though. Strong characters emerge through a process of discovery. You put them in scenes, set the scenes in motion, and let their personalities, dreams, fears, and values show themselves as you go. You may be surprised to find that the strongest characters you create are the ones least like yourself. This happens because, dependent on observation, you put the characters on the page visually and through dialogue, which allows readers to come to know them much as they experience people in their own lives, coming to their own conclusions along the way.

Creating characters based on yourself, you are more likely to write from inside your head, to shape them based on what you know—or think you know. This makes autobiographical characters less malleable than ones you invent. It's hard, but to create believable autobiographical characters you have to be willing to innovate: Give your characters memories that are different from your own, add or subtract a sibling, let characters behave differently than you would. If you're dead set on what you regard as the "true" version of yourself, your fictional alter egos will be wooden—and, worse, as stubborn as you become yourself when someone tries to make you do something you don't want to do.

Part of the problem is that you know too much about yourself to turn yourself into fiction; the other part is the opposite: You don't know enough. You can't observe yourself from the outside, so you can't know how you seem to others or what they think of you. You can't truly know the effect you have on their lives. You can't even count on your own inner voice to be reliable because, as E. M. Forster once observed, real people don't talk to themselves truthfully. We can't. Our secret happiness and misery proceed from causes we can't quite explain.

It is also true that you run out of material pretty quickly if you depend totally on your own experience. As Ha Jin says, "On the whole, my life is limited, and my own story cannot give enough room for imagination, so I don't write my personal story."

The same is essentially true when you make characters directly from people you know. Describing a breakthrough she made writing "Compassion," a story based on her mother's death, Dorothy Allison says, "From the moment the two sisters started talking they weren't my sisters. But they were the same *kind* of people and that made it happen."

Translating real people to fiction is tricky from a personal standpoint, as well. Your interpretation of another person, your willingness to tell his secrets may hurt him badly and do irreparable damage to your relationship. That's not to say you shouldn't use the people you love and loathe in your work. Great writers do it all the time. In fact, they'll do most anything to bring their work to the page. William

Faulkner said, "If a writer has to rob his mother, he will not hesitate. The 'Ode on a Grecian Urn' is worth any number of old ladies." Real people are a writer's best material. The strong feelings you have for them are in great part why you write, what you hope writing will help you understand. But be honest with yourself about the possible consequences. Your reaction to Faulkner's statement is probably a pretty good indicator of the degree to which you are willing to risk hurting real people by appropriating their lives for fiction.

Characters may be born of a religious or political conviction or intense interest in philosophical ideas. Speaking about politics as an integral part of her life, Grace Paley says, "It has to be there in one way or another. It's the way I see the world." But to create a character to prove a point or to promote some idea or way of life is a prescription for disaster. Your only agenda with characters should be to put real people on the page, and to do that you have to let go of all your stereotypes. If you don't, you'll create puppets that never break the strings that control them and so never come truly alive on the page. They'll be saints or villains, neither of which have much capacity to surprise you or your readers.

No matter where your characters come from, remember: It is the unexpected that fascinates. The Sunday school teacher who cheats a waiter out of a tip; the gang member who adores his little sister; the truck driver who listens to opera; the linguistics professor who loves auto racing. Talking about his decision to make the main character in "Sabateur" an intellectual, Ha Jin says, "Intellectuals often present themselves as victims. The truth is that no totalitarian regime could exist without the help of intellectuals. I wanted to show that an intellectual could also be an evildoer, given the situation." Characters must be as complex and paradoxical as real people—and, of course, believable. You must examine your characters' motivations, feelings, and beliefs and the actions that result from them to make sure they are psychologically sound.

Every story has a whole constellation of characters. While major characters naturally shine more brightly and demand more of the writer's attention, it is important to remember that minor characters are also important in creating the story's overall atmosphere and effect. Dan Choan finds a skeptical, critical minor character useful as an instrument for asking the main character questions that put her on the line; he throws minor characters in the way of major ones to test their weaknesses and illuminate their characters.

Minor characters may be crafted to serve a certain purpose in a story; they may appear in process by way of the writer's unconscious. Regardless of how they arrive in a story, they may be used in a variety of ways: to reveal information, move the plot, underpin the theme, or throw light on the setting. They will not be as deeply drawn as major characters, but they must be authentic and believable. They must be in the story for a reason, not just by happenstance or because the writer is fond of them.

Dialogue

When someone you know calls you on the phone, more often than not he doesn't bother to say his name but depends on your recognizing the sound of his voice, its timbre and pitch. If you don't recognize it right off, you'll figure it out pretty quickly by something he says. "Hey, you want to watch the Lakers tonight?" he asks, and you immediately rule out all the people in your life who *never* watch the Lakers—unless he says it a certain way, ironically maybe, that identifies himself as a person who knows watching the Lakers is the *last* thing you'd be likely to do.

If the caller is someone you don't know or don't remember, your mind scrambles for clues. Telemarketer, long-lost cousin, police, wrong number. Word choice, accent, syntax, tone of voice, reference points—all of these things, and more, help you figure out who it is and what he wants.

Dialogue in stories works the same way. If you're doing it right, readers will recognize each character's voice in the same way they recognize the voices of real people. In stories, as in real life, conversations reflect the personalities, upbringings, education, values, experiences, and motivations of the people speaking. They grow naturally from situations people find themselves in and play out in the writer's mind in what Russell Banks calls "auditory hallucinations."

People—real or imagined—talk to each other for all kinds of reasons: to clarify, persuade, reassure, amuse, impress, vent, control. *How* they talk—word choice, the rhythms of their sentences—is full of clues about the emotions and intentions driving what they say. "You look fabulous" can mean anything from, literally, you look fabulous, to you look absolutely ridiculous, depending on who says it and the tone in which it is said. Like negative space in sculpture, part of dialogue is also what characters *don't* say, whether it is from shyness or stubbornness, or because someone else is talking so much he never gets a chance.

Tape a dinner table conversation with your family or a conversation at a café among friends and then transcribe it. You'll quickly see how useful this is. In real life, people engage in pointless dialogue of assent. *"Hi, how are you doing?" "Okay, how about you?" "Not too bad. Bummer of a test, though." "No kidding."* They engage in small talk, commenting on the neighbor's lawn, wondering what's on TV tonight, gossiping about what happened at work. They start to say something and then digress. They're repetitive and inarticulate. They pace what they say with "uh" or "you know" or "like."

There are hot spots, though, when the conversation suddenly focuses on something that matters and you, the listener, perk up and lean toward the tape recorder in anticipation. That's what dialogue in stories is made of. It's distilled, the essence of real conversation—or in Amy Bloom's words, "conversation's greatest hits." Highlight the hot spots of conversation in the transcript of your tape; then write a dialogue that conveys the essence of the conversation. Don't worry about flow or transitions. Write as if you're writing dialogue for a play, identifying each speaker by name at the beginning of her speech.

There is no pointless dialogue in a story. Dialogue is a workhorse, serving to characterize, move the plot, clarify the situation, create tension, and convey information. Every bit of it is there for a reason. Pam Houston observes that dialogue is often about people with competing agendas. They aren't really talking *to* one another. They say what they want to say then wait, not listening to what the other person is saying, for the next opportunity to speak. This, she says, provides an excellent opportunity to create tension. Tobias Wolff believes good dialogue contains a lot of unspoken understandings between people. Characters, like real people, come to every conversation carrying all the baggage of the relationship they have with the person they're talking to. They make reference to past history, jump into ideas and issues midstream, knowing he will know exactly what they mean.

"What I really want you to do is to 'hear' someone speak," Dorothy Allison says. Believable dialogue is as much about the rhythms of language as it is about the particular words people use. Allison and many other writers experience dialogue as an auditory hallucination; writing it down feels like taking dictation. "If I can't hear it myself, then I can't expect any reader to hear it," Russell Banks says.

"It's all about paying attention," believes Amy Hempel. "I ask [my students] to write a sentence that they've overheard and bring it to class. Don't give it a context, just say the sentence. I want something that's just slightly skewed from the normal, so that we won't at first understand it." Then ask, "What if?"

If dialogue is hard for you, start with the voices you've heard all your life. "Everyone has a tune in their head of the way their families spoke when they were little," Grace Paley says. "There's some music in everybody's head who wants to write." So sit quietly awhile, let the voices of your childhood float into your head. What was it your mother always said? "You *kids.*" "Good night, *God bless.*" Whatever the voice inside your head says, write it down. *That's* what writing dialogue feels like. Once you get the hang of it with real voices, the voices of your characters will begin to clamor for your attention.

And when they start speaking, listen. What phrases do they use repeatedly? What words do they use to register surprise, anger, sadness, disgust? If, moving through a scene, you think a character will say, "Honey, it's so good to see you," and instead she says, "Well, it's about *time*," stop and think what that means and how it affects what you thought you knew about her and the relationship between the two characters—not to mention how what she says affects "Honey!"

Dialogue may reflect accents or dialect, but be careful. A little bit of that goes a long way. It's better to convey national or regional flavor through syntax, sentence rhythms, and word choice. The same is true in using shortened words such as "gonna" or "darlin'." "Why drop off the 'g'?" Carolyn Ferrell observes. "Won't the character's background come across with that 'g' intact if the setting truly does its work and the sentences do all they can to create and sustain the voice?"

You won't get dialogue down right the first time. Nothing works better than reading dialogue aloud to let you know where the problems are. Wrong words feel like wrong notes in music. Speeches that go on too long or are loaded with information bore you. You stumble over syntax gaffes, stop short in tangled logic. You feel breathless if the dialogue is happening too fast. There aren't exact rules for writing good dialogue, but there are practical considerations that apply to most dialogue and will help you as you tinker to get yours just right. Here are some suggestions.

✓ *Avoid weighing down dialogue with too much information.* Though good dialogue naturally conveys information, it should not be constructed solely for that purpose. At its worst, dialogue that is really exposition in disguise sounds something like this. "Have you heard about Darla?" "Do you mean Darla who works at the Farm Bureau and who was having an affair with the county agent who dumped her and ran off with the snake charmer from the circus?" Give your readers the pleasure of collecting bits of information about Darla by way of rich, sensory clues folded into the story rather than through stiff, clunky dialogue with no spark or tension in it. Trust them to be able to assimilate information along the way and come to the conclusions you want them to come to about her life.

✓ *More often than not, use tags to identify characters, even when their voices are distinctive.* Almost always use a simple "Tom said" or "Mary said." They are unobtrusive to the reader and may even be used as a kind of punctuation or pacing device to give dialogue a more authentic feel. Consider the difference between "'My God, I cannot believe this'" and "'My God,' Charles said. 'I cannot believe this.'" The tag both identifies the reader and intensifies the moment. Movement works to tag characters, too, and carries emotional clues. "'My God.' Charles dropped the phone and sank into the chair. 'I cannot believe this.'"

By all means, avoid melodramatic tags such as "Harvey spat" or "Gina hissed." Avoid the use of adverbs, as in "Chip said enthusiastically" or "Lisa said ominously," as a way of conveying mood or intent. Instead, let word choice and the rhythm of the sentences tell readers what they need to know.

✓ *Use movement and setting to enhance dialogue.* The way characters move and what they're doing as they speak, influences the effect of dialogue. So does the setting of the conversation and how the characters perceive it. In real life, people are almost always doing something as they speak—fixing dinner, fishing, dressing the baby, building a model airplane, doing their hair. They drink coffee, gulp soft drinks, nibble hors d'oeuvres. They fidget, pace, stalk. Rub an arthritic wrist, fling their arms out in joyful abandon. They turn on the radio and turn it off. Smooth a child's hair. Quickly put a wine glass out of sight. They bite their nails, mop their foreheads, wipe away tears. They respond midsentence to a sick, elderly parent calling from another room for attention. Sometimes what they do contradicts and complicates what they say. For example, "'I love you,' he said. And hit her."

✓ *Use description to develop dialogue.* What characters do, the body language they use doing it, provides clues to readers as they puzzle out what's happening in a story and why. Where characters are, how they respond to the atmosphere of the place and the objects surrounding them provides a wealth of information. Effective description of movement and place deepens the effect of dialogue, helps create the proper pace, and may even be used in place of tags to identify who's speaking.

Read a story that uses dialogue effectively and highlight the text, using different colors for speech, movement, and description. When you're finished, you'll probably see a weave of colors. Looking closely at the weave, you'll begin to perceive how the rhythm and balance of these three elements work together to create the effect of people talking on the page.

To see good dialogue in action, watch a single scene in a movie that involves people talking. Play it over and over, noticing facial expression, body language, the rhythm of verbal exchange, and how the camera moves between the characters and through the setting to record movement, create atmosphere, and move the dialogue at the proper pace.

Now go back to the simple dialogue you created from the taped transcript. Have a friend or classmate read it aloud to you, and listen for places where you might clarify or slow things down using tags or some kind of description. Sit a moment and bring the people who were talking into your mind's eye—where they were, what they were doing. Then rewrite the dialogue, tinkering until you capture the feel and pace of a real conversation.

Voice

What do people mean when they talk about *voice* in fiction? The question often bemuses students and writers alike, perhaps because voice works on so many levels in a story. Though it is impossible to isolate each kind of voice and define its function, it may be helpful to identify them and consider the ways in which they contribute to the story's overall effect.

Dialogue is made from the voices of characters who speak in a story, grown from the rhythms and experiences of the world they inhabit. But characters do more than speak to each other; they also speak to themselves. A character's inner voice complicates what she says and does on the page. The person who labors to be seen as someone who doesn't care reveals in her thoughts how much things really matter. A person who is sugary sweet may seethe on the inside, imagining exquisitely satisfying punishments for those who take advantage of her. Capturing a character's inner voice is just as important as capturing her spoken voice because it clarifies and deepens readers' understanding of her outward behavior. Terrible acts may make more sense once the character's inner logic is understood, just as virtuous acts may be revealed to be manipulative or even evil in intent.

If you keep a journal—an honest one—you know what your inner voice looks and sounds like on the page. It may also emerge in heartfelt letters to family or friends. Jill McCorkle suggests letting a character write journal entries, letters, and monologues as a way of establishing an inner voice. But make sure that the inner voice you're writing in is not, as Dave Eggers describes it, you "wearing some obvious mask."

The story itself has a voice; it is, essentially, how a story is told. Pam Houston observes that the second-person *you* is a particularly American way to tell a story. Stuart Dybek finds the mood and rhythms of music useful in discovering and bringing forth a story's voice.

"The voice of the story is the whole story," says Grace Paley. She is right. Rhythm, word choice, details of setting—every single thing in Eggers's "After I Was Thrown in the River and Before I Drowned" contributes to its "loopy breathlessness" and reflects the fact that it is about a dog and a dog's world. Describing his story, "Media Event," Charles Baxter says, "The story feels and sounds slightly schizoid, as [the main character] is."

Every writer has a voice, too. Particular to no one story but present in all of them, it is as recognizable and idiosyncratic as the spoken voice. Ernest Hemingway's voice comes to mind. Or William Faulkner's. This aspect of voice is virtually indistinguishable from style, about which Katherine Anne Porter astutely commented, "A cultivated style would be like a mask. Everybody knows it's a mask, and sooner or later you must show yourself—or at least, you show yourself as someone who could not afford to show himself, and so created something to hide behind. You do not create a style. You work, and develop yourself; your style is an emanation from your own being."

Point of View

Complete the exercise on the next page to help you understand point of view.

exercise

Think of a significant incident in your life, one that was fraught with tension and controversy. The Christmas your dad moved out of the house, your sister's engagement to a man you don't like, your mother's announcement that she was going to have a baby, a hospital visit to a cousin who's terminally ill, an argument you had with your best friend over a love interest. Sit for a moment, eyes closed, and bring the scene to mind. Where is it happening? Who's present? What are they doing, saying? Now freewrite everything you see in your mind's eye, everything you remember about the incident. Be honest, even brutal. Feel free to vent your emotions.

Now step into the consciousness of another person who was present—your father, your sister's fiancé, your mother, your aunt, your best friend. Again, sit for a moment, eyes closed. Try to imagine what this person was noticing, thinking, feeling as the incident unfolded and how it might be different from your own take on the scene. Consider what he had to lose or gain, what she hoped would happen, what he couldn't or wouldn't see about himself, the other people involved, the situation itself. Now write the same incident again, in that person's voice, expressing his or her concerns.

As you've seen from the above, point of view is essentially the writer's ability to experience the world through another person's consciousness. Each of us sees the world through a lens ground by experience, and to write believable fiction a writer must not only be able to separate his own experience—and the values, beliefs and assumptions that come of it—from the experience of another person (real or invented) but to be able to imagine how life might shape that person in a way that makes what he thinks and believes absolutely plausible to him. To be able to do this effectively, you must honor the experience of all people. You must look honestly and dispassionately at how a lifetime of personal, political, cultural, and spiritual experiences might have brought them to the moment in which you first encounter them in your story. You don't have to condone the behavior of a character you create; you don't have to like him. But you do have to be willing to try to understand him. Intolerance and judgment are luxuries a writer cannot afford. The students who murdered their classmates at Columbine High School, the terrorists who flew planes into the World Trade Center Towers on September 11, 2001: Challenge yourself to try to step into their shoes and experience those momentous events by way of their consciousness. You then will begin to understand the powerful insights that come from mastering this essential element of fiction.

Sometimes writers (and readers, too) are territorial about certain points of view. Men can't write about women, women can't write about men, a person of one race can't write about a person of another. If the story you are burning to tell demands a point of view drastically different from your own, approach it with humility and respect. Talking about a story written from the point of view of an African American girl, Grace Paley says, "I read it to the guy who told me the story three times. If he had told me it didn't sound right, I'd have changed it." Writing from a woman's point of view, Dan Chaon observes, "I find it very much like writing from a place you live in when you are a very little kid and you're not attached to any gender." The further a point of view is from your own, the more important it is to look and listen for details that will bring authenticity to your story.

More often than not, choosing the point of view of a story happens naturally. Charles Baxter says, "It all depends on how you hear the story coming to you." For Elizabeth Tallent, the point of view is as obvious to her at the outset as the fact that she will write the story in English. She says, "I've always been really startled when a student comes in and says, 'I've got to change this from third person into first,' because . . . I couldn't do that."

Writing "Night Train," based on the story of a woman raped by D. C. Stephenson, the Grand Dragon of the Ku Klux Klan, Susan Neville tried many points of view before telling the story from the point of view of the victim's friend. Russell Banks speaks analytically about his decision to tell "Sara Cole: A Type of Love Story" from the point of view of the male character. "The automatic sympathy goes to the woman," he says. "If you don't see it from [the man's] point of view, you don't have any sense of his struggle, of his interior drama, of its possible meaning for him. Therefore, I had to include his point of view."

Similarly, Joan Silber realized that she couldn't tell "Bobby Jackson" from the point of view of the real person the story is based on. "I knew him only in this peripheral way," she explains. "The guys were closer witnesses and had more access to him than I did, so I invented the person who narrates the story."

First and third person are the most commonly used points of view in the short story. Writing in the second-person *you* has gained popularity with the success of stories by writers like Pam Houston and Lorrie Moore. Occasionally, stories are written in the collective *we*.

First-Person Point of View. With first person, you literally step into the head of the character and tell the story as he experiences it. You can see only what he can see, know only what he can know. You interpret what's happening according to his experience, values, emotions, and beliefs. In this sense, every first-person narrator is an unreliable narrator. The way he tells a story, the conclusions he comes to about what people do, their motivations for doing it, and the place and time they're doing it in are completely dependent on his own personal worldview. An old hippie, a secretly gay schoolteacher, a skinhead, and a corporate lawyer, all regulars at a neighborhood bar, will almost certainly have very different views on why an altercation occurred between another bar patron and a gay couple and what exactly happened. They might lie, blatantly or by omission. More likely, they won't. They'll report what they saw and heard—or *thought* they saw and heard. They'll notice different details because of who they are. The fun of a first-person narrator for readers is in picking up on clues that give them the information they need to discover the underlying truth of the story.

Dan Chaon goes so far as to say that first person *depends* on the narrator having a perception of the world that's skewed. For him, first person has become almost the sole province of dramatic irony. Michael Martone is less interested in capturing a voice than in the way first person allows him to use exposition differently. "The way someone tells something is scenic," he says, "and so the telling becomes a kind of showing." It's connected to his nonfiction writing, too. "I inhabit a character in order to talk about things," he says. "I . . . borrow people and make them write essays."

For a beginning writer, first person is a good place to start. Its natural limitations in scope make it easier to know what should be in the story, and once you establish a strong voice, it talks back to you and lets you know if you are beginning to go astray. You're not likely to slip inadvertently into a different point of view. A good way to practice first-person narration is to write from the point of view of a child, real or invented, using only the words available to that child, reporting only what she sees, thinking the way she thinks. Talking about the way children see the world, Martone describes an incident that happened when his son was just beginning to speak. Early that spring, as the snow melted, a paper plate was revealed in a muddy patch. "Look." the child said. "Moon fall down." Having no understanding of what the moon really is, this made perfect sense to him. It is on understanding what and why things make sense to a particular child that writing successfully in his point of view depends.

Second-Person Point of View. Pam Houston likes the second person for its conversational rhythms and because it is a particularly American way to tell a story: "So, you know, you're in this bar and this guy comes up to you . . ." For her, a story written in this point of view is always about "a narrator who's ashamed of herself, afraid to say *I*." Using the second person washes a layer of shame over the story without the narrator ever having to admit to it. "It's a kind of diversion," explains Houston. "It's not me, it's you. It's unbelievable that we can fool ourselves so easily." Shame and denial breed a kind of underlying tension that lends to the power of this point of view. This narrator, too, is unreliable and affords readers the pleasure of puzzling out the truth behind the narration.

Writing her second-person story "Fish," Jill McCorkle was addressing her father. "I wasn't trying to put the reader in the story at all," she says. "It was more the way that you would write a letter to someone . . . very private . . . a confession of feelings." It is the feel of the confession and the tension surrounding it that fuels the second-person story written as a form of address. Using an accusatory *you* works similarly. In both, calibrating the voice is of utmost importance. Sentimentality and melodrama are the pitfalls here, and a tendency to tell rather than show emotions.

Narration using the first-person plural *we* has the personal attachment of first person, expanding it to bring a sense of all-knowing. "There's the feeling that this story happened and they all know it," Jill McCorkle says. "It works especially well when you are telling a story about a town and within a town." Using the first-person plural point of view successfully hinges on what the characters who constitute the *we* have in common. Tension and conflict arise in their relationships with characters outside the *we*. Fueled by the narrator's impulse to accept, understand, censor, or distance themselves, the narrative may explore questions like, "Why isn't he like us? Why should we accept him? How can we understand him? How can we help (or hurt?) him? How can we make him see things the way we do?"

Third-Person Point of View. Writing in the third person is more complicated than simply deciding you'll use *he* or *she* instead of *I*, *you*, or *we*. There are three kinds of third-person points of view: close-third, objective-third, and omniscient-third. Each one has its own requirements, and once you choose one you must stick with it throughout your story.

In close-third, the narrator resides inside the main character's head. He knows what the character thinks and feels. He knows only what the character knows about the other characters in the story, sees only what the character sees. In this point of view, you may work so closely with a character that the effect is very similar to a first-person point of view, or you may pull back and get a broader view.

Using objective-third, the narrator is like a camera positioned on the shoulder of the main character. He can record what the main character sees and hears, but is not privy to the character's thoughts or feelings. The details of the story must speak for themselves.

The omniscient narrator knows everything about everyone in the story. She can enter the thoughts and feelings of any character, skip to different places and times to fill readers in on what they need to know, and may even comment on the action of the story. But, although the omniscient point of view offers the writer great freedom, it is very difficult to maintain a consistent voice. Also, some readers find it impersonal. Not much used today, it is best illustrated by nineteenth-century writers like George Eliot, Leo Tolstoy, and Charles Dickens.

Multiple Points of View. For the beginning writer, working with a single point of view is probably a good idea. But some writers, beginners to professionals, find using multiple points of view the only possible way into a story they want to write. Elizabeth Tallent likes working with multiple points of views for the way they give readers an event "refracted through different sensibilities." She likes what multiple points of view do to structure because "right from the get-go, it rules out any kind of classic arc—conflict, crisis, resolution."

Characters don't perceive things the same way, and this raises interesting questions for her. If they don't perceive the same conflict, how could they see the same thing as a crisis? Can one character have a crisis that remains invisible to others, and what does that mean? Can one character come to closure when nobody else does? Or can everybody *but* one character come to closure?

Tallent compares moving from one point of view to another, writing a story, to crossing a stream going steppingstone to steppingstone. The gap between each one—where it is, the nature of it—informs the story, too. She writes one point of view until she feels she fully understands it. Making the switch to the next one "is like starting the story over," she observes. "It cannot be down time." She knows if the point of view that comes next is right if it somehow complicates the work she's done so far.

For the beginning writer, multiple-points-of-view stories can easily get out of hand. It's easy to jump from one character to another because you get bored or stuck, bringing the reader out of the fictional dream, uncertain and confused. Multiple points of view should complicate a story, not obscure it. Each point of view should be there for a reason. Both writer and readers should finish the story with the feeling that it could not have been told any other way.

Point of view, generally, is challenging for both inexperienced and experienced writers. In her usual pithy way, Flannery O'Connor observed, "Point of view runs me nuts. If you violate the point of view you destroy the sense of reality and louse yourself up generally."

Following are some commonsense questions to help you choose the right point of view for your story and use it effectively.

✓ Realistically, can you get into the head of the point-of-view character you've chosen? If your character is an Indian guru, do you understand Indian culture well enough to know how it would affect his thoughts and actions? If you are twenty and the character you imagine is ninety, how will you accommodate your differences in life experience?

- ✓ Can your point-of-view character be in all the necessary places at the right times to be able to recount what's needed to make the story clear to readers? If not, how will you provide readers with what they need to know?
- ✓ Is your point-of-view character the one most affected by the action in the story? If the action does not focus on her or even involve her, how will you make it her story?
- ✓ Is the point of view of one person sufficient to reveal the complexity of the story?
- ✓ If you discover that multiple points of view will best serve your story, how will you balance them so that readers will go willingly and without confusion from one to the next, never awakening from the fictional dream?

Scene

Complete the following exercise to learn more about scene.

exercise

Watch the first twenty minutes or so of *Witness*, until Harrison Ford appears and establishes himself as the detective/love interest in the movie. As you watch, jot down everything you know about the characters, setting, situation, and plot. Then, alone or with a group, consider how particular details in the movie work as clues to cause you to come to your conclusions.

Stories work the same way as movies. Characters come alive in scenes, revealing information about themselves and the situation through what they say and do. Details of setting enrich the action and enhance readers' understanding of what is happening. Reading a good scene is like looking through a keyhole, watching the drama of other people's lives unfold.

To write a good scene, you experience it in your mind's eye like a visual hallucination. Your goal is to create that same visual hallucination for the reader. Russell Banks observes, "If you can't see what you're describing, you can't expect the reader to see it either."

If you're lucky, that visual hallucination arrives full-blown into your mind and you just transcribe it. More often, you will have to imagine your way into a scene, working consciously toward the moment when it begins to move forward of its own volition.

exercise

To learn how to do this, choose a scene from the story you want to write. If you don't have a story scene in mind, try the exercise using a real scene, something that actually happened to you or someone you know. Sit a moment, let what you know or remember about the scene gather in your mind's eye. Then answer the following questions on separate 4″ x 6″ index cards to help jar your characters into motion and shape a living, breathing scene.

- ✓ **Who** is present in the scene? Observe how these participants look. What are they wearing? What is their body language? What catches your eye? Who is *not* there? Why not?
- ✓ **Where** does the scene take place? Write a physical description of the setting. What is the significance of the setting? Are there objects that are significant to the scene?
- ✓ **When** does the scene happen? Give the specific date if you can. Write a report for the day and consider if the weather might affect the outcome of the scene somehow. Is there anything significant happening just outside the scene (in another room, outside the window) that might affect how it plays out? Is there anything happening in the world at large that is important to the scene or at the periphery of it? (For example, a scene that took place on September 11, 2001, would very likely be affected by the events of that day.) What memories float up and come into play, affecting the outcome of the scene?
- ✓ **What** happens? Record the events of the scene—flying a kite, arguing with your mother, dining with your boyfriend. Describe what happens—give a little plot summary. How much time passes from the beginning of the scene to the end of it? What does each character bring to the scene that may affect its outcome? Mood? A history with the others involved? Some unrelated problem or joy?
- ✓ **Why** are these people together in this scene? What issues are involved? Where's the tension and/or conflict in it? What's at stake? If there's dialogue, what will the characters be talking about? Individually, what does each character want the outcome of the scene to be? Is there a difference between what they say they want and what they really want? Are they aware of the difference? Remembering that good stories deal with the yearnings of people, consider who in this cast of characters wants the most, longs for the greatest, is willing to go the farthest to get it.

Now write! Let what's happening in your mind's eye unfold on the page. Record it as a movie camera would, writing only what you can see or hear. Let your sense of the scene shift and change as you go. Be willing to let it surprise you. If you get stuck or if you find yourself lapsing into summary, take Stuart Dybek's advice: "Stop a second and think: What am I doing? How can I make a reader see it?" When you finish the scene, add description and exposition where it is needed, letting it work as a good soundtrack in a movie works, subtly manipulating readers' understanding.

A story may be made of a single scene, so the scene you just wrote may turn out to be the first draft of your story. A story may also be made of a series of scenes. There's no rule for the number of scenes a short story should have, and it doesn't usually help much to try to figure out ahead of time how many scenes the story you want to write will require. It's almost always best to jump in and write the first draft of a story as best you can, letting the process of writing it show you what it wants to be. But if you're stuck, try the following exercise.

exercise

It can be useful to make a list of scenes that *could* be in the story and then consider them one by one, answering the above questions. When you've finished doing that, lay the

4″ x 6″ index cards out and look at them as a way of generating new questions about the story. For example:

- ✓ Are all the scenes told from the same point of view?
- ✓ Does each scene have its own little plot, with clear movement from beginning to end?
- ✓ Does each scene move the plot and deepen readers' understanding of the story?
- ✓ Is each scene necessary?
- ✓ How many different ways could the scenes be sequenced in the story?
- ✓ Are there scenes that could be added?
- ✓ Are there any scenes whose information might be better revealed through exposition?

Even though scene is crucial to the short story, writers employ scene to a greater or lesser degree. In fact, it is possible (though very challenging) to write a story with no scenes at all. How much and the way a writer uses scene is primarily dependent on the needs of each story she writes: Some stories are more dependent on scene, others on narration. Complicating the matter is Jill McCorkle's observation that writers tend toward scene or summary. Scene writers set their characters in motion and follow them through a scene, recording all they say, do, and see so that the reader feels as if he is experiencing it. Writers who prefer summary tell readers about what happened in a scene, rather as they would in a spoken account. Writers who tend toward scene imagine different stories *and* imagine stories differently from writers who tend toward summary. Over time, good writers learn how to recognize what a story wants and the mix of skills they'll need to bring it to the page.

They learn, too, how to position themselves to best capture the essence of a scene. "You can see a wild fire or a house burning from far off," Russell Banks says. "In fact, it's probably best to see it from far off. But you can't see a heart breaking or a life crumbling from inside. . . . You have to get in its face."

Most lives, fictional or real, are composites of small moments, but not moments of small impact. Good writers find those small, crucial moments in their characters' lives and, in them, find their stories. "Why do you think all the hacks are writing true crime books?" Luis Urrea asks. "Because if a guy makes soup out of his grandma it's hard to go wrong with that material. But if you can have somebody kiss someone on the cheek and have your reader weep, then you're really writing."

In advising aspiring writers how to deal with material that is necessarily brutal, Ha Jin suggests, "Don't flinch. Write out any scene needed by the story. Be truthful but avoid vulgarity." Russell Banks would agree. "The hotter the moment, . . . the cooler the prose," he says. "You don't have to build it up; you don't have to make anything out of it because it's all there."

Plot

You know your character as well as you know your own sister. You know how she spends her days. You know what she thinks and feels about everything. But no matter how interesting the fixed actions and habits of her life are, something out of the ordinary must happen if you want to write a story about her. Plot forms around moving action. Something moves the character out of her fixed routine and offers the potential for change.

Essentially, plot is what happens in a story: Boy meets girl, boy falls in love and tries to make her love him back, boy wins or loses. It grows from character, evolves in process. It is more than what happens on the surface of a story, though. There's an emotional plot, too, humming along beneath the action, and for many writers the emotional plot is what a story is really about. "If it's a character-based story," Susan Neville says, "the plot has more to do with the arc of the character in that particular moment than it does with a chain of causality." Tobias Wolff assesses the direction a character is facing at the beginning of a story and then creates plot by slightly altering his angle of vision so that, moving forward, the character ends up "very far away" from where he would have been.

Ha Jin observes that discovering events that produce dramatic development is key in creating plot. "The first event emotionally pushes the story toward the second event, the ending," he says. Joan Silber tries "to have a rise, a crucial thing that happens. Often it's a crucial moment of reflection."

Plot and structure in a story are virtually indistinguishable, each completely dependent on the other. Structure is how a story is organized from beginning to end, how it moves through time. Scenes are the building blocks of structure. You might also think of them as vehicles that carry characters through the terrain of the story. Without them, plot and structure are no more than summary.

exercise

To begin to understand the function of plot in a story and its relation to the other elements of fiction, read the following column from the *Indianapolis Star* and then create the plot for a short story that uses the facts in some way. You may add to or subtract from the facts, but you may not change them. The plot must make sense, given the facts as they are presented in the published story. Feel free to imagine new characters and project beyond the time frame of the news story in exploring plot possibilities.

Prison Sentences Won't Stop Activists' Fight for Democracy

Busting a $12, taxpayer-paid-for padlock on a gate during a protest at a U.S. military school will cost Charity Ryerson 21, and Jeremy John, 22, six months in federal prison, along with a year on probation and a $1,000 fine. But it's a nothing price, they say, if Americans here and across the land get the message.

Or better yet, remember *the message. "Look at the precedents to our non-violent action," says the red-haired Ryerson. "Look at the Boston Tea Party, this country's earliest act of civil disobedience. Look at all the freedoms that have been fought for us by the military, by the labor movement, in civil rights, women's rights and the right to vote. Freedom is never given. It is taken," says the University of Chicago student, a political science major.*

Ryerson and John, who study cognitive science at Indiana University take their freedom with a good measure of joy—sentenced last month in a federal court in Georgia, they recently held a tongue-in-cheek jail-sentencing party at Ryerson's parents' suburban home. The party's theme? "Come Dressed as Something that Sucks Worse than Spending Six Months in Jail." Guests' costumes included a Texas oil tycoon and the Bush twins. Gilbert came as a middle school physical education teacher. Jones was rain on his own wedding. "I wore a veil and spritzed myself," he says, laughing.

But don't be fooled by their sense of the ridiculous. They're deadly serious when it comes to life in these United States today—they think our foreign policy is open season on the world's disenfranchised. They are determined to expose what they see as U.S.-driven corporate globalization, especially in countries where the poor and voiceless dwell.

And they are going to jail, gladly, they say, for those beliefs. Last fall, Ryerson, a graduate of Brebeuf Jesuit Preparatory School, and John, a South Central High alumnus, joined 11,000 others (including a half dozen or so from Indiana, mostly nuns) in what Ryerson calls "probably the nation's most spirit-filled protest."

The target, for the 12th year in a row, was the Western Hemisphere Institute for Security Cooperation, formerly known as the School of the Americas in Fort Benning, Ga.—a place that counts among its graduates Panama's Gen. Manuel Noreiga.

For years, marchers were permitted to express themselves nonviolently on fort property. However, after 9/11, tightened security was added, including a fence and gate. On Nov. 16, 2002, some chose to bypass that gate by wading across a nearby creek to get to the fort's grounds. Ryerson and John made up their minds—in advance—to use bolt cutters and open the gate. They were among 86 people arrested.

The gate, says John, is heavy with meaning. "It stands for lack of citizen involvement in government. It is a symbol of our lack of democracy."

By breaking the lock, they believe they open the fort to public scrutiny—exposing it and allowing people to question its activities.

That is what being a patriot is all about.

You will quickly see that the possibilities for stories are limitless. You might want to explore the emotional tensions around the pre-prison party. For example, what if Ryerson's parents are divorced and one of her parents is aghast that the other would allow such a party? Such a story might illuminate the differences between the parents and how they shaped Ryerson and brought her to this moment. You might move backwards and write a story from the point of view of one of the nuns, charting her involvement with Ryerson and John on the day of the protest, showing how it brought her to a moment of change. Or project forward to John's first moments in prison, when the consequences of his acts become reality. The arresting police officer, a college professor whose political beliefs influenced Ryerson or John, a sibling, one of the caterers, a family friend—each would tell a different story, depending on who they are. Ryerson and John might affect their lives profoundly; they might be only minor characters in the story they want to tell.

Once you've settled on the plot you want to work with, consider the following questions to assess and refine it.

- ✓ Whose story is this? Write a brief character profile of this person. In what way will the action of this story change his life? What do you learn about this situation from him that you wouldn't have learned from anyone else's point of view? How will this person's identity/voice affect your use of language in the story?
- ✓ If the story will be told from multiple points of view, say why each point of view is necessary and what it will contribute to the story.
- ✓ Where is the story happening? Why did you choose this particular setting? How does it enhance and clarify the action of the story? If there are several settings, what is the purpose of each?
- ✓ What is the time frame of the story? If the story is not chronological and/or if it involves multiple levels of time, how will the structure of the story accommodate this?

- ✓ Plot outline: In a few sentences, describe the beginning, middle and end of the story. Briefly describe the scene that sets up the beginning, the "big scene" (pivotal moment), and the scene at the end. If the story is only one scene, say how it begins and ends, identifying its climactic moment.
- ✓ Emotional outline: Briefly describe the emotional state of the point-of-view? character as she moves through the story.
- ✓ Where does the tension lie? What or who causes it? Are there several kinds of tension at work? What are they?
- ✓ What larger issues are reflected in the action of the story? For example: money, revenge, loss, divorce. Complete this sentence to clarify the story's theme: "This is a story about what happens when . . . "
- ✓ How would your story begin? Write the first line—or a first paragraph.

Now pare it all down to a basic outline, using this exercise developed by the Gotham Writers' Workshop. Answer the following questions one by one, without looking ahead. Number your responses.

1. Write the name and age of the main character (A).
2. Write the name and age of the character with whom he is in conflict (B).
3. What is their relationship? (Examples: siblings, coworkers, best friends, teacher/student, coach/athlete, parent/child.)
4. What does A need or want from B that B won't give? (This can be an object or an emotional need. The important thing is that A must want it badly and B must be absolutely unwilling to give it up.)
5. Why does A need or want (or think he needs or wants) this? Why is B unwilling to give it up?

6a. Show one way A tries to get what he wants.
 b. Show how B responds.
7a. Show another way A tries to get what he wants.
 b. Show another way B responds.
8a. Show the third and final attempt by A to get what he wants.
 b. Show B's response to this last attempt.
9. Does A get what he wants? Yes or no.
10. What does A discover about himself as a result of all this?
11. How is A changed forever? How is this reflected in his behavior?

Ideally, your answers to these questions will have formed an outline for a perfectly plotted story whose structure could be diagrammed using the traditional arc of rising and falling action.

#1 and #2 name the main characters.
#3 gives background and context.
#4 and #5 establish and define the conflict.
#6 and #7 chart development.
#7, #8, and #9 bring crisis and climax.
#10 and #11 are the denouement and resolution.

But remember! Stories evolve. If you actually decided to write this story, your original idea might change quite drastically in process. Jhumpa Lahiri's "A Temporary

Matter," a story about a marriage in crisis, was originally about a young woman renting a room in an old man's apartment. The only element consistent with the story in its final form is that it takes place in the dark. It's important not to be dead set on any one idea. Writing the story you just imagined, you'd work by trial and error, much as Dave Eggers worked on his story "Up the Mountain Coming Down Slowly. "It was really a matter of constructing it brick by brick," he explains. He wrote the basic narrative first and then threaded in the main character's background, developed subplots, created tension, and provided description of place—all the while careful to move the story along at just the right pace.

For Tobias Wolff, moving the plot forward, attending to its various tensions, feels like bringing a story to a boil. "And then and then and *then.*" It is instinctive, internalized. "So naturally built into the story telling enterprise," he says, "that I don't know how to detach it.

Of course, not all stories fit the traditional arc of rising and falling action produced by the plot exercise. Amy Hempel's stories hinge on a single moment. "Some of the concerns in writing a short-short are not unlike joke writing," she says. "You know you're going to have a punch line, a kicker—whether it's a funny one or not." Pam Houston works with "chunks" of writing, small scenes, and luminous moments. They "don't have a narrative line that drives them," she says. They bounce off each other, metaphorically, rhythmically; there is usually a plot line running underneath defined by time. In her story "How to Talk to a Hunter," the plot line is simply "Jane Coyote comes, she leaves." She wrote "The Best Girlfriend You Never Had," however, willfully avoiding any connective material. The story "begins fifteen times and ends fifteen times," she says. It was only very late in the process that she wrote the sentence that begins the story, "A perfect day in the city always starts like this," which serves to establish an artificial narrative line and a loose structure to hold the story together.

Early in his writing career, Michael Martone realized that he wasn't interested in trying to create John Gardner's fictional dream or to learn the tricks of realism that "make what you're writing look like a spontaneous utterance." What he liked to do was arrange, and so his stories most often take the form of collage, their structures like musical compositions, dependent on theme and variation.

Structure and Time

Considering Houston's "chunks" and Martone's collage illustrates how plot and structure merge in the actual creation of stories. Still, it can be useful to identify and define the aspects of structure, which dictate how a story is organized and how time works in it. For our purposes here, *form* and *structure* mean the same thing and are used interchangeably.

Writers approach structure differently—and for different reasons. "If I could have written a story with development in it, I would have," Grace Paley says. "I couldn't do it. I didn't know how." Susan Neville wants "each story to be an experiment into some new ground, formally, as well as . . . emotionally or intellectually." Stuart Dybek, whose stories sometimes mirror the structure of musical compositions, finds structure in process. "That's the fun of it, the beauty of it," he says. "The writer doesn't know where it's going. . . . That's what form is about."

The most traditional kind of short story begins at the beginning and moves chronologically to the end. In a variation of the chronological story, Carolyn Ferrell's

"Please Don't Erase Me" reverses time, progressing through a series of scenes that begins with the narrator's struggles with full-blown AIDS and ends with the moment when things might have gone another way for her.

A chronological story might cover years, a month, a week, a few days, a single day, an afternoon, a moment. It might be several scenes or a single scene. The narrator in Joan Silber's "My Shape" skates over time, settling here and there to render a scene or phase of her life, moving from her adolescence all the way into middle age. Another Silber story, "Ragazzi" covers a series of events that occur over several weeks during the narrator's visit to an old friend. Russell Banks's "With Che in New Hampshire" covers the few moments between the time the narrator imagines getting off the bus in his hometown and starting down the road toward his father's house. The time frame in Jhumpa Lahiri's "A Temporary Matter" is defined by a blackout.

Generally, the less time a story covers, the easier it is to write. It's clearer to the writer what needs to be in the story and what can be left out; there are fewer transitions to make, less risk of bringing readers up, blinking, from the fictional dream.

Another commonly used structure is the frame. A story begins in present time, jumps to the meat of the story in the past, and then circles back to the present, letting readers know how things turned out and conveying the sense that there has been some resolution. Dybek's "Pet Milk" surprised him, beginning in the now, jumping backwards first to a memory of the narrator's grandmother, and then to a remembered love affair. "The whole intention of that story was to create the simple circular story," he says. "It was supposed to come back with him sitting at the window. But again, by accident, I reached the last line of the story. When I was a kid in college, I read *Rabbit Run*, and I loved the ending that shoots out over the frame of the story. So . . . when I hit that el train . . . , it reminded me of he 'runs, runs, runs.' And I said, 'No, I'll let it go there.'"

Sometimes a story is structured to alternate between two or more equally important periods of time. The challenge here is to move readers from one to the next in a way that they go willingly and without confusion.

If the story you imagine doesn't fit any of these common structures, take heart—you're in good company. "Forget that appalling narrative business of the realist: getting from lunch to dinner," Virginia Woolf once advised. Forge ahead, wrestle with your material until the right form emerges and allows you to tell the story you want to tell.

The dense structure of Luis Urrea's story "Father Returns from the Mountain," one long paragraph with sentences divided by slashes allowing the reader no way to escape from it, mirrors Urrea's claustrophobic experiences surrounding his father's death. Michael Martone's "Watch Out" is constructed as a series of essays that imitate the essays the main character asks her English as a Second Language students to write. Dorothy Allison wrote a list of secrets, *verboten* topics in her family, and arranged them in what she called "stanzas" to create "River of Names."

Almost every story, no matter its form, makes use of flashback to enhance and clarify readers' understanding of the action that is occurring in present time. Past events are usually revealed through straight narrative all in a "chunk" that is blended into the text. But they may also be fed to readers bit by bit through dialogue or by the use of devices such as letters, diaries, and news articles.

Flashbacks may be as short as a sentence or as long as a whole scene. Just remember that every time you move backwards in time, you risk jarring readers from the fictional dream. So make sure that each flashback is absolutely necessary and take care to move readers smoothly from one time to another. If the flashback is a reminiscence, consider what triggers it. "There's a reason a character is recalling something," Amy Hempel says. "Often, students forget to indicate what in the present moment makes the character think back." Avoid extremely long flashbacks that deter the forward movement of the story; avoid flashbacks within flashbacks. Keep the various levels of time straight in your own mind so that you can keep them in good balance on the page.

As you can see, a story's architecture is very much defined by the way its events are framed in time. Time frame is crucial to discovering a story's focus, as well. Most lives, fictional or not, are composites of small moments—but not moments of small import. Find those for your character and you will find your story. For example, listing all the important moments in a story, you may find that a cluster of them take place around a certain time—a day, a few weeks, a holiday season. The arc of such a period—the beginning, middle, and end of it—often reveals the emotional issue at stake for the characters and the natural movement toward resolution. Writing each moment or scene on an index card and then moving the cards around to experiment with sequence can help you see where the ones outside the cluster might fit as flashbacks or reminiscences.

exercise

Unlike real time, story time can be expanded, compressed, and manipulated. To better understand how time works in a story, consider a day in your own life—today, for example. Take a sheet of paper and begin to record everything that has happened to you so far, from the moment your day began to now—this moment, contemplating this page. *Write every single thing.* Write what you thought and remembered as well as what you did.

You woke to an alarm or maybe your mom's voice or maybe a loud noise out in the street. You opened your eyes, stretched, thought about last night's date, dozed off, woke up for real, noticed the copy of *Be Here Now* on your bedside table, thought about Buddhist philosophy, got out of bed, put on your slippers, looked out the window, remembered planting that maple tree with your father and your sister Karen when you were five, brushed your teeth . . .

You'll pretty quickly feel the list becoming unwieldy. You'll think, who cares? But keep going anyway, at least for a page or two. Then look at what you've got and highlight what happened that was significant in some way. Maybe you wrote, "Karen called." If your sister Karen calls a lot just to chitchat, you probably won't highlight that. But if it's the first time she's called you since the two of you had that huge argument six months ago, you would. If a friend asked, "So, what happened today?" would you mention Karen's call? If so, would it be the first thing you mentioned or would you just mention it in passing? Would it be the *only* thing you'd tell? Would you go back in time and describe your relationship with Karen so that your friend would fully understand the importance of the call? Would the tree you planted together or Buddhist philosophy enter the conversation?

You choose the events and ideas to be included in a story in a similar way. You simply can't tell every single thing that happens to your characters within the time frame you've established for the story, so you identify the important ones and tell those, creating transitions to move readers from one to the next.

Transitions glue a story together. They work rather like the board game *Chutes and Ladders,* suddenly, painlessly moving readers to a time, place, or idea. (This just happened to you, reading. Notice how the word *transitions* in the last paragraph slid you right into this new element of fiction.) Rarely discussed in the literature classroom, transitions are often a topic among working writers. "You could spend a whole semester just looking at the beautiful transitions that certain poets and fiction writers made," Stuart Dybek says. "You could argue that the art of the short story is the art of transition."

Transitions that move readers backward and forward in time in a story may be indicated by a change in verb tense or by simply separating the two time periods by white space on the page. Sometimes a transition is made by carrying a word or idea through to the next time period. Good transitions are unobtrusive, often made with a single word or phrase: *now, yesterday, later that afternoon, the summer before I went to college.* They work rather like signs on a highway, directing readers' attention, keeping them on the path through the story.

The transitions in Daly Walker's "I Am the Grass" came late in the process of writing the story. They are simple and purposeful, often incorporating a bit of flavor of the story's setting. For example, "In the morning I walk from my hotel through steamy air, on streets boiling with people, to the hospital."

Creating transitions between larger gaps of time, Joan Silber treats habitual action as a scene. "Every day I walk down the street" becomes a single walk that she describes. Similarly, she gives summary the quality of scene. "You want to have as much sensory detail as you would have in a direct scene," she says. "You want to make it as immediate and particular as scene." Transitions are made from one subject to another, too. These transitions are the trickiest to achieve, and the best of them are magical, both for readers and the writer. Writing "Pet Milk," Stuart Dybek learned about transitions in a visceral way, surprised by his own leap from glancing from a coffee cup in the clutter of a still life he'd created to the el train across the street and how it looked against the sky. Asked how he made the transition in the story from the narrator's memory of his grandmother to the memory of a lost lover, he said, "It actually doesn't occur between the grandmother and the girl, it occurs between the coffee and the sky."

Transitions from one time, place, or idea to another in a story work very much like they do in our real lives. "The events in our lives happen in sequence in time," Eudora Welty observed, "but in their significance to ourselves, they find their own order, a timetable not necessarily—perhaps not possibly—chronological. The time as we know it objectively is often the chronology that stories and novels follow: It is the continuous thread of revelation."

Go back to the list of things that happened today and notice how many times memories and ideas surfaced. What events or thoughts triggered them? Studying the way your mind works, connecting one idea to the next, will help you see how to make strong transitions that mirror human consciousness.

World

"Learning to write is learning to see," says Susan Neville. To practice, she tells her students, "Every time you go for a walk or do anything, count up to a hundred. With each number, look at something different. Look at a hundred things. . . . Don't think about what they are. Just look. . . . If you do that everywhere you go, you've got 'stuff.' And without stuff, you don't have any meaning. You don't have metaphor. There's nowhere for the story to grow."

exercise

Beginning in your own neighborhood, walk with a notebook, jotting down details that you might use to describe the area to someone who's never seen it. You might ask yourself these questions: Are the houses mostly of the same size and architecture, or do they vary? Are they set close together or far apart? Are the yards all perfectly manicured, or are only some of them tended? Are there walls or fences? Gardens, porches? Are front doors open or closed up tight? Are there children, older people, animals present? What are they doing? Are cars parked on the street? What kinds of cars? Are they waxed, or dirty and in disrepair? What can you see glancing into open windows as you pass by?

Go deeper. If it's an ethnic neighborhood, say, Greek, what clues would signal this? Greek restaurants, a Greek food market—or, if the neighborhood is small, a special Greek section in a chain grocery store: big jars of olives, slabs of feta cheese, phyllo dough. There might be a Greek Orthodox church tended by old ladies dressed in black, images of Greece in the windows of businesses, Greek newspapers at the newsstand. You might hear Greek music wafting from an open window, voices speaking Greek on the street. Adapt these questions and techniques to your neighborhood and record as much detail as you can in your notebook.

Writers capture subtle details that carry information about a place. Old-timers in a diner in a small midwestern town are likely to be wearing baseball caps; in a small town out west, they'll have on cowboy hats. A diner in Mississippi will have grits on the breakfast menu; in New Mexico, you'll find a breakfast burrito; in California, something with sprouts.

The setting of a story is more than just colorful description of a place, however. It must evoke a whole world. The particular details used to describe the setting must carry with them a certain set of images and sensibilities that underpin the story. *Brownstone* calls up the image and sensibilities of a city. *Ranch house* calls up middle class suburbia: big yards, burgers on the grill, basketball hoops set above garage doors, bicycles in the driveways. "All art forms boil down to details," Jhumpa Lahiri says. "To me, details aren't ancillary to any given experience. They are the heart of the experience, and what endure most vividly over time."

The details you choose and how you render them must reflect the way the characters perceive the world of the story and their sense of where they fit into it. Setting must do its part in revealing character and moving the story forward, as well. The lyrical way the narrator in Stuart Dybek's "We Didn't" describes the Chicago Gold Coast contributes to readers' understanding of who he is; Lake Michigan provides the body of the drowned woman that sets the story in motion. In a number of Pam Houston's stories, characters navigate treacherous landscapes that mirror their inner lives and trigger action that allows them to confront personal issues.

A story setting may be real, imagined, or somewhere in between. If you choose to set your story in a real place that is utterly familiar to you, stay open to the possibility that during the writing process the place might reinvent itself to better suit the needs of the story; if you choose to set your story in an imaginary place, be sure to construct it so that readers believe it is real.

If you set your story in a real place that is well known, say, New York, make sure that you know more than simply looking at a map can reveal. A wrong detail is like a wrong note in music, jarring and unpleasant, and it brings readers out of the vivid, continuous dream. What do the various districts and neighborhoods of the city look like, and what does it mean to live or work there? How are the people, buildings, institutions, and places of business in Greenwich Village different from those on the Upper East Side or Wall Street, in Soho or Harlem? What bus or subway would you take to go from one district to the next? If you walked, what would you see, hear, and smell along the way? What sensory clues would show the transition between one neighborhood to another?

Dave Eggers took a tape recorder, camera, and notebook along when he climbed Mount Kilimanjaro, thinking it might make a good setting for an adventure story. The world he created in "Up the Mountain Coming Down Slowly" is "a pretty exact description of what it's like to climb the mountain on the Machame route," he says. "I didn't make up anything, in terms of details of the climb." The characters, their interactions with each other and the porters, and the conclusion are fiction. "That's usually how I work," he says. "I get the details of place correct, and then fabricate the rest."

If you want to set a story in a real place that's unfamiliar to you and the kind of onsite research Eggers did is out of the question, read travel books, novels, histories—any book that enriches your visual and intellectual understanding of the place. Look at photographs, watch movies, talk to people who've lived in or traveled to the place you want to write about.

Rosario, the village that provides the setting for many of Luis Urrea's stories, is a real place—and so much a part of his work that he considers the place itself as a kind of character. But in his mind it's mythic, imaginary. "It's just a little smelly Mexican town on the edge of the highway," he says. "There's nothing there." It's the overlay of stories he sees and remembers when he visits that brings the town to life and sets fictional stories in motion in his mind.

Russell Banks says that Catamount, New Hampshire, the imaginary setting for the story cycle in his collection, *Trailerpark,* was pieced together in the geography of his mind from memories of real New Hampshire towns, a kind of collage of his memories and experiences in those towns. Catamount seems "realer" to him than the real towns it is based on. He describes working as being similar to dreaming, when elements of real landscape and architecture blend to bring forth new images and assemble the dream's own vivid, believable world.

Settings can be smaller and more particular than geographical areas, cities, or towns—like schools, race tracks, trains, or archaeological digs. The narrator in Grace Paley's "Faith in a Tree" tells her story sitting up in a tree in her neighborhood park. Tobias Wolff has set a number of stories on military bases, a world he learned to know because he spent four years in the army. Daly Walker, a surgeon, likes to set stories in hospitals and doctors' offices, his "little niche of the world." Carolyn Ferrell often chooses a high school setting for her stories because high school "is a place of great learning where the pupils understand little and the adults understand even less . . . a world within a world, complete with ruling hierarchies, political prisoners, unrequited loves, and basic forms of torture and unfairness."

An era is a kind of setting, too. Creating the world of a story that occurs during the 1960s, World War II, or Elizabethan England presents a particular kind of challenge. Not only do you have to render the place accurately, you have to be accurate about both physical details and the sensibility of the time. Characters in a story set in fifteenth-century Florence can't be modern people dressed in Renaissance garb, but must act, speak, and think in ways that reflect the time and place they live in.

As for a fantasy or science fiction setting, you have to create a whole new world. You can't research it—it doesn't exist. But this doesn't mean you can build it by layering on details at your whim. Whether your world is a fairy glen or distant planet, there must be logic behind its creation. Things can't just happen randomly. They must be explainable and believable, governed by a structure you design. Characters must be believable based on the design of the story's imaginary universe, as well. While their world and the events unfolded in it may be completely imaginary, they must be believable people engaged with issues of the human heart.

Beginning writers are wise to avoid science fiction, fantasy, and stories set in past times and concentrate on the fundamental elements of fiction in stories that happen in places and times that are more easily rendered, preparing themselves for when they are ready to add the dimension these differently imagined worlds bring to their repertoire of skills.

Real or imagined, a story's setting should be an integral part of its overall effect. Don't set a story in a place you cannot imagine. But don't set a story in Vienna just because you visited there and collected lots of great details in your notebook, either. Set it there because Vienna seems to you the best—maybe the *only*—place in which the story could happen. Don't set a story in another era, a fantasy world, or a different galaxy unless the story can't be told any other way.

And By the Way . . .

The Way Writers Talk

When talking about reading and writing stories, English teachers use words and phrases like text and subtext, symbol, style, theme, structure, protagonist, outline, rising and falling action, figurative language, subject matter, sustaining point of view, author's intent. Writers almost always talk in a completely different way. Their subject matter is stuff, flotsam, chunks, slivers, shards, seeds, glimmers, ground, hard-wired obsession. They grope, shift, leap, dream, coalesce, tunnel their way toward a moment of combustion when they begin to sense the bones of a story, see it through some personal lens. They juggle, calibrate, distill, juxtapose, frame, trigger, lumber, weave, fiddle, embroider, bridge, creep, tinker, blast away, string along, thread, accumulate to bring a story into being. They hobble language, pop the point of view, consider angles of vision. They work brick by brick, go steppingstone by steppingstone. They bring to a boil, folding in details, creating byproducts, considering heft and resonance—all the while listening to the tune of dialogue in their heads.

There's no blueprint, they say. You drill for oil, hang ideas on a clothesline, follow a thin wire through the dark, bounce off walls until, suddenly, stories blossom into metaphor like pop-up books. They're like snapping turtles: the words on the page the shell and head above the water, what the author knows beneath in the hearts and guts and beating paddles of the feet. They're tarnish. Perfect, smooth river pebbles. Loose, baggy monsters. Heat and light.

All of which is to say, setting out to write (or read) a story, don't let academic language about stories limit the way you look and talk about it. Don't worry about sounding smart. Learn to think and talk like a craftsman and you will be surprised at the variety of ways stories will reveal themselves.

The Fictive Dream

The novelist John Gardner equated a story that works to a "vivid, continuous dream." Readers slip into it, "forgetting the room [they're] sitting in, forgetting it's lunchtime or time to go to work. [They] recreate, with minor and for the most part unimportant changes, the vivid and continuous dream the writer worked out in his mind (revising and revising until he got it right) and captured in language so that other human beings, whenever they feel like it, may open his book and dream that dream again."

It is an apt metaphor. Waking in the middle of a dream, the dreamer feels disoriented, maybe even angry to have been brought back to the surface. What was moments ago vivid and real has vanished with the realization that it was just a dream. Reading a word or phrase in dialogue that falls flat, a wrong detail of place, a character's inauthentic response brings readers to the surface of the story and makes them remember that the world they have been so immersed in is not real.

Language

If you want to write, chances are you love language. That, of course, is a good thing. But don't be so besotted with words that you forget that their purpose is to serve your story. Don't use a word just because you love it or, even worse, because you think using it makes you seem smart. Use it because it is the absolute best word to convey the meaning and spirit of your ideas.

Use figurative language with the same care. Metaphors and similes should reflect the characters and their circumstances. Used effectively, metaphors and similes reflect the characters and the situation of the story, deepening the effect. Used thoughtlessly, they are detritus readers have to slog through to get to the meat of the story. At worst, they are laughable, absurd.

Show, Don't Tell

This is the most fundamental lesson in writing fiction and, for most, the most difficult to learn. Stories are so often generated from our feelings about people, places, and events that the beginning writer's impulse is to tell readers those feelings. The girl was beautiful. The place was amazing. The event, awesome. In fact, the writer's job is to create the girl, the place, the event on the page in ways that make readers feel what he feels. The writer must trust readers to come to their own conclusions. In a sense, the writer is a detective in reverse, laying down clues for readers who (subconsciously) put them together in their minds until the meaning of the story emerges.

Adjectives are vague and judgmental. A *beautiful* girl may pop up as tall, thin, blond, and blue-eyed in one reader's mind and short, dark, and voluptuous in another's. The writer may judge a place *amazing* or an event *awesome*, while the reader might think it quite ordinary. Adverbs are bland. *He walked slowly* doesn't convey nearly the visual information as *He sauntered.* Or *limped, lumbered, strolled.*

Comb your first draft for adjectives and adverbs, highlight them, and then go back through and "translate" them to strong nouns and verbs. You'll be amazed how this will make your characters come to life and your settings resonate with sights, sounds, and meaning.

Look for places where you can replace summary with scene, where you can show, not tell. Some of what happens in a story may be told, of course. But, almost always, the bulk of a story should be shown in a scene or a series of scenes.

Symbols

Symbols are perhaps the most misunderstood aspect of fiction. They are almost never constructed and set into place by the writer, but grow organically in the process of writing a story. Once there, the writer usually recognizes them and works during revision to bring them more effectively to the page. Sometimes, though, she is quite surprised when professors and critics bring them to her attention.

Theme

Likewise, theme most often reveals itself in process. Often it is not until the first draft of a story is finished that the writer even considers it. Maybe he never does—academically. Usually a writer's understanding of a story's theme is directly connected to discovering what it is about and finding the story's focus. If you look at your story that way, mostly likely theme will take care of itself.

Beginnings, Middles, Ends

The beginning of a traditional, character-driven story has two functions: to capture readers' interest and make them want to go on reading, and to introduce the characters and establish the conflict between them. A good beginning has motion. A strong first sentence is especially important.

Inexperienced writers are tempted to use the beginning to give readers a lot of background information about the characters and the situation, which interferes with the forward motion of the story and makes readers lose interest. It's almost always best just to jump in and tell the story. Don't worry about what readers don't know. If you let them see what the characters see and hear them talking, most likely your readers will figure out all they need to know. A good rule of thumb is: Begin a story as close to the end as possible. Throughout the story, give information only when readers absolutely must have it to understand fully what's happening.

The middle of a story shows how the characters try to deal with the conflict or problem that was introduced in the beginning. It must maintain the tension, the forward movement of the story. To accomplish this, everything in the middle must be related in some way to what the beginning promised.

Near the end of the middle comes the big scene. It is the moment the author has been writing toward, what he really wanted to say all along. It is what the story is *about.* Inexperienced writers tend to underwrite this scene, so take care to render the scene fully. The success of the whole story hinges on it!

Near the end of a story, readers should reach a moment in which they think both "Aha!" and "Of course!" If the author maintains tension throughout the story, readers will be uncertain about what will happen in the end. When they find out what happens, their response will be, "Aha, so that's it." The author earns readers' "Of course!" by preparing them subconsciously for the surprise. Skillfully and subtly the author pulls all the promises he made in the beginning right through to the end, thus making the end at the same time startling and believable.

A story should stop as soon as possible after the "Aha!" moment. Inexperienced writers tend to want to moralize or to explain what happened in case readers didn't get it. Let the story speak for itself.

There are many different kinds of endings. Some are neatly tied up, with every question answered. Some are tricks. Some are open-ended, giving readers some leeway in imagining the outcome. But all good endings have some sense of emotional closure. They never leave readers confused.

Just Do It!

If you've gotten to here, you have a wealth of information about where short stories come from and the countless ways writers bring them to the page. Some writers write the first draft of a story in a kind of white heat, never stopping to consider what they've written until the draft is complete. Others stop and start, rethinking and revising as they go. Part of becoming a writer is discovering what kind of writer you are and using that knowledge to be able to use your writing time most productively. It is also true that each story will demand something different of you, constantly shifting your sense of what stories are and how best to approach them. "Every story teaches me how to write it," Eudora Welty said. "But it doesn't teach me how to write the one that comes after."

"[What students] often don't understand is how long it is from the mess to the story," Elizabeth Tallent says. Generally, writers say that a story takes them several weeks to several months to write. But there's no hard and fast rule about this either. Jamaica Kincaid finished "Girl" in a single sitting. Jill McCorkle had published "Snipes" in a literary magazine and then, several years later, reconsidering it for her collection, *Creatures of Habit*, opened it back up and discovered the story it was meant to be all along. All you can do is keep writing and stay open to possibilities, reminding yourself that, eventually—if you are stubborn enough—the story will come.

Susan Neville describes working through a story like this. "It's as if the character is in a completely dark space and there's a little tiny thread or wire and the character's groping along it somehow—not knowing what the wire is, where it will end, or why he's obsessed with it. There is some desperation. But there's complete and utter faith—it *is* faith—that it's going to lead you someplace. It's going to save the character's life somehow to follow it and yours as you're writing it."

Describing the internal compass that directs him through a story, Dan Chaon says, "In a story, you're in a room and you know that there are four walls. You can guide yourself by knowing that, okay, I've got to touch this wall and then I've got to touch that wall." The walls he's writing within are setting, character, plot, and theme. "I keep balancing those four things until I finally get to the end," he says.

Essentially, do whatever works to get the first draft on the page. *Keep writing.* Sitting and staring at the page, thinking about a story's problems, rarely bears much fruit. So turn to freewriting if you get stuck. Write everything you know about the story; then turn the tables on yourself and write all you can think of that you *don't* know. Write what the main character knows and doesn't know about himself and the situation he's in. Write at the top of a page, "Who are you and what are you doing in my story?" Let the character answer in his own voice. Describe the places in your story. Now describe them from each character's different point of view. Ask, "What if?" Ask it again.

In those moments of despair, when it seems the story will never, ever come, remember Ernest Hemingway's experience: "I would stand and look out over the roofs of Paris and think, 'Do not worry. You have always written before and you will write now. All you have to do is write one true sentence. Write the truest sentence that you know.' So finally I would write one true sentence, and then go on from there."

Of course, you must stop eventually and live your real life. It's what feeds your creative process, after all. In this, Hemingway instructs us, as well. "When I was writing, it was necessary for me to read after I had written. It was necessary to get exercise, to be tired in the body, and it was very good to make love with whom you loved. That was better than anything. But afterwards, when you were empty, it was necessary to read in order not to think or worry about your work until you couldn't do it again. I had learned already never to empty the well of my writing, but always to stop when there was still something there in the deep part of the well, and let it refill at night from the springs that fed it."

Forty Writing Exercises

Here's a roster of writing exercises to help you practice and hone your craft.

1. **Show, don't tell.** "Translate" these generalizations to vignettes that show what they mean. It's a small world. It was a false alarm. We couldn't stop laughing. The game was exciting. It was definitely time to speak up. I'm just not a very good judge of character. I underestimated the number of people who would show up.
2. **Write a scene placing two characters in this very fundamental conflict: One wants something the other does not want to give.** The something may be anything—money, respect, jewelry, sex, information—but be sure to focus on the one desire.
3. **Write a paragraph outlining the conflict between two characters.** Then write the crisis scene for this conflict, a scene in which one of the characters changes his mind because he understands something not understood before. Make sure the internal change is shown through external action.
4. **List four qualities that describe a character, real or imagined.** Then place that character in a scene, writing so that the qualities are conveyed through significant action and detail. Use no generalizations; make no judgments. No word on your list should appear in the written scene.
5. **Imagine a character you really don't like.** Then give her one mental habit, desire, fear, love, or longing that you have. Write a scene in which that trait plays out in a way that readers feels sympathetic toward her.
6. **Go to any public place—a mall, park, museum, ball game, church, school—and pay attention to human behavior.** Jot down what people do and say to make you

conclude how they feel. Pay attention to what they're wearing, their body language, how they interact (or avoid), how they move. Notice unusual mannerisms. Choose five details you collected and write about what each one seems to imply—and why. For example: What gestures imply impatience, anger, self-consciousness, love, anger, joy? In what ways are people's physical manifestations of emotions universal? In what ways are they idiosyncratic?

7. **Write a scene from the point of view of a peripheral narrator** who is not at all involved in the events he describes, but who is placed in a position from which he can observe them. Nevertheless, make the observing narrator the character who is moved by the action.
8. **Write about a character who begins at a standstill,** works up to great speed (in a vehicle or on foot, pursued or pursuing, competing in a sport—or let the rush be purely emotional) and then comes to a half again, either gradually or abruptly. Let the prose rhythm reflect the changes.
9. **Write about a boring situation.** Convince readers that the situation is boring and that your characters are bored or boring—or both. Use no generalizations, no judgments, no verbs in the passive voice. The trick is, *readers* can't be bored by this boring situation.
10. **Pick two contrasting or contradictory qualities in your own personality.** Create a character that embodies each, and set them in conflict with each other. Since you are not writing about yourself, but aiming at heightening and dramatizing these qualities, make each character radically different from yourself in at least one of these fundamental aspects: age, gender, nationality, or class.
11. **Describe your character's purse, backpack, or briefcase.** Make a list of everything inside it. Give the list to a friend or fellow student and ask her to tell you what she knows about the character based on these objects.
12. **Collect colorful words and phrases that people use in conversation.** Use them as clues to create the kinds of characters who could believably use them.
13. **Tape a dinner conversation at your house.** Transcribe the tape and *see* what it looks like on the page. Now write the dinner scene, removing parts of the dialogue that are repetitive or boring and adding anything you think will make it more interesting or more clear.
14. **Spend time with a dog, cat, horse, bird, or any other nonhuman creature.** Feel the fur or feathers and let yourself move into creature consciousness. Write a scene from this point of view.
15. **Choose a family photograph.** Consider each person in it and how his or her feelings about the occasion for the photograph might differ. Then write the story of the photograph from each person's point of view.
16. **Choose a fairy tale you love.** Tell it from a different point of view, for example, from that of the witch or parents in "Hansel and Gretel" or one of the dwarves in "Snow White."
17. **Write a scene from the point of view of a five-year-old child entering a park on one of the first spring days of the year.** Then write a scene from the point of view of a seventy-year-old widower entering the same park on the same day.
18. **Find a newspaper article that interests you.** Make a list of the "characters" in it and define the conflict between or among them. Using the facts in the article, write the beginning of a short story from the point of view of one of them. Then write a second beginning from another character's point of view. How do they differ?

19. **Listen to people talking in places like grocery stores, restaurants, basketball games, and shopping malls.** Build a story based on a bit of dialogue that intrigued you.
20. **Analyze the interests, speech rhythms, and word usage of a family member, teacher, or friend.** Write a speech in that person's voice. See if others can guess who it is.
21. **Present any two characters in conversation at an important moment in their lives, one that you might like to explore later in a story.** Try to establish two distinct voices. Sketch the setting, show them in action, and unobtrusively work in information about their appearance, expressions, feelings, and their history together.
22. **Imagine two people who are romantically involved with the same person** (they know it, but they don't like it!), who (a) get on an elevator going up to the 50th floor, (b) end up sitting next to each other on a plane, or (c) end up standing next to each other in a very long checkout line at the supermarket. Write the scene without allowing them to make any direct reference to the person with whom each is involved. What do they say to each other? What *don't* they say to each other? What is their body language like?
23. **Using third person, spend ten minutes writing a dialogue in which a character in the story you are working on gets into an argument with someone, anyone.** The argument should deal with something significant to the character. Be sure to locate the argument in time and space. Next, still in third person, explain how your character feels about the argument. What does he think about what happened? Next, pull back. Tell readers something about the character that he cannot admit out loud or that he does not recognize about himself. Next, write about what your character's face looks like during the argument. Finally, get behind your character's eyes and describe what he sees during the argument. Now reread the draft of your story. Can you use any of what you wrote in it? Look for spots to refocus and move readers through your story differently.
24. **Think about a place that has the mystery and beauty of a poem to you.** Close your eyes, sit for a few moments, and take yourself on an imaginary journey through that place. Then write.
25. **Think of a moment when you achieved or received a spiritual insight or epiphany.** Describe the place where that insight or epiphany occurred.
26. **Make a short list of the places that have mattered to you, from your earliest memories to now.** Write about them.
27. **Think of a setting that has been important to you.** This might be a room, a house, a landscape. Then think of a smell, taste, sound, texture, and visual image that summon up this setting for you.
28. **Write a scene with two characters in conflict over the setting.** One wants to go; one wants to stay. The more interesting the setting you choose, the more interesting the conflict will be.
29. **Think about a time when you felt deeply moved by contact with water—stream, river, ocean, lake, pond, puddle, rain.** Describe that encounter. Do the same for a time when you were deeply moved by contact with wind, earth, or fire.
30. **Remember objects you have collected from nature—shells, rocks, seeds, butterflies, autumn leaves.** Describe what moved you to do the collecting.
31. **Draw a map of your "home place," the natural and human surroundings that are saturated with memory, history, and meaning for you.** Is it a neighborhood,

town, city, watershed, bioregion? Write about the landmarks by which you navigate your home place.

32. **Study highway maps to find the name of a town or geographical feature that is intriguing to you.** Monkey's Eyebrow, Kentucky, perhaps. Or Yellow Jacket, Colorado. Maybe The Book Cliffs in Utah. Imagine what kinds of people might live there if the name of the place was pressed to its logical consequence. For example, the people in Yellow Jacket might be hostile, ill-tempered, buzzing with energy, addicted to sweets. Write about the place. What you write may be a description, a history, a dramatic monologue from one of the citizens, the story of a stranger's visit there— anything that conveys the essence of the place, its strangeness, its wonder.
33. **Identify the place you hate most in your life.** Write a scene set in that place from the point of view of a person who absolutely loves it.
34. **Analyze the structure of a story you admire.** Write a story of your own, mirroring that structure.
35. **Choose any simple event.** Describe it using the same characters and elements of setting in five completely different ways.
36. **Consider the way a story you admire is told.** Think of all the *other* ways it might have been told. Then rewrite the story using the one you like best.
37. **Make a list of every single thing you did and said from the moment you left your front door this morning until right now, the moment you are reading these directions.** The list will be long! Now write a paragraph describing that period of time, choosing only the most telling details and sequencing them effectively so that readers will feel they are experiencing it.
38. **Write the plot line of some experience in your life.** For example, a family vacation, Christmas Eve, a falling out with a friend, a grandparent's death. Consider character, setting, conflict, resolution.
39. **Summarize in a few sentences the plots of several stories you admire.** Try to figure out what it is about the plot of each one that makes it memorable.
40. **Think of a time in your life when you were made a fool of.** First, write a few paragraphs that relive the moment you became convinced you'd been made a fool of. Then go back in time and show the history of the way your perception developed. Be specific. You may want to use some short scenes or dwell for a long paragraph or two on one critical moment, combining those with summaries. You may want to stop and comment—say something that you, earlier, might not have been able to say about yourself. Whatever means you use, render this background information vividly, specifically, using a variety of elements of fiction in the process: scene, dialogue, description, narrative, flashback. If you don't want to use a personal experience, make up a character who's been made a fool of and follow the same pattern of revealing how it happened and why.

chapter 4

Revision

Revision is not simply recopying what you've written so that it looks neater! It is assessing your first draft in a variety of ways and then improving it. Here are some things to consider during the revision process.

- ✓ **Details:** Are your details vivid and specific? Look for places where your language is general and improve it by making it as specific as you can. Try to make your words create pictures or images in readers' minds.
- ✓ **Adverbs and adjectives:** These parts of speech trick us! We think of them as descriptive, yet they are most often ineffective in creating specific images. Search out *-ly* words and eliminate them wherever possible. If you have strong visual details, you won't need adverbs. Next, look at your adjectives and keep only those that help create vivid images. Avoid words such as *nice, pretty, good, bad, ugly.* They are too vague and allow readers to make generalizations based on their own ideas of what these words mean.
- ✓ **Verbs:** Have you used strong, descriptive verbs? A quick, easy way to improve your writing dramatically is to go through your first draft and circle all forms of the verb *to be* (*am, is, are, was, were*). Replace these with strong, active verbs. Choose your verbs carefully. They can carry a lot of meaning. For example, there are a multitude of ways of saying *walk.* He strode, sauntered, shuffled, ambled—these are just a few. Each verb gives a completely different visual image. Make sure the verbs you've used give the visual effect you want.
- ✓ **Clarity and coherence:** Are there places in your story where readers might be confused? Does each sentence logically follow the one before it? Do your sentences actually mean what you want them to mean? Are you certain that every word you've used means exactly what you think it means? Have you used the best possible word in every case? Do you make smooth transitions from one idea or action to the next?

✓ **Grammar and flow:** Awkwardness in writing is very often caused by grammatical errors. Are there run-ons that need to be broken up into several sentences? Are your sentence fragments purposeful, used to create a certain effect, or are they unintentional? Are there misplaced modifiers? Awkwardness is also caused by problems with flow. Is each sentence constructed so that it flows smoothly? Are any sentences carrying too many ideas? Reading your work aloud will help you easily spot awkward places and grammatical errors.

✓ **Dialogue:** Are there places where you could add or improve dialogue?

✓ **Unnecessary words, phrases, sentences, and sections:** Because we allow ourselves to write a first draft quickly, we often include redundancies. Cutting unnecessary words, phrases, sentences, and sections is an important part of the revision process.

✓ **Punctuation and spelling:** Any well-written paper is correctly punctuated in its final form. All words are spelled correctly.

✓ **Organization:** Make an outline of what you have so far, to help you decide whether your ideas proceed in a logical manner and whether some sections might be combined.

Complete the exercise below to practice the revision process.

exercise

Revise one of the fifty-five-word story drafts below, considering the questions that follow the drafts. Don't look for the correct answers at the back of the book when you've finished because there are none—which may be the most important thing you need to know about revision, after all. You tinker until you come upon something that works. The solution you come to will have the feel of inevitability, but seasoned writers know that the solutions they come to in revision might have gone any number of ways.

Last Words

"What is your defense?" the king asked, eyes glaring at the slave like two hot coals. "I was hungry. I had to eat!" he replied icily. "A man who eats his horse is no man at all!" "And a king who starves his people is not worth living under." How noble these, his last words.

Rejected

"Are you free after school today?" I asked. "Why?" He leaned against his locker. "I wondered if we could do something together," I said. "I can't. I'm going to my little brother's soccer game." How sweet, I thought. "Really?!" He laughed at me and started to walk away, glancing back to reply, "Nope. I lied."

Hindsight

"What's with you?" he retorted, sipping from his bottle. "One drink won't affect your driving. You're just being pussy about it." I didn't know why I had come to the party in the first place, but I'd do it if it would shut him up, I thought. Things sure look different from a morgue drawer.

- ✓ **"Aboutness":** What is the story about? Even as small a story as this must be *about* something to work. Does every single thing in the story contribute in some way to the story's "aboutness"?
- ✓ **Setting:** Does the story have one? What is it? How do readers know this is the setting? How could the setting be stronger?
- ✓ **Character:** Obviously, there are people in the story. But how does the story let readers know exactly who the characters are? What details and dialogue convey information about each character's uniqueness in the universe and his role in the story?
- ✓ **Conflict:** What happens in the story? What tensions are set it in motion, pique readers' interest and play out in the resolution?
- ✓ **Resolution:** What shifts in the story? What happens (or doesn't happen) that brings insight and leaves readers feeling satisfied? Is the resolution clear or are readers left confused? To answer these questions, you need to know what the little story is *about.*
- ✓ **Language:** Are there unnecessary repetitions? Are there adverbs that could be replaced with strong, visual verbs? Are sentence fragments used intentionally, for effect, or are they used only because you couldn't afford the words to make a complete sentence? Is every single word the right word? Could a different word deepen the effect of the story? Is the language perfectly clear? Is there anything that might be interpreted in a different way than you intended?

You might get a first draft of your own, longer short story down in a few hours, or it might take weeks—or more. As soon as it's completed—perhaps even before—the process of revision begins. Susan Neville works straight through the first draft of a story, often coming to the end with the realization that she's gone too far. Her most common revision is to cut off the last two pages and experiment until she writes a last line that feels right. Then she tweaks "until the story starts to shimmer."

Tobias Wolff revises as he goes. "By the time I get to the end of a story, I've rewritten every sentence," he explains. "Very little goes untouched. I rewrite every day; I rewrite when I finish the story."

Different writers face different tasks in revision. Charles Baxter revises with an eye toward extraneous details that might be removed to keep the story moving. Elizabeth Tallent most often revises toward expanding, opening up the story to new possibilities that bring it closer to the vision and sense of shape that inspired it. Pam Houston's revision is all about order. "I move chunks around for hours," she says. "I spend more time moving than I spend writing." Dorothy Allison reads her story drafts aloud, listening for problems in voice and diction.

Grace Paley says, "I go through a story for lies. I might discover the lie of trying to show off. Sometimes they're lies of character. Sometimes they're lies of writing the most beautiful sentence in the world that has nothing to do with the story."

Ultimately, each writer comes to his own way of revision and is prepared to adapt it to accommodate the special challenges of every story. Facing the revision of your story, it helps to revisit the idea of translation to remind yourself of why you need to revise and why you are not yet the best critic of your own story.

Words are a second language to your heart. Regardless of what draft of a story you're working on, there will be a gap between the story inside you and the words that you've managed to get down on the page. Revision is necessary to narrow that gap, so that the finished story is as close as possible to the one you imagined. But because the story you're trying to write is so clear and vivid inside your head, it is likely to be difficult for you to see *only* the words on the page and to be able to assess the nature of the gap between the two. It follows, then, that good criticism is a gift. A reader who knows how fiction works and who understands and respects your intent is invaluable for the way she raises questions and makes observations that help you see what's actually there, on the page. When you know what's there—and not there—you can begin to clarify and deepen the effect of your story.

In time, like Russell Banks, you may develop an objective inner voice that will give you reliable direction in the revision process and make you less dependent on the observation and advice of outside readers. "The best way to do that [when you're young] is to show your work to someone else and check [what they say] against your own perception," he says. In the end, "you have to face it honestly—and alone." But you have to get the tools that will allow that.

In receiving critique of your work and offering critique of others' work, it is crucial to recognize the difference between an objective and subjective reaction. An objective reaction is based on issues of craft and on an understanding of and respect for the author's intent; a subjective one is based on personal issues, interests, and beliefs. Effective criticism avoids making judgments about a piece of writing. Instead, it asks, "Does this piece of writing work?"

Check for Clear Focus

Stories by beginning writers often lack focus. Sometimes they take a turn and become completely different from what the writers originally imagined they would be. Sometimes they go off on tangents, muddying the story's intent. They may juggle too many issues, creating confusion. A good critic can help you decide whether it would be wiser to "re-vision" the story to incorporate a twist or tangent or to abandon it and get the story back on track. He can often point out which supporting ideas underpin the focus and which obscure it.

Focusing a story draft is best accomplished by first asking, "What is this story *about*?" It is entirely possible, even likely, that you won't have known the answer to this question when you began the story and still may not know it on completing the first draft. The observations of a good reader may be necessary to help you see what the story is about or, perhaps, what it "wants" to be about.

When you can answer this question in a sentence that begins, "This story is about what happens when . . . ," it's easier to identify what doesn't belong in the story—characters, scenes, details, plot twists. You see what's missing, too, and can begin to consider how the addition of new scenes or the fine-tuning of what's already there can enhance and deepen the story's focus.

Clarifying the story's theme or "aboutness" also helps you know whether the scenes you've written are in the best possible order, and if the end of the story makes sense based on what the beginning promised and set into play.

Though it is rarely even possible at the outset to make an outline that will direct you efficiently through a story from beginning to end, it may be very helpful to make one in the early stages of revision. Even if a story's focus is clear in the first draft, its various elements may not yet be in the right order or be fully realized. The effect can be chaotic. Making an informal outline may help you work out the story's shape and clarify how it should move. You may achieve the same results, or better, by cutting up a copy of your story draft and experimenting with order by moving parts of the story around on a large flat surface. The cut and paste functions on your computer will also allow you to explore a variety of ways to put the story together.

Check for Correct Sequencing

To help you see if the movement of a story makes sense, try listing what happens chronologically and consider whether one part of the story leads to the next in a logical fashion. To see if the emotional movement of the story is valid, jot down what emotions come into play in each scene and consider whether they match what's actually happening in the scene. Look, too, to see if the progression of conflict, emotion, and resolution makes sense, based on what information you've given readers.

Check Individual Sections

Once you decide on a story's focus and the sequence of scenes, your work changes. Now you must look at individual sections of the story.

- ✓ Is there a good, strong beginning, one that compels readers to continue and at the same time properly prepares them for what the story will be about?
- ✓ Is each scene fully rendered? Do readers *see and hear* the story happening through your use of detail and dialogue?
- ✓ Are there good, logical transitions from one scene to the next? Is the ending earned?

During the focusing stage, you most often have to take things out of a story; in the later stages, you'll probably have to expand your story to make it come alive. You may need to add sensory details to enhance the story's setting and atmosphere, or flesh out your characters with description, dialogue or reflection. You will look for places where you can work in the necessary exposition.

Polishing

The last task of revision is to polish your prose, sentence by sentence. The importance clarity plays in your ability to get the best possible story on the page cannot be stressed too much. Again, you ask a series of questions.

- ✓ Does this sentence really say what you mean?
- ✓ Does this word convey the tone and shade of meaning you intend?
- ✓ Do the similes and metaphors reflect the world of the story and the characters' experiences?

Grammar, punctuation, and style come into play here, but not in the abstract way you've probably considered them in the past. A good critic might observe, there are too many ideas in this sentence; break it up. This sentence is awkward, fix it. This fragment is not effective here. Get rid of this adverb and get a verb that *shows* what it says. This metaphor does not work because . . .

If you're in love with language and pride yourself on being a creative person, the criticism of your prose style is often the hardest criticism to accept. But correct grammar, punctuation, and spelling are a crucial part of the creative process, as worthy of your attention as a perfect metaphor. "Clarity *is* beauty," Leo Tolstoy once said. The determination to polish a manuscript toward perfection is the mark of a serious writer. It is the final measure of commitment to your vision.

Revision Checklist

The following checklist may be used by a writer revising her own story, in a workshop setting to help students offer useful critique to their peers, or in a literature class as a guide to discussing a published story.

✓ **Theme or "aboutness":** State what you think the story is about, completing the sentence "This story is about what happens when . . ." Is the story's aboutness "shown," not told?

✓ **Plot:** What moving action brought the characters to the point at which the story begins? In a few sentences, say what happens in the story. Does the plot reflect the story's "aboutness"?

✓ **Tension:** Where does the tension of the story lie? What or who causes tension? Are there several kinds of tension at work? What are they? Are there any tensions left unresolved?

✓ **Time:** How much time is covered by the "now" of the story? If there are multiple levels of time in the story, do you move readers through them smoothly? Why did you choose to treat time the way you did? Is there a better way?

✓ **Setting:** Is the setting rendered in strong sensory detail? Do the kind of details chosen create the desired atmosphere? Are they authentic and believable? Does setting and the author's treatment of it enhance readers' understanding of what the story is about?

✓ **Characters:** What complexities or paradoxes do they reflect? What details of their lives move you? Identify details, actions, or speeches that could belong only to that particular character, and explain why. Is there anything about the characters that doesn't ring true? Why? Is there some sense, perhaps implied, of aspects of the characters' lives that triggered the moving action of the story?

✓ **Dialogue:** Identify dialogue in which the characters' voices seem especially in tune with who they are. Then identify dialogue that doesn't ring true. Identify dialogue that works on multiple levels (to characterize, inform, move the plot.) Is there too much dialogue? Too little?

✓ **Voice:** Do the words and sentence rhythms used to tell the story suit the time, place, and characters involved? Is the tone of the story consistent throughout?

✓ **Point of view:** Who is the point-of-view character? What do you learn about this situation that you couldn't have learned if it had been written in another point of view? How does that relate to what you think the story is about? Is the point of view consistent throughout? If you use multiple points of view, do you move readers from one to another smoothly? Is there good balance in the different points of view? Is one more or less interesting than another? Consider other points of view from which the story might be told.

✓ **Scene:** List the scenes and consider how each one moves the plot and provides characterization. Is each scene fully rendered, with sensory detail? Are there enough scenes? Are there parts of the story that might be better rendered in scene?

✓ **Sequence of story elements:** What is the logic behind the order in which you present the events of the story to readers? Is there another sequence you might consider?

✓ **Emotional outline:** Identify the emotional states of the characters as they move through the story. Are they in synch with the movement of the plot?

✓ **Transitions:** Where are they? How do they work to make the story a vivid and continuous dream? Are there places that need stronger transitions?

✓ **The first sentence:** How does it prepare readers for what the story will be about? Does it set tone? Is there anything about it that will pique readers' interest and make them want to read on? How does it relate to the last sentence of the story?

✓ **The beginning in general:** What evidence of the "aboutness" of the story is found here? What promises does it make to readers?

✓ **The end:** In what way does the story come full circle? What elements of the beginning are present, and how, specifically, do they fulfill your promise to readers? Is the end satisfying? If so, why? If not, why?

✓ **Clarity of the prose:** Do the sentences actually say what you mean? Are there awkward sentences that you could improve? Do the words and rhythms of the prose underpin the story's meaning?

✓ **Title:** Why is—or isn't—it appropriate? How could it better reflect what the story is about?

When you've addressed every question and made all the changes you could think of to make, put the manuscript away. Let some time pass—the longer the better—and then take it out and consider all those questions again. Be patient. Don't let go of your story until you know it is as close as it can possibly be to the perfect story you see and sense inside your head.

chapter 5

Okay, It's Finished. Now What?

Dave Eggers says, "Publish as often as you can, anywhere you can. Don't be snobby, don't wait ten years holding your breath for *The Paris Review* or *The New Yorker* to take your story; get your work out there." He also says, "Be able to take any criticism. Ask for the most brutal criticism you can get." Taking the leap into the world of publishing, you would be wise to keep both bits of advice in mind.

For a student writer to submit a story to *The New Yorker* would be akin to a student actor auditioning for a Broadway play or a student vocalist auditioning for the Metropolitan Opera. They are almost certain to be disappointed—perhaps fatally—by the rejection they will almost certainly experience. So, yes! Get your work out there. But be realistic in your first efforts to find its best audience.

Traditional Publishing

Most universities' English departments publish literary magazines to showcase the best work of their undergraduate students. With the help of faculty sponsors, student editors set standards for submission and then select and edit the work for publication. These small magazines provide the first audience for many aspiring writers and help create a literary community on campus. Consider volunteering to help with your school's literary publication, where you will learn and practice editing skills that will benefit your own work and become a part of the literary community on your campus.

At the graduate level, students are usually ready to send their work out into the world of the "small magazine." There are hundreds of these literary magazines, from those stapled together in someone's kitchen, a labor of love, to beautifully produced, prestigious publications such as *Glimmer Train, Zoetrope*, and *Prairie Schooner.* The most accomplished short story writers publish in the best of these magazines; in fact, in most story collections you'll find a page of acknowledgments to the magazines in which the stories were first published. You won't get rich publishing in any of them. Even the best literary magazines rarely pay more than $100 for a story; most offer no more than several copies of the issue in which a writer's story appears. Nonetheless, placing your work in these magazines is worth the effort. Serious readers and writers will be your audience—and editors read the good ones regularly, hoping to discover wonderful writers to publish.

Editors also eagerly read *Best New American Voices,* an annual publication that showcases the most accomplished short stories written by full-time graduate students in American MA and MFA programs. Creative writing professors are invited to submit two stories to this anthology, which is edited by a different writer each year. Past editors include Sherman Alexie, Charles Baxter, Francine Prose, and Tobias Wolff.

Regardless of whether your work is published in *Best New American Voices,* the anthology is worth reading as way of assessing the short story market. Other anthologies that are invaluable to the aspiring writer include *The Pushcart Prize: Best of the Small Presses, The Best American Short Stories,* and *O'Henry Prize Stories.*

Most university libraries and some English departments subscribe to a selection of literary magazines and purchase a selection of anthologies every year, so do your research. Read! Pay attention to what kind of work each magazine publishes and be realistic about whether your work (1) seems compatible with the subject matter and style of the stories in them and (2) compares favorably in terms of craft.

Augment your research with publications such as the annual *Writers' Market, The Writer's Handbook,* and the *International Directory of Little Magazines and Small Presses.* These publications provide information about a variety of kinds of magazines, including what kind of stories they do and don't like to publish, past contributors, and submission guidelines. Periodicals such as *The Writer* and *Poets and Writers* offer general information about working with editors as well as suggestions for where to submit your work.

Many magazines have websites where a writer can go for information about submissions. Generally, though, magazines want to see just one story at a time. Your work should be presented professionally: double-spaced, 1″ margins, your name in the header on each page. A simple cover letter is best, introducing yourself and your work in no more than a half-page. Include publications, if you have them, and inform the editor if you intend to submit the story to more than one magazine at once. Avoid cute or boastful letters! Editors do not find them in the least amusing or impressive. Of course, always include a self-addressed-stamped envelope (SASE). To keep postage costs down, some writers ask the editor to recycle the manuscript and include a stamped postcard for reply. Increasingly, magazines are accepting e-mail submissions—another great way to get out from under the cost of submitting your stories. Go to a magazine's website for information on how to submit your work this way.

Keep track of your work. Establish a notebook or make a spreadsheet on your computer so you'll know where you sent a story, when you sent it, and what response you received.

Publishing on the Web

Increasingly, the Web offers publication opportunities for writers at all levels. Cyberspace is cheap. It's not limited by the space and time constraints of paper publications. So webzines can publish more writers, publish more frequently, and create archives to make writers' work available and easily accessible—forever.

As with conventional literary magazines, it's important to examine online publications to decide if your work is likely to be a good fit before submitting to them. Also, pay close attention to submission guidelines. For example, many publications do not accept e-mail attachments, so you must submit your text in the body of an e-mail message. If you use a lot of italics or line breaks, you may be required to provide editors with information about how you want your work formatted.

A few websites worth exploring:

- **www.writingworld.com/rights/erights.shtml** Electronic rights to written material differ from publication rights in printed literary magazines. This website offers an excellent discussion of this very complex topic.
- **www.all-story.com** This innovative webzine, founded by movie director Francis Ford Coppola, is dedicated to "supporting the brightest young voices in fiction." The website features a virtual studio where you can submit your stories, participate in a virtual workshop, and have your story considered for publication by the Zoetrope editors. Workshop membership is free.
- **www.clmp.org** Council of Literary Magazines and Presses website. Everything you ever wanted to know about small presses and literary magazines.
- **www.loft.org** Site of the prestigious Loft Literary Center, based in Minneapolis.
- **www.pen.org** Pen International. A nonprofit literary organization defending the freedom of writers all over the world.
- **www.pw.org** The website of Poets & Writers Inc., the nation's largest nonprofit literary organization.
- **www.webdelsol.com** A massive portal site with literary links to national and international print and online publications.

Remember!

You'll be rejected, probably many times. But if you're lucky, now and then you'll get a personal response from an editor who may give you some useful feedback about your story or simply a word of encouragement. Pay attention when that happens. It means the editor recognizes you as a serious writer and your story as one with potential.

Remember, too, that concentrating on publication takes time away from writing. If you use your best time becoming the best writer you can be, publication will almost surely follow.

part two

Stories and Conversations

Writers love to talk about writing! Each has his or her own writing community, which may be as small as one like-minded fellow writer, or large and far flung, including writers kept in touch with over coffee, by mail and e-mail, by phone. Writers talk about stories and how stories are made. They help one another solve problems in their work.

The student writer's community is usually limited to the classroom, where she learns to think and talk about writing by way of a good writing instructor and, with luck, a dozen or so classmates who look critically at one another's work and offer useful insights. Class members read and talk about stories by professional writers, too—but only very rarely, perhaps at a reading or book signing, do they have the opportunity to hear writers talk about the process by which those stories were made.

This section of *Story Matters* provides you with a variety of well-written, readable stories from which to learn. Best of all, it provides mentors in the voices of twenty-one successful short story authors who speak articulately and with great passion about their creative lives—a kind of writing community on the page.

The authors of this book prepared extensively for each of these conversations, reading the body of each writer's work in the short story and formulating very specific questions about their creative processes; then the authors talked with writers in cafés and hotel rooms, on university campuses, and in writers' living rooms or sitting at their kitchen tables—from Indiana and New Hampshire, to Boston, Chicago, San Francisco, and Cleveland, to a very snowy mountaintop in Vermont.

If only there had been room in the book for more of them! The vast number of wonderful writers working today made it difficult to choose twenty-one. In deciding, the authors considered writers whose stories they loved and wanted, themselves, to know more about; writers whose stories creative writing teachers love to teach; and—a crucial element—writers who were willing to take the time for an in-depth interview about their work.

You may not find your favorite writer included here, but it is a sure bet that at least one writer in *Story Matters* will seem to be speaking just to you. Listen! Then go back to those favorite stories and use your new insights to consider how the stories are made. Write or e-mail the writer you admire. If your questions and observations reflect an in-depth reading of the work, you might just receive an answer!

....

Dorothy Allison

Dorothy Allison (b. 1949) is the author of a collection of short stories, two novels, a collection of essays, and a memoir. She was born in Greenville, South Carolina, and was educated at Florida Presbyterian College and the New School for Social Research. Her honors include Lamda Literary Awards for Best Small Press Book and Best Lesbian Book, and a nomination for the National Book Award. Allison is a popular workshop teacher and lecturer. She lives in Guerneyville, California.

For Further Reading:
Trash (1988), *Bastard Out of Carolina* (1992), *Skin: Talking about Sex, Class, and Literature* (1993), *Two or Three Things I Know for Sure* (1996), *Cave Dweller* (1998).

River of Names

At a picnic at my aunt's farm, the only time the whole family ever gathered, my sister Billie and I chased chickens into the barn. Billie ran right through the open doors and out again, but I stopped, caught by a shadow moving over me. My cousin, Tommy, eight years old as I was, swung in the sunlight with his face as black as his shoes—the rope around his neck pulled up into the sunlit heights of the barn, fascinating, horrible. Wasn't he running ahead of us? Someone came up behind me. Someone began to scream. My mama took my head in her hands and turned my eyes away.

Jesse and I have been lovers for a year now. She tells me stories about her childhood, about her father going off each day to the university, her mother who made all her dresses, her grandmother who always smelled of dill bread and vanilla. I listen with my mouth open, not believing but wanting, aching for the fairy tale she thinks is everyone's life.

"What did your grandmother smell like?"

I lie to her the way I always do, a lie stolen from a book. "Like lavender," stomach churning over the memory of sour sweat and snuff.

I realize I do not really know what lavender smells like, and I am for a moment afraid she will ask something else, some question that will betray me. But Jesse slides over to hug me, to press her face against my ear, to whisper, "How wonderful to be part of such a large family."

I hug her back and close my eyes. I cannot say a word.

I was born between the older cousins and the younger, born in a pause of babies and therefore outside, always watching. Once, way before Tommy died, I was pushed out on the steps while everyone stood listening to my Cousin Barbara. Her screams went up and down in the back of the house. Cousin Cora brought buckets of bloody rags out to be burned. The other cousins all ran off to catch the sparks or poke the fire with dogwood sticks. I waited on the porch making up words to the shouts around me. I did not understand what was happening. Some of the older cousins obviously did, their strange expressions broken by stranger laughs. I had seen them helping her up the stairs while the thick blood ran down her legs. After a while the blood on the rags was thin, watery, almost pink. Cora threw them on the fire and stood motionless in the stinking smoke.

Randall went by and said there'd be a baby, a hatched egg to throw out with the rags, but there wasn't. I watched to see and there wasn't; nothing but the blood, thinning out desperately while the house slowed down and grew quiet, hours of cries growing soft and low, moaning under the smoke. My Aunt Raylene came out on the porch and almost fell on me, not seeing me, not seeing anything at all. She beat on the post until there were knuckle-sized dents in the peeling paint, beat on that post like it could feel, cursing it and herself and every child in the yard, singing up and down, "Goddamn, goddamn, that girl . . . no sense . . . goddamn!"

I've these pictures my mama gave me—stained sepia prints of bare dirt yards, plank porches, and step after step of children—cousins, uncles, aunts; mysteries. The mystery is how many no one remembers. I show them to Jesse, not saying who they are, and when she laughs at the broken teeth, torn overalls, the dirt, I set my teeth at what I do not want to remember and cannot forget.

We were so many we were without number and, like tadpoles, if there was one less from time to time, who counted? My maternal great-grandmother had eleven daughters, seven sons; my grandmother, six sons, five daughters. Each one made at least six. Some made nine. Six times six, eleven times nine. They went on like multiplication tables. They died and were not missed. I come of an enormous family and I cannot tell half their stories. Somehow it was always made to seem they killed themselves: car wrecks, shotguns, dusty ropes, screaming, falling out of windows, things inside them. I am the point of a pyramid, sliding back under the weight of the ones who came after, and it does not matter that I am the lesbian, the one who will not have children.

I tell the stories and it comes out funny. I drink bourbon and make myself drawl, tell all those old funny stories. Someone always seems to ask me, which one was that? I show the pictures and she says, "Wasn't she the one in the story about the bridge?" I put the pictures away, drink more, and someone always finds them, then says, "Goddamn! How many of you were there anyway?"

I don't answer.

Jesse used to say, "You've got such a fascination with violence. You've got so many terrible stories."

She said it with her smooth mouth, that chin nobody ever slapped, and I love that chin, but when Jesse spoke then, my hands shook and I wanted nothing so much as to tell her terrible stories.

So I made a list. I told her: that one went insane—got her little brother with a tire iron; the three of them slit their arms, not the wrists but the bigger veins up near the elbow; she, now *she* strangled the boy she was sleeping with and got sent away; that one drank lye and died laughing soundlessly. In one year I lost eight cousins. It was the year everybody ran away. Four disappeared and were never found. One fell in the river and was drowned. One was run down hitchhiking north. One was shot running through the woods, while Grace, the last one, tried to walk from Greenville to Greer for some reason nobody knew. She fell off the overpass a mile down from the Sears, Roebuck warehouse and lay there for hunger and heat and dying.

Later, sleeping, but not sleeping, I found that my hands were up under Jesse's chin. I rolled away, but I didn't cry. I almost never let myself cry.

Almost always, we were raped, my cousins and I. That was some kind of joke, too.
What's a South Carolina virgin?
'At's a ten-year-old can run fast.

It wasn't funny for me in my mama's bed with my stepfather, not for my cousin, Billie, in the attic with my uncle, nor for Lucille in the woods with another cousin, for Danny with four strangers in a parking lot, or for Pammie who made the papers. Cora read it out loud: "Repeatedly by persons unknown." They stayed unknown since Pammie never spoke again. Perforations, lacerations, contusions, and bruises. I heard all the words, big words, little words, words too terrible to understand. *DEAD BY AN ACT OF MAN.* With the prick still in them, the broom handle, the tree branch, the grease gun . . . objects, things not to be believed . . . whiskey bottles, can openers, grass shears, glass, metal, vegetables . . . not to be believed, not to be believed.

Jesse says, "You've got a gift for words."

"Don't talk," I beg her, "don't talk." And this once, she just holds me, blessedly silent.

I dig out the pictures, stare into the faces. Which one was I? Survivors do hate themselves, I know, over the core of fierce self-love, never understanding, always asking, "Why me and not her, not him?" There is such mystery in it, and I have hated myself as much as I have loved others, hated the simple fact of my own survival. Having survived, am I supposed to say something, do something, be something?

I loved my Cousin Butch. He had this big old head, pale thin hair, and enormous, watery eyes. All the cousins did, though Butch's head was the largest, his hair the palest. I was the dark-headed one. All the rest of the family seemed pale carbons of each other in shades of blond, though later on everybody's hair went brown or red and I didn't stand out so. Butch and I stood out then—I because I was so dark and fast, and he because of that big head and the crazy things he did. Butch used to climb on the back of my Uncle Lucius's truck, open the gas tank and hang his head over, breathe deeply, strangle, gag, vomit, and breathe again. It went so deep, it tingled in your toes. I climbed up after him and tried it myself, but I was too young to hang on long, and I fell heavily to the ground, dizzy and giggling. Butch could hang on, put his hand down into the tank and pull up a cupped palm of gas, breathe deep and laugh. He would climb down roughly, swinging down from the door handle, laughing, staggering, and stinking of gasoline. Someone caught him at it. Someone threw a match. "I'll teach you."

Just like that, gone before you understand.

I wake up in the night screaming, "No, no, I won't!" Dirty water rises in the back of my throat, the liquid language of my own terror and rage. "Hold me. Hold me." Jesse rolls over on me; her hands grip my hipbones tightly.

"I love you. I love you. I'm here," she repeats.

I stare up into her dark eyes, puzzled, afraid. I draw a breath in deeply, smile my bland smile. "Did I fool you?" I laugh, rolling away from her. Jesse punches me playfully, and I catch her hand in the air.

"My love," she whispers, and cups her body against my hip, closes her eyes. I bring my hand up in front of my face and watch the knuckles, the nails as they tremble, tremble. I watch for a long time while she sleeps, warm and still against me.

James went blind. One of the uncles got him in the face with home-brewed alcohol.

Lucille climbed out the front window of Aunt Raylene's house and jumped. They said she jumped. No one said why.

My Uncle Matthew used to beat my Aunt Raylene. The twins, Mark and Luke, swore to stop him, pulled him out in the yard one time, throwing him between them like a loose bag of grain. Uncle Matthew screamed like a pig coming up for slaughter. I got both my sisters in the tool shed for safety, but I hung back to watch. Little Bo came running out of the house, off the porch, feet first into his daddy's arms. Uncle Matthew started swinging him like a scythe, going after the bigger boys, Bo's head thudding their shoulders, their hips. Afterward, Bo crawled around in the dirt, the blood running out of his ears and his tongue hanging out of his mouth, while Mark and Luke finally got their daddy down. It was a long time before I realized that they never told anybody else what had happened to Bo.

Randall tried to teach Lucille and me to wrestle. "Put your hands up." His legs were wide apart, his torso bobbing up and down, his head moving constantly. Then his hand flashed at my face. I threw myself back into the dirt, lay still. He turned to Lucille, not noticing that I didn't get up. He punched at her, laughing. She wrapped her hands around her head, curled over so her knees were up against her throat.

"No, no," he yelled. "Move like her." He turned to me. "Move." He kicked at me. I rocked into a ball, froze.

"No, no!" He kicked me. I grunted, didn't move. He turned to Lucille. "You." Her teeth were chattering but she held herself still, wrapped up tighter than bacon slices.

"You move!" he shouted. Lucille just hugged her head tighter and started to sob.

"Son of a bitch," Randall grumbled, "you two will never be any good."

He walked away. Very slowly we stood up, embarrassed, looked at each other. We knew.

If you fight back, they kill you.

My sister was seven. She was screaming. My stepfather picked her up by her left arm, swung her forward and back. It gave. The arm went around loosely. She just kept screaming. I didn't know you could break it like that.

I was running up the hall. He was right behind me. "Mama! Mama!" His left hand—he was left-handed—closed around my throat, pushed me against the wall, and then he lifted me that way. I kicked, but I couldn't reach him. He was yelling, but there was so much noise in my ears I couldn't hear him.

"Please, Daddy. Please, Daddy. I'll do anything, I promise. Daddy, anything you want. Please, Daddy."

I couldn't have said that. I couldn't talk around that fist at my throat, couldn't breathe. I woke up when I hit the floor. I looked up at him.

"If I live long enough, I'll fucking kill you."

He picked me up by my throat again.

What's wrong with her?

Why's she always following you around?

Nobody really wanted answers.

A full bottle of vodka will kill you when you're nine and the bottle is a quart. It was a third cousin proved that. We learned what that and other things could do. Every year there was something new.

You're growing up.

My big girl.

There was codeine in the cabinet, paregoric for the baby's teeth, whiskey, beer, and wine in the house. Jeanne brought home MDA, PCP, acid; Randall, grass, speed, and mescaline. It all worked to dull things down, to pass the time.

Stealing was a way to pass the time. Things we needed, things we didn't, for the nerve of it, the anger, the need. *You're growing up,* we told each other. But sooner or later, we all got caught. Then it was, *When are you going to learn?*

Caught, nightmares happened. *Razorback desperate,* was the conclusion of the man down at the county farm where Mark and Luke were sent at fifteen. They both got their heads shaved, their earlobes sliced.

What's the matter, kid? Can't you take it?

Caught at sixteen, June was sent to Jessup County Girls' Home where the baby was adopted out and she slashed her wrists on the bedsprings.

Lou got caught at seventeen and held in the station downtown, raped on the floor of the holding tank.

Are you a boy or are you a girl?

On your knees, kid, can you take it?

Caught at eighteen and sent to prison, Jack came back seven years later blank-faced, understanding nothing. He married a quiet girl from out of town, had three babies in four years. Then Jack came home one night from the textile mill, carrying one of those big handles off the high speed spindle machine. He used it to beat them all to death and went back to work in the morning.

Cousin Melvina married at fourteen, had three kids in two and a half years, and welfare took them all away. She ran off with a carnival mechanic, had three more babies before he left her for a motorcycle acrobat. Welfare took those, too. But the next baby was hydrocephalic, a little waterhead they left with her, and the three that followed, even the one she used to hate so—the one she had after she fell off the porch and couldn't remember whose child it was.

"How many children do you have?" I asked her.

"You mean the ones I have, or the ones I had? Four," she told me, "or eleven."

My aunt, the one I was named for, tried to take off for Oklahoma. That was after she'd lost the youngest girl and they told her Bo would never be "right." She packed up biscuits, cold chicken, and Coca-Cola, a lot of loose clothes, Cora and her new baby, Cy, and the four youngest girls. They set off from Greenville in the afternoon, hoping to make Oklahoma by the weekend, but they only got as far as Augusta. The bridge there went out under them.

"An Act of God," my uncle said.

My aunt and Cora crawled out down river, and two of the girls turned up in the weeds, screaming loud enough to be found in the dark. But one of the girls never came up out of that dark water, and Nancy, who had been holding Cy, was found still wrapped around the baby, in the water, under the car.

"An Act of God," my aunt said. "God's got one damn sick sense of humor."

My sister had her baby in a bad year. Before he was born we had talked about it. "Are you afraid?" I asked.

"He'll be fine," she'd replied, not understanding, speaking instead to the other fear. "Don't we have a tradition of bastards?"

He was fine, a classically ugly healthy little boy with that shock of white hair that marked so many of us. But afterward, it was that bad year with my sister down with pleurisy, then cystitis, and no work, no money, having to move back home with my cold-eyed stepfather. I would come home to see her, from the woman I could not admit I'd been with, and take my infinitely fragile nephew and hold him, rocking him, rocking myself.

One night I came home to screaming—the baby, my sister, no one else there. She was standing by the crib, bent over, screaming red-faced. "Shut up! Shut up!" With each word her fist slammed the mattress fanning the baby's ear.

"Don't!" I grabbed her, pulling her back, doing it as gently as I could so I wouldn't break the stitches from her operation. She had her other arm clamped across her abdomen and couldn't fight me at all. She just kept shrieking.

"That little bastard just screams and screams. That little bastard. I'll kill him."

Then the words seeped in and she looked at me while her son kept crying and kicking his feet. By his head the mattress still showed the impact of her fist.

"Oh no," she moaned, "I wasn't going to be like that. I always promised myself." She started to cry, holding her belly and sobbing. "We an't no different. We an't no different."

Jesse wraps her arm around my stomach, presses her belly into my back. I relax against her. "You sure you can't have children?" she asks. "I sure would like to see what your kids would turn out to be like."

I stiffen, say, "I can't have children. I've never wanted children."

"Still," she says, "you're so good with children, so gentle."

I think of all the times my hands have curled into fists, when I have just barely held on. I open my mouth, close it, can't speak. What could I say now? All the times I have not spoken before, all the things I just could not tell her, the shame, the self-hatred, the fear; all of that hangs between us now—a wall I cannot tear down.

I would like to turn around and talk to her, tell her . . . "I've got a dust river in my head, a river of names endlessly repeating. That dirty water rises in me, all those children screaming out their lives in my memory, and I become someone else, someone I have tried so hard not to be."

But I don't say anything, and I know, as surely as I know I will never have a child, that by not speaking I am condemning us, that I cannot go on loving you and hating you for your fairy-tale life, for not asking about what you have no reason to imagine, for that soft-chinned innocence I love.

Jesse puts her hands behind my neck, smiles and says, "You tell the funniest stories."

I put my hands behind her back, feeling the ridges of my knuckles pulsing.

"Yeah," I tell her. "But I lie."

A Conversation with Dorothy Allison

In your essay, "Stubborn Girls and Mean Stories," you wrote, "Why write stories? To join the conversation. Literature is a conversation—a lively enthralling exchange that constantly challenges and widens our own imaginations." Would you talk about your continuing need to write stories and what that ongoing conversation which is literature means to you?

The reason to write stories changes all the time. When I was young, I was writing in self-defense, defending and honoring a despised nation, I was writing about my working-class family with this mix of anger and love and resentment and adoration. I wanted to put them on the table, because everything I read erased us. The first story that I ever wrote was about one of my cousins who had nine children in sets of three with different fathers, only to have them all taken away by the state for one reason or another. She just cracked. She was constantly talking to the kids that she had lost. I wrote this story because I adored her, and it was rejected. In part, I felt the rejection was about who I was paying serious attention to. I was writing about the kind of person that most people would say about, "Well, if she'd been the kind of mother she should have been, she wouldn't have lost those babies anyhow."

I was writing about me as a lesbian, too—all the lesbians that I knew. I am fifty-four years old, so I date back to the horrific and contemptible portraits of the people I loved. My writing about lesbians was shaped by reading my mother's Mickey Spillane and Ross McDonald novels. Isn't that weird? They have a style that's very matter-of-fact and staccato, paying attention to rhythms of language and how people talk, and I found that I really liked that way of writing about lesbianism. Now, it's an education that starts at Mickey Spillane and Ross McDonald and then goes on to Flannery O'Connor, Carson McCullers, and Grace Paley—then gets romantic and lyrical at some point. But life changes.

Now, it's an education that starts at Mickey Spillane and Ross McDonald and then goes on to Flannery O'Connor, Carson McCullers, and Grace Paley—then gets romantic and lyrical.

When I became a lesbian activist and moved into a lesbian feminist collective, I started writing lesbian feminist stories. And lesbian feminist bad poetry. That was an era of bad poetry and really bad short stories. Really reductive short stories.

But it was a voice that hadn't been heard, hadn't been refined, because it hadn't been out there—in every sense of the word.

Yes. I became an editor at a lot of little magazines, joined *Quest* in Washington, D.C., and moved up there. The primary short story that you read in all those little magazines was how love saves your life. You come out and then everything is fixed. Or in some situation of stress or denial, you find true love with some other lesbian remarkably similar to you. So romantic. But it wasn't my experience, because sex didn't save me. Sex is very complicated and difficult for me. My own romantic impulses, certainly at that time, tended to be pretty self-destructive. I fell in love with same kind of objects my sisters fell in love with: violent abusers. You can find them in girls as well as boys. I couldn't write that easy, romantic story. I hated that fairy tale gloss.

In that same essay, you say that you wanted to write so that you could join the conversation.

But there are different conversations going on, and it seemed to me that some of the conversations going on were shortsighted and temporary. The conversation that I wanted to join was one that would last. I wanted one that my nieces could read and not be horrified by, which is tricky because I've got a lot of hard-headed nieces in the category that this culture still holds in contempt. They are really scared by some of the stuff I write.

You said, too, that you wanted to challenge and widen the reader's imagination. But how do you get people to listen to stories about people whom they hold in contempt?

Language. You want to see it done perfectly? Read Tobias Woolf's story, "Bullet in the Brain." The character he's giving you is just an impossible jackass. But Toby's gift is that, not only is the character recognizable, but immediately also felt. A trick of the voice invites us to have contempt for him in the beginning of the story, to find him stupid and amusing and arrogant. But Toby's language, very slowly, subtly, sees deeper than what the man is saying. So that by the end, we are sympathetic. That's what you can do with language. That's what I try to do. I tend to be a more lyrical writer than Toby. I tend to echo the Bible—God help me. I grew up on the Bible. You have to find a language that is highly seductive, that can startle you occasionally. But it has to be beautiful, so beautiful that you can say painful things in a voice that people will listen to.

You have to find a language that is highly seductive, that can startle you occasionally. But it has to be beautiful, so beautiful that you can say painful things in a voice that people will listen to.

Sometimes when students start out to write beautifully that's a problem. You can be so enamored of words that you choose the beautiful word instead of the right one.

A lot of times, if writers are being "pretty," they'll put so many words around the speech that it buries it. You have to be pretty pared down and stark and you have to echo the pattern of how people speak in your description. It's easy to talk about, but hard to do. I hear it—and I hear it in paragraphs, which helps a whole bunch. I use the accordion technique. I write large, very expansive and lyrical, with lots of pretty words—and then cut it.

You once said that your characters come when people start talking to you. How do characters form for you?

There's almost always a visual. In fact, they are doing something and they are talking as they are doing. That's how you get a character. People talk in a way that reveals who they are. When I hear a character talking, literally, it's like they are dictating and I'm taking it down. I want the voice to be unique, recognizable, and true to my experience. I love the speech of southern working class people. I love the huge variety of it. I have an ear for it and I can get it on the page. What I really want you to do is to "hear" someone speak.

I have an anthropology degree. Not really useful, but sideways useful. Part of what I was fascinated with was literally taking down verbatim not only what people say but how they say it. I am fascinated not just with the particular words that people use, but the rhythms of language. There's a huge similarity in the working class of the South that crosses color lines. You can't tell from speech alone whether the person is white or black. There are boys I love—Larry Brown, Madison Smartt Bell—because they get that vernacular and they write it so that you can hear it.

What I really want you to do is to "hear" someone speak.

Would you talk about the character in "Steal Away," the formation of that character?

It's semi-autobiographical—I was that kid in that college. So, a lot of it is taken, literally, from journal entries. Going to the president's reception and stealing the cheese knife. And eating cheese—brie was a huge, startling thing to me. But falling in love with professors: I fell in love with one at a time. The trick of the story is that she falls in love with just one.

When the narrator says, "I went, instead, downtown to steal," that one word, instead, *tells the reader so much. How do you accomplish those nuances of language?*

It's the rhythm. I read it out loud over and over until I can pare it down, until it flows. It's a lot like music. What I want is that [loud clap of hands]. You only get there by being slightly seductive. The rhythm has to be reassuring. I heard, "I went." Then I listened again, and wrote, "I went, instead, downtown." If you listen to music, you hear this. I went comma—instead—comma, downtown to steal. It breaks it up. The first paragraph is very smooth, with longer clauses. That what I mean by the rhythm of language.

Another thing you do is stack, as in "Steal Away": "My sociology professor had red hair, 40 shelves of books, 4 children and an entirely cordial relationship with her ex-husband." Many times there are four things—three physical and then an emotional zinger.

Yes, I stack images and motifs. The last one in a series will be a longer clause, and that gives it more weight. It comes from reading a lot of poetry. At the time I wrote that story, all I read was poetry. People will follow the rhythm. You watch people listening to you as you read. You can seduce them. You'll see them nodding their heads and then you give them a sideways—and their heads go back. And that's what I want.

In a story, there has to be a lyrical pause where you'll get something that is gorgeous, that gives you a chance to catch your breath before you come back into something emotionally wrenching. "Don't Tell Me You Don't Know" is deliberately designed that way. It keeps giving you breaths, where you can wait. You get to where you like these people and then you get slapped in the face with really hateful material. They've all done something hateful to each other.

In a story, there has to be a lyrical pause where you'll get something that is gorgeous, that gives you a chance to catch your breath before you come back into something emotionally wrenching.

You do a lot of this "stacking," particularly in your short stories.

Yes, but there's something else, too. I do it in the story *itself.* If you look at how "Steal Away" is designed, there is this almost reassuring element. She is who you expect her to be. She's working class; she's a thief. She gets angry and she sneaks back into the office and she takes books. She doesn't do any real damage. She puts the books back; but she's written in them.

I'd like to know what she writes in those margins. You didn't include that. Why?

I want the reader to wonder. At the end, the story cuts sideways. Instead of some redemptive encounter with the professor, I bring in the mother and the stepfather, and what I want is for you to be devastated in a different way that you expected.

What about the particular books she steals—one by Jean Genet, one by Bataille? Genet was abandoned by his parents and spent much of his youth in a center for juvenile delinquents, where he was accused of stealing even though he was innocent. He said, later, that since he was declared a thief, he decided to be a thief—thus repudiating a world that had repudiated him. Bataille wrote of fusion of religion and eroticism and questioned the mystery of sin: what is it, what makes an action wrong? Did you consciously choose those books to mirror the questions that "Steal Away" explores?

Yes, of course, the choice of books and authors mentioned was deliberate! I loved Jean Genet when I was a college student. I was drunkenly, maddeningly, romantically convinced we were somehow the same kind of creature—outlaws on the outskirts of civilization. As you might imagine, much of that was my rather esoteric, romantic notion of theft, thieves, and prison life—far from Genet's reality, but I did not know that. I had copies of Bataille and Baudelaire. I think I originally intended to mention Baudelaire as well, but edited that out in the tightening process. The other truth is that I have a whole series of stories that I think of as thief stories, all following on Genet and to a lesser extent John Rechy. I liked Rechy's posture, but didn't much like the actual writing—but that is a longer conversation.

There's not a lot of dialogue in the story. Only two conversations with the professor and then the conversation with her mother.

All the conversations are about the narrator. They are all about her. She's more present telling you the story than in some of the other first-person stories in which the *I* is incidental. In "Don't Tell Me You Don't Know," the most important person in the story is the aunt and we get her story sideways, filtered through the first-person narrator. "Steal Away" is a tone poem. There are four in *Trash:* "River of Names," "Steal Away," "Lupus," and "Lesbian Appetite." They are lyric poems, but they are also short stories. I love that—using more poetry than stories.

Some describe a process of writing a story that feels organic but your process—particularly in terms of a story's structure—seems quite deliberate. Does that conscious understanding come early for you or does it reveal itself in revision?

I began as an organic writer. I had friends and I had good listeners, but I didn't have an editor to work with. I had to feel my way. After I started learning how to cut, how to edit, how to structure a story, then I became more deliberate.

So you're more deliberate when you start out now?

I know a lot more. But when I'm just writing, it's organic. It's people talking. You get the whole thing done and you look back and you say "Oh!" If the "Oh!" isn't there, sometimes if you just move things around a little bit, you'll say, "Oh, there, look at that!" There's stuff with language that happens that I'm not terribly conscious of until I'm almost done. *Bastard Out of Carolina* is absolutely about language. There were moments when I would realize that I was using the same motifs—all that language about Bone, bones, porous—took over the f___ing book. Only when I got to the end and started cutting and shaping did I make it deliberate.

In "River of Names," Jessie says, "You've got such a fascination with violence. You've got so many terrible stories." Most of your stories are concerned with violence within the family, but in this story, there's a kind of external violence that's very different from that. It's an emotional violence. In "Steal Away," the narrator is made invisible when the professor says, "We expect great things of your daughter," and says exactly the same thing to the mother of an African American student. That's brutal!

Yes. And it is the common experience of a whole class of kids who go to college. The professor has no clue, no idea that she's a brutal character.

In "River of Names," Jessie is described as having a face that's never been slapped, and in "Steal Away," the sociology professor reaches out to touch the narrator's face. In some ways, that gesture is the opposite, the other side of a slap.

Right. It's the contempt behind the gesture. It's easier to be slapped in the face than it is to be looked at with that kind of "Oh, you are just so surprising." What the f___ does *that* mean?

Generally, how much do you know about a story before you start?

The writing tells you. You start and then that person's not real. You start and the language is wrong. You start and then think, I don't want to tell that story. You start and then—you take off. Why does it click? It's not generally because of an idea; it's more about a feeling that you can get on the page. I can write as long as I can get the feeling on the page. When I come to the point where I'm editing and shaping, then I'm more about the idea that's there. In the beginning, though, it's what can I make work on the page.

The writing tells you. You start and then that person's not real. You start and the language is wrong. You start and then think, I don't want to tell that story. You start and then—you take off.

Most teachers would warn against introducing characters in the last three paragraphs, as you did with the parents in "Steal Away." But you did it—economically, with just the right detail: "My mother took the day off from the diner; my father walks slow because of the back brace." Usually, the adults in your other stories are huge.

The parents *are* huge here. They have to be there to counter the professor and the president, but in order for them not to overwhelm the story, there has to be just that little bit. They are never together in the same place in this world, or very rarely. Seeing them in the same place, you know so much more than can be articulated. And shouldn't be articulated, should be felt.

"Steal Away" is a story of emotional violence. The physical violence we so often see in your stories is not there.

But she's armored, calloused. We see a kid who's been slapped around and who has developed a poise and a pose that get her through. She's a person who expects to take damage. But she's a strong, truly muscular character and if they try to f___ with her, she'll take them out! That's the nature of scholarship kids in college—if they are conscious at all. Otherwise they'd break. Did you not know anybody going crazy while you were in college? I did! Some of it is self-hatred, some of it is self-violence. The only way that she, the mother, and the stepfather lose is the construction of the situation to begin with. They have no money. They have no reality: These people don't know who they are, they won't *recognize* who they are, so there's this big safe barrier. But the violence is so overwhelming. More in the stories where there's not *physical* violence.

So, when she throws all the ashtrays into the bay, that's a kind of sublimation of what she could do.

Right. It means she's not going to kill them.

In "River of Names," the violence is right at the surface. How did that story come to the page?

God, God, God. I don't know. I worked on that story for so long. I started it when my grandmother died. My mother kept it a secret, didn't tell me that she had died until many months afterwards. I was in college. She called me on the phone and mentioned that she'd seen one of my aunts. I asked, "When did you see her?" And she said, "At Granny's funeral." I said, "Granny died?" That just knocked my feet out from under me.

How did you deal with the news at the time?

I walked. When I was in college, sometimes I walked all night. I had insomnia and I'd go out for long walks and I'd argue with my family. I remember walking and walking and crying. I was so angry at how she'd died and at my mother for not telling me. But I knew that my mother actively keeping me away from the rest of the family was her way of keeping me alive.

The story started with a piece that's no longer in it. Then I tried writing it as a bad poem, going all out, stringing together all the stories that you can't tell. Who got raped and who raped them. Who died and how they died. All the grim details of the piece of glass, the baby in the microwave. Overwhelming, horrific details. There was enormous exhilaration about putting it down. The telling of secrets.

You once said that a good way to make a child a writer is to keep her in the dark about things.

You become a detective trying to figure it out. My mother wouldn't talk. She would give me just the barest sketch of something, just enough to make me completely hysterical. Granny would tell me. She would tell me things you should not tell children! My great-aunt was murdered, beaten to death—and her description of the body, I'll never forget that!

So I had these two poles, but I couldn't get to my granny very much. I can't say my mother didn't like her mother, but they were at always war. So she cut me off from her. Some of what remains in my memory is my grandmother's telling these stories with savage enjoyment in the brutal details. She was real piece of work! She was f___ed with early on, by her mother—they loved boys, and didn't like girls. That was part of her estrangement from my mother. That defined all of us. I loved my aunts, but it defined them, too. They loved their husbands; they loved their boys—but they treated their girls like inconvenient, difficult animals.

Yes. They're everywhere in your work, especially in "River of Names."

They have really powerful voices. So some of [making the story] was using their voices, in stanzas. "River of Names" is in stanzas. Not paragraphs. List poetry, if you really think about it. But it's different figures, my different aunts and my grandmother. They are really the ones talking.

Did you tinker a lot with the order of the memories in the story?

Yeah. I read it out loud until it worked—but not for anybody else. It was the only story that I never tried out on an audience. Couldn't do it. Literally, just couldn't do it.

There's such power in that first image in "River of Names," but you never return to it. We see the boy hanging and the mother putting her hand over the daughter's face—but we don't get the story. That's interesting in terms of what you've said about growing up with images and no one telling you what they mean.

It's maddening. At different points in your life, you learn a little more, but it never solves the mystery. About ten years ago, one of my cousins got in touch with me. She's two years younger than me and profoundly disabled and lives in a trailer park. But the Internet happened and she researched the family. I did some of that, but people wouldn't talk to me after they found out that I was writing stories. There was nobody to stop her, though, and now she knows all this stuff. She was one of the other kids who found him. We all found him. We were all standing there before the adults figured out what was going on.

The version that I heard years later was that the older kids had been swinging and he was too little. When he put the rope around him and swung, the rope slipped up. My cousin thinks that somebody put the rope around him and gave him a kick. Probably one of the older cousins. She's got reasons and she's told me the reasons and they sound plausible.

The narrator of "River of Names" is, in a sense, a victim. But victims aren't usually interesting. So how do you make them so?

Wait a minute! We have a whole lot of words around this label of *victim.* You can be a person to whom horrific things have happened, and you can be like my girl in "Steal Away," who is armored. The character in "River of Names" is armored. She's got layers of armor that are so defining and powerful that she can give you that litany. And she can give it in this brutal fashion so that it becomes, like my grandmother's story, a pornography of violence. A kind of licentious enjoyment of tsk, tsk, tsk. That's a damaged person, not a victim.

The information about the world of the narrator's childhood comes straightforwardly in the story, but the emotional information comes at the reader sideways, by way of her responses to her lover, Jessie. Would you talk about that?

Let's start at the beginning. The beginning is cross-class relationships—almost endemic in American culture. The engine of social change is that we fall in love with people who are radically different from us. As a young girl, I was always falling in love with these candy-smooth middle class girls. Sweet, gentle, tender—not sexually interesting—but, emotionally, they were just rare creatures to me. Now, the feeling that goes along with that is that I had great contempt for them, which is part of being a damaged person. But it is also a part of maintaining one's equilibrium in the world. They had so much more, but I could look at them and say, "I have something that they don't have. I know that any situation I'm in where terrible things can happen, I can come out on the other side. That's a strength they do not have." So I had contempt for the very things that the culture admired in them. When I look at it now, I'm kind of horrified at how simple it was. But you can't see it when you're young.

That kind of dynamic creates a terrific amount of tension in your stories.

It's my stuff. It's where I come from in the world. If that is your stuff and you are going to write from that pose, you have to have a complicated and deep understanding of where it is strength and where it is weakness and give it to the character. Otherwise, it becomes a pose that is pretty brittle.

If that is your stuff and you are going to write from that pose, you have to have a complicated and deep understanding of where it is strength and where it is weakness and give it to the character.

After reporting Jessie's comment about her fascination with violence, the narrator says, "So I made a list." And that list is a killer! In your mind, does she ever say the list aloud to her lover?

She isn't going to tell her. She's broken. It isn't going to work. So that's the other trick of the story. What the story plays with is, is she going to be honest with Jessie? Are they going to have a real relationship? You know she's not and they're not.

It's heartbreaking. She says, I know I have to tell if we are to survive—and then she lies.

The character in "River of Names" comes on as really tough. Very sexually aggressive, very strong, very matter-of-fact about her family, about all the stuff that's happened. Being so tough was a pose. That was one of the tricks I wanted in the story. She's not as brutal with Jessie as the girl in "Steal Away" is with the professor. She's much more tender. On some level, she does love Jessie, even though she holds her in contempt. But the contempt is also a pose, which is her defense against the contempt Jessie's world feels for her.

Talk about the end of that story and what you were trying to achieve with it.

It works on three different levels. It works as the story, and the story works as a conversation between the two of them. But the last line subverts everything that has happened so far. "But I lied." Which is the lie? Is it simply what it says on the page? That her funny stories are lies and the really horrible are the truth? Or is it, in fact, that she's been lying to herself about what she feels for Jessie and what she feels about her family? When I got the ending of that story, I had to walk for three days. I was, like, oh, this is perfect—because it was *everything* you have to think about, *everything* you have to question.

Writing is like really great sex. Let me be blunt. There's a whole lot of good storytelling in rhythm, in emotional focus, in intensity, in payoff that has that exact structure toward orgasm and release. When a story crests, when you get that lift-off at the end of a really good story, the exhilaration is enormous. And what you get immediately following is the little death where you are brought back to the real world and you see the story as a story. I am addicted to that. That's why I want to write. More, really, than any political motivation, any motivation of revenge, any motivation of honoring people and making real the world, there is that exhilaration in which everything has meaning. But then you drop back down and you've got to tell another story.

The world you give us is stark, frightening—for everybody. For the reader, for those involved, for you. *In your view, what redeems that kind of brutal reality.*

It's the subtext of everybody's lives. Even the unslapped girls. Even for Jessie. The subtext of her life is my life. This is part of widening the conversation. Let's put at the table all the people who haven't been there before—not in black-and-white caricatures, but fully emotionally complex, in a real world. Not the good poor. I *hated* the good poor. We were the complicated poor. The doing-the-best-they-can-and-failing-more-often-than-not-poor.

It was an act of love for me to tell that story. To put us at the table as our real selves, not our diminished selves. So much of the fiction I read as a girl that was about working class people was . . . diminished. I want the story where Mama comes in from taking a day off from her waitress's work and stands there next to these people who look at her like an animal. That has always been how it seemed to me. We were the animals, the workhorses of this culture. If you do it in a simple way, you get that cleaned-up, paragon, good-poor bullshit which honors nobody and makes me more ashamed of my people because we are not that. But if you give me someone like my mother, who for much of her life failed, but who tried, who risked her immortal soul, in which she absolutely believed, to save something—give me her *real* and I can forgive every place that she failed. Give me her diminished and we might as *well* be dray horses because we are not real. We don't have genuine human feelings. I hate the world of fiction where there are spear-carriers and walk-ons, whose only purpose is to be victimized in the third paragraph and vindicated in paragraph sixteen, where we—me, my sisters, my girlfriends, my boyfriends (I had a few)—are simply devices to prop up a John Cheever suburban reality. I hate that shit. Even John Cheever was miserable.

I hate the world of fiction where there are spear-carriers and walk-ons, whose only purpose is to be victimized in the third paragraph and vindicated in paragraph sixteen.

There are traces of Bastard *in all these stories. What is the relationship of "River of Names" to that novel?*

I was populating the world and I was teaching myself to write. The first chapter of *Bastard Out of Carolina* was a short story first. But "Gospel Song" and "Mama" were huge pieces of my trying to tell this larger story. I wanted to tell two different stories. I wanted to talk about this working class family, profoundly damaged, but full of resilient people. They'd love you and do you a little harm. I wanted to talk about incest in a different way. "River of Names" was the place I found to be angry on the page about incest. I couldn't do that in the story called "Mama," which is very blunt about the stepfather and the violence. Yet it has all those lyrical phrases where the mother says, "Don't say that, don't talk about that. We're not the ones who can." That was the voice of my whole childhood. "River of Names" was a way of finding a way to say, yeah, we were raped. In the first draft, I made a list of all the girls in my family that I knew had been raped. And I made a list of all the girls in my family who had children by members of their family. It's not in the story that you read now, but giving myself permission to make those lists was part of learning how to be a writer and deal with that material. And then to shape it into something different.

It's your stuff and you have to learn how to write about it. Remember, I was being shaped by the early women's movement, which in the beginning was completely inarticulate on class and incest, then began to grapple with it. It gave me a context to do something. There were a lot of stories of the moment that people would tell. You could write the victim story. You could write the story of a girl who goes to a women's center and stumbles into an incest survivor and realizes that she is an incest survivor, too. I wrote that story, too, but I wrote it about a character being the fourth person in the room to talk and changing what she's going to tell them based on what each person has already said. Not the simple story. I like the story that makes me, personally, uncomfortable.

In "Steal Away," the character becomes what "they" expect her to be.

If you are going to be what they expect you to be, then you are going to die. There's a kind of vindication of poor white trash that Americans love in the conscious, articulate, ironic, self-destructive voices of our writers. They really adore them. It's all through American history. Way back. It's what makes working class and black literature. We tell this culture terrible things about itself, and as long as we do it in a particular way, so that it has purpose and some kind of sense of style and glory of language, we can be enormously powerful and make huge differences. It's how our culture changes. I figured out that you can change the rules a lot faster if you can give people a story that they fall into against their will than you can by shouting slogans. So I started actively taking my time back from being a feminist revolutionary to being what I think is the kind of revolutionary I am now, a revolutionary writer.

How has that been for you? Your stuff changing as you change?

Cultural change in America is based on the active cultivation of the working class by the upper class. That goes from marrying across class relationships to constantly bringing in the working class into colleges on scholarships or with appropriations. To bring our desperation, our drive (a lot of which is manufactured by our desperate circumstances) to energize, strengthen, and revitalize a moribund culture. Because upper class culture in America is tedious. And empty. Shadow puppets. To bring in the blood and greed of the working class and their need and desperation, the desire, there's lots of energy there.

A lot of things that are published are about that middle class world, however.

Absolutely. Absolutely! However, the narrative stance is often a subversion of it. It's the outsider. Even the upper class has outsiders.

You say that about yourself. "I was born between two batches of babies."

Being an outsider gives you lots of power. Because you are the outsider, you can tell anything. It's also a pose. You want to be an insider, you want to be at the table. You want to talk to Toby Wolff and Amy Tan. Christ, Grace Paley! You want to also have something genuine to say, which is trickier because anytime you bring something genuine to the table, you're taking risks. You're telling secrets, but your secrets are not just that my daddy raped me and my mama slapped me around. Those are little secrets. The big secrets are your self-consciousness, your self-hatred, your horror of who you have been made to be and cooperated in becoming. When you go to college, you want to become something that your mama isn't. You want to be not-poor, not-powerless. But you start by saying, "I don't want to be what I've been." You have to cut yourself off from everyone you love, what you have been.

You want to also have something genuine to say, which is trickier because anytime you bring something genuine to the table, you're taking risks.

And what you can't know until you get there is that the price of finally arriving in the middle class is to that it creates a nearly unbridgeable gap between you and those you love. What has that been like for you?

It makes you look at your family—your parents, particularly. I'm ashamed of myself every time I do it. You don't ever become middle class, you never get really comfortable there. You always feel that you are there by permission. My mother desperately wanted me to become educated. She wanted me to get out. But getting out meant losing me—and me losing her. But she was getting educated, too. She was willing to go to college and stand beside me while those people looked at her with contempt, and that experience changed her profoundly. She looked into a world that she was not able to inhabit, and it made her sad. And angry. But it didn't break her love for me, and that made me *more* ashamed of myself and more defensive of her. It made me want to write more out of her. It's not easy and it's not what you think it's going to be. Huge emotional stuff happens that you can barely articulate.

The recent edition of Trash *includes a new story, "Compassion," which explores the tensions that arise among three sisters on the occasion of their mother's death. Would you talk about that story?*

"Compassion" happened in part because of *Cave Dweller.* In that book, I wanted to write about two sisters who hated each other. "Compassion" was a short story version with very different characters. But it's the same family dynamic. At this particular moment, my sister Barbara is not speaking to me, but most of my life, she and I have managed to communicate. My two sisters have not spoken to each other in fifteen years. They barely allow their children to wave at each other and they live in the same town. We are radically different kinds of women. Both of my sisters dropped out of high school. I was a hippie, June was a druggie, and Barbara was a throwback to the '50s—she ratted her hair right up to the '70s!

The thing is, we are completely broken. The times we have had to come together have been family crises. The place where it was most astonishing was when we came together for the last three months of my mother's life. After she died, during the process of the funeral, there was genuine detente. My sisters and I constructed a funeral. We made that thing happen between people who hated each other—my stepfather and some of his family, my uncles and some of my aunts, none of whom could stand each other—by how we behaved.

"Compassion" came out of that?

It came out of trying to write about when my mother died. She had cancer for nearly thirty years. She'd done so well, been sick for so long, but I knew she was dying when she got the last diagnosis. So I said, I'm moving back here because my sisters are not going to be able to handle this. They didn't recognize that she'd gotten the death sentence. My stepfather was a basket case. My lover quit her job and we went and visited my mother, stayed with her for a week. Got her into chemo, bought her a wig. Then we began to prepare to move back to Florida for a year. I was teaching at the Art Institute in San Francisco, writing *Bastard,* and got a call from my sister to tell me that my mother had had a stroke and she'd be dead in twenty-four hours. I arrived twenty minutes after she died. There were a couple of hours there where we were all so destroyed. I still haven't been able to write about what that was like. It was easier to start writing about the funeral. I would try, write a little bit, put it aside, try again. It just wouldn't work. It was too much autobiography, too much memoir.

What finally made it work?

I got to the part in the story where my stepfather brings the greasy hamburgers, and from the moment the two sisters started talking they weren't my sisters. But they were the same *kind* of people and that made it happen. Because they were not my sisters, I could treat them as fiction. And I could be someone on the page that's close to me but not me.

Did anything that happened in the process surprise you? Or enlighten you?

Very much! In our family, some of the dynamics are humiliatingly banal—childhood resentments. The person in the story for whom you have the greatest sympathy, Arlene, is the contemptible one. She's the broken one, she's the tender bird, she's the beloved younger child. But the older two girls hate her at some deep, resentful level. They're the fighters; she's the peacemaker. Everybody's got their roles. When the others fall apart, she gets strong.

When I was writing that, I began to see a dynamic in my own family that I had never admitted was going on.

I believe in the Baptist sense of grace. It is not something that you can work for. It's not something that you deserve. It's something that descends. When my mother died, my sisters and I experienced a series of moments of grace. We did not work for it; we didn't deserve it—and it happened. And I'm grateful. I wanted to write it on the page.

It took me almost as long to finish that one short story as it did to write *Bastard.* Sections of it were so powerful and true that I kept going back to it, but I just couldn't make it close out right. I couldn't get that lift off at the end until I could create a character who was at variance with my lived experience with my sisters. Arlene in this story isn't like any of us. But the grace that she brings to this story is the equivalent to the grace that my sisters and I found. That's the way it goes with a story. You keep writing it until you get an emotionally true portrait.

How did the right ending for the story finally come to you?

I brought a draft of the story to read at the Chicago Public Library. I still hadn't gotten quite the right ending, but I had an ending that worked—more or less. It was a thirty-page story. I'm reading, reading and I get to page twenty-eight and there's no twenty-nine or thirty. I had left the ending at home. I look up and there are a thousand people! I'm, like, okay—and I just closed my eyes and went. I spoke the ending. I walked off the stage and said, "Did they tape it?" But there was no tape. On the way home, I wrote it down.

Where did the spoken ending begin?

From where she's going "Ba, Ba, Ba, . . ." The rest of it, from when Arlene takes him out of the room, is the part I wrote down. The last two pages. I knew that Arlene would take him out and come back. But not "We held her until she set us free." Afterwards, I went into the bathroom and wrote down that line. I've done that a couple of times. I'll be traveling with a draft, get up there and I will have scribbled so much that I can't read. I have to invent. One or two times I've gotten the tape of what I read and found stuff that I've used in finishing the piece. If you can screw yourself up to this pitch of intensity, you can make connections and make jumps. The gift of it is that the language will mesh and you'll discover that what you come up with out of nothing echoes all the way back to the story.

What are you working on now?

A novel called *She Who.* I got in trouble and the story stopped. I'd always had this pose that I don't get writer's block because I'm always working on more than one thing. And if something goes cold, I can shift over to something else. I figured out that part of having that construction was because I was terrified that the engine would stop. And it did. It just stopped. That's not to say that I didn't write. I kept trying to write—but it was all drek. It only broke this fall, after two-and-one-half years. If I didn't have a child, I would have killed myself. I learned something that I kind of knew—which is that if I can't write, I go crazy. That, in fact, writing, for me, is making sense of everything. I can't tell you how grateful I am that I'm working again.

So much of your writing has come out of pain and hard times, and your life is so good now. Do you think that had anything to do with the block?

I think there's a lot of stuff around that. You know, for a Baptist, I'm amazingly Jewish. Layers of guilt on guilt. I've got so much I can be ashamed of. I can be ashamed of being ashamed!

But I've also learned—the hard way: You need a boring, uncomplicated life to write emotionally intense complicated stories. The secret of good writing is what I call necessary boredom. The world in your head has to be more interesting than the world around you.

What is your best advice to a young writer?

Write the stories you are most afraid of. You have to get your feet under you. You have to get your stance to grapple with the material in complicated ways. You don't want to tell the story *they* want you to tell. You want to tell the story that goes further than they want you to go, further than you yourself can stand in the writing. You will be different by the time it's done.

You want to tell the story that goes further than they want you to go, further than you yourself can stand in the writing. You will be different by the time it's done.

Once he's ready to face that material, how can he create a satisfying writing life?

You have to love the work. A lot of my life as a working class kid was spent trying to pass as middle class. I remember getting my apartment in Brooklyn, getting a couch, and sometimes setting a scene so that people would come in and see me as the person I wanted to be. I actually remember organizing my office so that people would walk into my office and see a writer's office. But I didn't write there. I wrote mostly in bed or on the couch with a blanket because I was freezing all the time, even in summer. I don't know why. With notebooks, by hand.

Do you still write by hand?

Yes. Then I type. The computer is my slave. I love the *writing*. If you don't like the writing, you're f___ed. There has to be some emotional satisfaction from the act of trying to craft a story. It can't be about pose, it can't be about getting the kind of notebook a writer's supposed to have or the kind of software or the office with a fax machine and two phones and all that . . . *bullshit*. It's about the place you are most comfortable and most yourself—with that notebook and that story that isn't finished.

Writing Prompts

READ: "River of Names" and the interview with **Dorothy Allison.**

PONDER: How Allison uses a list of memories to reveal character.

WRITE: Make a list of memories about an experience or event that happened to you and then project that situation on an invented you. Use that to write a beginning to a story in which all the memories play into the character's understanding of the present.

PRACTICE:

- Write about a time when you felt you were an outsider.
- What are you most afraid of? Address that fear in a story.
- Search through your journals for entries that might be made into stories.
- Remember a dialogue you had with a family member or friend and write it, giving yourself permission to let it surprise you and become something new.
- Create a list of memories for a character to help you understand the character's past.
- Identify a voice that you do not think is being heard today and write a scene in which that voice is heard.
- Write a scene in which a character does what's expected of her, even though it is against her best interests.

Russell Banks

Russell Banks (b. 1940) is the author of five collections of short stories and ten novels. Born in Newton, Massachusetts, he was educated at the University of North Carolina at Chapel Hill. His honors include a Woodrow Wilson fellowship, a Guggenheim fellowship, two NEA fellowships, the American Book Award, the St. Lawrence Award for Fiction, the John Dos Passos Award, the Fels Award, the O. Henry Memorial Award, the Ingram Merrill Award, the Best American Short Story Award, the American Academy and Institute of Arts and Letters Award for work of distinction, and two Pulitzer Prize nominations. Banks has taught at Columbia University, Sarah Lawrence College, the University of New Hampshire, New England College, New York University, and Princeton University. He lives in Keene, New York.

For Further Reading:
Searching for Survivors (1975), *Family Life* (1975), *Hamilton Stark* (1978), *The New World* (1978), *The Book of Jamaica* (1980), *Trailerpark* (1981), *The Relation of My Imprisonment* (1984), *Continental Drift* (1985), *Success Stories* (1986), *Affliction* (1990), *The Sweet Hereafter* (1991), *Rule of the Bone* (1995), *Cloudsplitter* (1998), *The Angel on the Roof: The Stories of Russell Banks* (2000), *The Darling* (2004).

With Ché in New Hampshire

So here I am, still wandering. All over the face of the earth. Mexico, Central America, South America. Then Africa. Working my way north to the Mediterranean, resting for a season in the Balearic Islands. Then Iberia, all of Gaul, the British Isles. Scandinavia. I show up in the Near East, disappearing as suddenly and unexpectedly as I appeared. Reappearing in Moscow. Before I can be interviewed, I have dropped out of sight again, showing up further east, photographed laughing with political prisoners outside Vladivostok, getting into a taxi in Kyoto, lying on a beach near Melbourne, drinking in a nightclub in Honolulu, a club known for its underworld clientele. Chatting amiably with Indians in Peru. When I drop out of sight altogether.

All this from the file they have on me in Washington. They know that somehow I am dangerous to them, but they are unable to determine in which way I am dangerous, for everything is rumor and suspicion, and I am never seen except when alone or in the cheerful company of harmless peasant-types. My finances are easily explained: I have none. I never own anything that I can't carry with me and can't leave out in the rain, and I am a hitchhiker wherever I go. I accept no money whatsoever from outside sources that might be considered suspicious. Occasionally, I find employment for a few weeks at some menial job—as a dockhand in Vera Cruz, a truck driver in North Africa, a construction worker in Turkey—and occasionally I accept lavish gifts from American women traveling to forget their wrecked lives at home.

Okay, so here I am again, wandering, and everything is different from the way it is now, except that I am alone. Everything else is different. And then one day late in spring, I turn up in Catamount, New Hampshire. Home. Alone, as usual. I'm about thirty-five, say. No older. A lot has happened to me in the interim: when I step down from the Boston-to-Montreal bus at McAllister's General Store, I am walking with an evident limp. My left leg, say, doesn't bend at the knee. Everything I own is in the duffle bag I carry, and I own nothing that cannot be left out in the rain.

Rerun my getting off the bus. The cumbersome Greyhound turns slowly off Route 28 just north of Pittsfield, where the small, hand-lettered sign points CATAMOUNT 1/2 MI., and then rumbles down into the heart of the valley, past the half dozen, century-old, decaying houses, past the Hawthorne House, past Conway's Shell station to McAllister's Gulf station and general store, where the bus driver applies the air brakes to his vehicle, which has been coasting since it turned off Route 28, and it hisses to a stop.

The door pops open in front of me, and I pitch my duffle down to the ground and ease my pain-racked body down the steps and out the door to where the duffle has landed.

A few old men and Bob McAllister, like turtles, sit in the late-morning sun on the roofless front porch that runs the width of the store building. Two of the men, one on each side of the screen door, are seated on straight-backed, soda-fountain chairs, which they lean back against the wall. One old man, squatting, scratches on the board floor with a penknife. The others (there should be more than three) are arrayed in various postures across the porch.

Even though the sun feels warm against my skin, the air is cool, reminding me of the winter that has just ended, the dirty remnants of snow in shady corners between buildings, snow that melted, finally, just last week, and the mushy dirt roads that are beginning to dry out at last. The old men seated on the stagelike platform stare down at me without embarrassment. They don't recognize me. Through the glass behind their heads I can see the semidarkness of the interior of the store and the shape of Alma McAllister's perpetually counting head. She is stationed at the checkout counter, which is actually a kitchen table. Beyond her, I can pick out the shapes of three or four parallel rows of canned foods, the meat locker, and the large refrigeration unit that holds all of McAllister's dairy products, his frozen foods, packaged bacon and sausage, eggs, cold drinks, and beer. And farther back in the store, I can make out the dim shapes of hoses, buckets, garden tools, work clothes, fishing rods, and the other items that finish out the store's inventory—Bob McAllister's guess at the material needs of his neighbors.

The old men staring at me wonder who the hell I might be. They don't recognize me at all, not yet anyway, although I was able to recognize them as soon as I saw their faces. It is I who have changed, not they, and I have thought of them many times in the last few years, whereas they probably have not once thought of me.

Bob McAllister, of course, is there. And old Henry Davis, he would have to be there, too. His sister died back in 1967, I recall as soon as I see his sun-browned, leathery face, remembering that I learned of the event from a letter my father wrote to me while I was in Florida waiting for instructions from Ché.

The others, now. There is John Alden, who claims he is a direct descendant of the original John and Priscilla Alden. He is. Gaunt, white-maned, and silent, except to speak of the time, and always dressed in a black suit, white shirt, and black necktie and drawing from his pocket the large gold watch that the Boston & Maine Railroad gave him when he retired back in 1962, drawing it out and checking its time against anybody else's—the radio's, the church's, Bob McAllister's, Timex's, anybody's who happens to walk into the store.

"What time you got, Henry?"

"I got ten-seventeen, John."

"Check it again, Henry, 'cause I got ten-twenty-one."

"Thanks, John, thanks a lot. Hell of a watch you got there. It ain't ever wrong, is it?"

"Not yet it ain't."

There are two or three others. There is Bob McAllister, who comes over to the bus as he has done every day for over twenty years and takes the bundle of Boston newspapers from the driver. There is Henry Davis, who plowed the few acres that my grandfather cultivated every year with corn and potatoes and the meadows that were hayed when I was a child—but that was before Henry and his horses got too old and Grandpa had to go to Concord and buy a John Deere tractor to replace Henry. And there is John Alden, who is a direct descendant of John and Priscilla. And there would be Dr. Wickshaw, too, because it's about ten years from now, and Dr. Wickshaw has retired, no doubt, has left his entire practice to that young Dr. Annis from Laconia, the new fellow from Laconia my father told me about in his letters.

That's four, which is enough. They don't recognize me. Although when Bob McAllister lifts himself off the porch and crosses between the Gulf gasoline pumps to the bus to receive the Boston papers, he stares at me quizzically, seeming to think that he knows me from some place and time, but he can't remember from where or when, so he merely nods, for courtesy's sake as well as safety's, and strolls by.

I bend down and pick up my duffle, heave it easily to my right shoulder—three years in the jungles of Guatemala have left me with one leg crippled and deep scars on my face and mind forever. But the years have also toughened me, and my arms and back are as hard as rock maple.

Close-up of the scar on my face. It starts, thin and white, like a scrap of white twine, high up on my left temple, and then runs jaggedly down to my cheekbone, where it broadens and jags suddenly back and down, eventually disappearing below my earlobe. I am reluctant to talk about how it happened, but anyone can see that it is the result of a machete blow.

The driver closes the door to his bus and releases the air brakes hurriedly, for he is no doubt relieved to be rid of a passenger whose silent intensity somehow unnerved him from the moment he left the Park Square Greyhound Bus Terminal in Boston until the moment when the man, without having said a word to anyone, finally rose from his seat immediately behind the driver and stepped down in Catamount. The driver closes the door to his bus, releases the air brakes hurriedly, and the big, slab-sided, silver vehicle pulls away, heads back to Route 28 for Alton Bay and Laconia, and then north to Montreal.

The cool, dry air feels wonderful against my face. It's been too long. I've been away from this air too long this time. I had forgotten its clarity, the way it handles the light—gently, but with crispness and efficiency. I had forgotten the way a man, if he gets himself up high enough, can see through the air that fills the valley between him and a single tree or chimney or gable miles away from him, making the man feel like a hawk floating thousands of feet above the surface of the earth, looping lazily in a cloudless sky, hour after hour, while tiny creatures huddle in warm, dark niches below and wait for him to grow weary of the hunt and drift away.

Leaving Mexico City. As I boarded the Miami-bound jet, I promised myself that, if I could make it all the way back home, I would not leave again. I renew this promise now while walking up the road, moving away from McAllister's store and the silent chorus on the porch, past the three or four houses that sit ponderously on either side of the road north of the bus stop and south of the white Congregational church and the dirt road just beyond the church on the left, the road that leads to the northern, narrow end of the valley. I am limping. Yes, right, I am limping, but while my disabled leg slows me somewhat, it doesn't tire me, and I think nothing of walking the three and one half miles from McAllister's in the village to my father's trailer in the park at the north end of the valley. With Ché in Guatemala I have walked from the Izabal Lake to San Agustin Acasaguastlán, crossing the highest peaks in Guatemala, walking, machete in hand, through clotted jungle for twenty days without stopping, walking from sunrise till sunset every day, eating only in the morning before leaving camp and at night just before falling into exhausted sleep. In three years we never set up a fixed camp, and that is why the Guatemalan Army, with their CIA and American Army advisers, never caught up with us. We kept on the move constantly, like tiny fish in an enormous, green sea.

I know that receding behind me, shrinking smaller and smaller in the distance, there are four old men who are trying to figure out who I am, where I've come from, and why I have come from there to Catamount. As soon as one of them, probably Dr. Wickshaw (he would be the youngest of the four, the one with the most reliable memory), figures out who I am and that I have come home to Catamount again, maybe this time for good, as soon as they have discovered that much of my identity, they will try to discover the rest—where I have been and what I have been doing all these years.

"How long's it been since he last took off, Doc? Five, six years?"

"No, no, longer. Close to ten, actually. As I recall now, he took off for parts unknown right after he come up from Florida to see his dad, who was all laid up with a heart attack, y'know. Angina pectoris, if my memory serves me correctly, was what it was. You remember when ol' Tom took sick, don't you? Paralyzed him almost completely. And the boy, he drove all the way up from Florida soon's he heard his dad was in trouble, even quit his fancy job with this big advertising company down there and everything. Just to make sure his dad was okay. Now that's a son for you. A damn sight better than most of the sons these days, let me tell you. The boy stayed around for a few weeks till his dad got back on his feet, and then he took off again. Nobody around here knew where he went to, though. Just dropped out of sight."

"How 'bout Boston, Doc? Used to live down in Boston, I heard. You think he went to Boston?"

"Naw, John, we'd a known it if he'd been in Boston all these years."

"Maybe this time the boy's come home for good. He sure looks like he's been through hell, don't he?"

"Smashed his patella, I'd say, Bob, though I couldn't offer as to how, or how he picked up that scar on his face. It sure does change his looks, though. I'd hardly recognized him if it wasn't for the fact that I was the one who brought him into the world in the first place."

No. Erase that remark. Wipe it out. Doc would never think such a thing, let alone say it, and Bob McAllister hates and distrusts me, I'm sure. Won't even give me a credit for a dollar's worth of gasoline. Be damned if I want to help those people out of their misery. If Doc Wickshaw ever saw me getting off a bus in Catamount, limping, scarred, back in town again after a mysterious three-year absence (five? ten?), he'd fear for my father's peace of mind, and, as soon as I was safely out of sight, he'd be on the phone, warning him to be careful, Buddy's back in town.

But that's okay, that's okay now, because everything is different. I'm about thirty-five, say. Maybe thirty-six, but no older. I'm wearing khaki trousers, a white shirt, open at the throat, and high, brown work shoes that have steel toes. My hair is cut fairly short, and my face and the backs of my hands are deeply tanned. I look like a construction worker, except for the limp and the scar, and when you are a tall, cold-looking man who looks like a construction worker, except that you limp badly and bear a cruel machete scar across your face, what do people think? They think they're looking at a veteran of guerrilla warfare, that's what they think.

Okay. So here's these four old turtles sitting in the sun on McAllister's porch, and the Boston-to-Montreal bus wheezes up, stopping ostensibly to let off the Boston papers as usual, but instead of just the wire-bound packet of *Boston Globes, Herald-Travelers,* and *Record-Americans* being pitched out the door, I get off, too, first chucking my duffle bag down the steps ahead of me. The bus driver, moving quickly to give me a hand, is sent back to his seat by my fierce, prideful glare, which silently says to him: I *can make it on my own.* "Okay . . . ," he says, almost calling me Soldier, but suddenly thinking better of it, sensing somehow that I have fought not for a nation, but for a *people,* and thus have worn no uniform, have worn only what the people themselves, the peasants, wear.

I like the idea of not having a car, of arriving by bus, carrying everything I own in a single duffle bag and owning nothing that can't be left out in the rain. No household goods are carried on *my* back, no, sir. Just a duffle, U.S. Army surplus, brought all the way home from the jungles of Guatemala. And inside it—two changes of clothing, a copy (in a water-proof plastic bag) of Régis Debray's *Révolution dans la Révolution?* which has been as a Bible to me. Also in a waterproof plastic bag: the notes for my book (Did I come back to Catamount for this, to write my own book, a book about my experiences with Ché in Guatemala, a book which in actuality would be a theoretical textbook thinly disguised as a memoir?). And the Ten Essentials: maps (of Belknap

County, New Hampshire, obtainable from the U.S. Geological Survey, Washington, D.C.), a good compass, a flashlight, sunglasses, emergency rations (raisins, chick-peas, and powdered eggs), waterproofed matches, a candle for fire starting, a U.S. Army surplus blanket, a pocketknife, and a small first-aid kit. That's it. Everything I own is there. The Ten Essentials. No, I need to have another. I need one of those one-man Boy Scout cooking kits. And maybe I should have a gun, a small handgun. A black, snub-nosed .38, maybe. I would've had trouble, though, with the customs officials in Mexico City—they would've been alerted that I might be coming through and would be carrying something important and dangerous, like secret instructions from Ché to supporters and sympathizers inside the U.S. Maybe I should leave Mexico from Mérida, after crossing overland from Guatemala through the low jungles of the Yucatán in hundred-degree heat, walking all the way, and then suddenly in the line of American tourists checking out of Mérida for Miami. It's when you arrive inside the United States that they check your baggage. They never bother you when you leave a place, only when you come back.

Say I picked up the gun *after* I arrived in Miami, picked it up in a pawnshop. Say I managed to lose the agent assigned to follow me, ducked into an obscure little pawnshop in the west end of the city, and purchased a.38 revolver for twenty-seven fifty. Later, at the airport coffee shop, I spot the agent. He's seated three tables from me, pretending to read his paper while waiting, like me, for his plane to Boston. He pretends to read, and he watches my every move. I get up from my chair, leaving a small tip, walk over to him, and say quietly: "I'm leaving now." Then smile. Probably they would arrest me at some point during my journey, but they would be unable to muster proof that I have been working in Bolivia with Ché for these three—no, five no, ten—years. They lost me in Mexico City, and so far as they can say for sure, that is, so far as they can legally prove, I've been in Mexico all that time. At least twice or three times a year, I slip back across the border to make my presence in Mexico known to the officials—I simply let myself be seen conspicuously drunk in a well-known restaurant—and then, taking off at night from a field near Cuernavaca in a small Beechcraft Bonanza piloted by a mercenary, a gunrunner from New Orleans, I return to the jungles of Bolivia. I am valuable to Ché for many reasons, one of which is my American citizenship, and so it is very important that I do not become persona non grata, at least not officially. "Conejo," Ché calls me, using my code name. "Conejo, you are valuable man to me y también a la revolución como soldad, pero también como norteamericano usted es muy borracho en los cafés. Comprendes, amigo?"

"Sí, Ché, yo comprendo." We embrace each other manfully, the way Latins will, and I leave with the pilot, slashing through the jungle to his plane, which he has cleverly camouflaged at the edge of a small clearing several miles down the valley from where we have camped.

Now, three thousand miles away. I have just disembarked, from a Grey-hound bus in Catamount, New Hampshire. I stand next to the idling bus for a few moments, gazing passively at the scene before me, and upon receiving the blows of so much that is familiar and so much that subtly has grown strange to me, I become immobilized. I remember things that I didn't know I had forgotten. Everything comes into my sight as if somehow it were brand-new, virginally so, and yet also clearly, reassuringly, familiar. It would be the way my own face appeared to me when, after having grown a beard and worn it for almost two years, I went into a barbershop and asked to have it shaved off. And because I had to lie back in the chair and look up at the ceiling, while the barber first snipped my beard with scissors and then shaved me with a razor, I was unable to watch my beard gradually disappear and my face concurrently appear from behind it, and when I was swung back down into a seated position and peered at my face for the first time in several years, I was stunned by the familiarity of it, and also by its remarkable strangeness.

A Conversation with Russell Banks

In the preface to your collected short stories, The Angel on the Roof, *you observe that we tell stories in lieu of what we're too fearful to say to those we love and even to strangers,—praying that they'll be transformed by the telling, made believable and about us all. By what process do you think this transformation occurs, and how is the teller-writer transformed himself in the telling?*

You had to start with a hard question, didn't you? In a sense, there is a very simple answer to it. Under the strictures and restrictions and rigors of fiction, the writer, when writing, is always more honest and more intelligent than at any other time. The requirements of art create a possibility of greater honesty and greater intelligence and greater insights, a greater access to one's unconscious, greater access to the world around us than at any other time in one's life. As a result, when engaged in storytelling, one is able to say things that are not available consciously to him at the time and to conduct a kind of relationship with strangers that is much more intimate than is possible any other time. It's really the requirements of art that make the transformation possible.

Do you believe that the story knows more than you do?

In a sense, yeah. The occasion to tell a story creates a space where one can know more than one knows at any other time. I prefer it that way.

Many of your stories take place in the fictional New Hampshire mill town, Catamount. Is the setting based on a real town?

It isn't based on any real town, although it's become in some real sense "realer" to me than whatever town it might be based on. It's like a dream town that's been created in my visual imagination. In the geography of my mind, it's pieced together from memories of Pittsfield, New Hampshire; Barnstead, New Hampshire; Plymouth, New Hampshire—I could come up with half a dozen and include, also, the town where I live today in upstate New York, Keene. It's not a literal portrait or even a distorted portrait. It's a kind of collage of my memories and experiences of those places.

It's not a literal portrait or even a distorted portrait. It's a kind of collage of my memories and experiences of those places.

You know how when you dream, there's always a landscape and often architecture that vaguely resembles places you know. Maybe one room resembles the room you grew up in, but you walk into another room and it's like the kitchen downstairs in your present house. They kind of get assembled that way. Because I go back to Catamount again and again, it gets reassembled freshly. New rooms, new buildings, new streets.

What is it about that particular kind of town that's so compelling?

Initially, when I started to locate stories there, I was mining my own personal past. There wasn't any plan to it. It was simply that I could go there and I could evoke feelings for myself and construct stories from the materials of my past. But then after a while, I began to see that it had the heavy advantage of being a small enough locale that I could make moral fables out of it. I could simplify it. I could draw it in my mind and on the page almost like a stained glass window. I wasn't so much interested, at the time, in the sociology of it, but that, too, started to become clearer to me when I realized that an awful lot of what I thought about and cared about in the world, in the United States, particularly, could be represented there. I think that's all any writer does. Cheever went to the suburbs not because he loved the suburbs but because he lived in the suburbs. He found the materials there that he could assemble into moral fables. The same is true of Updike.

There are certain motifs that show up again and again in the stories, like stones in a kaleidoscope shifting into endless patterns. Alcoholism, ruined families, irrevocable mistakes, the terrible grind of a working class life. What is your fascination with these particular aspects of life, why turn the kaleidoscope again and again to examine them?

I think the fascination initially came out of that attempt to order and make coherent to myself a lot of my own experiences. It wasn't really a case of writing what you know because I really didn't know it. In attending to that kind of material by writing fiction, I began to understand it and make it coherent to myself. But in the process, also, I developed a kind of compassion for human beings who endure these kinds of traumas and turmoils and are subjected to the violence of these kinds of domestic misarrangements and disarrangements. I think that the compassion replaced what was originally a kind of personal need. Then it became a kind of operating principle. So if I return again and again and again now, it isn't in order to comprehend so much as it is a straightforward feeling for other human beings of that ilk. I like to think that I have a fairly generalized sense of compassion. But you can't spread it around unless you're the Dalai Lama—at least, not that widely. You have to choose who you are going to exercise your compassion on. I ended up choosing that particular class of people—not always, but generally. Those particular kinds of dramas and sufferings are the ones that intrigue me the most. I think that's what you do, what any writer does. The initial attraction isn't what keeps you there—like in a marriage, you know? The initial attraction isn't what keeps you married. It can't. You come back to him or her again, again and again over the years for very different reasons and you stay there for very different reasons.

But do you learn, each time you write about those people, do you understand in some kind of different way that you didn't before each time you return to those people?

Yes. It's a little like peeling an onion You sense that if I do this one more time, I'm going to get some understanding that I didn't have before. I'm going to go to another layer, another level.

You sense that if I do this one more time, I'm going to get some understanding that I didn't have before. I'm going to go to another layer, another level.

Like that kaleidoscope? You turn it just a little each time and you get something different.

Exactly, exactly. So you have a different angle of vision on it.

And you have to keep being surprised by the story?

Sure. Otherwise there's no point. It's just compulsive repetition.

A number of stories in The Angel on the Roof *revolve around the community of people living in a small trailer park on the Catamount River, just outside the town. What was the genesis of this cycle of stories, how did they evolve?*

I wrote them in a fairly short period of time and in the order that they appear in *Trailerpark.* That book was consciously structured, deliberately structured. It was concept-driven initially. I really wanted to write a story cycle that participated in the tradition of story cycles like *Winesburg, Ohio* and *Dubliners*—going all the way back to *The Canterbury Tales*—just for the dramatic possibilities of it. You have a cast of characters and you can approach them from any angle. They can play major or minor roles. You can tell their stories at any point in time. To do that, you have to locate them physically together. I was living in New Hampshire and at that time something like 32 percent of the population lived in trailers. Trailer parks do mix people of different classes, in different stages of their lives together. You do get retirees living cheek-by-jowl with kids on the lam and runaways. I liked that possibility and was interested in a narrative without any single central consciousness—except the community's itself.

What was the first story?

"The Guinea Pig Lady." The last one was "The Fisherman." It's like the first act and the last act of an opera: you meet everybody that's going to be in the opera in the first act and then, in the last act, everybody comes back. The Guinea Pig Lady and the Fisherman are both outsiders. They are marginal characters. One is the wise man and the other is the crazy lady. They both play similar roles in the life of the community. The different characters are more or less worked out in an anthropological way in relation to the whole community. You have a warrior, a mother figure, the foolish counselor. I was playing with all those archetypal roles there.

Why didn't the cast of characters become a novel?

Every aesthetic position and every artistic decision has a political implication or meaning with it. I am a little "d" democrat, and I was interested in trying to find literary forms that would express that commitment that I have personally to community. The tension between individual needs and desires, on the one hand, and the needs and desires of the community, on the other, are very important to me. Just dramatically. I've had a persistent interest in finding a literary form that might explore and express that. *The Sweet Hereafter* and *Trailerpark* are the best I've been able to do so far. I'm not alone in this. The truth is that some storytelling traditions are different from the ones we inherit from Europe and are quite comfortable with there being no hero at the center of the novel or story. In recent American literature, you see it with African American, Native American, and Latino storywriters who are usually female. Whether it's *The Women of Brewster Place* or Louise Erdrich's cycles of stories, they often have no central consciousness. There is, instead, a kind of communal consciousness. I was very interested in that and saw it as a way of noting that the storytelling tradition that I grew up with and that I accepted passively wasn't the only one. There are other modes of telling stories and of gathering them together and organizing them into a larger narrative arc.

The tension between individual needs and desires, on the one hand, and the needs and desires of the community, on the other, are very important to me. Just dramatically.

Each story stands alone, yet also brings new insight to characters who have "starred" in other stories by allowing the reader to see them from a different point of view. Buddy, for example, has his own story, "With Ché in New Hampshire." He's an important character in his father's story, "The Burden." Leon and Captain Knox puzzle over him in "Comfort." When did he first appear in the constellation of characters, and how did he evolve in your mind?

A version of Buddy appeared way back, in the late '70s, maybe, when I was first writing the "Ché" story. I don't even remember whether he had that name or not. I just know that that kid with his grandiose fantasies, slightly manic manner, and charm was in my mind then. Later, when I was working on *Trailerpark,* I started to think about him from the point of view of his father and what a pain in the ass he would be. This may be coincident with when my own children were reaching adolescence—and I had one or two of them to pull some "Buddys" on *me!* So part of the evolution of the character was my own evolution. I could imagine him from another angle and see him freshly, see the other sides of his reality. In the first version of him, I could only see how other people impinged upon him. But by the time I was writing *Trailerpark,* he had become settled enough into my imagination, he had become real enough that I could see he impinged upon other people. He now populated the village that I was going to wander through.

There's a kind of thought pattern that recurs in some of your characters, one that's characteristic of working class people who long for more from life, but have no idea how to get it. You see it in its most common form in "Success Story," when the narrator's thoughts escalate from some small success to a grandiose idea of what will come of it. In Buddy's story, "With Ché in New Hampshire," it takes a different, much more complex form when Buddy imagines himself returning home after years of fighting with Ché Guevara. What was the genesis of this story? How did it evolve?

Actually, this is what happens when you interiorize a toxic image of that kind of romantic male and define yourself through the dream of behaving bravely under circumstances that require a love of violence and glamour. You inherit these images from the media, largely. It's not the occasion of your life to behave or react that way. The conditions of your life don't permit it or invite it. So, it's not an existential reality for you. It's an acquired essential reality and it's false and inauthentic at bottom. What often happens is that, as Buddy does, you glamorize it with a certain kind of preening dread. That's what Buddy has in that story—at least that's what I was hoping for or grasping at in that story.

Would you talk about the politics that shape your stories?

Inevitably, a story will carry a writer's political views. We all have them, whether we admit it or not. Mine are probably more consciously held than most in that I have a kind of political nature. It's an education and a kind of commitment that's necessary for me. The specific images that come into play are drawn from my own political romance, my own political personal critique. "Ché" arises out of that. He's a figure out of my generation, emblematic of certain values and longings that people who were engaged politically in the Sixties held. That's the reason he's there. I don't know who would be the equivalent today. Or even if there is an equivalent.

Inevitably, a story will carry a writer's political views. We all have them, whether we admit it or not.

"With Ché in New Hampshire" demands a close reading—and probably more than one reading—to be fully understood. The story is deceptive in a wonderful way.

Except that the suspension of disbelief gets broken when it says: *Stop. Rewind.* So by breaking the suspension of disbelief, you put that ripple into the glass, you see the glass. That's really what I was doing. Saying, "Wait a minute, this is an unreliable narrator. You have to perceive this differently than you might expect."

Those phrases do stop the reader and allow him to know what's going on—if he's paying attention. Did you always know that you were going to do that?

I was playing with the failed dissolute returnee. It's really a prodigal son story, and I felt like a prodigal son at that period in my life when I was writing it. At twenty, twenty-one years old, I felt I had wrecked my life. I was just playing with that memory. The image of the prodigal son, the returning boy or young man with his tail between his legs, and how he could deal with that or cope with that without hating himself: that's where it starts for me. Then I realized, I know how *I* would do it coming home like this: develop a limp, develop a false history. Start to try to believe in it for myself. When you think you have no future, you can create a vivid past to explain it. That's what he was doing. I was aware of that, but I wanted to make it real to me. I wanted to get as intimate with that fantasy and with that process as I could. The techniques of the story are designed to make that possible, to get that intimately engaged with the character's emotional situation or necessity. That's why you go into it and it plays as realistically as it does. But, of course, it is only a dream—in a sense. You have to remind the reader of that because that's part of the pathos of the story. It is only a dream. If it is fact, it's a kind of heroic fantasy of the writer, not really plausible. If it's just fantasy alone, then that's all it is—just fantasy. You have to find a way to dramatize the *need* for fantasy because that's what's interesting.

That's what breaks your heart.

Yeah, and you have to see both simultaneously: the fantasy and the need for fantasy. You have to be conscious of it at the same time you experience it. That's why those devices are there and why you have to break that suspension of disbelief to make the reader conscious of it as an artifice. But I didn't have them all in a little kit before I started, open it and say, "Oh, let's use these devices here." No, no. At a certain point you say, "No, wait a minute. If I go another paragraph on this, the fantasy is going to take over the story. I've got to find a way to get out of it without destroying it or critiquing it."

Crafting consciously, how do you decide how much of the process you want the reader to see? How do you find the balance between what to tell a reader and what to allow a reader to puzzle out for himself?

I don't think about trusting or not trusting the reader at all. It's really about trusting or not trusting myself. The reader comes into it afterwards and it's almost, in some ways, incidental to the process of writing. It's trusting language; it's trusting the tradition, trusting myself, and trusting the process, really, and its requirements and its demands.

The reader comes into it afterwards and it's almost, in some ways, incidental to the process of writing.

This seems to go back to your original idea that narrative is an attempt to make the world make sense. The story has to be able to do that.

Right—and you have to keep pushing against the incomprehensible. If you just stop and hold yourself against what is comprehensible, you're playing it very safe. You haven't gone anywhere out of any necessity. That's when writers are overconsidering the reader and not considering their own needs. I have no idea what the reader's needs are. I can't care what a reader's needs are.

A number of your stories reflect a fascination with the way stories are told. "Sarah Cole: A Type of Love Story" is good example. Would you talk about the genesis and evolution of the story, how it works?

Again, a story's inception is a character or a scene or an event. "Cow-Cow" came out of someone telling me the story of having shot his cow when he was drunk and not understanding why. Sometimes a story comes from a memory. Sometimes it comes from a kind of literary conceit. "Sarah Cole" came from two sources. The frog prince story has always mystified me in some way, and I always wondered what would happen if I reversed the genders so that it becomes a frog princess story. So it comes out of that. It also comes out of sitting in a bar, talking to a woman in the north of New Hampshire on a snowy night. She was a really nice woman, very poor, really struggling. She had just had a horrible day—you know, you have a conversation at the end of the day with someone who has had a much worse day than you've had in years and you realize that she has them *every day.* I was sitting there feeling sorry for her. She had several kids and she had to go home and fix supper for them and I watched her as she went out of the bar and into the parking lot—you know how those kind of blurry, snowy nights can feel in winter. She got out to her car—a beat-up old piece of shit car—and somebody had hit it and crinkled the door so that she couldn't get it open. I watched her walk around and get in on the other side and hitch her way over the hump in the middle. And I thought, oh, man, it can't get any worse than that. The story started there, literally. The literary conceit, on the one hand, and this tiny incident of this woman's life becoming humiliating for her.

Why was it necessary for you to tell it the way you did? Why not just tell the story straight?

It would have been an entirely different story. The automatic sympathy goes to the woman. It would have been almost impossible to have any kind of sympathy for the man. If you don't see it from his point of view, you don't have any sense of his struggle, of his interior drama, of its possible meaning for him. Therefore, I had to include his point of view. But I didn't want him to already have figured it out. The story has to be a process of discovery for him, otherwise it's not interesting—you would make up your mind one way or another about him in the opening paragraph. It's a story that in the telling makes itself a story about storytelling, of course—and in the telling it begins to lead him to the understanding of what he has actually done (his use of her, his justification of that) and its moral dimensions. The story is designed to make that possible for him and for the reader—and for me, of course, primarily—to come to an understanding through the telling of the story.

So, does that make it metafiction?

In a sense it is.

In your view, what is metafiction?

Well, the problem with metafiction is that usually it is *only* about storytelling. "Sarah Cole" is a story about human beings. I feel as though I have the right to draw on any technique or tradition available to me. I don't belong to any school, and whatever the materials that I'm trying to work with require—whether it's the techniques of naturalism, or realism or expressionism or metafiction, or folktale or parable or allegory—I feel that I have the right to draw on it with impunity. And I do. But it's the requirements of the materials that take me there and give me that permission. The requirements of this material obliged me to take from the techniques of metafiction in order to get the story told. Sometimes critics get a little confused. They can't put me into a box with the other metafictionists because I've only done a few stories that borrow from those techniques or a couple of short novellas. Otherwise, I've left them generally alone. And then the realists don't feel comfortable—the critics who want to put me in the realism box—because I'm not consistently a realist. The old-time Marxists can't make me a naturalist because I'm not consistently that, either. But that's not a problem for me. That's a problem for the critics.

It seems that you have many and varied ideas in your head for stories. How do you keep track of them?

Story ideas do pile up and you can go back and mine them later. I don't write stories constantly. I'll write a novel, and that will be a two- or three-year commitment. I'll come out of that and write short stories for six months or a year. Then a novel will take me over after that. In the meantime, stuff accumulates. At one time, with great delight, I was reading Hawthorne's journals and I saw that a good deal of his journals were taken up with story ideas. There'd be an image, two sentences or something, and question: story. And so on. A lot of my notes are like that. I write them down in my little pocket notebook. Also, clippings. I have a clipping file—well, it's not really a file, it's a box, a clipping box. A drawer really. It starts as a box and ends up as a drawer. It accumulates.

What makes one story emerge from all that stuff?

That's hard to say. That's what's wonderfully mysterious about it. You feel like you're walking through life as a blue serge suit, picking up lint. You can't predict what's going to stick and what's not going to stick—or why. The story isn't there yet; it's just the door to a story. You don't know what's on the other side, but the door has enough mystery to it that you know it's something interesting. That's why you are saving those things. A story can come from anywhere. It can come from an anecdote overheard in a bar or an incident like the one I've just described or from a newspaper clipping. Or from another story, sometimes. My story, "Black Man and White Woman in a Dark Green Rowboat" comes from "Hills Like White Elephants." It's an homage to that story—only with my cast of characters in it. In that one, the *man* is saying "Don't do that."

Can you teach someone how to look for a story?

I don't think you can teach it because it's so individualized, so particular to the experience of the writer. You can help the person once that person has made the selection to open that door. But the door has to be selected by the person.

What is talent, then? Where does it fit into the mix?

For me, it's a combination of curiosity and energy. You can't teach either one of those. You can't say, "If you work at this long enough, you'll work up enough curiosity to write it." That's not true. Nor can you say, "If you work at this long enough, you'll work up enough emotive energy to write it." They've got to bring that to the process, to the classroom, and to the text on their own. There are no shortcuts. I had the most brilliant students in the world, the most literary, literally, in the English-speaking

For me, it's a combination of curiosity and energy. You can't teach either one of those.

Those kids brought a kind of primitive curiosity to the process of life and to the process of writing. And a kind of tireless energy.

world when I was at Princeton—and as far as writers go, they were dead in the water. And I've had students who were inarticulate, bumbling kids who could barely get by, who don't test well, who are now widely published authors in their thirties and forties. Those kids brought a kind of primitive curiosity to the process of life and to the process of writing. And a kind of tireless energy.

Doggedness is a kind of talent, too.

Right. And the ego, which allows you to withstand rejection for years and years.

How do you approach revision?

I believe something that the writer John Berger said, which was that "all problems in writing arise from the writer's problems with the thing written about." If I see technical problems in a story—clumsy prose, structural confusion in the story, or something like that—I don't assume it's because I'm not smart enough to fix it or didn't see it coming. I assume that it has to do with my relation to what I'm writing about. There the clouds are. There's where whatever the denial or fear or turbulent and conflicted emotions I might have arise. So I go there. I go to the content rather than to the band-aid box.

Do you use other readers, or is the revision more a conversation about the story with yourself?

Occasionally, I use another reader, but only where I happen to be insecure about something. I don't do that very often with short stories. When I was younger, early on, I certainly did because you have to interiorize an objective point of view. The best way to do that is to show your work to someone else and check that against your own perception. In the process, over time, you create an objective inner self. That's part of the process of apprenticeship. That's why you need your peers; that's why you need your mentor—because you are building that imaginary self, in the early years, that's more objective than you are. You need both sides—the very subjective self and other more objective self—to read it and appraise it. I was able to do that over time and don't really need another reader since I carry that person around inside now.

You have to face it honestly—and alone. You cannot have someone else tell you where the false god or the true god is. You have to get the tools that allow you to be on your own. Creating this inner, objective self over time is one way. A writer with greater self-confidence and ego-strength finds it easier to create that person than someone who's insecure and afraid, someone who needs approval more than others. To talk about what tools you need in order to get to that point: You need to have to be extremely intimate and familiar with the tradition of storytelling. As many of the aspects of the tradition as possible.

You have to be a reader.

Yes, it's a simple requirement. You don't have to reinvent the wheel. Why bother? You've got tens of thousands of years of storytelling behind you. It's ridiculous for you to try to reinvent it. You need to be an intensive reader.

Telling stories, regardless of the tradition from which they're born, where in the process do you most often encounter surprise?

It almost always lies in the last page. I don't know where they are going to end. I don't want to know. If I knew where a story was going to end, I would know more than the reader, so why would I bother to write it? I think you have to *not* know. Now I can plot a story pretty nearly to the end, open it, initiate it—and as I go I can see where it's going, because with every paragraph you are narrowing your options down to two. Surprise, for me, always arises when I get to the point where the options are down to two. You don't know which it's going to be until you get there; otherwise, it has not been an interesting elimination of options. It's like the Final Four. You start with sixty-four options and then win or go home.

If I knew where a story was going to end, I would know more than the reader, so why would I bother to write it?

How do you go about discovering the end of a story, then make it happen on the page?

I remember saying once in a workshop that you have to bear down so hard that the smoke comes out your ears. That's the greatest moment in writing short stories: when you feel the smoke coming out of your ears. That is the point. You try to create a situation where the stakes are so high that whether you go right or left really matters as to how you view the world from here on out. You don't know ahead of time, but once you do know, then you are out of the story and you know it's done. Then you live with it. To me, it's the most exhilarating moment of writing fiction—getting to that point where the stakes are so high that who you are will emerge with those last couple of sentences. The writing process, for me, is designed, in many ways, to bring me there. If it can't do it, then I feel I've failed early on in the story somewhere.

Is that different from a novel?

Yes, completely different. It is such a fundamentally different process—they should be written in different colored ink! When you get to the end of a story, you should be able to remember the beginning. For me, that's absolutely essential. In a novel, it's the opposite. The idea is to forget the beginning. A novel has a mnemonic relationship to time—it imitates time; whereas, a short story is outside of time, it defies time. So it's a completely different mentality in the writing. There's not the cumulative effect that you have at the end of novels—like, ". . . and then the house fell on you."

Perhaps it's different, too, in the more literal sense of time. One can write more short stories than novels in a lifetime. So a short story writer's material can play out in greater variety than a novelist's does. In your stories, "Cow-Cow" and "Queen for a Day," for example, it's the same stuff in a different pattern.

Gee, I never put them together. They were written about thirty years apart. But, yeah—a different point of view. "Queen for a Day" is from the kid's point of view, of course, divorce and the abandonment from the kid's point of view. "Cow-Cow" is from the mother's point of view, and she's the one doing the abandoning; she's the one dismantling the marriage. I read it aloud recently. The audience quickly thought it was a comic story and they were laughing away, looking for the jokes. And slowly they began to realize, hey, wait a minute, this is really awful. Something really bad is about to happen to one or both of these parents. You know, those kids she's putting to bed—they have a story to tell, too. How does it feel to be that little girl who stayed up to watch Letterman and the parents come home and they're drunk—again? Then they shoot the cow.

"Queen for a Day" draws fairly heavily on my own personal memory. When I visualize it, I think of it as taking place where I lived at the time of my parents' breakup. "Cow-Cow" is recent and is set in my mind because it was told to me by a man in Keene, New York. A very different world. The stories do seem to overlap, in some way. It relates to the question about how the geography blurs in your mind, your distant past and your present. Your imagination is like a blender, pulling together all these different aspects of your awareness and mixing them together and reshaping them.

A lot of the tension in your stories revolves around incidents similar to the ones in those two stories: people caught in a desperate kind of love, bound to fail each other in the worst possible ways. How do you create that kind of tension on the page? What advice can you give the aspiring writer about how dialogue and gesture in such seemingly small moments can convey such intense emotion?

I have to get specific here, don't I? The hotter the moment, or scene, or situation, the cooler the prose. That's one of those generalizations, but it continues to be true. You don't have to build it up; you don't have to make anything out of it because it's all there. You know, you can see a wild fire or a house burning from far off. In fact, it's probably best to see it from far off. But you can't see a heart breaking or a life crumbling from inside, except from very much up close. You have to get in its face to see it. I think that's another truism. The more interior the event, the closer you have to get to it, the more intimate you have to become with it. A lot of it is the quality of tension that the writer brings—or doesn't bring—to the event.

The hotter the moment, or scene, or situation, the cooler the prose. That's one of those generalizations, but it continues to be true.

What you are talking about and describing are really interior events. If you are sitting at the next table, you don't see anything happening. The writer has to bring his or her tension right up close. You have to sit at the same table. You have to visualize it right up close. And listen right up close in order for it to unfold on the page. Writing so much of the time is almost a physical activity in that you are moving and arranging yourself in relation to the people and events that are unfolding in front of you. Where you stand—it's almost theatrical, cinematic. You say, where do we position the camera here? Where do I position my intelligence, my feelings here? What happens a lot, with writing students particularly, is that they don't know where to position themselves relative to the thing they are writing about. So if it's a blazing house, they get too close to it. They get burned and you can't *see* it. If it's a small exchange between a man and a woman over the hood of a car, where they are basically telling a terrible truth to each other, they show that from a great distance and you don't even hear the characters speaking. Because the *writer* didn't hear the characters speaking. That's the best answer I can give. And the most specific way I can give it.

What are your thoughts about dialogue, generally?

If I can't hear it myself, then I can't expect any reader to hear it. So I really need to hear it myself. And it has to be plausible and it has to be a voice that's distinctive. I have a general requirement and that is that I shouldn't have to say who said what. You should be able to tell it from the words on the page. From the dialogue itself. Obviously, one does occasionally, simply because one does lose track in long, extended dialogue. Generally, you shouldn't have to provide the tags. It should be obvious.

Just like you'd know in real life.

Exactly, or on the telephone. It really has to do with the ear. That goes back to what I was saying about how you position yourself relative to what you are writing about. Listening is part of that positioning. Sometimes an inexperienced writer will write dialogue, not with her ear, but rather with her eyes. So it just ends up on the page as words, but they are not heard words. What you are trying to do with dialogue, as opposed to what you are doing with exposition, is that you are trying to create an auditory hallucination. You are trying to make the reader and yourself hear something that isn't there. If you can't hear that noise, if it's not auditory hallucination for you, you can't expect it to be that for the reader either. Just like in exposition or descriptive writing, if you can't see what you're describing, you can't expect the reader to see it either. Because that's a visual hallucination you're trying to create.

Talk about that some more. You use a lot of exposition, a lot more than some writers do.

It's because I have a very strong visual imagination. Stronger than my auditory, I think. So I tend to see things when I'm writing. I do have visions when I'm writing. I'm not taken over by them, it's not a "visionary experience," but I do see what I'm writing when I'm writing. Basically I describe what I need in order to make it clear *to me* where I am.

That's interesting. You do it because you need it. Often students write exposition because they don't know what else to do.

Right. They think they are writing it to make someone else see something without having first seen it themselves. Oftentimes, that's when they fall into imitation instead of imagination. When they don't have the impressions for themselves, they begin imitating what they think it supposed to look like or supposed to sound like. You cannot bypass the medium. And you are a medium in this process.

Is it useful for a student writer to identify whether he works primarily from an internal voice or an internal vision?

The whole early years of writing are a process of mapping out one's own imagination. It's *terra incognito* when you are young.

You are unlikely as a student or a young writer to know that about yourself because you just simply haven't written long enough to know where your strengths are and learned to take advantage of them. The whole early years of writing are a process of mapping out one's own imagination. It's *terra incognito* when you are young. So you sail all around it. Then you begin to see what it is you are. I've learned over the years that I have a visual imagination. But I didn't know it for a long time.

Can the formal training of an MFA help people shortcut that process?

Yes, I think the process can be accelerated and rationalized as a writer's apprenticeship. But what you are rationalizing and, in a sense, packaging in an MFA or graduate creative writing program is basically the same elements that every writer, from the beginning of time, probably even Homer, went through. I've been able to isolate the three basic elements that worked for me in my own apprenticeship and that I think work for any beginning writer: The need to find a mentor, the need to find your peers for a period of time, and the need to get out of the economy for a while in order to buy time. It's usually a period of anywhere from—depending upon your life circumstances—two to five or eight years. It really varies according to the individual and what you bring to it and the kind of situation you're living in. If you're married and have kids, obviously that's a complication that makes getting out of the economy a little more difficult. If you are isolated, geographically, that makes finding your peers and mentor a little more difficult. I have no argument with MFA programs on principal, though I think that they are restrictive in a lot of ways. They make it harder for the apprentice writer to alter or change any of these elements in them—because it is a package. I was free to change the elements. I could to go to Boston or New York where there were other young writers who were struggling with the same issues that I was, who were excited about books and passing them back and forth. I didn't have a graduate teaching fellowship so that meant I could break away—hitchhike to Florida, or wherever. If I didn't have a mentor, I could find one. I could move. I had a more flexible and traditional apprenticeship in that sense.

The need to find a mentor, the need to find your peers for a period of time, and the need to get out of the economy for a while in order to buy time.

You have such vast interests. Everybody from Hogarth's wife to Ché to Simon Bolivar show up in your stories. The beginning of Continental Drift *is filled with archaeological data. How did you teach yourself? Where did all those interests come from?*

I didn't have a traditional education. I didn't go to college until I was twenty-four and was only there for two-and-a-half years. That was the extent of my formal education. So I am, in some ways, an autodidact. I think the truthful answer is I learned out of necessity. Having found myself, through purely reckless happenstance, at the age of nineteen, married and, at the age of twenty, a father and at the age of twenty-one, divorced—having already wrecked my life, I was out there on the margins. Of course, driven by a very real and needy curiosity about everything. I know that had I been smart enough or my family been educated enough when I was eighteen, I probably should have gone to Columbia University or the University of Chicago or Berkeley—a big university in an urban environment where a kid like me could just go crazy, and happily so, with guidance and instruction. Instead, I had to do it on my own and piece it together in a haphazard way, which worked out. And there are always older people, more educated who will take a bright kid under their wing and be helpful. That was certainly true for me. From the writer Nelson Algren to an older buddy here in Boston who was a sort of village-explainer type of guy who read everything and loved to make lists for me. "Now this is what you've *got* to read." And I'd say, "Yes sir," and I would do it. It isn't all that difficult, really, if you have insatiable curiosity and openness. In a way, it's almost easier if you are outside the conventional academy or academic institution because there aren't any rules. Nobody is saying you have to major in something. I didn't major in anything except for those two-and-a-half years at the University of North Carolina. Then I majored in English literature and American history—bounced back and forth between those two. I was just sorry I couldn't major in three or four other things as well. But I had to get on with my life.

Which you had already wrecked?

I can't tell you how trapped I felt at twenty-one and how I thought I had destroyed everything.

The narrator in "Assisted Living" observes, "For years, like an archaeologist attempting to reassemble a piece of pottery from a handful of shards, he'd turned the memories over in his mind, trying to construct a coherent narrative, a story with a beginning, middle, and end that would explain the intensity of emotion that he associated with that brief period of his life. He finally gave it up. It was adolescence, that's all. These emotions, like his brother's and sister's overall feelings toward their mother, were displaced from some other, still unexamined part of his life. There was no story here." If there's no story, you seem to be saying, there's no way of understanding our experience. No way of incorporating it, moving on. In the end, isn't this what writing fiction is?

Yeah. It's a way of making the inner mysteries manifest and more coherent to us. Flannery O'Connor talks about the process in that way, saying that the idea is to penetrate the mystery which will allow you to penetrate the next mystery as far as you can go.

Could you talk about penetrating those mysteries by way of fiction, how the stories themselves surprise you—whether it is being surprised by the stories themselves or by what you learn about yourself or someone else in the process of writing them?

You are, after all, your own reader. The simultaneity of the reading and writing process is really a fascinating one because it produces enough heat and enough light that it justifies itself and everything that goes with it. And that *is* where the heat and light

> The simultaneity of the reading and writing process is really a fascinating one because it produces enough heat and enough light that it justifies itself and everything that goes with it.

does come from—how you, the writer as reader, surprise yourself in the process. When you were just reading those sentences, I was listening because I haven't read them myself in some years. I was just following along and I have no memory of having written those sentences. But I was listening, thinking, yes, that does make sense. One couldn't say that ahead of time or think that ahead of time.

The story takes you there?

Yes. And that goes back to the beginning when I was saying that the story allows you to be more intelligent, more insightful, more honest than you can be normally—or in an interview!

Writing Prompts

READ: "With Ché in New Hampshire" and the interview with **Russell Banks.**

PONDER: How Banks reveals Buddy's character through the fantasy homecoming he imagines.

WRITE: Remember a time that you felt you had failed and were reluctant to tell the truth about it. Invent a lie that you might have invented to cover up your failure and write an imagined homecoming in which the lie comes into play somehow.

PRACTICE:

- Write the past that a character invents for himself.
- Assign a character a specific landscape. Describe it. What do you know about your character because she lives there? Then explore the satellite of characters in that landscape and imagine stories for several of them. How would their situations and perceptions of the place change readers' understanding of it?
- Write a story based on something someone told you. Feel free to imagine and embroider.
- Make a list of the 'motifs' that you feel will influence your writing: for example, a move to a new school, a death in your immediate family, a divorce, a triumph that brought great change to you or someone close to you.
- Retell a myth or fairy tale using contemporary characters, but invert it to open up possibilities for invention.
- Write a 'hot' moment using cool prose.

Charles Baxter

Charles Baxter (b. 1947) is the author of four collections of short stories, four novels, two collections of poems, and a collection of essays on fiction. Born in Minneapolis, he was educated at Macalester College and the State University of New York at Buffalo. His honors include the Lawrence Foundation Award, the Associated Writing Programs Award Series in Short Fiction, an NEA fellowship, a Guggenheim fellowship, a Reader's Digest *Foundation fellowship, the O. Henry Prize, the Award in Literature from the American Academy and Institute of Arts and Letters, and a National Book Award nomination. Baxter teaches at the University of Minnesota and Warren Wilson College. He lives in Minneapolis.*

For Further Reading:
Chameleon (1970), *Harmony of the World* (1984), *Through the Safety Net* (1985), *First Light* (1987), *Imaginary Paintings and Other Poems* (1990), *A Relative Stranger* (1990), *Shadow Play* (1993), *Believers* (1997), *Burning Down the House: Essays on Fiction* (1997), *The Feast of Love* (2000), *Saul and Patsy* (2003).

The Cures for Love

On the day he left her for good, she put on one of his caps. It fit snugly over her light brown hair. The cap had the manufacturer's name of his pickup truck embossed above the visor in gold letters. She wore the cap backward, the way he once had, while she cooked dinner. Then she kept it on in her bath that evening. When she leaned back in the tub, the visor hitting the tiles, she could smell his sweat from the inside of the headband, even over the smell of the soap. His sweat had always smelled like freshly broiled white-fish.

What he owned, he took. Except for the cap, he hadn't left much else behind in the apartment. He had what he thought was a soulful indifference to material possessions, so he didn't bother saving them. It hadn't occurred to her until later that she might be one of those possessions. He had liked having things—quality durable goods—around for a little while, she thought bitterly, and then he enthusiastically threw them all out. They were there one day—his leather vest, his golf clubs—and then they were gone. She had borrowed one of his gray tee-shirts months ago to wear to bed when she had had a cold, and she still had it, a gray tee in her bottom dresser drawer. But she had accidentally washed it, and she couldn't smell him on the fabric anymore, not a trace of him.

Her cat now yowled around five-thirty, at exactly the time when he used to come home. She—the cat—had fallen for him the moment she'd seen him, rushing over to him, squirming on her back in his lap, declawed paws waving in the air. The guy had had a gift, a tiny genius for relentless charm, that caused anything—women, men, cats, trees for all she knew—to fall in love with him, and not calmly, either, but at the upper frequencies.

Her clocks ached. Time had congealed. For the last two days, knowing he would go, she had tried to be busy. She had tried reading books, for example. They couldn't preoccupy her. They were just somebody's thoughts. Her wounded imagination included him and herself, but only those two, bone hurtling against bone.

She was not a romantic and did not like the word *romance.* They hadn't had a romance, the two of them. Nothing soft or tender, like that. They had just, well, driven into each other like reckless drivers at an intersection, neither one wanting to yield the right-of-way. She was a classicist recently out of graduate school, and for a job she taught Latin and Greek in a Chicago private school, and she understood from her reading of Thucydides and Catullus and Sophocles and Sappho, among others, how people actually fought, and what happened when they actually fell in love and were genuinely and almost immediately incompatible. The old guys told the truth, she believed, about love and warfare, the peculiar combination of attraction and hatred existing together. They had told the truth before Christianity put civilization into a dream world.

After she got out of the bathtub, she put herself into bed without drying herself off first. She removed the baseball cap and rolled around under the covers, dampening the sheets. *It's like this,* she said to herself.

She thought of herself as "she." At home she narrated her actions to herself as she performed them: "Now she is watering the plants." "Now she is feeding the cat." "Now she is staring off into space." "Now she is calling her friend Ticia, who is not at home. She will not leave a message on Ticia's machine. She doesn't do that."

She stood naked in front of the mirror. She thought: I am the sexiest woman who can read Latin and Greek in the state of Illinois. She surveyed her legs and her face, which he had praised many times. I look great and feel like shit and that's that.

The next morning she made breakfast but couldn't eat it. She hated it that she had gotten into this situation, loaded down with humiliating feelings. She wouldn't tell anyone. Pushing the scrambled eggs around on the plate, making a mess of them, the buttered wheat toast, and the strawberry jam, her head down on her arm, she fell into speculation: *Okay, yes, right, it's a mistake to think that infatuation has anything to do with personality, or personal tastes. You don't, uh,* decide *about any of this, do you?* she asked herself, half-forming the words on her lips. Love puts anyone in a state outside the realm of thought, like one of those Eleusinian cults where no one ever gets permission to speak of the mysteries. When you're not looking, your mouth gets taped shut. You fall in love with someone not because he's nice to you or can read your mind but because, when he kisses you, your knees weaken, or because you can't stop looking at his skin or at the way his legs, inside his jeans, shape the fabric. His breath meets your breath, and the two breaths either intermingle and create a charge or they don't. Personality comes later; *personality,* she thought, reaching for the copy of Ovid that was about to fall off the table, *is the consolation prize of middle age.*

She put the breakfast dishes in the sink. She turned on the radio and noticed after five minutes that she hadn't listened to any of it. She snapped it off and glanced angrily in the direction of the bedroom, where all this trouble had started.

She and he had ridden each other in that bed. She glowered at it, framed in the doorway of the bedroom, sun pouring in the east window and across the yellow bedspread. They had a style, but, well, yes, almost everyone had a style. For starters, they took their time. Nothing for the manuals, nothing for the record books. But the point wasn't the lovemaking, not exactly. What they did started with sex but ended somewhere else. She believed that the sex they had together invoked the old gods, just invited them right in, until, boom, there they were. She wondered over the way the spirit-gods, the ones she lonesomely believed in, descended over them and surrounded them and briefly made them feel like gods themselves. She felt huge and powerful, together with him. It was archaic, this descent, and pleasantly scary. They both felt it happening; at least he said he did. The difference was that, after a while, he didn't care about the descent of the old gods or the spirits or whatever the hell he thought they were. He was from Arizona, and he had a taste for deserts and heat and golf and emptiness. Perhaps that explained it.

He had once blindfolded her with her silk bathrobe belt during their lovemaking and she had still felt the spirit coming down. Blindfolded, she could see it more clearly than ever.

Ovid. At the breakfast table she held onto the book that had almost fallen to the floor. Ovid: an urbane know-it-all with a taste for taking inventories. She had seldom enjoyed reading Ovid. He had a masculine smirking cynicism, and then its opposite, self-pity, which she found offensive.

And this was the *Remedia amoris,* a book she couldn't remember studying in graduate school or anywhere else. The remedies for love. She hadn't realized she even owned it. It was in the back of her edition of the *Ars amatoria.* Funny how books put themselves into your hands when they wanted you to read them.

Because spring had hit Chicago, and sunlight had given this particular Saturday morning a light fever, and because her black mood was making her soul sore, she decided to get on the Chicago Transit Authority bus and read Ovid while she rode to the suburbs and back. Absentmindedly, she found herself crying while she stood at the corner bus stop, next to the graffitied shelter, waiting. She was grateful that no one looked at her.

After the bus arrived in a jovial roar of diesel fumes and she got on, she found a seat near a smudgy semi-clean window. The noise was therapeutic, and the absence on the bus of businessmen with their golf magazines relieved her. No one on this bus on

Saturday morning had a clue about how to conduct a life. She gazed at the tattered jackets and gummy spotted clothes of the other passengers. No one with a serious relationship with money rode a bus like this at such a time. It was the fuck-up express. Hollow and stoned and vacant-eyed people like herself sat there, men who worked in carwashes, women who worked in diners. They looked as if their rights to their own sufferings had already been revoked months ago.

Over the terrible clatter, trees in blossom rushed past, dog-wood, and lilacs, and like that. The blossoms seemed every bit as noisy as the bus. She shook her head and glanced down at her book.

Scripta cave relegas blandae servata puellae:
  Constantis animos scripta relecta movent.
Omnia pone feros (pones invitus) in ignes
  Et dic 'ardoris sit rogus iste mei.'

Oh, right. Yeah. Burn the love letters? Throw them all in the flames? And then announce, "This is the pyre of my love"? Hey, thanks a lot. What love letters? He hadn't left any love letters, just this cap—she was still wearing it—with "Chevy" embossed on it in gold.

Quisquis amas, loca sola nocent: loca sola caveto;
  Quo fugis? in populo tutior esse potes.
Non tibi secretis (augent secreta furores)
  Est opus; auxilio turba futura tibi est.

Riding the CTA bus, and now glimpsing Lake Michigan through a canyon of buildings, she felt herself stepping into an emotional lull, the eye of the storm that had been knocking her around. In the storm's eye, everyone spoke Latin. The case endings and the declensions and Ovid's I-know-it-all syntax and tone remained absolutely stable, however, no matter what the subject was. They were like formulas recited from a comfortable sofa by a banker who had never made a dangerous investment. The urbanity and the calm of the poem clawed at her. She decided to translate the four lines so that they sounded heartbroken and absentminded, jostled around in the aisles.

The lonely places
  are the worst. I tell you,
    when you're heart-
  sick, go
where the pushing and shoving
    crowd gives you
  some nerve. Don't be
    alone, up in your
burning room, burning—
  trust me:
    get knocked
down in public,
    you'll be helped up.

All right: so it was a free translation. So what? She scribbled it on the back of a deposit slip from the Harris Bank and put it into her purse. She wouldn't do any more translating just now. Any advice blew unwelcome winds into her. Especially advice from Ovid.

Now they were just north of the Loop. This time, when she looked out of the window, she saw an apartment building on fire: firetrucks flamesroof waterlights crowdsbluesky smoke-smoke. There, and gone just that rapidly. Suffering, too, probably, experienced by someone, but not immediately visible, not from here, at forty miles per hour. She thought: *Well, that's corny, an apartment fire as seen from a bus. Nothing to do about that one.* Quickly she smelled smoke, and then, just as quickly, it was gone. To herself, she grinned without realizing what she was doing. Then she looked around. No one had seen her smile. She had always liked fires. She felt ashamed of herself, but momentarily cheerful.

She found herself in Evanston, got out, and took the return bus back. She had observed too much of the lake on the way. Lake Michigan was at its most decorative and bourgeois in the northern suburbs: whitecaps, blue water, waves lapping the shore, abjectly picturesque.

By afternoon she was sitting in O'Hare Airport, at gate 23A, the waiting area for a flight to Memphis. She wasn't going to Memphis—she didn't have a ticket to anywhere—and she wasn't about to meet anyone, but she had decided to take Ovid's advice to go where the crowds were, for the tonic effect. She had always liked the anonymity of airports anyway. A businessman carrying a laptop computer and whose face had a WASPy nondescript pudgy blankness fueled by liquor and avarice was raising his voice at the gate agent, an African-American woman. Men like that raised their voices and made demands as a way of life; it was as automatic and as thoughtless as cement turning and slopping around inside a cement mixer. "I don't think you understand the situation," he was saying. He had a standby ticket but had not been in the gate area when they had called his name, and now, the plane being full, he would have to take a later flight. "You have no understanding of my predicament here. Who is your superior?" His wingtip shoes were scuffed, and his suit was tailored one size too small for him, so that it bulged at the waist. He had combed strands of hair across his sizable bald spot. His forehead was damp with sweat, and his nose sported broken capillaries. He was not quite first class. She decided to eat a chili dog and find another gate to sit in. Walking away, she heard the gate agent saying, "I'm sorry, sir. I'm sorry."

You couldn't eat a chili dog in this airport sitting down. It was not permitted. You had to stand at the plastic counter of Here's Mr. Chili, trying not to spill on the polyester guy reading *USA Today,* your volume of *Publius Ovidius Naso* next to you, your napkin in your other hand, thinking about Ovid's exile to the fringe of the Roman empire, to Tomis, where, broken in spirit, solitary, he wrote the *Tristia,* some of the saddest poems written by anyone anywhere, but a—what?—male sadness about being far from where the action was. There was no action in Tomis, no glamour, no togas—just peasants and plenty of mud labor. On the opposite side of Here's Mr. Chili was another gate where post-frightened passengers were scurrying out of the plane from Minneapolis. A woman in jeans and carrying a backpack fell into the arms of her boyfriend. They had started to kiss, the way people do in airports, in that depressing public style, all hands and tongues. And over here a chunky Scandinavian grandma was grasping her grandchildren in her arms like ships tied up tightly to a dock. You should go where people are happy, Ovid was saying. You should witness the high visibility of joy. You should believe. In . . . ?

Si quis amas nec vis, facito contagia vites
Right, right: "If you don't
want to love,
don't expose yourself to
the sight
of love, the contagion."

Evening would be coming on soon; she had to get back.

She was feeling a bit light-headed, the effect of the additives in the chili dog: the Red concourse of O'Hare, with its glacially smooth floors and reflecting surfaces, was, at the hour before twilight, the scariest manmade place she'd ever seen. *This airport is really manmade,* she thought, *they don't get more manmade than this.* Of course, she had seen it a hundred times before, she just hadn't bothered looking. If something hadn't been hammered or fired, it wasn't in this airport. Stone, metal, and glass, like the hyperextended surfaces of eternity, across which insect-people moved, briefly, trying before time ran out to find a designated anthill. Here was a gate for Phoenix. There was a gate for Raleigh-Durham. One locale was pretty much like another. People made a big deal of their own geographical differences to give themselves specific details to talk about. Los Angeles, Cedar Rapids, Duluth. What did it matter where anyone lived—Rome, Chicago, or Romania? All she really wanted was to be in the same room with her as-of-yesterday ex. Just being around him had made her happy. It was horrible but true. She had loved him so much it gave her the creeps. He wasn't worthy of her love but so what. Maybe, she thought, she should start doing an inventory of her faults, you know, figure the whole thing out—scars, bad habits, phrases she had used that he hadn't liked. Then she could do an inventory of his faults. She felt some ketchup under her shoe and let herself fall.

She looked up.

Hands gripped her. Random sounds of sympathy. "Hey, lady, are you all right?" "Can you stand?" "Do you need some help?" A man, a woman, a second man: Ovid's public brigade of first-aiders held her, clutched at her where she had sprawled sort of deliberately, here in the Red concourse. Expressions of fake concern like faces painted on flesh-colored balloons lowered themselves to her level. "I just slipped." "You're okay, you're fine?" "Yes." She felt her breast being brushed against, not totally and completely unpleasantly. It felt like the memory of a touch rather than a touch itself, no desire in it, no nothing. There: She was up. Upright. And dragging herself off, Ovid under her arm, to the bus back to the Loop and her apartment. Falling in the airport and being lifted up: okay, so it happened as predicted, but it didn't make you feel wonderful. Comfortably numb was more like it. She dropped the *Remedia amoris* into a trash bin. Then she thought, uh oh, big mistake, maybe the advice is all wrong but at least he wants to cheer me up, who else wants to do that? She reached her hand into the trash bin and, looking like a wino grasping for return bottles, she pulled out her soiled book, smeared with mustard and relish.

"Kit?"

A voice.

"Yes?" She turned around. She faced an expression of pleased surprise, on a woman she couldn't remember ever seeing before.

"It's me. Caroline."

"Caroline?" As if she recognized her. Which she didn't. At all.

"What a coincidence! This is too amazing! What are you doing here?"

"I'm, um, I was here. Seeing someone off. You know. To . . . ah, Seattle."

"Seattle." The Caroline-person nodded, in a, well, professional way, one of those therapeutic nods. Her hair had a spiky thickness, like straw or hay. Maybe Caroline would mention the traffic in Seattle. The ferries? Puget Sound? "What's that?" She pointed at the haplessly soiled book.

"Oh, this?" Kit shrugged. "Ovid."

More nodding. Blondish hair spiked here and there, arrows pointing at the ceiling and the light fixtures and the arrival-and-departure screens. The Caroline-person carried—no, actually pulled on wheels—a tan suitcase, and she wore a business suit, account executive attire, a little gold pin in the shape of the Greek lambda on her lapel. Not a very pretty pin, but maybe a clue: lambda, lambda, now what would that . . . possibly mean? Suitcase: This woman *didn't* live here in Chicago. Or else she *did*.

"You were always reading, Kit. All that Greek and Latin!" She stepped back and surveyed. "You look simply fabulous! With the cap? Such a cute retro look, it's so street-smart, like . . . who's that actress?"

"Yeah, well, I have to . . . it's nice to see you, Caroline, but I'm headed back to the Loop, it's late, and I have to—"

"—Is your car here?" A hand wave: Caroline-person wedding ring: tasteful diamond of course, that's the way it goes in the Midwest, wedding rings everyfuckingwhere.

"Uh, no, we took, I mean, he and I took the taxi out." Some-how it seemed important to repeat that. "We took a taxi."

"Great! I'll give you a ride back. I'll take you to your place. I'll drop you right at the doorstep. Would you like some company? Come on!"

She felt her elbow being touched.

Down the long corridors of O'Hare Airport shaped like the ever-ballooning hallways of eternity, the Caroline-person pulled her suitcase, its tiny wheels humming behind her high-heeled businesslike stride; and easily keeping up in her jogging shoes, in which she jogged when the mood struck her, Kit tried to remember where on this planet, and in this life, she'd met this person. Graduate school? College? She wasn't a parent of one of her students, that was certain. *You were always reading.* Must've been college. "It's been so long," the woman was saying. "Must be . . . what?" They edged out of the way of a beeping handicap cart.

Kit shook her head as if equally exasperated by their mutual ignorance.

"Well, I don't know either," Caroline-person said. "So, who'd you see off?"

"What?"

"To Seattle."

"Oh," Kit said.

"Something the matter?"

"It was Billy," Kit said. "It was Billy I put on the plane."

"Kit," she said, "I haven't seen you in years. Who's this Billy?" She gave her a sly girlish smile. "Must be somebody special."

Kit nodded. "Yeah. Must be."

"Oh," Caroline said, "you can tell me."

"Actually, I can't."

"Why not?"

"Oh, I'd just rather not."

A smile took over Caroline's face like the moon taking over the sun during an eclipse. "But you can. You can tell me."

"No, I can't."

"Why?"

"Because I don't remember you, Caroline. I don't remember the first thing about you. I know a person's not supposed to admit that, but it's been a bad couple of days, and I just don't know who you are. Probably we went to college together or something, classics majors and all that, but I can't remember." They had stopped near a Buick display, and Kit wondered for a moment how the GM people got the car, a large midnight blue Roadmaster, into the airport. People rushed past them and around them. "I don't remember you at all."

"You're kidding," the woman said.

"No," Kit said, "I'm not. I can't remember seeing you before."

The woman who said her name was Caroline put her hand on her forehead and stared at Kit with a what-have-we-here? shocked look. Kit knew she was supposed to feel humiliated and embarrassed, but instead she felt shiny and new and fine for the first time all day. She didn't like to be tactless, but that seemed to be the direction, at least right now, this weekend, where her freedom lay. She'd been so good for so long, she thought, so loving and sweet and agreeable, and look where it had gotten her. "You're telling me," the woman said, "that you don't remember our—"

"—Stop," Kit said. "Don't tell me."

"Wait. You don't even want to be reminded? You're . . . but why? Now I'm offended," the woman told her. "Let's start over. Let's begin again. Kit, I feel very hurt."

"I know," Kit said. "It's been a really strange afternoon."

"I just don't think . . ." the woman said, but then she was unable to finish the sentence. "Our ride into the city . . ."

"Oh, that's all right," Kit said. "I couldn't take up your offer. I'll ride the bus back. They have good buses here," she added.

"No," she said. "Go with me."

"I can't, Caroline. I don't remember you. We're strangers."

"Well, uh, goodbye then," the woman muttered. "You certainly have changed."

"I certainly have. But I'm almost never like this. It's Billy who did this to me." She gazed in Caroline's direction. "And my vocabulary," she said, not quite knowing what she meant. But she liked it, so she repeated it. "My vocabulary did this to me."

"It's that bad?" the woman said.

Standing by the Buick Roadmaster in O'Hare Airport, where she had gone for no good reason except that she could not stand to be alone in her apartment, she felt, for about ten seconds, tiny and scaled-down, like a model person in a model airport as viewed from above, and she reached out and balanced herself on the driver's side door handle and then shook her head and closed her eyes. If she accepted compassion from this woman, there would be nothing left of her in the morning. Sympathy would give her chills and fever, and she would start shaking, and the shaking would move her out of the hurricane's eye into the hurricane itself, and it would batter her, and then wear her away to the zero. Nothing in life had ever hurt her more than sympathy.

"I have to go now," Kit said, turning away. She walked fast, and then ran, in the opposite direction.

Of course I remember you. We were both in a calculus class. We had hamburgers after the class sometimes in the college greasy spoon, and we talked about boys and the future and your dog at home, Brutus, in New Buffalo, Minnesota, where your mother bred cairn terriers. In the backyard there was fencing for a kennel, and that's where Brutus stayed. He sometimes climbed to the top of his little pile of stones to survey what there was to survey of the fields around your house. He barked at hawks and skunks. Thunderstorms scared him, and he was so lazy, he hated to take walks. When he was inside, he'd hide under the bed, where he thought no one could see him, with his telltale leash visible, trailing out on the bedroom floor. You told that story back then. You were pretty in those days. You still are. You wear a pin in the shape of the Greek letter lambda and a diamond wedding ring. In those days, I recited poetry. I can remember you. I just can't do it in front of you. I can't remember you when you're there.

She gazed out the window of the bus. She didn't feel all right but she could feel all right approaching her, somewhere off there in the distance.

She had felt it lifting when she had said his name was Billy. It wasn't Billy. It was Ben. Billy hadn't left her; Ben had. There never had been a Billy, but maybe now there was. She was saying goodbye to him; he wasn't saying goodbye to her. She turned on the overhead light as the bus sped through Des Plaines, and she tried to read some Ovid, but she immediately dozed off.

Roaring through the traffic on the Kennedy Expressway, the bus lurched and rocked, and Kit's head on the headrest turned from side to side, an irregular rhythm, but a rhythm all the same: enjambments, caesuras, stophes.

My darling girl, (he said, thinner
than she'd ever thought he'd be,
mostly bald, a few sprout curls,
and sad-but-cheerful, certainly,
Roman and wryly unfeminist, unhumanist,
unliving), child of gall and wormwood (he pointed his
thin malnourished finger at her,
soil inside the nail),
what on earth
brought you to that unlikely place?
An airport! Didn't I tell you,
clearly,
to shun such spots? A city park on a warm
Sunday afternoon wouldn't be as bad. People fall
into one another's arms out there all the time.
Hundreds of them! (He seemed exasperated.)
Thank you (he said)
for reading me, but for the sake

of your own well-being, don't go there
again without a ticket. It seems
you have found me out. (He
shrugged.) Advice? I don't have any
worth passing on. It's easier
to give advice when you're alive
than when you're not,
and besides, I swore it off. Oh I liked
what you did with Caroline, the lambda-girl
who wears that pin because her husband
gave it to her on her birthday,
March twenty-first—now that
I'm dead, I know everything
but it does me not a particle of good—
but naturally she thinks it has no
special meaning, and that's the way
she conducts her life. Him, too. He
bought it at a jewelry store next to a shoe
shop in the mall at 2 p.m.
March 13, a Thursday—but I digress—
and the salesgirl,
cute thing, hair done in a short cut
style, flirted with him
showing him no mercy,
touching his coat sleeve,
thin wool, because she was on commission. Her
name was
Eleanor, she had green eyes.
The pin cost him $175, plus tax.
She took him, I mean, took him for a ride,
as you would say,
then went out for coffee. By herself, that is,
thinking of her true
and best beloved, Claire, an obstetrician
with lovely hands. I always did admire
Sapphic love. But I'm
still digressing. (He smirked.)

The distant failed humor of the dead.
Our timing's bad,
the jokes are dusty,
and we can't concentrate
on just
one thing. I'm as interested
in Eleanor as I am
in you. Lambda. Who cares? Lambda: I suppose
I mean, I *know*,

he thought the eleventh letter, that uncompleted triangle,
looked like his wife's legs. Look:
I can't help it,
I'm—what is the word?—salacious, that's
the way I always was,
the bard of breasts and puberty, I was
exiled for it, I turned to powder
six feet under all the topsoil
in Romania. Sweetheart, what on earth
are you *doing* on
this bus? Wake up, kiddo, that guy
Ben is gone, good riddance
is my verdict from two thousand
years ago, to you.
Listen: I have a present for you.

He took her hand.
His hand didn't feel like much,
it felt like water when you're reaching
down for a stone or shell
under the water, something you don't
have, but want, and your fingers
strain toward it.
Here, he said, this is the one stunt
I can do: look up, sweetie, check out
this:
(he raised his arm in ceremony)
See? he said proudly. It's raining.
I made it rain. I can do that.
The rain is falling, only
it's not water, it's
this other thing. It's the other thing
that's raining, soaking you. Goodbye.

When she awoke, at the sound of the air brakes, the bus driver announced that they had arrived at their first stop, the Palmer House. It wasn't quite her stop, but Kit decided to get out. The driver stood at the curb as the passengers stepped down, and the streetlight gave his cap an odd bluish glow. His teeth were so discolored they looked like pencil erasers. He asked her if she had any luggage, and Kit said, no, she hadn't brought any luggage with her.

The El clattered overhead. She was in front of a restaurant with thick glass windows. On the other side of the glass, a man with a soiled unpressed tie was talking and eating prime rib. On the sidewalk, just down the block, under an orange neon light, an old woman was shouting curses at the moon and Mayor Daley. She wore a paper hat and her glasses had only one lens in them, on the left side, and her curses were so interesting, so incoherently articulate, uttered in that voice, which was like sandpaper worried across a brick, that Kit forgot that she was supposed to be unhappy, she was listening so hard, and watching the way the orange was reflected in that one lens.

....

A Conversation with Charles Baxter

At the base of your work is the mystery of human love of all kinds, really the mystery of human existence. Yet nearly all of your stories are set in the Midwest, a part of the world known for its ordinariness. Would you talk about the ways in which the mysteries and ordinariness of life converge to make stories happen for you in this kind of setting?

Flaubert said that to find anything interesting, you merely had to look at it long enough. It's the business of the writer not to make extraordinary events interesting (they're interesting anyway), but to make the seemingly "ordinary" ones seem new again. Life anywhere, everywhere, is bewilderingly mysterious, fascinating, and worthy of our attention; the writer must simply put a strong pressure of close attention on it. An out-of-work man sitting on a sofa, a secretary calling her lover for a rendezvous somewhere, a woman recovering from a love affair—why shouldn't these common people and events be worth reading about?

How did the imaginary Five Oaks, Michigan, evolve in your mind? Why do you so often set stories in this imaginary setting, and how do you see the relationships among the characters who live their stories out, occasionally crossing paths with each other, in that setting?

The first time I used it, it was just a setting for a story ("Saul and Patsy Are Getting Comfortable in Michigan"). Then I used it again for "Gryphon." By that time I had realized that I had spent quite a bit of time in large towns and small cities, and I knew that particular town/city well enough to write about it repeatedly, and over a period of time, as it evolved during two decades. Every time I thought of Five Oaks, I imagined it as a model setting for events that were happening elsewhere: The city suffers from unemployment and outsourcing, and pollution, and trouble in its schools and among its young people. The relationships among the characters are often like relationships anywhere and everywhere, though those characters suffer from a particular kind of solitude. Not always, but often.

What makes you know that a story idea will best play out in this setting?

I don't always know. But I know I can't use it if some other particular feature of a community is needed for a story or novel. *The Feast of Love* my third novel, required talkers for its main characters, people telling their stories aloud, and so I used Ann Arbor, Michigan, as a setting, because it's a university town, and many people are unusually loquacious there. Five Oaks is more a setting that emphasizes solitude, isolation, a feeling of being cut-off, and an occasional refusal to speak aloud. Loneliness—and a reluctance to speak about it—is what that city has.

In what ways, if any, are the Five Oaks stories set apart from your other stories?

All the stories set in that community have as a common thread a character who is trying to find his or her way to a sense of where he or she "belongs"—a common subject for fiction.

Would you talk, generally, about how stories "gather" for you and finally make their way to the page? How do you recognize an idea or detail as your own—something from which you might make a story? Do you keep folders or have other ways of organizing incubating story ideas? How do you know when the moment is ripe to actually begin a story?

I don't keep folders. I just keep thinking and thinking about a story or a dramatic action that has some kind of interesting incongruity in it until I can see it well enough to start writing. I don't always know whether it will be a story; I have to write it *down to* find out. Usually I start when I have enough time to write, when I don't feel rushed.

I don't always know whether it will be a story; I have to write it *down to* find out.

How do you recognize the problems in the early drafts of your stories and go about solving them? Is there a particular kind of revision you find yourself faced with most often?

I read and reread and reread what I've written. I try to put myself in the position of a reader who is gamely looking for a good meaningful story with a feeling of some kind attached to it. If I feel that something is wrong with the story, something probably is, and I keep searching for it so I can fix it. If the story entertains me, causes me to laugh, keeps me interested after several rereadings, it might be okay. When I revise, I often have to take out extraneous images and details; I have to keep things moving.

When I revise, I often have to take out extraneous images and details; I have to keep things moving.

How do you know when a story is finished?

If, no matter how many times I have reread it, I can't think of anything else to do to it, it's probably finished. When nothing else seems to suggest itself, the story is done.

When people talk about your work, they almost always comment on your mastery of the third-person point of view. How do you explain the fundamentals of the third-person point of view to your students, and in what ways do you guide them toward being able to recognize when third person is the most appropriate way to tell a story?

I actually don't have any theories about third-person versus first-person narratives. It all depends on how you hear the story coming to you. Nevertheless, if you're going to

I like close-third person narratives because I have both some intimacy with, and some distance on, the character.

use third-person point of view, you have to decide what the character would notice, what the character would see, and you have to decide how much of his/her thoughts you're going to allow in the narrative. I like close-third person narratives because I have both some intimacy with, and some distance on, the character. First-person narratives don't give you the same kind of distance.

In your experience, what do students most often get wrong when attempting a story in the third person?

Sometimes they don't realize that a third-person point of view is a commitment. You can't suddenly change to someone else's point of view. Also, they sometimes become afraid of emotion and don't know how to express it through third person. They're afraid that any real drama will seem melodramatic. But if it's truthful and clear and logical, it won't be.

In "The Next Building I Plan to Bomb," Harry Edmonds, a banker, finds a scrap of paper with a drawing of what looks like a train station with "The next building I plan to bomb" scrawled on it. He proceeds to show it to various people, each of whom interprets it completely differently depending on the circumstances of his or her life. What makes this a story, as opposed to a kind of meditation on point of view? Would you talk about your sense of what a story is, the elasticity of the short story form?

The story is really about Harry Edmonds, and it's not about the note or the views of other people about the note; the note is a kind of calling card that Harry uses with people whom he meets. Harry doesn't want to be taken for granted. He doesn't want to seem ordinary (he's not, for example, the straight heterosexual that he seems, at first, to be). He wants people to notice him. But he feels invisible, and that's the central conflict, as it is in several of my stories. He's in a kind of crisis point of his life, and when people get into that condition, they're often story material. Something has happened to Harry that will tip his life over; the little slip of paper actually is a bomb, in a sense, and when people reach a crisis point, and their lives threaten to shatter, you have a story on your hands.

An early story, "Media Event," begins "This is his story." A single paragraph sets the reader up to know that the story that follows is being written by the protagonist himself in third person "for greater accuracy and objectivity," thus profoundly affecting the reader's perception of the unfolding events. Would you comment on the genesis and evolution of that story and what writing it taught you about the third-person point of view and point of view, generally?

> The psychological or psychic understanding of a character comes first, and that understanding then calls forth a writerly strategy to get it down dramatically on paper.

Well, that story begins with a central character who suffers, as Harry Edmonds does, from invisibility. That characterological feature dictated the point-of-view strategy: George, the narrator of "Media Event," would think of himself as a *he,* as a someone else. He's so unhappy inside his own skin and his own identity that he looks at himself all the time as if he himself were another person. The story feels and sounds slightly schizoid, as he is. The psychological or psychic understanding of a character comes first, and that understanding then calls forth a writerly strategy to get it down dramatically on paper.

Your often-anthologized "Gryphon," narrated by a fourth-grade boy, is the story of what happens when a strange substitute teacher is assigned to his class for several days. What made "Gryphon" a first-person story for you?

I felt the story required a kind of immediacy that I could only get from the first-person narrator who is remembering an event that happened a long time ago. The boy's reactions are crucial; these events are happening to *him.*

What do you feel a young writer can learn from writing from the point of view of a child?

How to write down the way things look and feel and sound without inserting a lot of commentary. Children often look very closely at events without commenting on them.

What was the genesis of "Gryphon," and how did it evolve in your mind and on the page?

I once taught fourth grade and, one day in springtime, spent an afternoon making up facts about ancient Egypt. I thought I'd be fired, but no one seemed to notice that I had done anything wrong. This happened during the era of the Vietnam War, when public officials were lying about what was going on. It gave me an idea. I wrote the story several years later.

What did you know when you began the story? What surprised you along the way?

I knew that I wanted to write a story about a substitute teacher who comes into class and begins to teach "substitute facts." The fourth graders can't argue with her because they don't know enough about the world to argue; besides, she's fun, at first. She's a relief from the usual grade school drudgery. The story was boiled down from a failed novel about lying. What surprised me was that I couldn't make her an out-and-out lunatic. That shouldn't have surprised me, but in the first draft she's much crazier than she is in the published version. She has to be a convincing borderline personality, and, for the most part, I think she is.

Would you talk about how a young writer can know the difference between a surprise in process that is useful and one that is likely to take the story off-track?

The surprise has to be integral to the materials. If you put in a surprise just to surprise the audience, you're doing it for rhetorical reasons, and it will probably look and sound phony. You can't know the difference until the story is done, and then, if you can't tell what the story is about, or if it seems to be about two incompatible subjects, you probably know that somewhere the story took a left turn. You may have to throw it away, or do a radical revision. But that's life.

Miss Ferenczi, the subsitute teacher, is among the first of a type of character that often appears in your work: a borderline crazy person who wreaks havoc in the main character's view of the way the world really is, rendering him alternately enlightened, empowered, frightened, angry, and confused. Would you talk about how you used Miss Ferenczi to convey something about the world of childhood in this story?

Children are at the mercy of authorities. All childhood is a condition of being in an authoritarian state. Most of the time, children are asked to see all authority as correct. But sometimes it's not correct, and if it isn't, then what's going to happen to the child's world? What's going to happen to reliability? Such a switch constitutes a small but genuine revolution. What if our authorities aren't telling the truth? That's a question worth asking, starting in childhood.

The story torques as Miss Ferenczi moves from being charmingly eccentric and intellectually provocative toward the moment when she does actual harm in reading the tarot cards and telling one of the children that he will die soon. The narrator reports, "She told me my future," but he does not say what she told him. Why did you decide against including that information in the story?

Fiction grows equally out of what we don't know and can't figure out as from what we do know.

Because by the time Tommy tells the story, he knows whether her prediction has come true. At the time, he didn't know, and neither should the reader. Miss Ferenczi should be somewhat undecidable, unknowable. Fiction grows equally out of what we don't know and can't figure out as from what we do know. That mystery is at the heart of fiction that we return to, that we can't help thinking about.

Would you talk, generally, about the power of what's left out of a story and how a writer can find the right balance between mystery and confusion?

What's left out of a story creates a gap for the reader's own imagination to fill. Readers like to imagine quite a bit for themselves. Confusion arises when a character knows some crucial piece of information at the time that he or she withholds from the reader (at the time that "Gryphon" takes place, Tommy does not know whether Miss Ferenczi's prediction came true). Tommy's not-telling the reader is not confusing. What would be confusing would be if he withheld information about what age his childhood protagonist was, or where he was, etc. You can't withhold important expository material. You have to play fair with the ground-situation of a story.

What's left out of a story creates a gap for the reader's own imagination to fill.

"The Cures for Love" is an incredibly intelligent story that is also funny, insightful, and compassionate. Would you talk about the genesis and evolution of the story, particu-

larly in regard to your use of Ovid as a way of defining your character and shaping the plot?

In high school Latin class, we read Ovid's *The Art of Love.* I found out later that Ovid had written a sequel, *The Cures for Love,* which is rarely read. In that book, Ovid explains how to get over a love affair that's ended. I'd gone through some love affairs myself, and I became interested in the whole problem of recovering your equilibrium after a relationship ends. So I mulled it over for a long time, and finally I wrote that story.

How did you go about crafting the story so that it could be thoroughly enjoyed, if not fully appreciated, by a reader without any knowledge of Ovid at all?

Almost everything in it is explained. A reader might not know Ovid's major works, but most of the historical background can be figured out from the exposition.

You called yourself an ex-poet in an essay in Burning Down the House, *yet near the end of "The Cures for Love," the voice shifts to Ovid speaking to Kit by way of a two-and-a-half-page poem. Would you talk about what brought you out of "retirement" to write it and also about the pitfalls a writer faces when original poetry is required to give a story the desired effect?*

It was a dare on my part, a piece of risky business. I wanted her to dream of Ovid speaking, and once I decided that he would speak, I decided that he had to speak in verse. The story seemed to require it. The pitfalls are obvious: If the poetry is lousy, it won't (of course) sound anything like Ovid. But I had read a lot of Ovid and thought I could do a cheap imitation of his ruefulness.

The poet in your story admits he couldn't help being the salacious "bard of breasts and puberty," and it got him exiled. The mature Ovid was obsessed with being read and remembered and he is, for The Metamorphoses. *Even for his exile letters, all written in verse. The Ovid of your story is proud when he waves his arm—transforms—and the rain is something else. Would you talk about this "other thing" and how it brings the reader to the final image of Kit in the story, listening and watching?*

I wasn't exactly sure what the "other thing" was, and, like the prediction in "Gryphon," wanted to leave it to the reader's imagination. But it's Ovid's small metamorphosis in the story: He waves his hand, and the rain turns into something it isn't, something (I think) that my protagonist needs.

"The Cures for Love" must have been fun to write, for all its risks and challenges. Would you talk about the things you like best about this story, and why?

It *was* fun to write. It wasn't like my other stories. I had a lonely sexy classicist in it, a Chicago setting, Ovid (who speaks in verse), a moment of social amnesia, and a real subject: how anyone ever gets over anything and gets on with his or her life. I especially liked that old person at the end of the story whom Kit sees when she gets off the bus. It means that Kit is starting to get interested in the world again.

What were the story's surprises in process?

I can't remember. Often when I write a story, I'm in a kind of dream world, and I can't remember the stages the story went through afterwards. I do remember that I was unusually happy (for me) while I was writing it. I reread Ovid's advice about getting over someone. He advises people to get out of the house, burn all images of the beloved, and to fall down in the street: People will help you up, Ovid says, and that's a good lesson.

What are the pitfalls of spinning such an esoteric topic into fiction? What mistakes do most writers make when they decide to create fiction from an area of academic expertise?

Some readers may think that the story is putting on airs or is trying to make them, the readers, feel stupid. But the story is not really about Ovid or *The Cures for Love* that Ovid actually wrote. It's about something most people have gone through: suffering after a love has ended. Everyone can get into the story through that door.

Young writers often create nameless characters, referred to as he *or* she, *hoping to achieve a certain effect but, instead, just creating confusion and/or a false sense of drama. You don't reveal the main character's name in "The Cures for Love" until ten pages into the story, when Caroline, the woman who recognizes her in the airport, speaks it. Why did you decide not to name Kit until halfway through the story, and why does it work? How can a writer know when it is and isn't appropriate to allow a character to remain nameless?*

The story is in such a close-third point of view that Kit wouldn't be thinking of her own name while she's hanging around her apartment, and because she's alone in her apartment, the name just didn't naturally come up. It doesn't come up until the encounter in the airport. She doesn't need a name until then. Also, she feels anonymous, because her boyfriend has broken up with her. She feels generic. She feels like a *she*—a lonely woman—and not like Kit.

There's a brief switch to first person just after Kit turns away from Caroline, in which she remembers intimate details of the friendship, ending with "I can't remember you when you're there." Why did you make that switch? Would you talk about that passage, upon which the story hinges?

It's a moment of self-reconnection, a moment of great intimacy—and the switch would have a sudden effect, I thought. It seemed to me that most readers wouldn't notice the switch except subliminally. It's a sign that Kit is less self-alienated to herself. She's an *I* again.

There's such pleasure reading this story, being smug and amused, knowing the truth in Ovid's "Love and dignity cannot share the same abode" while Kit is rolling around in bed without drying herself off, wearing the ex's baseball cap and pontificating about mutual love that "started with sex, but ended somewhere else.—" Yet at the same time, you're fully engaged in the story. Would you talk about the reader's role in this story—or in any story, for that matter. How much is it fair for a writer to expect a reader to bring to a story?

I'm not sure how interesting "The Cures for Love" would be to someone who has never been exalted with or has suffered from love. Love makes even smart people act stupid, act unlike themselves. Kit is going through a kind of anguish that is quite impersonal. The writer has to imagine that the reader will bring some experiences of his or her own to the story; what I have imagined will connect, with luck, to the reader's experience. Sometimes the reader will be interested in activities that he or she may have had no experience of, but much good art involves both something new, and something recognized.

The writer has to imagine that the reader will bring some experiences of his or her own to the story; what I have imagined will connect, with luck, to the reader's experience.

Everything Kit reveals about herself illustrates to the reader what a "high-maintenance" person she is, how impossible the failed relationship must have been, how unlikely it is that she could have a satisfying relationship with anyone. Yet the paradox in her intellectual distance from herself and the way she gives herself up to Ovid, letting things happen randomly and gain a kind of reckless momentum, makes her so appealing. Would you talk about how she evolved for you, and about the importance of contradiction, generally, in the creation of character?

First I fell in love with her. I imagined a beautiful naked woman in her bath, wearing a baseball cap. Then I gave her something to feel sorrowful about. Then I made her smart, but at her wit's end, helpless. She's contradictory, like many of us. She'd be hard to get along with, but I would have liked to have known her. The whole story is somewhat unstable because she doesn't know what to do with herself, so she has to get into motion, go somewhere, do something. So she goes to the airport, which I did, when I was in high school, and very lonely, just to kill time, and so I could imagine myself going somewhere else.

Talk, too, about Caroline: the deftness with which you created her in a few crucial details and the difference between bringing major and minor characters to the page.

Sometimes I've had the experience of meeting someone whom I was supposed to know, but whom I could not remember. For Caroline, all I needed was someone who seemed to have her life in order, and who was helpful, and sane, and all that which Kit isn't, at that particular moment. Kit doesn't want that kind of suburban competence just yet. She wants to be soulful in her unhappiness for a little while longer. She needs to grieve.

While we're on the subject of character, how did Saul and Patsy evolve from short story characters to characters in the novel Saul and Patsy?

They wouldn't leave me alone. They wouldn't die. They kept creeping back into my imagination. They wanted to be characters in a novel, not in a group of short stories. These things happen.

Is there a guideline for recognizing the difference between an idea for a short story and one that should become a novel—or a novella? In what ways do you consider both characters and plot differently when writing a short story, a novella, and a novel?

Short story characters are often ruled by impulse, and they rarely create what you might call a history. Novel characters make decisions and plans, and those decisions and plans have consequences that keep the novel going, like a set of dominoes falling. When you map out a novel, you have to think of long-term consequences of actions that your characters commit. You are, in effect, creating a kind of history for them.

Short story characters are often ruled by impulse, and they rarely create what you might call a history.

Though you've written novels, novellas, essays, and poetry, you've worked most in the short story form. What drew you to the short story as a young writer, and what keeps you interested in it now, both as a writer and a reader?

I wrote three apprentice novels that were never published, and I realized that I wasn't learning how to write by writing them. I only buckled down to specific details and real characters when I started writing short stories. It seemed to me a kind of minority art form, with somewhat marginal characters, an art form for the down-and-out, and I liked that. I came to dislike or at least to distrust some of the big bow-wow effects of novels and was drawn to the quietness and subtlety of the short story form.

What do you think aspiring writers least understand about the process by which stories are made, and what is your best advice to them?

In stories, as in novels, something has to happen, and the more momentous these events are to the character, the better. Young writers, who have watched a lot of TV and seen many movies, may be drawn toward the subject of violence as a subject for their stories in order to keep the reader's attention, but stories do not need violence: What they need instead is emotional intensity, pitched at the highest possible believable level. Emotional intensity is actually harder to write than violence, and you put more on the line and risk more when you get it on paper. You can be ridiculed for it. But it is at the heart of much of the literature I care about, the literature that concerns what men and women do to each other under conditions of stress, and how they behave when confronting one another.

But stories do not need violence: What they need instead is emotional intensity, pitched at the highest possible believable level.

Writing Prompts

READ: "The Cures of Love" and the interview with **Charles Baxter.**

PONDER: How Baxter uses his knowledge of Ovid to create a character and to color her responses to lost love.

WRITE: Create a character who has some kind of specific knowledge or expertise. Then write a scene in which that knowledge comes into play to reveal something about the character's present situation.

PRACTICE:

- Write a scene in which your character remembers an object or an event at two different stages in his life.
- Imagine a story that could take place only in one particular setting—for instance, a college town, a rural farming community, a hotel, a nursing home, or a prison. Consider the ways in which the place and the people in this setting might shape the action and resolution of the story.
- Let your character find or receive something unexpected, startling. Write a scene in which the found thing reveals something about her.
- Create a character in crisis and then imagine events that might bring the crisis to a head and provide material for a story.
- Write a scene from a child's point of view, expressing the way things look, feel, and sound without commenting on them.
- Create a borderline crazy character and set him in motion in the midst of people going about their day-to-day lives.
- Write a beginning for a story using Baxter's first line: "This is his story."
- Write a story about someone who feels invisible.

Dan Chaon

Dan Chaon (b. 1964) is the author of two collections of short stories and one novel. Born in Omaha, Nebraska, he was educated at Northwestern University and Syracuse University. His honors include the Raymond Carver Memorial Award, the Chiocote Foundation Fiction Award, the A. B. Guthrie, Jr. Short Fiction Award, and a National Book Award nomination. His stories have been anthologized in The Best American Short Stories, The Pushcart Prize: Best of the Small Presses, *and* The O. Henry Prize Stories. *Chaon is the Houck Associate Professor of Humanities at Oberlin College. He lives in Cleveland Heights, Ohio.*

For Further Reading:
Fitting Ends and Other Stories (1996), *Among the Missing* (2001), *You Remind Me of Me* (2004).

Big Me

It all started when I was twelve years old. Before that, everything was a peaceful blur of childhood, growing up in the small town of Beck, Nebraska. A "town," we called it. Really, the population was just less than two hundred, and it was one of those dots along Highway 30 that people didn't usually even slow down for, though strangers sometimes stopped at the little gas station near the grain elevator, or ate at the café. My mother and father owned a bar called The Crossroads, at the edge of town. We lived in a little house behind it, and behind our house was the junkyard, and beyond that were wheat fields, which ran all the way to a line of bluffs and barren hills, full of yucca and rattlesnakes.

Back then I spent a lot of time in my mind, building a city up toward those hills. This imaginary place was also called Beck, but it was a metropolis of a million people. The wise though cowardly mayor lived in a mansion in the hills above the interstate, as did the bullish. Teddy Roosevelt–like police commissioner, Winthrop Golding. There were other members of the rich and powerful who lived in enormous old Victorian houses along the bluffs, and many of them harbored dreadful secrets, or were involved in one way or another with the powerful Beck underworld. One wealthy, respectable citizen, Mr. Karaffa, turned out to be a lycanthrope who preyed on the lovely, virginal junior high school girls, mutilating them beyond recognition, until I shot him with a silver bullet. I was the city Detective, though I was often underappreciated, and, because of my radical notions, in danger of being fired by the cowardly mayor. The police commissioner always defended me, even when he was exasperated by my unorthodox methods. He respected my integrity.

I don't know how many of my childhood years existed in this imaginary city. Already by the age of eight I had become the Detective, and shortly thereafter I began drawing maps of the metropolis. By the time we left Beck, I had a folder six inches thick, full of street guides and architecture and subway schedules. In the real town, I was known as the strange kid who wandered around talking to himself. Old people would find me in their backyard garden and come out and yell at me. Children would see me playing on their swing sets, and when they came out to challenge me, I would run away. I trapped people's cats and bound their arms and legs, harshly forcing confessions from them. Since no one locked their doors, I went into people's houses and stole things, which I pretended were clues to the mystery I was trying to solve.

Everyone real also played a secret role in my city. My parents, for example, were the landlord and his wife, who lived downstairs from my modest one-room flat. They were well-meaning but unimaginative people, and I was polite to them. There were a number of comic episodes in which the nosy landlady had to be tricked and defeated. My brother, Mark, was the district attorney, my nemesis. My younger sister, Debbie, was my secretary, Miss Debbie, whom I sometimes loved. I would marry her if I weren't such a lone wolf.

My family thought of me as a certain person, a figure I knew well enough to act out on occasion. Now that they are far away, it sometimes hurts to think that we knew so little of one another. Sometimes I think: If no one knows you, then you are no one.

In the spring of my twelfth year, a man moved into a house at the end of my block. The house had belonged to an old woman who had died and left her home fully furnished but tenantless for years, until her heir had finally gotten around to having the estate liquidated, the old furniture sold, the place cleared out and put up for sale. This had been the house I took cats to, the hideout where I extracted their yowling confessions. Then finally the house was emptied and the man took up residence.

I first saw the man in what must have been late May. The lilac bush in his front yard was in full bloom, thick with spade-shaped leaves and clusters of perfumed flowers. The man was mowing the lawn as I passed, and I stopped to stare.

It immediately struck me that there was something familiar about him—the wavy dark hair and gloomy eyes, the round face and dimpled chin. At first I thought he looked like someone I'd seen on TV. And then, as I looked at him, I realized: He looked like me! Or rather, he looked like an older version of me—me grown up. As he got closer with his push lawn mower, I was aware that our eyes were the same odd, pale shade of gray, that we had the same map of freckles across the bridge of our nose, the same stubby fingers. He lifted his hand solemnly as he reached the edge of his lawn, and I lifted my opposite hand, so that for a moment we were mirror images of one another. I felt terribly worked up and began to hurry home.

That night, considering the encounter, I wondered whether the man actually *was* me. I thought about all that I'd heard about time travel, and considered the possibility that my older self had come back for some unknown purpose—perhaps to save me from some mistake I was about to make, or to warn me. Maybe he was fleeing some future disaster, and hoped to change the course of things.

I suppose this tells you a lot about what I was like as a boy, but these were among the first ideas I considered. I believed wholeheartedly in the notion that time travel would soon be a reality, just as I believed in UFOs and ESP and Bigfoot. I used to worry, in all seriousness, whether humanity would last as long as the dinosaurs had lasted. What if we were just a brief, passing phase on the planet? I felt strongly that we needed to explore other solar systems and establish colonies. The survival of the human species was very important to me.

Perhaps it was because of this that I began to keep a journal. I had recently read *The Diary of Anne Frank*, and had been deeply moved by the idea that a piece of you, words on a page, could live on after you were dead. I imagined that, after a nuclear holocaust, an extraterrestrial boy might find my journal, floating among some bits of meteorite and pieces of buildings and furniture that had once been Earth. The extraterrestrial boy would translate my diary, and it would become a bestseller on his planet. Eventually, the aliens would be so stirred by my story that they would call off the intergalactic war they were waging and make a truce.

In these journals I would frequently write messages to myself, a person whom I addressed as Big Me, or The Future Me. Rereading these entries as the addressee, I try not to be insulted, since my former self admonishes me frequently. "*I hope you are not a failure*," he says. "*I hope you are happy*," he says.

I'm trying to remember what was going on in the world when I was twelve. My brother, Mark, says it was the worst year of his life. He remembers it as a year of terrible fights between my parents. "They were drunk every night, up till three and four in the morning, screaming at each other. Do you remember the night Mom drove the car into the tree?"

I don't. In my mind, they seemed happy together, in the bantering, ironic manner of sitcom couples, and their arguments seemed full of comedy, as if a laugh track might ring out after their best put-down lines. I don't recall them drunk so much as expansive, and the bar seemed a cheerful, popular place, always full, though they would go bankrupt not long after I turned thirteen.

Mark says that was the year that he tried to commit suicide, and I don't recall that either, though I do remember that he was in the hospital for a few days. Mostly, I think of him reclining on the couch, looking regal and dissipated, reading books like *I'm Okay, You're Okay*, and taking questionnaires that told him whether he was normal or not.

The truth is, I mostly recall the Detective. He had taken an interest in the mysterious stranger who had moved in down the block. The Stranger, it turned out, would be teaching seventh-grade science; he would be replacing the renowned girl's basketball coach and science teacher, Mr. Karaffa, who'd had a heart attack and died right after a big game. The Stranger was named Louis Mickleson, and he'd moved to Beck from a big city: Chicago, or maybe Omaha. "He seems like a lonely type of guy," my mother commented once.

"A weirdo, you mean?" said my father.

I knew how to get into Mickleson's house. It had been my hideout, and there were a number of secret entrances: loose windows, the cellar door, the back door lock, which could be dislodged with the thin, laminated edge of my library card.

He was not a very orderly person, Mr. Mickleson, or perhaps he was simply uncertain. The house was full of boxes, packed and unpacked, and the furniture was placed randomly about the house, as if he'd merely left things where the moving men had set them down. In various corners of the house were projects he'd begun and then abandoned—tilting towers of stacked books next to an empty bookcase, silverware organized in rows along the kitchen counter, a pile of winter coats left on the floor near a closet. The boxes seemed to be carefully classified. Near his bed, for example, were socks—underwear—white T-shirts—each in a separate box, neatly folded near a drawerless dresser. The drawers themselves lay on the floor and contained reams of magazines that he'd saved, *Popular Science* in one, *Azimov's Science Fiction* magazine in another, *Playboy* in yet another, though the dirty pictures had all been fastidiously scissored out.

You can imagine that this was like a cave of wonders for me, piled high with riches, with clues, and each box almost trembled with mystery. There was a collection of costume jewelry, and old coins and keys; here were his old lesson plans and grade books, the names of former students penciled in alongside their attendance and grades and small comments ("messy"; "lazy"; "shows potential!") racked up in columns. Here were photos and letters: a gold mine!

One afternoon, I was kneeling before his box of letters when I heard the front door open. Naturally, I was very still. I heard the front door close, and then Mr. Mickleson muttering to himself. I tensed as he said, "Okay, well, never mind," and read aloud from a bit of junk mail he'd gotten, using a nasal, theatrical voice: " 'A special gift for you enclosed!' How lovely!" he mocked. I crouched there over his cardboard box, looking at a boyhood photo of him and what must have been his sister, circa 1952, sitting in the lap of an artificially bearded Santa. I heard him chuckling as he opened the freezer and took something out. Then he turned on the TV in the living room, and voices leapt out at me.

It never felt like danger. I was convinced of my own powers of stealth and invisibility. He would not see me because that was not part of the story I was telling myself: I was the Detective! I sensed a cool, hollow spot in my stomach, but I could glide easily behind him as he sat in his La-Z-Boy recliner, staring at the blue glow of the television, watching the news. He didn't shudder as the dark shape of me passed behind him. He couldn't see me unless I chose to be seen.

I had my *first* blackout that day I left Mickleson's house, not long after I'd sneaked behind him and crept out the back door. I don't know whether "blackout" is the best term, with its redolence of alcoholic excess and catatonic states, but I'm not sure what else to say. I stepped into the backyard and I remember walking cautiously along a line of weedy flower beds toward the gate that led to the alley. I had taken the Santa photo and I stared at it. It could have been a photograph of me when I was five, and I shuddered at the eerie similarity. An obese calico cat was hurrying down the alley in front of me, disappearing into a hedge that bordered someone else's backyard.

A few seconds later, I found myself at the kitchen table eating dinner with my family. I was in the process of bringing an ear of buttered corn to my mouth and it felt something like waking up, only faster, as if I'd been transported in a blink from one place to another. My family had not seemed to notice that I was gone. They were all eating silently, grimly, as if everything were normal. My father was cutting his meat, his jaw firmly locked, and my mother's eyes were on her plate, as if she were watching a small round television. No one seemed surprised by my sudden appearance.

It was kind of alarming. At first, it just seemed odd—like, "Oh, how did I get here?" But then, the more I thought about it, the more my skin crawled. I looked up at the clock on the kitchen wall, a grinning black cat with a clock face for a belly and a pendulum tail and eyes that shifted from left to right with each tick. I had somehow lost a considerable amount of time—at least a half hour, maybe forty-five minutes. The last thing I clearly recalled was staring at that photo—Mr. Mickleson or myself, sitting on Santa's knee. And then, somehow, I had left my body. I sat there, thinking, but there wasn't even a blur of memory. There was only a blank spot.

Once, I tried to explain it to my wife.

"A *blank* spot?" she said, and her voice grew stiff and concerned, as if I'd found a lump beneath my skin. "Do you mean a blackout? You have *blackouts?*"

"No, no," I said, and tried to smile reassuringly. "Not exactly."

"What do you mean?" she said. "Listen, Andy," she said. "If I told you that I had periods when I . . . lost time . . . wouldn't you be concerned? Wouldn't you want me to see a doctor?"

"You're blowing this all out of proportion," I said. "It's nothing like that." And I wanted to tell her about the things that the Detective had read about in the weeks and months following the first incident—about trances and transcendental states, about astral projection and out-of-body travel. But I didn't.

"There's nothing wrong with me," I said, and stretched my arms luxuriously. "I feel great," I said. "It's more like daydreaming. Only—a little different."

But she still looked concerned. "You don't have to hide anything from me," she said. "I just care about you, that's all."

"I know," I said, and I smiled as her eyes scoped my face. "It's nothing," I said, "just one of those little quirks!" And that is what I truly believe. Though my loved ones sometimes tease me about my distractedness, my forgetfulness, they do so affectionately. There haven't been any major incidents, and the only times that really worry me are the times when I am alone, when I am driving down one street and wake up on another. And even then, I am sure that nothing terrible has happened. I sometimes rub my hands against the steering wheel. I am always intact. There are no screams or sirens in the distance. It's just one of those things!

But back then, that first time, I was frightened. I remember asking my mother how a person would know if he had a brain tumor.

"You don't have a brain tumor," she said irritably. "It's time for bed."

A little later, perhaps feeling guilty, she came up to my room with aspirin and water.

"Do you have a headache, honey?" she said.

I shook my head as she turned off my bedside lamp. "Too much reading of comic books," she said, and smiled at me exaggeratedly, as she sometimes did, pretending I was still a baby. "It would make anybody's head feel funny, little man!" She touched my forehead with the cold, dry pads of her fingertips, looking down into my eyes, heavily. She looked sad, and for a moment lost her balance slightly as she reached down to run a palm across my cheek. "Nothing is wrong," she whispered. "It will all seem better in the morning."

That night, I sat up writing in my diary, writing to Big Me: *I hope you are alive, I wrote. I hope that I don't die before you are able to read this.*

That particular diary entry always makes me feel philosophical. I'm not entirely sure of the person he is writing to, the future person he was imagining. I don't know whether that person is alive or not. There are so many people we could become, and we leave such a trail of bodies through our teens and twenties that it's hard to tell which one is us. How many versions do we abandon over the years? How many end up nearly forgotten, mumbling and gasping for air in some tenement room of our consciousness like elderly relatives suffering some fatal lung disease?

Like the Detective. As I wander through my big suburban house at night, I can hear his wheezing breath in the back-ground, still muttering about secrets that can't be named. Still hanging in there.

My wife is curled up on the sofa, sipping hot chocolate, reading, and when she looks up she smiles shyly. "What are you staring at?" she says. She is used to this sort of thing, by now—finds it endearing, I think. She is a pleasant, practical woman, and I doubt that she would find much of interest in the many former selves that tap against my head like moths.

She opens her robe. "See anything you like?" she says, and I smile back at her.

"Just peeking," I say brightly. My younger self wouldn't recognize me, I'm sure of that.

Which makes me wonder: What did I see in Mickleson, beyond the striking resemblance? I can't quite remember my train of thought, though it's clear from the diary that I latched whole-heartedly on to the idea. Some of it is obviously playacting, making drama for myself, but some of it isn't. Something about Mickleson struck a chord.

Maybe it was simply this—*July 13: If Mickleson is your future, then you took a wrong turn somewhere. Something is sinister about him! He could be a criminal on the lam! He is crazy. You have to change your life now! Don't ever think bad thoughts about Mom, Dad, or even Mark. Do a good deed every day.*

I had been going to his house fairly frequently by that time. I had a notebook, into which I had pasted the Santa photo, a sample of his handwriting, and a bit of hair from a comb. I tried to write down everything that seemed potentially significant: clues, evidence, but evidence of what, I don't know. There was the crowd of beer cans on his kitchen counter, sometimes arranged in geometric patterns. There were the boxes, unpacked then packed again. There were letters: "I am tired, unbelievably tired, of going around in circles with you," a woman who signed herself Kelly had written. "As far as I can see, there is no point in going on. Why can't you just make a decision and stick to it?" I had copied this down in my detective's notebook.

In his living room, there was a little plaque hanging on the wall. It was a rectangular piece of dark wood; a piece of parchment paper, burned around the edges, had been lacquered to it. On the parchment paper, in careful, calligraphy letters, was written:

I wear
the chain
I forged
in life.

Which seemed like a possible secret message. I thought maybe he'd escaped from jail.

From a distance, behind a hedge, I watched Mickleson's house. He wouldn't usually appear before ten o'clock in the morning. He would pop out his front door in his bathrobe, glancing quickly around as if he sensed someone watching, and then he would snatch up the newspaper on his doorstep. At times, he seemed aware of my eyes.

I knew I had to be cautious. Mickleson must not guess that he was being investigated, and I tried to take precautions. I stopped wearing my favorite detective hat, to avoid calling attention to myself. When I went through his garbage, I did it in the early morning, while I was fairly certain he was still asleep. Even so, one July morning I was forced to crawl under a thick hedge when Mickleson's back door unexpectedly opened at eight A.M. and he shuffled out to the alley to dump a bag into his trash can. Luckily I was wearing brown and green and blended in with the shrubbery. I lay there, prone against the dirt, staring at his bare feet and hairy ankles. He was wearing nothing but boxer shorts. I could see that his clothes had been concealing a large quantity of dark, vaguely sickening body hair; there was even some on his back! I had recently read a Classics Illustrated comic book version of *Dr. Jekyll and Mr. Hyde*, and I recalled the description of Hyde as "something troglodytic," which was a word I had looked up in the dictionary and now applied as Mickleson dumped his bag into the trash can. I had just begun to grow a few hairs on my own body, and was chilled to think I would end up like this. I heard the clank of beer cans, and then he walked away and I lay still, feeling uneasy.

At home, after dinner, I would sit in my bedroom, reading through my notes, puzzling. I would flip through my lists, trying to find clues I could link together. I'd sift through the cigar box full of things I'd taken from his home: photographs, keys, a Swiss army knife, a check stub with his signature, which I'd compared against my own. But nothing seemed to fit. All I knew was that he was mysterious. He had some secret.

Once, one late night that summer, I thought I heard my parents talking about me. I was reading, and their conversation had been mere background, rising and falling, until I heard my name. "Andrew . . . how he's turning out . . . not fair to anybody!" Words, rising through the general mumble, first in my father's, then my mother's voice. Then, loudly: "What will happen to him?"

I sat up straight, my heart beating heavily, because it seemed that something must have happened, they must have discovered something. I felt certain that I was about to be exposed: my spying, my breaking and entering, my stealing. I was quiet, frightened, listening, and then after a while I got up and crept downstairs.

My mother and father were at the kitchen table, speaking softly, staring at the full ashtray that sat between them. My mother looked up when I came in and clenched her teeth. "Oh, for God's sake," she said. "Andy, it's two-thirty in the morning! What are you doing up?"

I stood there in the doorway, uncertainly. I wished that I were a little kid again, to tell her that I was scared. But I just hovered there. "I couldn't sleep," I said.

My mother frowned. "Well, try harder, God damn it," she said.

I stood there a moment longer. "Mom?" I said.

"Go to bed!" She glared.

"I thought I heard you guys saying something about that man that just moved in down the block. He didn't say anything about me, did he?"

"Listen to me, Andrew," she said. Her look darkened. "I don't want you up there listening to our conversations. This is grown-up talk and I don't want you up there snooping."

"He's going to be the new science teacher," I said.

"I know," she said, but my father raised his eyebrows.

"Who's this?" my father said, raising his glass to his lips. "That weirdo is supposed to be a teacher? That's a laugh."

"Oh, don't start!" my mother said. "At least he's a customer! You better God damn not pick a fight with him. You've driven enough people away as it is, the way you are. It's no wonder we don't have any friends!" Then she turned on me. "I thought I told you to go to bed. Don't just stand there gaping when I tell you something! My God, I can't get a minute's peace!"

Back in my bedroom, I tried to forget what my parents had said—it didn't matter, I thought, as long as they didn't know anything about me. I was safe! And I sat there, relieved, slowly forgetting the fact that I was really just a strange twelve-year-old boy, a kid with no real playmates, an outsider even in his own family. I didn't like being that person, and I sat by the window, awake, listening to my parents' slow-arguing voices downstairs, smelling the smoke that hung in a thick, rippling cloud over their heads. Outside, the lights of Beck melted into the dark fields, the hills were heavy, huddled shapes against the sky. I closed my eyes, wishing hard, trying to will my imaginary city into life, envisioning roads and streetlights suddenly sprouting up through the prairie grass. And tall buildings. And freeways. And people.

It has been almost twenty years since I last saw Beck. We left the town in the summer before eighth grade, after my parents had gone bankrupt, and in the subsequent years we moved through a blur of ugly states—Wyoming, Montana, Panic, Despair—while my parents' marriage dissolved.

Now we are all scattered. My sister, Debbie, suffered brain damage in a car accident when she was nineteen, out driving with her friends. She now lives in a group home in Denver, where she and the others spend their days making Native American jewelry to sell at truck stops. My brother, Mark, is a physical therapist who lives on a houseboat in Marina del Rey, California. He spends his free time reading books about childhood trauma, and every time I talk to him, he has a series of complaints about our old misery: At the very least, surely I remember the night that my father was going to kill us all with his gun, how he and Debbie and I ran into the junkyard and hid in an old refrigerator box? I think he's exaggerating, but Mark is always threatening to have me hypnotized so I'll remember.

We have all lost touch with my mother. The last anyone heard, she was living in Puerto Vallarta, married to a man who apparently has something to do with real estate development. The last time I talked to her, she didn't sound like herself: A Caribbean lilt had crept into her voice. She laughed harshly, then began to cough, when I mentioned old times.

For a time before he died, I was closest to my father. He was working as a bartender in a small town in Idaho, and he used to call me when I was in law school. Like me, he remembered Beck fondly: the happiest time of his life, he said. "If only we could have held on a little bit longer," he told me. "It would have been a different story. A different story entirely."

Then he'd sigh. "Well, anyway," he'd say. "How are things going with Katrina?"

"Fine," I'd say. "Just the usual. She's been a little distant lately. She's very busy with her classes. I think med school takes a lot out of her."

I remember shifting silently because the truth was, I didn't really have a girlfriend named Katrina. I didn't have a girlfriend, period. I made Katrina up one evening, on the spur of the moment, to keep my dad from worrying so much. It helped him to think that I had a woman looking after me, that I was heading into a normal life of marriage, children, a house, et cetera. Now that I have such things, I feel a bit guilty. He died not knowing the truth. He died waiting to meet her, enmeshed in my made-up drama—in the last six months of his life, Katrina and I came close to breaking up, got back together, discussed marriage, worried that we were not spending enough time together. The conversations that my father and I had about Katrina were some of the best we ever had.

I don't remember much about my father from that summer when I was twelve. We certainly weren't having conversations that I can think of, and I don't ever recall that he pursued me with a gun. He was just there: I walked past him in the morning as he sat, sipping coffee, preparing to go to work. I'd go into the bar, and he would pour me a glass of Coke with bitters "to put hair on my chest." I'd sit there on the bar stool stroking Suds, the bar's tomcat, in my lap, murmuring quietly to him as I imagined my detective story. My father had a bit part in my imagination, barely a speaking role.

But it was at the bar that I saw Mr. Mickleson again. I had been at his house that morning, working through a box of letters, and then I'd been out at the junkyard behind our house. In those unenlightened times, it was called The Dump. People drove out and pitched their garbage over the edge of a ravine, which had become encrusted with a layer of beer cans, broken toys, bedsprings, car parts, broken glass. It was a magical place, and I'd spent a few hours in the driver's seat of a rusted-out Studebaker, fiddling with the various dashboard knobs, pretending to drive it, to stalk suspects, to become involved in a thrilling high-speed chase. At last I had come to the bar to unwind, to drink my Coke and bitters and re-create the day in my imagination. Occasionally, my father would speak to me and I would be forced to reluctantly disengage myself from the Detective, who was brooding over a glass of bourbon. He had become hardened and cynical, but he would not give up his fight for justice.

I was repeating these stirring lines in my mind when Mr. Mickleson came into the bar. I felt a little thrum when he entered. My grip tightened on Suds the cat, who struggled and sprang from my lap.

Having spent time in The Crossroads, I recognized drunkenness. I was immediately aware of Mickleson's flopping gait, the way he settled heavily against the lip of the bar. "Okay, okay," he muttered to himself, then chuckled. "No, just forget it, never mind," he said cheerfully. Then he sighed and tapped his hand against the bar. "Shot o'rum," he said. "Captain Morgan, if you have it. No ice." I watched as my father served him, then flicked my glance away when Mickleson looked warily in my direction. He leveled his gaze at me, his eyes heavy with some meaning I couldn't decipher. It was part friendly, that look, but part threatening, too, in a particularly intimate way—as if he recognized me.

"Oh, hello," Mr. Mickleson said. "If it isn't the staring boy! Hello, Staring Boy!" He grinned at me, and my father gave him a stern look. "I believe I know you," Mr. Mickleson said jauntily. "I've seen you around, haven't I?"

I just sat there, blushing. It occurred to me that perhaps, despite my precautions, Mr. Mickleson had seen me after all. "Staring Boy," he said, and I tried to think of when he might have caught me staring. How many times? I saw myself from a distance, watching his house but now also being watched, and the idea set up a panic in me that was difficult to quell. I was grateful that my father came over and called me son. "Son," he said, "why don't you go on outside and find something to do? You may as well enjoy some of that summer sunshine before school starts."

"All right," I said. I saw that Mickleson was still grinning at me expectantly, his eyes blank and unblinking, and I realized that he was doing an imitation of my own expression—Staring Boy, meet Staring Man. I tried to step casually off the bar stool, but instead stumbled and nearly fell.

"Oopsie-daisy!" Mr. Mickleson said, and my father gave him a hard look, a careful glare that checked Mr. Mickleson's grin. He shrugged.

"Ah, children, children," he said confidingly to my father as I hurried quickly to the door. I heard my father start to speak sharply as I left, but I didn't have the nerve to stick around to hear what was said.

Instead, I crept along the outside of the bar; I staked out Mickleson's old Volkswagen and found it locked. There were no windows into the bar, and so I pressed myself against the wall, trying to listen. I tried to think what I would write in my notebook: that look he'd given me, his grinning mimicry of my stare. I believe I know you, he'd said: What, exactly, did he know?

And then I had a terrible thought. Where was the notebook? I imagined, for a moment, that I had left it there, on the bar, next to my drink. I had the horrifying image of Mr. Mickleson's eyes falling on it, the theme book cover, which was decorated with stylized question marks, and on which I'd written: ANDY O'DAY MYSTERY SERIES #67: THE DETECTIVE MEETS THE DREADFUL DOUBLE! I saw him smiling at it, opening it, his eyes narrowing as he saw his photo pasted there on the first page.

But it wasn't in the bar. I was sure it wasn't, because I remembered not having it when I went in. I didn't have it with me, I knew, and I began to backtrack, step by step, from the Studebaker to lunchtime to my bedroom and then I saw it, with the kind of perfect clarity my memory has always been capable of, despite everything.

I saw myself in Mickleson's living room, on my knees in front of a box of his letters. I had copied something in the notebook and put it down on the floor. It was right there, next to the box. I could see it as if through a window, and I stood there observing the image in my mind's eye, as my mother came around the corner, into the parking lot.

"Andy!" she said. "I've been calling for you! Where the hell have you been?"

She was in one of her moods. "I am so sick of this!" she said, and gave me a hard shake as she grabbed my arm. "You God damn lazy kids just think you can do as you please, all the God damn day long! This house is a pigsty, and not a one of you will bend a finger to pick up your filthy clothes or even wash a dish." She gritted her teeth, her voice trembling, and she slammed into the house, where Mark was scrubbing the floor and Debbie was standing at the sink, washing dishes. Mark glared up at me, his eyes red with crying and self-pity and hatred. I knew he was going to hit me as soon as she left. "Clean, you brats!" my mother cried. "I'm going to work, and when I get home I want this house to shine!" She was in the frilly blouse and makeup she wore when she tended bar, beautiful and flushed, her eyes hard. "I'm not going to live like this anymore. I'm not going to live this kind of life!"

"She was a toxic parent," Mark says now, in one of our rare phone conversations. "A real psycho. It haunts me, you know, the shit that we went through. It was like living in a house of terror, you know? Like, you know, a dictatorship or something. You never knew what was next, and that was the scariest part. There was a point, I think, where I really just couldn't take it anymore. I really wanted to die." I listen as he draws on his cigarette and then exhales, containing the fussy spitefulness that's creeping into his voice. "Not that you'd remember. It always fell on me, whatever it was. They thought you were so cute and spacy, so you were always checked out in La-La Land while I got the brunt of everything."

I listen but don't listen. I'm on the deck behind my house with my cell phone, reclining, watching—my daughters jump through the sprinkler. Everything is green and full of sunlight, and I might as well be watching an actor portraying me in the happy ending of a movie of my life. I've never told him about my blackouts and I don't now, though they have been bothering me again lately. I can imagine what he would come up with: fugue states, repressed memories, multiple personalities. Ridiculous stuff.

"It all seems very far away to me," I tell Mark, which is not true exactly, but it's part of the role I've been playing for many years now. "I don't really think much about it."

This much is true: I barely remember what happened that night. I wasn't even there, among the mundane details of children squabbling and cleaning and my mother's ordinary unhappiness. I was the Detective!—driving my sleek Studebaker through the streets of Beck, nervous though not panicked, edgy and white-knuckled but still planning with steely determination: the notebook! The notebook must be retrieved! Nothing else was really happening, and when I left the house I was in a state of focused intensity.

It must have been about eleven o'clock. Mark had been especially evil and watchful, and it wasn't until he'd settled down in front of the television with a big bowl of ice cream that I could pretend, at last, to go to bed.

Outside, out the door, down the alley: It seems to me that I should have been frightened, but mostly I recall the heave of adrenaline and determination, the necessity of the notebook, the absolute need for it. It was my story.

The lights were on at Mickleson's house, a bad sign, but I moved forward anyway, into the dense and dripping shadows of his yard, the crickets singing thickly, my hand already extended to touch the knob of his back door.

Which wasn't locked. It didn't even have to be jimmied, it gave under the pressure of my hand, a little electrical jolt across my skin, the door opening smooth and uncreaking, and I passed like a shadow into the narrow back foyer that led to the kitchen. There was a silence in the house, and for a moment I felt certain that Mickleson was asleep. Still, I moved cautiously. The kitchen was brightly fluorescent and full of dirty dishes and beer cans. I slid my feet along the tile, inching along the wall. Silence, and then Mickleson's voice drifted up suddenly, a low mumble and then a firmer one, as if he were contradicting himself. My heart shrank. Now what? I thought as I came to the edge of the living room.

Mickleson was sitting in his chair, slumping, his foot jiggling with irritation. I heard the sail-like snap of a turning page, and I didn't even have to look to know that the notebook was in his hands. He murmured again as I stood there. I felt light-headed. The notebook! I thought, and leaned against the wall. I felt my head bump against something, and Mr. Mickleson's plaque tilted, then fell. I fumbled for a moment before I caught it.

But the sound made him turn. There I was, dumbly holding the slice of wood, and his eyes rested on me. His expression seemed to flicker with surprise, then terror, then annoyance—before settling on a kind of blank amusement. He cleared his throat.

"I believe I see a little person in my house," he said, and I might have fainted. I could feel the Detective leaving me, shriveling up and slumping to the floor, a suit of old clothes; the city of Beck disintegrated in the distance, streets drying up like old creek beds, skyscrapers sinking like ocean liners into the wheat fields. I was very still, his gaze pinning me. "A ghostly little person," he said, with satisfaction. He stood up for a moment, wavering, and then stumbled back against the chair for support, a look of affronted dignity freezing on his face. I didn't move.

"Well, well," he said. "Do I dare assume that I am in the presence of the author of this—" and he waved my notebook vaguely "—this document?" And he paused, thumbing through it with an exaggerated, mimelike gesture. "Hmm," he murmured, almost crooning. "So—imaginative! And—there's a certain—*charm*—about it—I think." And then he leaned toward me. "And so at last we meet, Detective O'Day!" he said, in a deep voice. "You may call me Professor Moriarty!" He made a strange shape with his mouth and laughed softly—not sinister exactly, but musing, as if he'd just told himself a good joke and I was somehow in on it.

"Why so quiet?" he exclaimed, and waggled the notebook at me. "Haven't you come to find your future, young Detective?" I watched as he pressed his fingers to his temples, like a stage medium. "Hmm," he said, and began to wave his arms and fingers with a seaweedlike floating motion, as if casting a magic spell or performing a hula dance. "Looking for his future," he said. "What lies in wait for Andy O'Day? I ask myself that question frequently. Will he grow up to be . . ." —and here he read aloud from my journal— ". . . 'troglodytic' and 'sinister'? Will he ever escape the sad and lonely life of a Detective, or will he wander till the end of his days through the grim and withering streets of Beck?"

He paused then and looked up from my journal. I thought for a moment that if I leapt out, I could snatch it from him, even though the things I had written now seemed dirty and pathetic. I thought to say, "Give me back my notebook!" But I didn't really want it anymore. I just stood there, watching him finger the pages. He leaned toward me, wavering, his eyes not exactly focused on me, but on some part of my forehead or shoulder or hair. He smiled, made another small effort to stand, then changed his mind. "What will happen to Andy O'Day?" he said again, thoughtfully. "It's such a compelling question, a very lovely question, and I can tell you the answer. Because, you see, I've come through my time machine to warn you! I have a special message for you from the future. Do you want to know what it is?"

"No," I said at last, my voice thick and uncertain.

"Oh, Andy," he said, as if very disappointed. "Andy, Andy. Look! Here I am!" He held his arms out wide, as if I'd run toward them. "Your Dreadful Double!" I watched as he straightened himself, correcting the slow tilt of his body. "I know you," Mr. Mickleson said. His head drooped, but he kept one eye on me. "You must be coming to me—for *something*?"

I shook my head. I didn't know. I couldn't even begin to imagine, and yet I felt—not for the last time—that I was standing in a desolate and empty prairie, the fields unraveling away from me in all directions. The long winds ran through my hair.

"Don't you want to know a secret?" he said. "Come over here, I'll whisper in your ear."

And it seemed to me, then, that he did know a secret. It seemed to me that he would tell me something terrible, something I didn't want to hear. I watched as he closed my notebook and placed it neatly on the coffee table, next to the *TV Guide*. He balanced himself on two feet, lifting up and lurching toward me. "Hold still," he murmured. "I'll whisper."

I turned and ran.

I once tried to explain this incident to my wife, but it didn't make much sense to her. She nodded, as if it were merely strange, merely puzzling. Hmmm, she said, and I thought that perhaps it *was* odd to remember this time so vividly, when I remembered so little else. It *was* a little ridiculous that I should find Mr. Mickleson on my mind so frequently.

"He was just a drunk," my wife said. "A little crazy, maybe, but . . ." And she looked into my face, her mouth pursing. "He didn't . . . *do* anything to you, did he?" she said awkwardly, and I shook my head.

"No—no," I said. And I explained to her that I never saw Mr. Mickleson again. I avoided the house after that night, of course, and when school started he wasn't teaching Science 7. We were told, casually, that he had an "emergency," that he had been called away, and when, after a few weeks, he still didn't return, he was replaced without comment by an elderly lady substitute, who read to us from the textbook—*The World of Living Things*—in a lilting storybook voice, and who whispered "My God," as she watched us later, dissecting earthworms, pinning them to corkboard and exposing their many hearts. We never found out where Mr. Mickleson had gone.

"He was probably in rehab," my wife said sensibly. "Or institutionalized. Your father was right. He was just a weirdo. It doesn't seem that mysterious to me."

Yes. I nodded a little, ready to drop the subject. I couldn't very well explain the empty longing I felt, the eager dread that would wash over me, going into the classroom and thinking that he might be sitting there behind the desk, waiting. It didn't make sense, I thought, and I couldn't explain it, any more than I could explain why he remained in my mind as I crisecrossed the country with my family, any more than I could explain why he seemed to be there when I thought of them, even now: Mark, fat and paranoid, on his houseboat: my mother in Mexico, nodding over a cocktail; Debbie, staring at a spider in the corner of her room in the group home, her eyes dull; my father, frightened, calling me on the phone as his liver failed him, his body decomposing in a tiny grave in Idaho that I'd never visited. How could I explain that Mickleson seemed to preside over these thoughts, hovering at the edge of them like a stage director at the back of my mind, as if he'd done me a favor?

I didn't know why he came into my mind as I thought of them, just as I didn't know why he seemed to appear whenever I told lies. It was just that I could sense him. *Yes,* he whispered as I told my college friends that my father was an archaeologist living in Peru, that my mother was a former actress: *Yes,* he murmured as I lied to my father about Katrina: *Yes*, as I make excuses to my wife. When I say I am having dinner with a client when in fact I am tracing another path entirely—following a young family as they stroll through the park, or a whistling old man who might be my father, if he'd gotten away, or a small, brisk-paced woman, who looks like Katrina might, if Katrina weren't made up. How can I explain that I walk behind this Katrina woman for many blocks, living a different life, whistling my old man tune?

I can't. I can't explain it, no more than I can admit that I still have Mickleson's plaque, just as he probably still has my notebook; no more than I can explain why I take the plaque out of the bottom drawer of my desk and unwrap the tissue paper I've folded it in, reading the inscription over, like a secret message: "I wear the chains I forged in life." I know it's just a cheap Dickens allusion, but it still seems important.

I can hear him say, "Hold still. I'll *whisper*."

Hmmm, my wife would say, puzzled and perhaps a bit disturbed. She's a practical woman, and so I say nothing. It's probably best that she doesn't think any more about it, and I keep to myself the private warmth I feel when I sense a blackout coming, the darkness clasping its hands over my eyes. It's better this way—we're all happy. I'm glad that my wife will be there when I wake, and my normal life, and my beautiful daughters, looking at me, wide-eyed, staring.

"Hello?" my wife will say, and I'll smile as she nudges me. "Are you there?" she'll whisper.

A Conversation with Dan Chaon

There's always something or someone missing in your stories. In your collection, Among the Missing, the narrator of "Prodigal" says, "We are already lost, even to ourselves." Would you talk about the issue of loss, how and why it seems to be the central issue in this collection and in your work, generally?

The collection formed around two really central events in my life, which were having kids and realizing how wrong I was about just about everything that I thought about my parents. The very act of having children suddenly frames you in time in a way that I think makes you become aware of yourself moving through stages in life. And through the generations. Then there was the death of my parents, which happened quite suddenly. Both of them died in 1996, and most of the stories were written in the two or three years after their deaths. I'm not advocating stories as therapy, but I certainly think the mood of the collection, the directions that it took were influenced by coming to grips with grief and with saying goodbye to my parents.

There's often a disconnect between parents and children in the stories. Is there an autobiographical element in that?

I was the only person in my family who went to college. I grew up in a very working class family, and there was a lot of weird tension about that. I remember once one of my aunts asking what I did for a living and I told her I was a teacher. She said, "Oh, what grade?" I said, "I teach college." She looked at my father and said, "How can you stand him?" The very act of becoming a college professor was making this pretentious statement, showing off. She said it jokingly, but really *not.*

Along with that—and also reflected in the stories—goes a kind of sadness and longing rooted in the knowledge that the people you love can't love you the way you need to be loved because they don't know you.

Yes. In parenthood and marriage there is, to a certain extent, a character that you are playing for people that's taking up a part of your life that's *not* what's happening in your head. The first four years of my kids' life, I was a stay-at-home daddy, which is a weird thing, coming from the background that I came from. It's a weird thing for a man to do. It may be why, for the first time, I tried writing from a woman's perspective. This was really attractive to me because it felt like I could talk about things that were happening to me internally and not feel like I was getting too close to myself. I felt like there was a mask that allowed me to talk about certain aspects of emotion that made more sense in a female voice than in a male voice.

Sometimes writers—and readers—are territorial about certain points of view. Did you worry that you might have been criticized for writing from a woman's point of view?

It doesn't bother me. There was a review of Colson Whitehead's first book, *The Intuitionist,* which was written in the voice of a woman, and the reviewer implied that there was always something sexual about writing from the point of view of a different gender. I don't find that at all. I find it very much like writing from a place you live in when you are a very little kid and you're not attached to any gender.

It's also true that the farther away you get from yourself in creating a character, the more you have to rely on observation, which can make for a stronger character. Your stories are full of the most amazing details: the tooth in the ashtray in "Safety Man," the evil parrot in "I Demand to Know Where You're Taking Me," and the inflatable doll in "Safety Man." How did those stories gather, and how did the details find their way into them?

There's a center of gravity, and it's always sort of frightening when all of the pieces start to come together.

Gathering is exactly the right word. There's a center of gravity, and it's always sort of frightening when all of the pieces start to come together. "Safety Man" started with a desire to write a story about a haunted house, which never made it into the story. Originally, it was about a man whose wife had died.

That's a long way from a story about a woman whose husband has died and who has bought an inflatable man to ride home from work with her.

Yeah, it is. I was on an airplane and found an advertisement for Safety Man in the "Sky Mall." I clipped it out, put it into my file, and the guy changed into a woman so that I could incorporate Safety Man. Then, the year my parents died, I was teaching down at Ohio University. I was there all week, then driving back home on the weekends. Living in graduate housing, which is like living in a motel room—very thin walls. I was very emotionally high-strung like the character Sandi is. One night some song came on the radio and I got all teared up; then I lost it and I was sobbing. The woman who lived next to me was a graduate student in math. She was from China and didn't speak English very well. I remember her knocking on the wall, saying, "Hello, hello, are you all right?" And I didn't say anything. Then the next morning when we were both taking out the trash, and I said, "Hello, how are you?" I didn't say anything about what had happened the night before, and I was thinking about the ways that you are able to put on a certain kind of face no matter how emotional you are. So the story started coming together: the idea of somebody who is really feeling crazy but who is completely functional. The other thing about Sandi is that I gave her one of the problems that has plagued my life and that is that I do have small hallucinations. I usually catch them. I did see a tooth in the ashtray. It was actually a piece of dried-up Wrigley's Spearmint gum, but I *thought* it was a tooth for a moment and it made me panic.

You mentioned a folder as part of your gathering process. What's in it?

Usually, there's a lot of story beginnings. I feel that they are connected, but I'm not sure how they are connected.

Each story possibility has its own folder?

Yes. There was the haunted house folder, and I knew that the tooth was going in there. And an old Popeye cartoon from the '30s. Popeye is warning about going out into deep water and he says, "Don't you know what a terrible feeling it is, kids, to stick out your toe and think there's a bottom and there is no bottom?" It doesn't actually appear in the story. But later in the story, Safety Man is sort of like a noble sea captain who says something along that line. The cartoon was an inspiration for that.

This is kind of a silly question, but it's hard not to visualize all those folders with bits and pieces of stories in them. What would happen if one of those pieces got in the wrong folder?

They're always getting in the wrong folders.

Do you ever take something out of one folder and put it in another?

Yeah. That parrot in "I Demand to Know Where You're Taking Me" hopped around from story to story. In a lot of the early versions of things, it was just a small detail. That happens to me a lot. A small detail in one story can get magnified in another one. There are a number of images in the collection that hopped from story to story. There are things that happen in several of the stories that probably are too similar.

In that gathering process, there's a moment of combustion where you've got all kinds of things— among them in "Safety Man" a haunted house, a grieving spouse, the Popeye cartoon—but it was finding the ad for Safety Man, the inflatable doll, that made the story become what it ended up being.

Right. Usually for me it's an opening line or an opening set of actions that gives me a tunnel through a story, like the image of Sandi blowing up Safety Man or letting the air out and being ashamed of it. In that story, I had the tension—she has this secret—and it pulled me through the story. With "Big Me," it was the blackouts. "It all started when I was twelve years old" was the first line that came to me.

Usually for me it's an opening line or an opening set of actions that gives me a tunnel through a story, like the image of Sandi blowing up Safety Man or letting the air out and being ashamed of it.

Do the first lines like that one usually remain the first lines of the stories?

Yes. There's all this stuff that's out there, pieces and images and character details. Maybe they belong in one story, maybe they don't. It's like flotsam. The first line is a little clothesline that I can start hanging the stuff on.

Your first lines give the reader an entrance into the world of the story. When the narrator in "Big Me" says, "It all started when I was twelve years old," the reader is grounded in that moment. Somebody is telling a story and whatever it is, it happened a while ago. It gives the reader a place to stand, a way to enter the story. It's very deft. Do you think short story writers have to do that since they don't have the space a novel offers for rambling around?

My biggest problem as a writer has always been that I don't think in terms of narrative as much as some people do. I have never been able to write a kind of stripped-down, one scene classical story like "A Worn Path," where it starts at two o'clock and ends at five o'clock. For me, a story doesn't proceed chronologically and it doesn't proceed with a single line of coherent action, as in Poe's classic idea of "unity of effect." I've never been able to figure that out. Actually, the stories that I like and the ones that have inspired me have been the ones that are really wasteful and profligate stories. Like Cheever's "A Country Husband," Tony Earley's "A Prophet of Jupiter." Basically anything by Alice Munro. These great stories of explosive wastefulness just keep piling on detail and piling on layers of narrative and layers and layers of possibility. That's what compels me about story.

These great stories of explosive wastefulness just keep piling on detail and piling on layers of narrative and layers and layers of possibility.

How do you recognize the difference between a big, "wasteful" story like that and what really needs to be a novel?

There's a kind of internal compass. In a story, you're in a room and you know that there are four walls. You can guide yourself by knowing that, okay, I've got to touch this wall and then I've got to touch that wall. With the novel, you're not in a small room, you're in a great big field or a desert, and there are no walls. You can keep going in one direction forever. For me, the process of learning to write stories was learning what my own walls were, the walls I was writing within. Those generally have to do with the sociology of the story and the sense of place, a character in some sort of anxiety, some sort of plot line, and theme or mood. I touch one wall, then go to another one, then back to the first. I keep balancing those four things until I finally get to the end. Ends are hard for me. With all of these stories, I got to the point where I was at a climax, but it took me forever to figure out what the right thing to happen was.

Why do you think that ends are so difficult for you?

I have a tendency to say, okay, I got them here, and not have a climax. With "Big Me," for example, I really resisted that scene where he actually confronts Mickleson. It took a really long time for me to get up the guts to do that scene. I tried every single thing I could think of to get around it.

Why didn't you want to write the scene?

It had such huge potential to be corny, and I'm always afraid of being corny. But I knew in my heart that that was just avoidance behavior. Most of the time I know I have to have those scenes and I just have to figure out a way to get to them.

"Big Me" reflects all the central issues of your work, generally. Where did it come from? How did it evolve?

You'll think this is ridiculous, but it started out with a song by the Fu Fighters, "Big Me," that I kept hearing on the radio when I was driving back and forth from Cleveland Heights to Ohio University. It's strangely cheerful, but it's got an underlying menace to it. I do a lot of things to try to generate stories. One of the things I play around with is to find a title and then burrow into it. I have my students do this. You take a title, you try to figure out what that title evokes for you, where it takes you in terms of character or plot or image. So, I started with the title and I came up with these early freewriting pieces that had to do with what I was like as a boy.

I had recently reread *The Diary of Anne Frank*. There's a passage in the story about it, probably the first stuff that I wrote. It's about the future person that he is imagining. About the future people we could become. There are so many people that we could become, and we leave such a trail of bodies through our teens and twenties that it's hard to tell which one is us. With that as a grounding philosophical point, I thought about the idea of this kid writing to a future self. I found it interesting to play with identity and with my own desire to write a story that was full of unreliable narrator trapdoors. It got really ridiculous for a while. He was finding bodies in his trunk and then when he would open the trunk they weren't there. Stupid stuff. The idea of the blackouts was also something I was interested in. Something we talked about with the Sandi character in "Safety Man" is seeing things that aren't there and not seeing things that are there. Again, this was right after my parents had died. There was a lot of arguing between my brother and sister and I, including stuff like what happened and what *really* happened—everybody, as a sibling, has had those conversations. Everybody has a different version of reality. That fed into the story, too. It made the Mark character a little more extreme. He has a completely different reality than the narrator.

As fast as the reader thinks one thing, he enters and offers a completely different point of view.

Everyone had a different version and everyone was lying to one another. They were so scattered that they could never come together and put together the story of the family. It's kind of like what I was going through at the time. You know how things can go insane, even things like the cleaning out of the house. My sister had a great line, and I have to find a way to put it in a story. We were talking about who was going to get the house. My brother wanted to live there and my sister said, "Danny, I just keep thinking I would rather see that house burnt to the ground than have him live there. Do you think that's selfish of me?" Some of that stuff fed into the mood of the story.

Each character in the story gives the reader useful information about the narrator and his problems. The wife, for example.

My wife hates my wives. I very often have useful wives who ask the right questions and dispense wisdom and are critical of the precisely right things. She asks, "You don't think of *me* that way." There are a few stories, especially in a sort of memoir style, where you've got a big sweep of time and you can use a character who's skeptical and critical to ask the exact right questions so you don't have to go round about it. That's her function.

It seems you're saying that the trick is in choosing the particular aspects of the character that you put on the page. How does that work with minor characters, people who aren't involved in the central action of the story but somehow help trigger or clarify it?

Central characters get defined by their observations. The more you have them observe things, the more you get to know them. Then when you're going back with the second and third and the fourth draft, you start to see, oh, that's the wrong thing for him to think. One of the things you always want to do is throw people in the way of the main character that are going to test their particular weaknesses and illuminate their character. Very often, a student whose story goes astray isn't testing the character hard enough or they can't let go of something—I want to have this mother in here.

One of the things you always want to do is throw people in the way of the main character that are going to test their particular weaknesses and illuminate their character.

Do you think creating character in short stories is different from creating character in the novel?

The only thing I can say about the difference is that you get in and out so much faster. It's like with a short story you had a week-long fling; with the novel, it's like you had a long marriage that ended in divorce. You remember them both very vividly, but you remember them in very different ways. Novels are always about trying to understand the world, whereas stories are always about why the world is so unexplainable. With a story you can make somebody come vividly alive with a couple of strokes as long as the reader is willing to have a ton of white space all around him.

Does the writer always know what's left out about the people in a story?

No. *I* don't know. People will say, "What happened to the mother at the end of 'Among the Missing'?" I don't have any idea. "Is Wendell guilty?" I don't know.

Once you know who the central character is, how do you make the choice to tell the story in first or third person?

For me, the first person has become almost sole province of dramatic irony. Maybe that's because I got so tired of that memoir/first-person voice as it is practiced currently. Certainly there are writers whose first-person narrators are trustworthy; but for me, first person has to have something to do with the way the guy or the woman perceives the world that's skewed. Third person for me is not that different from first person. Mainly, perspective is less of a concern for me in the third person.

Would you talk about the imaginary city in "Big Me"? Where did it come from?

I played Dungeons and Dragons, so I had a lot of maps that were based on this little town where I lived, which only had, like, fifty people in it.

So you actually had an alternate reality like the narrator's Beck, when you were growing up?

Yes. I did. And I had different things happen in it that were sort of comic-book-like.

And you kept a folder with the maps.

I don't have the maps or the folder anymore, but I did at one time.

Was Beck always part of the story?

Yes. Once I started thinking about where the setting was, it was always in the story. When pieces started to fall together, that was one of them.

So you had the song and you liked the title and started fooling around with it. Then you went to the idea of a diary and how many people we could have been. You were thinking about family. Were you writing the story in sections, not chronologically?

Right. Again, it's those four walls for me, and one of the walls is, where is it? What's the sociology of this place, what does it look like? My process tends to be fragmented. A story never comes this scene, this scene, this scene. I think, where is this place? What has this person's childhood been like? I'll write a paragraph about each thing and then shuffle them around and feel them. Those are usually my first five or ten pages.

Is that shuffling around physical, like working with the pieces of a mosaic?

Yeah. I can't compose on the computer for that reason. I usually do it in longhand. I'll start the story and then I'll write the next paragraph. Tear that off. Then I'll go back, write a different paragraph, and if it works, I'll go on to the next. Pretty soon I have a big stack of things that have the same paragraphs on them, but they also have several alternate versions of different paragraphs and different approaches. I'll write two paragraphs and then I'll think, oh no, this paragraph is actually where it starts and so I'll tear the paper off and start with that paragraph. I do a lot of rewriting of the same sentences and paragraphs. Over and over. I usually don't

Pretty soon I have a big stack of things that have the same paragraphs on them, but they also have several alternate versions of different paragraphs and different approaches.

work on stories all at once. I'll work on a story for a while, like for an eight-hour period one night. Then the next night I'll work on a different story.

What surprised you writing "Big Me?"

Mark, the brother, surprised me all the time. When he said, "Don't you remember the time Dad chased us with the gun?" I was, like, oh man! I can't believe you just said that. And then that final scene with Mr. Mickleson totally surprised me.

Why?

Because it was like being possessed by somebody. I actually did write it by acting it out. Up in my office, on the third floor, sitting there, I'd say the line, I'd write it down, then I'd think about it. I'd try out different responses. There was a point where, acting out Mickleson's responses, my voice changed.

Like Dr. Jekyll and Mr. Hyde.

Yes! And I suddenly, sort of, loved him. He's such a crazy, weird guy.

You had all these things: the song, the place, your geeky childhood self, but Mr. Mickleson is the moving action that turned a bunch of stuff into a story. When did he enter the mix?

It was after I got to the point where I thought about the kid writing to "Big Me." The plot urge was: You, know what? I'm going to send somebody back just to scare that kid to death. And that was when Mr. Mickleson appeared. He came to the town, and the kid, because he's such a weird kid, thinks, Oh, he looks like me. I wonder if he *is* me. For me, personally, the easiest plot to work is the mystery plot. You've got somebody who wonders about something, so you send them off to find clues about it and that keeps the tension going.

It's interesting the way time works in the story. The structure mirrors the sense of the narrator thinking it through. How did you come to that?

One of my favorite stories of all time is Sherwood Anderson's "Death in the Woods," which is about someone trying to sort out what's true about a story. I think that was certainly an aspect of "Big Me." I didn't want this piece to be located simply in the past. I wanted to have that other layer of the adult looking back on the child who's looking at a different adult who the child thinks is himself. So there was a little bit of a hall of mirrors. One of the things I wanted to do with time was to have the looking back and looking forward happening at once. I wanted to have a sort of mini-plot that follows the present time guy, which would be minimal. He doesn't have a whole lot to do, but he's investigating his past at the same time the kid is investigating this guy he thinks is from the future.

And the deeper he gets into it, the more the narrator talks about in this matter-of-fact way—he had blackouts, he stole things, he tortured the cat, he broke into the house—the more the reader realizes how unreliable he is. You talked earlier about the bottom falling out of the story. Was it falling out for you, as a writer, too? It was, wasn't it? You were being surprised all along.

That was the thing that was the most fun. Like I said, there were points were I had to sort of rein myself in. There was a point where I thought, oh, this guy's going to turn out to be a serial killer. And then, I though, no, I hate that idea. It's so corny.

The story could have been corny, but you never let it happen. There's tension all over the place. Reading it feels like the process you described, kind of like bouncing off the story's walls. How did you come to the story's ending?

I kind of knew that I wanted it to end with the character coming out of a blackout. There were other versions, where it was a little more extreme—coming out of the blackout and entering into a life that was golden, but he didn't know how he got there exactly. I also sort of wanted him to meld a little with Mickleson, so there's the sense that his last line has a kind of Mickleson-like quality.

Ultimately, what would you say "Big Me" is about?

I think it's about the fear that we are not really the same person over time, and that what we are is really some sort of monster that has taken over for the real us that used to exist. Or, vice versa. That the real us that used to exist was a monster that we aren't anymore—but may become again. It is an examination of the question, "Who is the real me?"

Those little diary entry things, where I was saying, "I hope that I will become . . . " That was something I did when I was a kid. From a less philosophical point, the story's about wanting to go back and scare the shit out of that kid I used to be: You will become this whacked-out, scary person. That was kind of fun.

What did you learn, going through the process of writing the story? Generally, what does writing teach you?

In terms of craft and process, sometimes I'm thinking of specific things that I want to be able to do that I can't do until I set myself a goal. The things I just love about somebody else's writing; I want to be able to do that. Like the Sherwood Anderson story. I wanted to do that. And I wanted to do something with a really unreliable narrator. So there is the technical element. Then there's also this very personal stuff. I'm finding a way to fit these things together. The thing that I'm always learning is that when you find the right kind of electric, magnetic match for one image and another or one piece of story and another it changes both pieces. There are some that have magnetic repellent and they don't work. When they hook together there's something that's better than a drug.

The thing that I'm always learning is that when you find the right kind of electric, magnetic match for one image and another or one piece of story and another it changes both pieces.

Combustion.

Yeah. It is like that. Whatever that stuff chocolate gives off, some drug in it, that really warm, ooohhh, that's-so-great feeling. You're learning something there, but it's hard to say what it is. It's very subconscious in some ways. It's not like a moral. It's about—oh, you now understand why clouds and stop signs fit together. The greatest pleasure you can get from a story is the moment when somebody comes alive and is outside of your control. They're not characters anymore. They're people.

What's your history as a writer? What kind of training made you the writer you've become?

I started out writing very young because I grew up in the country and I didn't have a lot of other entertainment. I was very book-oriented, so a lot of the stuff I was interested in as a kid had to do with making up pretend games.

Were you the Andy O'Day of "Big Me"?

In some ways, yeah, I was that kind of kid. But I think most writers were. I had a lot of interest in fantasy as a genre. Ray Bradbury was one of my favorite writers. When I was in junior high, one of my teachers encouraged me to write to one of my favorite writers. I wrote to Ray Bradbury, and he wrote back to me. I sent him some stories and he was very encouraging. So at a very early age, thirteen or fourteen, I began to have a sense of myself as a writer. And to really want to do craft-oriented things.

I think for me a lot of the training had to do with imitation—reading and imitation and learning how stories work technically. I think once you begin to learn how stories are put together, then you can vary from that and play around with the form. By the time I was in high school, I had started sending my work out—ridiculous as that was, but I didn't know it at the time. I sent a story to Reginald Gibbons at *Tri-Quarterly*. He wrote back and said, "We can't publish this, but have you ever considered coming to Northwestern as a student?"

How did you even know about Tri-Quarterly?

From *Writers' Market,* which I bought every year.

How did you know about that?

The lady at the bookstore in Sidney, Nebraska—a very small town of about five thousand people. There was a small writers' group that met there, and it was all women who were writing poetry and short stories. They were in their forties and fifties. The lady at the bookstore suggested that if I was interested in writing I should join this writers' group. So I did. That was where I learned about *Writers' Market* and *Writers' Digest* magazine. They were very serious about getting their work published, so I learned a lot from them, especially about the market. There are people like that in every small town. They are determined to be writers, and they may have gotten a few publications here and there. I got encouraged by them. I suppose I was like a weird little mascot.

So that led you to Reginald Gibbons and ultimately to Northwestern.

He suggested that I look at Northwestern—and my family was very upset about that, by the way. They were very upset that this man would write me and want to take me some place far away from home. They were suspicious of him. I applied and I got money to go there and I did, though everybody in my family felt that I should go to the University of Nebraska.

And after Northwestern?

I wandered around Chicago for two or three years, then went on to do creative writing at Syracuse, where I worked with Toby Wolff for two years. I got an MA there.

What can't *a graduate degree in writing teach?*

It's like Gardner talks about in *The Art of Fiction,* when he says that there are some people who can't look at a puppy without seeing a cute puppy, who can't look at a child without seeing rosy apple cheeks, who can't look at a grandma without seeing a dear old lady. I think maybe you can't teach someone how to see the world in a complicated way when they are just not inclined to. I think you can teach someone how to write a good sentence. I think you can teach someone those simple things like "show, don't tell." Everybody has something to talk about.

I think maybe you can't teach someone how to see the world in a complicated way when they are just not inclined to.

But just because they have something to talk about doesn't mean what they say will be interesting. So often student stories are technically proficient, yet flat somehow. They have a good idea, but there's nothing in it that's going to bring them up against their own best material.

That's the other thing. I think there is a difference when you write a story because you want to write a story, any story, and writing a story because you want to write that particular story.

And the need to write that story.

I always worry about saying need, but there is that.

What do you think an aspiring writer could best learn from reading "Big Me?" What does it offer a student of contemporary literature?

I guess I would want young writers to know that they don't have to answer every question and sometimes it's more fun if you don't.

I'm proud of what it does with the issue of an unreliable narrator, and I'm proud of the way of it has a memoir/mystery story. I wouldn't mind if they read it alongside

"Death in the Woods." I guess I would want young writers to know that they don't have to answer every question and sometimes it's more fun if you don't.

. . . .

Writing Prompts

READ: "Big Me" and the interview with **Dan Chaon.**

PONDER: How Chaon layers time to show the connection between the story of how the narrator's obsession with an alternate reality shaped both the events of his childhood and his present life.

WRITE: Create a character whose life now reflects what an alternative reality allowed him or her to escape as a child, and write a scene that illustrates the means by which the character copes or escapes in his present life.

PRACTICE:

- Think of a song that brings a vivid memory of a certain moment or period in your life. Freewrite about what it makes you remember. Is there some possibility for a story there?
- Create a character of the opposite gender to your own and write a scene from this character's point of view.
- Give a character one of the major or minor problems that has plagued your life, but make that the *only* thing you have in common. Write a scene in which that problem plays out in a way that could not happen in your life.
- Find a cartoon that makes you laugh. Write the scene. Then imagine how it might fit into a whole day in the life of one of the characters portrayed.
- Write a story that begins with "It all started when I was . . ."
- Look a story you are having difficulty with. Are there scenes that you are resisting writing? Why?
- Make a map of the town where your character lives. Draw her house plan. What do you learn from that?
- Come up with a title you like and write the story it suggests to you.
- Remember a family argument and write each person's account of what happened and why. How do they differ?
- Imagine a character who assumes something about another character. Write a beginning scene in which the assumption is revealed without actually stating what the assumption is. Consider ways in which the assumption might play out in a story.

Stuart Dybek

Stuart Dybek (b. 1942) is the author of three collections of short stories and two collections of poetry. Born in Chicago, he was educated at Loyola University of Chicago and the University of Iowa. His writing is frequently anthologized and has appeared in numerous periodicals including The New Yorker, The Atlantic Monthly, Harper's, Poetry, The Paris Review, *and* Tri-Quarterly. *His honors include the Whiting Writers' Award, the PEN/Bernard Malamud Prize, the Academy Institute Award in Fiction from the American Academy and Institute of Arts and Letters, a Guggenheim fellowship, two NEA Fellowships, the Nelson Algren Award, and four O. Henry Prizes. Dybek teaches in the writing program at Western Michigan University. He lives in Kalamazoo, Michigan.*

For Further Reading:
Brass Knuckles (1979), *Childhood and Other Neighborhoods* (1980), *The Coast of Chicago* (1990), *I Sailed with Magellan* (2003), *Their Own Ink* (2004).

We Didn't

> We did it in front of the mirror
> And in the light. We did it in darkness,
> In water, and in the high grass.
>
> —Yehuda Amichai, "We Did It"

We didn't in the light; we didn't in darkness. We didn't in the fresh-cut summer grass or in the mounds of autumn leaves or on the snow where moonlight threw down our shadows. We didn't in your room on the canopy bed you slept in, the bed you'd slept in as a child, or in the backseat of my father's rusted Rambler, which smelled of the smoked chubs and kielbasa he delivered on weekends from my uncle Vincent's meat market. We didn't in your mother's Buick Eight, where a rosary twined the rearview mirror like a beaded, black snake with silver, cruciform fangs.

At the dead end of our lovers' lane—a side street of abandoned factories—where I perfected the pinch that springs open a bra; behind the lilac bushes in Marquette Park, where you first touched me through my jeans and your nipples, swollen against transparent cotton, seemed the shade of lilacs; in the balcony of the now defunct Clark Theater, where I wiped popcorn salt from my palms and slid them up your thighs and you whispered, "I feel like Doris Day is watching us," we didn't.

How adept we were at fumbling, how perfectly mistimed our timing, how utterly we confused energy with ecstasy.

Remember that night becalmed by heat, and the two of us, fused by sweat, trembling as if a wind from outer space that only we could feel was gusting across Oak Street Beach? Entwined in your faded Navajo blanket, we lay soul-kissing until you wept with wanting.

We'd been kissing all day—all summer—kisses tasting of different shades of lip gloss and too many Cokes. The lake had turned hot pink, rose rapture, pearl amethyst with dusk, then washed in night black with a ruff of silver foam. Beyond a momentary horizon, silent bolts of heat lightning throbbed, perhaps setting barns on fire somewhere in Indiana. The beach that had been so crowded was deserted as if there was a curfew. Only the bodies of lovers remained, visible in lightning flashes, scattered like the fallen on a battlefield, a few of them moaning, waiting for the gulls to pick them clean.

On my fingers your slick scent mixed with the coconut musk of the suntan lotion we'd repeatedly smeared over each other's bodies. When your bikini top fell away, my hands caught your breasts, memorizing their delicate weight, my palms cupped as if bringing water to parched lips.

Along the Gold Coast, high-rises began to glow, window added to window, against the dark. In every lighted bedroom, couples home from work were stripping off their business suits, falling to the bed, and doing it. They did it before mirrors and pressed against the glass in streaming shower stalls; they did it against walls and on the furniture in ways that required previously unimagined gymnastics, which they invented on the spot. They did it in honor of man and woman, in honor of beast, in honor of God. They did it because they'd been released, because they were home free, alive, and private, because they couldn't wait any longer, couldn't wait for the appointed hour, for the right time or temperature, couldn't wait for the future, for Messiahs, for peace on earth and justice for all. They did it because of the Bomb, because of pollution, because of the Four Horsemen of the Apocalypse, because extinction might be just a blink away. They did it because it was Friday night. It was Friday night and somewhere delirious music was playing—flutter-tongued flutes, muted trumpets meowing like cats in heat, feverish plucking and twanging, tom-toms, congas, and gongs all pounding the same pulsebeat.

I stripped your bikini bottom down the skinny rails of your legs, and you tugged my swimsuit past my tan. Swimsuits at our ankles, we kicked like swimmers to free our legs, almost expecting a tide to wash over us the way the tide rushes in on Burt Lancaster and Deborah Kerr in *From Here to Eternity*—a love scene so famous that although neither of us had seen the movie, our bodies assumed the exact position of movie stars on the sand and you whispered to me softly, "I'm afraid of getting pregnant," and I whispered back, "Don't worry, I have protection," then, still kissing you, felt for my discarded cutoffs and the wallet in which for the last several months I had carried a Trojan as if it was a talisman. Still kissing, I tore its flattened, dried-out wrapper, and it sprang through my fingers like a spring from a clock and dropped to the sand between our legs. My hands were shaking. In a panic, I groped for it, found it, tried to dust it off, tried as Burt Lancaster never had to, to slip it on without breaking the mood, felt the grains of sand inside it, a throb of lightning, and the Great Lake behind us became, for all practical purposes, the Pacific, and your skin tasted of salt and to the insistent question that my hips were asking your body answered yes, your thighs opened like wings from my waist as we surfaced panting from a kiss that left you pleading *Oh, Christ yes, a yes* gasped sharply as a cry of pain so that for a moment I thought that we *were* already doing it and that somehow I had missed the instant when I entered you, entered you in the bloodless way in which a young man discards his own virginity, entered you as if passing through a gateway into the rest of my life, into a life as I wanted it to be lived *yes* but Oh then I realized that we were still floundering unconnected in the slick between us and there was sand in the Trojan as we slammed together still feeling for that perfect fit, still in the *Here* groping for an *Eternity* that was only a fine adjustment away, just a millimeter to the left or a fraction of an inch farther south though with all the adjusting the sandy Trojan was slipping off and then it was gone but *yes* you kept repeating although your head was shaking *no-not-quite-almost* and our hearts were going like mad and you said, *Yes. Yes wait . . . Stop!*

"What?" I asked, still futilely thrusting as if I hadn't quite heard you.

"Oh. God!" You gasped, pushing yourself up. "What's coming?"

"Gin, what's the matter?" I asked, confused, and then the beam of a spotlight swept over us and I glanced into its blinding eye.

All around us lights were coming, speeding across the sand. Blinking blindness away, I rolled from your body to my knees, feeling utterly defenseless in the way that only nakedness can leave one feeling. Headlights bounded toward us, spotlights crisscrossing, blue dome lights revolving as squad cars converged. I could see other lovers, caught in the beams, fleeing bare-assed through the litter of garbage that daytime hordes had left behind and that night had deceptively concealed. You were crying, clutching the Navajo blanket to your breasts with one hand and clawing for your bikini with the other, and I was trying to calm your terror with reassuring phrases such as "Holy shit! I don't fucking believe this!"

Swerving and fishtailing in the sand, police calls pouring from their radios, the squad cars were on us, and then they were by us while we struggled to pull on our clothes.

They braked at the water's edge, and cops slammed out, brandishing huge flashlights, their beams deflecting over the dark water. Beyond the darting of those beams, the far-off throbs of lightning seemed faint by comparison.

"Over there, goddamn it!" one of them hollered, and two cops sloshed out into the shallow water without even pausing to kick off their shoes, huffing aloud for breath, their leather cartridge belts creaking against their bellies.

"Grab the sonofabitch! It ain't gonna bite!" one of them yelled, then they came sloshing back to shore with a body slung between them.

It was a woman—young, naked, her body limp and bluish beneath the play of flashlight beams. They set her on the sand just past the ring of drying, washed-up alewives. Her face was almost totally concealed by her hair. Her hair was brown and tangled in a way that even wind or sleep can't tangle hair, tangled as if it had absorbed the ripples of water—thick strands, slimy looking like dead seaweed.

"She's been in there awhile, that's for sure," a cop with a beer belly said to a younger, crew-cut cop, who had knelt beside the body and removed his hat as if he might be considering the kiss of life.

The crew-cut officer brushed the hair away from her face, and the flashlight beams settled there. Her eyes were closed. A bruise or a birthmark stained the side of one eye. Her features appeared swollen, her lower lip protruding as if she was pouting.

An ambulance siren echoed across the sand, its revolving red light rapidly approaching.

"Might as well take their sweet-ass time," the beer-bellied cop said.

We had joined the circle of police surrounding the drowned woman almost without realizing that we had. You were back in your bikini, robed in the Navajo blanket, and I had slipped on my cutoffs, my underwear dangling out of a back pocket.

Their flashlight beams explored her body, causing its whiteness to gleam. Her breasts were floppy; her nipples looked shriveled. Her belly appeared inflated by gallons of water. For a moment, a beam focused on her mound of pubic hair, which was overlapped by the swell of her belly, and then moved almost shyly away down her legs, and the cops all glanced at us—at you, especially—above their lights, and you hugged your blanket closer as if they might confiscate it as evidence or to use as a shroud.

When the ambulance pulled up, one of the black attendants immediately put a stethoscope to the drowned woman's swollen belly and announced, "Drowned the baby, too."

Without saying anything, we turned from the group, as unconsciously as we'd joined them, and walked off across the sand, stopping only long enough at the spot where we had lain together like lovers, in order to stuff the rest of our gear into a beach bag, to gather our shoes, and for me to find my wallet and kick sand over the forlorn, deflated Trojan that you pretended not to notice. I was grateful for that.

Behind us, the police were snapping photos, flashbulbs throbbing like lightning flashes, and the lightning itself, still distant but moving in closer, rumbling audibly now, driving a lake wind before it so that gusts of sand tingled against the metal sides of the ambulance.

Squinting, we walked toward the lighted windows of the Gold Coast, while the shadows of gapers attracted by the whirling emergency lights hurried past us toward the shore.

"What happened? What's going on?" they asked without waiting for an answer, and we didn't offer one, just continued walking silently in the dark.

It was only later that we talked about it, and once we began talking about the drowned woman it seemed we couldn't stop.

"She was pregnant," you said. "I mean, I don't want to sound morbid, but I can't help thinking how the whole time we were, we almost—you know—there was this poor, dead woman and her unborn child washing in and out behind us."

"It's not like we could have done anything for her even if we had known she was there."

"But what if we *had* found her? What if after we had—you know," you said, your eyes glancing away from mine and your voice tailing into a whisper, "what if after we did it, we went for a night swim and found her in the water?"

"But, Gin, we didn't," I tried to reason, though it was no more a matter of reason than anything else between us had ever been.

It began to seem as if each time we went somewhere to make out—on the back porch of your half-deaf, whiskery Italian grandmother, who sat in the front of the apartment cackling at *I Love Lucy* reruns; or in your girlfriend Tina's basement rec room when her parents were away on bowling league nights and Tina was upstairs with her current crush, Brad; or way off in the burbs, at the Giant Twin Drive-In during the weekend they called Elvis Fest—the drowned woman was with us.

We would kiss, your mouth would open, and when your tongue flicked repeatedly after mine, I would unbutton the first button of your blouse, revealing the beauty spot at the base of your throat, which matched a smaller spot I loved above a corner of your lips, and then the second button, which opened on a delicate gold cross—which I had always tried to regard as merely a fashion statement—dangling above the cleft of your breasts. The third button exposed the lacy swell of your bra, and I would slide my hand over the patterned mesh, feeling for the firmness of your nipple rising to my fingertip, but you would pull slightly away, and behind your rapid breath your kiss would grow distant, and I would kiss harder, trying to lure you back from wherever you had gone, and finally, holding you as if only consoling a friend, I'd ask, "What are you thinking?" although of course I knew.

"I don't want to think about her but I can't help it. I mean, it seems like some kind of weird omen or something, you know?"

"No, I don't know," I said. "It was just a coincidence."

"Maybe if she'd been farther away down the beach, but she was so close to us. A good wave could have washed her up right beside us."

"Great, then we could have had a ménage à trois."

"Gross! I don't believe you just said that! Just because you said it in French doesn't make it less disgusting."

"You're driving me to it. Come on, Gin, I'm sorry," I said. "I was just making a dumb joke to get a little different perspective on things."

"What's so goddamn funny about a woman who drowned herself and her baby?"

"We don't even know for sure she did."

"Yeah, right, it was just an accident. Like she just happened to be going for a walk pregnant and naked, and she fell in."

"She could have been on a sailboat or something. Accidents happen; so do murders."

"Oh, like murder makes it less horrible? Don't think that hasn't occurred to me. Maybe the bastard who knocked her up killed her, huh?"

"How should I know? You're the one who says you don't want to talk about it and then gets obsessed with all kinds of theories and scenarios. Why are we arguing about a woman we don't even know, who doesn't have the slightest thing to do with us?"

"I *do* know about her," you said. "I dream about her."

"You dream about her?" I repeated, surprised. "Dreams you remember?"

"Sometimes they wake me up. In one I'm at my *nonna*'s cottage in Michigan, swimming for a raft that keeps drifting farther away, until I'm too tired to turn back. Then I notice there's a naked person sunning on the raft and start yelling, 'Help!' and she looks up and offers me a hand, but I'm too afraid to take it even though I'm drowning because it's her."

"God! Gin, that's creepy."

"I dreamed you and I are at the beach and you bring us a couple hot dogs but forget the mustard, so you have to go all the way back to the stand for it."

"Hot dogs, no mustard—a little too Freudian, isn't it?"

"Honest to God, I dreamed it. You go back for mustard and I'm wondering why you're gone so long, then a woman screams that a kid has drowned and everyone stampedes for the water. I'm swept in by the mob and forced under, and I think, This is it, I'm going to drown, but I'm able to hold my breath longer than could ever be possible. It feels like a flying dream—flying under water—and then I see this baby down there flying, too, and realize it's the kid everyone thinks has drowned, but he's no more drowned than I am. He looks like Cupid or one of those baby angels that cluster around the face of God."

"Pretty weird. What do you think all the symbols mean?—hot dogs, water, drowning..."

"It means the baby who drowned inside her that night was a love child—a boy—and his soul was released there to wander through the water."

"You don't really believe that?"

We argued about the interpretation of dreams, about whether dreams are symbolic or psychic, prophetic or just plain nonsense, until you said, "Look, Dr. Freud, you can believe what you want about your dreams, but keep your nose out of mine, okay?"

We argued about the drowned woman, about whether her death was a suicide or a murder, about whether her appearance that night was an omen or a coincidence which, you argued, is what an omen is anyway: a coincidence that means something. By the end of summer, even if we were no longer arguing about the woman, we had acquired the habit of arguing about everything else. What was better: dogs or cats, rock or jazz, Cubs or Sox, tacos or egg rolls, right or left, night or day?—we could argue about anything.

It no longer required arguing or necking to summon the drowned woman; everywhere we went she surfaced by her own volition: at Rocky's Italian Beef, at Lindo Mexico, at the House of Dong, our favorite Chinese restaurant, a place we still frequented because when we'd first started seeing each other they had let us sit and talk until late over tiny cups of jasmine tea and broken fortune cookies. We would always kid about going there. "Are you in the mood for Dong tonight?" I'd whisper conspiratorially. It was a dopey joke, meant for you to roll your eyes at its repeated dopiness. Back then, in winter, if one of us ordered the garlic shrimp we would both be sure to eat them so that later our mouths tasted the same when we kissed.

Even when she wasn't mentioned, she was there with her drowned body—so dumpy next to yours—and her sad breasts, with their wrinkled nipples and sour milk—so saggy beside yours, which were still budding—with her swollen belly and her pubic bush colorless in the glare of electric light, with her tangled, slimy hair and her pouting, placid face—so lifeless beside yours—and her skin a pallid white, lightning-flash white, flashbulb white, a whiteness that couldn't be duplicated in daylight—how I'd come to hate that pallor, so cold beside the flush of your skin.

There wasn't a particular night when we finally broke up, just as there wasn't a particular night when we began going together, but it was a night in fall when I guessed that it was over. We were parked in the Rambler at the dead end of the street of factories that had been our lovers' lane, listening to a drizzle of rain and dry leaves sprinkle the hood. As always, rain revitalized the smells of smoked fish and kielbasa in the upholstery. The radio was on too low to hear, the windshield wipers swished at intervals as if we were driving, and the windows were steamed as if we'd been making out. But we'd been arguing, as usual, this time about a woman poet who had committed suicide, whose work you were reading. We were sitting, no longer talking or touching, and I remember thinking that I didn't want to argue with you anymore. I didn't want to sit like this in hurt silence; I wanted to talk excitedly all night as we once had. I wanted to find some way that wasn't corny sounding to tell you how much fun I'd had in your company, how much knowing you had meant to me, and how I had suddenly realized that I'd been so intent on becoming lovers that I'd overlooked how close we'd been as friends. I wanted you to know that. I wanted you to like me again.

"It's sad," I started to say, meaning that I was sorry we had reached the point of silence, but before I could continue you challenged the statement.

"What makes you so sure it's sad?"

"What do you mean, what makes me so sure?" I asked, confused by your question.

You looked at me as if what was sad was that I would never understand. "For all either one of us knows," you said, "death could have been her triumph!"

Maybe when it really ended was the night I felt we had just reached the beginning, that one time on the beach in the summer when our bodies rammed so desperately together that for a moment I thought we did it, and maybe in our hearts we did, although for me, then, doing it in one's heart didn't quite count. If it did, I supposed we'd all be Casanovas.

We rode home together on the El train that night, and I felt sick and defeated in a way I was embarrassed to mention. Our mute reflections emerged like negative exposures on the dark, greasy window of the train. Lightning branched over the city, and when the train entered the subway tunnel, the lights inside flickered as if the power was disrupted, though the train continued rocketing beneath the Loop.

When the train emerged again we were on the South Side of the city and it was pouring, a deluge as if the sky had opened to drown the innocent and guilty alike. We hurried from the El station to your house, holding the Navajo blanket over our heads until, soaked, it collapsed. In the dripping doorway of your apartment building, we said good night. You were shivering. Your bikini top showed through the thin blouse plastered to your skin. I swept the wet hair away from your face and kissed you lightly on the lips, then you turned and went inside. I stepped into the rain, and you came back out, calling after me.

"What?" I asked, feeling a surge of gladness to be summoned back into the doorway with you.

"Want an umbrella?"

I didn't. The downpour was letting up. It felt better to walk back to the station feeling the rain rinse the sand out of my hair, off my legs, until the only places where I could still feel its grit were in the crotch of my cutoffs and each squish of my shoes. A block down the street, I passed a pair of jockey shorts lying in a puddle and realized they were mine, dropped from my back pocket as we ran to your house. I left them behind, wondering if you'd see them and recognize them the next day.

By the time I had climbed the stairs back to the El platform, the rain had stopped. Your scent still hadn't washed from my fingers. The station—the entire city it seemed—dripped and steamed. The summer sound of crickets and nighthawks echoed from the drenched neighborhood. Alone, I could admit how sick I felt. For you, it was a night that would haunt your dreams. For me, it was another night when I waited, swollen and aching, for what I had secretly nicknamed the Blue Ball Express.

Literally lovesick, groaning inwardly with each lurch of the train and worried that I was damaged for good, I peered out at the passing yellow-lit stations, where lonely men stood posted before giant advertisements, pictures of glamorous models defaced by graffiti—the same old scrawled insults and pleas: FUCK YOU, EAT ME. At this late hour the world seemed given over to men without women, men waiting in abject patience for something indeterminate, the way I waited for our next times. I avoided their eyes so that they wouldn't see the pity in mine, pity for them because I'd just been with you, your scent was still on my hands, and there seemed to be so much future ahead.

For me it was another night like that, and by the time I reached my stop I knew I would be feeling better, recovered enough to walk the dark street home making up poems of longing that I never wrote down. I was the D. H. Lawrence of not doing it, the voice of all the would-be lovers who ached and squirmed. From our contortions in doorways, on stairwells, and in the bucket seats of cars we could have composed a Kama Sutra of interrupted bliss. It must have been that night when I recalled all the other times of walking home after seeing you, so that it seemed as if I was falling into step behind a parade of my former selves—myself walking home on the night we first kissed, myself on the night when I unbuttoned your blouse and kissed your breasts, myself on the night when I lifted your skirt above your thighs and dropped to my knees—each succeeding self another step closer to that irrevocable moment for which our lives seemed poised.

But we didn't, not in the moonlight, or by the phosphorescent lanterns of lightning bugs in your back yard, not beneath the constellations we couldn't see, let alone decipher, or in the dark glow that replaced the real darkness of night, a darkness already stolen from us, not with the skyline rising behind us while a city gradually decayed, not in the heat of summer while a Cold War raged, despite the freedom of youth and the license of first love—because of fate, karma, luck, what does it matter?—we made not doing it a wonder, and yet we didn't, we didn't, we never did.

A Conversation with Stuart Dybek

Your book, I Sailed with Magellan, has been called a novel-in-stories by some critics. Did you conceive of it as a kind of novel, or did the collection just turn out that way?

I, personally, could care less what anybody calls anything. I just care about the character of the piece. On the other hand, sometimes the character of a piece does have to do with the conception of the genre. In this case, the confusion arises because the term *novel-in-stories* gets reduced down to *novel,* and people put expectations on a hybrid form that the form in itself never wanted to have. So it ends up arguing about this distracting notion: Is it a legitimate novel, is it not a novel? The whole point of hybrid forms—the prose poem, the short-short—is that they are in-between forms. I always have a notion of a hybrid form in mind—just because I have always gravitated toward them. I write a lot of short-shorts, a lot of prose poems.

I think, often when somebody writes a book, there's a homage concealed inside of it. A lot of my favorite books are what I would call novels and stories or linked story collections. *Winesberg, Ohio, Dubliners,* all of Isaac Babel's books—*Red Calvary, Odessa Tales*—Eudora Welty's *Golden Apples,* Hemingway's *In Our Time.* All of those were critical books for me and remain some of my favorite books. They are also some of the most seminal books in literature in the twentieth century. One of my favorite writers of the century was Italo Calvino. I don't know that Calvino ever published a book that couldn't be defined as a novel-in-stories, with the exception of his first book, which was a conventional novel. His sources were Boccaccio and Chaucer. If you put it in its proper historic context, then it becomes clearer that *Last Exit to Brooklyn,* Tim O'Brien's *The Things They Carried,* and all those books are not novels, they're not collections of stories; they're this hybrid form of novel-in-stories.

In what ways do you think I Sailed with Magellan *does work as a novel?*

A novel needs this overarching arc, and a novel-in-stories is a way out of that arc.

I don't think it works as a novel. A novel needs this overarching arc, and a novel-in-stories is a way out of that arc. You can have all kinds of novels, but essentially, for me, a novel is the form that most implements the cause and effect that is inherent in chronological narration. Even if you break it up.

A novel-in-stories is saying there are huge links to experience. But I don't believe that our experience is as coherent as narrative line makes you think, particularly, if what you are writing about is remembered experience. We don't remember in narrative lines, we remember in these bursts. So that's one thing. Another thing is that if you look at those writers that I talked about, they're all noted stylists. What made them noted stylists is that they are writers that work very well in a lyrical mode. The beauty of the novel is rising and falling action, and what lyrical writers don't want to do is fall.

The beauty of the novel is rising and falling action, and what lyrical writers don't want to do is fall.

So the novel-in-stories is this opportunity to create linked stories, but to try to keep that lyrical intensity. Welty seems to be particularly exemplary in that regard. Certainly Joyce, as well. The form isn't trying to duplicate the novel. It's trying to mimic the novel's sense of unity but arrive at that unity in a different way. The story collection has no desire, whatsoever, to do that. It might happen as a byproduct, but the point of a story collection is not to create some kind of unified story of a platoon in Vietnam or a neighborhood in the Bronx or the city of Dublin. You know, it's interesting. The place is frequently the organizational principle in a lot of these books.

The Coast of Chicago *is a certain kind of a collection, too, with those longer stories juxtaposed with the really short ones. It has the feel of music to it. Music seems to have been as great an influence on you as the work of other writers.*

For me, albums like *Sketches of Spain, Kind of Blue,* and concept albums like *Sergeant Pepper* were a huge influence on me. Those are novels-in-stories of music. With *The Coast of Chicago,* I was trying to mimic the way those little intense musical moments are connected. I love *Sergeant Pepper.* What makes it different than so many other Beatle albums is some connecting force that still allows those to be intense, individual songs.

You once said, "What I hear in music, I find later in literature." What, exactly, did you mean by that?

I never quite understood Kafka, in the context of the culture he was writing in, until I heard music that reminded me of Kafka. This is entirely subjective. I'm certainly not arguing that anybody else would listen to Zolten Kodali, a Hungarian influenced by Transylvanian folk music, and hear Franz Kafka, a Jew from Prague, in that music. But, I did. Another way music works for me is like what I did, in fact, when I taught sixth grade. You walk in one day with your tape recorder and you say, "Kids we're gonna write poems today. Get ready." Then you press the button and out of the tape recorder comes [whistles a tune] and they're all writing. You know, the dromedaries are marching across the desert. It gives you that soundtrack that you create.

I never sat down consciously to write about Chicago, but it was a natural thing to write about. The tradition I was educated in, like most Americans, was pretty militantly realistic, and so I was writing this little story that was absolutely without any kind of self-examination and would have just been a realistic story about Chicago, except that I happened to have this music by Zolten Kodali on the record player. Something about that music changed my perception, my imagined perception of the city, so that rather than writing from this American bias—that has behind it Andersen and Hemingway and all those writers—the emotional elements that were arising in me from listening to that sort of gypsy sound of the cello made me suddenly see the city from the perspective of ethnicity. It just so happened that I grew up in an Eastern European neighborhood. And so, without even knowing it, because I was in that kind of semitrance of listening to music and writing, stuff I had never thought before just jumped out on to the page. Once I got to that place, I wanted to go back to that place, but the only way I could get back there for the first three or four stories that followed that one was to put that music on again. By this time I was accumulating other kinds of music: Shostakovich and Bartok. When I thought back to it, the first writer that wasn't American that really, really just blew me out of my socks was Dostoyevsky—and that was several years before this thing with the music. So there was always something there in that direction, but I never had a coherent notion of what it was. The music supplied that coherence.

Did you study music?

Yeah. It's the art form that I feel the greatest reverence toward, and I think that great reverence can work against you. Your disappointment with your own clumsy attempts is so great because you have invested such religious fervor that it makes failure almost too difficult to put up with—and with any art you have to put up with failure. But that might be a fancy way of saying I just plain don't have enough talent.

Do you see parallels in the learning the craft of writing and learning the craft of music?

I do, indeed. The craft of writing is much slyer, sleeker, though. Let's just say if you went to a university to study music, you would expect that you were going to learn the craft. You would expect that you were going to be in a fine arts department, and one of the reasons you would expect that is that in something like music you have to learn another language. If it's painting, you've got to learn how to mix colors. You've got smells and scents of canvas and all kinds of palate knives. If it's photography, you're going to learn digital this or darkroom that. Whereas, writing has none of that. It's all invisible—and, not only that, but it's taking place mostly in the English departments, where the huge emphasis is on reading. The vocabulary that you're given to talk about what you're reading is the vocabulary of literary interpretation rather than the vocabulary of composition. I'm not saying it in any critical way. Reading is absolutely essential to writing, but they're not the same thing. In fact, one of the things about writing that I think is so interesting is how mysterious it gets when you try to figure out what the

The vocabulary that you're given to talk about what you're reading is the vocabulary of literary interpretation rather than the vocabulary of composition.

difference between reading and writing *is*. I always get lost in there somewhere. Where does writing even take place? It's really a very mysterious art—and it's the most abstract of the arts. I think it's that very abstraction that creates that mystery, and part of the mystery is figuring out what in the world craft is in the first place.

Because we write our stories with the same language that we order pizza?

Absolutely right. So everybody *thinks* that they already know about language, and yet hardly anyone has written dialogue. How often do you go around constructing scenes? Not only that, but a lot of people don't come to it until they're in college, and because they get this notion of language in their literature classes that they can become powerful critics already, they don't realize that the kid who made it as a rock star when he was twenty-two probably might have had piano lessons from the age of five, finally weaseled out of piano lessons when he was twelve and bought his first guitar, locked himself in a room with about five million records and his parents never saw him again until he emerged when he was eighteen. He was teaching himself the craft in his little basement or his bedroom, playing six to seven, eight hours a day, thinking, living, and breathing music. How many people come to writing like that? I'm sure there were a bunch of writers that wrote their way through high school. I'm not one of them.

So everybody *thinks* that they already know about language, and yet hardly anyone has written dialogue.

Would you talk about the short-short story, a genre you've written in a lot. How would you define it, what dictates it, how do you know when it's the right form for a story?

I came to it in part through the prose poem. No one was publishing those short pieces but poetry editors in the late '60s and '70s. A hundred years after Europeans had made the prose poem just another part of the continuum of literature, Americans discovered it with a vengeance in the late '60s and '70s. Everybody was writing them. I loved them from the time I first read those grand old prose poems. But I never really felt the need to make a huge differentiation between those things and what Hemingway was doing in those little vignettes in *In Our Time*—and the more I read and studied the prose poem, the more reservations I had about clearly defining what I was doing as a prose poet. My largest reservation came out of the fact that, historically, the prose poem is an anti-poem, which I applaud. That's all interesting. But for an anti-poem to work, you have to have a reader that is very conversant to what a poem is, and I really didn't want to be writing something that needed readers so conversant with the genre that they could see the anti nature of it. So I started thinking, maybe they're more like little stories—and as soon as I thought that the stuff I started writing became more American.

But at the same time there must have been a bunch of different writers independently arriving at the same kind of conclusions, because on the tail end of that little tiny bit of prose poem hysteria, this new short-short stuff started. Suddenly, there were places where you could publish short fiction, whether you called it a prose poem or not. In my first book of poems there are a bunch of prose poems, but now I would consider them short-shorts.

Some writers believe that the short story is more closely related to the poem than it actually is to the novel. Would you agree with that?

Yeah, I agree with that. A story, because of its length, could be sustained by an image. It's really difficult, unless your image happens to be the great white whale, to sustain a novel entirely on the exploration of a single image. Prose poems are a way for me to study compression in prose, which I think takes place on a different scale than compression in verse takes place. In verse, you're talking about haikus, sonnets; in fiction, the short form was the short story before the short-short came along. So compression is in some degree a relative term. The thing that interests me most about the short-short is that it lends itself to interesting sequences. I think the same thing is true about the Rimbeau poems and Hemingway's *In Our Time.* There is a tendency to forget that each one of those is a chapter number rather than a title, and what that chapter number indicates is that these are sequential. It's really hard for me to sort out "masterpieces" in the short-short form. The first one that comes to mind is Kawabata, a writer I love. He wrote over a hundred what he called "palm of hand stories" and out of that hundred—and this a Nobel Prize winner—I'd sort out three or four that I would say are little masterpieces. So I don't think this is a form that necessarily lends itself to the individual masterpiece.

The thing that interests me most about the short-short is that it lends itself to interesting sequences.

In all of your collections, the sequence of stories is very important. How do you come upon the right sequence?

I've heard discussions on this subject. Somebody says, "You didn't lay out the overall art," as if the fact that you didn't perceive it in its entirety from the start somehow negates it as a unified form. But it's just the opposite. That's the fun of it, the beauty of it. The writer doesn't know where it's going. We all do this, that's what form is about. You create something on the page and, suddenly, even though it's your creation, it's now asking you to surrender to it. It's demanding that you have a dialogue with it. That's what sequential writing is. You've written a couple pieces that you hadn't even thought had a connection, and then you see some vague connection and you say to yourself, I've got A and I've got D. I could write C. Now the sequence is calling you to write something that you would have never thought of writing had you not seen the sequential possibilities—and once you write C, suddenly B jumps in the pile. So what happens is that you're having this dialogue with the pieces as if it's outside of yourself, even though you've created it. It's this interesting dialectic between what everybody wants to think a writer has, which is control, but what every writer wants to actually do, which is surrender.

Do you usually come to the end of a collection with all the pieces in their right sequence as a result of talking back and forth with the pieces, listening to them as you go along?

Well, hopefully. It's a totally organic, instinctive process—and I can tell you from reviews that I got on this last book, some readers enjoy it and some don't. One young woman wrote in an alternative newspaper in Seattle, "*I Sailed with Magellan* is an aerobic reading workout." It wasn't said in an admiring way. She was wondering why the hell I didn't do a bit more of the work for her. When you put these sequential things out, you are asking the reader to participate the way you did, finding the coherence between them.

When you put these sequential things out, you are asking the reader to participate the way you did, finding the coherence between them.

"Nighthawks" does what you've described, but in the context of a single story. Or is it a novella?

I don't know what it is. It's a little collection within a collection. It was for me an opportunity to really play with sequence. It was a desire for me to try to put myself in a situation where I really didn't know what I was writing.

What was the genesis of it?

Images that seemed mysterious to me. I had written a story called "Chopin in Winter," and I began that story to the collective Rubenstein Chopin. But the longer I wrote it, the more and more Rubenstein pieces that I was listening to were the preludes—in particular, the nocturnes—and at some point it occurred to me that a nocturne is not a formal piece like a sonata. It's a mood piece. And mood interests me enormously. The American writers that I am hugely attracted to are Hawthorne and Melville, and to some smaller degree Poe, because mood was such central element in those writers. Twain, who Hemingway credits as the first modern American voice, is really a tonal writer—and what happens in the twentieth century is that tone replaces mood as the central defining element for a lot of writers. There are exceptions—Welty—and I tend to gravitate toward those exceptions. Anyway, back to noctures, mood pieces. For a while "Nighthawks" was called "Nocturnes." Why I changed the name, I'm not even sure. I think I finally felt I was getting more out of the image than the music.

The Edward Hopper painting of the same name?

Yeah, the painting. And nighthawks being actual birds. All of the different resonances in meaning. "Nocturnes" had served the purpose of getting me started, but on the page I just felt that with the word '*nighthawks*' I was getting more for my buck.

Your stories find their locus in the Chicago neighborhood where you grew up. Would you talk about the relationship between the real neighborhood and the fictional one?

I just gave a reading yesterday at Loyola and a guy showed up from my old hood. He said, "In that story of yours, 'The Cat Woman,' you called the character Swantek. That's me." I actually just used the name from the neighborhood; it never occurred to me that anyone in the neighborhood would read the story. It's not a particularly attractive portrait of Swantek, but he was delighted. In fact, I have reimagined the city. I have taken total imaginative liberties with that neighborhood. I have heightened certain things and muted others. But people who live there think it *was* like that. They say, "You really caught that." I'm really happy to hear it. In one sense, the neighborhood is very much the same as it always was because it never got gentrified or yuppified; it only got rougher. The neighbors I'm writing about are still intensely ethnic. They are one giant barrio.

There are what might be called elements of magical realism in some of your stories—"The Pulaski Man" is a good example. Another writer, Luis Urrea, suggested that the magical realism so prevalent in Latino literature is rooted in the mystical aspects of the Catholic faith.

That's an absolute bull's eye. I think Catholicism had a gigantic effect on my imagination. To this day, what puzzles me about the mystery about being a human being is how thoroughly we compartmentalize religion. We make these little compartments where we keep the magical and impossible elements that we wouldn't believe in any other aspect of our lives and then we go and visit them at prescribed times. But they keep bleeding out of their borders, so you end up killing people in the name of this faith or that faith. In a lot of my stories, the folkloric, mythological elements start bleeding into the real world, which is supposed to be practical, brutal, capitalistic. But I'm not really fond of that term, "magical realism." "The Pulaski Man" was written well before Gabriel Marquez's stuff ever came out. I'm worshipful toward that writer, but the term itself seems to me to be at once reductive and so abstract that's it's all but useless.

To this day, what puzzles me about the mystery about being a human being is how thoroughly we compartmentalize religion.

In addition to the idea of being bound by Catholicism, do you think that in ethnic neighborhoods there's a sense that people are bound to something bigger than just their immediate families—and that storytelling is a natural result of that, a way to contemplate the magical people you encounter, people that nobody ever understood and who keep coming up like ghosts in conversations at the dinner table?

Yes. In fact, what I'm working on now are ghost stories. That's my next book, both because I like the genre and because it's a connection with exactly what you are talking about: that, at the end of the day, there's a sudden vision of this huge connection. It's not just Catholicism. There are two American writers who crossed that border that were really important to me. One was Cheever, with stories like the "Enormous Radio" and "Torch Song" and "Swimmer." Stories that there was a lot of pressure on him *not* to write. *The New Yorker* did not want this guy writing ghost stories, they wanted him to be a chronicler of realistic Long Island and Connecticut upper middle class Americans. The other one is Malamud, who figured out how to bring folkloric elements of Judaism into his work.

Your stories resist the conventional, as well. For one thing, they are full of digressions. In "Blue Boy," for example, there's a page and a half of dialogue between two men at the little boy's wake. They raise these huge theological questions, then disappear. Poe's single effect would tell you that you can't do that, but you get away with it at every turn. How?

I don't know how. I was aware of taking that liberty. It seemed okay, so I left it in. I would have cut it if the few people who saw it had jumped on me about it. I think it was allowable because that really is not a story about the kid, the blue boy. It's the neighborhood's story. And because it's the neighborhood's story you could suddenly have a couple of guys just yakking out of the blue here and a couple of women over there. In fact, it's a way, a compressed way of trying to suggest to the reader just how crowded this neighborhood is.

The world of your Chicago stories is vivid and concrete, but the emotional truth most often comes to the reader sideways. What advice do you give students about how to reveal information in a story?

That kind of oblique writing has always been attractive. But I would have to have a student writing a specific story to speak to it, because a lot of that stuff for me is actually byproduct. Emphasis for me is always on the image. If you keep creating and recreating the image, there will be all of these byproducts. Theme will be a byproduct. Some writers start writing with all of the answers, where for other writers everything is about questions. If you teach, isn't it true that it is way harder to ask a good question than it is to tell them everything it is that you want them to know?

Emphasis for me is always on the image. If you keep creating and recreating the image, there will be all of these byproducts. Theme will be a byproduct.

I keep going back to image, but it really is tremendously central to me. I think that is one reason why I have stuck with the neighborhood that I write about. It never occurred to me about my own work, but it occurred to me any number of times when I read Ralph Ellison. God, if you just write about the everyday life of an African American in the United States, you are writing about the grandest, most important themes you can. That's the magic of writing. Then it suddenly occurred to me that, by making this working class blue-collar neighborhood on the page, you couldn't *not* write about ethnicity, assimilation, class. You don't have to go there with this huge desire.

It's not so different from English professors looking for symbols everywhere, assuming the writer is crafting a story with symbols in mind, when in fact it's an organic process.

Exactly. Because creative writing is often taking place in the context of literature, students are often, not surprisingly, approaching their stories with the desire to have all of these themes. Somebody really feels terrible about the homophobic nature of our society, so they sit down and write a story about how bad homophobia is. But it isn't like you're hiding symbols for an Easter egg hunt. It's happening naturally because you are creating images in this believable resonant way, and all of this other stuff is just byproduct.

To move onto something a little bit different, you've spoken about your closeness with your Polish-speaking grandmother. Do you think her use of language influenced your work?

I think it dovetailed with nonverbal aspects of music that so fascinated me and that it led me to feel comfortable with the paradox that the aim of a verbal arc might be to reach nonverbal places. Even though you wanted me to change the subject, it goes back to the idea that, emphasizing nonagenda parts of writing, you are emphasizing the parts of writing which are the least verbal. It's true you are creating an image out of language, but it's also true that that aspect of the art of writing is the farthest away from the expository mode.

You've described a moment in your childhood when you looked out of a window, observed that the tall buildings were "scraping the sky," and suddenly understood the power of words. Critics often comment on the beautiful language in your stories. "We Didn't" is deliciously lyrical, but it never goes over the top. How did you find that balance?

One thing that was really important to me in that story was the sentence rhythms. I felt like if I could connect the reader with those sentence rhythms, they would drive him through the story. I must have been in a phase like that because that story was written close to the time of "Paper Lantern." In both of those stories, I wanted that rhythm driving the reader through—but only in a subliminal way. I didn't want the rhythm so strong that it seemed incantory.

I felt like if I could connect the reader with those sentence rhythms, they would drive him through the story.

What is the genesis of that story, and how did it evolve?

It's a failed poem. I loved Yehuda Amichai's writing, and at that time thought that *Magellan* was a collection of love stories. One of the puzzles for me with the love story is how to portray sexuality. Part of the question of how to do it came out of a very critical feeling I had about the way our culture does it. Particularly movies. It's almost a banality to say that we have an anti-erotic culture that is more interested in violence than it is in eroticism. One day I just sat down and I wrote about all of things about sexuality in

American movies that I don't like. Then I tried to think, What's the opposite of this? What is the relationship of sex to a story? Number one is that sex is action. It should be good action writing. Often I'll have a student who is a good describer, but when they reach action the whole story goes right down the tubes. Sometimes the simplest thing to do is to stop a second and think: What am I doing? How can I make a reader see it? Previously, it had occurred to me that action writing is a kind of description unique to itself, so I started reading writers whose action appealed to me, like Elmore Leonard. Pam Houston. I saw that the scene *itself* should be an image, that it's action. And you never have the scene unless it advances the character.

Sometimes the simplest thing to do is to stop a second and think: What am I doing? How can I make a reader see it?

I also had the antennas out, which is a long way round to the Amichai poem. Here's this poem by this poet that I really love and the translation of its title is "We Did It." I hate this word, '*it.*' I think that it is one of the tackiest phrases. It made me think, What kind of language *does* a writer want to use? What is erotic language? Do I use language from a hygiene class? Do I use language from a bodice ripper, which for me is the dirtiest language? So here's this writer that I really love, using this tacky phrase, but the poem's beautiful! So, I decided I would write a poem in response. I played around with that for a couple of years, and it never went anywhere, but I accumulated a bunch of lines and images. Then it broke into characterization and dialogue. When that happened, I decided I would develop it into a story. By that point, though, it already had poetry DNA in it—in the rhythms of the verse lines transposed to sentences and the images I'd collected. I do that a lot—loop my poems for fiction images. "Nighthawk" burned up about half a book's worth of poems.

You see that poetry DNA here: "Along the Gold Coast, high-rises begin to glow, window added to window, against the dark. In every lighted bedroom, couples home from work were stripping off their business suits, falling to the bed, and doing it. They did it before mirrors and pressed against the glass in streaming shower stalls; they did it against walls and on the furniture in ways that required previously unimagined gymnastics, which they invented on the spot. They did it in honor of man and woman, in honor of beast, in honor of God. . . .

Those are Amichai's lines. I took them right from the poem. Then once I did that, I thought, I'll wink at the reader and let him know. You've got the obvious reference to Molly Bloom's "Yes." But I also went back to Neruda's early books where he's a strapping young man of twenty-two or twenty-three, an assistant consulate stuck in some backwater, and he writes these twenty-one love poems, where he thinks the whole world is getting laid, but not him. That's what behind "all along the Gold Coast." So, I was actually having fun with allusion.

You were playing.

In a way I don't usually do. He is stupid in that story, by the way. Sometimes people think that it's a story about a guy who's been failed by his girlfriend. But, really, it's just the other way around. When she says, "You don't get it," he really doesn't. He doesn't get it that she is so much more deeply haunted than he is by the murder because of her connection as a woman.

Your "Pet Milk" story seems related to "We Didn't." The intensity around lost love, the sensuality, even the image of the el train at the end. It's a completely different kind of story, though. It begins with a little meditation on Pet Milk, segues to a memory of his grandmother, then leaps—in the simplest transitions—to the meat of the story, which is the memory of an early love. Would you talk about that leap, the connection in your mind between the grandmother and the young woman in his past?

I didn't have that relationship in my mind.

Then how did it get there?

It's just a byproduct. You're a good reader, a very good reader. I honestly didn't have that connection. I'm *happy* you read it that way. I will answer your question, but by going back to the real early question about writing and craft. There used to be that thing in the '60s about participatory democracy; writers have that. The enormous participation on the part of the reader is like dancing to music. With the other arts it isn't the same. Of course, there's a relationship between the viewer and a painting, but it's a far more passive relationship than the relationship with language, the abstraction of language. When you came up with that connection, I didn't really see it. But that doesn't mean it's not there. You write in order to be smarter than yourself. You hope that what you make is smarter than you are.

You write in order to be smarter than yourself. You hope that what you make is smarter than you are.

Still, it's such a huge leap! What made you believe that it worked?

The process of it, as I remember it, was that at the start all I wanted to do was to talk about painting. I love still lifes. I thought, I can write a poem that's just a still life, and the still life I selected was a kind of clutter on a table that had a can of Pet Milk and a coffee cup. I tried for about two years—I don't mean every day. Every once in a while I'd take that poem out and mess with it. It was just flat and dead and static, but there was something about it that kept making me mess around with it rather than throw it away. Then, I guess, one day I just asked myself why the hell do I have can of Pet Milk out there anyway? And it reminded me of my grandmother, my *Boucha*. As soon as I remembered her, that rush of feelings that I always have about her rushed out into the poem. Then, suddenly, the poem was a story. A lot of times writers learn things from their stories, usually from an accident, that they can use. The accident from that story that I learned from was transition. You could argue that the art of the short story is the art of transition. You never, ever will sit in a literature class and hear that, though. It just does not interest an academic.

Generally, they don't care seem to care about how a story works.

They don't care how it works, they really don't. Maybe they don't even know. And yet you could spend a whole semester just looking at the beautiful transitions that certain poets and fiction writers made. Anyway, I learned at a visceral level from this story. To transition between looking at the cup of coffee, looking up at the sky above the train, across the street, was for me a moment like the tree-scraped skies. I mean, I *really* learned something—and it was something I wanted to repeat. From the writing of that story on, for whatever it's worth, I've been much more aware of what transition is. That first sentence is a transition out of silence. So when you ask me, what's the jump from the grandmother to the girl, I would say that it actually doesn't occur between the grandmother and the girl, it occurs between the coffee and the sky.

That first sentence is a transition out of silence.

What makes the memories so powerful is how they grow from the "now" of the story. Yet the now, the day it started snowing, is never revisited. The story doesn't come full circle as students are so often taught that it must.

The whole intention of that story was to create the simple circular story; it was supposed to come back with him sitting at the window. But again, by accident, I reached the last line of the story. When I was a kid in college I read *Rabbit Run,* and I loved the ending that shoots out over the frame of the story. So even though my intention was to circle back when I hit that el train shooting out of the frame of the story, it reminded me of he "runs, runs, runs." And I said, "No, I'll let it go there."

Writing Prompts

READ: "We Didn't" and the interview with **Stuart Dybek.**

PONDER: The influence of Yehuda Amichai's poem both on the page and between the lines of the story.

WRITE: Pick a poem that you love, look at it closely, reread it several times, and then freewrite about how it makes you feel the way it does. Write the beginning paragraphs of a story in which the poem's influence can be seen both in subject matter and style.

PRACTICE:

- If there's a poem you've tried and failed to write, look at it and see if you can turn it into a story. Or turn a perfectly good poem (your own or someone else's) into a story.
- Write four paragraphs, describing you childhood neighborhood with concrete, sensory details. Consider the stories that happened or might have happened there. Write one of them.
- Write a story that involves people from your neighborhood, but is actually *about* the neighborhood itself.

- Listen to music that you feel is connected somehow to the subject matter you want to write about and allow insights and images to float up as you listen. Write with that same music as a backdrop and be open to whatever it suggests as you go.
- Go to an art gallery or a museum. Find a still life. Write about it. Who has gathered these things together? Why? What kind of active life does it represent?
- Create a still life in your mind's eye that reflects your character's life and his sensibilities.
- Contemplate two or more unlike objects and freewrite, allowing your brain to make connections and transitions between them.
- Identify your character's former selves and write a scene that reveals one of them.

Dave Eggers

Dave Eggers (b. 1970) is the author of a novel, a collection of short stories, and a memoir and the editor of numerous books. Born and raised near Chicago, he was educated at the University of Illinois. His honors include the Independent Book Award, the Addison Metcalfe Award, and nominations for the Pulitzer Prize and the National Magazine Award for Fiction. His work was cited as a New York Times Book Review *Editors' Choice and named Best Book of the Year by the* Los Angeles Times, *the* San Francisco Chronicle, *the* Washington Post *and* Time. *His fiction has appeared in* Zoetrope, Punk Planet, *and* The New Yorker. *Eggers is the editor of* McSweeney's *and the founder of 826 Valencia, a writing lab for young people located in the Mission District of San Francisco, where he teaches writing to high school students and runs a summer publishing camp. With the help of his workshop students, he edits a collection of fiction, essays, and journalism called* The Best American Nonrequired Reading. *He lives in the San Francisco Bay Area.*

For Further Reading:
A Heartbreaking Work of Staggering Genius (2000), *You Shall Know Our Velocity!* (2002), *How We Are Hungry* (2004).

After I Was Thrown in the River and Before I Drowned

Oh, I'm a fast dog. I'm fast-fast. It's true and I love being fast I admit it I love it. You know fast dogs. Dogs that just run by and you say, "Damn! That's a fast dog!" Well that's me. A fast dog. *Hoooooooo!* I'm a fast fast dog. *Hoooooooooooooo!* You should watch me sometime. Just watch how fast I go when I'm going my fastest, when I've really got to move for something, when I'm really on my way—man do I get going sometimes, weaving like a missile, weaving like a missile between trees and around bushes and then—pop!—I can go over a fence or a baby or a rock or anything because I'm a fast fast dog and I can jump like a fucking gazelle.

Hoooooooo! Man, oh man.

I love it, I love it. I run to feel the cool air cool through my fur. I run to feel the cold water come from my eyes. I run to feel my jaw slacken and my tongue come loose and flap from the side of my mouth and I go and go and go my name is Steven.

I can eat pizza. I can eat chicken. I can eat yogurt and rye bread with caraway seeds. It really doesn't matter. They say, "No, no, don't eat that stuff, you, that stuff isn't for you, it's for us, for people!" And I eat it anyway, I eat it with gusto, I eat the food and I feel good and I live on and run and run and look at the people and hear their stupid conversations coming from their slits for mouths and terrible eyes.

I see in the windows. I see what happens. I see the calm held-together moments and also the treachery and I run and run. You tell me it matters, what they all say. I have listened and long ago I stopped. Just tell me it matters and I will listen to you and I will want to be convinced. You tell me that what is said is making a difference, that those words are worthwhile words and mean something. I see what happens. I live with people who are German. They collect steins. They are good people. Their son is dead. I see what happens.

When I run I can turn like I'm magic or something. I can turn like there wasn't even a turn. I turn and I'm going so fast it's like I was still going straight. Through the trees like a missile, through the trees I love to run with my claws reaching and grabbing so quickly like I'm taking everything.

Damn, I'm so in love with all of this. I was once in a river. I was thrown in a river when I was small. You just cannot know. I was swimming, trying to know why I had been thrown in the river. I was six months old, and my eyes were burning, the water was bad. I paddled and it was like begging. The land on either side was just a black stripe, indifferent. I saw the gray water and then the darker water below and then my legs wouldn't work, were stuck in some kind of seaweed or spiderweb and then I was in the air.

I opened my burning eyes and saw him in yellow. The fisherman. I was lifted from the water, the water was below me. Then shivering on their white plastic boat bottom and they looked at me with their moustaches.

I dried in the sun. They brought me to the place with the cages and I yelled for days. Others were yelling too. Everyone was crazy. Then people and a car and I was new at home. Ate and slept and it was dry, walls of wood. Two people and two girls, thin who sleep in the next room, with a doll's house between them.

When I go outside I run. I run from the cement past the places and then to where the places end and then to the woods. In the woods are the other dogs.

I am the fastest. Since Thomas left I am the fastest. I jump the farthest too. I don't have to yell anymore. I can go past the buildings where the people complain and then to the woods where I can't hear them and just run with these dogs.

Hoooooooooooooooo! I feel good here, feel strong. Sometimes I am a machine, moving so fast, a machine with everything working perfectly, my claws grabbing at the earth like I'm the one making it turn. Damn, yeah.

Every day on the street I pass the same people. There are the men, two of them, selling burritos from the steel van. They are happy men; their music is loud and jangles like a bracelet. There are the women from the drugstore outside on their break, smoking and laughing, shoulders shaking. There is the man who sleeps on the ground with the hole in his pants where his ass shows raw and barnacled and brown-blue. One arm extended, reaching toward the door of the building. *He sleeps so much.*

Every night I walk from the neighborhood and head to the woods and meet the others. It's shadowy out, the clouds low. I see the blues jumping inside the windows. I want all these people gone from the buildings and moved to the desert so we can fill the buildings with water. It's an idea I have. The buildings would be good if filled with water, or under water. Something to clean them, anything. How long would it take to clean all those buildings. Lord, no one knows any of this. So many of the sounds I hear I just can't stand. These people.

The only ones I like are the kids. I come to the kids and lick the kids. I run to them and push my nose into their stomachs. I don't want them to work. I want them to stay as they are and run with me, even though they're slow. I run around them and around again as they run forward. They're slow but they are perfect things, almost perfect.

I pass the buildings. Inside, the women are putting strands of hair behind their ears, and their children are standing before the mirror for hours, moving tentatively to their music. Their fathers are playing chess with their uncles who are staying with them for a few months while things straightened. They are happy that they are with each other, and I pass, my claws ticking on the sandpaper cement, past the man laying down with his arm reaching, and past the steel van with the music, and I see the light behind the rooftops.

I haven't been on a rooftop but was once in a plane and wondered why no one had told me. That clouds were more ravishing from above.

Where the buildings clear I sometimes see the train slip through the sharp black trees, all the green windows and the people inside in white shirts. I watch from the woods, the dirt in my nails so soft. I just cannot tell you how much I love all this, this train, these woods, the dirt, the smell of dogs nearby waiting to run.

In the woods we have races and we jump. We run from the entrance to the woods, where the trail starts, through the black-dark interior and out to the meadow and across the meadow and into the next woods, over the creek and then along the creek until the highway.

Tonight is cool, almost cold. There are no stars or clouds. We're all impotent but there is running. I jog down the trail and see the others. Six of them tonight—Edward, Franklin, Susan, Mary, Robert and Victoria. When I see them I want to be in love with all of them at once. I want us all to be together; I feel so good to be near them. We talk about it getting cooler. We talk about it being warm in these woods when we're close together. I know all these dogs but a few.

Tonight I race Edward. Edward is a bull terrier and he is fast and strong but his eyes want to win too much; he scares us. We don't know him well and he laughs too loud and only at his own jokes. He doesn't listen; he waits to speak.

The course is a simple one. We run from the entrance through the black-dark interior and out to the meadow and across the meadow and into the next woods, along the creek, then over the gap over the drainpipe and then along the creek until the highway.

The jump over the drainpipe is the hard part. We run along the creek and then the riverbank above it rises so we're ten, fifteen feet above the creek and then almost twenty. Then the bank is interrupted by a drainpipe, about four feet high, so the bank at eighteen feet is gapped for twelve feet and we have to run and jump the gap. We have to run and feel strong to make it.

On the banks of the creek, near the drainpipe, on the dirt and in the weeds and on the branches of the rough grey trees are the squirrels. The squirrels have things to say; they talk before and after we jump. Sometimes while we're jumping they talk.

"He is running funny."

"She will not make it across."

When we land they say things.

"He didn't land as well as I wanted him to."

"She made a bad landing. Because her landing was bad I am angry."

When we do not make it across the gap, and instead fall into the sandy bank, the squirrels say other things, their eyes full of glee.

"It makes me laugh that she did not make it across the gap."

"I am very happy that he fell and seems to be in pain."

I don't know why the squirrels watch us, or why they talk to us. They do not try to jump the gap. The running and jumping feels so good—even when we don't win or fall into the gap it feels so good when we run and jump—and when we are done the squirrels are talking to us, to each other in their small jittery voices.

We look at the squirrels and we wonder why they are there. We want them to run and jump with us but they do not. They sit and talk about the things we do. Sometimes one of the dogs, annoyed past tolerance, catches a squirrel in his mouth and crushes him. But then the next night they are back, all the squirrels, more of them. Always more.

Tonight I am to race Edward and I feel good. My eyes feel good, like I will see everything before I have to. I see colors like you hear jet planes.

When we run on the side of the creek I feel strong and feel fast. There is room for both of us to run and I want to run along the creek, want to run alongside Edward and then jump. That's all I can see, the jump, the distance below us, the momentum taking me over the gap. Goddamn, sometimes I only want this feeling to stay.

Tonight I run and Edward runs, and I see him pushing hard, and his claws grabbing, and it seems like we're both grabbing at the same thing, that we're both grabbing for the same thing. But we keep grabbing and grabbing and there is enough for both of us to grab, and after us there will be others who grab from this dirt on the creek bed and it will always be here.

Edward is nudging me as I run. Edward is pushing me, bumping into me as we run. All I want is to run but he is yelling and bumping me, trying to bite me. All I want is to run and then jump. I am telling him that if we both just run and jump without bumping or biting we will run faster and jump farther. We will be stronger and do more beautiful things. He bites me and bumps me and yells things at me as we run. When we come to the bend he tries to bump me into the tree. I skid and then find my footing and keep running. I catch up to him quickly and because I am faster I catch him and overtake him and we are on the straightaway and I gain my speed, I muster it from everywhere, I attract the energy of everything living around me, it conducts through the soil through my claws while I grab and grab and I gain all the speed and then I see the gap. Two more strides and I jump.

You should do this sometime. I am a rocket. My time over the gap is a life. I am a cloud, so slow, for an instant I am a slow-moving cloud whose movement is elegant, cavalier, like sleep.

Then it speeds up and the leaves and black dirt come to me and I land and skid, my claws filling with soil and sand. I clear the gap by two feet and turn to see Edward jumping, and Edward's face looking across the gap, looking at my side of the gap, and his eyes still on the grass, exploding for it, and then he is falling, and only his claws land above the bank. He yells something as he grabs, his eyes trying to pull him up, but he slides down the bank.

He is fine but others have been hurt. One dog, Wolfgang, died here, years ago. The other dogs and I jump down to help Edward up. He is moaning but he is happy that we were running and that he jumped.

The squirrels say things.

"That wasn't such a good jump."

"That was a terrible jump."

"He wasn't trying hard enough when he jumped."

"Bad landing."

"Awful landing."

"His bad landing makes me very angry."

I run the rest of the race alone. I finish and come back and watch the other races. I watch and like to watch them run and jump. We are lucky to have these legs and this ground, and that our muscles work with speed and the blood surges and we can see everything.

After we all run we go home. A few of the dogs live on the other side of the highway, where there is more land. A few live my way, and we jog together back, through the woods and out of the entranceway and back to the streets and the buildings with the blue lights jumping inside. They know as I know. They see the men and women talking through the glass and saying nothing. They know that inside the children are pushing their toys across the wooden floors. And in their beds people are reaching for the covers, pulling, their feet kicking.

I scratch at the door and soon the door opens. Bare white legs under a red robe. Black hairs ooze from the white skin. I eat the food and go to the bedroom and wait for them to sleep. I sleep at the foot of the bed, over their feet, feeling the air from the just-open window roll in cool and familiar. In the next room the thin twins sleep between their doll's house.

The next night I walk alone to the woods, my claws clicking on the sandpaper cement. The sleeping man sleeps near the door, his hands praying between his knees. I see a group of men singing on the corner drunkenly but they are perfect. Their voices join and burnish the air between them, freed and perfect from their old and drunken mouths. I sit and watch until they notice me.

"Get out of here, fuck-dog."

I see the buildings end and wait for the train through the branches. I wait and can almost hear the singing still. I wait and don't want to wait anymore but the longer I wait the more I expect the train to come. I see a crow bounce in front of me, his head pivoting, paranoid. Then the train sounds from the black thick part of the forest where it can't be seen, then comes into view, passing through the lighter woods, and it shoots through, the green squares glowing and inside the bodies with their white shirts. I try to soak myself in this. This I can't believe I deserve. I want to close my eyes to feel this more but then realize I shouldn't close my eyes. I keep my eyes open and watch and then the train is gone.

Tonight I race Susan. Susan is a retriever, a small one, fast and pretty with black eyes. We take off, through the entrance through the black-dark interior and out to the meadow. In the meadow we breathe the air and feel the light of the partial moon. We have sharp black shadows that spider through the long gray-green grass. We run and smile at each other because we both know how good this is. Maybe Susan is my sister.

Then the second forest approaches and we plunge like sex into the woods and take the turns, past the bend where Edward pushed me, and then along the creek. We are running together and are not really racing. We are wanting the other to run our fastest. We are watching each other in love with our movements and strength. Susan is maybe my mother.

Then the straightaway before the gap. Now we have to think about our own legs and muscles and timing before the jump. Susan looks at me and smiles again but looks tired. Two more strides and I jump and then am the slow cloud seeing the faces of my friends, the other strong dogs, then the hard ground rushes toward me and I land and hear her scream. I turn to see her face falling down the gap and run back to the gap. Robert and Victoria are down with her already. Her leg is broken and bleeding from the joint. She screams, then wails, knowing everything already.

The squirrels are above and talking.

"Well, looks like she got what she deserved."

"That's what you get when you jump."

"If she were a better jumper this would not have happened."

Some of them laugh. Franklin is angry. He walks slowly to where they're sitting; they do not move. He grabs one in his jaws and crushes all its bones. Their voices are always talking but we forget they are so small, their head and bones so tiny. The rest run away. He tosses the squirrel's broken form into the slow water.

We go home. I jog to the buildings with Susan on my back. We pass the windows flickering blue and the men in the silver van with the jangly music. I take her home and scratch at her door until she is let in. I go home and see the thin twins with their doll's house and I go to the room with the bed and fall asleep before they come.

The next night I don't want to go to the woods. I can't see someone fall, and can't hear the squirrels, and don't want Franklin to crush them in his jaws. I stay at home and I play with the twins in their pajamas. They put me on a pillowcase and pull me through the halls. I like the speed and they giggle. We make turns where I run into door frames and they laugh. I run from them and then toward them and through their legs. They shriek they love it. I want deeply for these twins and want them to leave and run with me. I stay with them tonight and then stay home for days. I stay away from the windows. It's warm in the house and I eat more and sit with them as they watch television. It rains for a week.

When I come to the woods again, after ten days away, Susan has lost her leg. The dogs are all there. Susan has three legs, a bandage around her front shoulder. Her smile is a new and more fragile thing. It's colder out and the wind is mean and searching. Mary says that the rain has made the creek swell and the current too fast. The gap over the drainpipe is wider now so we decide that we will not jump.

I race Franklin. Franklin is still angry about Susan's leg; neither of us can believe that things like that happen, that she has lost a leg and now when she smiles she looks like she's asking to die.

When we get to the straightaway I feel so strong that I know I will go. I'm not sure I can make it but I know I can go far, farther than I've jumped before, and I know how long it will be that I will be floating cloudlike. I want this so much, the floating.

I run and see the squirrels and their mouths are already forming the words they will say if I don't make it across. On the straight-away Franklin stops and yells to me that I should stop but it's just a few more strides and I've never felt so strong so I jump. I float for a long time and see it all. I see my bed and the faces of my friends and it seems like they already know.

When I hit my head it was obvious. I hit my head and had a moment when I could still see—I saw Susan's face, her eyes open huge, I saw some crisscrossing branches above me and then the current took me out and then I fell under the surface.

After I fell and was out of view the squirrels spoke.

"He should not have jumped that jump."

"He sure did look silly when he hit his head and slid into the water."

"He was a fool."

"Everything he ever did was worthless."

Franklin was angry and took five or six of them in his mouth, crushing them, tossing them one after the other. The other dogs watched; none of them knew if squirrel-killing made them happy or not.

After I died, so many things happened that I did not expect.

The first was that I was there, inside my body, for a long time. I was at the bottom of the river, stuck in a thicket of sticks and logs, for six days. I was dead, but was still there, and I could see out of my eyes. I could move around inside my body like it was a warm loose bag. I would sleep in the warm loose bag, turn around in it like it was a small home of skin and fur. I could look every so often through the bag's eyes to see what was outside, in the river. I never saw much through the dirty water.

I had been thrown into the river, a different river, when I was young by a man because I would not fight. I was supposed to fight and he kicked me and slapped my head and tried to make me mean. I didn't know why he was kicking me, slapping. I wanted him to be happy. I wanted the squirrels to jump and be happy as we dogs were. But they were different than we were, and the man who threw me into the river was different. I thought we were all the same but as I was inside my dead body and looking into the murky river bottom I knew that some are wanting to run and some are afraid to run and maybe they are broken and angry for it.

I slept in my broken sack of a body at the bottom of the river, and wondered what would happen. It was dark inside, and musty, and the air was hard to draw. I sang to myself.

After the sixth day I woke up and it was bright. I knew I was back. I was no longer inside a loose sack but was now inhabiting a body like my own, from before; I was the same. I stood and was in a wide field of buttercups. I could smell their smell and walked through them, my eyes at the level of the yellow, a wide blur of a line of yellow. I was heavy-headed from the gorgeousness of the yellow all blurry. I loved breathing this way again, and seeing everything.

I should say that it's very much the same here as there. There are more hills, and more waterfalls, and things are cleaner. I like it. Each day I walk for a long time, and I don't have to walk back. I can walk and walk, and when I am tired I can sleep. When I wake up, I can keep walking and I never miss where I started and have no home.

I haven't seen anyone yet. I don't miss the cement like sandpaper on my feet, or the buildings with the sleeping men reaching. I sometimes miss the other dogs and the running.

The one big surprise is that as it turns out, God is the sun. It makes sense, if you think about it. Why we didn't see it sooner I cannot say. Every day the sun was right there burning, ours and other planets hovering around it, always apologizing, and we didn't think it was God. Why would there be a god and also a sun? Of course God is the sun. Simple, good.

Everyone in the life before was cranky, I think, because they just wanted to know.

A Conversation with Dave Eggers

Aside from being daring and unconventional in form, the forty-page preface and acknowledgments section of your book, A Heartbreaking Work of Staggering Genius, *works as a kind of primer for the aspiring fiction writer—which is kind of ironic, since the book is a memoir. Would you talk about the increasingly blurred line between fiction and nonfiction in terms of how a writer might look at the material that compels him and decide in which general category it belongs?*

You know, I'm not sure if the line is increasingly blurry, or increasingly sharp. I think there's always been a very moveable line between fiction and memoir, for example. In the modern era, people have written a lot of semiautobiographical fiction, which in many cases was pretty much memoir with a few names changed. I would venture that it's a more recent phenomenon, though, to have younger writers writing their stories as memoir, which is why, I guess, we're talking about what's fiction and what's nonfiction. Anyway, I occasionally moderate seminars for adults writing memoirs, or considering doing so, and I usually try to talk them out of it. The stakes are just so much higher with memoir, and the form is much more volatile, more dangerous. You can hurt a lot of people by telling your story, unless that story takes place on an island or a cave—and no real people are involved. I always recommend the good old semiautobiographical fiction way. It's freeing, it's easier, and you have more room to create and write a good book.

How did writing the preface serve the process of writing the story of those years you spent raising your younger brother after your parents' deaths—the story you set out to write? What parts did you write before actually beginning the book, what parts did you write in process? In what ways was it revised after the book was finished and ready to go into print?

I wrote about 99 percent of the preface before beginning the book. It was an exercise in stalling for me, and also an attempt to work out why I was writing it, and how I'd go about it. While writing the preface, I wasn't completely sure it would end up in the book, though. The editor, Geoff Kloske, and I debated it a bit. Not that he was against it, but neither one of us knew if it worked or was just annoying and getting in the way. I guess there's still some debate about that.

I wrote about 99 percent of the preface before beginning the book. It was an exercise in stalling for me, and also an attempt to work out why I was writing it, and how I'd go about it.

You've joked about including the preface as a way of insuring a small readership for the book, but would you talk about what actually made you decide to do something so unusual and also the larger question behind that, which relates both to your own work and the work you do with McSweeney's, *a magazine that celebrates and nurtures the unconventional: What do you think makes experimenting with form work for writers, what do you think makes it fall flat?*

McSweeney's has always sought to put a less pretentious and even good-humored face on formal experimentation. I think the thing that kills a lot of great groundbreaking writing is when the author takes him- or herself too seriously, and the work then becomes a slog, like a lot of performance or conceptual art. I think a sense of humor can make the departure from standard linear narrative less grating. I can't say that *McSweeney's* has any hard and fast rules about its writing being funny—because only about a quarter of what we publish attempts that—but we do prefer writing that's both not afraid to depart from standard form and, at the same time, not incredibly self-impressed and self-serious.

Your story "After I Was Thrown in the River and Before I Drowned" certainly tests the bounds of fiction, in that it's told from the point of view of a dog.

That's pretty much the first short story I ever finished. At the time, I was writing a series of letters to Fortune 500 CEOs from the point of view of that same dog, Steven. Around then, Nick Hornby asked me to contribute to *Speaking with the Angel,* so I just kind of went off with Steven for a while. And of course the story is a pretty direct allegory for the relationship between people who run and people who watch those who run, so to speak—those who judge them.

The voice of the story is irresistible. In the first line alone, you use the word fast *four times, establishing the, well, dogness. And also the story's tone.*

It's a tone that I'd love to use more often, because I think its loopy breathlessness is how our heads work sometimes, but it would sound odd coming from human-writer-me, whereas it seems totally logical that a dog, especially one named Steven, would think and talk that way. It's really liberating speaking through Steven. When I teach high school writing, I often ask the students to adopt a voice of an animal or bird or insect or fish. And the stuff they produce is incredible; often it's the first time they've broken free of their standard human law-obeying voice, and they feel very free. It gives you license to observe things you normally wouldn't.

It's the first time they've broken free of their standard human law-obeying voice, and they feel very free. It gives you license to observe things you normally wouldn't.

What is voice, after all? What gives it such power, when it's good? What does an aspiring writer need to know about how voice works in a story?

I can't really answer all those questions, but I'll relay another anecdote. I'm in the middle of a biography of a Sudanese man named Dominic Arou, a refugee from the civil war between the north and south. And while his English is very good, it's not perfect. But because the primary English text he knows is the Bible, his sentences have a very biblical rhythm to them, a very clear sense of the weight of words. So early on in the process of telling his story, I wasn't sure whether I'd tell it in a straight narrative/journalistic voice or what. But when I transcribed our conversations, it became clear that the story took on a much more memorable tone when I let his syntax stand. So instead of my way, "It was a cold night, and the lions were growling, hungry for human flesh," it might be Dominic's way: "The lions, they were roaring. They roar when they are hungry for boys. It was cold, the night. So cold." Much more interesting, I think.

What comes first for you, character or voice? Would you talk about how your characters evolve, both in your head and on the page?

I always figured voice would come first, but so far, it hasn't worked out that way. Seems like, with the exception of the Steve story, I've written stories with a fairly unobtrusive narrator. I would love to write more stories where the voice is more central; I guess I should get on that. I did actually attempt one such story recently, but the readers I showed it to really didn't like this particular voice, and after a while I agreed it was getting in the way of an otherwise strong story. So I flattened the voice out a bit on that one. That is a pitfall: It's really hard for most writers to create a voice that's believable, distinctive, appealing, and not obstructing of the story. It requires a very careful calibration, and obviously, the easier way would be to remove voice, and just leave the writing unvarnished, uninflected.

How is all this linked to point of view? "After I Was Thrown in the River and Before I Drowned" processes the world from a dog's point of view—and it works. How did you do that? What are the requirements of point of view, in your opinion?

I think I was just writing while keeping in mind what I share with a dog's point of view. As kids—and that story masquerades as a fable, ostensibly for kids—running around in the woods, there's not so much difference between how we run and process the information flying by, and how we would imagine a dog would. At least I don't remember there being a difference. When you run, you can only think so much, and the language of your moving brain is limited to shapes, colors, good, bad, life, and death. But inhabiting a dog's head, or a killer's head, or a 400-pound Appalachian woman's head—should any of that be so difficult? Not if you keep in mind the thoughts we share, as opposed to focusing on what's exclusive to each person (or dog). I also got talked out of a novel written from a woman's point of view, in first person, and I still wonder if I did the right thing by abandoning that. I don't want to think that a man's brain absolutely must be, and always is, mechanically

But inhabiting a dog's head, or a killer's head, or a 400-pound Appalachian woman's head—should any of that be so difficult? Not if you keep in mind the thoughts we share.

different than a woman's. But inhabiting another head does get easier the further we get from that of a human. I wrote for a time from the point of view of a seal, and that was very entertaining, and seemed to come pretty easily.

There are places where the sheer pleasure of the language and the wonderful absurdity of detail make the reader laugh out loud. Yet, there's such poignance in what Steven sees, what he knows. At one point, he says, "We're all impotent but there is running." This seems to sum up what all your work is about, really: the precarious balance of hopelessness and joy. Would you talk about your sense of what your material is and your use of humor in expressing it?

I guess I do spend a lot of time thinking about how little we can change, in relation to the things we want to change. And in lieu of remaking the world in a way we would find more just, we have our eyes and our legs and we can run.

The end of the story is both lyrical and surprising: Steven speaking after his death.

I love writing the narrator's death into a story. The narrator of *You Shall Know Our Velocity*! is dead, too. But the whole collection, *How We Are Hungry,* deals a lot with death, given the period during which much of it was written. Steven dies, but then lives on. He goes to some better place. In my mind I picture it as Iceland, where I'd lived for a month or so right before writing that story. Steve dies and leaves the city where he lives, and then is in a place where there are endless hills and where he never has to turn around, never has to go home. I see it as a fairly optimistic ending, actually, for a dog named Steven.

McSweeney's *devoted an entire issue to genre fiction, a kind of fiction that's mostly disparaged by "serious" writers. Edited by Michael Chabon, whose literary credentials are impeccable, the anthology includes a roster of stories by writers from Stephen King to Aimee Bender. Why do you think genre writing gets such a bad rap by most literary types, and why did you decide to publish* McSweeney's Mammoth Treasury of Thrilling Tales?

It was mostly Chabon's idea, because as much as I was a fan of the whole project, I haven't ever been such an avid reader of genre fiction. Actually, until recently, I rarely read books to find out what happened to any of the characters. I was just never very interested in the artifice of who did what to whom. I've always just read for the sentences, the imagery, the dialogue, innovations in form, or epiphanic moments in the text. I'm pretty much speculating, but I think genre's bad rap comes from those who feel that a few of the writers of genre fiction aren't really trying very hard when it comes to the writing. That there's a certain laziness to it, a tendency to fall into cliché, to take the easy way out because, these writers might assume, the reader's reading to find out what happens, as opposed to enjoying the art of the sentences. But

I guess those who malign the form are really separating work that comes from a rupture in the soul, which I would hope the best fiction would, as opposed to books that are more about craft.

then a guy like Elmore Leonard proves that you can have both. His writing is incredibly tight, sharp, as witty as anything out there, and on top of that it's well plotted and people get murdered and all the things you'd want in genre fiction. I guess those who malign the form are really separating work that comes from a rupture in the soul, which I would hope the best fiction would, as opposed to books that are more about craft.

Your story in the anthology, "Up the Mountain Coming Down Slowly," couldn't be more different in form and content from "After I Was Thrown in the River and Before I Drowned." What was the genesis of that story, and how did it evolve?

Chabon was starting to put the collection together around when I was about to climb Kilimanjaro, so I went up the mountain with a tape recorder and camera and notebook, thinking it might make a good adventure story. I come from a journalism background—I studied it for a few years in college, got my degree in that field, and worked as a feature writer for a while, including a lot of travel writing—so most of the fiction I've written so far has a good deal of foundation in real experience, in travel. Sometimes I'll go somewhere hoping to come across a story, and sometimes I'll set a plot line in a place I've been recently; I guess most writers do some combination of those methods. But the creation of Rita and her backstory was really pretty organic. She wasn't based on anyone I knew, or anyone on the trip I took (with about twenty hikers). I pretty much pasted her together from random thoughts, and what the story demanded. Why would this woman want to climb the mountain? I couldn't think of exactly why, so I made the trip something her sister had planned for the two of them, and then backed out of. That way, she's on the trip, but it wasn't her idea, and she's alone. Then I added the part about her having lost two foster children, due to her lack of maturity. So then she's got something to prove, in a way. She thinks that maybe, if she can finish this, get to the top, then it would prove to whomever that she's strong, that she's capable of managing her life, raising these kids.

Having climbed Mt. Kilimanjaro yourself, what role did your imagination play in constructing the vivid world of the story?

Not much. That's a pretty exact description of what it's like to climb the mountain on the Machame route. I didn't make up anything, in terms of the details of the climb. The fictional elements were the characters, the interactions with the porters, Rita's story, and of course the conclusion. That's usually how I work: I get the details of place correct, and then fabricate the rest.

I get the details of place correct, and then fabricate the rest.

As you go about your life, both at home and in your travels, how do you recognize a detail as something that's "yours," something that you know will or at least might find its way into your fiction?

It happens at least a few times a day. I take a lot of notes while I drive, especially while traveling alone in new places. But I'm really trying to get away from basing anything I write on actual events. It can get very limiting, especially for me, because I just have all these journalism teachers' voices in my head, yelling at me about truth and accuracy. When I start borrowing things from my own life, suddenly I find myself just transcribing real events, and then the plot suffers. "Up the Mountain" and *Velocity* each were struggles, because in both cases I took trips knowing I'd fictionalize them, and in both cases I had a hard time departing from what actually happened. I'm getting better at that now.

The story has a well-constructed plot, perfectly paced, with lots of torques along the way that usually occur when some new bit of information is revealed. How do you decide what information a reader needs at any given point in a story and how it is best conveyed?

It's just trial and error, I think. That story was the most traditionally paced one I've written; I was trying to keep it moving, up the mountain, while at the same time having the tension build slowly. To that end, it was really a matter of constructing it brick by brick. I wrote the basic narrative first, with everyone getting up the mountain, and then began threading in Rita's background and subplots, tension between the hikers, all that. It's a challenge to deepen our understanding of the principal characters, too, without stopping the action and explaining things too much. That story really was a clinic for me, where I had to learn a lot about a multicharacter story, keeping a reader interested in the plight of eight different people, while keeping things moving, because the story's damned long to begin with—about 18,000 words, I think. So you really have to be economical about it.

What about pace? Are there tricks to unfolding a story so that it doesn't happen too quickly or too slowly?

I think you know it when you see it. About once a month, I can get a good cold read on a story. That is, I can't read it objectively unless I get some distance from it. So after I let it sit for a while, I can come back and say Ah! Now I see the problems, now I know what it needs or what needs to be removed. But I've learned that if I don't fix that story right after that good cold read, I'm dead. You have to do it while it's fresh in your head. In general, I revise a lot. I cut probably 3,000 words from that story, when I realized no one really cared about every last detail of Kilimanjaro—not for a story like that.

What is the process, generally, by which your stories gather and move toward completion— either fiction or nonfiction?

Well, I just finished this first story collection, and I have to say that all of those stories were written very differently. The dog story was written in about three days, and I didn't have to revise it much. I guess that one I knew in my bones and it was just a matter of throwing it onto the page. The Kilimanjaro story took forever—about three months on and off. I struggled with it, and just revised it again for the collection." The Only Meaning of the Oil-Wet Water," probably my favorite thing I've written, started out as a chapter in a novel I never published. I took the setting and action, Costa Rica and surfing, and used new characters—actually, I used one old one, Hand, from "*Velocity*"—and wrote it with really no clue about what the plot would be. I love it now for some of the language—it's one of the very few things of my own I can read without cringing—and because in that story, nothing really happens. Lots of small things happen, sure, but there's no main arc, the story doesn't build to any one event, and neither character undergoes some transformation. God, I hate that rule, that a character needs to be *changed in some fundamental way* by the end of the story. I got that in college, and lord, what bullshit that is. I'm all for it when it works, but forcing it into every 4,000-word story is just silly. So in "Oil-Wet," I wanted to describe the relationship between two people who have known each other for a long time, but have never been alone together for a week at a time. No one dies, no one falls in love, and there's no real ending to the story. But in between, I think some things are learned. Speaking of which, I have no idea if I answered your question.

God, I hate that rule, that a character needs to be *changed in some fundamental way* by the end of the story.

What are the problems you most frequently find in your own work? How do you identify and correct them through revision? How do you know when a story is finished?

The main problem, oddly enough, is reducing the intereference of my own voice. I'm in a tough spot, because I wrote a memoir, and a lot of people know my own voice by now. That makes it hard to write first-person fiction, first of all, and when I do, I really have to be careful that the narrator isn't clearly *me* wearing some obvious mask. Not sure I've been convincing yet. Working on that. The other thing my friends and editors save me from is getting too cute. I tend to make lame jokes sometimes in my fiction, and to go off on the same sorts of tangents again and again. Good editors pull me back from the brink. As for knowing when a story's finished, I always know when it's 99 percent done, but count on editors to tell me to quit. Otherwise I'd revise eternally.

As for knowing when a story's finished, I always know when it's 99 percent done, but count on editors to tell me to quit. Otherwise I'd revise eternally.

How does your work as an editor inform your work as a writer?

If you apply the same standards to your own writing that you do to those you're editing, then it's very helpful. The problem is seeing your own work clearly and being honest with yourself about it. I haven't always been successful at either, but sometimes I get a good clean read on something. The other benefit is when you're reading so much new work, you can get excited about what's out there, what's being done on the forefront of fiction—and I think the submissions to *McSweeney's* really represent that—and that can get you energized. At the same time, seeing

The problem is seeing your own work clearly and being honest with yourself about it.

developing writers make mistakes is helpful, too. I'll never do that, you think to yourself, ha ha. But of course you do, and worse.

What does your background in graphic design add to the mix? How are the words in process shaped by your visual sense of what a book will be? Your novel, You Shall Know Our Velocity!, *for example. There's no title on the front cover, no author credit—just text defining the perameters of the story—"after Jack died and before my mom and I drowned in a burning ferry." The book ends before those deaths, yet they complicate and bring weight to the story in a subtle way. The effect would have been completely different with another design.*

Before I started writing that book, I knew it would begin on the cover. Sometimes a design idea, like the cover of the first issue of *McSweeneys,* will occur to me pretty early on in the process. Sometimes the design idea doesn't work out, in terms of its gelling with the actual content. In the case of *Velocity,* I wanted it to have the opposite feel as *Heartbreaking.* The first book stalls for sixty pages before it gets to talking about my parents' deaths. *Velocity,* because it's about speed and wanting everything now, had to start on the cover and eschew all front matter altogether.

Oddly, the language on the cover of You Shall Know Our Velocity! *and the structure of that book echo the structure of "After I Was Thrown in the River and Before I Drowned." There's a similar feel to them, as well. Will and Hand move through the world, giving away money, with a reckless abandon similar to the way Steven runs. How are the two stories related in your mind?*

They're both about speed, first of all. They're both about wanting to live forever and to know and love and punch and kiss everyone in the world. And they're both about how likely those desires are to lead to disappointment and death. They're similar in pretty much every way.

The success you've achieved, both as a writer and an editor, is the kind of success most aspiring writers hope for. What advice would you give writers just beginning to consider publishing their work?

I always tell aspiring writers of any age the same mix of things. In no particular order: publish as often as you can, anywhere you can. Don't be snobby, don't wait ten years holding your breath for *The Paris Review* or *The New Yorker* to take your story; get your work out there. The most important thing is to get feedback, work with editors, get yourself in a conversation with readers. Don't spend five years holed up without any feedback. Be able to take any criticism. Ask for the most brutal criticism you can get. But—and this is important—I'm not a huge fan of group critiques. I only had one of those, in my one creative writing class in college, and it was horrific. Just humiliating for everyone. I'm not sure that helps anyone. Lots of edits are

The most important thing is to get feedback, work with editors, get yourself in a conversation with readers.

good, lots of comments, but one-on-one is best, I think. But don't expect your friends to like your work. Stay away from negative influences—people who discourage you, compete with you in an unhealthy way, or have a creepy way of giving you comments. I've never had this problem, with bad editors, but I know lots of people (and have had some students) who have, and I always tell them to run away from those influences. It's hard enough, without dealing with the issues of some loony editor/writing group member.

Along with success, comes the inevitable labeling. Some call you a postmodernist. Would you define yourself that way?

I've never read a definition of *postmodernism* that I found very compelling or accurate in describing any contemporary art I know, so I would have to excuse myself from that group. I do think there are many American writers under forty or so who share many aesthetic goals and tools, but I wouldn't know what to call them and wouldn't cripple them with a label.

I still haven't met anyone who had any idea what the term *postmodern* really means in relation to contemporary writing, so I just can't feel good sitting under that umbrella. Labels are for students to use, when they're trying to make sense of a given field. Grouping people and labeling them is comforting, and it creates a sense of order. But do they help us understand the work? Do they enhance our enjoyment of it? I think that's rare.

As a young writer, still at the beginning of your career, what do you hope for? How do you imagine yourself, your writing life, at—say—sixty? What might your body of work look like by then?

Man, I have no idea. I can see about four years into the future, and after that, I don't have a clue. In the next few years I'd love to finish a few books I'm working on, one the biography of Dominic Arou, the other a sprawling political novel. In the meantime, I'm hoping to write more stories, taking "Oil-Wet Water" as my starting point. I want to get back into that rhythm, write some good sentences, try to open up the short story form a bit more. After a decade of expansion, lots of experimentation from a wide swath of writers, I feel like it's contracting again, people getting conservative again, the form getting a bit stolid. So we should all be fighting back a bit.

I want to get back into that rhythm, write some good sentences, try to open up the short story form a bit more.

Writing Prompts

READ: "After I Was Thrown into the River and Before I Drowned" and the interview with **Dave Eggers.**

PONDER: The words and language rhythms Eggers uses to create a believable canine voice.

WRITE: A scene from an animal's point of view, using language in a way that reflects its characteristics and the way it lives.

PRACTICE:

- Think of a fable or a myth and then write it using animals instead of people.
- Write a series of letters from an animal to a corporation or institution.
- Write a scene in first person narrated by a person who has already died.
- Take a notebook on a trip, record detailed observations about the place, the people, and what happens there. Then transform your travel experience into fiction.
- Write the simple narrative layer of a story and then return to it again and again, layering in description, exposition, and tension.

Carolyn Ferrell

Carolyn Ferrell (b. 1962) is the author of one collection of short stories. Born in Brooklyn, she was educated at Sarah Lawrence College and the City College of New York. Her honors include the Art Seidenbaum Award of the Los Angeles Times *Book Prize, the John C. Zachiris Award given by* Ploughshares, *the Quality Paperback Book Prize for First Fiction, an NEA fellowship and a Fulbright fellowship. Her stories have been anthologized in* The Best American Short Stories of the Century, Rise Up Singing: Black Women Writers on Motherhood, Dream Me Home Safely: Writers on Growing Up in America, Giant Steps: The New Generation of African American Writers, and Children of the Night: The Best Short Stories by Black Writers, 1967 to the Present. *Ferrell teaches at Sarah Lawrence College. She lives in the Bronx.*

For Further Reading:
Don't Erase Me (1997).

Can You Say My Name?

We have two facts in front of us. One: babies, once they're here, stay, and can do our work for us; and two: men love love. Bri threw up in homeroom almost every day and it seemed like a awful commotion. But whenever she turned around and saw Roc two rows back and felt his blue eyes reciprocating love and understanding, it was like it was *his* hands that were wiping up her mouth, all the baby throw-up, and not the teacher's, Mr. Hancock's, who was scared shitless, and so Bri didn't have anything to fear. Me, I'm still waiting. I'm trying to reciprocate, but I'm doing it alone. Boy Commerce bops past me in the hall on his way to practice and sometimes has a stone frown, or sometimes he laughs all in my face when he catches me rubbing my belly. He don't talk to me anymore. He pretends to dis me any chance he gets. Like when he knows I'm following him down the hall, he'll put his hand up some other girl's ass and say, "Did I do that? Sorry," like it's supposed to really make the girl laugh, like I'm supposed to get jealous and shit.

He pretends to dis me. But it ain't no real disrespect, cause it's strange, but you know deep in your heart that one day your waiting will come to an end. My plan is gold. I can even go so far as to say this: that whenever I look at Boy Commerce, I see him as the black ship sailing out to the wide free sea, and me as one of the slaves in the hold. Like we learn about in school and are supposed to feel proud of. The waves are crashing against the side of the boat and the dolphins are trying to catch the sun rays in their open mouths with their tiny rows of teeth and I am licking the toes of the other slaves lying around me. Maybe there is something else out there, but I am the one who dies in the hold, on the trip to the New World, the new life. I will never leave. I will stay on the ship. There is not a damn thing to fear.

Do you like tongue kissing a dog? No, I ain't tried that shit. *Would you try it for me?* Hell, are you crazy? *No, I ain't, it's real simple, all you do is pretend you got someone in your arms that is ready for you to do just about anything, and you're hot tonight.* Shit, that's some sick shit, I will never put my mouth on a dog's. *Then you won't ever put your mouth on mine.* Don't say that. *I just did.* Why you treat me like this, don't you know my loving is all for you, you my number one, ain't nothing gonna come between us? *Look, I'm not asking for too much, just something little and crazy, you want to prove you will do anything I say, that's what I call love!* But that dog been licking his ass. *The dog's mouth is clean, and I just want to see you do it, please baby.* I only want your kisses. *I just want to see.* Will you promise to never leave me, I'm doing this crazy shit only for you and you better not fucking go nowhere. *I just want to see.* Look, I'm the boss now, and I want you to promise you will never leave, because you can't imagine how much I love you. Please. *Please.* Please.

Bri and me decided in ninth grade that we were going to be wives in school. The homegirl cheerleaders turned up their noses and shook their asses at us. One of them, Sam, said to me, "You got to lose that shit, girl! There *are* other ways to get out, and the one you doing is crack open for a dick and get a public assistance check shoved up there instead. Don't get it too wet or they won't cash it." Vulgar. Another one, Mandy with the imported African box braids, said, "Become a cheerleader! This way you can save yourself all by yourself, and *then* the shit that the adoring homeboys serve up to you is choice!" Teeny, cornrow cheerleader, said, "Geez Christ, mens do pain us!" The last time any one of them said anything, it was Marge, real name Margarita Floretta Inez Santamaria, who really could've had any boy in the whole damn school: "You will go through all that work but you ain't gonna have the reward. You gonna be two women sitting alone in the laundromat, dreaming about humping a tube of toothpaste when you get home."

Me and Bri laughed them off. *Yo yo:* we are homegirls and you know we know the deal better than anyone else and their mama and their mama's mama.

The teachers didn't think we were so crazy. One of them, the old science lady, puckered up: You folks are all the same. Laying up under men like that. It's a God-honest shame. Don't you ever wonder where you'll be?

Mrs. Mary, the Irish teacher who used to be in Catholic school, chimed in: No, they sure as hell don't. We show them the history of the world, and they are doomed to repeat all the mistakes. They just want to spend the rest of their born days right here!

Mrs. Faulkner, Elizabeth Taylor lookalike, sewing homeroom: Here? But they'll just wind up statistics! Heavens! Don't you think we should perhaps guide them . . . at least a little into the light?

Blond sissy-ass Mr. Hancock, math teacher and homeroom: You mean *our* way! Are you kidding, Althea? We don't want them our way! Let them stay the fuck where they are. They ain't got a clue. And I ain't gonna be the one to give it to them.

(*Wrong*, of course, because that dumb fake-English-accent ass was the one who didn't have the clue! We had the clues, we were on the money. Somehow. Still, all this talk tended to make Bri get all nervy, and she would start asking, "Toya, do we know what we're actually gone do? I mean, should we have babies or become junior-year cheerleaders?" Bri was always the unsteady one. I started to get sick of that shit, but then again: I didn't want to do it all alone. So I calmed her down, because she couldn't figure a damn thing out. The only thing she seemed to get together was this Africa thing. Wearing the African-looking clothes, gold bamboo earrings, a map of Africa on her jacket. She was really into that before-slavery shit. She called me her sister under the skin. She even wanted us to give each other African names, like Tashima and Chaka, Myesha, Zenzile, Aminata, and things. Like that is going to solve some shit! Sometimes she made me sicker than the baby throw-up.)

Bri was always freaking about the baby, but I managed to talk her out of her commotion and even got her to make a compromise: she relaxed her hair like the cheerleaders but wore T-shirts that said BABY = 1 + 1 and SOMEBODY DOWN THERE LOVES ME.

There was no question for me. I was going to be a wife in school. Boy Commerce was planning on a basketball scholarship so I'd have me an educated man. I *do* have a clue. It's just that people have clouded-up, fucked-up minds, and they refuse to see the truth and they live like snails underground in a garden, slimy. Blind. Dark. Like that hold.

Why you being so good to me all of a sudden, I thought you was mad at me, baby. Me, hell no, I just think I'm finally ready to give you all my loving. What's that supposed to mean, what I ain't already got? Me, the whole me, my heart. Well then, hurry up and give it. It's yours for the taking. *I like that shit, lemme feel your lovin.*

My Uncle Marion busted his best pair of glasses upside my head. "You what?" He rammed me into the refrigerator, so hard the door popped open and the milk crashed on the floor. *Big-time dis!* "Ho, ho, you been ho'ing in my house!" He had the wooden spoon, the one that used to belong to my mother and me on Delancey Street, and he was drumming out a funeral march on my ears. (I admit, it was hard not to bust out crying, but I kept my plan in mind, and that was like my light at the end of the tunnel.) "Ho! You get what you deserve! Grinding up neath that boy! You worse than a African! Is that how I raised you? Is that how I done?" Uncle Marion grabbed one of my cheeks and tugged till his nails left his permanent mark of love on me. "Ho! What was you thinking?"

Don't say nothing till it's too late to have an abortion.

It took a lot out of me to try and learn this scared-ass Bri the basics. I told her to keep on going to gym class, keep on doing the fifty warm-up pushups, hundred situps. Volunteer to be the kickball team captain, not just a regular player! Keep on wearing Wah Wah lipstick and doing your hair up like if someone better came along, you'd go for him and leave that other sorry ass—the one who was going to be your husband—behind. Don't put your head down on the desk because you say you're tired, or other kinds of baby-related shit. Be like you were in the old days and get the right answers and say them in front of the rest of the class: *you are still a genius like before.* Just don't zip up your pants, just wear a big sweater over so nobody sees you can't bend over no more. The gold plan. That's how you become a wife in time for Homecoming and Thanksgiving break.

I have been in love since the seventh grade. One day I sat in Reading with my large-print version of *Tale of Two Cities* propped up on my lap and dreamed of what I am doing now: being big with somebody's love. My destiny was as clear to me then as it is now. You might say that since I was a child then, I was illing because I was thinking I would be Boy Commerce's wife in tenth grade. But not so. You're only illing when you dream of things that can't possibly come true.

Bri took it upon herself to fall in love with Roc, and at first the cheerleaders said they wouldn't even consider looking at me or Bri because of this move of hers. Sam said that Bri was taking some white girl's boy away, and they didn't go for that, man-snatching, the cheerleaders. The only way the girls could be sure you wasn't playing dirty was if you had some homeboy or some Puerto Rican dude as yours. But I ask you: what do a white boy want with one of us for? What do Roc want with Bri, who's dark and not the prettiest girl you ever seen? That's some fucked-up shit. In my opinion, men like that only see the girl as a dark-skinned beauty, like some Pam Grier in the action movies, and they want to experience some bad pussy. Bri ought to have known that shit. And if it ain't that, then some white girl is crying her eyes out because her boy has left her for some dark ass. And that ain't right, because it's the same thing as man-stealing, and that goes against all cheerleader rules of order. We *are* all sisters when you get down to it.

Bri said love never happened like it was planned. She said love was a flower with no name in the garden of mankind. A flower like the kind that grew in the Motherland, *Africa.* She said, "You all are *illing.* This man wants me for me!" So she said she was going to prove it. Roc followed her around like a puppy. Once I caught them in the science lab, and it was like Roc's hands was straightening Bri's whole body like a relaxing comb. Smooth, broken, knotting-out movements. I laughed out loud. Bri flushed and was ashamed, and Roc said, "You can't stop me!" He looked scared like a true skinny white boy, but he did put his arms around big Bri to try and cover her up. I think that was the real reason Bri said she was going to be with Roc as his wife in school. Maybe if I hadn't a caught them planting the seed, maybe she would have left him afterwards. I had wanted to apologize, but they ran off dragging their clothes down the hall.

Bri was ashamed, and so I made it my job to convince her to stay with him because first: I knew she would never get a man like him (who loved love) again in this world, and two: I didn't want to be alone.

You know, I feel like I want to open up to you, ain't that weird? *Why? I feel the same way*. Nah, really, I'm not used to that kind of shit, and now I'm feeling like: hey, I want this girl to know a part of the real me. *I'm all ears, forever*. You know my father, he ain't raised me to be a sissy, he raised me to be a real man, and so it's hard, it's hard. *You want to lay your head on my shoulder?* I got things to do, I got places to see—but don't talk to me about any of that when I'm lying next to you making some good love. *What do you mean, places to go?* Baby, I got feelings, sometimes I just look at all the people in the street lying around, or sometimes I see my father dealing out a deck of cards and kissing my mother's cheek, and I start feeling so low. *Don't worry, you always got me.* Do you know I feel like killing my fucking self, getting on the track and touching the third rail? *Baby, don't say that shit, don't!* Word. *Don't.* That's how it gets to me sometimes, and I wonder: am I going to get a chance to kill myself, or will I just be buried alive? *BUT WHERE YOU TALKING ABOUT GOING, AM I GONNA BE WITH YOU, HOW DO I FIT IN BABY?* There you go talking all that shit, you don't listen to a word I say, do you? *Sure I do, baby, it's just I don't know where you thinking about going, that's all, and I always want to be there with you, understand?* I ain't talking about you, I'm talking about staying the fuck alive! *Don't worry, baby, with me, you will always be alive to the one who matters, now go on.*

I used to be five-foot-six with pretty box braids, skin the same color as the singer in that movie *Mahogany* and a nice voice. I could sing me some beautiful songs, like "Reveal Him to My Soul" and "Precious Is the Son." I used to be skinny and used to could dance to music. I used to go to parties with my mother's, then with Uncle Marion's permission. My nose came out in a perfect point, and I used to have dimples. Cute, you could've called me, or even a fox.

Then there is this time where everything disappears, everything. I make up my mind, I look in the mirror and make up my mind. Tired of all this being alone and shit. They all think they can book whenever they like.

Therefore, now I am five-foot-three with relaxed hair in a runt ponytail. I travel with a belly now. My face is spread out like a ocean, with rocks and seaweed in every wave. I always have throw-up in my mouth, sometimes I carry a little cup with me in the train. I don't dance at parties to the record player no more. I dance underneath a boy who says, "Put your butt this way, I am almost *there*."

I look into the mirror and still see a fox. Hell, I will go so far as to say: I am badder than bad.

I took Bri to the new Stop-One Supermarket and to Tiny-town's. She had to learn the good sides that were to come.

This was part of the gold plan. It's like we learned about in school: this was a science.

Look, I'ma show you what you don't learn in Home Economics. This here is the most important aisle: Borax, Mr. Clean, 2000 Flushes, Fantastic. You got to know how to keep your man happy, and this is gold. This is the surefire way. This is the way so that when his boys come over to check out the crib and hang and smoke some herb, you earn a A+ .

This aisle is the lifesaving ring to the new wife and mother: Alpo, KittyKat Delight, Friskies, Yum Pup. Now, you can bet your bottom dollar that once you're in, the husband is going to want to get you a pet so you have some hobby to take your mind off the kid sometimes, because you don't want to go having a nervous breakdown on me, right? If it's a cat, then you also got to think about kitty litter, and somehow boys don't like cats too much, all that rubbing up on you and shit. Boys get jealous when they see the cat laying up with you in the bed and then they act like: it's them or me, and you about ready to fall out laughing because they sure as hell don't seem like grown husbands but like spoiled kids. But you don't laugh, you take the cat to a shelter. Let em get you a dog. Boys like to be around dogs because it makes them into men faster. It's the kind of thing where they can go out on a Sunday morning to the park and jog and run and play catch and think in the back of their minds: Hey, this shit is *down*, I'm feeling good. Husbands need to feel good. And that's when they thank their lucky stars they got us back at home. Dogs' breath sure do smell like shit, but just think of him in the park. You take the dog out for a walk in the weekday morning and let it protect the baby.

Here's my favorite aisle, because it always changes: diet foods and ethnic. They got all these Slim Control foods, like Slim Control Salad Dressing, Slim Control Apple Snack'ems, Slim Control Malted Milkshake. Slim Control is what's going to keep us going, girl! And they keep on getting more: Slim Control Ketchup, Slim Control Jelly. You can eat all this shit, then take one or two of their Slim Control Diet Pills and you aren't hungry for three days. Get it? You lose weight that's really not weight at all. And you can laugh at the men getting their beer bellies in front of the TV, because you ain't going to be in the same boat. Then the homies that come by the crib start checking you out. Wouldn't you love to stay skinny forever? Not blow up the way all those mothers do? We got to hold on to our world, honey, and this is the way we going to do it. I want Boy to fucking love me forever. I love Slim Control Cheddar Cheese Popcorn.

Bri, like I had figured, loved Tinytown's. She kept saying, "Oooh, I'ma get me this for the baby, oooh, I like this toy machine gun if it's a boy." Bri held the black baby dolls like they were her own and kissed their cheeks. She said they looked like African goddesses! I was thinking. This store is too goddamn expensive. My child will do like me in the old days: play in the bathtub with the spatula, the wooden spoon, the rice pot, the strainer. Man, I had me some good times once.

Bri asked the Tinytown saleslady how much the black baby doll was that said, "Can you say my name?" The saleslady said eighty-nine fifty. And do you believe Bri was thinking about asking her mother for the money for that thing? *Typical.* Ugly-ass doll. *Can you say my name!* But at least I got Bri to look for a moment at the positive side of motherhood and being a wife in school. I told Margarita Santamaria in the school cafeteria, Yeah we know what the hell we are doing.

Listen up I'm only gonna say this once I know I done some fucked-up things in life but it's never too late to make things change for the better, *you ain't done anything that fucked up and listen we got more important things to talk about like what's gonna be the name and when you coming over to spend the night with me again*, shit Toya you ain't gonna let me get a word in is you, *sorry*, sorry my ass, sorry.

Listen up we can still be together but don't you want to go to college like me or you was talking about that business school where you could learn something useful, *man all that stuff's in the future we got other things to think about*, no THIS IS WHAT

WE NEED TO THINK ABOUT, *no this is what we need to think about: are you always gonna be there for me in other words are you always gonna be faithful?*

I want you to be happy even if I been doing some fucked-up shit, *you mean with them other girls*, yeah I mean like that, *shoot I know you don't really care about them*, yeah you right I don't, *so why you bring them up?*

Because I want the chance to care about them, baby.

Listen up you: I ain't going to college or business school or nothing, when it comes you are gonna give it a name or else!

Else what?

Don't do like that because I know that what you really want deep inside is love love love and that's what I got to give let me show you again.

Listen to me, LISTEN TO ME, listen to me, listen to me.

In seventh grade, my mother was still alive. The house on Delancey Street was cold indoors because the bricks were falling off outdoors. When I came home from school, I used to have to feed her applesauce and overcooked vegetables from a spoon. Uncle Marion called from his house on the other side of the city, Washington Heights. He used to check on us and ask how my mother's breasts were doing. I used to have to hold Mother's head in my arms like a warm ball and smooth out her hair with my hands, she couldn't take no brush. She would ask me to sing "Unforgettable you" and "Breakaway" to her so she could sleep better. My voice was high in those days. I was in the after-school gospel singers. I used to love to sing, but only songs like "In Times Like These" and "Send a Message" — songs that gave you a good feeling, like you *are* in seventh grade and your whole life *is* spread out in front of you like a red carpet, but I hated it when her head dozed off in my arms. It made me too ancient.

Her favorite animals were fishes. She dug them all, angelfish, blue whales, sharks, dolphins. She liked the free way they swam the ocean. They moved without seams, without giving a thought to where their next breath was going to come from. They traveled light and always in a direction. They never dreamed about getting caught, about being on a dinner plate, about swimming in a tank before hundreds of hungry eyes. They let the currents brush them along, and they tasted ocean water the way we tasted the air in the room with the air conditioner on. Mother had the kind of wishing talking that cut deep when she spoke and when I held her head in my arms.

It was going okay, I thought. I did take good care of her. But then one day, sure as shit, Mother announced like she was a loudspeaker in a subway station, I am going to kill myself. She said, I won't be here for you when I do that, but you will have Uncle Marion. You can hold on to him.

I said, under the water of tears, "Don't you think you could change your mind? Don't you think you could think again and decide to stay with me till I am a grown-up? I want to hold on to you."

She said, You just don't understand the pain, Toya. It has to give way. I have to make it give way.

So she sent me off to Uncle Marion's house and she drowned herself in poison air with her head laying in the gas oven. Uncle Marion said that was because her breasts were on fire on the inside, that's how he explained that shit to me then.

She couldn't stay for me. Damn, she couldn't even do it in the water, take her life where I knew she'd like to do it the most.

Mandy with the imported box braids said, "You *gots* to be crazy, baby! I ain't giving up being a cheerleader for nothing! And I don't want to have stretched-out legs!" Mandy had seven brothers and sisters and you could understand that she needed to spend all that time at cheerleader practice to get the hell away from them.

Margarita Santamaria said, "Bri, you aren't stupid. Do like I did."

Sam, head cheerleader, told us, "Naw, I see things different now. You girls is *on!* Lemme be the godmother, okay? I can give it a godname, right?"

Boy Commerce got cheerleader Sam's boyfriend, Big Daddy Dave, to let us into the biology lab. He had some big secret for me, Boy, he even held my hand on the way there from the boys' locker room. Big Daddy unlocked the door, and Boy held it open as I walked on through. He was like a real gentleman when he said to Big Daddy, "Catch you in a sec, bro."

I made sure to keep my hands off my belly. I didn't complain one time about my big swelled-up feet. I wore my old raincoat so Boy wouldn't have to notice my shape if he didn't want to. One time I even linked my arm in his and pressed a little and said, "Are we really here?" Boy lit up a cigar in the lab and just let the smoke out his mouth like a chimney. In the dark I could see the outline of his pick sticking out the front of his afro.

So I asked him, "Do you want my loving now, baby?"

So he waited a moment and pulled me by the hand over to a table with glass jars and beakers on it. There was a row of fat glass cylinders. When he went to turn on the light, I saw little baby mice bodies in the cylinders. They were just little baby mice floating in gray water. They were holding their hands in prayer.

Boy Commerce said, "If you have this kid, it might come out all twisted and small like this, Toya. Why you want to do some nasty shit like that?"

He said, "Toya, you think you gonna trap me like this baby here? You gonna tie my hands up? Well, *think again*. That's some stupid-ass shit. And you're a stupid-ass girl." It looked for a second like he was going to put his hand on one of the cylinders.

His eyes were red-lined. By accident, the basketball under his arm slipped out and fell on another table and knocked a beaker to the floor. "You see what you made me do, asshole?" He swept the broken pieces under the table with his foot. The smell of something fierce hit my nose, but it wouldn't make me do something stupid like cry. That was the way to lose them. Wives in school didn't cry. They just carried their load and thought their thoughts just like old women. I didn't say a word. Silence was the golden plan.

Boy switched off the light and opened the door. "Toya, get this fact through your head: I won't let you end my fucking life. I always thought you were smart."

Silence.

"So forget it, bitch. You ain't nothing but a animal." He left.

But he never said he wouldn't change once the baby got here. He had turned off the lights and I was alone in the dark lab. I slipped off my shoes and put my hands just like the praying babies and thought: God, I do love him. Let him recognize my love for what it is. Let him follow Roc's example of loving love.

Then I let my own damn self out.

Boy is the ship, I am in the hold. Mrs. Mary taught us in history that that was how the slaves traveled. They couldn't see the outside, they were in chains. (They could maybe hear it, though. Maybe it was a dolphin flying through the air, telling them that their iron buckles would be off in about four hundred years, and maybe they were grateful for that dream from the fish. They might've even got so happy, they woulda wanted to kiss each other, this shit wasn't going to be forever, but the chains wouldn't reach, so the one who was able to slip the chains went around kissing the others for joy. She kissed their feet. That made them more together. But then the smell was bad.)

Mrs. Mary told us that the slaves had been a primitive people. That's why they didn't rebel — they had been too primitive. And sure, they had the hardships of slavery to endure before them, but that would be only a short chapter in their history, and then they would be free! Mrs. Mary said that Negro people in our country had always had it so much better than the Africans that were still in Africa. Some of them still didn't even live in houses. The Negro has definitely come a long way in America. The Negro has become — *sophisticated.*

All I knew was that Bri was wrong. I couldn't have no African name. I had me my slave name, and I wasn't going away from it never.

Bri called me up all hysterical and shit, and I wanted to say: Like I don't have enough of my own problems, but I didn't say that. She cried so hard I thought the phone would melt.

"Toya," she whimpered, "what if I wake up one day and realize I don't love Roc?" Her crying was impossible. We had agreed not to do it.

I said, "Bri, calm the hell down. You haven't come to that point. Wait till you get married before you start in with all the soap opera shit. By that time you will need to have an affair, maybe we can fix you up with Big Daddy Dave." I was still grateful to him for that night in the lab.

She screamed, "But I don't love Roc *now!* The day in the future was this morning, and the baby throw-up almost choked me! Fuck!"

I told her to calm the hell down, but secretly I was afraid. Bri had heard about a place that would get rid of it almost at the same time it could be born, and she was going around school trying to get the information. She didn't have to become a school wife, I had told her before, because she could just *be* with him and *be* his woman. But she had to go through with the kid. How the hell could she have her anchor if she backed out now? And Roc was a white boy, an ugly one by white girl standards, flat nose and a caved-in chest, only he had this thing for Bri's hair when it wasn't relaxed, just natty afro and shit, and he had this thing for her African ass, and logically we all knew that that meant he would be easier to keep. Even the cheerleaders knew it, even if they were too stuck up to admit it. That white boy was not going back.

"Bri, just think about it for a moment. He won't ever make you work a day in your life. All he will want is children. Baby, most people would say you got it made."

She must a fallen out her seat because the phone hit the floor and I could hear her sniffling close by. "Toya, he told me that he got me pregnant on purpose, that I didn't have a damn thing to do with it! He wanted to have me forever! That's some sick shit! I don't want his fucking hands to touch me again. I'ma throw me down the bleachers at school."

I said, "It doesn't matter who got who. Point of the matter is, you got the prize at the end of the rainbow. You got your whole life ahead of you."

Bri whispered, "I don't want his fucking hands to touch me."

I ain't your goddamn vacation home! You think you can come and go if you like? YOU THINK I'MA ALWAYS BE HERE? Look me in the eye! I got feelings, too. You think you can come and go and it ain't gonna make me break inside? No, don't be looking at me like that! I got pride, damn you, and I got me, yeah that's right, ME! And it's about time I took care of me! Yeah, I know you been fucking with Margarita Santamaria, and I know she told you she came after the first time! Well, that's bullshit! It's hard for girls to come, they only say that to make you feel like a man! Yeah, I'd like to see you try and make me come! Try it! Just remember: when you're done, you ain't gonna have me to push around no more. That's not how my mama raised me! She raised me with good loving! What you talking about: good loving? Is that what you been wanting all this time? Good loving from a good woman?

Well, baby, that's what I been offering you all this time, you just been too blind to see. Let me love you. Let me show you what loving is all about. It's all in here, just for you. Just relax on me. Let's you and me reciprocate. Let me be sure. Let's reciprocate. You don't have to make me come, neither.

Boy Commerce wrote a poem for the school newspaper. Well, that was about the craziest shit I ever heard! He don't even know how to spell, and he hates English class! He hates books and he hates using your brains to do what you can do with your mouth in two seconds flat.

He wrote a poem, and he had all the cheerleaders sighing in the hallway. Bet they wished they was in my shoes.

FOR YOU

I want to say
but then I stop and think
Did you think I
could keep this song
in the bottom of my heart
with my everlasting love?
Don't keep me
let me run my wild manly course free.
I'm just an ordinary man,
doing all I can.
Wandering around
till it's true love I found.
Where's my future?
Is it you?
I'm a bird
but you want to be the sea.
So let me spread my wings, you done
yours.
Let's stay that way
And I'll never forget you down there
If you ever learn to forget me.

Mother, Mother, Mother, Mother.

(I want you.
I am in the ship.
I need you.)

(This was the beginning of my own poem. I would never show it to anybody cause there ain't anybody.)

I don't want a African name. I know we should be proud. Bri calls herself "Assata" and when she isn't thinking about the future, she is feeling proud like there is something else to live for. I know we should be proud.

But face it, why don't you? Here Mr. Hancock is telling me that I could get a vocational diploma and go on to do work in food service like he used to say I could do when I was back in his class reading *Tale of Two Cities* and not paying attention really. Here he is. He said, "Toya, you still have a chance for an okay future, you don't have to throw it all away." Right? Only a primitive person would turn their nose, like I did. *Right?* Fuck Mr. Hancock. Shit, I knew damn straight I wanted a better future than in food service.

Slave of a slave. I don't want a African name. I'll keep my slave name.

Boy was voted Most Valuable Player. Margarita Santamaria was voted Homecoming Queen. Bri went and had the secret abortion but promised me she would always be my friend. Big Daddy Dave asked her to check out a private party at his crib and she said yes she would sneak out her mother's house at four A.M. in the morning. Mr. Hancock asked me if I would want Boy's newspaper poem dedicated to me in the year-book, as someone had anonymously requested, and I said, What the hell, it's his loss. Roc called me up late one night at Uncle Marion's and asked me if he could start coming over and shit, and I said, Why the hell not? Sam the cheerleader came up with Katherine as the godname. She is down with the program. She and I are going over to Tinytown's next week to check out what's new and happening.

A Conversation with Carolyn Ferrell

The stories in Don't Erase Me *are about young African Americans, mostly young women, struggling not only to find themselves, but quite literally to survive, not to be erased. Are there images, moments in your own young life that you think made you want to explore these issues through fiction?*

There is the smell of lilacs, coming from a bush on the side of the house I grew up in. I would stand in that bush, staring through its foliage to the clouds swimming past (was it more like a tree towering over me, separating me from heaven?). And I'd breathe in that fragrance which, from then on, I'd come to associate with the beginning of summer, though there would be many more agonizing days until summer arrived. But standing in this bush, breathing in its deliciousness, brought to my mind the coming of long school-free, boiling days, full of water, carefree behavior, and secret summer yearning. Perhaps in the summer I would have new friends. Perhaps the old ones would forget how much they didn't like me. This was not usually the case. Often I went friendless straight from autumn to winter through spring until the long hot months of July and August, and then to the beginning of school in September.

Sometimes I stood in that lilac bush loving my aloneness. Many other times, though, I stood there, cowering, afraid of being seen, and chased, and beaten by other children. Race was understood and misunderstood by everyone on North Ronald Drive. I can remember my parents coming to visit me in my second grade class; I felt an overwhelming shame spread through my body, a lot like lava. I knew the other children sitting at their desks were busy studying the black man and the white woman: The children probably wondered how these grownups came to be in the world, like this, together. I myself can't remember when I learned that they were simply all wrong, that the sight of a black man and a white woman together in a loving way was an unwelcome one—but that day I understood the eyes of my schoolmates too well, and bowed my head deep into the construction paper. A bad thing. I pretended not to see them, and I overheard my father say to my mother, "She's pretending not to see us." I was stung. I wouldn't recover from his words until I learned to write fiction—many years later, of course.

As a child I was wildly in love with spelling, which I believed was the foundation of the world.

As a child I was wildly in love with spelling, which I believed was the foundation of the world. You had to know how to spell if you wanted the teacher to place a halo around your head made of pure, unadulterated love or if you wanted a gasp of envy to escape from the mouths of the children in your class, or from the school cafeteria monitor watching you eat your sardine in tomato sauce sandwich, or from the janitor whom you secretly worshiped. A highlight of my life came when, in the fifth grade, my teacher asked that we do a different exercise with spelling words each day, culminating in Friday's assignment: a spelling story. It didn't matter that she had no real interest in reading the stories, that she marked each of them indiscriminately with a star and gave them back with the same smile—spelling stories were a life-changing event for me. My imagination was given a chance to dust itself off from the mountain of dittoes and workbooks and breathe. I was in heaven. I would *be* something.

To what degree are the stories in the collection autobiographical? Where do they draw from your personal experience as a literacy teacher?

Everything we write is autobiographical. That doesn't mean our work comes directly from our life experiences, but rather, from the lens though which we see the world. In her engrossing autobiography, the New Zealand writer Janet Frame describes a place she calls Mirror City, where people and events and memories are transformed by the creative process into works of art. There is the daily city in which we live our regular, unnarrative lives; and then there is Mirror City, where mere "slices of life" cease to exist. Everything is in service of the story, of the work of art. Mirror City is a place where "nothing is without its use," where "memories are resurrected, reclothed with reflection and change, and their essence [left] untouched." It is, in short, the city of the imagination.

My personal experiences must be filtered through the lens of Mirror City if I am to write the kind of story I want to read. I must become a citizen of Mirror City if the work can have meaning beyond experience. If I write a piece set on Jupiter, it will have a kernel of myself in it, and the same is true if I write a story set in the South Bronx. I draw on my own experiences to create that story, but all is transformed and revitalized and given narrative coherence. When I wrote "Proper Library," I drew in large part on people and experiences from my childhood on Long Island, a fact that has been frustrating to some people. When I was on a reading tour with *Don't Erase Me*, I at times sensed a kind of disappointment in readers who desperately wanted me to have come from a war-torn urban ghetto, just like in the movies. How could I write the way I did if I hadn't really lived there?

If I write a piece set on Jupiter, it will have a kernel of myself in it, and the same is true if I write a story set in the South Bronx.

In real life, I spent several years working in the South Bronx. I often kept late hours, so it sometimes felt like I lived there. But I didn't. I was a teacher in an adult basic education school, teaching day and evening classes to people who often toiled hard at jobs and children and who could write only their name. I listened to my students; I listened to my coworkers; I walked up and down Longwood Avenue countless times and observed traces of loveliness and failure and sorrow and vivacity. Again, I listened. Then I walked back to the number 2 train at Prospect Avenue and made notes. The train would come, and I'd return to Manhattan, a more "cosmopolitan" setting. Hell's Kitchen. My neighborhood was infected with Broadway theaters and tourist attractions and drooped underneath the weight of failed gentrification. I'd climb the four stories to my minuscule apartment, sit at my kitchen table and start to write. Everything is a product, finally, of Mirror City.

Would you talk about the ways in which elements of your real life made their way into "Proper Library"?

Once, as I stood on the subway el platform waiting to go home, I watched a group of children torture each other in what looked like "fun." I was on the opposite side, waiting for the train to take me back to Manhattan, out of the South Bronx. The children organized themselves into groups, breaking out now and again into merciless laughter. A boy sat off to the side, and his look was dejected, desultory—had he been left out of the festivities for a reason? Why? The children were busy dropping bottles down into the tracks (and thus into the street underneath the el) and occasionally they looked back at him, laughing. He did nothing except sit there. Watching them conjured feelings in me. Something came alive in my heart, a memory, a wound. I went home, took out my notebook, and began "Proper Library."

The story was influenced by the details of a person I knew from childhood, Arthur "Cookie" Thompson, a boy whom I secretly loved, though he was often harsh and indelicate. These are the true facts of his story: He was dark-skinned, overweight, a foster child, liked instantly by everyone he met, a bully. He went by the name Cookie. Everyone was wild about him; he was incredibly alone. He loved boys more than he did girls, and for that his foster father swore he would tear him up if he ever caught Cookie walking down the street with anyone other than his sister (who happened to be my best friend). "I love you like my own," his foster father told him. "But I will kill you if I have to." When I first sat down to "Proper Library, I was fueled by a mixture of vengefulness, rage, sorrow, and confusion. I'd been writing this story for some time, trying to make sense of its direction, but often my emotions got in the way of things. You can have all the ingredients, and still come up short. Just as a story can have many midwives or fairy godparents, it can also have a living, breathing soul, one that is composed of mystery.

Cookie's story was one ingredient to the story I was trying to write. Then there was Sherwood Anderson's "A Death in the Woods," which affected me deeply. The protagonist, Mrs. Grimes, a poor immigrant to the cold Midwest, lives a miserable life of service until her death. It is then that she is "honored" by a pack of dogs that circle her body, protecting it from the world that had hurt her in life. There was also the poem "More Girl Than Boy," a haunting piece written by Yusef Komunyakaa which seemed to ring in my ears at all times. "You'll always be my friend/Is that clear, Robert Lee?" That was the name of my father. The poem immediately brought to my mind my childhood with Cookie Thompson.

All those years later; and I did not possess the vocabulary to express my sadness when I heard about his end. All I had were details. New York, the destination he'd dreamed of since a child, the place he wound up running away to; the dresses he wore as a prostitute; the crack cocaine he ate for breakfast lunch and dinner; the rolls and rolls of luscious obesity he shed in those years. There was the way his skeleton peeked through his skin like an actor peeking out from a stage curtain—I saw pictures of him from time to time. In the late 1980s he died in the arms of his boyfriend, bruised, skeletal, and HIV positive, in an apartment in Hell's Kitchen. All these sources helped "Proper Library" come into being. Everything resonated with feeling, with memory, with creativity, and, in my eyes, with honesty. Cookie's story haunted me for years, and drove me not only to create, but to revise. What I am talking about is a kind of creative reenvisioning that allows me to get to the truth of a story, to what I believe is its emotional center. In "Proper Library," I took Cookie's life and my own and re-envisioned them, just the way Komunyakaa's poem instructed me to, just as that poem had earlier revised *me.* I searched for words to most honestly tell his story.

The voice in that story is so strong. How did you find it?

When I finished the first draft of the story that would eventually become "Proper Library," I spent a lot of time thinking about voice and character. Who was I to write the story of a gay teenaged black boy—and from his point of view? How could I make such a story authentic? Meaningful? What gave me the right? Naturally I didn't want to create a stereotypical character; I did not want him to be representative in a way that might be myopic, mawkish, sentimental, homophobic, careless, or in any other way false. How could I be sure I was truly speaking in his voice?

If I were to draw on my own experiences to create this character, he would naturally have to share something of my own background; but how could that be, since my growing up story had been so much different from Lorrie's? I was one of four children of a German mother and a North Carolina black father. We lived in a house that was just like the rest except that ours was blessed (or burdened) with a few extra creature comforts: a swimming pool, a swing set, a monkey bar set, a balance beam (for my gymnast sister), and a playhouse (built by my father for me). One or two extra cars sat in our driveway, as my father was an amateur auto mechanic and liked to fix their engines as a hobby. Unlike other families on the block, our family went on vacations to places other than relatives', and we kept a great assortment of books in our house, books that went beyond the obligatory encyclopedia and nature volumes. We were not rich, but by the standard of the block, I think we often seemed to be. A neighbor woman once remarked that we were "too big for our britches." Our ambiguous racial status as well as our ambiguous class status set us apart, painfully so.

What I had in common with my character Lorrie was a memory of being marginalized. My mother struggled to raise her children in an environment that was often hostile to her, unaccepting, a place where the slogans of the Black Consciousness Movement stirred me, her eldest child, but threatened to eat me alive as well. My sense of marginalization fueled my dreams, my nightmares, and my questions. For me, there was something bad about being a black and white family, just as later there would be something bad about Lorrie being a gay (and intelligent and black) boy. Was I being politically incorrect, insensitive, irresponsible in writing this story? Though I wrestled with these questions as I continued revising the draft of "Proper Library," I found that my fears would not prevent the story from emerging.

My sense of marginalization fueled my dreams, my nightmares, and my questions.

What I did not realize at the time was that Lorrie was me, and that this was also my story emerging in his.

The narrator in "Tiger-Frame Glasses" is a writer. In what ways does she bear witness to your experience?

When I was six years old, my mother bought me a small composition book, and I filled its pages with poems of a generally sunny nature. It was a red speckled composition book, on the small side, open and ready for action—I felt it fit my personality perfectly. The poems I composed were about kindness, thoughtfulness, and the wish to end pollution of any kind. In kindergarten, the first grade, I felt the sun was shining on me every second. But a few years passed, and life became harder for me. I came to see contradictions, moments of hypocrisy, complications in everyday life that confused me.

My family lived in a black community—lower middle class, some welfare—that during my early childhood existed in the heat of the Black Power Movement and the Vietnam War. It was not easy to have a white, German mother and a black, North Carolina father, who seemed to toss their heads indignantly at the world around them. Everyone on North Ronald Drive went to church, but they eschewed organized religion. They rejected many middle class trappings, such as color televisions, brand new cars, and sturdy, pressed clothes. My father was not kind to the women and children on the block. My mother was kind, but was often used by the other mothers who saw in her a cheap babysitter. There were no friends. The neighborhood was so suspicious of us that once a family got together a petition against our family and took it all the way to Town Hall! They simply hated the fact that we existed. When my parents divorced and my mother bought a house in another section of town—racially mixed but predominantly white—another petition was drawn against her. One white neighbor had felt offended and betrayed when, after the sale, he saw my mother's four brown-skinned children walk freely in her house!

When I was a child, it was hard to come to terms with the racial climate, particularly because those bad feelings, those kinds of hatreds, were inexplicable to me. I had difficulty understanding what the fuss was all about but I knew something was wrong—*we* were wrong. How to articulate my confusion? When I was nine years old I turned to fiction. Poetry seemed to be lacking in some way, maybe it was not vengeful enough, too righteous. I wanted action out of my words. I wanted to feel better.

I wanted action out of my words. I wanted to feel better.

There was one particular girl on my block who'd made my life a living hell—I wanted my red speckled composition book to take care of her somehow. Bellerina Brown tortured me as I walked to and from the school bus stop each day, making fun of my lukewarm good looks, threatening to kick my butt. She couldn't understand why I took a sardine in tomato sauce sandwich to school each day. Black people didn't take sardine sandwiches to school—they ate hot lunch! Bellerina got together with the Walker girls and the Benymon girls and plotted my demise. Once when we were waiting for a bus to take us to an elementary school in the white part of town, Bellerina even got a distant cousin of mine to join her in delivering threats. Once, a shy new girl (who had, in the hallways, become a new friend) suddenly shouted at me as the bus rounded the corner: "Your ass is grass!"

Something had changed in my sensibility, thanks to Bellerina Brown. I needed to write a story. The "true facts" of Bellerina's life deserved a tougher and (in my eyes) more honest literary vehicle, because just how could a poem convey the fact that Bellerina was a fat, hideous, unlovable girl who made life in general pretty miserable? (A harsh assessment, yes, but I was learning even then that "true facts" often bring out the harshest in us.) I was, in part, writing out of revenge, but I was also thinking about the shape of my work. Bellerina couldn't fit into a poem, even though she was, to my thinking, a form of pollution in my eyes. But a *poem?*

My composition book made me feel better about the world; I was confident that the story I was writing would change things, would make the world nicer if I just got down all the horror that was Bellerina Brown and all the good and angelic that was myself. It felt good to get the details in place, the hopes and victories. The children pure of heart, and those who could not possibly be loved by anyone on earth. Bellerina turned out, however, to play a rather small part in the story I began in my composition book. All along I had craved the feeling of vindication I would get by having Bellerina destroyed in a fire or suffering in an orphanage. But in my story, she took a back seat to the good characters, whose ideal lives sparkled underneath my pencil. The "chapters" of my story seethed with good deeds and Girl Scout medals and shapely girls whose names rang like bells: Vanessa Goodwin, Gorgea Gorgeous. There was a fire, but luckily there was also a fire escape and a ladder and a lifesaver's award from a firefighter by the name of Mr. Handy. Of course, Gorgea and Vanessa and Mr. Handy turned out to be the fine, upstanding members of the black community. They lived in a town called Ocean Dreams. They helped others, they were sweet in the face of destruction, they served a purpose (could I have already been thinking of racial uplift, or were my goals purely selfish?). Ultimately, they were flat characters. In writing the story, I felt a bit vindicated, but I also grasped somehow (deep in my unconscious) that what was missing from my work was conflict.

There is very little of the actual me in "Tiger-Frame Glasses." Everything is a composite, a remodeling, a challenge to the past, to the way things were. Adrienne Rich wrote that the imagination "has to question, to challenge, to conceive of alternatives, perhaps to the very life you are living at the moment. You have to be free to play around with the notion that day might be night, love might be hate; nothing can be too sacred for the imagination to turn into its opposite or to call experimentally by another name. For writing is renaming." The story has a struggle between Bellerina Brown and the narrator at its heart—a hard thing for me to tackle since I needed to divorce myself from my own experiences and really create Bellerina. As a character in my fiction, she deserves to be dealt with as honestly as possible—though Vanessa Goodwin and Gorgea Gorgeous might disagree.

In a fiction workshop I once attended, the wonderful Edna O'Brien said that yearning was the greatest ingredient of literature.

In a fiction workshop I once attended, the wonderful Edna O'Brien said that yearning was the greatest ingredient of literature. I still love that line, and hold onto it as tightly as I hold onto my memories of Bellerina Brown at the bus stop. Bellerina has a small bit of room to move about in my mind. But on the page? There she roams freely, she becomes someone else entirely—someone I don't know I know.

Generally, how do stories form for you? Where do ideas come from, how do they evolve, what kinds of surprises occur during the writing process?

Stories come to me in many ways. Memories, grudges, perceptions, dreams, conversations overheard, the sense of déjà vu. Of course, not every story comes to fruition. Grudges, for instance, are poor motivators for fiction. But often there is a kernel, a tiny bit from real life, whether the experience was pleasant or earth-shattering or sorrowful, and that kernel will allow itself to be spread throughout the soil and later be harvested. By the time it comes to fruition on the page, it bears no trace of a grudge. And thank goodness for that.

Some people will say to me, "Oh, you should really write about so-and-so, he really did you wrong!" My mother, for another example, can't seem to forgive the East Hampton matron who employed me for a month when I was in college and who treated me like a professional slave. "Write about Mrs. M—!" she will tell me. "You have such incredible stories about her!"

Which is why I haven't been able to write about Mrs. M. As my six-year-old son would say, she's "too real." I can't yet write about Mrs. M.'s monstrous cook either, a woman who'd been fired at one time in her life by a world famous pianist. I can't yet write about Mr. M., her husband, who believed education was a large waste of time. I can't yet write about their social circle, who drank Midori liquor like it was going out of style and still didn't believe the races should mix.

I am still angry! Not a good reason to write. Probably it will take another twenty or so years before traces of East Hampton make their ways into my work. Or perhaps they are already there, transformed by my journey to Mirror City. The important thing, as I often tell my students, is to go for honesty. Because you can be honest without being truthful. Writers should steer away from "real life" as much as they can—are there any sadder words to hear from a writer than, "But this is the way things really happened"?

Writers should steer away from "real life" as much as they can—are there any sadder words to hear from a writer than, "But this is the way things really happened"?

The stories in Don't Erase Me *certainly reflect what you teach. They are sometimes almost brutally honest in confronting the hard issues that plague the African American community—sexuality, teenage pregnancy, domestic violence, AIDS. You never flinch! What do you hope to accomplish with that kind of honesty? What is the responsibility of the African American writer in creating a picture of her people that will be read by blacks and whites alike?*

I don't have an agenda. I want my work to live and breathe. I want it to interest an audience. I want it to change the world in a good way. I want it to relate to others, all others. I have met writers, both black and white, who do take issue with certain forms of subject matter. There are, of course, black writers who take offense at certain characters or situations because they do not serve the greater purpose of "bettering" the black community. I am not one of these writers. First of all, because I believe that writing with an agenda is dangerous, and can lead to boorish, polemical, leaden work. And secondly, because the black community is always being redefined. It is not a monolith. Of course, there is writing that is out-and-out racist, or so filled with stereotype, it hurts the soul. I am against that!

Luckily, I know other writers who are not burdened with ideas of social or racial uplift. They don't intend to lecture or model good behavior or write things that won't offend. These are writers who see a purpose in dirty laundry. They don't believe there are some subjects which should not come to light in the larger world—AIDS and drugs and sex and violence—what the larger world might see as stereotypical. They write what they feel most passionate about, what most urgently needs to be put on paper. They think about developing authentic characters, settings, voices, and conflicts. They don't censor themselves. I don't censor myself. The world will be full of interpretations. How can I possibly control those?

I don't censor myself. The world will be full of interpretations. How can I possibly control those?

What we must do as writers is be as vigilant as possible. We have to always check our work, but we should never stop taking risks. We have to become informed readers and writers. We have to let the story do its work.

Your work is so right-on in its depiction of adolescents. Have you found a readership among teens and young adults?

I don't think my book was marketed for the young adult world. I enjoyed sculpting the world of those stories, hearing those young adult voices and seeing the world through their eyes. But on a practical level, there are far too many expletives in the prose. Plus, there are far too many teens having sex and enjoying it.

After the book came out, I was been invited to give a keynote address for a large writers' event at a high school on Long Island, but the invitation was rescinded once the superintendent read the stories. I was devastated to be dropped. I wondered if my version of things would truly be detrimental to the teens, especially given the amount of violence and "gratuitous" sex they are already exposed to? Could my stories possibly speak to teens in a meaningful way? I thought so then, but didn't fight their decision.

How do you think good fiction—yours and that of others—might change the way young African Americans see themselves and are seen by others?

I'd like to think my fiction is changing the world in some small (minuscule) way. One of the greatest joys in reading literature is somehow seeing yourself in the pages, relating to the work in your own, personal way, and then perhaps conjuring up new thoughts based on what you've read—new dreams, new outlooks, new ideas.

But if you set to change how people think, you may invoke a kind of "uplift" literature that merely oppresses, even when it's as cheerful as cheesecake. I remember a particular television show where all the black characters were well-dressed and well-meaning and only slightly troubled; by the show's end, each carefully pressed and manicured character had his or her problems resolved in a way that taught the World a lesson, that invited the World to look on and learn. I always felt depressed after watching that show.

Your stories are very creative with language. Your sentence rhythms mirror the grammatical characteristics of black speech. You use slang a lot, both in dialogue and narration.

I am not a big fan of vernacular in writing. I could take it when Zora Neale Hurston wrote out the language of her characters in *Their Eyes Were Watching God*, but I can't take it when my students attempt the same sort of thing. We see language issues differently now, I suppose. I prefer actual words to play on punctuation. It is possible to create a world without using language (in a contemporary sense, and nothing against Hurston) as a crutch or prop. Why drop off the "g?" Won't the character's background come across with that "g" intact if the setting truly does its work and the sentences do all they can to create and sustain the voice?

"But why are there too many curse words?" I asked her. "That is how they talk in real life." "Don't let that cussing try and do your work for you," my friend told me.

I once struggled with the weight of curse words in a story I was writing. I showed the draft to a friend who told me, "You have those characters cussing too much." I knew this was true, but at the time, I didn't understand what to do about it. "But why are there too many curse words?" I asked her. "That is how they talk in real life." "Don't let that cussing try and do your work for you," my friend told me. And after I thought about it, I realized how right she was.

"Country of the Spread Out God" does make use of a kind of vernacular. Would you talk about that story?

The story began with an entire sonnet from Wordsworth: "Surprised by Joy." I was in love with that poem for many years, and decided the best way to honor it was to write a story and steal the title. I toiled for a number of years with Wordsworth's ghost looking over my shoulder but came up with nothing. I recited the sonnet in my sleep, during my waking hours, and invoked the sorrow and intuition I believed were its hallmarks—but alas, nothing worked. The story was as stale as a bag of potato chips in a Midtown deli. There was a great deal of pain in my story, and I was searching for a way to make this pain real to the reader. It was not your average pain. It was a Wordsworthian pain!

But how many people knew that sonnet? I placed the sonnet up top on the page, like an epigraph, and prayed to it each time I began to revise. The lines flowed like blood in my veins. If Wordsworth could break a reader's heart with these words, why couldn't he at least help me? Sadly, that was not to be. It was only after I let the sonnet go and explored the characters in their own distinct ways that I was able to grasp the story. The poem evoked a deep feeling. But it was not the story. It did not go into particulars, it did not shed light on the voices, it did not establish a sense of purpose for my characters. That was all work I had to do.

When I took the poem off the page, I was able to complete "Country of the Spread Out God" in a relatively short time. I had been working on it for years without really knowing it. The title came to me from another work of literature, Olive Senior's short story, "The Country of the One-Eyed God," which, again, struck me as something of a small miracle. The elegant manner in which she moved from one code of language to another—from standard Jamaican English to a sort of biblical Jamaican English to what the poet Brathwaite calls "nation language"—was brilliant. The story was devastating—a combination of unsympathetic characters whose histories and motives nevertheless challenged and moved the reader. It was an honest story, a variation, in my eyes, of Flannery O'Connor's "A Good Man Is Hard to Find."

I once heard Russell Banks say, "Writers borrow." I believe he was talking about writers learning from one another, giving one another ideas, creating, perhaps, as a way to help others learn to create. An image, a slip of dialogue, a setting—the color of a woman's hair, the sound of a grandmother's voice, the reemergence of a hole in a mother's darned sock, the flicking of a toothpick in a man's mouth—we see these things and they stay with us, hopefully in the best, most honorable way possible. We learn from those details: The way they are written should haunt us at night and during the day.

What were the haunting details that generated "Can You Say My Name?"

There was a cheerleader two years ahead of me in high school who was bright and beautiful in unconventional ways and who made it her business to warn younger girls (like me, completely ignorant of the hearts of boys) about possible dangers that lay ahead. She'd given birth her junior year and was still (in spite of it all) in love with the father of her baby, a cad. After a long suffering of unrequited love, this cheerleader wrote a poem and printed it in the school paper. It moved everyone—and I mean everyone. There were few secrets in this setting, and so after the poem appeared, all the school waited for was to see whether this boy would come around and love her back, the way he should have from the beginning. Of course, he was too beautiful to love her back. He was selfish, conceited, mercenary. He liked his son from a distance. He was busy with basketball, failing grades. The mother of his child would have to manage without him—but how could he remain impervious to the poem, I asked myself, wiping away my tears. So what if the poem was corny? She loved him!

After the poem, this cheerleader went on a mission to save others. She gave out advice and stories with sense and urgency, in her calm way. When she spoke to me—at our Homecoming game—she warned me about the boy I was dating, who happened to be the best friend of her cad. I had no idea at the time what she was talking about: I didn't understand anything about boys who got you pregnant on purpose, or who only wanted one-night-stands, or who were not interested in dedicating their souls to you. I thanked her in my measly way, and then went on to enjoy a perfectly miserable, unrequited high school life. I did not go on to have a baby, but I was ever after aware of the suffering of girls at the hands of boys. This cheerleader had been a shoo-in for Homecoming Queen, but because she'd had a baby, the glorious world of popularity, of good state colleges and their athletes, and romantic alcoholic nights on the beach, was denied her forever. I coveted that world—even as I sat at its sidelines, touching the gates that eternally kept me on the other side.

So much for real life. If you read "Can You Say My Name?" you'll notice the differences. What intrigued me while writing the story was Toya's ruthless, aching logic. I wanted to write the cheerleader I'd known, but then Toya came out, a composite of many cheerleaders and boys and girls. And Toya had to have a plan, or else she would not survive the cruelties of this world. (Which is the world you and I live in, no matter who we are.)

That logic is brilliantly rendered, often with humorous effect. Toya is the classic unreliable narrator!

Some things she says sound funny, but only because she tries relentlessly to adhere to her logic. Ultimately it is a sad story, one of resignation and impossible yearning, but there has to be humor in the piece as well. Every character, no matter how dire their situation, needs an escape route. I loved the idea that Toya chose to be a wife and mother in school. At the time I wrote the story, it didn't seem that far-fetched; it still doesn't. Hopeless, for the most part, but believable. I had to have her operate under a set of assumptions that could go either way: They could bolster her esteem and help her make something of herself, or they could destroy her. As I was writing her, I didn't initially think of her as an unreliable narrator. Maybe I had gotten a bit too sucked up into her worldview; at any rate, once I recognized the signs of unreliability, I rejoiced. I was incredibly sad.

Every character, no matter how dire their situation, needs an escape route.

Her way of thinking and of doing often precludes real-life players. That is, she is so caught up with the myriad details that go into being a wife and mother, she almost has no need for the actual people to exist. She needs the order of Stop-One Supermarket and Tinytown's children's store, but not the people who inhabit those settings. She speaks of slavery, but in a limited way. It's a subject she has read about in school, and a piece of what she's learned has stuck with her, and is now in service to her larger story: that of a girl-woman who wonders, agonizingly, about her potential. What is her right? Her due?

Boy Commerce behaves badly toward Toya, but he is a wholly sympathetic character. How did he evolve for you?

Boy Commerce came easily to me. He was not drawn from the real-life cad—everyone knows how oppressive it is to read one-dimensional characters. For me, there was a wealth of feeling and aspiration and sorrow in Boy Commerce. His ambiguities, like

Toya's, are perhaps the closest thing I had to an ambition for the story: I wanted to deliver those ambiguities to the reader with as much life and authenticity as possible. His character belongs, to an extent, to Toya's world and her system of knowledge, and if we feel sorry for Toya, we also feel sorry for him. At least I did.

The dialogue between Toya and Boy Commerce is done very unconventionally. Why did you do it that way?

I had some difficulty creating the dialogue between Toya and Boy. There is a way that sort of unattributed dialogue can seem forced, derivative; my editor helped me a great deal in terms of sorting out the speech. What I had envisioned was a kind of dream world in which a dream language was spoken as softly as rain but then constantly banging, like worn shutters, against the windows of the outside world. I wanted this dream language to be understood by its speakers in bits and pieces. In other words: One speaker could not truly understand what the other was saying, in part because by understanding and acknowledging what the other was saying, they were in some way negating themselves, their place in the world.

Would you talk about the passages about Toya's mother's death and how her life used to be? Why were they crucial for the overall effect of the story?

I wanted her mother to haunt her every waking moment. The past underlies everything here: her mother, a different sort of life, her old home. It may not be possible to get the past back, but it is possible to sculpt a new future for oneself using what seem to be the most stone-like, unyielding materials.

In this and other stories, much that happens in the characters' lives takes place at school, yet school itself is, at best, incidental in the way their lives play out. What is it that appeals to you about a school setting?

I love setting stories in school because it often is a place of great learning where the pupils understand little and the adults understand even less. So much goes on at school. It is a world within a world, complete with ruling hierarchies, political prisoners, unrequited loves, and basic forms of torture and unfairness. I'm not saying anything new. Schools over the world are their own microcosms of good and evil. It's this dynamic that I find inexhaustible in terms of subject matter. It's the balance of hope and loss that I find intriguing about a school setting. It's also a phrase like, "I'll never forget you" or "I know you'll be a success" that is scribbled onto every page of every yearbook that I find inviting as a writer. Sure, they're meant well, but what do people actually do with such clichés? Why are such empty words seen as such a great goodbye gift? It's especially pertinent when you come back to your high school reunion twenty years later and realize what lies those words actually were.

I love setting stories in school because it often is a place of great learning where the pupils understand little and the adults understand even less.

Generally, how do you approach the task of revision?

I generally work on a story for about a year, though I worked on "Country of the Spread Out God" for several years; "Proper Library" had many beginnings, starting from my senior year in college to way past graduate school, when I finally completed the piece. I revise constantly; there are no hard and fast rules for revision. I'd like to say I instinctively know when a story is finished, but even that's not true. Sometimes I just get tired of a piece, realize it can go no further, and put it to rest. Maybe in months or years to come the story will rise from the ashes. Sometimes not. You can't underestimate the power of time and distance when you are writing.

You can't underestimate the power of time and distance when you are writing.

Don't Erase Me *is dedicated to the memory of your mentor, Doris Jean Austin. Would you talk about your relationship with her?*

When I got out of graduate school, I still felt as if I needed to belong to a larger writing community. I found the name of the New Renaissance Writers, a group led by Doris Jean Austin. I remember going a few times to their meetings (they were held in a room at the Schomburg), but was feeling oppressed by a few of the regulars who liked to talk the talk. I confided my feelings to Doris Jean, telling her I was about to drop out, but she begged me to stay. I couldn't understand why; we barely knew each other. But that was her intuition. She and I wound up meeting by ourselves, and then becoming great friends, and then sharing our work with each other. She was an intelligent reader, and a fantastic writer. She introduced me to Elizabeth Nunez and Arthur Flowers, also members of the group, who were tremendous talents and have received recognition for their work.

Here is a line that is really true: If Doris Jean had lived, this world would have been a better place. She left behind a beautiful novel, some stories, and fragments; but she also left behind many who loved her deeply and who were inspired by her insights on writing. In an introductory essay to a book she was working on when she died, she wrote, "Working writers can usually see through talkers who haven't begun their project, but who want to tell you the whole story as it will be written. Working writers have learned that talking is not writing. Reading, also, though imperative, is not writing. Only locking one's butt to the seat of the chair and writing, is writing. I write every day, sometimes a page, sometimes a sentence or a chapter. . . . Writing is work. A consuming, debilitating orgy of passion, intellect, and skill."

But everything, she told me, could be overcome when you sat at your desk and began your other life.

She taught me so much in such a short time. I loved simply being her friend. There was that one time we strolled through northern Central Park and talked about all things writerly—we could not stop being thrilled that Toni Morrison had won the Nobel Prize. Doris Jean spoke with interest to passersby, probably culling material for stories;

eventually we turned into one of her favorite restaurants, Teachers Too, and talked as if each moment were our last together. She gave me hope when it came to writing. She'd had disappointments. But everything, she told me, could be overcome when you sat at your desk and began your other life.

Writing Prompts

READ: "Can You Say My Name?" and the interview with **Carolyn Ferrell.**

PONDER: How Ferrell creates the logic of an unreliable narrator.

WRITE: A monologue in the voice of a character trying to persuade the listener that something utterly absurd actually does make sense.

PRACTICE:

- Identify a fragrance associated with your childhood and then freewrite a memory or memories associated with that fragrance. Is there some emotional truth associated with the memories the fragrance evokes? Write about that emotional truth.
- Write about a moment in which you were ashamed or embarrassed by your parents.
- What were you good at as a child? Write a scene that reflects your talent without saying what the talent is.
- Write a dialogue between two people who are incapable of hearing one another.
- Write an imagined scene in the life of someone you lost track of after childhood or adolescence, but have never been able to forget.
- Identify a strong feeling that shaped your childhood and/or adolescence—a sense of marginalization, a sense of being brilliant, anything. Create a character who has that same feeling but is nothing like you. Write a scene that illustrates the feeling and its effect on his life. Don't name the feeling.
- Were you a writer as a child or adolescent? If so, write a scene that reflects your writing life then.
- Identify a classmate who had a negative effect on your life as a schoolchild. Write a letter to that person saying how her behavior affected you. Then imagine you are the person receiving it and write back from her point of view. Let yourself be surprised by the classmate's response.
- Write a story in which you do not censor yourself in telling a hard, even brutal, truth about something that matters deeply to you.
- Tape the speech of someone with a heavy accent, someone whose speech is connected to a particular culture, or someone who frequently uses slang or profanity. Transcribe the tape and then edit it to create dialogue that, without resorting to dialect, reflects the speaker's sentence rhythms and grammatical characteristics.
- Write a scene set in a high school in which the pupils involved understand little and the adults understand even less.

Amy Hempel

Amy Hempel (b. 1951) is the author of four collections of short stories. Born in Chicago, she was educated at Whittier College, San Francisco State University, and Columbia University. Her work is widely anthologized and has appeared in numerous publications, including Vanity Fair, Harper's, Mother Jones, The Quarterly, GQ, Vogue, *and* Playboy. *Her honors include the Silver Medal from the Commonwealth Club of California and a Pushcart Prize. She lives in New York City.*

For Further Reading:
Reasons to Live (1985), *At the Gates of the Animal Kingdom* (1990), *Tumble Home: A Novella and Short Stories* (1997), *The Dog of the Marriage* (2005).

Going

There is a typo on the hospital menu this morning. They mean, I think, that the pot roast tonight will be served with buttered noodles. But what it says here on my breakfast tray is that the pot roast will be *severed* with buttered noodles.

This is not a word you want to see after flipping your car twice at sixty per and then landing side-up in a ditch.

I did not spin out on a stretch of highway called Blood Alley or Hospital Curve. I lost it on flat dry road—with no other car in sight. Here's why: in the desert I like to drive through binoculars. What I like about it is that things are two ways at once. Things are far away and close with you still in the same place.

In the ditch, things were also two ways at once. The air was unbelievably hot and my skin was unbelievably cold.

"Son," the doctor said, "you shouldn't be alive."

The impact knocked two days out of my head, but all you can see is the cut on my chin. I total a car and get twenty stitches that keep me from shaving.

It's a good thing, too, that that is all it was. This hospital place, this clinic—it is not your City of Hope. The instruments don't come from a first-aid kit, they come from a toolbox. It's the desert. The walls of this room are not rose-beige or sanitation-plant green. The walls are the color of old chocolate going chalky at the edges.

And there's a worm smell.

Though I could be mistaken about the smell.

I'm given to olfactory hallucinations. When my parents' house was burning to the ground, I smelled smoke three states away.

Now I smell worms.

The doctor wants to watch me because I knocked my head. So I get to miss a few days of school. It's okay with me. I believe that ninety-nine percent of what anyone does can effectively be postponed. Anyway, the accident was a learning experience.

You know—pain teaches?

One of the nurses picked it up from there. She was bending over my bed, snatching pebbles of safety glass out of my hair. "What do we learn from this?" she asked.

It was like that class at school where the teacher talks about Realization, about how you could realize something big in a commonplace thing. The example he gave—and the liar said it really happened—was that once while drinking orange juice, he'd realized he would be dead someday. He wondered if we, his students, had had similar "realizations."

Is he kidding? I thought.

Once I cashed a paycheck and I realized it wasn't enough.

Once I had food poisoning, and realized I was trapped inside my body.

What interests me now is this memory thing. Why two *days*? Why *two* days? The last I know is not getting carded in a two-shark bar near the Bonneville flats. The bartender served me tequila and he left the bottle out. He asked me where I was going, and I said I was just going. Then he brought out a jar with a scorpion in it. He showed me how a drop of tequila on its tail makes a scorpion sting itself to death.

What happened after that?

Maybe those days will come back and maybe they will not. In the meantime, how's this: I can't even remember all I've forgotten.

I do remember the accident, though. I remember it was like the binoculars. You know—two ways? It was fast and it was slow. It was both.

The pot roast wasn't bad. I ate every bit of it. I finished the green vegetables and the citrus vegetables too.

Now I'm waiting for the night nurse. She takes a blood pressure about this time. You could call this the high point of my day. That's because this nurse makes every other woman look like a sex-change. Unfortunately, she's in love with the Lord.

But she's a sport, this nurse. When I can't sleep she brings in the telephone book. She sits by my bed and we look up funny names. Calliope Ziss and Maurice Pancake live in this very community.

I like a woman in my room at night.

The night nurse smells like a Christmas candle.

After she leaves the room, for a short time the room is like when she was here. She is not here, but the idea of her is.

It's not the same—but it makes me think of the night my mother died. Three states away, the smell in my room was the smell of the powder on her face when she kissed me good-night—the night she wasn't there.

A Conversation with Amy Hempel

You're probably best known for your mastery of the very, very, very short story. Your story "Housewife" is only one sentence; many others are only a few pages long, so how did you come to this form and what appeals to you about it?

I wish I could write poetry, but I can't—so some of my short-shorts are in the blur between the two genres. It's as close to poetry as I can get. I write fiction with a poet's concerns, always paying attention to the acoustics, the image, the line, and a sort of distillation. In a short-short you are looking at a defining moment. There's not usually cause and effect. Something shifts, something becomes clear. I assemble longer stories, novellas moment by moment. It's how I experience life, in these moments, so it's natural to use them in fiction.

How do you know that you have a moment from which a story might grow?

One of my first short-shorts grew from something that happened to a friend of friend of mine. He was kidnapped and held for three months, during which time the captors put him on a diet and made him quit smoking. He had a heart condition. He wasn't going to be any use to them if he died. When the ransom was paid and he was released, he was in the best shape he'd been in for years. What occurred to me when I heard this became the last line in the story, "How do we know what happens to us isn't good?" So there was that moment. It was just handed to me. If you are listening seriously and paying attention, this stuff does get handed to you all the time.

I write fiction with a poet's concerns, always paying attention to the acoustics, the image, the line, and a sort of distillation.

If you are listening seriously and paying attention, this stuff does get handed to you all the time.

"The Rest of God" came from a small moment at the end of a long weekend. The men haven't been shaving and when they go to kiss their wives goodnight the wives cringe, thinking it's going to hurt, it's going to scratch. Then it doesn't. The thing that attracted me was just that: Something you expect to hurt doesn't.

Talk about that one-sentence story, "Housewife," a little bit and how you came to that.

I wrote that sentence and looked at it for two years. Then I thought, maybe I can't think of the next line because it's done. I had discovered some one-sentence stories by Gertrude Stein and Ernest Hemingway. Gertrude Stein's story, titled "Longer," goes, "She stayed away longer." You see the effect that that produces.

So the moment in your story is when the narrator thinks, "French Film, French Film." Justifying what she's doing.

Exactly.

How would you define a story?

Ken Kesey had a great simple definition, which was, "What someone wants and is going through to get it." But my former teacher Gordon Lish has a wonderful definition that I look to the most. It's twofold: "It's not what happens to people on the page, it's what happens to the reader in his heart and mind." He said that what's interesting in a story is not the situation, but who's in it and what they're making of it. A story happens when two equally appealing forces, or characters, or ideas try to occupy the same place at the same time, and they're both right.

A story happens when two equally appealing forces, or characters, or ideas try to occupy the same place at the same time, and they're both right.

What are the special considerations of the short-short story?

Some of the concerns in writing a short-short are not unlike joke writing. You know you're going to have a punch line, a kicker—whether it's a funny one or not. I wanted a close call that ended with something very evocative.

In your short-short "Going" you have this kid in a hospital who miraculously survived a bad accident contemplating eating an evening meal. Yet somehow that story conveys all the reader needs to about his parents' deaths. Where did that story come from?

My brother had an accident in Mexico, in which he was injured badly. He was driving *my* new car, looking through binoculars.

There's one of those details you could never make up!

It never would have occurred to me. But my brother did it, and he was injured really badly.

The binoculars are interesting as a metaphor because they underpin the way the story moves close up to memory, then backs off. The way time can be fast and slow.

The binoculars are entirely emblematic. The big thing that I pulled from what my brother did in my car in the desert in New Mexico was how many things are at the same time close and far away in memory and experience. Again, I have to give credit where it's due. This came from Gordon, as well. He said, "Be aware that the more literal you are on the page, the more metaphorical people think you are being." It's very true. People have read big meaning into some of the most flatfooted things I've said on the page, and then I get to say, "I meant that."

People have read big meaning into some of the most flatfooted things I've said on the page, and then I get to say, "I meant that."

The voice in that story is so strong. Is it his voice?

It was inspired by my brother's caustic, cavalier manner. It's scary. I'm lucky in having very amusing brothers, and maybe I've made a point of having close friends who say the kind of things I can use. I believe in just following certain people around with a notebook!

Did he actually say "severed noodles"? It's so funny.

I think I made that up, but the stance was very much him.

Metaphor grows naturally from the story itself, then—the situation, the characters. It's part of your fundamental thinking about the story. "Going," like nearly all of your stories, makes use of a kind of dark humor. One, "Three Popes Walk into a Bar" is actually about stand-up comics. Does humor work the same way as metaphor for you?

I put a premium on it in my life. I have tremendously funny friends. I prize that in people and, reading, I tend to like the really dark humor. Denis Johnson's incredible story, "Emergency." A lot of Mark Richard's work. I spent a lot of time in my twenties in San Francisco hanging out with comics. I'd go to comedy clubs five nights out of the week, and in the course of watching my friends do the same material time after time, I realized how subtle it was. If the emphasis is on this word, you get the laugh; if it's on that word, you don't get the laugh. That was an incredible influence later, when I started writing. This isn't in the story, but I remember watching other comedians or comics watching one another perform. They'd go, "That's funny. That's funny." But they weren't laughing. It's exactly how you read as a writer. You're looking at how the author got the effects. The end of Stephanie Vaughn's "Dog Heaven" always puts me in tears no matter how many times I read it: "It was a good day. It was a good day. It was a good day." I think, how did she make me cry? How brilliant, but how did she *know*?

So, fundamentally, good writing is about paying attention in every kind of way as you go about your day-to-day life.

It's all about paying attention. I often have my students eavesdrop. I ask them to write a sentence that they've overheard and bring it to class. Don't give a context, just say the sentence. I want something that's just slightly skewed from the normal, so that we won't at first understand it. A sentence that has some mystery. I tell them to read their dialogue aloud. Does it sound like people talking or does it sound like somebody making something up, writing about people talking? Dialogue is one of the hardest things for people to do, which is odd because they are always listening to people talk. Why should it be so hard? People clutch up. They think they have to have a kind of elevated speech. So the dialogue they write tends to fall into the formal. Hearing better, that's something I think we can teach.

I often have my students eavesdrop. I ask them to write a sentence that they've overheard and bring it to class.

What can't be taught?

Nerve. Gordon Lish he used to tell his class, "The three things we need: obsession, nerve, the grounds worth recording." You can't make someone say a thing that they're unwilling to say.

Your stories often have a kind of "Chutes and Ladders" effect, deftly moving the reader from one moment to another very different one. Would you talk about how the transitions work in "Going"?

Especially in short-shorts, anything that is not essential goes. I felt I had a little latitude in "Going" because the person narrating had a head injury. So, given that, he could swim around in his thoughts a little more.

So the transitions actually mirror what's happening in the story and what's happening in the person's head. Do transitions come easily for you?

Yes. I'm not a linear thinker in any situation, in any time. So jumping from one thing to the next seems normal to me.

In "Going," as in many of your stories, nothing comes to the reader directly. Would you talk about how you create that balance of humor and seriousness that "crabwalks" the reader toward the truth in your stories.

I like history; I like indirection. In any kind of reminiscence piece, there's a reason the character is recalling something. Often, students forget to indicate what in the present moment makes the character think back. It seems obvious, but this is something that's often missing. A story I always use when teaching is Tillie Olsen's "I Stand Here Ironing." It's beautiful, absolutely gorgeous, and such a heartbreaker. You see in the first line what makes her look back at the history of the daughter's life and the family's life. She opens it up into

There's a reason the character is recalling something. Often, students forget to indicate what in the present moment makes the character think back.

the country's life and the Depression and it just gets bigger and bigger. Then she goes right back to the daughter. A note from the teacher about her daughter is all it takes for her to explain why she can go back into the whole history of this child and this family. It's the thing that sends someone back that always interests me. Everyone has had the experience of hearing a certain song that takes them back. Or an olfactory trigger.

Like the worm smell in "Going." People generally don't write about the way things smell.

You can write just as you can live, from different points of departure. Some people respond to everything from an intellectual base. I don't. I work out of a sensory base.

You can write just as you can live, from different points of departure.

Often, in "Going," sensory triggers bring the narrator right up against something serious. Then he swerves away, usually with a joke

It's a narrative strategy. I really like not hitting a thing head on, but glancing off of it, then coming back and glancing off of it again in another spot. To me, that underscores the power of the central thing, the core of what's going on there. It's so big that you can't face it head on. You have to look at it and look away, look at it and look away. Make a joke about it. But if you *only* did that, it wouldn't be really satisfying. In classes that I teach, people often, often want to be clever. They enjoy being clever on the page. But it's not enough. "Going" ends with that moment where he lets down. That's important.

The power is in just leaving the character—and the reader—with the knowledge of the huge thing, his parents' death. It's there; it resonates. It's absolutely unsentimental. How do you write about real emotion, things that matter, without being sentimental?

I define sentimentality as unearned emotion or inauthentic emotion. Students can often catch it when they lapse into cliché. Also, I love reversals—like in "Going." Making jokes and dodging what the cause of the accident was until he lets down and reverses his stance in the very last lines.

I define sentimentality as unearned emotion or inauthentic emotion.

There's the same kind of movement in "In the Cemetery Where Al Jolson Is Buried," which is a much bigger story and probably the most well known of all your stories.

That was the first story I wrote. It's the most anthologized and the one most translated into foreign languages. I say that to point to what brought that story out. I never would have written about that if it hadn't been an assignment that Gordon Lish gave in a class at Columbia. Write your worst secret, the thing that dismantles your own sense of yourself. Oh, boy. Just what we *really* want to look at! I knew right away what that would be. I felt I had failed my best friend when she was dying. People would say, "Oh, no, you didn't." But I really felt I had. It's a hell of a thing to look at and present to other people, but that was the way I saw it. So "In the Cemetery Where Al Jolson Is Buried" is the story that came out of it.

To what degree is the story on the page autobiographical?

The situation was true. My best friend was dying, and did die. Certainly the emotion is true. There is not, however, a single line in that story the either one of us actually said. It's all about emotion and situation.

Where did the title come from?

My friend had worked in the film industry, and everything there is couched in terms of stars. When I heard where she was buried, I thought, oh, that's perfect. She's buried in the cemetery where Al Jolson is buried. That's how people refer to the cemetery. It's so the way Hollywood is. And I also like the rhythm: The cemetery where Al Jolson is buried. It had a nice feel. It sent a signal to the reader, but didn't give the story away.

You have many good titles.

I like titling. I find the writing very difficult, but titles are fun, first lines are fun, last lines are fun.

Would you talk about the first and last lines? How do they usually come to you?

When I'm attracted to a first line, I make a note of it, and it will stay with me. When an ending occurs to me—and a last line—then I start writing.

When I'm attracted to a first line, I make a note of it, and it will stay with me. When an ending occurs to me—and a last line—then I start writing.

Do you ever get the last line first?

No. First, last, then I can start writing it.

You know where you start, you know where you're going.

I need to know I'm going over . . . *there.* I don't know how. To get the last line doesn't mean I've figured out how to get to that last line. I know this is where it starts, this is where it ends. Now I'll figure out the rest.

What makes a good ending?

John Gardner said endings should be both inevitable and surprising. They should amplify all that came before. Endings are not hard for me. Often, teaching, the real last line of somebody's story just leaps out, and then they go on for another half page or page and a half. When I point it out, they go, "Oh, that's much better!" Usually it's a lack of confidence. They don't give themselves credit for having made the point, having done the right thing, and so they keep on. Or they don't give the reader credit for being smart enough to see things.

What are you mostly surprised by in process?

I'm surprised by logic. I find, when a story is finished, that it's logical in its own terms.

I'm surprised by logic. I find, when a story is finished, that it's logical in its own terms.

Would you call it sensory logic? It's the senses that pull the reader from one thing to the next in your stories.

That's very accurate. Sensory logic, that's a great term. It makes sense to *me.*

Animals appear in many of your stories. In fact, one of your collections is called At the Gates of the Animal Kingdom. *What is it about animals that's so compelling to you?*

The animal stories come from another question that was put to us in class by Gordon Lish. "Where in your life are you most yourself? Can you sound like that on the page?" It's a great question. It's really useful to identify that place. I'm instantly myself with animals. I'm not self-conscious, nothing is extraneous. I'm not encumbered by anything. There's no fear. I am entirely present in the moment. So, okay, how do you sound like that? That's a little harder.

You speak so often of Lish and his influence on you. He is legendary among writers for his unconventional ideas about what writing should be and the passion with which he promoted them. What were the pros and cons to having a mentor like that?

For me, only pros. I knew that if anybody could get me to become a creative writer it would be him. I was reading everything contemporary, starting back in the early '70s, and every time I read a story that just turned on the lights for me, he had published the writer—either in *Esquire* or, later, at Knopf. So I felt entirely aligned with his take, especially in short fiction. I still run stuff by him. He's an amazing teacher.

Your common interest in unconventional fiction is obvious. "Tom-rock Through the Eels" is, essentially, a list of the mothers the narrator most remembers from her girlhood and what she remembers about them. She talks very little about her own mother, yet there's such longing in the story, so much implied about what her mother was not. How did you come upon that device, and what makes it work?

The story is certainly empowered by longing. When I moved to New York, I wrote the bulk of the California story. I was yearning for the West Coast, for everything about it. When I was actually living there, I didn't write about it. It was listing;

I was adding them up, accumulating the power of all these little ideas of the ideal mother, making an ideal mother from what was around me.

again, little defining moments. I was adding them up, accumulating the power of all these little ideas of the ideal mother, making an ideal mother from what was around me.

Mothers, the idea of mothering, is an idea you look at again and again in your work. In fact, there's a description of the mother's body, how it looked in death, in "Tom-rock Through the Eels" that is used again—verbatim—in your novella, Tumble Home. *Most students would think, "I can't do that. It's cheating." But you did it.*

I saw a lot of writers who did that and I figured, well, I can do it, too. I came to a place in the novella where I recognized the need to describe the position of her body. I thought it seemed dumb to resay it in a different way just to say it in a different way, when the way I had already said it was the right way. We do often tell the same story. We turn it this way, we turn it that way. We're coming at it up here or down there.

What is that story for you?

I think mine is, largely, how do you survive now—and that can be anything. How do you get to this? How do you understand what happened to you? How do you continue? Sometimes it is how do we know what happens to us isn't good? Sometimes it is I'm going to die for love.

Grief is always in the mix.

There's been a lot of it in my life, but it's in everybody's life. It's always there, for everyone. I've only written a couple of stories where people have everything they want and are perfectly happy.

What do you get from looking at grief up close?

I'll answer that with something Raymond Carver said. "It's what I can do."

The happiness in those couple of stories you mentioned is seen against something darker. The narrator in "The Day I Had Everything" tells the story of a party being thrown for a woman about to have surgery for breast cancer. Everyone there is unhappy about something. It's a courageous act, at the end, to say, "I met someone. I'm happy. I'm probably in love."

That story started with a real party for somebody who was going in for surgery. This was years ago, in Berkeley. It wasn't a gloomy affair at all. It was very upbeat, and I was moved by how supportive everyone was, that it was *fun.* I remember thinking how odd it was that you felt you should hide the things that were going really well for you. It felt unseemly to be pleased with your own life at a moment like that. But the beautiful thing in the real situation, the thing that moved me to write the story was that, in fact, no matter how unpleasant or frightening some situations, you were happy in your own happiness. It's darker in the story, but even though there was some bitterness and some anger in the characters, they rallied in genuine gladness for good news.

That brings to mind the narrator of "Beg, Sl Tog, Inc, Cont, Rep," who says, "The worst of it is over now, and I can't say that I am glad. Lose that sense of loss, you have gone and lost something else." How does this apply to the writer and her material?

I wrote that and then I read this wonderful poem by Sharon Olds, ["After 37 Years My Mother Apologizes for My Childhood,"] with the line, "I hardly knew . . . who I would be now that I had forgiven you." There it is said more eloquently than I could ever say it. What I was trying to get at is that when you lose something, even a bad thing, it redefines you.

And with that redefinition comes a shift in the way you see your material.

You do what Mark Doty described. "When you look at a thing long enough, it takes you over and eventually the thing you're looking at becomes the lens through which you see the world." That's what happens. William Maxwell has written two stories, both about mother figures, about thirty years apart. I think that's so interesting. I wish every writer would do that—write the same story again, years later

Right now I'm putting together a class I'm going to do at Columbia, based on a kind of call and response: stories that were written to answer other stories or poems. My story "Today Will Be a Quiet Day" is really a response to Mary Robison's story "Widower." I love the idea that there can be continuity and conversation between stories—your own and the stories of other writers.

The father in that story is so compelling. He's so honest with his children and at the same time so tender.

That's my father. It's funny. There's no mention of the mother in that story, but some reviewers refer to the divorced father and some refer to the widowed father. That's absolutely what *they're* bringing to it.

Why did you leave any mention of the mother out of the story?

It wasn't important.

The father's relationship with the children is so . . . there. He'd be that same father regardless of who or where their mother is.

Exactly. *Exactly.*

What you wanted the reader to look at was the man.

Right. The mother's just not there. It's another reversal of expectation. It reverses again, at the end of the story. The kids are bracing for the bad news and I thought, oh, wouldn't it be an incredible gift for there not to be bad news just for that one moment.

But there's so much implied in his response to the daughter's request to hear the bad news first. The fact that she knows there's bad news out there to be heard and she's prepared herself for it make him think she's okay.

I dedicated my third book to my brothers. I didn't tell them I was going to do it, and when I handed them each a finished book I watched them turn to the page. I got to watch their expressions as they saw the dedication. Almost instantly, one of them turned to me and said, "What did you do in here that you had to dedicate this to me?"

Prepared for the bad news, right?

That makes it sound like I'm having a hard life, and it's not that at all.

But you are curious about bad news, yours and the bad news of others. Maybe curiosity is the most important thing for writers, after all.

Yes. But most people are curious about the Roman Empire or Vermeer—or whatever. Writers' curiosity is more like this: You don't know it until you see it. It's situational. You'll see a person or overhear a conversation and then you'll become curious around something you never could have predicted.

Writers' curiosity is more like this: You don't know it until you see it. It's situational.

Writing Prompts

READ: "Going" and the interview with **Amy Hempel.**

PONDER: How Hempel uses humor and reversals to bring the reader to the last line in which the narrator reveals his emotional state and brings insight to how he ended up in the hospital because of an automobile accident.

WRITE: A scene that is the aftermath of an event that is linked to the narrator's emotional state. Don't name the narrator's emotional state or let the reader know the reason for it until the last line.

PRACTICE:

- Identify a defining moment in the life of a character and write it in three pages or less.
- Make a list of defining moments around an important relationship in your life. Order those moments to make a story.
- Write a story about a character for whom a bad experience turns out to have a single positive consequence.
- Write a story in a single sentence.
- Create an olfactory trigger and write the memory that comes of it.

- Write a scene in which two equally appealing characters are at odds about something that really matters to both of them—and both of them are right.
- Eavesdrop in a public place. Listen to a sentence that is slightly skewed from the normal, slightly mysterious. Then invent a dialogue that includes it.
- Write your worst secret, the thing that dismantles your sense of yourself. Then use it to write a story that may or may not be autobiographical.
- Where in your life are you most yourself? Can you sound like that on the page?
- List all of the senses in "Going" besides sight.
- Write about something or someone you lost and how that loss redefined you.
- Write a story in response to a story you admire.

Pam Houston

Pam Houston (b. 1962) is the author of two collections of short stories, a novel, and a memoir. Born in Trenton, New Jersey, she was educated at Denison College and the University of Utah. Her honors include the Western States Book Award and the Willa Cather Award for Contemporary Fiction. Her stories have been selected for The Best American Short Stories, The O. Henry Prize Stories, The Pushcart Prize: Best of the Small Presses, *and* The Best American Short Stories of the Century. *She teaches in the graduate writing program at the University of California at Davis and at many summer writers' conferences and festivals in the United States and abroad. She lives in Davis, California, and in Colorado, near the headwaters of the Rio Grande.*

For Further Reading:
Cowboys Are My Weakness: Stories (1992), *Waltzing the Cat* (1998), *A Little Bit More About Me* (1999), *Sight Hound* (2005).

How to Talk to a Hunter

When he says "Skins or blankets?" it will take you a moment to realize that he's asking which you want to sleep under. And in your hesitation he'll decide that he wants to see your skin wrapped in the big black moose hide. He carried it, he'll say, soaking wet and heavier than a dead man, across the tundra for two—was it hours or days or weeks? But the payoff, now, will be to see it fall across one of your white breasts. It's December, and your skin is never really warm, so you will pull the bulk of it around you and pose for him, pose for his camera, without having to narrate this moose's death.

You will spend every night in this man's bed without asking yourself why he listens to top-forty country. Why he donated money to the Republican Party. Why he won't play back his messages while you are in the room. You are there so often the messages pile up. Once you noticed the bright green counter reading as high as fifteen.

He will have lured you here out of a careful independence that you spent months cultivating; though it will finally be winter, the dwindling daylight and the threat of

Christmas, that makes you give in. Spending nights with this man means suffering the long face of your sheepdog, who likes to sleep on your bed, who worries when you don't come home. But the hunter's house is so much warmer than yours, and he'll give you a key, and just like a woman, you'll think that means something. It will snow hard for thirteen straight days. Then it will really get cold. When it is sixty below there will be no wind and no clouds, just still air and cold sunshine. The sun on the windows will lure you out of bed, but he'll pull you back under. The next two hours he'll devote to your body. With his hands, with his tongue, he'll express what will seem to you like the most eternal of loves. Like the house key, this is just another kind of lie. Even in bed; especially in bed, you and he cannot speak the same language. The machine will answer the incoming calls. From under an ocean of passion and hide and hair you'll hear a woman's muffled voice between the beeps.

Your best female friend will say, "So what did you think? That a man who sleeps under a dead moose is capable of commitment?"

This is what you learned in college: A man desires the satisfaction of his desire; a woman desires the condition of desiring.

The hunter will talk about spring in Hawaii, summer in Alaska. The man who says he was always better at math will form the sentences so carefully it will be impossible to tell if you are included in these plans. When he asks you if you would like to open a small guest ranch way out in the country, understand that this is a rhetorical question. Label these conversations future perfect, but don't expect the present to catch up with them. Spring is an inconceivable distance from the December days that just keep getting shorter and gray.

He'll ask you if you've ever shot anything, if you'd like to, if you ever thought about teaching your dog to retrieve. Your dog will like him too much, will drop the stick at his feet every time, will roll over and let the hunter scratch his belly.

One day he'll leave you sleeping to go split wood or get the mail and his phone will ring again. You'll sit very still while a woman who calls herself something like Janie Coyote leaves a message on his machine: She's leaving work, she'll say, and the last thing she wanted to hear was the sound of his beautiful voice. Maybe she'll talk only in rhyme. Maybe the counter will change to sixteen. You'll look a question at the mule deer on the wall, and the dark spots on either side of his mouth will tell you he shares more with this hunter than you ever will. One night, drunk, the hunter told you he was sorry for taking that deer, that every now and then there's an animal that isn't meant to be taken, and he should have known that deer was one.

Your best male friend will say, "No one who needs to call herself Janie Coyote can hold a candle to you, but why not let him sleep alone a few nights, just to make sure?"

The hunter will fill your freezer with elk burger, venison sausage, organic potatoes, fresh pecans. He'll tell you to wear your seat belt, to dress warmly, to drive safely. He'll say you are always on his mind, that you're the best thing that's ever happened to him, that you make him glad that he's a man.

Tell him it don't come easy, tell him freedom's just another word for nothing left to lose.

These are the things you'll know without asking: The coyote woman wears her hair in braids. She uses words like "howdy." She's man enough to shoot a deer.

A week before Christmas you'll rent *It's a Wonderful Life* and watch it together, curled on your couch, faces touching. Then you'll bring up the word "monogamy." He'll tell you how badly he was hurt by your predecessor. He'll tell you he couldn't be happier spending every night with you. He'll say there's just a few questions he doesn't have the answers for. He'll say he's just scared and confused. Of course this isn't exactly what he means. Tell him you understand. Tell him you are scared too. Tell him to take all the time he needs. Know that you could never shoot an animal; and be glad of it.

Your best female friend will say, "You didn't tell him you loved him, did you?" Don't even tell her the truth. If you do you'll have to tell her that he said this: "I feel exactly the same way."

Your best male friend will say, "Didn't you know what would happen when you said the word 'commitment'?"

But that isn't the word that you said.

He'll say, "Commitment, monogamy, it all means just one thing."

The coyote woman will come from Montana with the heavier snows. The hunter will call you on the day of the solstice to say he has a friend in town and can't see you. He'll leave you hanging your Christmas lights; he'll give new meaning to the phrase "longest night of the year." The man who has said he's not so good with words will manage to say eight things about his friend without using a gender-determining pronoun. Get out of the house quickly. Call the most understanding person you know who will let you sleep in his bed.

Your best female friend will say, "So what did you think? That he was capable of living outside his gender?"

When you get home in the morning there's a candy tin on your pillow. Santa, obese and grotesque, fondles two small children on the lid. The card will say something like "From your not-so-secret admirer." Open it. Examine each carefully made truffle. Feed them, one at a time, to the dog. Call the hunter's machine. Tell him you don't speak chocolate.

Your best female friend will say, "At this point, what is it about him that you could possibly find appealing?"

Your best male friend will say, "Can't you understand that this is a good sign? Can't you understand that this proves how deep he's in with you?" Hug your best male friend. Give him the truffles the dog wouldn't eat.

Of course the weather will cooperate with the coyote woman. The highways will close, she will stay another night. He'll tell her he's going to work so he can come and see you.

He'll even leave her your number and write "Me at Work" on the yellow pad of paper by his phone. Although you shouldn't, you'll have to be there. It will be you and your nauseous dog and your half-trimmed tree all waiting for him like a series of questions.

This is what you learned in graduate school: In every assumption is contained the possibility of its opposite.

In your kitchen he'll hug you like you might both die there. Sniff him for coyote. Don't hug him back.

He will say whatever he needs to to win. He'll say it's just an old friend. He'll say the visit was all the friend's idea. He'll say the night away from you has given him time to think about how much you mean to him. Realize that nothing short of sleeping alone will ever make him realize how much you mean to him. He'll say that if you can just be a little patient, some good will come out of this for the two of you after all. He still won't use a gender-specific pronoun.

Put your head in your hands. Think about what it means to be patient. Think about the beautiful, smart, strong, clever woman you thought he saw when he looked at you. Pull on your hair. Rock your body back and forth. Don't cry.

He'll say that after holding you it doesn't feel right holding anyone else. For "holding," substitute "fucking." Then take it as a compliment.

He will get frustrated and rise to leave. He may or may not be bluffing. Stall for time. Ask a question he can't immediately answer. Tell him you want to make love on the floor. When he tells you your body is beautiful say, "I feel exactly the same way." Don't, under any circumstances, stand in front of the door.

Your best female friend will say, "They lie to us, they cheat on us, and we love them more for it." She'll say, "It's our fault; we raise them to be like that."

Tell her it can't be your fault. You've never raised anything but dogs.

The hunter will say it's late and he has to go home to sleep. He'll emphasize the last word in the sentence. Give him one kiss that he'll remember while he's fucking the coyote woman. Give him one kiss that ought to make him cry if he's capable of it, but don't notice when he does. Tell him to have a good night.

Your best male friend will say, "We all do it. We can't help it. We're self-destructive. It's the old bad-boy routine. You have a male dog, don't you?"

The next day the sun will be out and the coyote woman will leave. Think about how easy it must be for a coyote woman and a man who listens to top-forty country. The coyote woman would never use a word like "monogamy"; the coyote woman will stay gentle on his mind.

If you can, let him sleep alone for at least one night. If you can't, invite him over to finish trimming your Christmas tree. When he asks how you are, tell him you think it's a good idea to keep your sense of humor during the holidays.

Plan to be breezy and aloof and full of interesting anecdotes about all the other men you've ever known. Plan to be hotter than ever before in bed, and a little cold out of it. Remember that necessity is the mother of invention. Be flexible.

First, he will find the faulty bulb that's been keeping all the others from lighting. He will explain, in great detail, the most elementary electrical principles. You will take turns placing the ornaments you and other men, he and other women, have spent years carefully choosing. Under the circumstances, try to let this be a comforting thought.

He will thin the clusters of tinsel you put on the tree. He'll say something ambiguous like "Next year you should string popcorn and cranberries." Finally, his arm will stretch just high enough to place the angel on the top of the tree.

Your best female friend will say, "Why can't you ever fall in love with a man who will be your friend?"

Your best male friend will say, "You ought to know this by now: Men always cheat on the best women."

This is what you learned in the pop psychology book: Love means letting go of fear.

Play Willie Nelson's "Pretty Paper." He'll ask you to dance, and before you can answer he'll be spinning you around your wood stove, he'll be humming in your ear. Before the song ends he'll be taking off your clothes, setting you lightly under the tree, hovering above you with tinsel in his hair. Through the spread of the branches the all-white lights you insisted on will shudder and blur, outlining the ornaments he brought: a pheasant, a snow goose, a deer.

The record will end. Above the crackle of the wood stove and the rasp of the hunter's breathing you'll hear one long low howl break the quiet of the frozen night: your dog, chained and lonely and cold. You'll wonder if he knows enough to stay in his doghouse. You'll wonder if he knows that the nights are getting shorter now.

A Conversation with Pam Houston

"How to Talk to a Hunter," the first story in your first book, Cowboys Are My Weakness, *establishes the "bad boys/smart girls" theme that is prevalent in much of your early work. It has in it, too, other hallmarks of your work: the funny, sensible voice of a good female friend, a loyal dog, the yearning to be cherished, to feel at home, the disconnect between men and women, the gap between what we know, intellectually, and how we are actually able to live. What was the genesis of that story, how did it evolve?*

I had just read "Self-Help" and I love it, so I was trying to write my Lorrie Moore story, basically, as a graduate student experimenting. I say that to students: Try imitating. I wish *I'd* had a teacher that said that. But anyhow, I was doing it—with no thought of it ever being published. Unlike every story I've ever written, I wrote it in one sitting and I changed very little. It was sort of a gift-from-the-gods story. That was at a time when everyone said, "Pam writes eleven days behind her life." Almost everything in it actually happened, and I came home and wrote it down, pretty much all in one holiday malaise rush. I kind of puked it up. I honestly can't tell you what the initial push was to write it—whether it was the question "skins or blankets" or the fact of the coyote woman. When I think about its form—the Lorrie Moore kind of second-person element of it, the cadence, the best girlfriend, the best boyfriend, and the dog—the people who weigh in in the story—well, in a way, that's how it feels to be twenty-seven, which is how old I was when I wrote the story. The idea that life is sort of coming at you and people are telling you "No, you should do this, you should do that." It feels very authentic to my life at the time. And taking into account how absolutely stupid my narrator was about her own personal life through this entire book, I really feel in the last lines of that story the first sliver of understanding—that she at some point is going to have to take responsibility for her own life. She begins to see the things that will feed her rather than the things that will hurt her. But it's a lot of pages before she gets anywhere near that!

Were there any surprises when you were writing the story?

In all of my own stories that I still feel good about and that I most value, there's always a ton of surprises. A surprise is what identifies a short story for me as a really worthwhile endeavor. If I do manage to write a story that doesn't surprise me at all, I hope I have the sense to throw it away or put it away until one day when it might. One of the things that surprised me about this story was the insertion of all the philosophies. I wasn't trying to impress my theory teacher; they seemed to fit. Then pop psychology. Someone had given me, pathetically, *Love Means Letting Go of Fear* at the time. It's not the kind of thing you want to admit, but I read it—and it worked into the story.

There's a line I especially like: "Why can't you ever fall in love with a man who will be your friend?" I didn't really have a best female friend who was saying these wise things then, and I realized that the best female friend was my own wise voice, which had nothing to do with the way I was living at the time.

The whole story was a surprise, in the sense that it was the first story that I ever made in the way that I have come to make stories all the time now, by taking what I call "glimmers," chunks of the physical universe that seem to speak to each other and putting them down on the page. "How to Talk to a Hunter" has a lot of double-double spaces that aren't filled in between the various elements of the story, and that has become the way I write now—even if the finished story doesn't look like this on the page. I just pull all these things together. I don't worry about the order at all. Now it's second nature to me. It's what I do as an artist. But at the time, I had no idea of what I was doing.

Do the stories usually end up in the order they come out?

No. I move chunks around for hours. I spend more time moving than I spend writing.

After all these years, do you still like "How to Talk to a Hunter"?

Yes, I do like it. I remain committed to it in a way that I'm not to some of the stories in *Cowboys Are My Weakness.*

Your graduate school experimentation with second-person voice turned out so well in that story. It's a voice that students are attracted to, but their experimentations with it don't usually turn out as well as yours did. What do you think is the greatest mistake writers make when they want to use the second person?

I don't know that more of them go wrong with second-person stories than with first person. I think certain voice and certain stories lend themselves to that point of view. That's why Lorrie Moore is so successful at it, her voice lends itself to it. I'm a fan of the second person. One reason is that the second person is the first person who's ashamed of herself. She's a narrator who's afraid to say 'I.' The second person takes this layer of shame and washes it over the story without her having to say "I am ashamed." It's a kind of diversion—it's not me, it's you. It's unbelievable that we can fool ourselves so easily. The other reason that I like second person and don't discourage my students from writing in it is that it's such an American way to tell a story. "So, you know, you're in this bar and this guy comes up to you . . ." It's the rhythm of American storytelling. We do it all the time, conversationally. So, the fact that a lot of writers get uppity about it and say that it's an invalid method is a kind of elitism.

I'm a fan of the second person. One reason is that the second person is the first person who's ashamed of herself. She's a narrator who's afraid to say 'I.'

Interesting that this experimentation led you to a big breakthrough in terms of seeing for the first time how the creative process would work for you.

I wrote a story before "How to Talk to a Hunter" called "Whole," which was a little bit the same. I couldn't tell you what it was about because I wrote it twenty years ago, but if I were being completely honest, I would say that *that* story was the first time I caught a glimpse of that process. It wasn't a successful story, but it was my first attempt at that form. It got thrown out of this book *Cowboys Are My Weakness.* I don't think it was ever published, but it had its moments, and I see it as the beginning of me figuring out how it was best for me to make stories. "How to Talk to a Hunter" was certainly the first time that I really *committed* to this idea. There are a lot of different metaphors I can think of to describe it. It's like a weave—the best girlfriend, the best female friend, what's going on with the dog, what's going on with Coyote Woman—all of these pieces that don't have a narrative line driving behind them but are bouncing off each other, metaphorically, rhythmically. There's an essential plot line: Jane Coyote comes, she leaves.

This story, ten years later, is "The Best Girlfriend You Never Had." In those two stories, I think I'm honoring my own esthetic. I'm doing what I claim to do in a kind of pure way. Now, "Selway," which happens to come next in the collection [*Waltzing the Cat*], doesn't *look* like those stories. You have a put-in and take-out on the river and you have that narrative line of "here comes the next rapid." You cannot avoid the narrative line of that story. Or the hurricane story—you can't avoid it. But I still made it the same way. I said, OK, what happened in that hurricane? But I didn't *write* it in a line.

Sometimes, particularly in "The Best Girlfriend You Never Had," which I do remember writing, I was willfully not making any connective material. If you look at that story, it begins fifteen times and ends fifteen times. The artificial narrative line is the day, the opening line is "A perfect day in the city always starts like this." But that came very, very, late to the writing process. All the other pieces were there, and it was my goal to see how many disparate objects I could juggle in the story. Juggling is another metaphor I use to think about this process. I love it best when a juggler juggles a toaster, a chain saw, and an apple! That's what writing that story was like for me—trying to see how many objects that are not like each other can fit into one story and still cohere in some way.

That's what writing that story was like for me—trying to see how many objects that are not like each other can fit into one story and still cohere in some way.

This story has the feel of a jump-cut in film. Do you think of it that way?

I hadn't thought about it "filmically." What I do think of is photo ops. It's like flipping through photographs. I think of them as little glimmers, too. Things in the world that glimmer in a way that say, "Are you writing? Hel-lo? Are you paying attention?" It could be a terrible thing or a wonderful thing. I certainly don't mean to assign value by saying "glimmer," just that these are things that go "Whooooo" and you go "Ohhhhh!"

If one of those glimmers holds somewhere in your peripheral vision for a while, do you know it's going to fall into a story at some time?

Yeah, I think that's true.

How do you keep up with the glimmers? Do you keep folders? Files?

Until about two years ago, I had a pretty good memory, but then I turned forty. I used to be able to remember, but I just can't anymore. So I think now I'll be more rigorous about writing down— oh, this happened and that happened—several times a week. I think I will keep a "glimmer" file!

These glimmers, how do they most often appear to you?

I think that there are things in the physical world—and I include in that conversations, atmosphere, light in the trees—that resonate with some sort of deep emotion. I want to say pain, but it's not always pain. It's emotion that wants to be expressed, some truth that I have not yet been able to articulate either because of fear, or not understanding the language for it, or it being too complicated, too contradictory, or multiple to articulate. Somehow that thing in the world—whether it's a dog, three lines of dialogue, a boat, or the way a mother is treating a child, whatever it is—glows because it's an articulation of something.

Really, you're talking about metaphor.

Of course, I am. There's a deep emotional reason something glimmers. The diversion through the physical world makes it accessible and palatable. Happily it's what the reader wants, too. We can so much more tell the truth about it when it's made into a part of the physical world.

Sort of putting a distance between you and the deep emotional thing?

Yeah. You can be more honest about it. The minute your analytical brain starts to work on it, forget it. It's not fiction anymore, it's not art anymore; it's therapy. You're just trying to protect yourself. Using the diversion of it in the physical world, you can lie to yourself and say I'm not talking about me, I'm talking about that baseball. I feel like so much of writing is tricking my analytical brain into the closet. I have a very good analytical brain and I'm happy for it, but during writing, everything is absolutely about shutting her down and locking her up. It's back to surprise. The analytical brain does not like surprises and once she's in charge of a story, that story is not going anywhere.

The analytical brain does not like surprises and once she's in charge of a story, that story is not going anywhere.

One of the reasons I focus so much on the physical world when I write and the reason that I employ metaphor so much—that's my entire focus when I'm writing—is that I believe so much in the "glimmering." I have absolute faith that if I can write it well enough, the emotional truth that made it glimmer will distill out of it.

For the reader?

Yes, but also for me. I don't necessarily know why something is glimmering, but I can imagine.

Would you talk about your story "Waltzing the Cat" in terms of the relationship between the central metaphor of the story and the emotional truth of the story?

I have to tell you that that cat started out as a cat. Not a metaphor at all. That cat exists—or did.

What were the glimmers there?

The big glimmer in that story, the seminal glimmer, was after my mother's funeral. My father and I were back at the house and I was thinking, oh, my God, we will have to cope with each other without my mother in the middle. I was doing things around the kitchen. We weren't even looking at each other. And I heard him say, "I love you so much." That was not something that he had ever said to me, and I turned and he had the cat. That was the absolute beginning of the story. There was no waltzing. I added the waltzing.

That was the obvious end for that glimmer.

Yeah, but there were lots of things. It's also true—and isn't this the writer's life? You are at your mother's funeral and you are writing a story. My father had paid his $2,000 or whatever to have my mother's ashes put in this little round garden. It's starting to rain and my mother's going into the ground and he says to the priest, "So, really there's no limit to the number of people you could put in there." The priest said, "Oh, two or three hundred thousand, I guess." And I knew what my father was thinking—$2,000! He was talking about money. I just knew. It was such a moment. My mother was going into the ground, and I was thinking this is my family!

I just knew. It was such a moment. My mother was going into the ground, and I was thinking this is my family!

Aside from the waltzing, what else did you invent for the story?

Everything to do with music. I never volunteered at a homeless shelter. And Leo, frankly, wasn't there when I got the news.

Is the Leo in the story the architect of the same name in "The Best Girlfriend You Never Had"?

No, he's a different Leo. That's all sort of . . . invented. He never mowed my lawn!

In terms of craft, what's left out of the story is as interesting as what's left in it. The funeral, for example. Why didn't you include it? How do you know what can and should be left out of a story?

I went through that whole event in shock. I look back and think, funeral? The only thing I remember was having to give my little talk and thinking about halfway through it that it wasn't very complimentary. When I wrote the story, I probably wasn't ready to admit that. Also, it appeals to me to leave out the most obvious event. Though, in this case, I just don't think it glimmered. This story, in a way, is not about the funeral at all. It's about the cat. It's about the displacement of love. To answer the question more generally, you leave out what's generic. If nothing happened that's of interest, you leave it out.

To answer the question more generally, you leave out what's generic. If nothing happened that's of interest, you leave it out.

Generally, how do stories gather and evolve for you?

I have a sense that I have a rich metaphorical field. For example, I went on a cruise with my father through the Panama Canal. A cruise ship, as awful as it is, is an extremely rich metaphorical field. Especially since this one was going through the Panama Canal, which is *itself* a rich metaphorical field. The very idea of cutting a continent in half! Birth canal, me with my father. Absolutely! There are so many absurd things that happen on a cruise ship and a lot of them are physically represented—pumpkins carved into the heads of the ethnicities of the foods that are being served that evening. I had dinner with a guy—we were on the equator and there was this amazing, amazing sunset. At dinner, with these strangers, we asked if they had watched the sunset and they said that they had watched it on TV. There's a camera that's mounted on the back of the ship and they sat in their room with a balcony and watched this amazing sunset on TV! So I come home from a cruise, with a file in the computer that's called "cruise absurdities." One hundred and twenty-seven of them! That's what I call a rich metaphorical field. For me, that's how it works.

So how will a story emerge?

I will take each one of these and write them to their length and then leave them alone awhile. Then there's this juggling act of where they all go. Of course, you lose some along the way and you invent some out of thin air. These are my chunks: carved heads, man who watched sunset on TV, DJ Doug in the Stratosphere Lounge. Granted, the cruise was seven years ago and I'd be doing a lot of inventing. Usually I write quicker after an event. But I have my list.

How do you know which chunks are going to show up in the story?

I don't. People always say, "Oh, your characters, your characters." But my characters are so secondary to this process that I'm describing. In one of these scenes from the cruise, I was sitting in a lounge chair and my horrible father was sitting beside me. The only woman on the cruise ship who was under sixty came up to me and said, "Hi, where are you from?" I turned to start talking to her and my father stood—he's ninety-two—and he said, "What kind of a daughter would turn her back on her father?" So, all of a sudden, I've got a father. And there was this pool with fountains and this crazy German woman. She'd get into the hot tub that was on this platform in the middle of the pool and hump the bubbles. In fact, that's the working title of the story: "Humping the Jets." Everywhere she was, I was. She wore these really flowing dresses with these big plastic flowers pinned to them and she would disrobe at any excuse. When we got into the locks of the Panama Canal, she was out there waving to the Greek sailors. I try not to think this far in advance about things like this, but she's the ghost of my dead mother come back to be on this cruise with my father and me in the story that will eventually come out of all of this. I'll write everything about her and in the process some other woman who was in the scarf-tying class might get folded into her. The characters grow out of the glimmers.

Nearly all your stories, one way or another, involve women and sexuality. You articulate desire and need, the enjoyment of sex without being lascivious about it. Where does that fit into the mix?

It may boil down to my attitude toward sex. It's not that big a deal to me. I like it a lot, but I also really like skiing. I really like horses and travel. It's not fraught and weighted in my life and it isn't in my fiction. It's another thing that my characters do and it's equal to every other thing. I don't think, Oh, I'm writing sex now! If sex was in the glimmer, then there it is. If peaches were in the glimmer, then they'd be there, too.

There's so much that I don't think about when I write. I think about the glimmers. I try to write into them as far as they will go until they start to become boring. Often when I start to write the glimmer, it will start to do a thing that it didn't really do in real life and the surprise is there already. When I'm writing a story, I'm a trained observer, a recorder of these things in the world that have suggested themselves to me. I don't think about character or plot. I don't think about whether I'm being a good feminist or a bad feminist or whether I'm representing women in any way at all. I don't think until very late in the game how the story going to work out.

When I'm writing a story, I'm a trained observer, a recorder of these things in the world that have suggested themselves to me. I don't think about character or plot.

Your second collection of stories, Waltzing the Cat, *is a cycle of stories about a single character, a photographer named Lucy O'Rourke. Would you talk about how these stories are different from the ones in* Cowboys Are My Weakness?

I think, quite honestly, I'm never going to write a usual collection of short stories. In a way, both collections are story cycles. I was writing the stories in *Cowboys Are My Weakness* when I had no idea how to write. I was reading, I was in grad classes, and I was certainly engaged in the pursuit of learning how to write. But I had no consciousness of my own process. In some ways, that's a good thing. That's a moment in a writer's career, a really great moment, before you become self-conscious and recognize your own tricks. When I was writing these stories, I really thought they were all different. I know that sounds idiotic, but I did. I thought, I'm writing all these different stories about all these different women who bear no relationship to each other. At some point, I remember my editor saying, "Where are we going to leave her? We've got to get her somewhere." Then it was not hard to realize that she was she and she was me. Really, this was a story cycle.

Do you think these story cycles happen because you are so much a daughter of place?

What my editor would say—and I've had the same editor for everything—is that's why I have to write stories and not novels, because I'm so peripatetic. That came up in the novel I just finished. Carol kept saying, "She can't move around." But I'm so driven by place. I'm not willing to say that what actually happened in Tibet happened in southeastern Colorado. I won't do it. So I think that's both why the characters stay consistent and why a novel is difficult.

Why didn't Waltzing the Cat *become a novel?*

Certain reviewers called it a novel. I'm not invested in what people call it.

But this new book is actually a novel, though.

Yeah. But I started out thinking of it as stories. I envisioned twelve stories from these twelve narrators, all around a series of related events. I wrote about eighty pages of it and ran up against the problem of time. I realized that I wanted the characters to be able to speak again. Even though I should have been able to do this, they couldn't say everything they needed to say and remain fixed at one point in the story. Anyway, I got frustrated. So imagined a two-tier book of short stories with twenty-four stories where everyone got to speak twice. But by the time I got to the third tier and had thirty-six stories, I thought, hey, wait! This must be what they mean when they say "novel." This was such a slow dawning and I was so dense about it.

The stories in Waltzing the Cat *take the character, Lucy, through a phase in which the reader sees her finally learning a lot of the lessons suggested by the lives of the characters in* Cowboys Are My Weakness. *Your own life lessons, too.*

There was some resistance to *Waltzing the Cat* from my editor and my agent. They felt that the audience would not be the same as for *Cowboys Are My Weakness.* Dopey as this may sound, I feel that I'm here on earth to work my shit out—and so what I hope is that, coincidentally with that, my narrators will get a little better at working their own shit out. It's certainly true in book four. Rae, the main character, is further along. Still struggling, still trying to figure it out, but in a better place than Lucy, a better place than hunter-woman.

So writing fiction is a way of looking at yourself, growing, moving forward.

You know that Cathy Bates movie where she wraps up in cellophane? *Fried Green Tomatoes?* I guess I feel that that's kind of the process of my life. I think that cowboys are my weakness, and then I discover, oh, no, they're not. There's a constant unwrapping of all these partial truths, trying to get deeper. I think, I *thought* that was true, but it's not—not the whole truth. Writing is a huge part of that, and there are other parts too, like walking around with my dogs, thinking. There's therapy, there's being with friends. But writing fiction is a huge part of reorganizing events so that I can understand them better.

But writing fiction is a huge part of reorganizing events so that I can understand them better.

Music shows up a lot in your work. Where does it fit in the process?

Music is extremely important to me and to my life. I owe so much of who I became as a writer to the music I listened to as a young person. My first Jackson Brown album sort of explained myself to me in ways that I didn't have words for. The sound track for *Waltzing the Cat* is the Counting Crows album "August and Everything After." Music is really integrated in how I move through the world and, therefore, for obvious reasons, it's important to my characters, too. A lot of times in the assembling of the glimmers and the decisions about where the glimmers go, I think of it rhythmically. I think of a kind of cadence. Often the titles of songs or lyrics of songs become another thread, another kind of downbeat in the cadence of like pieces repeating every third or fourth chunk.

Dialogue is part of cadence, too. Talk about that.

I like to think about dialogue as two people with competing agendas. I am always saying to my students, "People never talk to each other, they never listen." The key to understanding dialogue is remembering that it's a great opportunity for tension in a story.

Your stories always have great first lines. How do you find them?

I have a sense of wanting to start strong when I'm moving all the pieces around. But the first line could be written anywhere in the process. Several times in my storywriting life, what turned out to be the first chunk came very late in the process.

Titles?

Sometimes they just come to me. Most often I find them in the text—three or four words strung together that suggest themselves when I'm just reading and looking for a title. After the fact. Sometimes, actually, a title will suggest itself before I have any idea where the story is. That's rare.

Your book of essays, A Little Bit More About Me *came out very close to publication of* Waltzing the Cat *and uses a lot of the same material. Would you talk about the relationship between those two books?*

I was writing both books at the same time, and in many places they do talk to the same issues. The idea of home and what that means, learning how to take responsibility for your own life, coming to terms with who I am as opposed to who I might want to be. I like *A Little Bit More About Me* and I'm glad that it exists. But I don't feel about it . . . like a book. Almost all the pieces were all written for something else. If somebody pays me to write an article or personal essay for a magazine, then I'll say okay. When I think about writing nonfiction, I think *pay.* This is what I do for money. I teach for money, I give a talk for money. But when I'm in this oh-this-may-never-work-out-and-I-can-do-anything-I-want space, that means fiction.

The essay, "In Bhutan There Is No Way to Be Famous" brings so many of your personal issues full circle and makes readers heave a sigh of relief as you begin to see yourself as the person we've known you could be all along. There's this beautiful Buddhist wrestling all through your work, fiction and nonfiction, such honesty, such yearning to get it right, such willingness to go back at it again and again, each time spiraling deeper into your material. "Epilogue," the last story in Waltzing the Cat, is a reflection of the idea that a writer's best work is made directly from that kind of wrestling. In it, considering her work as a photographer, Lucy observes, "The world's greatest work is all self-portraiture, the artist as subway, as mountain, as sky."

That line was a surprise when I wrote it. I'm not sure about the tone of that statement: I don't know whether it was defensive or relieved. The year that I wrote that story, I was teaching in Provincetown with a visual artist who has devoted her entire life to making half-sized images of herself. She has an optic nerve guy who does the eyes, and the fingers move. I never spoke to her, but seeing her work and hearing her talk about her work made me realize, this is what I do.

I don't think of myself as an imaginative person. I think of myself as a very keen observer.

I was on a panel with Sherman Alexie around that time and he said, "In my culture, if you steal someone else's story, it would be like stealing their car. Your story is the story you have to tell." That's how I feel. It's the way I write. I don't think of myself as an imaginative person. I think of myself as a very keen observer.

You've mentioned being a keen observer and a reporter several times. How does that figure in with that elusive thing that some people call talent. What do you think talent is?

That's a tough one. I think there are a lot of different ways to "have it." All of us who teach know that there are people who clearly don't. They can work really hard and can reach a level of adequacy but they are never going to be great—or even really good. I think where *my* talent lies is in the way my mind wants to recombine objects. I don't think I'm particularly talented with language. I don't think I'm a particularly great storyteller, in the traditional sense. I have a collagist's artistry. I think my talent is to combine unlike objects.

I don't think I'm a particularly great storyteller, in the traditional sense. I have a collagist's artistry. I think my talent is to combine unlike objects.

Can you teach someone to write fiction?

It's one of those questions that you can spend hours on and, in the end, it doesn't really matter. There are many things about writing that can be taught and several things that can't. But so much of what we do as teachers is to put students in the path of their own possible discoveries. We recruit somebody great and they get better and then go off and publish something great and that's fabulous. But the real moments in teaching are with the people that you are not so sure about and all of a sudden, one day, they write this piece, and you're asking, "What happened?" Was it something I did? Not necessarily. Was it anything that one of their fellow students did? Something they read at the right time? I have a student right now and all of a sudden, she wrote this fabulous story. Why did that happen? I don't know. I don't think that it's something that I or anyone else has taught her, but something came together in her head.

Student or professional, whatever talent we do or don't have, the prospect of actually beginning a story is daunting. What finally brings you to the moment when you know it's time to begin trying to bring a story to the page?

I won't let myself write until the chunks are pretty good. I don't throw out much but I will avoid my computer for weeks and weeks and weeks. I don't like myself well enough to write badly. I won't go near the box if I don't have an idea. Don't confuse this with my saying that I have an outline or idea what I am going to write. But I have to get a tremendous amount of courage up and a tremendous amount of confidence in my metaphorical field and I can't go near the machine until I have that. A lot of times I'll make a list of the chunks before, so I have that to refer to. But they are just a couple of words. I envy people who write and write and write and then say, Oh, that's good! I can't do that. That means a lot of times I can't write at all. I'm so afraid that I'll write badly.

Writing Prompts

READ: "How to Talk to a Hunter" and the interview with **Pam Houston.**

PONDER: The way Houston uses the second person to wash a layer of shame over the story and subtly reveal the narrator's sense of self.

WRITE: A second-person story about a character who tells something about herself that she is ashamed of.

PRACTICE:

- Write a question similar to "skins or blankets?" that could define a relationship.
- Create a character whose wise inner voice most often goes unheard.
- Consider a rich metaphorical field in your own life and make a list of moments and images within it that glimmer. Write each one to its length and then move them around until you find the right sequence for a story.

- Write a story with a straight narrative line. For example, begin with the moment a group of characters put their whitewater rafts into the river and end with the moment they take them out at the end of the trip.
- Create the artifical narrative line of a single day and then create a story that moves back and forth in time within it.
- Brainstorm a list of completely unrelated things; then write a believable story that includes as many of them as you can.
- Think of a single experience you had with one of your parents that might act as a metaphor for your whole relationship. Use it as the basis of a story, changing the real experience to suit the story's needs.
- Make a CD of a character's favorite songs. Write the memories that go along with each one.
- Make a CD of songs that create a soundtrack for a story.
- Write a dialogue between two people who don't listen to each other.

Ha Jin

Ha Jin (b. 1956) is the author of three collections of short stories, four novels, and four collections of poems. Born in Liaoning, China, he was educated at Heilongjiang University and Shangdong University. He came to the United States in 1986 to study at Brandeis University and decided to emigrate after the Tiananmen Square Massacre. His honors include the National Book Award, the PEN/Hemingway Award for First Fiction, the Flannery O'Connor Award, the PEN/Faulkner Award for Fiction, the Townsend Prize, and three Pushcart Prizes. Ha Jin teaches at Boston University. He lives in Foxboro, Massachusetts.

For Further Reading:
Between Silences: A Voice from China (1990), *Facing Shadows* (1996), *Ocean of Words: Army Stories* (1996), *Under the Red Flag* (1997), *In the Pond* (1998), *Waiting* (1999), *The Bridegroom* (2000), *Quiet Desperation* (2000), *Wreckage* (2001), *The Crazed* (2002), *War Trash* (2004).

Love in the Air

After the political study, Chief Jiang turned on both the transmitter and the receiver and started searching for the station of the Regional Headquarters. Half a minute later a resonant signal emerged calling the Fifth Regiment. Kang Wandou, who had served for two years, could tell it was an experienced hand at the opposite end. The dots and dashes were clean and concrete; the pace was fast and steady.

"He's very good," Shi Wei said.

"Of course, Shenyang always has the best hands," Chief Jiang said, returning the call. This was their first direct communication with the Headquarters of Shenyang Military Region. In no time the two stations got in touch. Jiang telegraphed that from now on they would keep twenty-four-hour coverage.

"Understood. So long," Shenyang replied.

"So long," Jiang tapped. He turned off the transmitter, but left the receiver on. "Shun Min, it's your turn now. Little Kang will take over in the evening."

"All right." Shun moved his chair close to the machine.

Though the middle-aged chief called him Little Kang, to the other soldiers Kang was Big Kang. His whole person was marked by abnormal largeness except for his voice, which was small and soft. Whenever he spoke, he sounded as though he was mumbling to himself. If his neck were not so long, his comrades would have believed he had suffered from the "big-joint" disease in his childhood. His wrists were thick, and his square thumbs always embarrassed him. But everybody was impressed by the beautiful long lashes above his froggy eyes.

After dinner Kang replaced Shun. The evening shift was not busy. Since all news stations broadcast at dusk and there was too much noise in the air, few telegrams were dispatched or received during these hours. Kang's task was to answer Shenyang's call every hour, and for the rest of the time he had to attend to the receiver in case an emergency arose. Having nothing else to do, he opened the fanlight and watched the night. Gray streaks of clouds were floating rapidly beneath the crescent moon and the glimmering stars. In the air there was a mysterious humming, which seemed to come from the constellations. Except for the swarms of lights in Hutou Town, it was dark everywhere. Even the silhouette of those mountains in Russia had disappeared.

Cold wind kept gushing into the office, Kang closed the fanlight and sat back on the chair. Again, nothing could be seen through the window, on whose frosty panes stretched miniature bushes, hills, caves, coral reefs. He picked up a pencil, turned over a telegram pad, and began drawing pictures. He drew a horse, a cow, a dog, a pig, a rooster, a lamb, a donkey, and a hen leading a flock of chicks.

After taps at nine, the quiet grew intolerable. If only he could have something interesting to do. In one of the drawers there was a volume of Chairman Mao's selected works and a copy of Lenin's *What Is to Be Done!*, which Chief Jiang would browse through at night, but these books were too profound for Kang. He missed the picture stories he had read when he was a boy. Those children's books could no longer be found anywhere, because they had been burned at the beginning of the Cultural Revolution. Kang took out his tobacco pouch and rolled a cigarette. Smoking was the only way to prevent himself from dozing off. Then he stretched his legs, rested his feet on the table, and leaned against the back of the chair as if lounging on a sofa. Soon the small office turned foggy.

Shenyang began to call at ten sharp. Kang turned on the transmitter and was ready to reply. It was another radio operator at the other end now. The signal was fluctuating at a much faster speed, approximately 130 numerals a minute. Because of the noise, the dots and the dashes didn't sound very clear, though they were distinguishable.

"Please answer," it ended.

Immediately Kang started to call back. His large hand held the button of the sending key and pounded out the letters one after another. He was a slow hand and could tap only eighty numerals a minute. But his fingers and thumb were powerful—whenever he telegraphed, the key with its heavy steel base would move about on the table. Holding the base with his left hand, he was repeating the reply signal in a resolute manner. His thick wrist was moving up and down while a little red light was flashing nervously at the top of the transmitter.

The operator at the opposite end did not hear Kang and resumed calling. Now there was less noise in the air and the signal became distinct. The call sign, composed of eight letters, was repeated again and again, it formed a crisp tune, flowing around and around. Kang pricked up his ears. This must be the chief of the station. He had never met such an excellent hand. There were automatic machines that could produce 180 numerals a minute clearly, but those dead instruments always sounded monotonous. They didn't have a character. The more you listened to them at night, the more likely you would fall asleep. But this fellow was one of those "machine defeaters."

"Please answer," the other side asked again.

Once more Kang went about calling back. Affected by the dexterous hand at the other end, he tried hard to speed up. The chair under his hips creaked while he was struggling with the bakelite key button, which turned slippery in his sweating hand.

Unfortunately this was a bad night. The other side simply could not find him. It called him time and again; Kang replied continually, but they could not get in touch. Forty minutes passed to no avail. By now, the other operator had become impatient. The melodious signal gradually lost its rhythm and flowed so rapidly that the letters were almost indistinguishable. It sounded like raindrops pattering on metal tiles. Patient as he was, Kang began to worry.

Around eleven, the telephone suddenly rang. Kang picked up the receiver and said, "Hello."

"Hello," a tingling female voice said. "This is the Military Region Station. Wake up, comrade. Have you heard me on the machine?"

"Ye-yes." Kang paused with surprise, his heart kicking and his throat tightening. Who could imagine a woman would call you on the border at night? "I-I've heard you," he managed to say. "I ne-never dozed off. I've been calling you all the time."

"Sorry, don't take it to heart. I was teasing you. Shall we switch to the second set of frequencies?" She sounded so pleasant.

"All righ-t." His tongue seemed not his own.

"Bye-bye now, meet you on the machine."

"Bye."

She hung up. Kang was dazed, still holding the receiver.

The sweet voice went on echoing in his ears, "Sorry, don't take it to heart. . . ."

The call sign appeared again. This time it repossessed its elegance and fluency, but to Kang every dot and dash was different now, as though they were tender, meaningful words the young woman sent to him alone.

"Switch frequency please," she ended.

Kang jerked his head and rushed to look for her on the new frequency. Without much effort, he found her again. His body grew tense as he became engrossed in the sways and ripples of the heavenly melody. How wonderful to work with a woman at night. If only she could call him like this for an hour. But she stopped and asked, "Please answer."

Kang's hand began to tremble. It settled on the sending key like a small turtle, shaking out every letter brokenly. He cursed his hand, "Come on, you coward! This is not a battle yet." He wiped his wet forehead with a telegram sheet.

What a pity. She heard him in less than a minute and replied promptly: "No business. Meet you at twelve o'clock. So long."

"So long." Kang had to agree, because it was a rule that an operator must never transmit an unnecessary dot or dash. The longer you stayed on the air, the easier it was for the Russians to locate your position.

Kang felt at a loss. He raised his head to look at the clock on the wall—eleven-ten, so he would meet her in fifty minutes. His imagination began to take wing. What was her name? How stupid he was, having forgotten to ask her. How old was she? She sounded so young and must have been around twenty. A good person, no doubt; that pleasant voice was full of good nature. What did she look like? Was she beautiful? Well educated? Intelligent? That voice told everything—all the best a woman could have. But what did she look like exactly? Tall and slim, with large black eyes? Of course he could not find out much about her through only one meeting. It had to take time. He believed that eventually he would get to know her well, because from now on they would meet every night.

The clock moved slowly, as though intending to avoid an ominous ending. Kang kept watching it and longed to arrive at the midnight rendezvous in the twinkling of an eye.

Suddenly somebody knocked at the door. Chief Jiang came in. "You can go to bed now, Kang. I happened to wake up a few minutes earlier tonight." He yawned.

Kang stood up and didn't know what to say. He tried to smile, but the effort distorted his face.

"What happened?" the chief asked. "You look as awake as a lynx."

"Nothing, everything is fine." Kang picked up his fur hat, with enormous dismay he slouched out. He forgot to take an apple, which was his night snack.

How could he sleep? Every inch of his skin was affected by a caressing tingle he had never experienced before. At the other side of the room, Shun was snoring and Shi murmured something in his dream.

"I was teasing you. . . ." The voice spoke to Kang again and again. He shut his eyes tight, he shook his head many times in order to get rid of her and go to sleep, but it was no use. She was so close to him, as if sitting right beside his bed in the dark, whispering and smiling.

Little by little, he gave up and allowed her to play whatever tricks she wanted to. The most unbearable mystery was what she looked like. He tried to think of all the women he knew, but he could not recall a pretty one. Surely he had aunts and cousins, surely he remembered some girls who had hoed the cornfields and cut millet together with him, but none of them differed much from his male relatives or from the men in his home village. Every one worked like a beast of burden, and none could speak without swearing.

The prettiest women he had ever seen were those female characters in the movie copies of the Revolutionary Model Plays, but most of them were too old, well beyond forty. How about the girl raped by the landlord in *The White-Haired Girl?* Yes, she was a wonderful ballerina, slim and good-looking. How deft her toes were. They capered around as if never touching the ground. She could swing her legs up well beyond her head. And the slender waist, which was full of rebellious spirit. What a wonderful body she had! But did she have a wonderful voice? No one could tell, because she kept quiet in the ballet.

No, she wouldn't do. He would not accept a woman who might lack that charming voice. Besides, that actress had long white hair like an old crone's. She must have been weird, or her hair wouldn't be so silvery.

How about the revolutionary's daughter in *The Story of the Red Lamp?* Well, that was a good one. But did she not seem too young? She was seventeen, old enough to be somebody's wife. A marriageable girl indeed. What he liked most about her was that long glossy braid, which reached her buttocks. But she was too thin and must have been too feeble to work. Her aquiline nose was narrow, that was not a sign of good fortune. Even worse, her voice was sharp. It was all right for singing Peking Opera to a large audience, but who dared to quarrel with a girl like that? In real life, she must have been a "small hot pepper." No, he had to look for another woman.

Now he had it—the female gymnastic athlete he had seen in a documentary film. She performed on the uneven bars. Her body was so supple and powerful that she could stretch, fly, and even somersault in the air. No doubt, that was a healthy energetic woman, not a bourgeois young lady who would fall in a gust of wind. What did she look like? He had not seen her face clearly in the film and could not tell. Then this woman had to go too, at least for the time being.

The radiator pipes started clinking and whistling gently. The boiler room pumped steam at four. With dawn approaching, Kang was worried and tried to force himself to sleep. But that voice would not leave him alone. "Wake up, comrade. Have you heard me on the machine? . . ." It sounded even more pleasant and more intimate. You fool, he cursed himself. How stupid you are—bewitched by an unknown voice! Forget it and get some sleep.

Soon he entered another world. He married a young woman who was also a telegrapher. They worked together at the post office in his hometown. They lived in a small house surrounded by a stone wall that had a gate with iron bars. Their garden was filled with vegetables and fruits. The beans were as broad as sickles, and the peaches as fat as babies' faces. Poultry were everywhere, three dozen chickens, twenty ducks, and eight geese. Who was his bride? He didn't know, for he only saw her back, a tall, sturdy young woman with a thick braid.

At breakfast he felt giddy. He could not tell if he had slept at all. Neither was he sure whether the prosperous domestic scene was his dream or his fantasy. How absurd the whole thing was. He had never loved a woman before, but all of a sudden he'd fallen in love with a voice. His first love was an unknown voice. He was scared, because he could not determine whether it was real love or merely a delusion from mental illness. Did people feel this way when they were in love? He felt sick and beside himself. How long would it take for him to grow used to this thing or get over it?

He could not sleep that morning when he was supposed to have a good rest to make up for the previous night and prepare himself for the evening shift. That voice, mixed with the call sign, whispered in his ears constantly. Time and again, he forced himself to think of something else, but he could not summon up anything interesting. He dared not smoke, for fear that Chief Jiang, who slept in the same room, would know he had remained awake for the whole morning.

In the afternoon, during the study of Chairman Mao's "Combat Liberalism," Kang was restless, longing for the arrival of the evening. The words grew blurred before his eyes. When he was asked to read out a page, he managed to accomplish the task with a whistling in his nose. His comrades looked at him strangely. When he finished, Shun said, "Kang, you must have a bad cold."

"Yes, it's a bad one." Kang blew his nose with a piece of newspaper. He was both miserable and hopeful. Probably the more he worked with her, the better he would feel. Everything was difficult in the beginning; the end of suffering was happiness. At the moment he must be patient; a few hours later, he would be in a different world.

How ruthless Heaven was. She did not show up in the evening. It was a different operator at the other end. Kang spent the six hours racking his brains about what kind of schedule she had. The following three evenings passed in the same fruitless way. Kang was baffled. Every night he could not help thinking of that mysterious woman—all women—for several hours. In the daytime he was very quiet. Although pining away, he dared not talk to anyone about it. How shameful it would be—to have it known that you were enchanted by a woman about whom you didn't know anything. How silly he was! That woman must have forgotten him like used water. No, she had never bothered about knowing him. How could she, a pretty young woman in the big city and perhaps surrounded by many smart officers in the headquarters, be interested in a soldier like him, who was so dull, so homely, and so rustic? He knew he was the toad that dreamed of eating a swan, but he couldn't help himself.

On Saturday morning, Kang was roused from his catnap by Shi Wei. "Big Kang, come and help your younger brother."

"What's up?"

"Too many telegrams this morning. I've been copying for three hours and can't handle it anymore."

"All right, I'm coming." It was almost eleven o'clock anyway. Kang got up and wiped his face with a wet towel.

There she was! He had hardly entered the office when Kang froze stock-still. The pleasant signal, for which he had been yearning for days, was singing proudly as though to a large audience. The dots and dashes sounded like amorous messages inviting him to decode their secret meanings. How magnificent her telegraphic style was in broad daylight. Kang lost himself in an imaginary melody composed of both the electric signal and the tingling voice—"Hello, this is the Military Region Station. Wake up, comrade. Have you heard me on the machine? . . ."

"What's the matter with you?" Shi rapped him on the shoulder.

"Oh nothing," Kang muttered, moving to the desk. "Never met such a good hand."

"True, he has gold fingers."

There was no time to tell Shi that it was she, not he, because the receiver was announcing: "Please ready."

Kang started writing down the numerals rapidly. In the beginning it went well, but soon his attention began to wander. He was distracted by his desire to appreciate the rhythm and the personal touch in the sounds, and he had to drop some numerals now and then. More awful, that voice jumped in to trouble him—"Sorry, don't take it to heart. I was teasing you. . . ."

"Repeat?" she asked, having finished the short telegram.

"Yes, noise," Kang pounded nervously. "Group eight in line four, from group three to eight in line six . . ."

Meanwhile, Shi Wei watched him closely. He was surprised to find Kang, a better transcriber than himself, unable to jot down the telegram sent out so clearly. There was no noise at all, why did he tap "noise" as an excuse? Kang was aware of Shi's observing and was sweating all over. He rushed to bring the receiving operation to an end.

"Are you all right?" Shi asked, after Kang signed his name on the telegram.

"I don't know." He felt sick. He got up and hurried out of the office.

Another fruitless evening and another sleepless night. Kang could no longer contain himself. On Sunday evening, he revealed the truth to Shi and Shun, who happened to be in the office.

"Shi Wei, you know, the Shenyang operator with 'gold fingers' is a woman, not a man." He had planned to say a lot, to make a story, but he was bewildered, finding that he completed the project in just one sentence. He blushed to the ears with a strange emotion.

"Really?" Shi asked loudly. "No kidding? Why didn't you tell me earlier, Brother Kang?"

Kang smiled. Shun was not sure who they were talking about. "Which one?"

"The best one," Shi said with a thrill in his voice. "I can't believe it. A girl can telegraph so well. Tell me, Big Kang, how did you get to know her?"

"She called me, because she couldn't hear me," he declared proudly.

"What's her name?" Shi asked.

"I have no idea. Wish I knew."

"Must be a good girl. I'll go to Shenyang and get her."

"Come on, don't brag," Shun said. "I want to see how you can get her."

"You wait and see."

Kang was shocked that Shi was also interested in her. He regretted telling them the truth. If Shi made a move, Kang would have to give ground. Shi was an excellent basketball player and had in his wallet the pictures of a half dozen young women, who he claimed were all his girlfriends. In addition, his father was a divisional commissar in the navy; Shi had grown up in big cities and knew the world. Most important of all, he spent money like water. How could Kang compete against such a smart, handsome fellow?

It was this new development that made him fidgety that evening. He paced up and down in the office, chain-smoking for two hours. Finally, he decided to investigate who she was. He picked up the telephone and called the Shenyang Miliary Region. It took half an hour for the call to get through.

"Hello, this is Shenyang, can I help you?" an operator asked sleepily.

"Ye-yes," he struggled to say. "I want to speak to—to the wireless station, the one that communicates with Hutou?"

"What's 'Hutou'? A unit's code name?"

"No, it's a county."

"Oh, I see. Please tell me the number of the station you want to speak to."

"I don't know the number."

"I can't help you then. We have hundreds of stations, and they are in different cities and mountains. You have to tell me the number. Find the number first, then call back. All right?"

"Uh, all right."

"Bye-bye now."

"Bye."

It was so easy to run into a dead end. All the clever questions, which he had prepared to ask the radio operator on duty about that woman, had vanished from his mind. How foolish he was—having never thought there could be more than ten stations in the Regional Headquarters. What was to be done now? Without an address, he could not write to her; even with an address, he didn't know how to compose a love letter. Why was Heaven so merciless? It seemed that the only way to meet her was through the air, but he had not figured out her capricious schedule yet.

It did not make much difference after they rotated the shifts. Now Kang worked afternoons. No matter how exhausted he was when he went to bed at night, he would lie awake for a few hours thinking of one woman after another. His dreams ran wilder. Every night the pillow, which contained his underclothes, moved from beneath his head, little by little, into his arms. He was tormented by endless questions. What was it like to kiss and touch a woman? Did women also have hair on their bodies? Was he a normal man? And could he satisfy a woman? Was he not a neurotic, drenched in sweat and burning away like this in the dark? Could he have children with a woman?

Whenever he woke up from his broken sleep that mysterious voice would greet him, "Wake up, comrade. Have you heard me on the machine? . . ." The sounds grew deeper and deeper into him, as though they were sent out by his own internal organs. During these frantic nights, he discovered that Chief Jiang had to rouse Shi Wei at least three times every night. Shi worked the small hours.

Kang's skull felt numb in the daytime. He was convinced that he was a lunatic. How panicked he was when receiving a telegram, because that melodious signal and that tender voice, again and again, intruded themselves into his brain and forced him to pause in the middle of the transcribing. How good it would be to have peace once more. But peace of mind seemed remote, as though it belonged only to a time that he had outgrown and could never return to. Even the exercises in the mornings became a torture. He used to be able to write down 160 numerals per minute with ease, but now he had to struggle with 110. When they sat together reading documents and newspapers, his comrades often waved their hands before his eyes to test if he could see anything. Somebody would say, "Big Kang, why do you look like you lost your soul?" Another, "What do you see in your trance? A goddess?"

On these occasions Kang would let out a sigh. He dared not tell anybody about the ridculous "affair." He was afraid that he would be criticized for having contracted bourgeois liberalism or become a laughingstock.

One morning during the exercises, the telegraphic instructor, Han Jie, looked at Kang's transcription and said under his breath, "No wonder the Confidential Office complained."

Suddenly it dawned on Kang that he had become a nuisance in the Wireless Platoon. A pang seized his heart. No doubt, the confidential officers in the Regimental Headquarters were dissatisfied with his work and had reported him to the company's leaders. It was this stupid "affair" that had reduced him to such a state. He had to find a way to stop it—forget that woman and her bewitching voice—otherwise how could he survive? Although in his heart he knew he had to get rid of her, he didn't know how. Neither did he want to try.

On Thursday evening two weeks later, Chief Jiang held an urgent meeting at the station. Nobody knew what it was about. Kang was scared because he thought it might be about him. The secret would come out sooner or later. Had he babbled it during his sleep at night? He regretted drawing three pictures of women on the back of a telegram pad. Chief Jiang must have seen them. What should he say if the chief questioned him about those drawings?

The meeting had nothing to do with him. When Jiang asked Shi Wei to confess what he had done in the small hours, Kang at last felt relaxed. But like Shun, he was baffled about what had happened. Shi protested that he had not done anything wrong.

"You're dishonest, Comrade Shi Wei," the chief said.

"No, no Chief Jiang." Shi looked worried. "I did all the work well."

"You know our Party's policy: Leniency to those who confess, severity to those who refuse. It's up to yourself."

"Why?" Shi seemed puzzled. "This policy applies only to the class enemies. I'm your comrade, am I not?"

"Stop pretending you're innocent. Tell us the truth."

"No, I really didn't do anything wrong."

"All right, let me tell you what happened." The chief's voice grew sharper. "You were caught by the monitoring station. You thought you were smart. If you didn't want us to know, you shouldn't have done it in the first place. Look at the report yourself." He tossed the internal bulletin to Shi and handed Shun and Kang each a copy.

The title read: "Radio Operators Proffered Love in the Air." Kang's heart tightened. He turned a page and read "From February 3 on, from 1:00 A.M. to 5:00 A.M., a radio operator in the Fifth regiment and an operator at the 36th station of Shenyang Military Region have developed a love affair in the air. . . ."

Kang was stunned, and his thick lips parted. He could never imagine Shi would make such an unlawful move. A small part of their love talk was transcribed in the report:

I am Shi Wei. Your name?
Lili. Where are you from?
Dalian. And you?
Beijing.
Your age?
Twenty-one. And you?
Twenty-two. Love your hand.
Why?
It is good.
Why? Not love me?
Yes, I do.
!
Love me?
Maybe.
. . . . . .

Kang wanted to cry, but he controlled himself. He saw Shi's face turn pale and sweat break out on his smooth forehead. Meanwhile Shun bit his lower lip, trying hard not to laugh.

"Now, what do you want to say?" Jiang asked.

Shi lowered his eyes and remained silent. The chief announced that the Communication Company had decided to suspend Shi Wei from his work during the wait for the final punishment. From now on, Shi had to go to the study room during the day and write out his confession and self-criticism.

Though he was working two more hours a day to cover for Shi, Kang no longer expected to meet Lili, whose family name was not revealed in the bulletin. Obviously she was also suspended from her work and must have been doing the same thing as Shi did every day in the company's study room. But the tune created by her fingers and her charming voice were still with him; actually they hurt him more than before. He tried cursing her and imagining all the bad things that could be attributed to a woman in order to pull her out of himself. He thought of her as a "broken shoe" which was worn by everyone, a bitch that raised her tail to any male dog, a hag who was shunned by all decent men, a White Bone Demon living on innocent blood. Still, he could not get rid of her. Whenever he was receiving a telegram, her voice would break in to catch him. "Sorry, don't take it to heart. I was teasing you. . . ." It was miserable. The misery went so deep that when he spoke to his comrades he often heard himself moaning. He hated his own listless voice.

Shi's punishment was administered a week later. Both Shi Wei and Wang Lili were expelled from the army. This time the woman's full name was given. To Kang's surprise, Shi did not cry and seemed to take it with ease. He ate well and slept well, and went on smoking expensive cigarettes. Kang figured there must have been two reasons why Shi did not care. First, with the help of his father, he would have no problem finding a good job at home; second, the expulsion gave him an opportunity to continue his love affair with Wang Lili, since they were now two grasshoppers tied together by one thread. Lucky for Shi, he didn't lose his military status for nothing. It seemed he would go to Shenyang soon and have a happy time with her.

The station planned to hold a farewell party for Shi Wei. Though it was not an honorable discharge, they had worked with Shi for almost a year and had some good feelings about him. For days Kang had been thinking what souvenir he should give Shi Wei. He finally chose a pair of pillow towels, which cost him four *yuan*, half his monthly pay. In the meantime his scalp remained numb, and he still could not come to himself. Not only did the task of receiving a telegram frighten him, but any telegraphic signal would give him the creeps. He had developed another habit—cursing himself relentlessly for his daydreaming and for having allowed himself to degenerate into a walking corpse for that fickle woman, whose name he would now murmur many times every night.

Four older soldiers from the Wireless Platoon were invited to the farewell party. Chief Jiang presented an album to Shi, and Shun gave him a pair of nylon socks. When Kang's pillow towels were displayed, everybody burst out laughing, for on each towel was embroidered a pair of lovely mandarin ducks and a line of red characters. One said: "Happy Life," and the other: "Sweet Dreams." Peanut shells and pearstones fell on the floor because of the commotion the garish towels caused.

"You must be joking, Big Kang," Shi said, measuring one of the towels against his chest. "You think I'm going home to get married?"

"Why not?" Kang smiled. "Won't you go to Shenyang?"

"For what? I don't know anyone there."

Kang stood up. The floor seemed to be swaying beneath his feet. Tears welled up in his eyes. He picked up a mug and gulped the beer inside, his left hand holding the corner of the desk. He put down the mug, then turned to the door.

"Where are you going?" Chief Jiang asked.

Without replying, Kang went out into the open air. He wanted to bolt into the snow and run for hours, until his legs could no longer support him. But he paused. On the drill ground, a dozen soldiers from the Line Construction Platoon were practicing climbing telephone poles without wearing spikes. Behind the brick houses stood the thirty-meter-tall aerial, made of three poles connected to one another, which had been raised for their station by these fellow men. In the northeast, the Wusuli River displayed a series of green, steaming holes along its snow-covered course. On the fields and the slopes of the hills, a curtain of golden sparks, cast by the setting sun, was glittering. The gray forests stretched along the undulating mountain ridges toward the receding horizon. The sky was so high and the land so vast. Kang took a deep breath; a fresh contraction lingered in his chest. For the first time he felt a person was so small.

That evening he wrote a letter to the company's Party branch, imploring the leaders to transfer him to the Line Construction Platoon. He did not give an explicit reason, and merely said that somehow his mind was deteriorating and that he could not operate the telegraphic apparatus anymore. The letter ended as follows:

> If I can no longer serve the Revolutionary Cause and our Motherland with my brain, I can at least work with my hands, which are still young and strong. Please relieve me from the Wireless Platoon.

After writing the letter, he wept, filling his hands with tears. He used to believe that when he was demobilized he could make a decent living by working as a telegrapher at a post office or a train station, but now he had ruined his future. How painful it was to love and then give it up. If only he could forget that woman's voice and her telegraphic style. Whether he could or not, he had to try.

A Conversation with Ha Jin

You were a poet in China before coming to the United States to study. Would you talk about the writing you did before you left China, your political motivation to write about Communist China, and how your American experience shaped the writer you have become?

I began to write seriously since 1990. I have never been a political writer. In fact, for years I was half-hearted about writing. Before I came to the States, I had been trained to be a translator of American literature. I had just graduated from a Masters program and hadn't really started to do any professional work, that is, writing criticism and translating literary works. Regardless of my experience in China, it's the American experience that forced me to be a writer. I have to survive and exist here. After the Tiananmen Massacre, I decided to emigrate but psychologically I was not ready to live in this country. I didn't know what I could do. Having failed to find employment related to Chinese, I concluded that English was the only means of my survival since all my degrees were in English. Also, I realized that I wouldn't starve here as long as I worked and was in good health, but what was hard would be how to live meaningfully. It took me more than a year to decide to write in English only. Before coming to the States, I had written some poems in Chinese, but I had never had an audience. It would have been suicidal for me to write in Chinese here. In this sense, I began to write out of necessity.

In your opinion, how does writing in a second language affect both the nature and quality of the stories you write? How would your work be different if you were writing in Chinese?

In English I have to be very careful and patient. If I wrote in Chinese, I might have to invent a different kind of language. Even in Chinese, I wrote in a simple, straightforward style. I hate flowery stuff. That's why my wife often says that the Chinese won't accept my way of writing, which is too plain and too honest. Probably because I study poetry and write poetry, I tend to be more selective than inclusive. This cannot be helped. I am this kind of writer.

Probably because I study poetry and write poetry, I tend to be more selective than inclusive. This cannot be helped. I am this kind of writer.

Why did you decide to focus mainly on fiction, instead of poetry?

After I published my first book of poetry, *Between Silences,* I thought that some of the material would be more effective if I put it into fiction. Soon I began writing short stories, which later were included in *Ocean of Words.* I was hired to teach poetry writing by Emory University in 1993, but I had a terrible time getting my second poetry book published. Short stories were easier to get published than poems, at least in my case. So I published some stories in order to meet the academic requirement.

Though you said that you are not a political writer and it is true that your stories don't feel as if they have a political agenda, your work has had a political effect in the way it reveals the often brutal, dehumanizing nature of life in Communist China. What advice would you give to a writer who might hope to effect political change through literature?

Auden says, "Poetry makes nothing happen." I don't believe in the social effect of literature. I write to tell a good story, which first must delight. To instruct is much less important. On the other hand, we should keep in mind that literature lasts longer and that our work can be more significant work than politics if we write literature.

I don't believe in the social effect of literature. I write to tell a good story, which first must delight.

Your stories are full of violence—rape, beatings, deprivations—and you use a deceptively simple style to describe these events. Often the most brutal moments turn on small moments and details, as in "Man to Be," when the rapist looks into his victim's eyes. What advice would you give to aspiring writers about when and how to write about violence in their stories?

Don't flinch. Write out any scene needed by the story. Be truthful but avoid vulgarity.

You have said, "As for the subject matter, I guess we are compelled to write about what has hurt us most." To what extent is your work autobiographical? How and why do bits of the real world, things you have seen, heard, read, or experienced make their way into your stories?

Occasionally, I may give my experience to a character, but my fiction is never autobiographical. For example, in the story "Love in the Air," all the knowledge and experience of telegraphy are my own, but I used them only to produce the texture of the protagonist's life to make him convincing. On the whole, my life is limited, and my own story cannot give enough room for imagination, so I don't write my personal story. At the same time, almost all details in my fiction are factual. I create a special order for them. That order is my invention. For many years, I was hurt by China. Because of that stubborn, mad country, I landed here, having to struggle for a different kind of existence. Then, gradually, China became less overwhelming. The

At the same time, almost all details in my fiction are factual. I create a special order for them. That order is my invention.

immigrant experience is essentially a traumatic experience to most people, which involves truncation of one's old life and the painful creation of a new life. Often I feel crippled, but I am not complaining. The American experience has toughened me up and turned me into a different man.

Yet you go "home" in a sense, writing fiction. Would you talk about how returning to China again and again by way of writing your stories has brought insight and perhaps even closure to the experience of growing up and coming of age there? Writing, do you understand things about China and about yourself that you could not have understood otherwise?

The writing act does take me back to the past and help me see things I didn't understand before, but it is not an exactly nostalgic act. I write in English, which keeps a kind of barrier between China and me and also some distance. This is necessary and beneficial. I can be more objective and depend more on universal references. In fact, the processing is somewhat like a distilling one—what is not essential can be left out. So the return to China is halfway.

In fact, the processing is somewhat like a distilling one—what is not essential can be left out.

Perhaps all writers are immigrants, in a way: It is in their nature to be uneasy in the world, to feel a disconnect with what others experience as ordinary, and to find themselves at any given time trying to make sense of the bits and pieces of the real world that connect inside their heads. Perhaps that kind of alienation might even be considered an aspect of talent. What do you think talent is? How do you recognize talent in a student writer?

The alienation is necessary. It makes a writer look at life from the side. But I don't think it is talent itself. Flaubert says, "Talent is a long patience." Over the years I have found that most of my students are talented, but not many of them have the patience to complete a book. Talent doesn't matter much. It's the ability to continue that makes a writer.

Talent doesn't matter much. It's the ability to continue that makes a writer.

Back to the story you mentioned earlier, "Love in the Air"—what was it about the work that you did as a telegraph operator that triggered the idea for this particular character in this particular situation?

Actually the conception of the story was inspired by Chekhov's "The Kiss." I was very moved by that story and wanted to write one about a kind of unrequited love as well. I wrote it for Leslie Epstein's workshop. When we began workshopping the story, one of my classmates recognized the connection with Chekhov's story. I was flattered by that, because such a connection often guarantees some literary merit.

Once you had the idea for that story, how did it evolve?

I was familiar with the work of telegraphy, so I could come by those details without difficulty. As for the dramatic pattern, I depended on some events that were factual. For example, when I was in the Chinese army, there were two telegraphers who flirted in the air and were caught. They were disciplined and discharged. It was a scandal. Also, when we couldn't get in touch with headquarters through the air, sometimes we would receive phone calls from the other end. On rare occasion, the caller was a woman. Whenever a woman called, the men would get excited for several days. So I was familiar with their emotion, though I was too young at that time to be like them.

You have not returned to China since you emigrated in 1985, yet the world in this story and in all your stories is so vividly drawn. Are there techniques you use for remembering, for placing yourself back in the world you once knew?

Details. Through the accumulation of authentic details we can bring out the material sensation of the place and we create the texture of the characters' lives. Sometimes I feel that a story has its own source of vitality. If you hit on the right source, a lot of details will come up automatically.

Through the accumulation of authentic details we can bring out the material sensation of the place and we create the texture of the characters' lives.

The idea that a "hand" of a telegraph officer could be recognized by the clarity, pace, and rhythm of her strokes reflects a depth of characterization student writers hope to achieve. The reader has only this information about Lili—and the sound of her voice, yet she is so present in the story! Kang, on the other hand, is vividly described. How do characters evolve for you? How do you know which details will work best to make them come alive on the page?

Most telegraphers have their own personal touches and rhythms of tapping out signals. You can follow them like listening to voices in a way. The presence of Lili's telegraphic style creates the aura of her presence in the story. At the same time, she is also a creation of the men's imagination. When that brief piece of transcription is shown to the men, we, as readers, can see she is just a regular woman. But to Kang she is everything. The character, Shi, helps bring out a lot of pathos in the story. Shi is a contrast to Kang and doesn't give thought to the woman at all after the affair is exposed.

As you said earlier, the basic plot of "Love in the Air" is unrequited love. But the story is also about the dangers of imagination. Add to the mix that it takes place in a repressive society where human relationships are tightly controlled and people are allowed to make few choices about their life paths and you've got a story fraught with all kinds of tensions. Would you talk about how you created the various levels of tensions in this story on the page and also comment on how a student might take an "ordinary" plot and make it extraordinary, as you did here?

I didn't think much about all the levels of tension when I was writing it, though I was aware of them. I tried to focus on Kang's psychology in the particular situation. In other words, try to walk in his shoes. Once we have given enough attention to a character, many nuances can be brought out naturally.

You have said, "Very often I feel that the stories have been inside me for a long time and that I am no more than an instrument for their manifestation." How do these stories gather inside you, present themselves, and take shape?

Most of the time when I am bothered by something, I write about it to let the emotion out. Usually I don't have enough time to write what is in my mind, so the seed of a story will stay a long time in me until I begin to work on it. Mostly they have the form of a key event, which gradually sprouts into the shape of a story. For instance, the story "Saboteur" originated from two key events I had heard and read long ago. One is that some workers in Shanghai contracted hepatitis, and that the moment they knew they were victims of the disease, they went out to eat at different restaurants to spread the virus. The other event was reported in a newspaper. In a country town, the police chief had a lawyer tied to a tree and let his men slap the lawyer by turns because the lawyer represented a man they had arrested. I strung these two events together and created an intellectual as the main character. Of course, I added a lot of other happenings to flesh the story out.

Usually I don't have enough time to write what is in my mind, so the seed of a story will stay a long time in me until I begin to work on it.

What was it about the two events that made them seem connected in your mind?

The two are key dramatic details, the kind of details that produce dramatic development. The connection between the two events is that the police's abuse of power creates the desire for vengeance in Mr. Chiu. In other words, the first event emotionally pushes the story toward the second event, the ending.

Why an intellectual? What made that kind of person right for what you hoped to accomplish with the story?

This is purely my decision. Intellectuals often present themselves as victims. The truth is that no totalitarian regime could exist without the help of intellectuals. I wanted to show that an intellectual could also be an evildoer, given the situation.

Would you talk generally about how "Saboteur" evolved once you'd made the connection between the two events and decided who the main character would be?

The dramatic development here is how to make a victim gradually change into to a victimizer. As the story continues, we can see that Mr. Chiu's temper gets worse and worse, and so does his hepatitis. He gradually becomes a shady character. This development is necessary for his final act. Without it, the ending would not feel logical.

You used the incident with the lawyer exactly as you heard it, yet you reshaped the incident about the Shanghai workers to suit Mr. Chiu's circumstances. Would you talk about why you made that change?

The function of our imagination is not just to create details, but also to unify details by reshaping some of them. In this case, the story is set in a smaller city, Muji, and the protagonist is an intellectual. These changes required the adaption of that factual detail.

The function of our imagination is not just to create details, but also to unify details by reshaping some of them.

In the beginning of the story, Chiu is an accomplished, sheltered man, eating lunch with his bride. At the end of the story, hungry for revenge, he is no better than those who harmed him, and his student for the first time thinks of him as an ugly man. Would you talk about the evolution of Chiu's character through the story and also about the abrupt, chilling end that you accomplish with the last paragraph? Did you know from the start that the story would end with that abrupt switch from Chiu's personal story to an objective statement of fact?

I knew for sure how the story would end. The difficult part was how to make the story move to the final point dramatically and emotionally. Mr. Chiu's evolution reflects how evil can beget evil. People who got hurt often hurt others in return. In truth, I don't think Mr. Chiu's character changes much. His student's view of him is a manifestation of the evil within him. The short story as a form doesn't have enough space to develop a character fully. The best way to reveal a character is through drama.

The best way to reveal a character is through drama.

Generally, what is it about an incident or piece of information that draws your attention to it and makes you think it's something that might be spun into fiction? Is there a way you collect and keep track of bits of the real world that you think you might use in a story?

As I said, I am often bothered by things and events. To create a story, you need some key dramatic details. Once you have one or two, you begin to look for more either in your memory or through research. Once you have enough dramatic details, you find the connections among them, trying to give them a dramatic order. By connecting them causally, you create a plot or a dramatic pattern. In this sense, a good writer must be sensitive to things around him.

Could you give some advice to aspiring writers about how to spin fact into fiction?

Facts in isolation are meaningless. A writer's strength lies in creating a unique order that organizes facts. That order is your message.

A writer's strength lies in creating a unique order that organizes facts.

Would you talk a bit about how you go about revising your stories?

Because I always teach, I often have a sense of urgency in writing my first draft. But it's important for me to have the black on the white. After that, I will have something to work on. The revision process is also an interpretive process—I will find nuances and possibilities I missed. So it is an organic part of writing.

The revision process is also an interpretive process—I will find nuances and possibilities I missed.

My first draft is awfully rough, embarrassingly bad, but I do rewrites and revise heavily for a long time. For every piece of work, I have reached the point where I can't do anything more, though I know that if I put the manuscript aside for a while, I will be able to return to it with a fresh mind and can surely do more revision. In this sense, revision is endless, but we have to stop somewhere. I stop at the point where I cannot improve anything for the time being. In truth, that's not enough. Sometimes I lay a piece aside for later revision.

How do you think living and working in the United States has affected the way you see China and/or how you write about it?

Living here makes it possible for me to treat China just as a subject. The distance and the feeling of alienation help me become objective and detached. Above all, America has given me a free state of mind. I haven't returned to China since I came. Contemporary China is unfamiliar to me now, so the more meaningful subject for me is the American experience. Up to now, I have written about the immigrant experience only in my poetry. In the future I will write about it in my fiction. But this cannot be rushed, and I have to be patient.

Is there a reason that writing about your immigration experiences has thus far seemed more possible in poetry than in fiction?

Yes, poetry often responds to immediate events and things. It doesn't have to be elaborate and comprehensive. Very often a poem is an impression. But fiction is different. It requires the deeper understanding and full mastery of your material. What's more, fiction is closer to reality, which is sometimes hard to present, especially if you are a new arrival in the place you describe.

"After Cowboy Chicken Came to Town" has some of the characteristics of an immigrant story in the way Chinese workers in an American-owned fast-food restaurant find themselves at odds with the culture of capitalism. Would you talk about that story—where it came from, how it evolved, and in what ways it might reflect your experiences working in restaurants during your early years in America?

It originated from a newspaper article I read. The policy of burning leftover chicken bothered me. So I created this story. At another level, the story was influenced by Chekhov, who in his later years wrote some long, plotless stories, which are just pieces of life. "After Cowboy Chicken Came to Town" strives to be a piece of life. It has no plot. Its ending seems to be a beginning. My work at Friendly's helped me know the inside of a fast-food restaurant, so I didn't have to do any research.

If you were to write a story about a Chinese immigrant doing similar work in the United States, how might it be the same and/or different from this story, set in China?

It would be very different, because the immigrants would face different kinds of frustrations. They wouldn't band together against the capitalist way. They would be homesick and feel handicapped socially and emotionally. In brief, their psychology would be totally different.

Camus wrote, "A man's work is nothing but a long journey through the detours of art to the two or three simple and great images which first gained access to his heart." What are those images for you? How do you think they will come into play as you shift focus and begin to write about your American life? What facts about your life in America and observations about American life generally interest you in terms of writing fiction about your American experience? What subject matter might those stories explore?

Camus must be right, though I don't have that many images. When I was young, before my teens, I often saw in my mind's eye a stonecutter. Every morning that young man would go to a mountain and cut stones alone. I never saw his face, always his back and with a long hammer on his sunburned shoulder. Later when my wife and I began to date, she once asked what my idea was, I said, "To be a stonecutter." I guess, I was longing to leave home and to be solitary. I haven't begun to write short stories set in America yet. But as a first-generation immigrant, I think language would be one of my main subjects. There are also alienation, home, the past, and the present.

While your work focuses on the ways in which the control and corruption of the Communist bureaucracy bring out the worst in people, the perceptive reader looks beyond the extremes and sees all of humanity reflected in your characters' greed and paranoia, their quickness toward cruelty when cruelty is rewarded—or simply ignored. "The Bridegroom," for example, explores homosexuality in a way that any honest reader will see echoes the treatment of homosexuality in our own culture. Would you talk about that story?

I write about similarities not differences. That story is the last piece I wrote in the collection. After finishing all the other stories, I felt the book needed something else to make it broader in scope. Since homosexuality was rarely written about in the Chinese setting, I decided to write a story about this. I began to do research, reading books and articles on the subject and picking the details I might use for the story. Gradually a story emerged in my mind. I wanted to create a prejudiced but decent narrator, who told a story about a gay man. In a way, this story is also about the narrator, about the failure and limitation of his compassion.

To what extent do you think it reflects attitudes about homosexuality that Western culture and Chinese culture have in common?

Homosexuality is often treated as abnormal or a disease. Human compassion is often limited by our mores.

Would you comment on the ways all of your work transcends its specific subject matter and becomes about all people, everywhere?

Literature operates on the principle of similarity and identity. I believe in universals and try to make my work speak to similarities. This isn't to say I ignore differences. We do need different details to make a piece of writing fresh and interesting, but at core, meaningful work should rest on the bedrock of humanity.

Literature operates on the principle of similarity and identity. I believe in universals and try to make my work speak to similarities.

Writing Prompts

READ: "Love in the Air" and the interview with **Ha Jin.**

PONDER: The way Ha Jin creates character and plot using the quirky details of a profession.

WRITE: List words, phrases, duties, relationships, and situations that are unique to a job with which you are familiar. Write a story that hinges on something that could not happen in any other kind of job.

PRACTICE:

- Create a character who falls in love with a voice. Write the scene in which the person behind the voice surprises the character and complicates his life.
- Remember or invent the most difficult, painful scene you can imagine. Write it using simple language. Don't flinch.
- Write a story that is an homage to a story you admire.
- Look for news reports for key events that might be combined to make a story. Consider how one event might emotionally push toward the other event to create a climax and ending.
- Identify a factual event or series of events that interests you. Then reorder, adapt, and invent around the facts to create a story.

Jamaica Kincaid

Jamaica Kincaid (b. 1949) is the author of one collection of short stories, four novels, one nonfiction book, and three collections of essays. Born in St. John, Antigua, as Elaine Potter Richardson, she came to New York as an au pair *in 1965. In 1973 she changed her name to Jamaica Kincaid and soon afterwards began writing for* The New Yorker.

*Her honors include the Morton Dauwen Zabel Award from the American Academy and Institute of Arts and Letters, the Lila Wallace–*Reader's Digest *Fund Writer's Award, and the Boston Book Review Fisk Fiction Prize. Her work has been nominated for the National Book Critics Circle Award, the National Book Award, and the PEN/Faulkner Award. Kincaid teaches at Harvard University. She lives in North Bennington, Vermont.*

For Further Reading:
At the Bottom of the River (1983), *Annie John* (1985), *A Small Place* (1988), *Lucy* (1990), *The Autobiography of My Mother* (1995), *My Brother* (1997), *My Garden (Book)* (1999), *Talk Stories* (2000), *Mr. Potter* (2002).

Poor Visitor

It was my first day. I had come the night before, a gray-black and cold night before—as it was expected to be in the middle of January, though I didn't know that at the time—and I could not see anything clearly on the way in from the airport, even though there were lights everywhere. As we drove along, someone would single out to me a famous building, an important street, a park, a bridge that when built was thought to be a spectacle. In a day-dream I used to have, all these places were points of happiness to me; all these places were lifeboats to my small drowning soul, for I would imagine myself entering and leaving them, and just that—entering and leaving over and over again—would see me through a bad feeling I did not have a name for. I only knew it felt a little like sadness but heavier than that. Now that I saw these places, they looked ordinary, dirty, worn down by so many people entering and leaving them in real life, and it occurred to me that I could not be the only person in the world for whom they were a fixture of fantasy. It was not my first bout with the disappointment of reality and it would not be my last. The undergarments that I wore were all new, bought for my journey, and as I sat in the car, twisting this way and that to get a good view of the sights before me, I was reminded of how uncomfortable the new can make you feel.

I got into an elevator, something I had never done before, and then I was in an apartment and seated at a table, eating food just taken from a refrigerator. In the place I had just come from, I always lived in a house, and my house did not have a refrigerator in it. Everything I was experiencing—the ride in the elevator, being in an apartment, eating day-old food that had been stored in a refrigerator—was such a good idea that I could imagine I would grow used to it and like it very much, but at first it was all so new that I had to smile with my mouth turned down at the corners. I slept soundly that night, but it wasn't because I was happy and comfortable—quite the opposite; it was because I didn't want to take in anything else.

That morning, the morning of my first day, the morning that followed my first night, was a sunny morning. It was not the sort of bright sun-yellow making everything curl at the edges, almost in fright, that I was used to, but a pale-yellow sun, as if the sun had grown weak from trying too hard to shine; but still it was sunny, and that was nice and made me miss my home less. And so, seeing the sun, I got up and put on a dress, a gay dress made out of madras cloth—the same sort of dress that I would wear if I were at home and setting out for a day in the country. It was all wrong. The sun was shining but the air was cold. It was the middle of January, after all. But I did not know that the sun could shine and the air remain cold; no one had ever told me. What a feeling that was! How can I explain? Something I had always known—the way I knew my skin was the color brown of a nut rubbed repeatedly with a soft cloth, or the way I knew my own name—something I took completely for granted, "the sun is shining, the air is warm," was not so. I was no longer in a tropical zone, and this realization now entered my life like a flow of water dividing formerly dry and solid ground, creating two banks, one of which was my past—so familiar and predictable that even my unhappiness then made me happy now just to think of it—the other my future, a gray blank, an overcast seascape on which rain was falling and no boats were in sight. I was no longer in a tropical zone and I felt cold inside and out, the first time such a sensation had come over me.

In books I had read—from time to time, when the plot called for it—someone would suffer from homesickness. A person would leave a not very nice situation and go somewhere else, somewhere a lot better, and then long to go back where it was not very nice. How impatient I would become with such a person, for I would feel that I was in a not very nice situation myself, and how I wanted to go somewhere else. But now I, too, felt that I wanted to be back where I came from. I understood it, I knew where I stood there. If I had had to draw a picture of my future then, it would have been a large gray patch surrounded by black, blacker, blackest.

What a surprise this was to me, that I longed to be back in the place that I came from, that I longed to sleep in a bed I had outgrown, that I longed to be with people whose smallest, most natural gesture would call up in me such a rage that I longed to see them all dead at my feet. Oh, I had imagined that with my one swift act—leaving home and coming to this new place—I could leave behind me, as if it were an old garment never to be worn again, my sad thoughts, my sad feelings, and my discontent with life in general as it presented itself to me. In the past, the thought of being in my present situation had been a comfort, but now I did not even have this to look forward to, and so I lay down on my bed and dreamt I was eating a bowl of pink mullet and green figs cooked in coconut milk, and it had been cooked by my grandmother, which was why the taste of it pleased me so, for she was the person I liked best in all the world and those were the things I liked best to eat also.

The room in which I lay was a small room just off the kitchen—the maid's room. I was used to a small room, but this was a different sort of small room. The ceiling was very high and the walls went all the way up to the ceiling, enclosing the room like a box—a box in which cargo traveling a long way should be shipped. But I was not cargo. I was only an unhappy young woman living in a maid's room, and I was not even the maid. I was the young girl who watches over the children and goes to school at night. How nice everyone was to me, though, saying that I should regard them as my family and make myself at home. I believed them to be sincere, for I knew that such a thing would not be said to a member of their real family. After all, aren't family the people who become the millstone around your life's neck? On the last day I spent at home, my cousin—a girl I had known all my life, an unpleasant person even before her parents forced her to become a Seventh-Day Adventist—made a farewell present to me of her own Bible, and with it she made a little speech about God and goodness and blessings. Now it sat before me on a dresser, and I remembered how when we were children we would sit under my house and terrify and torment each other by reading out loud passages from the Book of Revelation, and I wondered if ever in my whole life a day would go by when these people I had left behind, my own family, would not appear before me in one way or another.

There was also a small radio on this dresser, and I had turned it on. At that moment, almost as if to sum up how I was feeling, a song came on, some of the words of which were "Put yourself in my place, if only for a day; see if you can stand the awful emptiness inside." I sang these words to myself over and over, as if they were a lullaby, and I fell asleep again. I dreamt then that I was holding in my hands one of my old cotton-flannel nightgowns, and it was printed with beautiful scenes of children playing with Christmas-tree decorations. The scenes printed on my nightgown were so real that I could actually hear the children laughing. I felt compelled to know where this nightgown came from, and I started to examine it furiously, looking for the label. I found it just where a label usually is, in the back, and it read "Made in Australia." I was awakened from this dream by the actual maid, a woman who had let me know right away, on meeting me, that she did not like me, and gave as her reason the way I talked. I thought it was because of something else, but I did not know what. As I opened my eyes, the word "Australia" stood between our faces, and I remembered then that Australia was settled as a prison for bad people, people so bad that they couldn't be put in a prison in their own country.

My waking hours soon took on a routine. I walked four small girls to their school, and when they returned at midday I gave them a lunch of soup from a tin, and sandwiches. In the afternoon, I read to them and played with them. When they were away, I studied my books, and at night I went to school. I was unhappy. I looked at a map. An ocean stood between me and the place I came from, but would it have made a difference if it had been a teacup of water? I could not go back.

Outside, always it was cold, and everyone said that it was the coldest winter they had ever experienced; but the way they said it made me think they said this every time winter came around. And I couldn't blame them for not really remembering each year how unpleasant, how unfriendly winter weather could be. The trees with their bare, still limbs looked dead, and as if someone had just placed them there and planned to come back and get them later; all the windows of the houses were shut tight, the way windows are shut up when a house will be empty for a long time; when people walked on the streets they did it quickly, as if they were doing something behind someone's back, as if they didn't want to draw attention to themselves, as if being out in the cold too long would cause them to dissolve. How I longed to see someone lingering on a corner, trying to draw my attention to him, trying to engage me in conversation, someone complaining to himself in a voice I could overhear about a God whose love and mercy fell on the just and the unjust.

I wrote home to say how lovely everything was, and I used flourishing words and phrases, as if I were living life in a greeting card—the kind that has a satin ribbon on it, and quilted hearts and roses, and is expected to be so precious to the person receiving it that the manufacturer has placed a leaf of plastic on the front to protect it. Everyone I wrote to said how nice it was to hear from me, how nice it was to know that I was doing well, that I was very much missed, and that they couldn't wait until the day came when I returned.

One day the maid who said she did not like me because of the way I talked told me that she was sure I could not dance. She said that I spoke like a nun, I walked like one also, and that everything about me was so pious it made her feel at once sick to her stomach and sick with pity just to look at me. And so, perhaps giving, way to the latter feeling, she said that we should dance, even though she was quite sure I didn't know how. There was a little portable record-player in my room, the kind that when closed up looked like a ladies' vanity case, and she put on a record she had bought earlier that day. It was a song that was very popular at the time—three girls, not older than I was, singing in harmony and in a very insincere and artificial way about love and so on. It was very beautiful all the same, and it was beautiful because it was so insincere and artificial.

She enjoyed this song, singing at the top of her voice, and she was a wonderful dancer—it amazed me to see the way in which she moved. I could not join her and I told her why: the melodies of her song were so shallow, and the words, to me, were meaningless. From her face, I could see she had only one feeling about me: how sick to her stomach I made her. And so I said that I knew songs, too, and I burst into a calypso about a girl who ran away to Port-of-Spain, Trinidad, and had a good time, with no regrets.

The household in which I lived was made up of a husband, a wife, and the four girl children. The husband and wife looked alike and their four children looked just like them. In photographs of themselves, which they placed all over the house, their six yellow-haired heads of various sizes were bunched as if they were a bouquet of flowers tied together by an unseen string. In the pictures, they smiled out at the world, giving the impression that they found everything in it unbearably wonderful. And it was not a farce, their smiles. From wherever they had gone, and they seemed to have been all over the world, they brought back some tiny memento, and they could each recite its history from its very beginnings. Even when a little rain fell, they would admire the way it streaked through the blank air.

At dinner, when we sat down at the table—and did not have to say grace (such a relief; as if they believed in a God that did not have to be thanked every time you turned around)—they said such nice things to each other, and the children were so happy. They would spill their food, or not eat any of it at all, or make up rhymes about it that would end with the words "smelt bad." How they made me laugh, and I wondered what sort of parents I must have had, for even to think of such words in their presence I would have been scolded severely, and I vowed that if I ever had children I would make sure that the first words out of their mouths were bad ones.

It was at dinner one night not long after I began to live with them that they began to call me the Visitor. They said I seemed not to be a part of things, as if I didn't live in their house with them, as if they weren't like a family to me, as if I were just passing through, just saying one long Hallo!, and soon would be saying a quick Goodbye! So long! It was very nice! For look at the way I stared at them as they ate, Lewis said. Had I never seen anyone put a forkful of French-cut green beans in his mouth before? This made Mariah laugh, but almost everything Lewis said made Mariah happy and so she would laugh. I didn't laugh, though, and Lewis looked at me, concern on his face. He said, "Poor Visitor, poor Visitor," over and over, a sympathetic tone to his voice, and then he told me a story about an uncle he had who had gone to Canada and raised monkeys, and of how after a while the uncle loved monkeys so much and was so used to being around them that he found actual human beings hard to take. He had told me this story about his uncle before, and while he was telling it to me this time I was remembering a dream I had had about them: Lewis was chasing me around the house. I wasn't wearing any clothes. The ground on which I was running was yellow, as if it had been paved with cornmeal. Lewis was chasing me around and around the house, and though he came close he could never catch up with me. Mariah stood at the open windows saying, Catch her, Lewis, catch her. Eventually I fell down a hole, at the bottom of which were some silver and blue snakes.

When Lewis finished telling his story, I told them my dream. When I finished, they both fell silent. Then they looked at me and Mariah cleared her throat, but it was obvious from the way she did it that her throat did not need clearing at all. Their two yellow heads swam toward each other and, in unison, bobbed up and down. Lewis made a clucking noise, then said, Poor, poor Visitor. And Mariah said, Dr. Freud for Visitor, and I wondered why she said that, for I did not know who Dr. Freud was. Then they laughed in a soft, kind way. I had meant by telling them my dream that I had taken them in, because only people who were very important to me had ever shown up in my dreams. I did not know if they understood that.

A Conversation with Jamaica Kincaid

You began your career as a writer as a reporter for The New Yorker *magazine's "Talk of the Town." Would you talk about writing those "Talk" stories and about how your time at* The New Yorker *trained you to be a writer?*

I went to *The New Yorker.* I was taken there by a man named George Trow in 1973. I didn't really know anything about *The New Yorker.* I didn't know anything about writing. I just decided that I wanted to write. That I was a writer. I'd left college. I had no formal background. There's no tradition of writing in my family or where I'm from. But I just decided I was going to be a writer. I seemed unable to do anything else. So I went to New York and said, "I'm a writer." I started to write little things for the *Village Voice,* reviews of television shows, even before *The New Yorker.* I was also always quoted in "Talk of the Town." One day I went to the West Indian Day in Brooklyn and I jotted down my thoughts about it, put my quotes after my observations, and gave them to George, who took them to Mr. Shawn. I thought Mr. Shawn would have George rewrite it, because I didn't recognize it as writing. It was just my thoughts in my head. And my observations. Things I would just *say,* you know. It didn't seem to be my writing. But he published it just as I gave it to him and that's when I realized that the way I said things or the way I thought about things was the way I would write. That my thoughts and my observations were important to a reader. I think I would have spent a great part of my life trying to be a *writer,* maybe not understanding that my authority and my sense of self-possession were a profound part of my expression and worthy of consideration. I probably would not have known that, if ever. So when I saw this thing I had done in print, I literally just thought, Ah! I see!

But I just decided I was going to be a writer. I seemed unable to do anything else.

Then Mr. Shawn hired me as a "Talk" reporter. But that meant I had to start using the *we,* and I didn't like it at all. It felt constrained to me, it felt phony. I didn't—*don't*—like being a *we* in that regard. I like being a *we* when I'm crossing the street, I like being *We the people.* But when I'm writing I don't like being a *we* at all. So I started to invent this way of avoiding saying *we.* I just would start to talk. I would somehow place the voice in the story to eliminate the *we* or *I.* For example, "Crossing the street is the policeman." I could write a letter or I could write my own voice and say, "We have a letter from our friend, Jamaica Kincaid." A lot of those talk stories were ways of avoiding saying *'we'.* I would write them as plays, I would write them as dialogue, I would try to be funny with them. My friend, Sandy Frasier, and I would just sit there and try to come up with a way to write this *we* without *we*.

One of them I wrote in the form of an expense account. I hated the person I was writing about. It was Milton Friedman. At that time, even I knew that he was involved in Chile and economic destabilization in other places, and I absolutely hated his free market theories. He and his wife published a book, and I wanted to write about them with contempt. But I knew Mr. Shawn would not accept it if I said, "I find these people contemptible." He didn't think you had a right to say that about anybody, to make fun of people. So I knew he would never publish it if I put it that way. So I found this way of, in my mind, belittling them by reducing their efforts to an expense account. Eventually, the event, their ideas, their book, all their endeavors were overwhelmed by the finer line, which was the cost of the building. I called up and asked how much their clothes and shoes cost, how much their breakfast cost—even how much Mr. Friedman's tie cost. I wrote everything down, everything, in terms of cost, and was belittling. Even more belittling was to have them be overwhelmed by the building, because I thought that's the kind of people they were. And it was published. I look at it now with awe, that they would have published a "Talk" story in the form of an expense account.

Experimenting with the "Talk" stories had to be a big part of the transition into writing the stories in "At the Bottom of the River."

If you look at those stories, you'll see the beginnings of how I came to write fiction by, in a way, transgressing the normal bounds of what a story is.

What about the first story in that collection, "Girl"? There are no pronouns in the story; the speaker never refers to herself. Was there anything in particular that you were experimenting with or trying to avoid in writing it?

That form evolved out of my tinkering with forms in "Talk of the Town." I absolutely hated the kind of fiction *The New Yorker* published then. Not because it was bad. I thought it wasn't adventurous. I thought, if you were going to sit down and write, how could you allow your writing to become these shallow things? I won't mention the writers, but the only person I admired was Donald Barthelme. I loved him. But generally I thought the fiction was weak and not interesting at all. So when I started to write, I was determined—arrogantly, mind you, to a degree that you can only forgive because I was so young—to write in a certain way so that when the other people who were writing saw what I had written they would say, "Oh! My writing is abominable, I'll never write again." I really thought that they would all stop writing that terrible writing and they would write something interesting, whatever it was. Well, of course, my writing appeared and the world continued on its axis. Everything was the same. I was quite astonished.

If you look at those stories, you'll see the beginnings of how I came to write fiction by, in a way, transgressing the normal bounds of what a story is.

But you found a voice, and you found a place to publish.

I did. And I look at those stories and wonder, how did they publish them? They're very strange stories. But they were written out of an impulse to break some mold. They're the only stories I've ever really written. They come out of the experience of just trying to do something else with "Talk of the Town." When I first started to write I thought writing was the most sacred thing in the world and you just had to die for it, really. All of those attempts in that first book, all those short stories, were an attempt to see if I could survive a certain kind of experience, a certain kind of dying. I really felt that it was life and death every time.

Was "Girl" the first story that you wrote?

Yes. "Girl" was the first story. I used to have this New Year's wish. You know how you wish on New Year's for a wonderful year; I would wish that this was the year I'd write fiction. It was '78 that year. Somebody had given me a book by Elizabeth Bishop called *Geography Three.* I read it, but more important I read the first poem in it, "In the Waiting Room," and after I read that I sat down and wrote "Girl" in one sitting. I knew how to write after I wrote "Girl." I just knew.

I read the first poem in it, "In the Waiting Room," and after I read that I sat down and wrote "Girl" in one sitting. I knew how to write after I wrote "Girl." I just knew.

It really came directly from that poem?

Yes. I'd never heard of her. I didn't know she was important. I had just been given this book for Christmas, and I read it. It was as simple and direct as that.

So "Girl" was a story that just came to you, all of a piece?

Oh, yes. Also, in that period, was the time when I was most obsessed with my mother. I hadn't seen her in over ten years, and we hadn't talked. We'd stopped corresponding. I had refused to write to her anymore, I refused to open her letters. But I would talk about her obsessively. And I would dream about her. I could hear her voice all the time. And that story is a distillation of my entire childhood, how I came to be a woman. What was expected of me.

And that story is a distillation of my entire childhood, how I came to be a woman. What was expected of me.

It seems to have in it the seed for everything else that came afterwards.

It does.

That first collection, At the Bottom of the River, *feels like it's coming from some primal place—like you're right there in this really strange world, reporting on it. It's particularly evident in the story, "My Mother." Some people would call that magical realism. Students often want to write like that, and it so often falls flat. Why did it work for you there and in your other work?*

I don't know about the mysteries of these things. Many things contribute to that particular story. A certain moment in my childhood when the world did seem magical—and, by the way, I had never heard of the term *magical realism* at the time. It was a memory of a childhood, not necessarily my own, even, but certainly of a childhood as I would have heard of it in Pre-Raphaelite writing or Romantic poetry. It comes out of somebody's childhood, including my own, or I should say many childhoods imagined, real. I think there was a moment in my own life experience where I was in paradise. I was an only child, I lived a magical life with my mother. That story, "My Mother," is a pretty accurate description—I could practically say that's an autobiography of my childhood, as a metaphor.

I was always, especially when I first started to write, interested in paradise and losing it. Many things would contribute to that, not least of all that when I was about seven I misbehaved in class and my punishment was to copy out Books One and Two of *Paradise Lost.* I had read the Bible a lot—the story of Genesis, Adam and Eve in the garden. Those things made a tremendous impression on me. The idea of once there was some golden moment that was my life and then I lost it or I was kicked out of it. That's actually a motif that repeats in my life, of having something and then losing it. The first time it happened was when my brothers were born. Suddenly, I lost my mother—not her love, really, her attention. But I didn't know the difference.

The idea of once there was some golden moment that was my life and then I lost it or I was kicked out of it. That's actually a motif that repeats in my life, of having something and then losing it.

Much in "Poor Visitor" reflects how uncomfortable the new can make you feel; early on, the narrator observes that some of the New York landmarks she's seeing for the first time seem like "lifeboats to [her] small drowning soul" because she's imagined them so many times. Being uncomfortable with the new and searching for "lifeboats" are elements that show up again and again in your stories.

Yes. That line! You make me realize how much I was thinking of Milton and *Paradise Lost* when I wrote that book. I was thinking of, actually, mainly two—or maybe three—things. Probably, I was thinking of *Jane Eyre.* But most certainly I was thinking of Wordsworth and Milton—in a rather innocent way. Not as a scholar at all, but just as an influence on my imagination. I would say that I very much thought of my imagination as shaped by English sensibilities, traditions.

Annie John *followed* At the Bottom of the River. *The prose in that book and in* Lucy, *which followed it, seems to bring the two worlds together, in terms of your writing style. The sense of strangeness and wonder of the island world is rendered in the kind of simple, clear, honest sentences that* New Yorker *writers were known for during that time. Would you talk about the evolution of your writing style reflected in your first novel?*

Her voice, the way it is written, she's young. It has more a sense of discovery. She says very complicated things, but in a simple way. That was not hard to do at all. That girl's life was so familiar to me, her voice was so familiar. Lucy, too, would call for that kind of straightforward, though very probing voice—saying complicated things, but in a very innocent way. Also at the same time I was discovering *my* voice, the way I could say things. Having written *At the Bottom of the River,* I could see that I could do all sorts of dramatic things. I had a command of language and sentences and emotion. I knew I could do that. So now I could simplify. And in the later books, the two later novels and the book about my brother, I come back to do that more complicated thing. Now I'm at the stage where I want to do more complicated things, and I'm trying to do that. But to talk about the evolution of my style, I think that what drives it is trying to find a way of saying something new. I always want to do something new. So if I wrote *Lucy* today, or something like it, it would be different. And I probably will write it again, and in another way, because all I write is the same thing.

It seems all writers do that. Your material is like a kaleidoscope—a set stones inside and you just shake it just a bit, see it again and again in brand new patterns.

That's right. I love that. I'm accused of, "Oh! Her mother *again.*" I suspect that if I were a man—and I say this not looking for sympathy, but as a clear observation—that these things would be considered wonderful. No one says, "*Dublin* again!" Not to compare myself. But you see what I mean. I probably will write Lucy again. I love that world. But it's not just that I love it. It yields so much of how I see the world, that I could find a metaphor for the powerful and the powerless in *that,* that is satisfying to me. I needn't go on a slave ship to find the relics of master/slave—or master/subordinate. I can find it in my own family. The power is the same. It's complicated. You die, you *die.* But how you die yields all sorts of questions and answers for me. So I probably will revisit it.

But you don't often go back—physically—to Antigua, do you?

I didn't for a long time—twenty years, and then when I had my first child, a daughter, I was afraid that if I didn't speak to my mother I would repeat my childhood. So I went back in 1986, and then I went back a couple of times and my mother and I again repeated our catastrophic, disastrous behavior to each other. So I didn't go for a while, and she and I were not speaking again. But then my brother got ill and I started to go back a lot to take care of him. That was between '92 and '96. After he died, I went a couple of times to see my mother. Then she and I fell out and that was the last time I ever spoke with her. So far I don't regret it. It was a very . . . unmanageable relationship. Actually, my mother died, and her three children were not speaking to her. It was sad.

The relationship is reflected in your character, Lucy. It's heartbreaking when she gets the letters from her mother and knows that if she reads them she will die of the longing. The reader, at that point, knows exactly what she's going through. It's a very complicated set of emotions to give over to a reader. The stories, novels are really all about love, aren't they?

Yes, they are. People often think they are about anger, but not at all. You can't hate unless you love. They are the same. Always, a lot of the stories in the past—including *Autobiography of My Mother*—you could see them all as one person. You could go back to Annie John, who learns that love is a dangerous emotion. It can immolate you. It can make you disappear, it can destroy you. She loves this sun of a mother, this great sunlight, but it always threatens to extinguish her. Love is everything. It is an emotion that you have to be very careful with. Certainly, that's what happens in *Autobiography of My Mother.* This person carefully controls her feelings, and it's very important to her that she remain in control of her entire world. That really narrows you. That's the price.

People often think [the stories] are about anger, but not at all. You can't hate unless you love.

What was it about your early life that made you a writer? What makes people writers?

What is it? In my case, I believe very strongly that being alone was crucial. I was alone for a long time. Perhaps also crucial was, early on, my mother found my attachment to her—she loved it, but it was also demanding. She read a great deal and I was always interfering with her reading. No other mother I knew read. None of my friends' mothers read. But my mother read a lot of things. Obsessively. I felt neglected. She thought that if I could read I would leave her alone, so she taught me to read. By the time I was three-and-a-half, I could read so well that she sent me to school. But you could only go to school if you were five. So she told me to say I was five, and they believed it because no one younger than five could read so well. In fact, I read so well that the other parts of my education suffered. They were always impressed by how well I could read and they were always putting me in a higher class, but I didn't know how to do the other things. But anyway, that's the beginning of something writerly. That, my books and love. And lying—I was told all the time, "Never lie, never lie," but I was asked by this great person to lie, to say that I was five, and that began a whole set of things. I was too young to know how to behave properly, so from the very beginning of school I got in trouble. I was overly curious, I didn't behave well, I spoke out of turn. And I was alone. So I go home. I'm alone with my mother and I remember the day. I remember missing her. I was quite thin and fragile. I didn't know how to defend myself. I would get in trouble and people would beat me up. Oh! It was one long thing after the next. It must have been only two years, but it all left an impression on me. I can remember the first primer I read, and that must have been when I was three-and-a-half years old. But something I remembered from it—and I've told this story many times. It was about a man who was a farmer, who had a cat, whose name was Tibbs, and a dog named Mr. Dan, a cow—I think she was just a cow—and a hen, a mother hen. She had twelve chicks; eleven of them were yellow and chick-like, and one, the twelfth one, was bigger and black. His name was Percy. The sentence that stayed in my mind about all that was, "Percy, the chick, had a fall." Only much later I could understand why it would stick in my mind. He was black, he was in trouble. He had a fall, like Lucifer. Only much later I could put it together and look at the things I retained, the things I chose to remember.

Perhaps that is the definition of a writer's material, her "stuff." The things that you remember, whatever makes you keep asking the questions, Why do people do this? Why did this happen? Perhaps it's that innate curiosity, a desire to understand that makes one a writer.

Yes. *How* could this be? *Why* was he bigger? *Why* was he in trouble? Why was he black? And he was the only one who had a name. And he had a fall. "Percy, the chick, had a fall." He was always in trouble. Not so long after that I began to read the Bible. I read what's called the Old Testament obsessively, because it was, actually, the only thing I had to read in our house. I had my own Bible, and I would read it and read it and read it. I didn't like the New Testament so much. It was just about this main character and his friends. You can't underestimate how boring it is for a reader, those stories, after a while. The beheading, the fishes, the this, the that. Whereas, the drama of the people and crossing the Red Sea! The Commandments. Oh, it was endless! Even the prophets were about the people. Really, I could exhaust the New Testament rather quickly, until I got to Revelations. I loved Revelations. I would read it over and over and feel so terrified.

What do you think can and can't be taught about writing? How do you work with young people who want to become writers?

I think you can't teach writing at all, even though I'm a writing teacher. But I don't think I'm teaching writing. The way I begin class often is to bring in something that I think is wonderful and read it to my students. I insist they read. Mainly, I go over their writing with them in the class, and we have a conversation about writing and about their writing. I edit things with them in the class. I come across a word and say, "Is this the right word?" What does this word mean, and is this how you should use it? Wouldn't a comma be better there? Someone was just writing about being on a train and seeing things go by, but it was all jumbled. I asked her to explain and she said, "Well, you know how when you're on a train . . ." And it occurred to me, of course, when you're on a train and things are going by that fast, they *do* go by that fast, but *you* make the effort to make each scene still. You say, "I saw a building, it had windows, windowpanes." So I could make her slow down each frame. It was a useful thing to teach—not just them, myself: what it is you see when you're writing.

I think you can't teach writing at all, even though I'm a writing teacher.

It was a useful thing to teach—not just them, myself: what it is you see when you're writing.

I had in William Shawn someone who gave me an opportunity to write, and guidance. Who, when he heard something I had done said, "This is it." And was loving. That's the most you can give a young writer: encouragement and love and kindness. And listen to them and say, "That sounds like your voice." Or, "That doesn't." You could be wrong, mind you. Mr. Shawn often didn't like things that I wrote, and I said, "Well, I'm going to write it anyway," and then he would publish it. He'd ask me to remove something and I'd say no. He would beg me to remove something. He'd say, "If you could just change it and then you could change it back when you put it in a book," and I'd say, "No, no, no." And he would publish it. But part of being a teacher is to allow the person being taught to defend the idea that they have a responsibility for their voice, too. And part of your teaching is to be respectful to hear what the person is saying. But, generally, I think it is impossible to teach such an individual thing. It's not like painting where, you know, you have to learn how to draw. The difficulty with writing is that it's common to all of us. All of us *might* be able to write. But there's simply no way all of us can paint.

The difficulty with writing is that it's common to all of us. All of us *might* be able to write. But there's simply no way all of us can paint.

We share the currency of writing. It's what we use to order a pizza.

Yes. Or the instructions on a tin of soup. It's a very dramatic thing to do: to decide that you are a writer. You decide, I am going to separate myself and make art of a thing that is common to all of us. I find it weird.

Many excerpts from your novels that followed At the Bottom of the River *were published as short stories in* The New Yorker. *They work as short stories.*

I know!

You sound surprised.

I am surprised. I never knew how the novels would end, even though sometimes I'd write the end first. I never knew what the whole thing would turn out to be. I was always writing for Mr. Shawn. So much of what I wrote up until *A Small Place* was simply written to get his attention, like my mother. So I would write something and I'd say, "Here." And he would publish it.

Did you feel you were working on novels when you were writing those pieces, or did you feel you were writing a cycle of short stories?

I didn't feel I was working on a novel, I didn't feel I was working on a short story. I had no thought of shape to anything, simply that I would give it to Mr. Shawn. For instance, my book, *A Small Place,* was written as something to give Mr. Shawn. I gave it to him and he absolutely loved it and was going to publish it in *The New Yorker* as an essay. He was fired, and Bob Gottlieb hated it. He said it would antagonize the advertisers, and he didn't publish it. Mr. Shawn was really heartbroken and said, "I'm going to call Robert Straus and tell him to publish it as a small book." That's how it became a book. It would never have been a book if Mr. Shawn had remained at *The New Yorker.*

Do you have a definition of what a story is?

No, not for myself. One of the things that I really didn't want to do when I first started to write was to think something was fiction or not-fiction. I used the same material in both places. I didn't want to know what I was doing. I obviously had to know *how* to do what I was doing, but I didn't want to say, here's a short story, here's fiction. I simply wanted to write. Whatever I was thinking, I wanted it to be on the paper, but I didn't want to know that it had a name. Because if it had a name it would affect the style, and I didn't want it to do that. For instance, the style of *My Brother* is not really applicable for nonfiction. It's very peculiar as a piece of reportage. It's manipulative. I wouldn't have been able to let myself do that if I had *said* it was reporting. But it *was.* I never let myself have the category in mind while I'm doing it. But, clearly, when I'm done, I see what it is.

You said that when you were working on Lucy *and* Annie John, *those stories did not come to you chronologically.*

No, they didn't. In *Annie John,* the last story did come last. But that's because I had to finish the book. I had gotten pregnant and I just at that moment really turned against the character. I found her extremely annoying and I didn't want the voice in my head at all, because I was now becoming a mother. I thought, it has to come to an end *now.*

There are so many ways that stories gather and evolve toward their final form. Would you talk about "Poor Visitor," the first chapter of Lucy, *which was published as a short story in* The New Yorker?

It *was* written first. I wanted to write about that period in my life. It actually is very autobiographical. When I first came to America, I lived as a nanny with a family where the father was a writer for *The New Yorker.* But I didn't know anything about the magazine then. I left, went to school, came back to New York, and the next time I saw him was in the halls of *The New Yorker.* It made him very uneasy. He was very distant. And then I started to write about this part of my life. I didn't think of it as writing about them, but about what it was like. He said he didn't care. But it made the family very upset—the ex-wife and children. The mother in the family has since told me that she's so glad I wrote it because it made her understand her life. But I just wanted to understand my *own* life. I found it astonishing that I was sent off to this place in the cold. In less than ten years—really eight years—I'd gone from this poor visitor to writing for *The New Yorker.* So it was part of my anger toward my mother. I was trying to figure out, *How did she do this to me?* But of course, as she had often pointed out, it was for the best. But I have to say, *I* made it for the best. I had to rescue myself. Now I was trying to understand that part of what had happened to me. I could have done it as a memoir, but I was interested in language and form and feeling—being true to the feeling that I—that girl I was—had. She was very upset at the way she had been treated. She makes the reference to slavery, about cargo. She was like a thing. So, in a way, I start not only at the beginning of my own presence in the book, but I start basically at 1492. Partly, I wanted to retell an ancient story of my ancestors. I could have written the big drama, I suppose, about being an au pair. But I was and still am interested in condensing.

There's a wonderful little incident in the story with the black maid. She doesn't like Lucy, so it's a double not-belonging. She doesn't fit with the white people and she doesn't belong with the black people. Would you talk a little bit about yourself as African American writer—though you're not really African American, are you?

No, I'm not. Not by birth, but by adopting. A lot of Africans don't like to be African Americans because they don't like how African Americans are treated. Where they come from they're not treated that way. They are the majority. But I decided that when I became an American citizen I was going to call myself an African American and attach myself to that American narrative, because I benefit so much from the African American presence.

That isn't true for Lucy, though.

No, Lucy does not do that. She does not yet have the language of race. A lot of people criticized the book because she never says she's black.

There's that beautiful passage, where she speaks of her skin as the color of a nut. So she does know, but she sees her skin in a beautiful way. She doesn't come thinking there's something wrong with her. When she's treated differently, she's startled.

Yes. And then she locates the difference in the way she's treated with the imbalance in power. It's not her race. It's not something that is meant to be. It's just a quirk that you are in the position to deny her something. She understands, I think, that it's all a matter of where you're sitting when the music stops. Sometimes she might be sitting down and you might be standing up. The idea of race, she rejects it.

What about the dream that she shares at the end with them at the end of the story. To Lucy, it's about how they've become important to her. But Mariah says, "Oh, Dr. Freud!"

Yes, and a snake is sexual. That actually really did happen. I innocently told them at the dining table. I used to eat with them. I was the nanny, so we all ate together. And I told them this dream and they were just. . .

It got very quiet.

Yes.

When you're writing autobiographically as you do, where are the places where you make the leap into fiction? How does that feel? Are those the surprising moments, when you're working on a story and it takes a turn and then it's not your own life anymore?

I do this very self-deceiving thing when I'm writing—and also ruthless thing. I don't have any morals about it. I don't say, oops, mustn't cross that line. I take whatever I can get. If it's a real thing that will bring me to this point that I want to get to, I will take it. For instance, in the chapter "The Long Rain" in *Annie John,* all the things I described of the illness of the girl actually took place when I was seven and had whooping cough and then maybe typhoid.

I do this very self-deceiving thing when I'm writing—and also ruthless thing. I don't have any morals about it.

I had a few serious illnesses when I was a child. Another thing I suspect led to an influence on my imagination was all the time I was alone, sick. I was often very sick and delirious. I had worms, I had parasites. I had fevers, whooping cough, measles. I was often sick and I would be alone and I would read. I often couldn't tell what was the book and what was real.

That's true in the story, "My Mother." Annie John is in the darkened room and she's not sure what's real. Her mother begins to shape-change. It feels almost like a fevered dream.

When I was writing that chapter, the one before she's sent off to America, I understood that I needed her to metamorphose. But what form should she take going from this child into adulthood? How should I do it? So I took this incident of being seven and remembered certain things about being seven—the fever, my illness. I remembered another scene of rain. It was raining so much and the sound of the rain on the roof and the darkness of the storm. There are many things that I just reached and made them into what I needed.

Changed the order?

Yes, and heightened them. You have to remember, I write so much out of memory—either real memory or imagined memory.

In process, are you often surprised by your work?

Oh, yes. I'm often surprised how it all will make a whole. It makes me think that one's psyche or your mental state, your unconscious is whole. It's just waiting to reveal itself as a whole to you, if you will just let it. Whereas, you experience yourself in fragments. That moment of realizing how to take this and this and this and make it go through transitions into the last chapter is truly wonderful. I would say that in every book I've written there has been something of that kind. It makes me feel like my own psychiatrist.

You once said, "When I look at someone's library, I wish could put my head to it and just absorb it." Would you talk about the importance of reading for aspiring writers.

I would say one thing school gives the writer a chance to do is read. When people say, "I'm having a writer's block," I say, "Read." If you're reading, you're writing. Read anything. It's just essential that you never stop reading.

Writing Prompts

READ: "Poor Visitor" and the interview with **Jamaica Kincaid.**

PONDER: The way Kincaid shows "how uncomfortable the new can make you feel" through scene and detail, cranking the tension as the story moves toward the dramatic moment at the dinner table when Lucy reveals her dream.

WRITE: Remember a time when you didn't know the rules, when you felt isolated or lonely because of what you did not know. Write a scene that shows your alienation (or that of a fictional character) and hinges on the revelation of a dream. Avoid explaining why you feel alienated.

PRACTICE:

- Create an expense account that illuminates a character.
- Write a story that is inspired by the essence or truth of a poem you love.
- List all the things your mother said to you throughout your childhood and adolescence and string them together, paying attention to rhythm and tone, to convey the essence of that relationship.
- Remember a place that felt magical and describe it so that readers will feel the magic. Avoid the impulse to explain.
- Generate a cluster of memories around a certain age and then write a story from the point of view of a character that age, changing and heightening your own memories and creating new ones to serve the story.
- Identify a book that influenced you in your childhood. Consider its subject matter and the kind of words and language rhythms used to tell the story. Freewrite about the book, ranging backwards to moments in your life that are connected to it, and see if a story idea emerges.
- Write a scene in which a character gets a letter she feels she cannot open.
- Write a story that you hope will please a person whose opinions about literature are important to you.

Jhumpa Lahiri

Jhumpa Lahiri (b. 1967) is the author of one collection of short stories and one novel. Born in London and raised in Rhode Island, she was educated at Barnard College and Boston University. Her honors include the Pulitzer Prize for Fiction, the O. Henry Prize, and the Transatlantic Review Award. Her work has been selected for The Best American Short Stories *and short-listed for the M. F. K Fisher Distinguished Writing Award.* The New Yorker *named her one of the twenty best young writers in America. She lives in New York City.*

For Further Reading:
Interpreter of Maladies (1999), *The Namesake* (2003).

A Temporary Matter

The notice informed them that it was a temporary matter: for five days their electricity would be cut off for one hour, beginning at eight P.M. A line had gone down in the last snowstorm, and the repairmen were going to take advantage of the milder evenings to set it right. The work would affect only the houses on the quiet tree-lined street, within walking distance of a row of brick-faced stores and a trolley-stop, where Shoba and Shukumar had lived for three years.

"It's good of them to warn us," Shoba conceded after reading the notice aloud, more for her own benefit than Shukumar's. She let the strap of her leather satchel, plump with files, slip from her shoulders, and left it in the hallway as she walked into the kitchen. She wore a navy blue poplin raincoat over gray sweatpants and white sneakers, looking, at thirty-three, like the type of woman she'd once claimed she would never resemble.

She'd come from the gym. Her cranberry lipstick was visible only on the outer reaches of her mouth, and her eyeliner had left charcoal patches beneath her lower lashes. She used to look this way sometimes, Shukumar thought, on mornings after a party or a night at a bar, when she'd been too lazy to wash her face, too eager to collapse into his arms. She dropped a sheaf of mail on the table without a glance. Her eyes were still fixed on the notice in her other hand. "But they should do this sort of thing during the day."

"When I'm here, you mean," Shukumar said. He put a glass lid on a pot of lamb, adjusting it so only the slightest bit of steam could escape. Since January he'd been working at home, trying to complete the final chapters of his dissertation on agrarian revolts in India. "When do the repairs start?"

"It says March nineteenth. Is today the nineteenth?" Shoba walked over to the framed corkboard that hung on the wall by the fridge, bare except for a calendar of William Morris wallpaper patterns. She looked at it as if for the first time, studying the wallpaper pattern carefully on the top half before allowing her eyes to fall to the numbered grid on the bottom. A friend had sent the calendar in the mail as a Christmas gift, even though Shoba and Shukumar hadn't celebrated Christmas that year.

"Today then," Shoba announced. "You have a dentist appointment next Friday, by the way."

He ran his tongue over the tops of his teeth; he'd forgotten to brush them that morning. It wasn't the first time. He hadn't left the house at all that day, or the day before. The more Shoba stayed out, the more she began putting in extra hours at work and taking on additional projects, the more he wanted to stay in, not even leaving to get the mail, or to buy fruit or wine at the stores by the trolley stop.

Six months ago, in September, Shukumar was at an academic conference in Baltimore when Shoba went into labor, three weeks before her due date. He hadn't wanted to go to the conference, but she had insisted; it was important to make contacts, and he would be entering the job market next year. She told him that she had his number at the hotel, and a copy of his schedule and flight numbers, and she had arranged with her friend Gillian for a ride to the hospital in the event of an emergency. When the cab pulled away that morning for the airport, Shoba stood waving good-bye in her robe, with one arm resting on the mound of her belly as if it were a perfectly natural part of her body.

Each time he thought of that moment, the last moment he saw Shoba pregnant, it was the cab he remembered most, a station wagon, painted red with blue lettering. It was cavernous compared to their own car. Although Shukumar was six feet tall, with hands too big ever to rest comfortably in the pockets of his jeans, he felt dwarfed in the back seat. As the cab sped down Beacon Street, he imagined a day when he and Shoba might need to buy a station wagon of their own, to cart their children back and forth from music lessons and dentist appointments. He imagined himself gripping the wheel, as Shoba turned around to hand the children juice boxes. Once, these images of parenthood had troubled Shukumar, adding to his anxiety that he was still a student at thirty-five. But that early autumn morning, the trees still heavy with bronze leaves, he welcomed the image for the first time.

A member of the staff had found him somehow among the identical convention rooms and handed him a stiff square of stationery. It was only a telephone number, but Shukumar knew it was the hospital. When he returned to Boston it was over. The baby had been born dead. Shoba was lying on a bed, asleep, in a private room so small there was barely enough space to stand beside her, in a wing of the hospital they hadn't been to on the tour for expectant parents. Her placenta had weakened and she'd had a cesarean, though not quickly enough. The doctor explained that these things happen. He smiled in the kindest way it was possible to smile at people known only professionally. Shoba would be back on her feet in a few weeks. There was nothing to indicate that she would not be able to have children in the future.

These days Shoba was always gone by the time Shukumar woke up. He would open his eyes and see the long black hairs she shed on her pillow and think of her, dressed, sipping her third cup of coffee already, in her office downtown, where she searched for typographical errors in textbooks and marked them, in a code she had once explained to him, with an assortment of colored pencils. She would do the same for his dissertation, she promised, when it was ready. He envied her the specificity of her task, so unlike the elusive nature of his. He was a mediocre student who had a facility for absorbing details without curiosity. Until September he had been diligent if not dedicated, summarizing chapters, outlining arguments on pads of yellow lined paper. But now he would lie in their bed until he grew bored, gazing at his side of the closet which Shoba always left partly open, at the row of the tweed jackets and corduroy trousers he would not have to choose from to teach his classes that semester. After the baby died it was too late to withdraw from his teaching duties. But his adviser had arranged things so that he had the spring semester to himself. Shukumar was in his sixth year of graduate school. "That and the summer should give you a good push," his adviser had said. "You should be able to wrap things up by next September."

But nothing was pushing Shukumar. Instead he thought of how he and Shoba had become experts at avoiding each other in their three-bedroom house, spending as much time on separate floors as possible. He thought of how he no longer looked forward to weekends, when she sat for hours on the sofa with her colored pencils and her files, so that he feared that putting on a record in his own house might be rude. He thought of how long it had been since she looked into his eyes and smiled, or whispered his name on those rare occasions they still reached for each other's bodies before sleeping.

In the beginning he had believed that it would pass, that he and Shoba would get through it all somehow. She was only thirty-three. She was strong, on her feet again. But it wasn't a consolation. It was often nearly lunchtime when Shukumar would finally pull himself out of bed and head downstairs to the coffeepot, pouring out the extra bit Shoba left for him, along with an empty mug, on the countertop.

Shukumar gathered onion skins in his hands and let them drop into the garbage pail, on top of the ribbons of fat he'd trimmed from the lamb. He ran the water in the sink, soaking the knife and the cutting board and rubbed a lemon half along his fingertips to get rid of the garlic smell, a trick he'd learned from Shoba. It was seven-thirty. Through the window he saw the sky, like soft black pitch. Uneven banks of snow still lined the sidewalks, though it was warm enough for people to walk about without hats or gloves. Nearly three feet had fallen in the last storm, so that for a week people had to walk single file, in narrow trenches. For a week that was Shukumar's excuse for not leaving the house. But now the trenches were widening, and water drained steadily into grates in the pavement.

"The lamb won't be done by eight," Shukumar said. "We may have to eat in the dark."

"We can light candles," Shoba suggested. She unclipped her hair, coiled neatly at her nape during the days, and pried the sneakers from her feet without untying them. "I'm going to shower before the lights go," she said, heading for the staircase. "I'll be down."

Shukumar moved her satchel and her sneakers to the side of the fridge. She wasn't this way before. She used to put her coat on a hanger, her sneakers in the closet, and she paid bills as soon as they came. But now she treated the house as if it were a hotel. The fact that the yellow chintz armchair in the living room clashed with the blue-and-maroon Turkish carpet no longer bothered her. On the enclosed porch at the back of the house, a crisp white bag still sat on the wicker chaise, filled with lace she had once planned to turn into curtains.

While Shoba showered, Shukumar went into the downstairs bathroom and found a new toothbrush in its box beneath the sink. The cheap, stiff bristles hurt his gums, and he spit some blood into the basin. The spare brush was one of many stored in a metal basket. Shoba had bought them once when they were on sale, in the event that a visitor decided, at the last minute, to spend the night.

It was typical of her. She was the type to prepare for surprises, good and bad. If she found a skirt or a purse she liked she bought two. She kept the bonuses from her job in a separate bank account in her name. It hadn't bothered him. His own mother had fallen to pieces when his father died, abandoning the house he grew up in and moving back to Calcutta, leaving Shukumar to settle it all. He liked that Shoba was different. It astonished him, her capacity to think ahead. When she used to do the shopping, the pantry was always stocked with extra bottles of olive and corn oil, depending on whether they were cooking Italian or Indian. There were endless boxes of pasta in all shapes and colors, zippered sacks of basmati rice, whole sides of lambs and goats from the Muslim butchers at Haymarket, chopped up and frozen in endless plastic bags. Every other Saturday they wound through the maze of stalls Shukumar eventually knew by heart. He watched in disbelief as she bought more food, trailing behind her with canvas bags as she pushed through the crowd, arguing under the morning sun with boys too young to shave but already missing teeth, who twisted up brown paper bags of artichokes, plums, gingerroot, and yams, and dropped them on their scales, and tossed them to Shoba one by one. She didn't mind being jostled, even when she was pregnant. She was tall, and broad-shouldered, with hips that her obstetrician assured her were made for childbearing. During the drive back home, as the car curved along the Charles, they invariably marveled at how much food they'd bought.

It never went to waste. When friends dropped by, Shoba would throw together meals that appeared to have taken half a day to prepare, from things she had frozen and bottled, not cheap things in tins but peppers she had marinated herself with rosemary, and chutneys that she cooked on Sundays, stirring boiling pots of tomatoes and prunes. Her labeled mason jars lined the shelves of the kitchen, in endless sealed pyramids, enough, they'd agreed, to last for their grandchildren to taste. They'd eaten it all by now. Shukumar had been going through their 'supplies' steadily, preparing meals for the two of them, measuring out cupfuls of rice, defrosting bags of meat day after day. He combed through her cookbooks every afternoon, following her penciled instructions to use two teaspoons of ground coriander seeds instead of one, or red lentils instead of yellow. Each of the recipes was dated, telling the first time they had eaten the dish together. April 2, cauliflower with fennel. January 14, chicken with almonds and sultanas. He had no memory of eating those meals, and yet there they were, recorded in her neat proofreader's hand. Shukumar enjoyed cooking now. It was the one thing that made him feel productive. If it weren't for him, he knew, Shoba would eat a bowl of cereal for her dinner.

Tonight, with no lights, they would have to eat together. For months now they'd served themselves from the stove, and he'd taken his plate into his study, letting the meal grow cold on his desk before shoving it into his mouth without pause, while Shoba took her plate to the living room and watched game shows, or proofread files with her arsenal of colored pencils at hand.

At some point in the evening she visited him. When he heard her approach he would put away his novel and begin typing sentences. She would rest her hands on his shoulders and stare with him into the blue glow of the computer screen. "Don't work too hard," she would say after a minute or two, and head off to bed. It was the one time in the day she sought him out, and yet he'd come to dread it. He knew it was something she forced herself to do. She would look around the walls of the room, which they had decorated together last summer with a border of marching ducks and rabbits playing trumpets and drums. By the end of August there was a cherry crib under the window, a white changing table with mint green knobs, and a rocking chair with checkered cushions: Shukumar had disassembled it all before bringing Shoba back from the hospital, scraping off the rabbits and ducks with a spatula. For some reason the room did not haunt him the way it haunted Shoba. In January, when he stopped working at his carrel in the library, he set up his desk there deliberately, partly because the room soothed him, and partly because it was a place Shoba avoided.

Shukumar returned to the kitchen and began to open drawers. He tried to locate a candle among the scissors, the eggbeaters and whisks, the mortar and pestle she'd bought in a bazaar in Calcutta, and used to pound garlic cloves and cardamom pods, back when she used to cook. He found a flashlight, but no batteries, and a half-empty box of birthday candles. Shoba had thrown him a surprise birthday party last May. One hundred and twenty people had crammed into the house—all the friends and the friends of friends they now systematically avoided. Bottles of vinho verde had nested in a bed of ice in the bathtub. Shoba was in her fifth month, drinking ginger ale from a martini glass. She had made a vanilla cream cake with custard and spun sugar. All night she kept Shukumar's long fingers linked with hers as they walked among the guests at the party.

Since September their only guest had been Shoba's mother. She came from Arizona and stayed with them for two months after Shoba returned from the hospital. She cooked dinner every night, drove herself to the supermarket, washed their clothes, put them away. She was a religious woman. She set up a small shrine, a framed picture of a lavender-faced goddess and a plate of marigold petals, on the bedside table in the guest room, and prayed twice a day for healthy grandchildren in the future. She was polite to Shukumar without being friendly. She folded his sweaters with an expertise she had learned from her job in a department store. She replaced a missing button on his winter coat and knit him a beige and brown scarf, presenting it to him without the least bit of ceremony, as if he had only dropped it and hadn't noticed. She never talked to him about Shoba; once, when he mentioned the baby's death, she looked up from her knitting, and said, "But you weren't even there."

It struck him as odd that there were no real candles in the house. That Shoba hadn't prepared for such an ordinary emergency. He looked now for something to put the birthday candles in and settled on the soil of a potted ivy that normally sat on the windowsill over the sink. Even though the plant was inches from the tap, the soil was so dry that he had to water it first before the candles would stand straight. He pushed aside the things on the kitchen table, the piles of mail, the unread library books. He remembered their first meals there, when they were so thrilled to be married, to be living together in the same house at last, that they would just reach for each other foolishly, more eager to make love than to eat. He put down two embroidered place mats, a wedding gift from an uncle in Lucknow, and set out the plates and wineglasses they usually saved for guests. He put the ivy in the middle, the white-edged, star-shaped leaves girded by ten little candles. He switched on the digital clock radio and tuned it to a jazz station.

"What's all this?" Shoba said when she came downstairs. Her hair was wrapped in a thick white towel. She undid the towel and draped it over a chair, allowing her hair, damp and dark, to fall across her back. As she walked absently toward the stove she took out a few tangles with her fingers. She wore a clean pair of sweatpants, a T-shirt, an old flannel robe. Her stomach was flat again, her waist narrow before the flare of her hips, the belt of the robe tied in a floppy knot.

It was nearly eight. Shukumar put the rice on the table and the lentils from the night before into the microwave oven, punching the numbers on the timer.

"You made *rogan josh,*" Shoba observed, looking through the glass lid at the bright paprika stew.

Shukumar took out a piece of lamb, pinching it quickly between his fingers so as not to scald himself. He prodded a larger piece with a serving spoon to make sure the meat slipped easily from the bone. "It's ready," he announced.

The microwave had just beeped when the lights went out, and the music disappeared.

"Perfect timing," Shoba said.

"All I could find were birthday candles." He lit up the ivy, keeping the rest of the candles and a book of matches by his plate.

"It doesn't matter," she said, running a finger along the stem of her wineglass. "It looks lovely."

In the dimness, he knew how she sat, a bit forward in her chair, ankles crossed against the lowest rung, left elbow on the table. During his search for the candles, Shukumar had found a bottle of wine in a crate he had thought was empty. He clamped the bottle between his knees while he turned in the corkscrew. He worried about spilling, and so he picked up the glasses and held them close to his lap while he filled them. They served themselves, stirring the rice with their forks, squinting as they extracted bay leaves and cloves from the stew. Every few minutes Shukumar lit a few more birthday candles and drove them into the soil of the pot.

"It's like India," Shoba said, watching him tend his makeshift candelabra. "Sometimes the current disappears for hours at a stretch. I once had to attend an entire rice ceremony in the dark. The baby just cried and cried. It must have been so hot."

Their baby had never cried, Shukumar considered. Their baby would never have a rice ceremony, even though Shoba had already made the guest list, and decided on which of her three brothers she was going to ask to feed the child its first taste of solid food, at six months if it was a boy, seven if it was a girl.

"Are you hot?" he asked her. He pushed the blazing ivy pot to the other end of the table, closer to the piles of books and mail, making it even more difficult for them to see each other. He was suddenly irritated that he couldn't go upstairs and sit in front of the computer.

"No. It's delicious," she said, tapping her plate with her fork. "It really is."

He refilled the wine in her glass. She thanked him.

They weren't like this before. Now he had to struggle to say something that interested her, something that made her look up from her plate, or from her proofreading files. Eventually he gave up trying to amuse her. He learned not to mind the silences.

"I remember during power failures at my grandmother's house, we all had to say something," Shoba continued. He could barely see her face, but from her tone he knew her eyes were narrowed, as if trying to focus on a distant object. It was a habit of hers.

"Like what?"

"I don't know. A little poem. A joke. A fact about the world. For some reason my relatives always wanted me to tell them the names of my friends in America. I don't know why the information was so interesting to them. The last time I saw my aunt she asked after four girls I went to elementary school with in Tucson. I barely remember them now."

Shukumar hadn't spent as much time in India as Shoba had. His parents, who settled in New Hampshire, used to go back without him. The first time he'd gone as an infant he'd nearly died of amoebic dysentery. His father, a nervous type was afraid to take him again, in case something were to happen and left him with his aunt and uncle in Concord. As a teenager he preferred sailing camp or scooping ice cream during the summers to going to Calcutta. It wasn't until after his father died, in his last year of college, that the country began to interest him, and he studied its history from course books as if it were any other subject. He wished now that he had his own childhood story of India.

"Let's do that," she said suddenly.

"Do what?"

"Say something to each other in the dark."

"Like what? I don't know any jokes."

"No, no jokes." She thought for a minute. "How about telling each other something we've never told before."

"I used to play this game in high school," Shukumar recalled. "When I got drunk."

"You're thinking of truth or dare. This is different. Okay, I'll start." She took a sip of wine. "The first time I was alone in your apartment, I looked in your address book to see if you'd written me in. I think we'd known each other two weeks."

"Where was I?"

"You went to answer the telephone in the other room. It was your mother, and I figured it would be a long call. I wanted to know if you'd promoted me from the margins of your newspaper."

"Had I?"

"No, But I didn't give up on you. Now it's your turn."

He couldn't think of anything, but Shoba was waiting for him to speak. She hadn't appeared so determined in months. What was there left to say to her? He thought back to their first meeting, four years earlier at a lecture hall in Cambridge, where a group of Bengali poets were giving a recital. They'd ended up side by side, on folding wooden chairs. Shukumar was soon bored; he was unable to decipher the literary diction, and couldn't join the rest of the audience as they sighed and nodded solemnly after certain phrases. Peering at the newspaper folded in his lap, he studied the temperatures of cities around the world. Ninety-one degrees in Singapore yesterday, fifty-one in

Stockholm. When he turned his head to the left, he saw a woman next to him making a grocery list on the back of a folder, and was startled to find that she was beautiful.

"Okay," he said, remembering. "The first time we went out to dinner, to the Portuguese place, I forgot to tip the waiter. I went back the next morning, found out his name, left money with the manager."

"You went all the way back to Somerville just to tip a waiter?"

"I took a cab."

"Why did you forget to tip the waiter?"

The birthday candles had burned out, but he pictured her face clearly in the dark, the wide tilting eyes, the full grapetoned lips, the fall at age two from her high chair still visible as a comma on her chin. Each day, Shukumar noticed, her beauty, which had once overwhelmed him, seemed to fade. The cosmetics that had seemed superfluous were necessary now, not to improve her but to define her somehow.

"By the end of the meal I had a funny feeling that I might marry you," he said, admitting it to himself as well as to her for the first time. "It must have distracted me."

The next night Shoba came home earlier than usual. There was lamb left over from the evening before; and Shukumar heated it up so that they were able to eat by seven. He'd gone out that day, through the melting snow, and bought a packet of taper candles from the corner store, and batteries to fit the flashlight. He had the candles ready on the countertop, standing in brass holders shaped like lotuses, but they ate under the glow of the copper-shaded ceiling lamp that hung over the table.

When they had finished eating. Shukumar was surprised to see that Shoba was stacking her plate on top of his, and then carrying them over to the sink. He had assumed she would retreat to the living room, behind her barricade of files.

"Don't worry about the dishes," he said, taking them from her hands.

"It seems silly not to," she replied, pouring a drop of detergent onto a sponge. "It's nearly eight o'clock."

His heart quickened. All day Shukumar had looked forward to the lights going out. He thought about what Shoba had said the night before, about looking in his address book. It felt good to remember her as she was then, how bold yet nervous she'd been when they first met, how hopeful. They stood side by side at the sink, their reflections fitting together in the frame of the window. It made him shy, the way he felt the first time they stood together in a mirror. He couldn't recall the last time they'd been photographed. They had stopped attending parties, went nowhere together. The film in his camera still contained pictures of Shoba, in the yard, when she was pregnant.

After finishing the dishes, they leaned against the counter, drying their hands on either end of a towel. At eight o'clock the house went black. Shukumar lit the wicks of the candles, impressed by their long steady flames.

"Let's sit outside," Shoba said. "I think it's warm still."

They each took a candle and sat down on the steps. It seemed strange to be sitting outside with patches of snow still on the ground. But everyone was out of their houses tonight, the air fresh enough to make people restless. Screen doors opened and closed. A small parade of neighbors passed by with flashlights.

"We're going to the bookstore to browse," a silver-haired man called out. He was walking with his wife, a thin woman in a windbreaker, and holding a dog on a leash.

They were the Bradfords, and they had tucked a sympathy card into Shoba and Shukumar's mailbox back in September. "I hear they've got their power."

"They'd better," Shukumar said. "Or you'll be browsing in the dark."

The woman laughed, slipping her arm through the crook of her husband's elbow. "Want to join us?"

"No thanks," Shoba and Shukumar called out together. It surprised Shukumar that his words matched hers.

He wondered what Shoba would tell him in the dark. The worst possibilities had already run through his head. That she'd had an affair. That she didn't respect him for being thirty-five and still a student. That she blamed him for being in Baltimore the way her mother did. But he knew those things weren't true. She'd been faithful, as had he. She believed in him. It was she who had insisted he go to Baltimore. What didn't they know about each other? He knew she curled her fingers tightly when she slept, that her body twitched during bad dreams. He knew it was honeydew she favored over cantaloupe. He knew that when they returned from the hospital the first thing she did when she walked into the house was pick out objects of theirs and toss them into a pile in the hallway: books from the shelves, plants from the windowsills, paintings from walls, photos from tables, pots and pans that hung from the hooks over the stove. Shukumar had stepped out of her way, watching as she moved methodically from room to room. When she was satisfied, she stood there staring at the pile she'd made, her lips drawn back in such distaste that Shukumar had thought she would spit. Then she'd started to cry.

He began to feel cold as he sat there on the steps. He felt that he needed her to talk first, in order to reciprocate.

"That time when your mother came to visit us," she said finally. "When I said one night that I had to stay late at work, I went out with Gillian and had a martini."

He looked at her profile, the slender nose, the slightly masculine set of her jaw. He remembered that night well; eating with his mother, tired from teaching two classes back to back, wishing Shoba were there to say more of the right things because he came up with only the wrong ones. It had been twelve years since his father had died, and his mother had come to spend two weeks with him and Shoba, so they could honor his father's memory together. Each night his mother cooked something his father had liked, but she was too upset to eat the dishes herself, and her eyes would well up as Shoba stroked her hand. "It's so touching," Shoba had said to him at the time. Now he pictured Shoba with Gillian, in a bar with striped velvet sofas, the one they used to go to after the movies, making sure she got her extra olive, asking Gillian for a cigarette. He imagined her complaining, and Gillian sympathizing about visits from in-laws. It was Gillian who had driven Shoba to the hospital.

"Your turn," she said, stopping his thoughts.

At the end of their street Shukumar heard sounds of a drill and the electricians shouting over it. He looked at the darkened facades of the houses lining the street. Candles glowed in the windows of one. In spite of the warmth, smoke rose from the chimney.

"I cheated on my Oriental Civilization exam in college," he said. It was my last semester, my last set of exams. My father had died a few months before. I could see the blue book of the guy next to me. He was an American guy, a maniac. He knew Urdu and Sanskrit. I couldn't remember if the verse we had to identify was an example of a *ghazal* or not. I looked at his answer and copied it down."

It had happened over fifteen years ago. He felt relief now, having told her.

She turned to him, looking not at his face, but at his shoes—old moccasins he wore as if they were slippers, the leather at the back permanently flattened. He wondered if it bothered her, what he'd said. She took his hand and pressed it. "You didn't have to tell me why you did it," she said, moving closer to him.

They sat together until nine o'clock, when the lights came on. They heard some people across the street clapping from their porch, and televisions being turned on. The Bradfords walked back down the street, eating ice-cream cones and waving. Shoba and Shukumar waved back. Then they stood up, his hand still in hers, and went inside.

Somehow, without saying anything, it had turned into this. Into an exchange of confessions—the little ways they'd hurt or disappointed each other, and themselves. The following day Shukumar thought for hours about what to say to her. He was torn between admitting that he once ripped out a photo of a woman in one of the fashion magazines she used to subscribe to and carried it in his books for a week, or saying that he really hadn't lost the sweater-vest she bought him for their third wedding anniversary but had exchanged it for cash at Filene's, and that he had gotten drunk alone in the middle of the day at a hotel bar. For their first anniversary, Shoba had cooked a ten-course dinner just for him. The vest depressed him. "My wife gave me a sweater-vest for our anniversary, he complained to the bartender, his head heavy with cognac. "What do you expect?" the bartender had replied. "You're married."

As for the picture of the woman, he didn't know why he'd ripped it out. She wasn't as pretty as Shoba. She wore a white sequined dress, and had a sullen face and lean, mannish legs. Her bare arms were raised, her fists around her head, as if she were about to punch herself in the ears. It was an advertisement for stockings. Shoba had been pregnant at the time, her stomach suddenly immense, to the point where Shukumar no longer wanted to touch her. The first time he saw the picture he was lying in bed next to her, watching her as she read. When he noticed the magazine in the recycling pile he found the woman and tore out the page as carefully as he could. For about a week he allowed himself a glimpse each day. He felt an intense desire for the woman, but it was a desire that turned to disgust after a minute or two. It was the closest he'd come to infidelity.

He told Shoba about the sweater on the third night, the picture on the fourth. She said nothing as he spoke, expressed no protest or reproach. She simply listened, and then she took his hand, pressing it as she had before. On the third night, she told him that once after a lecture they'd attended, she let him speak to the chairman of his department without telling him that he had a dab of pâté on his chin. She'd been irritated with him for some reason, and so she'd let him go on and on, about securing his fellowship for the following semester, without putting a finger to her own chin as a signal. The fourth night, she said that she never liked the one poem he'd ever published in his life, in a literary magazine in Utah. He'd written the poem after meeting Shoba. She added that she found the poem sentimental.

Something happened when the house was dark. They were able to talk to each other again. The third night after supper they'd sat together on the sofa, and once it was dark he began kissing her awkwardly on her forehead and her face, and though it was dark he closed his eyes, and knew that she did, too. The fourth night they walked carefully upstairs, to bed, feeling together for the final step with their feet before the landing, and making love with a desperation they had forgotten. She wept without sound, and whispered his name, and traced his eyebrows with her finger in the dark. As he made love to her he wondered what he would say to her the next night, and what she would say, the thought of it exciting him. "Hold me," he said, "hold me in your arms." By the time the lights came back on downstairs, they'd fallen asleep.

The morning of the fifth night Shukumar found another notice from the electric company in the mailbox. The line had been repaired ahead of schedule, it said. He was disappointed. He had planned on making shrimp *malai* for Shoba, but when he arrived at the store he didn't feel like cooking anymore. It wasn't the same, he thought, knowing that the lights wouldn't go out. In the store the shrimp looked gray and thin. The coconut milk tin was dusty and overpriced. Still, he bought them, along with a beeswax candle and two bottles of wine.

She came home at seven-thirty. "I suppose this is the end of our game," he said when he saw her reading the notice.

She looked at him. "You can still light candles if you want." She hadn't been to the gym tonight. She wore a suit beneath the raincoat. Her makeup had been retouched recently.

When she went upstairs to change, Shukumar poured himself some wine and put on a record, a Thelonius Monk album he knew she liked.

When she came downstairs they ate together. She didn't thank him or compliment him. They simply ate in a darkened room, in the glow of a beeswax candle. They had survived a difficult time. They finished off the shrimp. They finished off the first bottle of wine and moved on to the second. They sat together until the candle had nearly burned away. She shifted in her chair, and Shukumar thought that she was about to say something. But instead she blew out the candle, stood up, turned on the light switch, and sat down again.

"Shouldn't we keep the lights off?" Shukumar asked.

She set her plate aside and clasped her hands on the table. "I want you to see my face when I tell you this," she said gently.

His heart began to pound. The day she told him she was pregnant, she had used the very same words, saying them in the same gentle way, turning off the basketball game he'd been watching on television. He hadn't been prepared then. Now he was.

Only he didn't want her to be pregnant again. He didn't want to have to pretend to be happy.

"I've been looking for an apartment and I've found one," she said, narrowing her eyes on something, it seemed, behind his left shoulder. It was nobody's fault, she continued. They'd been through enough. She needed some time alone. She had money saved up for a security deposit. The apartment was on Beacon Hill, so she could walk to work. She had signed the lease that night before coming home.

She wouldn't look at him, but he stared at her. It was obvious that she'd rehearsed the lines. All this time she'd been looking for an apartment, testing the water pressure, asking a Realtor if heat and hot water were included in the rent. It sickened Shukumar, knowing that she had spent these past evenings preparing for a life without him. He was relieved and yet he was sickened. This was what she'd been trying to tell him for the past four evenings. This was the point of her game.

Now it was his turn to speak. There was something he'd sworn he would never tell her, and for six months he had done his best to block it from his mind. Before the ultrasound she had asked the doctor not to tell her the sex of their child, and Shukumar had agreed. She had wanted it to be a surprise.

Later, those few times they talked about what had happened, she said at least they'd been spared that knowledge. In a way she almost took pride in her decision, for it enabled her to seek refuge in a mystery. He knew that she assumed it was a mystery for him, too. He'd arrived too late from Baltimore—when it was all over and she was lying on the hospital bed. But he hadn't. He'd arrived early enough to see their baby, and to hold him before they cremated him. At first he had recoiled at the suggestion, but the doctor said holding the baby might help him with the process of grieving. Shoba was asleep. The baby had been cleaned off, his bulbous lids shut tight to the world.

"Our baby was a boy," he said. "His skin was more red than brown. He had black hair on his head. He weighed almost five pounds. His fingers were curled shut, just like yours in the night."

Shoba looked at him now, her face contorted with sorrow. He had cheated on a college exam, ripped a picture of a woman out of a magazine. He had returned a sweater and got drunk in the middle of the day instead. These were the things he had told her. He had held his son, who had known life only within her, against his chest in a darkened room in an unknown wing of the hospital. He had held him until a nurse knocked and took him away, and he promised himself that day that he would never tell Shoba, because he still loved her then, and it was the one thing in her life that she had wanted to be a surprise.

Shukumar stood up and stacked his plate on top of hers. He carried the plates to the sink, but instead of running the tap he looked out the window. Outside the evening was still warm, and the Bradfords were walking arm in arm. As he watched the couple the room went dark, and he spun around. Shoba had turned the lights off. She came back to the table and sat down, and after a moment Shukumar joined her. They wept together, for the things they now knew.

A Conversation with Jhumpa Lahiri

There is a wonderful metaphor for the intense connection that Indian immigrants feel for their homeland in "When Mr. Pirzada Came to Dine," when Mr. Pirzada rests his silver watch, set to Dacca time, on his napkin before beginning to eat his supper. In that same story, the narrator, an Indian American girl, is at the same time fascinated by and removed from her parents' and Mr. Pirzada's preoccupation with Indian politics. Would you talk about that story and about how having been raised in America by parents so firmly rooted in Indian culture shaped the geography of your own heart and fed your imagination?

The story is based on a period in my family's life when a scholar from Bangladesh did indeed visit my parents' home on a fairly regular basis during the Pakistani civil war. I was alive at the time but was too young to have any memories of the man or of the historical situation. It was many years later that I learned of our guest's circumstances. Afterward, I was curious and also felt somewhat ashamed of my own obliviousness. I wrote the story in my twenties, as a way of trying to understand an experience that happened literally in my own living room but which I had no comprehension of. Generally, growing up, I was always aware that my parents were rooted in a different part of the world, that they cared deeply about people and events far removed from their everyday reality.

In a way, all writers are immigrants—never quite belonging, constantly trying to bridge the gap between the "real" world and the world inside their heads. That inherent sense of being an outsider is intensified for a writer straddling two cultures, exploring the lives of characters set down in a foreign country, suffering a kind of emotional exile from everything that's familiar, as you do in your stories. What is the history of your impulse to write fiction and your education as a writer?

I began writing at about the same time I began reading, at around six or seven years of age. I was inspired to imitate what I read. Writing was a way for me to avoid socializing in large groups. I was extremely shy as a child and preferred one-on-one relationships. I wrote my first "stories" with a friend, and the collaboration was both a creative act and a way of connecting with her. I continued to write creatively throughout grade school. During my adolescence I stopped writing fiction but was very involved with my school paper. I wrote a bit of fiction in college but I felt quite self-conscious and secretive about it. It wasn't until I

I began writing at about the same time I began reading, at around six or seven years of age. I was inspired to imitate what I read.

graduated from college and felt free of the demands of a full-time education that I began writing fiction in a serious, dedicated way. Although eventually I returned to graduate school, by then, fiction had become the priority and the focus of my life.

Whether they are set in the United States or in India, your stories are rich with information about Indian culture. "When Mr. Pirzada Came to Dine" gives the reader a great deal of background about the Indian/Pakistani struggles in the early 1970s, and "The Third and Final Continent" is a primer for how a whole generation of Indians made their way to the United States. But the information in the stories doesn't make the reader feel as if you have an agenda, or as if he is being spoon-fed. How do you know which information is necessary for the reader to fully understand a story? How do you know what can be left out?

Almost all the details in my work are a part of me: things I've seen, tasted, experienced. I am drawn to the small details of life, as most writers are. I believe that all art forms boil down to details. Still, in writing a story, one must be careful to choose the essential, most illuminating ones. To me, the details aren't ancillary to any given experience. They are the heart of the experience, and what endure most vividly over time.

I am drawn to the small details of life, as most writers are. I believe that all art forms boil down to details.

In addition to providing information, you create the atmosphere of Indian culture on the page by way of dozens of small but significant sensory details. Would you talk about how you find and choose the details with which you create this world—and about the effective use of details in fiction, generally?

The world I write about never feels exotic to me. I write about what I know and sometimes about what I don't know, but the general world of the story always feels familiar. If a reader inexperienced with India or Indian culture nevertheless connects with my work, I'm grateful. I never write for a specific audience. While I write a lot about Indian subjects, I myself have always felt at a remove from both the Indian and the American sides of myself. It is a frustrating aspect of my life, but I think that as a writer it provides me with a proper perspective, a combination of alienation and intimacy.

One of the most compelling traits of your work is that there is such ordinariness, such a sense of real people going about their lives within what seems to the reader an exotic world. Would you talk about the ways in which you think your work transcends its focus on India and Indians and, perhaps, too, the pitfalls an aspiring writer might face in his desire to create another culture on the page.

As I mentioned earlier, "When Mr. Pirzada Came to Dine" is essentially autobiographical, and yet it is totally imagined at the same time. There are pieces of myself and my

There are pieces of myself and my life in everything I write, every character. I've never written anything that I would consider predominantly autobiographical.

life in everything I write, every character. I've never written anything that I would consider predominantly autobiographical. I based "The Third and Final Continent" on my father's experiences. So that is a biographical story, if not an autobiographical one.

Generally, how do stories gather and evolve for you?

I can't really explain. Ideas come and go. Some stick in the head and begin growing. It's a very slow, very long process.

What about characters? How do they first appear in your mind? How do they evolve in process? In what ways do they most often surprise you?

Sometimes characters come to me more or less fully formed. Other times they are extremely vague. I need to spend a great deal of time with them, think about them and write about them, in order to understand them.

Do you have a method for keeping track of story ideas?

I try to jot them down on a piece of paper

What do you need to know about a situation and a set of characters to feel that it's time to begin writing a story?

If I'm inspired to start writing a story, I don't question it. There are times when I begin something totally blind, without a clue about the characters or the plot. Stories can begin in very oblique, inchoate ways.

Your stories have wonderful first lines—at the same time simple and evocative. Where, in process, do you usually discover what the first line of a story will be? What do want the first line of a story to do?

Sometimes the first sentence is the first one I happen to write. Other times the beginning disappears and things get radically rearranged. Ideally, the first line of a story should make you want to read the second.

The stories in Interpreter of Maladies *are varied in structure. The title story covers an afternoon in the Das family's first visit to India, "Mr. P Comes to Dinner," a season of shared dinners, "The Third and Final Continent" ranges from the narrator, Mr. Pirzada's, departure from India in 1964 to the present time. Would you talk about how you decide where to "stand" to tell a story and the extent to which this decision shapes the plot?*

Again, it depends on the story, the sensibility of it, the pace and the tenor, the situation at hand. Some stories feel more concentrated in terms of time, covering a day or a few days, while others seem to be able to move through longer periods of time and still feel credible.

The time frame of "A Temporary Matter" is a five-day period in which electricity will be cut off for one hour each evening to allow for repairs, and that brief period of darkness triggers a series of exchanges between a young couple who've grown apart since their first child was stillborn some months ago. How did you come to use such a small, really insignificant inconvenience as an organizing structure to reveal the flaws in a marriage that really should have made it? What was it about that situation that seemed particularly appropriate for the story you wanted to tell about these characters? What was the genesis of that story, and how did it evolve in process? Were there any surprises for you along the way?

The detail about the lights going off for a few days is from my life. I thought it might make an interesting frame for a story. When I first starting writing that story it was about something totally different—a young woman renting a room in an old man's apartment. The only consistent element was that the story was taking place in the dark. Eventually I thought of a set of characters and a situation I wanted to work with, and the story grew from there.

When I first starting writing that story it was about something totally different—a young woman renting a room in an old man's apartment.

The story in the "now" is deepened by flashback and memory. Would you talk about how you accomplished that?

I don't know how I accomplished it. The present action is determined by an event in the past, so I tried to balance those two elements.

The power of the secrets Shukumar and Shoba reveal during those dark hours lies not in their drama but in the fact that they are so idiosyncratic—all but Shoba's secret plan to move out and Shukumar's secret about holding the baby are exactly like the seemingly small secrets all married people keep from one another. How did you come to those particular secrets, and what do you think they reveal about the characters and their marriage?

The secrets seemed to be a part of who they were as characters. I was curious about the information people withhold from one another, even in the most intimate and loving relationships.

Sometimes, suffering a loss will bring a married couple closer. For this particular couple, though, it seemed to have been more than the marriage could bear. Why?

I don't know. I just felt that for those characters, the loss was insurmountable.

Would you talk about the end of the story, particularly the last line: "They wept together, for the things they now knew." It is the moment in the story when they are closest, yet it feels like the end of the marriage rather than the beginning of a new phase of it.

Yes, I think the end of the story signals the end of their marriage. They have stayed together by withholding information from one another. Now that things are out in the open they fall apart.

What do you think "A Temporary Matter" says about the fundamental mystery at the center of marriage itself: Why do people stay together, what makes a marriage dissolve?

Marriages succeed and fail for hundreds of different reasons. I couldn't possibly generalize. The story is just a single example of two people suffering a loss who become estranged as a result.

Other stories in the collection look at marriage, too. The characters in "A Temporary Matter" made a love match, coming together by accident at a reading of Bengali poetry. All of the other marriages are to some degree or another "arranged." In fact, the happiest marriage in the book is the arranged marriage in "The Third and Final Continent." Would you talk about that story—where it came from, how it came to hinge on that one lovely moment of connection that was the beginning of the true marriage between the characters?

As I mentioned earlier, "The Third and Final Continent" is largely based on the experience of my father's arrival and first few months in the United States in 1969, right around the time of the moon landing. At the time, I'd already been born, but I was only two. I was in India with my mother that summer while my father moved from London to Boston and got settled. The details about Mrs. Croft, her house, her conversations with my father about the man on the moon are all based on stories my father told me. The moment of connection between husband and wife in the story is invention, considering that my parents had already been married for three years and had a child.

To look at the opposite pole, the marriage in "Interpreter of Maladies" is the most troubled of all the marriages in the book, its characters the most Americanized. What was the genesis of that story, and how did it evolve?

The story began with the title. I thought of it after bumping into an acquaintance who told me he was working as an interpreter in a doctor's office in Brookline, Massachusetts, on behalf of a large Russian-speaking patient base. I was struck by what he did, and a few minutes after we parted ways the title came into my head. I wrote down the phrase but didn't think of the story until years later. I was partly inspired by a trip I once took with my family in India, and being driven to see various tourist attractions. I've never come up with a title before I've written a story, apart from that one instance.

In what ways do you think all the stories in the collection are interpretations of their characters' maladies? Might the title be an apt description for what fiction writers do, generally?

I chose the title to represent the collection as a whole because I think each of the stories touches on the difficulties of communicating, across cultural divides, generations, and individuals. I suppose all writers are interpreters in that they have to communicate, to readers, what their characters are thinking and feeling.

I suppose all writers are interpreters in that they have to communicate, to readers, what their characters are thinking and feeling.

"Sexy" and "Mrs. Sen" are in some ways mirror images, each dealing with marriage obliquely, through observers who are children. In "Sexy," the child is Indian, the babysitter, American; in "Mrs. Sen," the child is American, the babysitter Indian. Would you comment on sources of those stories and their similarities?

I hadn't thought of the stories being mirror images until now. "Mrs. Sen" was inspired in part by the fact that my mother used to look after young American children in our house when I was growing up. I wondered how she might appear through the eyes of a child who wasn't her child, but who was nevertheless close to her. "Sexy" came about because I once heard a little boy use that word, and I wondered what would lead him to do so.

Why do you find Indian marriage such rich material for fiction? What has looking at it through the prism of fiction taught you?

All marriages are rich material for fiction, and countless novels have a marriage at their heart or as their culmination. Just look at Jane Austen. I don't know if my writing about marriages has taught me anything new. I write about arranged marriages and nonarranged marriages because I've been exposed to both. Either variety can fail or succeed.

"The Treatment of Bibi Haldar" and "A Real Durwan," set in Calcutta, are the only two stories in the collection that are purely about India and Indians. The stories have a different diction from the others and feel mythic. Would you talk about these stories, where they come from and how, in your mind, they relate to the others in the collection?

I'd read Faulkner's story, "A Rose for Emily," which uses the first-person plural, and was curious to try to write from that perspective. I felt that it was right for this story because it's about a group of people collectively involved with the protagonist, but all of them are somehow distanced from her as well.

The first-person plural seems an apt way to tell a story from an Indian point of view since sense of community is strong within the culture. Why, particularly, did you feel it was right for telling "The Treatment of Bibi Haldar"? Did you imagine a particular person telling the story?

I imagined the housewives of the building telling the story.

What advice would you give an aspiring writer who'd like to try working in first-person plural? What mistakes do you think writers most often make working with a we *narrator?*

The only advice is to try and see if it's credible and suitable to the story. I don't think people use it very often, and I've never read anything where it didn't work. Jeffrey Eugenides, in *The Virgin Suicides*, uses a similar narrative technique quite beautifully.

The story has the feel of a fable, yet the ending—the birth of Bibi's illegitimate child and how it makes her pull herself together to make a life—comes as something of a surprise.

On the one hand, it has a kind of American "can-do" feel to it; on the other, it may be that the shame of bearing an illegitimate child sets Bibi free from cultural constraints around marriage and allows her to live her own life. Would you talk about how you came to the ending of the story and in what ways it reflects the realities of Indian culture?

I can't really speak for the realities of Indian culture—that's a terribly broad concept. I have a difficulty thinking of life in broad terms.

I wasn't conscious of writing a fable. It surprises me when readers refer to it that way. To me, all the elements in the story are very realistic. In imagining the ending I tried to come up with something that was both surprising and inevitable and changed the character's life. I can't really speak for the realities of Indian culture—that's a terribly broad concept. I have a difficulty thinking of life in broad terms.

Your novel, The Namesake, *charts the life of an American Indian family much like the one in "The Third and Final Continent." Would you talk about the particular challenges of writing a novel and how they differ from those of the short story?*

In general the work is the same: imagining characters and events and working with sentences. That said, a novel is different from a story in that it is a longer and generally more complicated form, with far more variables than a short story. A novel can explore characters and ideas with more depth, more leisure, and more dimension. It also required more sustained concentration on my part. Usually I work on two or three stories at once. But when I was working on my novel, after a certain point, I devoted myself to it exclusively.

"Gogol," an excerpt of the novel, was published as a short story in The New Yorker. *How did you work with the novel to shape it that way? What is the difference between the focus and effect of the story and of the novel?*

The excerpt was shaped entirely by my editor at *The New Yorker.* She read the novel and fused together a condensed version of the first few chapters. I read the condensed version and thought it worked very well. I think it would have been much harder for me to do what my editor did.

Generally, what are your strategies for revision? Do they differ for the story and the novel? What kinds of revision do your stories most often need?

It seems as if everything I've ever written has gone through literally hundreds of drafts. I have no specific strategies. I just work on whatever needs improving.

As most writers will tell you, revision is 95 percent of the work. It is certainly true in my case. It seems as if everything I've ever written has gone through literally hundreds of drafts. I have no specific strategies. I just work on whatever needs improving.

Interpreter of Maladies, *your first collection of stories, won the Pulitzer Prize and thrust you into the limelight. Such success, while wonderful, is not all blessing. Would you talk about the challenges of that experience in terms of balancing your public life and your writing life and what you learned from it? Did you feel pressured to compete with yourself to write a second book that would be as good and popular as the first? What advice would you give to writers just starting out about the differences between writing and the business of writing?*

I try to block out the public aspects of writing as much as possible. By the time I received the Pulitzer Prize I was already involved with another book, and I knew that no amount of prizes was going to help me write it. You are on your own each time. I associate the success of my first book with that book exclusively. I was very humbled by all the attention, but after a month or two I simply stopped thinking about it. I wanted my next book to be a decent first novel, and I wanted it to be somehow stronger than my previous work. I think every writer hopes to move forward, not backward. So there was pressure in that regard, but it was pressure coming from myself. I can't control how something I write will be received, and as long as I write, I have to remember that fact. The business of writing—reviews, readings, book tours—can be exhilarating, but it can also be devastating and distracting. The real work of writing has nothing to do with it. One has to love the pursuit of writing and the process, and be willing to endure the solitude and the struggle.

Writing Prompts

READ: "A Temporary Matter" and the interview with **Jhumpa Lahiri.**

PONDER: How Lahiri uses the occasion and time frame of a blackout to create the structure for a story.

WRITE: A story in which a conflict between two people is revealed and resolved in the box of time created by a situation that is beyond their control.

PRACTICE:

- Write a story about some aspect of your parents' lives that you've always been curious about but never understood.
- Research a historical incident recent enough to have affected a living person's life. Then write a story in which a character's life in the present is somehow affected by that historical time. Take care to use only the necessary historical details.
- Write about a time in your life in which you felt like an exile.
- Write a story about two people who have a conflict that cannot be resolved.
- Write a story about two people who have survived by withholding information from each other—until now.
- Write a monologue in the first-person plural in which a group of people tell the story of someone who is both like and not like them.
- Identify ten characteristics of a group or culture. Then write a scene in which these characteristics are not named, but are shown through detail and dialogue.

Michael Martone

Michael Martone (b. 1955) is the author of five collections of short fiction and two collections of poems, and the editor of two collections of essays. Born in Fort Wayne, Indiana, he was educated at Butler University, Indiana University, and Johns Hopkins University. His honors include two NEA fellowships, three Pushcart Prizes, the Margaret Jones Fiction Award, the Ingram Merrill Foundation Award, the Story Magazine *Short-short Story Prize, and the Associated Writing Programs Award for Creative Nonfiction. Martone is a Professor of English and Director of the Creative Writing Program at the University of Alabama. He lives in Tuscaloosa, Alabama.*

For Further Reading:
Dark Light (1973), *At a Loss* (1977), *Alive and Dead in Indiana* (1984), *Return to Powers* (1985), *A Place of Sense: Essays in Search of the Midwest,* ed. Michael Martone (1988), *Safety Patrol* (1988), *Fort Wayne Is Seventh on Hitler's List,* (1990), *Pensées: The Thoughts of Dan Quayle* (1994), *Seeing Eye* (1995), *Flatness and Other Landscapes* (2000), *The Blue Guide to Indiana* (2001), *Extreme Fiction: Fabulists and Formalists,* ed. Martone and Robin Hemley (2004).

Watch Out

My Story

I will write my story using English only, as my students should do. I will write about our new home and how we live. I will write about the class I teach and my very good students who will read this and who are pleased to be here in Indiana. There is the church to write about too and our Bishop Leo. But most of all I will write in English about learning it and not using my own tongue or French because we are here now and must learn this one way to talk.

Things You Must Know

I am a woman. I am five feet high. My Christian name is Catherine. In my country, I lived with the Sisters of the Sacred Heart and the Sisters of the Most Precious Blood and I remember the white, black, and gray colors of their clothes and how hot it must have been. With them, I learned French and English and the ways to teach others these languages. I worked hard and had a good time. My hair is black. My eyes too. I can drive a car. I can run a typewriter. I was afraid, of course, when I came to America. But with the help of the Diocese of Fort Wayne-South Bend and the Fort Wayne Community Schools everything is fine now. I have no family in this country, but I have a father, a mother, two brothers, a sister, two uncles and their wives who are my aunts, and several cousins. All of my grandparents are no longer living.

My Health Problem

In America there is food. In America there are all kinds of food. When I arrived in America there were signs everywhere that said Eat. But when I came here to this country with all this food, I cannot eat. The food looks like wood and tastes like mud to me. Even the food of my country that we make here no longer tastes good to me now. I lose so much weight that my boss, Mrs. Anthis, is startled each time she sees me. She pretends everything is fine, but I can see.

Where I Work

I work for the public schools under a title from the President of the United States. "We are lucky to find you," Mrs. Anthis says. This is after she pretends not to worry about me. "We were lucky to find her," she says to her bosses when I am introduced to them. These men are kind and they want to shake my hand all the time. They don't know much about my country except for the war and they don't talk about that. They say, "Why, you are so little!" I laugh. I teach English to the children of my country so that they can go to regular school one day. Everyone knows America is the land of opportunity. Here is an example.

Where We Live

Our Bishop Leo lets us live in the Central Catholic High School. Let me tell you that it is not a high school now with students and teachers. It is called CC. There are other high schools where Catholic boys and girls go to learn. Those schools are far away, on the edge of the city. Many families live here. We are waiting to find houses of our own and for the children without families to be adopted. We have made curtains for the big windows at CC. The lights are tubes filled with gas. They hum. There are many places for the children to hide. They hide in the old desks. They run down the halls and hide in the lockers in the wall. Often they will jump out at me as I walk by. There is a gym and a greenhouse on the roof where people have planted seeds they brought with them. Each family has a classroom of its very own. I live in the room with many sewing machines, refrigerators, sinks, and ovens. It was decided that it would be best if I lived here since I am alone. Now, no woman with a family will be jealous of another. Each family has its own oven and a place to put food. Water is in this room, so the washing is done here too. It dries on the roof. There are smells of cooking in my room and much laughter among the women. It is okay because I work in school in the days and on the days I don't work I talk to the children or take them to places so they will hear English. There is a room of typewriters, too. I am there now. Every room has a clock on the wall. The thin hand is always moving. My room is quiet at night but for the refrigerators. I think to myself that they talk to one another. I hear the bells of the churches every fifteen minutes, and I hear the pigeons near the windows making their soft noises.

The Churches of Fort Wayne

There are many beautiful and interesting churches in the city. Many of the churches are near downtown, and we walk to them to hear daily mass. Sometimes we travel to the churches farther away, taking the black cars of the priests. Then we meet the people there in the new churches. We sit in the front pews with ushers standing by. The people talk to us slowly and give us boxes of cans. These are the new churches where there are many people and where they wear bright clothes and the ceilings are low and sparkle. I am thinking of St. Jude's and St. Vincent's, where the statues are smooth wood and never painted. Near to CC are the old churches. There is the cathedral of our Bishop Leo. It is called Immaculate Conception. There the stations of the cross are twice as big as life and there are banks of votive candles kept burning by the older people. There are side altars. The building is white and Mary has a crown of pure gold on her head. We have heard stories about a workman who caught on fire and fell burning from the steeple we can see from our windows at CC but lived. Nearby is a big rock where the Indians converted. There is St. Mary's made out of red sandstone. It is a church built in the old way. There are bats that live here high up near the painted ceiling. There is St. Peter and St. Paul, which is made with red brick. There is St. Patrick with one steeple. There is Precious Blood, which has two steeples and beautiful bells. There is Queen of the Angels, which is in an old gym since they are so poor. There is colored paper in the windows. And there is a shrine to the Virgin near the wrecking yard and power plant where the orphanage is and near the place where football is played. Near to CC is a chapel. It is open all the time. But someone must be there praying day and night. You can see the body of Christ. There it is in the center of a golden cross inside a round window. I go to this chapel often to hear mass at noon with the workers from the banks who are not having dinner. The chapel might not remain open at night. People are afraid to be alone in the early morning. I have spent many happy hours visiting these places and talking to the friendly people.

Worry

I believe I am not doing a very good job. This happens when the children call out the windows of CC at Americans on the street. The children use their own language and slam the windows. They do not want to leave the building but play games in the hallway near the glass cases that have old awards for sports. They play near the fountains and waste water. I speak to them in English and they don't understand. I know they know some English but they are afraid too. They do not want Americans to lose patience with them. They try to tell me how things are, but I shake my head. "Say it in English, please!" If I were bigger, I could do a better job.

In the Classroom

When they are not working, the parents of my students visit the classroom. They sit in the little chairs with the children on their laps. Or they sit next to the children on the floor and try to read the simple English. Then I hear them asking the children what this word is or what that one is. And I hear the children say the word in the old language. *Ball* or *dog.* I don't feel so bad then. The parents tell me it is too late for them to learn. Then they fall into silence. Then they tell the children to try harder. I say, "Let's sing a song!" With the children singing it is very nice and everyone is happier.

At CC I Am Very Busy

We all wait for the mail to come in the big bags brought by a man in a truck. People want me to read to them the letters that have come in English. Often these letters suggest buying things such as records, magazines, spoons, seeds, and food. There are other letters from leaders. Once a week, our Bishop Leo writes. And I read the *Sunday Visitor* for everyone when we all eat together. There are papers to fill out for others. And I talk to the operator when the family heads are called in other cities. I write notes for the men to take to the bank with their checks. On Sunday when Father Hamilton says mass in the little chapel, I translate the words for him. It makes me very happy to help.

Sunday Brunch

Mrs. Anthis took me to a Sunday brunch. She wanted to put meat on my bones. The Sunday brunch was at a restaurant owned by Mr. Hall. Many of the men from CC wash dishes there. There was much to eat. Bacon, ham, beef, chicken, fish, lamb, sausage, and eggs which were fried, scrambled, boiled, and eggs made a special way and given names. There was fruit. Apples, oranges, grapes, cherries, bananas, pineapples, berries, grapefruit, and many juices. There were potatoes with onions that were sliced or in long strips. There were breads that were sweet and had icing, and cakes, and bread in paper, and loaves of bread with three types of butter, one that had strawberries inside it. There was honey, and syrup for pancakes, and yellow corn bread. You could drink all the coffee you wanted. You could go back to the food tables as many times as you liked. People walked around the big room with two plates. Mrs. Anthis said, "This is our favorite place." Her husband was there and her children and other teachers. Some of the men from CC waved to me when no one else was looking. They were carrying dishes from the tables. "No wonder," Mrs. Anthis said, "Are you sure you don't want anything more?" she said. I was listening to all the English in the room, and that was enough for me.

I Become Sicker

I have gone again to the doctor. He wears a white coat, and there are folds at the bottom of his pants. There are bars on the windows, and the table where I sit is covered by a thin piece of white paper. The sister pulls out a new piece of paper from the end of the table. She pulls it tight and shiny. I am always afraid to sit on this new piece of paper and put wrinkles into it. I remember the women at CC with the hot irons and the steam and the stiff legs of their husbands' checkered pants. The women go back and forth with irons. "Go on. Sit down. It's only paper," the sister says. "You must eat," the doctor says. "Why don't you eat?" But I don't have the words to tell him why. They both look at me and I am so afraid. My hand goes back and forth on the paper. Then I cut my finger on the edge of the paper. There is some blood on the white paper and we are all surprised.

Downtown

The children are like sparrows. We go downtown and they run and follow one another. They all land at one spot. They all look into the mirror the Murphy's has on their building, and then they fly, one after another, to the boxes that have newspapers. We are about the only people downtown. The people work in offices high up in the tall buildings. The children like to stop in front of the wig shop. In the window of the wig shop are black heads with all different kinds of hair that shines in the light. Most store windows are painted white and have old signs that say Closed. The clocks have stopped on the store signs. In the street I see where a railroad track has been covered over by new paving. This city is so different from the old cities. The children run from one place to another. There are only big green buses in the streets. Without the buses the streets would be empty. "Where are the people?" the children ask. "Say it in English," I say. "Hiding! They're hiding!" the children say. The children are jumping at a string of lights in a small tree without leaves. "They are up there, the people, in all of those windows. They are speaking English to one another." That is what I say to them.

In Another Classroom

I have been to the Catholic high schools to talk to students there. I tell them stories like these about what we do and how we live and about my students. Mrs. Anthis stands in the back of the room and smiles. After awhile, a bell rings and the students collect their books from the little shelves under their chairs. They go. And new students come in and sit down. I say the same things about Fort Wayne and the beautiful churches and the children and CC and the green buses. The students listen closely. They smile and look at each other. They listen hard to me. They look hard at me. I feel as if I am talking softer and softer, and I am afraid that I have not said something I said before to another class. "What, dear?" Mrs. Anthis says. "What is it?" And I can't explain with these students watching me.

The Children's Zoo

The zoo of Fort Wayne has only young animals. There are the cubs of lions and monkeys and bears and kangaroos. There are baby elephants and turtles and pigs. Everywhere there are the chicks of birds scratching the ground. The small rabbits live in a big shoe. In one building, many tiny snakes, like noodles, were under an orange light wrapped around and around each other on a bed of sawdust. My students and I rode a small train around a lake. We went into a yard where kids and lambs ran after us and sucked our fingers until we gave them bottles of milk. I pointed and called every animal by name. I told the children that the zoo was a place for children. The grown-up animals must go to other zoos. "These animals you can play with now." And my students rubbed the fur and held the animals tight, and then they tried to carry the animals away while the animals made such loud crying noises. We fed the seals also. We bought food from a machine like the candy machines at CC. I pulled on a handle and the food arrived. The noise we made with the machine was heard by the seals, and they came up out of the cold green water onto the rocks and sang as their fur dried in the sun. The children threw food to them through the air, and the heads of the seals and their long necks moved back and forth following the food as it fell.

Our Country Will Not Go Away

Near CC is a garden enclosed in glass so that the flowers and the trees will grow even in the winter. All of us love to go there on Sunday after mass. The first room changes with the seasons. Pine trees grow there at Christmas. Lilies grow there at Easter. In the fall, there is colored corn and on the floor are leaves. Sometimes there are only tulips and roses. The next room is a desert, and it is filled with stones and bushes. It is very dry, and the plants are small. We must look for them but there are bright red flowers in the thorns. The last room is like our home. There is a mist shooting from the glass roof, and there is the sound of water everywhere. There is the smell in the mud. The roots of the trees wrap back up around the trunks and soon become the trunk. The leaves are big and dark green and heavy with water. The little stream is green. There is rice in the paddy and the bamboo is thick. The men talk to each other and point at how this or that plant has grown. The women watch the waterfall. The children, in their good clothes, sleep under the trees. Goldfish float in the pools. I read the small red signs and look for one that says this plant is from our home. I live to breathe in and out in this place. It would be great to live only by breathing.

One Night

One night the children were crying. Outside it was snowing, and the trucks that never stop were going by the building. The windows shook in the wind. The air in my room was hot and dry. It was very dark. I heard the children cry. The children were in their rooms and their crying came in under the door of my room. Then I heard mothers and fathers awake. The voices were low and they sang songs. It was like being rocked again by my mother's voice so far away. It was so hot and dry in my room. I wanted to move my bed to the floor. There near the ground would be cool air. I took off my nightshirt, which was red and pretty. I got it from the people of the church we visited. When I pulled the nightshirt over my head, I saw a flash of light. The light ran around my body and arms and legs and fingers and into my hair. Every time I moved there were more sparks and a sound like sitting on the paper in the doctor's office. The light was blue and green and it did not hurt. When I shook my head against my nightshirt there would be more sparks. I watched this for a long time. And that is why the children cried. One child woke that night and saw the light playing on the bodies of his mother and father and sisters and his brothers as they turned in bed against the sheets and blankets. He was frightened and called out. When everyone woke up and moved in the bed there was more light flashing in the dark and they thought they were on fire and cried for help. The next family woke up and the same thing happened. Then everyone was awake and screaming for help. But it was nothing. It was the new clothes, something in the new clothes, that made this happen. The women came into my room to wash the clothes in the dark.

Watch Out

The next day in class, I told the children how to ask for help in English. Help me. How to say I am hurt. I am hurt. I taught them to say be careful. Be careful. I taught them to say I am afraid. I am afraid. I taught them to say I'm scared. I'm scared. They learned the words *run, move, duck.* I told them don't look and I didn't see it and be calm and get out of the way. I taught them none of your business and leave me alone and I am okay and I can't walk. I taught the children to say I am sick. I am sick. And let me sit down and rest. Let me sit down and rest. And I can't go on. I can't go on. I taught them bad, evil, wrong, pain, and death. Yes, I told them the word for death. Death. And I said, "Watch out." "Say it. Watch out." "You say it now," I said. I said, "Watch out." And the children said, "Watch out." I said, "That's good." And the children said, "Watch out! Watch out!" as loud as they could.

In the Middle of Another Night

I go to the small chapel to sit and think. The people who must sit there sit together away from me in one pew. They turn to look at me when they think I am not looking but praying. I think of my family. Where they are and what they must be doing because it is day on the other side of the world. And I think at times in the old language when I think of my mother and father and I pretend they can hear me like it was a prayer. When the new people come to take the place of the people who have been sitting and watching, they all turn to look at me and to whisper to each other. Then I think I am really safe here in Fort Wayne.

Later

No one is out in the downtown. There are no sounds. Nothing is open. I am not afraid to walk around. Why should I be afraid? There is no one here. I asked Mrs. Anthis this. "Why do people stay away?" And she said, "They are afraid." I said, "Afraid of what?" "Of what is downtown." I said, "Are they afraid of us?" "No, no, my dear," she said, "they are just afraid." But there is no one here but us. There is no one here at all but us. I know because I walk around at night. "You, you tiny thing?" she said. "Yes," I said. I never see anyone else. But the lights that direct the traffic still work. There are big piles of snow in the corner of the parking lots where the buildings used to be, and in the middle of the parking lots are little houses that are empty. Inside the houses, I see through the window a light is on and the cash register is open and empty. When the wind blows snow off the piles, it flows over the black ground of the empty lots like a clear shallow river, white and running fast.

A Disease

The doctor told me of a disease he thinks makes me not eat. I cried in his office sitting on the paper on his table. I cried because I am not hungry and because I am fading away to nothing. That is what the sister said when I stood on the scale. "You are fading away to nothing." I cried because I am doing something wrong. I cried because I have no one to talk to. The doctor said it was something in the air, this disease. He said that very many American girls who cannot eat are sick with it. Girls in America, he said, want to look good in bathing suits. "Do you want to look good in a bathing suit?" I cried because I had never thought of bathing suits before. The doctor can think of nothing else it can be. "That must be it," he said and then he said good-bye and left me in the little room to get dressed.

Tet

It is our first new year in America. At CC we have a party in the gym. We play records and the sound comes out of the speakers in the ceiling. The children are running around the tables. Ribbons and colored paper sail along behind them when they run. Everyone is happy. We are using white paper plates for our food, the rice cakes and pork and lemon grass and milk. And Mrs. Anthis is here and Mr. Hall and all the bosses and the man who brings the mail. And our Bishop Leo is here too blessing everything. When I go up to him for a blessing I take his hand to kiss his ring and I cannot lift his hand in my two hands. He tells me to stand next to him on the stage and he asks me to tell him a phrase to say in celebration. He leans over and I tell him and he says it a few times to himself. Everyone is quiet when he speaks in English and then he speaks in the old language and everyone cheers. And our Bishop Leo says I am a good teacher. And I look at the faces. They are eating and drinking. They do not understand what has been said and they are waiting for me to translate, to say that I am a good teacher. But I say in the old language that all of you are my family, that we are here together, one body, and that we must eat all the food and not waste a bit of it.

In Another Building

We went to the top of one of the tall buildings. My students ran through the empty restaurant that is there. They ran from one big window to another and looked down carefully at the city. The restaurant was closed, so we could come in and see and not trouble anybody. Windows were everywhere and they were so big it seemed you could walk right out into the sky. Outside we saw the steeples of the churches and the green rivers way off in the distance. Below we saw the tops of the green buses and the parking lots filled with cars. We saw CC below us and the washing on the roof. Below us too were many gray pigeons flying together from one building to another. And the children asked quietly in the old language where the people were now, and I tried to show them the houses all around. But the trees made everything disappear. And the children said, "They're hiding. They're hiding." Some men from CC who work in this place were putting knives and forks and spoons on the table. The metal made a pretty sound. The children stood very close to the windows all in a line looking out. The lights of the houses and cars came on like stars in the sky. And with us in the sky, the stars began to show up. I could smell the food in the kitchen and I told everyone it was time to go. There were more and more lights all around the city, long straight lines of lights where the roads were. Why should I be this lucky one in America?

A Conversation with Michael Martone

You work a lot with first-person narratives, many of which feature real people—Dan Quayle, Heinrich Schlieman, James Dean's drama teacher—speaking by way of your imagination. What is it about a person that compels you to try to see the world through his or her eyes?

I always tell my students that you have two basic tools, exposition and scene. What I like about first person doesn't have so much to do with the "personalness" of the person. I'm not so interested in exploring the people or trying to capture their voice or be close to them, but in the formal thing that it allows you to do—and that is the exposition. The way someone tells something is scenic and so the telling becomes a kind of showing. Also, I think it's connected to my nonfiction writing in that basically what I do is borrow people and make them write essays. I inhabit a character in order to talk about things.

I inhabit a character in order to talk about things.

In "Everybody Watching and Time Passing Like That," James Dean's drama coach describes what happened when she found out about his death. But what she describes in your story is completely different from what the drama coach actually told you about that moment. What did she tell you, and why didn't you use it?

Hers was actually a better story than what I could have imagined. She was a young teacher at the time, not that much older than James Dean. After he had made it to Hollywood, he gave her money to go to New York to study drama and to try to get on the Broadway stage. So she had become a kind of colleague, collaborator. She was actually in New York City working in a hotel, trying to make ends meet, and when she heard she knew her life had changed. She immediately knew she had become a keeper of Dean's memory. That's a great story. But I didn't want to put it in the book because it's *her* story.

To tell the truth would have been like a kind of presumption.

Yeah, that's right.

But that's wonderfully paradoxical.

But that's always the case. At conferences and in classrooms, it comes up a lot—the preemptive taking of other people's stories. Whose story are you using and for what purpose? Especially when it comes to, say, a man writing in the voice of a woman or a white human writing in the voice of a black. It's exploitative. I became more sensitive to that during the publication of *Alive and Dead in Indiana* because the lawyers got involved.

You were a young writer then.

I was twenty-five, using these quasi-public figures, and it really surprised me about issues of privacy. From the lawyer's point of view, everyone is open and exposed. But if you write a story that's about your mother and you change slight things and all that and she wants to take you to court—she can.

So how do you negotiate that fine line between truth and fiction?

For me, fiction is disengaged from the idea of truth or falsehood. Fiction has to do with things that are done and finished. And things that are made. When you work with a foreign language there's always that verb that translates as "to do" or "to make." If you think about it, it's weird. How are those two things related? But in our own language the words *fact* and *fiction* are both derived from the Latin; the one means "to do" and the other means "to make." Fact is a thing done and a fiction is a thing made. So even though we think of facts as hard, solid, actual real things and fiction as made-up, lies, in reality, a fact, once it happens, is nonexistent. It's gone. All that is left is its residue. I always use the example of the battle of Chancellorsville. That's a fact, right? It happened in the Civil War and it's important because Stonewall Jackson was killed there. The beginning of the end. His arm was buried, or his leg was buried. But how would you go proving that happened? We talk about primary sources and secondary sources and eyewitnesses and evidence, but those documents can be fake; those artifacts can be fake. All of it can be fake. But if you take *The Red Badge of Courage,* which is about the battle of Chancellorsville, once it is made, it has a reality. Even though it is fiction, you can hold it. It has presence. You can reread it. You can smell it, taste it. It is, in that sense, more real than the fact that it represents. So to answer the question, what interests me is this: In this life that we all lead, we believe that we have these two concepts figured out, when in fact they're much more complex and confused. That leads into the other thing, where *The Blue Guide to Indiana* comes in. Writers have to make the frame for the way you are seeing something as well as making the thing itself. For example, if a story shows up in *People* magazine, unless you understand the frame of the magazine, you really don't know how to read it.

For me, fiction is disengaged from the idea of truth or falsehood.

Writers have to make the frame for the way you are seeing something as well as making the thing itself.

Do you remember that movie *The Piano?* It's set in New Zealand and there's a moment in the movie where Europeans and aboriginal people are watching a Western play. In the play, someone is murdered. The Europeans understand the frame. They are watching a murder, getting the excitement of watching it. They know it's a play, so they know it's real and not real. But the aboriginal people don't understand plays; they can't see the frame. So they rush the stage and try to stop the murder that's happening. To me, that's really truth and fiction. I use it to remind students that we live in a world where frames are manipulated constantly, and that that's also part of your job as a writer.

Your story, "Highlights," is clearly about the Olympic swimmer, Mark Spitz. You don't name him, though. Would you talk about how that story deepens and complicates what you were doing with those earlier stories?

It was one that was really contested by the lawyers. Spitz had been famous but now was receding into private life, so they really wanted him to give permission. But he didn't. So for a while I couldn't publish it. Finally, I just said the heck with it. If he wants to sue me, let him sue me.

Is that why he's not named?

That was one way of trying to sneak that through, but it is more complicated than that. In the Dan Quayle stories, for example, [his misspelling of the word] *potato* is never mentioned. There are advantages and disadvantages to using real people, and one of the advantages of using real people is the character is already made. I don't need to mention potato because I assume my readers are bringing to the table the idea of potato. In fact, I sort of work against it. So with the Spitz case, I knew he never was a dentist, but I also knew that the audience out there would widely, widely believe he was a dentist. And they did. I walked through a mall in Fort Wayne and in Indianapolis and I just stopped people and asked, "Whatever happened to Mark Spitz?" Most of them said, "Didn't he become a dentist?" He did enter dental school right after he stepped down as a swimmer, but the fact is, he stayed in one semester and then went into real estate. So back to truth and fiction—part of the fun of that for me was knowing that the truth of the world says that he was a dentist, when, in fact, he never was.

There are advantages and disadvantages to using real people, and one of the advantages of using real people is the character is already made.

"Watch Out" is an anonymous voice—a series of "essays" written by a woman employed by the Catholic Diocese in Fort Wayne, Indiana, to teach English to a community of Vietnamese immigrants living together in an old school building. Would you talk about the genesis and evolution of this story? Were there any surprises writing it?

I had one semester off where I could have gone to Paris, I could have gone to Vietnam, but no, I decided on Fort Wayne, Indiana. I lived downtown. Teresa, my wife, was at McDowell at the time, so I was really alone. I would walk around downtown at night. This was in the early '80s, not that long after the mass exodus from Vietnam, and Catholic Diocese all over the Midwest were taking in Catholic Vietnamese refugees.

There was an old high school in downtown Fort Wayne that wasn't being used, and they were housing immigrants there. As I would walk around downtown, I would see their laundry on top of the high school building. I would see them as they were beginning to assimilate. So the impetus of the story was there. Of course, most all my stories are about homesickness, from going away from Indiana, and here was another example of homesickness that I could shift the air around. I think about it as that paradox of mathematics, where you have a bounded space, but within that bounded space there's an infinite amount of points. Students initially resist that because they think, no, I want to be open to write about anything. The paradox is that once you actually put boundaries on what it is you're writing about, it opens up.

The paradox is that once you actually put boundaries on what it is you're writing about, it opens up.

And for you it's homesickness.

I think it is. I think it also has to do with the invisibility of the Midwest. If you are a southern writer and you say, "I'm going to write about Alabama," the response is, "Well, why shouldn't you?" The place is seen as something to write about. That's not the case in the Midwest. When I say I write about the Midwest, they say, "Why? There's nothing here."

How did you find the voice for the story? How was the story that evolved on the page different from the one you had in your head?

I have a theory about Hemingway—and Beckett as well. Beckett will write in French, then translate it into English, and you get a certain effect. If you look at Hemingway's "A Clean, Well-Lighted Place," it actually looks like a hobbled translation. What's great about a bad translation is you don't have the vocabulary, so you have to settle for less. I call it hobbling, like hobbling a horse. Raymond Carver also did this with voice. If you read the *Big Book of AA* and then you read Raymond Carver's stories, you realize what he was looking at were amateur narrators. They are trying to recover from alcoholism, they're at a moment when they are really trying to narrate their lives, but they're not professional narrators. They don't have the language. That's what I really dig about Raymond Carver. There's that huge kind of rage that happens when you don't have the language—you see it in little children when they are trying to talk. They're so frustrated, and you feel that for his narrators. Aesthetically, it submerges. That Hemingway-esque idea of an iceberg. It's all in between the lines. We get this suppressed poetry made out of this limited or forced-limited thing.

In this character's case it's even more so. I think it's dramatically interesting that she herself doesn't understand the language that she's now in charge of teaching other people. She's trying to find the words to use, and the story is about the inability to do this. All stories are about storytelling, really. I think

All stories are about storytelling, really.

the actual physical wandering around the deserted city that's not a city anymore is a representation of this.

Using hobbled language is risky, though, because if it's wrong it's really wrong. It's kind of like writing from the point of view of a child, figuring out what they can know and what language is available to them to talk about it.

Exactly. There's something about trying to go back to children that has to do, for me, with categories. We're fixated with categories in our lives. Creation isn't like an act of God. That is, we don't make something out of nothing, right? Instead, we take things that are already in existence and rearrange them into categories. A great poet sometime in our past said, "It is raining cats and dogs." We know what rain is, we know what cats and dogs are—and we juxtapose those things. And that transforms the world.

We don't make something out of nothing, right? Instead, we take things that are already in existence and rearrange them into categories.

The way I try to break students out of their categories is to use the categories *good* and *bad*. This is especially anxious in a workshop because the underlying idea is that you're coming here to get better. The first assignment I give when they come to class is to write something bad. They laugh, because they are already beginning to think about the problem. I'm surrounded by southern Baptists, so I say, "We live in a fallen world. You're already corrupted and the whole idea is that you're going to get better. So it should be easy for you to go home, be yourself, write badly." Their strategy usually is to take a rule of thumb, like don't use too many adjectives or use active verbs or show not tell. But often the mere fact that they're exaggerating this thing makes it become interesting in and of itself. The reason for this is that the way you really mark goodness and badness is in intention. So they bring these things in and we're reading them and people say, "That's pretty good." Bad becomes good because they actually meet their intention, which was to write badly. That's the successful thing.

One time a person, a thirty-year-old woman, went and got her journal from when she was ten, twelve years old and transcribed it word for word. And it was bad, right? It was bad writing. But all I did was reframe it. I said, "If this was a fiction class and this was a story, a fictional story, in the voice of a twelve-year-old girl, in the form of her journal, we'd all be saying, 'This is terrific! You really captured it.'"

I talk a lot about camouflage, how military camouflage was invented about the same time cubism was invented. In fact, Picasso and Braque were both *camofleurs* for the French army. About that time, the first theory of camouflage in nature was written by an American guy named Thayer. It was about the same time as gestalt theory. So, again, it was all about categories. Settling into categories and then breaking up those categories, fusing them: This tree over here is really a tank. That's what camouflage does. I talk about playing with a baby, giving a baby your keys and he drops them. What I really love about a child is when they drop the keys they really are concentrating when they see them fall down. They do it again and again. What you want to say to them is, "Gravity works." But of course for them gravity is not a category that's fixed yet. The next time they do it, the keys might go up. And they don't know that. That's why you can't take a kid of a certain age to a magic show. Because if the guy levitates, it's just a piece of information. I always tell students something my son said when he was a baby in Syracuse. Syracuse has a lot of snow, and he wasn't speaking when it started snowing but he had started speaking by the time the snow stopped. Underneath all that snow there was all this garbage, and when it melted there was a paper plate in a muddy patch. He looked at the thing and he said, "Look. Moon fall down." Isn't that amazing? In what way can we get back to seeing the world that way, I don't know.

Do you know the book *Mr. Wilson's Cabinet of Wonders* by Lawrence Welcher? Do you know about the museum of Jurassic technology, in California? David Wilson has created this museum. It's not only a natural history museum. There'll be a local China painting, all kinds of wonderful and bizarre things. Well, he recreates them, except some of them are real and some of them are not. Before museums there were things called "cabinets of wonder." Lawrence Welcher, the essayist, goes to see this guy, and he actually gets Wilson out there and he says, "Come on, this isn't real." And Wilson gives him more labels and papers that are written about these various wonders. One of them is about an ant that inhales a spore. This is in the Amazon. The ant grows antlers, and then it goes crazy. It climbs a tree, and at a certain height it bites into the tree and its head explodes and more spores float down for other insects to inhale. Another display is a huge block of granite that's cut away, and there's a bat that's caught in the middle of it. The label says that this bat has so developed its echo location possibilities that it can fly through solid objects, and this particular bat got caught halfway through this block of granite. Welcher says, "Come on, this isn't true," and David Wilson says, "No, it is. Here's some more data on it." So Welcher goes to Harvard to the guy who is the bat specialist and shows him all this material, and the guy says, "This is really good." He says it's not *true,* but it's really good. There is folklore about this. Of course, no bat can fly through solid objects. But the scientist said, "You know, when we first proposed the idea that bats had echo location nobody believed that either." Then Welcher says to him, "Well, what about this ant thing?" and he says, "That's true."

Going back to the real/unreal world of "Watch Out," the form of the story mirrors the kind of essays the narrator's ESL students would write.

That was part of it. I studied with John Barth, and John Barth is very, very good at explaining the narrative pattern: the rising action, the climax, denouement. I never could do that. Barth told me in our conference, "You don't write stories. Technically, you do not write stories. What you do is different." I said, "I know that." What I was doing, really, was using what Donald Barthelme says is the art form of the twentieth century, which was collage. Have you seen the Cordell boxes at the Art Institute of Chicago? They're incredible. Joseph Cordell. As an artist, he does not paint, he does not draw, he does not sculpt. All he does is arrange. That's a sort of standard form for me. My default position would be to do collage. So that's part of the basic structure of the story. The other part does have to do with language, trying to write these small essays. One common experience that our culture puts us all through is the five-paragraph theme. You know, the composition class. It's those two streams.

I have this new anthology with Robin Hemley called *Extreme Fiction.* Our argument is that for the last thirty years, the dominant form in instruction has been narrative realism. But there are also these other things that Robin and I identified as fabulism and formalism. I don't think of myself as a realist, even though I can render something as good as any other realist. I think of myself as a formalist. So what always interests me is the form of something. Now that's really difficult when you're a narrative realist, because the main trick of realism as a form is to make what you're writing look like a spontaneous utterance. I was reading Elmore Leonard, who said, "If looks like writing, rewrite it." There's great talk about entering the dream, not wanting people to realize they're reading. But that's not what I'm up to. I want people to know that this is an artifice.

Because the main trick of realism as a form is to make what you're writing look like a spontaneous utterance.

It's a made thing.

Right. It's a made thing. But then that becomes some of its subject matter. It's like the Pompideau Center. All the insides of the building are on the outside, as opposed to on the inside where we pretend they're not there.

So in "Watch Out," you wanted all the electrical cords to show.

Yeah, that's right.

The artful clutter.

The artful clutter. That's part of that story too.

Talk about artful clutter.

The story goes from thinking about one thing to thinking about another. This is related to, again, the story replicating its content in its form. You have people living out of boxes. They're making a new world out of bits and pieces of things. The narrator is interesting to me, too, because she's in the border. There's no American invention in fiction that is more compelling than the mitigated hero. There's that terrific moment in John Ford's *The Searchers.* The credits are rolling up a black screen, and on the black screen, as soon as the credits stop, a door opens and there's sunlight. In the doorway is John Wayne, the mitigated hero. What happens is, the Indians have captured some family member and he goes searching and finds her and brings her back home. In the last scene, the family is reunited. They go from the porch into the house, but he cannot enter. So the door closes on him. You have civilization here and the chaos here. In *Shane,* it's the farmers against the ranchers, and Shane is the mitigated hero there. He doesn't want to do it, but because he is a gunfighter he finally straps it on. It's Paladin as well. It's Natty Bumpo. They can exist in a civilized area, but they also know the chaos area—and because they know the chaos area, they can never fully get back to the domestic area. In Indian mythology, it's the raven or the trickster. In mythological terms, it's Hermes, the patron of the thief, who can operate in both those worlds. In "Watch Out," that's who she is. She's an essential part of the community, but because she's mitigating between these two communities, she can be part of both but not truly part of either.

So she's alone.

It's all about loneliness, which goes back to your original question about the first person and the basic aloneness of that character, which fascinates me.

"Watch Out" very much deals with the specifics of the immigrants' life in the school building. But there are a lot of things left out, too. You never say where she's from or the circumstances that brought her there. The reader never knows for sure why she is losing so much weight. How do you know what can be left out?

In creative writing programs, the assumption is that the writer is in complete control of meaning, and what's happening in new critical theory is that the reader is also participating in the making of meaning. Collage really, really needs that part because the white space is a kind of graphic representation of the reader reading. The writer's not there, but the reader is going to make some kind of connection between the section above and the section below. So figuring out what can be left out really is trying to psyche out what the reader can do. How big a jump the reader can make. Like in a photo booth. Twenty-four still pictures going by our eyes in a second will give the illusion of motion. But will twenty-three? Yeah, but it will be a little choppier. The reader will have to work a little bit more. But what's great about the use of collage here—the choppiness and the lack of information—is, again, it replicates her position. She doesn't know. There are a lot of gaps for her, and so I'm placing the reader in the position to translate this story the way she is translating the world.

In creative writing programs, the assumption is that the writer is in complete control of meaning, and what's happening in new critical theory is that the reader is also participating in the making of meaning.

You mirror her frustration and momentary illuminations, too. They happen in the gaps.

Right, right. For me, it's a matter of heft. What often happens in collage is that you have to put arbitrary numbers into it, arbitrary armatures. I just wrote an essay in the collage form about pregnancy. I arbitrarily said this is going to have nine sections. I'm going to do all I think I have to do in nine sections. I wrote something about May in Indiana for an anthology that was called *A Year in Place.* They wanted twelve writers, and I got May. So of course I wrote about the Indianapolis 500 and about Memorial Day and about going around in circles. Arbitrarily, though they didn't know why I chose it, it came out in thirty-three sections. The reason is there are thirty-three cars in the race. In a way, your question is simple for me: Arbitrarily I limit myself to this amount of information, only to give it a kind of beginning, middle, and an end.

But how did you know which *thirty-three bits to use, and how did you figure out the right order for them?*

I think it has to do with musical composition in some way. When I'm working in collage, I'm thinking in terms of sort of theme and variation. In the essay about Indiana in May, I knew I was going to be working Memorial Day, the race, and going around in circles. So in each section I want that to be present. In another anthology, I have this story called "The Moon over Wapaganeta." It's in twenty-four sections because there are twenty-four hours of the day. I remember saying that in every section I would mention the words in the title, *Wapaganeta* and *moon.* It became almost a kind of poetic exercise in finding all the variations.

It's playful. But also very cerebral.

It is a cerebral process, and that's the rap against this kind of literature. The rap against, say, metafiction. In the '70s, this stuff was riding high. John Barth wrote a book in 1980 called *LETTERS.* It was his seventh book. "Letters" is seven letters. It was a book made up of letters—six characters from his six previous books writing to each other, plus, a new seventh character. It's completely unreadable. The *New York Times* called it the tombstone of literary modernism—and, in part, it was. At the same time, in 1980, Raymond Carver writes the essay that says, "No more tricks." Let's get back to the sort of Chekovian realism that looks like a spontaneous utterance and that comes from the heart. John Gardner wrote one of the cerebral books in *Grendal,* taking another book and then redoing it from a different point of view, and John Barth invited John Gardner to his class. This is such a great moment in literary history. Gardner turns to Jack Barth and says, "You know, we wasted our lives." He says, "What we should have been doing is Dickensian realism all this time. This is just a bunch of trick-playing, it's bloodless, it's clueless." Barth went on to call it "literary kneecapping." And here's the great thing. Gardner said, "What we should all be aspiring to is the moment in *The Iliad,* where Prium goes to Achilles and begs for Hector's body back." And Barth says, "No." He says, "There's another moment. It's in *The Aeneid.*" We know that book less. Aeneas, who is the brother of Hector, has been traveling all around the Mediterranean and comes to Carthage. He gets out on the Carthage shore and they're building a temple. On the temple, they are showing Prium on his knees, begging Achilles for the body of Hector. Barth's thing is, here's an aesthetic moment, an artifice, and yet we are emotionally engaged even though this isn't the *real* moment. What you have with Aeneas standing there with all the pain of a brother losing a brother, watching his father not exactly being humiliated, but realizing his father has feet of clay. So there's double layers of emotion there. It invokes the previous emotions. So Barth argues that it's actually a more complicated and more interesting emotional moment because it's a layered moment as opposed to the pretended, transparent moment.

I think it's that way with Brecht as well. It is for me an incredible emotional moment when Mack the Knife is rescued in *Three Penny Opera* and he turns to the audience and says, "This is just a story. Outside people are being killed all the time, and you just sit here watching this fake stuff." To me, that's an incredible emotional thing. Brainy stuff. The *real* interesting thing about the cerebral stuff is that you can get away with it. But the rap is always against it. On the other hand, the rap against the danger of a narrative realist is sound and valid, too. They know they are in emotional territory. They don't want to go to excessive emotional stuff. The whole idea in narrative realism is that you have to experience things. But I have no experience in the world except in books. Since I was four years old, I've been in the classroom. I'm forty-eight. For me, books are more real than the world. I enjoy them much more. I often go to places that I've read about and find them incredibly disappointing.

The whole idea in narrative realism is that you have to experience things. But I have no experience in the world except in books.

Obviously, a lot of the reading you've done has been about history—particularly, World War II and the '50s. A number of the stories in your collection Seeing Eye *turn on odd details from that time—bombs that the Japanese sent toward America attached to hot air balloons, the use of human hair in the manufacture of the windows of bombers, the long-term effects of working with radium—and illuminate "ordinary" life in the most extraordinary ways. What is it about a particular detail that triggers a story? How do those stories evolve?*

What always interested me, growing up, were the albums my grandfather kept. He cut out the headlines from the paper and put them in these albums, and so every time I would visit my grandparents, I would look at these things. They were completely, completely out of order. Collage. I would start in 1943 and go back to 1941. Then '45.

What was in them?

Whatever caught his attention. Totally random. But then that's what a newspaper is. That was my first experience reading. I loved those little cut out papers. There's the story about Hemingway coming up with his style, which is that he was a newspaper correspondent, he had to send his stories back and because each word was charged on telegraph he compressed and compressed, finding the essence of things. That makes sense for a story. Barthelme also worked for the newspapers, but he worked as an editor. I always tell my students, "You guys don't remember this but it's still there in your computer: cut and paste." You literally, physically had to cut those galleys and paste them on a light board. So here's Donald Barthelme, the great collage writer, who did that. You have spaces open, and so you need those fillers. He often did the little fillers for *The New Yorker,* too. I think you hone that instinct. You look for the quirky thing. But it's also a sensitivity to what collage does, which is juxtaposition. Cats and dogs and rain: Put it together and you do get a spark. As in "Blue Hair." The fact that the gun site is actually called the "cross hairs," that they *are* hair, that there was a human who provided that hair. All this you put together and—!

So it's as if you have this album in your head, like the one your grandfather had, and you can mix and match at random.

When you talk about this stuff in your book, students and your colleagues will say, "No, no, people won't understand this. They don't get it. They want linearness. They need it all connected." Yet all of us now watch television in this exact manner: with a remote control. You're watching a game, clipping by, say, the marketing channel, and then you go to somebody who's saying five people were killed today in Iraq. Every once and a while you get some interesting juxtapositions. On the *Today Show,* you get Katie Couric saying, "Today we are going to be making Bundt cake, and then later we'll be going to Bosnia." So we *do* make sense of this kind of thing, and it comes from newspapers originally. The great thing about a newspaper is that every day it has to be put together. There's a moment that I like in *Blue Guide to Indiana.* In Rising Sun, Indiana, they make the sun rise every day, and every night it falls apart. They have to remake it every day. That, I think, is the excitement of collage: It falls apart, and you have to put it back all together. Then it falls apart again.

That, I think, is the excitement of collage: It falls apart, and you have to put it back all together. Then it falls apart again.

Maybe the closest you come to the traditional story is with some of the stories in the collection Safety Patrol. *There's a cycle of stories about a family in it. What relationship does that family have to your own?*

The safety director is based on my father. He really was a safety director. He knew he was too old to rewire himself when things were going from the mechanical to electronic, so he looked around the company for the place where he could make it to retirement and thought it would be safety, because people are always going to be having accidents. So he got himself transferred into safety, but there was a paradox there. Because AT&T was reorganized and General Telephone was reorganized in this huge revolution and even safety wasn't safe.

Could those stories have become a novel?

Yeah, in a way. Those stories are my attempt to demonstrate that if you want a realistic narrative, I can do that. I understand what I should do and what I can't do. I think that it *could* have been a novel. The bigger question about novels, being a novelist, is I'm just not like that. I'm really coming out of poetry. I think of myself as a poet who writes in prose. A novel for me is like a forest fire. You've got all these fires you're fighting, all this combustion that's happening. What's great about a short form is it also is combustion, but it's like tarnish. I rust something. For me, it's a more intimate form.

What's great about a short form is it also is combustion, but it's like tarnish. I rust something. For me, it's a more intimate form.

. . . .

Writing Prompts

READ: "Watch Out" and the interview with **Michael Martone.**

PONDER: How Martone "hobbles" language and uses structure to mirror the tensions in the narrator's life.

WRITE: A story in which the central tension in a character's life is mirrored in its structure and its use of language.

PRACTICE:

- Create a character whose language is limited and portray how that affects the character's life.
- Write an essay from a character's point of view.
- Create a character who lives on the border between two very different worlds and create a scene in which she mitigates between them.
- Inhabit the mind of a famous or quasi-famous person and talk about something that matters.
- Write a character monologue in a language in which you are moderately fluent. Ask someone to translate it to English for you and then "tweak" it to create Martone's hobbled effect in the voice.
- Write something bad. By what standards will you judge whether your bad writing is good?
- Choose a topic and set some arbitrary requirements that encourage theme and variation. Write a series of short pieces and then create a story with them, using techniques of collage.
- Consider the scene in *The Iliad* in which Prium goes to Achilles and begs for Hector's body. Write a scene that mirrors that kind of transparent moment. Now consider the scene in *The Aeneid* in which Aeneas, years later, comes on the same scene commemorated in stone on the side of a temple. Use the stuff of your first scene to write a second one that similarly deepens and complicates the emotion of the first by layering time.
- Play with the remote control on your television to discover interesting juxtapositions or images or ideas.
- Use a small, quirky historical detail as the launching point of a story.

Jill McCorkle

Jill McCorkle (b. 1958) is the author of three collections of short stories and five novels. Born in Lumberton, North Carolina, she was educated at the University of North Carolina and Hollins College. Her honors include the New England Booksellers' Association Award, the North Carolina Award for Literature, and four Notable Book of the Year citations from the New York Times. *She was named to the* Granta *list of Best of Young American Novelists. McCorkle has taught at Harvard University, Tufts University, and the University of North Carolina at Chapel Hill. Currently, she teaches at Bennington College. She lives near Boston.*

For Further Reading:
The Cheerleader (1984), *July 7th* (1984), *Tending to Virginia* (1987), *Ferris Beach* (1991), *Crash Diet* (1992), *Carolina Moon* (1996), *Final Vinyl Days* (1998), *Creatures of Habit* (2003).

Hominids

"I'm thinking I will have myself a restaurant known as Peckers, and as my model I will use Hooters, where one of Bill's buddies likes to go on Friday night. I will have a wood-pecker instead of an owl and waiters instead of waitresses. They will wear uniforms that are, shall I say, a bit revealing below the belt and as manager my job will be saying who looks good in the outfit and who doesn't. Sorry, that's business. It's not harassment if you say right up front that Peckers is all about peckers. The Pecker Burger, the Pecker Shake, the foot-long Peckerdog, the Pecker who serves you. There will be lots of cute puns about wood, redheaded, etc. I think it will be a huge success."

I make this speech to the group—Bill's old friends and their wives—gathered for the golf weekend Bill pulls together every year. Golf is the excuse for the get-together even though sometimes only a couple of them actually play. Most of the time is spent drinking and telling tales. Bill has just told how he and the boys could not help but pull off of I-95 and check out Cafe Risqué, which advertises all up and down the highway. I also say, "So why not South of the Border? They have lots of billboards on the highway, too, and they have liquor by the drink. They even have fireworks you can buy. Sombreros. Enchiladas. As a matter of fact, you can buy just about anything at South of the Border, except for the señoritas, *unless,*" I add, feigning great surprise, "that's why you went to Cafe Risqué instead."

The signs say that Cafe Risqué is open all night and that the women are topless. The women on the signs look like supermodels—shiny healthy hair and white well-cared-for teeth. I'm certain that what's on the billboards is not what you find inside, especially at eight o'clock in the morning, or two o'clock in the afternoon. Or any time, for that matter. I'm betting you find track marks, illiteracy, scars of at least one abusive relationship. At least that would be my uneducated guess.

I'm guessing stretched-out titties, the children who stretched them cold and alone at home waiting for mama to get off work. Or maybe the women have no children and they eye every man who comes in through that darkened glass door as a potential future, a ticket to a better, cleaner existence. Men, for instance, like my spouse, Bill, who is college educated and should know better, and his sidekick, Ed, an old fraternity brother who has flown in from Atlanta and who chooses to spend part of his day this way while his wife and newborn are back at home.

I voice my sadness at this scene. I politely question Bill's participation in this event and ask how he will explain such a place, should the question ever arise, to our son and daughter, who are on the threshold of adolescence. And still the conversation in the room turns to breasts. Ethan—former college fraternity brother from Winston-Salem—just can't get over the whole scene. He is imitating, swinging his pathetic khaki-clad body side to side. He discusses ta-ta size like you might a pumpkin, while his wife stands there and giggles. I catch her eye and she stops cold. She knows better but like many of us she has learned that it's easier to look the other way, pretend that you really did not see or hear what you thought you did.

You can learn a lot on a weekend like this. I look around the room—my dining room—as they gather here for cocktails and hors d'oeuvres, and I might as well be on another planet even though it's a scene I have lived through for over a decade by now.

There is always at least one man going through the motions of separation or divorce. That one normally arrives with a woman twenty years younger or comes alone and flirts with all the wives. This year it is Dennis, from D.C., who grew up in this very town but has gone to great lengths to rid himself of any traces of his native origin. It is as if he has no memory of a mother or a childhood or an education here. He would have the world believe that he simply sprang forth in a business suit with a fat wallet boasting membership in the NRA, a Rolex on his wrist, and a BMW parked by the curb. Right now he seems to be checking out everyone's cleavage. I watch him and keep thinking that before the night is over, I will go and get my high school yearbook and pass it around so everyone can check out when he was a Future Farmer of America and a Teen Dem and a relatively decent guy. I will ask how his mother—a woman who put in forty years as a receptionist at the courthouse and who raised a child all by herself—is faring out at Turtle Bay Nursing Home, which he visits only at Christmas if then. He keeps trying to catch my eye and wink like the two of us are somehow in on something. My glance back at him says *You suck.*

I tell everybody that I think men who are attracted to breasts in a major way are still yearning to suckle their mamas. Isn't it true there's a whole generation of formula-fed men who never had that opportunity and now they are suffering? They want to latch on; they want to make their mothers draw sharp breaths in with the tight wrench just before that glorious letdown. I say that knowing that they are all Enfamil men with mamas who claim they couldn't nurse when the truth is nobody taught them how. I don't think evolution would have allowed a whole generation to die out; it certainly hasn't happened that way in the animal kingdom. You don't see animals making fun of teats and udders. I doubt if it happens among humans in Third World countries either. But maybe this was the period in history when society began to look at the breast in a whole different way. Maybe this is when the breast went from a source of nourishment for the young to something for men to pinch and make jokes about.

I can tell that they are tiring of my lecture; I can feel the tension rising so I choose to sink back and away. I ask them to tell us all about their games that day, no one even noticing that this is a way of defusing the situation, a way for me to sit and sip my drink and fade off into my own thoughts. Like the time I accompanied my son and his third-grade class to the science museum where we stood before the model of Lucy—our first woman—her thumb visible, her body emerging from a previous simian form. She was only three and a half feet tall, her head the size of a softball. She was only in her twenties when she died and already her backbone was deformed; she suffered a terrible form of arthritis. She was found at the edge of a lake and scientists are unsure if she drowned or if she simply died of an illness. Did anyone even consider the possibility that perhaps she grew so tired, her heart so heavy, that she simply lay facedown on the shore and waited for the water to carry her into an eternal sleep? Did such a desire even exist in this early human form or was it the result of years of domestication, demands that went far beyond what life out in the wild would have required? Lucy's breasts were not huge; they were thin and stretched. The kids pointed at her nipples and butt crack. They were children and had that right. They still had every opportunity to grow up and imagine the infant kept alive by Lucy's milk—a whole world's population nourished by Lucy's milk.

The discussion of golf comes around to the old story about Johnny Carson asking Arnold Palmer what he did for good luck before a match. Palmer replied, "My wife kisses my balls," to which Carson said, "Bet that makes your putter stand up." No one in the room actually saw the interview so we're not sure how much if any of it is true. The discussion of Ethan's swing leads right back into the swing of the hips of the woman who was clearly attracted to him at Cafe Risqué. Then the swing of her breasts, which Ethan said made him think of Loni Anderson. "Not the face, of course," he said. "Jesus Christ."

"Can you give it a rest?" Ethan's wife finally says. She is on her third cosmopolitan and feeling strong if only momentarily.

"So men like breasts," Dennis says and looks around to get moral support. "Is that news? What's the big deal?"

I say that if there were a disease the cure of which required men to have their penises removed they would be a bit more sensitive to body parts. I say this knowing that Dennis's mother had a double mastectomy when he was still in high school; there she was, a divorced mother, not so common at the time, working a forty-hour week, with a disease no one ever mentioned. There were no support groups, no magazine articles in which other women told their stories.

Ethan, who is lounging back on my sofa with his shiny little loafers propped on one silk-upholstered arm and who has had one too many, tells us, apropos of nothing, that he takes Viagra. There is absolute silence. Ethan's wife, Joyce, who had gone to the bathroom (she said, though I know that really she slipped by the liquor cabinet to freshen her drink), now returns to silence.

"What's up?" she asks.

"Ethan apparently," I say, and after the roar of laughter dies down, I continue. "He was just telling us about how he takes Viagra."

"Ethan!" There is horror all over her face. I am horrified just to imagine the man tuned up like an Eveready. Horrified that poor Joyce has to live with him. And now horrified at myself for making a joke at her expense as well as his.

"Do you see blue?" one man asks. "I've heard it can affect your vision."

"Temporary," Ethan answers smugly. Mr. All Knowing. Mr. Thinks He's Big. Nothing can slow him down.

"And it works?"

"Oh, *yeah,* it works." Ethan is enjoying his five minutes in the sun as he and Joyce knock back the liquor for very different reasons.

"So this was for a medical reason?" I ask.

"You mean impotence?" Dennis yells.

"No," Ethan spits. He wants to call me something really really bad, but he thinks better with Bill there beside me. He can't call Dennis anything because Dennis is a rung or two higher than he is on the man's man ladder. "I was just curious."

"Oh," I say. "Curious."

Bill catches my eye and I can't tell if it's to apologize or to say *Give me a break, I only entertain these guys once a year, let us act like boys. Let us have some fun.* I've heard it all before. And there were the years when the women thought the way we could compete was to act just like them, to go to clubs and drink too much and watch men strip. Scream out things like *Wooo wooo woo, shake it baby yeah,* whistle wolf calls, salivate like Pavlovian dogs. You know, you never really do get into that and you sure get tired of trying to. Personally I'd rather be watching old movies—Bette Davis, Charles Boyer. I'd rather be in my nightgown with a mug of hot chocolate and my children snuggled under a down comforter watching reruns of *Andy Griffith* or *Leave It to Beaver.* I can't imagine Andy Taylor or Ward Cleaver going to Cafe Risqué. The long and short of it (no pun intended) is that very often at the end of a day, I am tired. My breasts are tired. My legs, back, brain. I would like nothing better than to stretch out and close my eyes, disappear, if only briefly.

The men, in spite of everything that has been said, return to the Cafe Risqué topic. Apparently there was one sexy waitress who was considerably overweight. (Ethan: "See? We aren't prejudiced against fat ones. The one that really liked me was the *fat* one.") Another skinny Asian one, Dennis informs us, needs a good orthodontist. (Plus her G-string was nasty looking; her thighs had purple stretch marks.) The one pouring coffee had a tattoo of a snake wrapping around her throat. A really fat ass. I am about to comment about how they all must have left nose prints on the glass of her cage when I walk over and stand next to Bill just in time to hear Ethan deliver his punch line about how to screw a fat girl: "Roll her in flour and look for the wet spots."

"What a hoot!" I slap him on the back as hard as I can. "Aren't you *funny?*" I avoid looking at Joyce, who I have known for a very long time. She was in my wedding. Bill is the godfather of their son. She drinks a little bit more, I notice, at each gathering.

"I've got one for you," I say. "Where do men go after they go to Hooter's?"

"Where?"

"The Hootel. And why don't women date Wood*peckers?*" I emphasize the last two syllables.

"Why?"

"Always boring." The women like that one. "And why does a dog lick his balls?"

"Wait, I know this one," Ron says. "Because he can."

"And did you hear about what happened when the woman showed her size 36C breasts? No? None of you guys have heard this one?"

They all shake their heads, Bill included, as they wait for the punch.

"God, this is an old one. I hear it at least once a week. And I can follow it with the one about the 36B and the 32A and the 48DD."

"So tell us already," Dennis says. He and Ethan are standing there nudging each other like prepubescent boys.

"Well, they all had cancer. They all had to have their breasts surgically removed." The women look down at my rug, the lovely intricate pattern of color. I'm sure there's at least one bad Pap smear in this room. One lump that has caused fear and worry. "Like your mother, Dennis."

They are all quiet now. The women are moving toward the warm yellow glow of my kitchen, where I have promised them a comfortable seat and a glass of good wine while I finish preparing the meal. "Maybe this is the reason the women go to the kitchen," Ron's wife, a relatively new wife, says quietly. "I wish we had done it sooner."

Now you can hear a pin drop. Now you can hear the cars passing on the highway, a rise and fall like ocean waves, and my mind is there by the highway with those women walking around inside Cafe Risqué. And wouldn't any one of them give everything she owned to be standing in this very room, in this privileged life where people actually have hobbies and children fuss about the full plate of good food you put before them and men take for granted the women they married, the bodies they like to roll on top of in the middle of the night, the breasts they pinch and knead like dough.

"Honey," Bill says and calls me back to the doorway. "Let it drop, okay? This is a party, not some New Age awareness group."

Tears spring to my eyes and I have to look away. I look out the window into our backyard at the array of Little Tikes apparatus that no longer gets used. He looks over at all of his buddies, especially Dennis, and laughs as if to apologize for the interruption. I can tell he wants to whisper all of the choice words—*hormones, premenstrual, girl things*—but to me he says, "I'm sorry. It was all a joke." He grips my hands in his. "Truce?"

The men are talking in low cautious voices. They are talking about birdies and bogeys and woods and irons, which in many ways is the same conversation with different nouns. The women have sprung to action and have begun setting my dining table with crystal and silver and Wedgwood china, all wedding presents eighteen years ago. They are laughing now about things their children have said and done. They are talking about their perennial beds, knowing that soon enough I will have to join in. The peonies are just on the verge of bursting into full bloom and Joyce knows that next to the first breath of autumn this is my very favorite time of the year.

When my son and I stood in front of the model of Lucy, it was as if the world stopped for just a second, just long enough for us to take note of how far we had come and how far we had to go. He waited until his classmates ran off in hysterical laughter and then—could he have sensed my great respect for this ancient little hominid?—took my hand and whispered, "I bet she was real pretty for her time." My heart leapt forward a couple of millennia. This boy, this future man, was evolution in action. I tell this story and the women all smile; they relax in a way that they haven't all night long. It begins a whole ring of conversation around topics of love and warmth, desire and longing. I am easily drawn into the circle but a part of me is still thinking about bare breasts and day-old coffee, empty bank accounts and biopsies, neglected children and scar tissue. I am thinking of Lucy as she limped her way to the water's edge seeking rest; I am thinking of her as she lay there millions of years ago staring out at this world for the very last time.

A Conversation with Jill McCorkle

All the stories in your most recent collection, Creatures of Habit, *have simple titles—each one an animal name. The animals in the titles don't always play an important part in the action of the story, but the defining traits of animals provide a weird and wonderful way of looking at human behavior—and that's what the stories are really about. How did you fall into this pattern of observation?*

Originally, the stories all stood alone, more or less. I think the only ones that had animals in the title were "Cats" and "Dogs," which was originally "Mad Dogs." I started to see, as I was working, that there was this thing emerging about animal behavior. When I'm writing fiction, I spend a lot of time reading nonfiction. I love those Desmond Morris books, and I read a lot about animals and nature. Somehow the two fused. Once I had the idea and realized what was coming out, it did, and in the revision process, the idea certainly found ways to grow within the stories where there hadn't been much activity. I wrote "Billy Goats" as a way of capturing a small town during a particular time, to get a sense of these children out on their bikes. I wrote it as an exercise for myself, as the backdrop for the stories. Then it became its own story. When I had that, it felt sort of like a loose bookend. "Billy Goats" truly was my voice. I felt really exposed in it because I had written it as an exercise, and I remembered that I had another piece that I had never intended to use, a meditation on my dad's death. When I pulled it out, I saw that it worked as the other bookend and various parts of it became the final story, "Fish." "Billy Goats" introduces a whole cast of characters and the population of that entire town, and "Fish" narrows it down to that teeny pinpoint of one life, passing.

So you discovered the pattern as you wrote?

I discovered it in the revision process. I worked on the stories the same way I would have worked on a novel. I really never let go of anything, even though they were separate stories. Every one was done with a rough draft and then revision and revision. I was working on a lot of them at the same time. So the bleeding process of one story into another was a natural part of the process. In keeping with my animal theme, I have referred to them as a "litter" of stories.

So the bleeding process of one story into another was a natural part of the process.

One of the stories in the collection, "Hominids," is about the annual reunion of a group of college friends. It's an edgy, very funny story that addresses and connects such complex topics as breast cancer, men's disrespect of women's bodies (and their cluelessness about why this matters), marriage, friendship, and evolution. Would you talk a bit about this story—where it came from, how it evolved?

The idea of that story was twofold. One, I felt that I knew all too many young women who were experiencing breast cancer, either themselves or with their mothers, and I was struck by how there's this hideous disease robbing so many women in our society. They have husbands, they have sons, and they have fathers who are, for the most, part there. Yet you still, in this same society, can go into a party or a gathering or turn on the radio and hear these same men in a disturbing level of humor and discussion about women's bodies. I'm like, how can the brain be so divided that the two are not connected for them? Sometimes I start off because I realize that something has really pissed me off. I sit down and do a tirade to sort of explain it to myself. So "Hominids" started with that. But also—this part of the story is real—I had taken my son and a lot of his friends to the Science Museum in Boston. They have a little model there of Lucy. I guess my son was eight at the time, and all these kids were pointing to her butt and her breasts and laughing. Then they moved on to whatever the next exhibit was and I was standing there and Rob stood right there beside me and he really did say, "I bet she was real pretty for her time." I looked at him and said, "You are evolution in the making. I feel so proud right now to have a son who sees this." I thought, as a mother, I have to write this down so that I will never ever forget it. It just seemed natural to bring it in as part of this story.

Did the experience with your son come during the time you were working on the story?

No, it had already happened. But I always store many scraps of ideas in my head, and it was floating up there.

When the story started to come to you, did you know that that would be a part of it?

Not at all. All I had were all the jokes about opening a restaurant called "Peckers." I had figured out this whole parallel to "Hooters," and I was just going at it in an aggressive, nasty way, having a lot of fun. Then the story turned.

What kind of revision did you do on that story?

The main thing was toning her down somewhat. She was much more vicious in the first draft. My editor, Shannon Ravenal, always tells me, "This is too mean." The first draft of "Monkeys" was really, really angry as well. Then I slowly worked beyond it, because I think that kind of anger and sounding off can be very one-dimensional.

It can feel like an agenda.

Yeah. I was so horrible to those men. That's when Shannon's vision made all the difference. I began to think it was Dennis's mother in the nursing home in the story, "Turtles," that he was the kid at home, doing his homework, ashamed his father had left. It doesn't excuse his behavior, but it does explain it. To a degree. I guess that's what I'm always looking for, those patterns within development. As a writer and as a person, I'm real interested in understanding how somebody gets from point A to point B. I guess, personally, I do hope that we get recycled and that we get to try it all over again. And do it a little better. That's the part in fiction that attracts me the most, reaching some level of understanding or acceptance of the things people do. It's easier to see on the page than you would ever be able to see it in life.

I guess that's what I'm always looking for, those patterns within development.

There's a lovely little moment in the story when the husband apologizes, grips her hand, and says, "Truce?" You know a lot about the characters and their relationship in that small exchange. In fact, a lot of life plays out in small, undramatic, but crucial moments just like that one, and there's a lot of those in your stories. How do you find them?

Sometimes they naturally come in and other times they happen along the way. I'm thinking of "Cats," probably the most direct animal connection idea that I had [in which a man in the early stages of Alzheimer's regularly appears at his ex-wife's home]. I had in mind that you would have a person like an old cat going back home. But what I didn't know was the enormous amount of tenderness and desire that the first wife was going to feel, that she would want to keep him. That surprised me. It was one of those little moments: just the turn of a body, the natural physical impulse to touch this other person, even though it had been years. I was expecting more of a feeling of justice for her, and it wasn't there at all.

Would you talk about the importance of surprise in stories?

Most of my stories surprise me. Like "Toads"— the story of the woman who has inherited the stepfather. I had already published it in some literary magazine, which I should not have done. It ended with the very despondent line, the daughter saying, "He was her white noise, third martini, Demerol in the vein," just not understanding what her mother ever saw in this man. Later, Shannon and I were talking, and she said, "How do you feel about this story?" I said, "It's never felt complete to me. I know it's not one of my best stories." She said, "Well, that's because it isn't finished. You just need to go back and think about it." And all it took was for me to give a name and a memory to his first wife in that brief little bit. Then it all opened up behind it. Suddenly this daughter sees that he didn't want this either. Instead of seeing him as the polar opposite of her father, there's much more of a connection that leaves the blame, really, on her mother, a very sad person. There was this wave of forgiveness and acceptance that surprised me. It made a very different story.

Most of my stories surprise me.

You said you knew the original published story wasn't right. How did you know that?

I had that sentence in my mind—the one about Demerol—and it had the feel of a last sentence to me. But I knew the story hadn't resolved its way to it.

It hadn't earned that last line?

Right. Sometimes on the way to the end of the story I do find what feels like that last line, then in revision I have to make sure that everything that comes before it has set it up right. An example of that is a story called "Intervention." It's rare for me that a story begins with the end, but that one did. The idea for that story was that there would be someone who clearly should not be driving and that this person's spouse would knowingly, almost sacrificially, get in the car and not fasten her seat belt. And then I started thinking, now why would she do that? Of course, then it was the whole restructuring of the marriage that they had had, the realization that in all the early years, she had been the person causing all the problems and he'd covered it all. Even her children had no clue. So, at the end, it's kind of like paying him back. I was pleased. I read it at Sewanee last summer, and some women who are in AA came up to me and said, "We didn't know where you were going and we were surprised. We were pulling for this man, hoping that people would just leave him alone." I felt that was good, then, because I wasn't trying to make any kind of comment on interventions. To me, it was more about what would make someone knowingly sacrifice her life for another person. That's an example where the ending was clear from the start.

Do first lines often come to you as first lines?

Sometimes the idea comes with that first line. The first line of "Dogs" came that way. I was having a really bad day and I was talking to a friend and I said "God, if I was a dog, somebody would have shot me by now." I knew I'd use it some day.

Humor plays an important part in all your work. "Hominids," for example, is hilarious. It makes you laugh out loud in parts, but at the same time there's this underlying tension in the situation that might explode at any moment. Would you talk about the use of humor in your work, how you use it to bring the reader to consider the serious issues your stories explore?

I love using humor. I really think that there's humor always to be found. The saddest thing can be happening in the world, and people still say and react in ways that are humorous. Humor is a lifesaving device. It enables people to go further into what is dark and complicated than they would be able to otherwise. So, for me, the funny makes the serious more serious and vice versa. The struggle for me as a writer is keeping the balance and not lapsing into too much on either side. It's like a tightrope walk. You see something that strikes you as funny and yet you know that if you explore and discover the rest of it, it won't be nearly as funny. Or at least there will be the flip side. As a writer, that's what I'm looking for—the other part.

Humor is a lifesaving device. It enables people to go further into what is dark and complicated than they would be able to otherwise.

Maybe because there is so much humor, there's also a lot of dialogue in your stories.

Dialogue is such a good way to get to know the characters. The more you have them talk, whether it's in a scene with another character or whether it's in the form of a letter, a journal entry, the better you get to know them. I enjoy doing that kind of first-person monologue. I love to read plays. I read a lot of them. If I was ever going to attempt another genre, that would be what I'd want to do.

Dialogue is such a good way to get to know the characters.

Sometimes beginning writers shy away from dialogue. I always say to my students that I think writers have a natural tendency toward either scene or summary. The scene writers very often—and I empathize because I did this for years—get in and they can't get out. I can remember working on stories where I would go ahead and have the character get in the car and drive across town, even though what I really needed to do was end and then restart. All too often students give scene and dialogue to parts of a story that aren't too important and it has the effect of watering down whatever strength the story has. I tell my students that they ought to "draw" a story. Look at it on paper. Look at the number of scenes. When I was a student at Chapel Hill, my first writing teacher, Max Steele, would have us read a story and then we were responsible for knowing how many scenes the story had—and to pay close attention to the transitions between them. "Three years later in Albuquerque . . ." You can do that. And, especially as present tense became more and more popular, people often didn't understand that you could still use a simple word like *now* to return the action to the present. A lot depends on the story. There are stories that need more scenes than others. There are stories that work just in the telling.

What is a story, in your view?

In my teaching, I always use a more classical definition: A story is a series of events leading to an emotional change. For me the key word is *emotional.* Some little shift in the universe. It doesn't have to be anything big. It's just a shift.

As in "Snipes," when the children realize that their mother doesn't love their father anymore. Or in "Snakes," when the narrator realizes that her husband has had an affair. Do you often have the sense of what those moments will be before you write a story?

Oftentimes, I have a vague idea, but it's not always right. For instance, "Snipes." It's based on a dear friend's story from childhood, where she and her siblings were taken on a snipe hunt—except that the adults took it one step further and had a tape recorder up in the tree. I heard the tape of my friend Emma saying, "I gotta pee." Her brother said, "Just pee in your pants." In my mind, that was going to be the horror of the moment—when these children, this brother and sister, realize what the adults have done to them and how betrayed they feel. What developed along the way was the relationship of the parents, so that the real betrayal is what's happening in the home.

What's interesting to me is that I've had people say, "Oh, that mean older brother." I see him as solicitous. I felt that what he was doing to her was a natural response to being the big brother and knowing what was going on. I felt that at the end, where she's leaning into him, that what she's feeling is that he's what she has. I did feel that he was there for her and that it was more the betrayal of the adult world that hurt her—and not just the snipe hunt, but the bigger picture of things not being what you expect.

Could you talk about writing from the we *point of view, as you did in "Billy Goats"? When do you think that's an appropriate way to tell a story?*

The story I always send my students to right off the bat is "A Rose for Emily." You're getting the viewpoint of the whole town. Unlike omniscient, *we* has the personal attachment that a first-person narrator does. You feel like you're getting it firsthand. You're bridging first-person attachment and closeness with this kind of all-knowing. There's the feeling that this story happened and they all know it. I do think there's a time and place for it. It works especially well when you are telling a story about a town and within a town.

What about the you? *As in "Fish."*

I was absolutely picturing the recipient of my *you* so I wasn't trying to put the reader in the story at all. It was more the way that you would write a letter to someone.

What was it about "Fish" that made it impossible to write it any other way?

I would have been so self-conscious if I had even said "my dad." I was not acknowledging an audience other than my dad. It felt more like the way a confessional poet addresses what feels very private. That's what it felt like to me—a confession of feelings. I'm not a poet, but I try every now and again, and much of that story had been written in little vignettes. Of course, every time I try to write a poem, I give up and finally put it in a paragraph.

I'm not a poet, but I try every now and again, and much of that story had been written in little vignettes.

There's such sadness and longing in the pages of Creatures of Habit. *Yet the book is such a celebration of what life is: difficult, heartbreaking, rich, complex, hilarious, and strange. How did you come to view life this way, and how has the process of writing fiction brought you to see life the way you do?*

I had a wonderful childhood, but it was one where I was privy to a lot that was sad. I had a lot of old relatives that I visited and I was aware of a lot of the problems that people have. I witnessed a lot. In a small town—and I think this comes out in "Billy Goats"—it's kind of hard not to hear about the deaths and the sadnesses of other people. So I was always aware of the sadness, and I was a child who *liked* sadness. I loved reading all those old Eugene Fields sad poems, and "The Little Match Girl." I just ate them up. For me, discovering that I had the power to control my emotions that way was remarkable. By reading and writing I could make myself laugh or cry or scare myself to death. And then I started trying it out on other people. Other children.

Is there a writer's sensibility, something that shows up even during childhood?

I think that most writers do feel like observers. Oftentimes there is a kind of detachment that comes in. I think it's why there's the need to write. I think it's a way of placing yourself back in life. I feel like I'm someone who's had this vicarious life on the page. It is the balance for me.

I think that most writers do feel like observers. Oftentimes there is a kind of detachment that comes in. I think it's why there's the need to write.

How do you begin the process of revision, how do you help a student who's stuck?

I ask a lot of questions. It's much easier for me to find those questions with students' work, because there's that "cold eye." I usually have a series of questions. Why is this scene here? What did I learn that I didn't already know? I ask myself the same questions.

Do you ever get through with a story and then decide it's not that character's story, after all?

Yeah, but I usually still think it's a story, just maybe not the best story out of the material. That's an exercise that I think is fun to use in class. Let them take the same situation and tell it from several different angles.

Is there anything that you cannot be taught as a writing student?

You can compare writing to teaching the basics and rules of any physical endeavor. You can teach somebody how to hold a baseball bat, how to stand, and you can position them perfectly, but whether or not they are going to hit it nobody knows. In writing, you can be taught technique—what we've been talking about in terms of scenes, transitions. You can be taught— and to me this is so important—to be a better reader. You can be taught a kind of open-mindedness. I'm always a bit wary of the students who are very quick to say, "I don't like that kind of story; I don't read that kind of story; I don't write that kind of story." I hesitate to cut people off because I've seen students many semesters into a writing program have this major brain change where, suddenly, they are thinking in stories. But when I've got somebody who's sitting there saying, "Oh, I really want to write, but I can't think of anything," that's when I'm thinking, well, you might want to find something else to do! *This* is a problem! I feel like I can't live long enough to write it all. I encourage students to keep journals and to keep ideas with the understanding that rarely does a whole story fall into place.

I feel what's most important for a student to learn is the power of revision and the willingness to stay open while the piece is growing and changing and developing. People who are not willing to take it to the next step are likely to be stuck, except for those once-in-a-blue-moon lucky stories that fall from the sky. Revision is such an important part of the process, and I find that I revise far more with stories than I do with a novel. I look at every word and comb back through and comb back through. And I feel like I'm getting more and more obsessive. It takes longer and longer with the revision. I don't know if that's good or bad.

I feel what's most important for a student to learn is the power of revision and the willingness to stay open while the piece is growing and changing and developing.

It seems that's what people who want to write least understand about the process of creating stories. There's no formula, you have to find your own way.

People want to be told definitely *How To Do It.* I'll never forget when I was teaching at Harvard, there was this student, a very talented writer, who came to my office one day and asked, "What is the equivalent for a writer to a doctor doing his residency?" I said, "There isn't one. A doctor doing his residency is already a doctor and unless he really screws up, they are going to call him 'doctor' and they are going to pay him like a doctor. And that's not true for a writer." He got this horrible look on his face and said, "What am I going to tell my parents?" I think that writing, like any venture in the arts, is such a leap of faith.

What's your best advice to aspiring writers?

Just to do it! There is no other way to learn. Just do it and keep doing it even if they know it's not working. The analogy that I cling to is that it's like drilling for oil. There is no fast way to get there, you just start digging and know that you are going to go through a lot of material that is worth nothing.

A lot of layers of shale and sand?

And shit! You bet! That's my advice. Be open to what a story will naturally do. Relinquish that control and to be able to revise. I think about it in the same way I think about life. Imagine if every time we made a mistake, it sealed our life in a way that didn't allow us to change and move in another direction. Who would want to live past twenty-five if that were true? You have to be open to the idea that change can be for the best. Cutting those sacred parts that people have such a hard time cutting is oftentimes the best thing that they can do. I often tell students and I feel this about my writing: What's there could not have been there without the original work. I just think of those things as phantom scenes that haunt the story.

Cutting those sacred parts that people have such a hard time cutting is oftentimes the best thing that they can do.

Writing Prompts

READ: "Hominids" and the interview with **Jill McCorkle.**

PONDER: How McCorkle creates a story that takes place in a single evening, folding in the memory of an incident with her young son to bring it to resolution. Note how anger and humor characterize the narrator, convey information about the group of lifelong friends, and crank the tension among them.

WRITE: A story that takes place over the period of a few hours, using a flashback to bring it to resolution.

PRACTICE:

- Identify a group of people who are bonded together by place and let them collectively narrate a story about something that happens there.
- Write with humor about something that enrages you.
- Consider the dark side of something you think is hilarious.
- Invent a story around a sentence that you said or heard.
- Write a story that has a politically incorrect resolution.
- Write a monologue, letter, or journal entry in a character's voice.
- "Draw" a story you want to write: List the scenes and show how you will make transitions from one to the next. Consider which parts of the story might work best as summary—and why.
- Write a monologue in which you or an invented character addresses a specific *you.*
- Consider all the points of view from which you might tell a story based on a situation that interests you. How would the focus of the story be different for each one?

Susan Neville

Susan Neville (b. 1951) is the author of three collections of short stories and two collections of creative nonfiction. Born in Indianapolis, she was educated at DePauw University and Bowling Green State University. Her honors include the Flannery O'Connor Award for Short Fiction, the Richard Sullivan Prize in Short Fiction, the Pushcart Prize, and an NEA fellowship. Neville is the Demia Professor of English at Butler University. She lives in Indianapolis.

For Further Reading:
The Invention of Flight (1984), *Indiana Winter* (1994), *In the House of Blue Lights* (1998), *Fabrication: Essays on Making Things and Making Meaning* (2001), *Iconography: A Writer's Meditation* (2003).

Night Train

At the trial they said that Madge had been abducted. But there were little details that didn't fit: the doorman at the Claypool Hotel who saw her waiting in the car without an escort. She waved at him in the light from the gas lamps. He remembered her hair, so black it was almost blue, and the wet shine on the pavement, veined by the metal tracks from the trolley. He said the smell from coal dust was thick that night, he said he'd been washing down the beveled glass in the door to the hotel for hours.

Steve had a will larger than this city, the kind of will it's almost impossible to escape from. I've known men like him. All it takes is single mindedness and narcissism and—what. Once I knew a cook who would put a speck of ground glass in the soup or cigarette ash in a sauce, just to know that he could. Not enough to hurt anyone, just so he would know it was there and he could watch an old man sip down bowls of chowder knowing there was that brittle bit of something that, if it were bigger, would begin to wear a hole inside large enough for his life to seep through.

This cook would look at the wet ground in the spring and watch the entire landscape loosen, unbuckle belts and fasteners and start to ooze around his feet, and he wanted to be the one who caused that loosening. Because he knew he could. He was a cook and when he looked at the world he saw it pressed into a fine string and woven through the bodies of people who knew in this world they would always be hungry. Once you know that, anything is possible.

That's how I see Stephenson and how I see Madge with him and that's how I think it happened. And I feel enormously guilty when I say that, going against the story of her abduction and rape by a man fully consciously evil. Who in this world ever sees himself as evil finally? No one. I think it was, instead, a loosening in the face of an enormous will, that she felt herself lifted into a whirlwind and then his voice, Steve's voice, saying, *listen girl, believe me when I tell you to close your eyes and fly and believe me when I say my arms are larger than the state, larger than God's, so large I can hold you up here where nothing will touch us, and I absolutely will not let you fall.*

He didn't say he loved her, just that and the fact that it was a quick shot to Chicago, the straight humming rails with car after car all coupled in a chain like the cells of her body like all the human beings and animals and atoms in the world coupling, separating, and reforming always with a kind of violence. And there she was, he said, maybe about to be left out of it or about to let go as she should, to take the freedom he was offering her. I'm sure his argument had something to do with courage. I'm sure she heard heroic music playing. Otherwise where would she be? Straight rows of church pews, of moment following moment, of stitches in the hem of her good winter coat. The cemetery was filled with row after straight fixed row of sinking stones.

They do sink, you know, after awhile, like rocks to the bottom of a creek bed.

So Steve's driver took them to Union Station, and they walked into that huge vault of arches and stained glass and Madge felt something rise up in her as dear and high as that ceiling, a giddiness or expansion of her self, like a cathedral. You know I'm mad about you, he'd said, or something like that, and they were heading for the train to Chicago and some bit of work I'm sure he'd said they had to do there, so the whole thing was this heady mixture of passion and duty. She could picture all the rest of us, her sisters, sleeping in our dull beds in the dull Midwestern night, the moon a fake mother of pearl with the plastic peeling off the surface, sleep-walking through our lives. When they, Madge and Steve, were in fact the ones sleepwalking. You know I'm mad about your body, he said, and in this much he was conscious: he knew he was seducing her.

I have to say this. The prosecuting attorneys painted her as wholly innocent. I believe she was. But not in the way they meant it. I do think that she started on this trip at least partially willingly, that there were times, even in Chicago, that she remained willingly. That doesn't make Steve less culpable. It just makes it more human, something you could see yourself being somehow sucked into. It's why it doesn't work to tell kids not to do something because they'll die. Then they're not prepared for the seduction, for how good it feels, how much they might want it, and when they find that out they think that everything they've been told has been a lie. So I think that a woman hearing the story of Madge dragged and bound in the middle of the night on a train to Chicago won't be prepared for anything. The dragged and bound kind of abduction—you can't see it coming, there's nothing you can do but work for some escape. But the kind that comes with power and charm, you think of it as a story outside and beyond you, not there in this particular smiling man. You know? Everyone loves him, even the governor. You feel so lucky that he turned to you. You! Madge Oberholtzer. A stenographer, working girl, with a life suddenly here in the dull center of the country like any New York flapper, the kind of life you read about in the magazines.

She had a beaded purse on her lap, with a handkerchief, some lipstick and powder, a pocket mirror. Why does that break my heart?

At one point on the train, maybe early on, maybe she felt the lens shift slightly from romance to something darker. And she laughed and said no to something he suggested, still living in that version of herself as the good Victorian girl with jazz-age courage, a difficult fiction to live behind as many girls like Madge discovered at that time, like a paper doll cut from paper made in two different centuries, the difficulty being that you have to find a man who isn't looking for the seam where the papers are joined, too flimsily, with makeshift glue. Madge and I were in the same sorority in college. I know what it was like then. The 1920s. We were born with the century. We really thought we'd invented sex. It's hard to believe now how innocent we were.

Why do I keep talking about innocence? Because this is a trial, and I have to come down on one side or another and I know that what I'm talking about is too human for that sort of certainty. Everyone has his own story, a story that's woven as tightly, that fits as warmly, as those footed pajamas that children wear.

Years ago I went rafting on the Little Pigeon River in Tennessee. It was a brilliant July day, not a cloud, everything shimmering like money. I was with a whole group of people, bobbing around on the Little Pigeon, a lot of chatting between rafts, a lot of falling and splashing in the water.

For a while I talked and then for a while listened and then finally, after an hour or so I just lay back on the raft and relaxed absolutely, letting the river and my fellow travellers take the raft and my thoughts without any direction from me—no paddling, no pushing against the shore, nothing—and after a half an hour there was this one moment when suddenly everything dissolved—the sky became the river, the river bled into the trees, I felt my body start to disintegrate into glittering pieces, or rather, I didn't feel my body as mine at all, what the Eskimos call kayak sickness, and I felt like I was falling into the sky. And suddenly there was this physical start, like the yank of a bridle, the bit in the corner of my mouth. That's up, that's down, this is upstream, that's downstream. These are the hard edges that separate one thing from another.

This has something to do with all of this, bear with me. I'm an old woman and allowed to wander.

My lover was with me on that trip, and that night when we came in from the carnival nightlife of Gatlinburg, the Little Pigeon outside the window of our room, I thought about the river and how there's a letting go that's terrifying. That if you could throw off the bridle, if you could trust that dissolution, if you trusted that your body was an especially strong and natural swimmer, then there would be this joy that might feel like drowning, like pain for a while but would eventually build this pressure and thrust you up through the endless water, or rather, through the brilliance of all the shimmering light, and you would rise up like the spouting foam of a great whale.

Or you could take something, a cup, and hold it in the fountain of that light, and drink it down, drain it into every cell.

I was madly in love, madly madly in love, and on that trip with my lover to the mountains and the thundering river. I started noticing when the bit of fear pulled me back, said that's good but enough, and I consciously, in the middle of each wave let go even more, a greater and greater letting go, and I swear to you one night I just stayed there floating on top of this sea for an entire evening, and it was something like coming, but deeper.

You don't want to hear this about an old woman, do you, but there you have it.

And you may think I'm getting back to Madge and Steve and that I'm going to say that's what Steve wanted. But what I'm going to say is that it's what Madge wanted, what she sensed and couldn't articulate, and that, in her innocence, she thought had nothing at all to do with love, that love was in fact the binding cord, the bridle.

And what Steve wanted? Not this letting go at all, that's exactly what he was most terrified of, no matter what he said. If he felt someone like Madge taking him close he'd feel like he was floating on a raging river and right ahead, with no turning back, the endless, pounding, falls. And that's when he sank his teeth into her, to pull himself back onto the shore. The autopsy showed them, on her breast. Puncture wounds caused by human teeth.

Did you know that at one time there were falls on the Ohio River? We domesticated them with locks.

I can't let go of the fact that she didn't tell her parents she was going to Chicago, that she didn't take anything with her for the trip. She left the house in her black wool coat, even though the day had been sunny and spring-like, and she didn't take a hat. She'd been out dancing with a friend, had come into the house at 10 P.M. Her parents had both been ill for a week with the flu; despite the early spring weather, and the crocuses along the foundation of the house, they'd been closed in, the windows still sealed tight, and the house had that sickroom smell, and all week she'd noticed the dust in the cracks of the wood floors and the sticky film on the furniture. They were old, her parents, and she lived there with them, and when she shut the door on the night and felt the contrast between the gay dance she'd left and the closed-in house, and the flesh of her parents, and when her mother said that Steve's secretary had called for her, had said for her to call no matter what time she came in, Madge got on the phone and said she'd be right there. There was moonlight coming through the lace curtains in the entry hall, and the dim chandelier glowed like cool stars. He needs me right away, she told her mother, some papers I need to prepare. He's leaving later on the train for Chicago.

She didn't say anything about going with him. How could she?

Though maybe she was angry with them for some reason, maybe she told herself she would call them the next morning, and in fact she sent a telegram from a hotel in Hammond. Or maybe it was kidnapping, and everything else I've said applies to some other woman, not this particular one.

However it was, she was in the car outside the Claypool with no one watching, thinking to herself maybe that she shouldn't be doing this, that she would tell Steve that when he came back to the car, she would tell him and he would keep her on; they would still work on that project together, she'd still have the excitement of carrying messages for him, of being associated with the most powerful man in Indiana.

There was the yellow light from the inside of the hotel, all refracted into pieces like flower petals or gold glitter, and the light in the streetlamps and the headlights of cars, the light caught in the bracelet on her wrist, a ring on her right hand, some silver threads in her dress fabric. I wonder if she thought about crosses burning out in the country, the gangs of young men that Steve set in motion, I wonder what or if she thought about those crosses, or if she even knew. She worked in the department of education, it's said she was compassionate, liberal. I wonder if she didn't know about the things the Klan was doing, or what it was Steve told her to stop her from worrying. Or if that was something she thought she might change in him, if it was part of their banter when they talked, something that attracted him to her—the fact that she had her own mind.

The train station was busy, loud and dirty, even that late at night, and the train to Chicago was almost full. He got two private rooms, and for a while she thought that maybe it was going to be all right, but when they walked through the railroad car in the warm domestic light of the stopped train, and Shorty went into one room and Steve followed her to hers, and he came inside with her, and locked the door behind him, she knew that it wasn't going to be all right, but she realized she didn't care.

And then the roaring of the train on its bright rails, metal against metal like sharpened knives, and Steve came toward her in the dim light of the car. They were moving, and outside the window, all of Indiana was dark and somehow oceanic, unfixed, a wilderness of fields waiting for spring seeding. If she were outside, she knew, she could smell the mud from spring thawing, in the morning there would be the early sound of birds, it was March. She'd been waiting months for the feel of spring, for the damp ooze of spring, but here in the railroad car there was only speed and metal, and the hard oilcloth seats and the thin mattress on what served as a bed, like the beds, she thought, that men slept on in prison.

I'm thirsty, she said, still feeling like a seduced one, which implies a moment of giving in, thinking she had a choice still, still not believing that she could be in any real danger. It was a *game* of danger they were playing, and at any moment she could say enough, let's stop this now, it was an adventure, but I want to go home, I want the feel of my own soft bed, the smell of clean sheets, my mother's voice and in the morning the bell of the phone and my girlfriends calling, and the story I could tell them of how much you wanted me.

He turned out the light in the car, and there was only the reflected light from the moon on his face, an ashen grayish light, and from then on there would be only the occasional light from a farmhouse or small town. His face was round as the moon in fact, floating above her, his lips were too full. He took a flask from his pocket and made her drink; he wouldn't ask the porter for any water. In the dim light he looked boyish with his pale blonde hair, boyish and swollen, like someone's child. And she, Madge Oberholtzer, wasn't there at all for him, she could tell that right away, his boyish face, lost, his eyelids closing over the pale blue eyes, the half smile on his face as he touched her. She was something just ordered up on the table, a woman with wide hips and pink aureoles large as platters. That's all he saw, or, rather, all he felt. She believed she had an awkward face. It didn't matter. Maybe she should accept this as the adventure it was. But wasn't he at least supposed to say he loved her?

He had a baby face, dark shadows around his eyes, oval shadows like the slits in the white hoods of the Klansmen.

She hoped that he would grow to love her.

The last thing she remembered being excited by was his face, by the picture she had of herself as brave, by the romance of the long dark train thundering like a river through the country. She was a little bit scared, but that was part of it. If pushed to the wall, she'd have to say she still trusted him.

I saw her two days later, an hour or two after Steve's bodyguard brought her into her parent's house. There were scratches all over her body. She was barely breathing. She told the story, whispered it. For three days the lawyer had her tell the story slow. There was a stenographer who typed it up at night and read it back the next day. Madge's dying statement. She had to say she knew that she was dying before she signed it. I was a witness to her signature.

At one point, in Chicago, she'd found his gun lying on a table. She stood in front of a full-length mirror and lifted the gun to her head. She thought about her mother then, the disgrace this kind of suicide would bring and somehow in her confusion, the lawyers said, decided on another way.

That's when she talked Steve into letting her go out with his assistant to buy the hat, and she went into the hat shop unescorted. This is another part of the story that never fit. And she tried hats on, several of them, perhaps looking for one that would cover the marks on her face, hoping to go back on the train maybe like any woman out for the day, not like the woman she felt was at that point, with the sky as blue and absolutely flat as enamel, red buds coating all the trees and somewhere a metallic bell-like sound that seemed to rise up out of the day itself, like that sound you get when you run a wet finger around the top of a crystal goblet, that kind of sound. She looked at herself in the mirror at the hat store and she saw a Madge whose life would never be the same again. She felt nauseous and brittle, and there wasn't even the tiniest bit of magic in the hat. The mirror's glass was a yellow greenish gold. She looked like an old woman to herself, and she couldn't imagine living. This part is all conjecture. The lawyer only had the time and Madge the strength to gather facts.

She went into the pharmacy then, unescorted, by telling the bodyguard that she needed some female things, that she was bleeding. He'd been kind to her in the hotel room. He'd soaked white towels in warm water and applied them to the scratches and the bites, washing the towels out in the sink when they got too cool, the blood a pale pink. He was a kind man. He was clumsy with his nursing, embarassed and slightly deferent, the way she imagined a husband might be, so different from Steve. All that was closed off to her now. Steve gets like this, he said, I'm so sorry, but it's just the way he is, you know. We all have our failings, and this is his. He might have called the police or a doctor, but he was also a weak man, she could tell, and he owed everything to Steve, and he was slightly afraid of him. And he probably told himself that Madge wasn't a whole woman anyhow, not one of the women the Klan was defending, she was one of the other kind, slightly less than a woman since this had happened to her, a good woman who'd allowed herself to become a whore.

But he let her go into the pharmacy alone. And there was clearly no thought of escape. She could have leaned over to whisper a word to the pharmacist, but she didn't.

If she'd lived, we agreed, no one else would ever hear a word of this story. It would have just meant shame for her. She knew shame.

Mercury chloride is the drug she bought in the pharmacy. Maybe she had been a virgin before that night; maybe she was terrified of pregnancy only, her mind so clouded at that point with the beating that the only real shame she could imagine was the one she was familiar with. The physical evidence, like some disease. Mercury chloride was used in those days to induce abortions.

Maybe Steve's story was partially right. Maybe the initial tragedy had been compounded by the beating. He was a man for whom beating women came naturally, it was part of what he did with women; it was the only way he could let go completely. There were parties at his house where he dressed like a satyr and beat women with whips. He paid them to ask for more. Like a little dog who takes hold of the female with his teeth and shakes and shakes her in between coming.

However it was, he didn't mean to have a dying woman on his hands, and suddenly he did. That's when he was fully conscious of the harm he'd done and he chose it again and again. Each minute he waited to get help for her, he was choosing to let her die.

How do I know all this?

When we were in our thirties, my lover married someone else, and I painted my apartment red. Not a rust color or a burgundy, this was the most fake food dye maraschino red that I could find. I painted it myself, spread the bright stain over the light switches, the vents, the electrical outlets, even the ceiling.

Only six months after his wedding, my lover started coming by again. I was a woman he would sleep with but not one he would marry. It hadn't of course seemed that way to me. It was the 1920s. I loved him.

It was different after. Sometimes we made love when I was bleeding. He would turn me over on my belly where we couldn't see each others' faces. I heard him groan, he could watch it all and he felt, he said, like an animal. You could forget you were human, he said, the blood, it was so good to watch. You see? What a relief it was to him, this man who thought too much. Face down on the bed, I would tilt my head and look for a mirror where I could catch a glimpse of his face. All I saw was red. He took a shower before he went back home to his wife; there was blood underneath his nails, smears of it on his thighs and arms. How could he have explained it? When he left, I made a smear over the red paint, and at first it blended in but in the morning there was a brownish stain.

I felt shame then, actually, and I couldn't wait for him to call the next day, to reassure me that he'd loved it. Me. Had I loved it? I'm a strong woman in most areas of my life, but it occurs to me now that I didn't ask myself that question. I asked myself very few questions when it came to him. I loved that he loved it. I'm ashamed of that as well. Or not ashamed. If I had it to do over, I'd do it the same way.

The red walls of my apartment would glow in the afternoon sun like the inside of a heart. The rhythm of his life brought him to that apartment over and over again. You see? The rhythm of *his* life.

I've been obsessed for years with what kind of hat it was. I wish the jurors had asked to see it, I wish I'd looked in Madge's closet. It didn't occur to me until the middle of the trial that it was the key to knowing why and how things happened. A large hat, veiled, would have meant something different than a straw hat with fruit. Was she still a woman with enough sense of a self that would continue to live and need a hat, or was she a woman who wanted to cover the bruises just long enough to buy the poison that would kill her?

Or maybe there was the tiniest bit of hope, and when the hat didn't do its work, that was the end of it.

Whatever hat it was, I feel like Madge has sent the memory of it spinning through the years to me, to any woman who would hear this story, and if I could only see it clearly, only latch onto the meaning of it, I would know how to get through my own grief, my own anger. She was a young woman then and had no idea what she was doing, but it was a gift somehow, her purchase of that hat. I would have read that hat for days to find its meaning. If it was the right hat, I thought, it would give me the courage I needed, a kind of hat I could use to demand things or to whisk him out the door.

In the end, Steve went to prison for his crime. Though it was clear from the trial that no one really cared about Madge. At that point he had become simply an embarrassment to everyone, even the Klan, and they had to get rid of him. In that sense, Madge was a martyr.

You know how, during the plague, they locked up the house when someone in the family became infected? And even after the infection was in the house, the people would do anything they could to escape that confinement, so there were guards at the doors who had to steel themselves to the screaming, the bribes, the tricks of those trapped inside? I'm not sure why I'm bringing this up, I'm old, but somehow I think that what they wanted to escape was not the house, but the disease, even after it was within them. There's always some disease we're trying to escape, and the night train is easy transportation. In my lover's case, it was the house of his body, its limits. He was desperately afraid of dying. In my case, it was the closed-in house of what I knew. I wanted mystery. And maybe in the end that was true of Madge as well.

A trial is just an attempt to make a story out of the facts. Both sides wedge their stories into the cracks in the other one, like scientific theories, like religion, like any stories. But maybe in the end the night train never makes sense in the light of day. It roars through the orderly towns and farms and graveyards and breaks them up like children's toys. We all wear masks at night. Maybe hers was a large-brimmed hat to cover the face that seemed unmasked and fragile in the light. Which face was the real one? Me, I rode that train for most of my adult life, no brakes on, the wind so harsh through the open windows. I rode the train and at the same time never left that room. Who am I now? There were Stephensons coming to power then all over Europe. Madge and I standing beside each other in our college yearbook. So innocent, we thought, so trusting. Hearts open, hands clutching the fare.

A Conversation with Susan Neville

What's your definition of a short story?

When I think about the difference between a story and a novel, I think of it in geometric terms. Any single character's life can go on infinitely in one direction or another—a line. With a novel you pick an inch or two inches on the line, or a quarter of an inch here and a quarter of an inch there. But a story—a certain kind of story—is more a point that implies the rest—the plane. It's a point; it's the moment. But that's a character-based kind of story. There are stories that are closer to poetry, or work as extended metaphors. There are so many different kinds of stories. But when a student asks me, "How do I know?" I generally say, "Find the point."A lot of time the best point is not the one you think of first.

For example, Michael Martone wrote this story when he was an undergraduate, called "The Spirit of St. Louis." It's about a child whose mother has just died. Most students would choose the point at the funeral or the point in the hospital when she's dying. He chose the point after they leave the funeral. What do they do next? They go to a toy store and buy a model airplane to put together—the father and the son, together. Everything comes into play. Because it's the *Spirit of St. Louis,* there's the idea that Lindbergh had to fly by himself. It's the point that had the most metaphorical resonance. It gives you a sense of that character in that moment.

There are so many different kinds of stories. But when a student asks me, "How do I know?" I generally say, "Find the point."

Plot?

The standard answer is that it's the moment in which a character changes or misses his last chance to change. If it's a character-based story, the plot has more to do with the arc of the character in that particular moment than it does with a chain of causality.

I become obsessed with a word or an image or a place—something, anything. It becomes this kind of sticky substance and things start coming in and glomming on.

How does material gather for you and become recognizable as an idea for a story?

I become obsessed with a word or an image or a place—something, anything. It becomes this kind of sticky substance and things start coming in and glomming on. There *is* a gathering. It seems that most writers work that way.

How do you know when it's time to begin?

Unlike a novel, which has to gather for quite a while before you start, just the feeling I associate with a word or the feeling I associate with a place—if I feel it strongly—makes me know it's time to start a story. Right away!

You mean, if the image, place—whatever—stays in your mind.

Yes. Short story writers—and perhaps poets are the same—are always getting a new idea. You get the feeling that you're ready to take that idea and use it as a lens through which you look at the world. And you just start writing. If I don't do something with an idea in a week or so, it'll be gone. It'll be time to do something different. After two weeks, I'll have a draft of a story—or I won't even remember why what I was thinking about was interesting. Novelists become obsessed with something over a period of time and get fewer ideas that don't have to do with that one thing.

You get the feeling that you're ready to take that idea and use it as a lens through which you look at the world.

If a promising idea or phrase comes to you, do you write it down?

I probably will. But sometimes I go back to it and have no clue what I meant. There's a difference between having just a word, a point where things might gather, and actually having gotten as far as writing a first page, though. Sometimes I'll start a first page and abandon it because it's not working. Later, I go back to it, rework it, and it will go on to become something completely different. But the phrase itself I wouldn't remember. It interested me because it had something to do with that particular day—the weather, what's going on that week.

So you see stories everywhere. You see the world that way.

I do. And constantly. When I'm working on stories, that's a problem. I can't wait to get done with one so that I can go on to the next one, because I'm in that storywriting mode. They come in clusters. The next one comes almost immediately.

It also seems that as the stories come, they bounce off of one another, triggering new ideas and possibilities.

Yes. It's why I can't do novels. Because when I start to do one, I get all these other ideas and I think, Whoa! I can't do that. In a novel, you can't abandon the obsession with one idea in order to go with a new obsession. If they were combinable, maybe, but they're hardly ever combinable. They're completely different things. Like litters of puppies that have separate parents. They don't even come out looking alike.

One thing all of your stories have in common is a killer last line. Reading them brings to mind Poe's comment about the short story form, "A story should be written for the sake of the last sentence."

I agree with that completely. Of course, we're talking about a certain *kind* of story, a character-driven story. What you hope happens is that the last line will make you have to go back to look at the story again, from the beginning. It's like striking a match in terms of your experience writing it. You go backwards and it all catches fire—like setting a match to light a stick of dynamite. It goes back along the fuse and then the explosion or experience of the story happens.

What you hope happens is that the last line will make you have to go back to look at the story again, from the beginning.

It's light, but it's also—poof! Combustion. Explosion. Striking the match finds that thread or fuse and powers it through the story.

Yes, and it connects the images you've been stringing along. It's like you've got this hidden wire and you don't know what it is and the reader doesn't know what it is until you light it up with the last line. And then you see, oh yeah, it was about that all the way through. Flannery O'Connor said that if you can summarize a story, it's probably not right because it's the last line that illuminates it and makes the rest of it fall into the pattern. You can't do that when you just summarize. Which is also why you can't say what it's about when you begin writing it. You have to follow that thread and following the thread to the end will tell you what it's about. I've heard a poet say that the last line of a poem causes the whole thing to blossom into metaphor. Like opening up a pop-up book.

You have to follow that thread and following the thread to the end will tell you what it's about.

That hidden line. What does it feel like you're following? A feeling, a shape?

If it's a shape, it's a line that you're following through the dark. A lot of times it feels like you're following the character, what the character is feeling. It's as if the character is in a completely dark space and there's a little tiny thread or wire and the character's groping along it somehow—not knowing what the wire is, where it will end, or why he's obsessed with it. There is some desperation. But there's complete and utter faith—it *is* faith—that it's going to lead you someplace. It's going to save the character's life somehow to follow it and yours as you're writing it. It really is discovering in the dark, and that's hard. It's a hard thing to teach: Trust the line. Trust the image.

When does that all-important last line usually come to you? How do you recognize it?

Usually I work harder on the last line than on any other part of the story. I rarely know the last line when I start, but I know it's out there. I'm always writing toward it and when I get to it I know it. But a lot of times I end the first draft of story and I know the last line isn't right yet. It's not the right ending. So my most common place to revise is to cut off the last two pages and do something completely different until I get the last line that seems right.

I rarely know the last line when I start, but I know it's out there.

When you've discovered the last line, do you go back and make everything connect to it?

Yes. Although, usually it already does. If the last line is right, and you've followed it correctly to get there, then you see it catch on fire, too. You don't go back and throw in four images of WWII—or whatever—because you realize at the end that that's what the story about. It's tweaking what you have until the story starts to shimmer.

Do you ever have that experience of coming to the end and seeing that the story could be about something else that's more interesting or more compelling to you? If that happens, do you try to change the story or just abandon it?

I've had the experience where I've worked on a story too long and realized that what I'm doing is layering a new idea into the original one. Sometimes that works, but a lot of time it's like putting too many patterns together.

How long does it usually take you to bring a short story to completion?

It usually takes about six weeks. Sometimes that's pretty constant, working on it every day. Sometimes a story will come and it'll just take a couple of days or a week. It's always really nice when that happens.

Does it feel different when a story comes full-blown that way?

It feels like the same process, it just feels faster.

You've talked about the difference between a story idea and a novel idea. How are story and essay ideas different?

In both essays and stories, I'm concerned with language and with metaphor. In an essay, I'm more interested in fact. I like to be able to read and to quote other people. But I've done a lot of things where I've used the same material in a story and in an essay. In a couple of cases, I've used the same paragraph, which I try not to do, but I have done. It's like Borges's story, "Pierre Menard, Author of Don Quixote." They become different things within the different forms.

The essay "In the Suburbs" and the short story "Your Own Most Quiet Voice" make use of the same material: your mother's mental illness. Would you talk about the differences and similarities in the process by which you created them?

They felt completely different to write. In the story, I was focusing more on character and place, which I made up. The scene in the beginning, in the jeweler's shop—all the parts and the fan. It never happened. In an essay, I don't allow myself to imagine.

It was a desperate act to write the essay. I either had to write it or stay in bed for weeks. I wanted to understand what had happened to my mother, intellectually and logically. So I was reading everything I could read, like William James and Emerson—just everything—to bring the intellectual resources to my experience. I wanted to understand what had happened rather than to just evoke it. I wrote the story first.

That's surprising. It seems that looking at the material straightforwardly in the essay would've freed you to write the story. That the intellectual understanding would make emotional understanding possible.

I needed to know what it meant in order to control what it felt like.

I had the emotional understanding—or *not* understanding. I knew what having a mother who suffered from mental illness felt like, so I could follow the feel of it. But I didn't know what it *meant.* I needed to know what it meant in order to control what it felt like.

I had been writing about the experience since I was in graduate school. The first story I wrote was called "Three Mothers," and I don't even know where it is anymore. I kept trying to figure out how to deal with that particular material, but you know how your attitude toward your parents—or towards anything—changes as the years go on. So about ten years after I wrote the first story I was still dealing with the problem, only now I was becoming my mother's caregiver. That was a different point of view and, since my father was out of the picture, it was a more difficult point of view. That's when I wrote "Your Own Most Quiet Voice"—and I haven't had to write another story about it since.

Writing "In the Suburbs" finally freed me from the material. I'll mention it in other essays occasionally. But it's not like I feel I *have* to write about it anymore. I even teach a class at Butler in madness and literature, but it's not personal or difficult to teach. It's like writing the essay cured me of something. Which is what you hope writing will do.

The essay "Hey John" and the short story "Jubilee" are both about the rock singer, John Mellencamp. In "Hey John" you, the writer, search for the essence of him in his songs, his paintings, and his hometown. In "Jubilee," two young people spend the summer actually searching for him. But the story turns on a contest that awards a new car to the person who can stay awake, keeping his hand on it, longer than all the others.

I was living in a small town—New Castle, Indiana—when I wrote "Jubilee," and I felt, not what it was like to look for John Mellencamp, but what it would feel like to be in a place, a small, industrial town where your options are very limited. Where holding onto a car all summer might seem like a good idea, because you have nothing else to do. It might give you a purpose in life—and a car.

The story came before the essay again. So is it that you work from feeling to intellect? The story following a feeling, the essay following the intellect?

There's something weirder that happens in a story. "Jubilee" was about what it feels like to hold on to the concrete world or to let go of it and be able to see something a little bit more magical. At the end, the guys who hold on to the car became for me a metaphor for holding on to the industrial landscape. The women are able to go out and see this kind of magical being. "Hey John" was about trying to understand what Mellencamp means to people who live in Seymour and what his art means—why he chose German Expressionism as a form as opposed to abstract or impressionism, or—anything. How German Expressionism is tied to rock and roll. All of those things.

If you could pick one of your stories to teach, which one would it be—and why?

"Night Train." I had so many problems with point of view with that story. Getting it started, I did a lot of early drafts using different points of view, so it was just such a triumph to me to finally figure out how to get into that material about D. C. Stephenson and the Ku Klux Klan in Indiana. I could have done it as an essay, but I wanted to understand how it felt to be the woman who Stephenson raped and who then either committed suicide—or didn't. That was part of the question and mystery. No one will ever know, so there was no way I could do an essay. In some ways, though, the narrator who's writing the story is writing it in the form of an essay. She's trying to figure out what she thinks about something. I tried doing it from Madge Oberholtzer, the victim's, point of view. It just didn't work. I tried doing it from the point of view of Stephenson's friend—Sonny—and that didn't work. I tried doing it from omniscient point of view and that didn't work. Madge Oberholtzer graduated from Butler University, so finally I just went to a Butler yearbook from that time. I opened it up and I picked a face and decided that would be her friend. That she would tell the story. So I got the point of view, but then she had to have a reason to tell the story.

Which is the whole idea of discovering the story.

Yes. The paragraph I worked really hard on was the last one, when the narrator discovers—in her threading through the dark—that it matters what kind of hat Madge was wearing. If it were this kind of hat it would mean one thing; if it were this kind of hat it would mean something else. Then she's thinking about her own lover and his power over her, and Stephenson's power over the secretary and over the state, and it suddenly occurs to her that there were Stephensons rising up all over the world then. (It was at the same time as Hitler and Stalin and Mussolini.) And she realizes that no matter what happened it was Madge's courage in speaking, in finally saying, "Yes, Stephenson did this to me" that was the important thing. The reason for telling the story. I don't know whether she shows any courage in speaking out herself about her own experience, or if she's just trying to figure it so that she can withdraw and put it to rest. Also, now that she knows what she knows, she can escape from being in a similar emotionally abusive relationship.

The story is so chilling. There's such malevolence underneath it. What drew you to the material?

I'm really interested in Indiana history. We tend to think of Indiana as sycamores, moonlight on the Wabash, and all that—the Pacers and the Colts. But the dark side is more interesting to me. The history of the Klan is interesting to me. But to be perfectly honest, the thing that was really fascinating to me was how that woman could have been drawn in.

The idea of seduction?

Yeah, the idea of seduction. How she could possibly have *not* known? It comes up again and again. I thought about it again in terms of Gary Condit and Chandra Levy, or with Joyce Carol Oates' *Black Water.* Young girls who are seduced by that kind of power and who don't *see.* The O.J. trial was going on when I wrote the story, too.

"The Increasing Distance" was inspired by something that actually happened, too. A series of murders of young men, whose bodies were found buried in the back yard of a suburban home. It's told in the voice of a victim's sister.

It's about the serial killer who lived in my neighborhood. It underlies the putting together of that whole collection, *The House of Blue Lights.* I was thinking about this guy, who looked like the father in the *Brady Bunch.* He and his wife lived in this house in the suburbs with their beautiful children, and he drove them to games and activities. And he was a serial killer of vast proportions—of other men. I think there was something in his splitting off, the *Dr. Jekyll and Mr. Hyde* thing. Because he had to have this way of presenting himself to the world, it became more and more important for parts of himself that he didn't consider proper to go into the darkness.

I started to write "An Increasing Distance" as an essay. I interviewed the FBI profiler for the essay and I listened to an interview with the wife. I was infinitely fascinated with her, and still am. I also talked to a friend of their maid. But there was really no way of understanding how or why somebody could live that divided, that double a life. It was just too bizarre. And I also realized that there were places I didn't want to go into in my own voice. I just couldn't do it. I couldn't *let* myself go there.

The voice of the sister is like a keen, a wail. Her despair—the man who killed my brother, this person who took so much away from me—is almost like a refrain. Her sorrow almost ameliorates what happens. Because the reader can side with her, it makes the story tolerable somehow.

I thought, if I try to channel through the sister of one of the victims who feels as though they haven't gotten their story told, then maybe I can think about what

> I thought, if I try to channel through the sister of one of the victims who feels as though they haven't gotten their story told, then maybe I can think about what happened.

happened. It actually worked. And there was political motivation, too. I was angry that the victims in this case were truly lost. They were and they still are. There were dozens of them, possibly up to forty.

So, what did you get out of the process of writing the story?

I freaked out—big time, major. I can't stand to read it myself. I just don't go back and look at it.

When you read a news story like that one, what happens that makes you know it's fertile material for fiction?

The same way I know—I'm going to buy that vase! It touches something, connects with something. Honestly, to get back to the essay about my mother, to be psychoanalytical about it, anybody who grows up in a house where you have to keep up one kind of appearance and then there's something else really going on every day, underneath, becomes fascinated with secrets and doubleness. All the stories in *In the House of Blue Lights* have to do with secrets and doubleness—and the house of the imagination. You know, the box inside the head.

Did you know at the outset that the book would be about secrets?

I didn't know until I saw all the stories from that litter. Sometimes it's clear to me what a collection is about; sometimes it's not. A collection comes together in the same way that a story comes together.

What about The Invention of Flight, *your first collection—and winner of the Flannery O'Connor Award for Short Fiction? That book has a number of characters, mostly women, who feel trapped in their lives, afraid to move forward, to change.*

Yes. Maybe it's a midwestern thing, that longing for safety. To ignore the risk, the danger in being. Just being alive is dangerous, I think. I really wanted "Indiana Winter" to be in that first book, too, but I revised and revised and couldn't get it right in time. It's from the same place. When I got out of graduate school, I moved back to Indiana and lived in Newcastle, a small industrial town. Isolation and wanting to get away from there were my strongest emotions while I was living there.

Related to that is another theme that runs through the collection: the sheer strangeness of being alive. The boyfriend in "Quinella" expresses it very well when he says, "I feel like I'm skating over the surface of something. And then I'll think it doesn't matter. It really doesn't matter. We're all dead anyway. We're nothing but light. We just fade away." There's the sense that if we looked, really looked, at the nature of human life we wouldn't be able to go on.

It shows up in my work a lot. I was in my early twenties when it hit me. I suddenly realized just how weird life is. I thought I was going mad; I thought I was going down that road. I think I still carry it around with me. Sometimes I think—we're on this ball that is floating in nothingness! What keeps it going? I can really understand agoraphobia, how just going out would frighten you. The ground could disappear! So you wash the dishes, fold the clothes. But underneath you know there's just this one life and you have to live it. Maybe the weirdness is the rapture.

I suddenly realized just how weird life is. I thought I was going mad; I thought I was going down that road. I think I still carry it around with me.

Some of your stories feel musical, like riffs or variations. "Rondo," for example.

I was a music major in college. I love the sound of language and what you can do with musical devices.

What is it that makes you decide to write an "experimental" story like that one?

When I first started writing, I told myself—though I didn't keep it up—that everything I would do would be completely different from the last thing. That's probably a modernist aesthetic: to make it different, make it new. Something I probably absorbed in college. I consciously did that. I wanted each story to be an experiment into some new ground, formally, as well as some kind of discovery, emotionally or intellectually. I do like doing things different with form, like having *In the House of Blue Lights* start with a prose poem.

Eudora Welty once said, "Every story teaches me how to write it, but not the one afterward." Is that true for you?

I agree with Welty, though I do learn things from each story that I take to the next. I don't throw away as many five-page beginnings as I used to. Now I pretty much know where the story starts. It gets easier in some ways because you do learn some things about craft, but in other ways it's always just as hard. You're always sitting down, feeling completely blank. And there are so many ways of writing a story. Eudora Welty's a good example of stories that are extended metaphor. Like "A Worn Path." As you grow and get interested in doing different things, you discover how plastic the genre is and what we can do with it. I'm writing stories now that are metaphors of place. They are spatial, like boxes. It's hard to describe. But nothing I've written before helps me with these stories.

Your fiction reflects an unusual breadth of knowledge— everything from rock stars to astronomy to Shaker villages. Would you talk a bit about how curiosity—reading, exploring ideas, feeding your head—is important for a person who wants to write fiction?

You'll get lost, you'll get completely stuck if you stop reading and learning. You will go over the same ground, over and over again, because you have these sort of hard-wired obsessions. But you have to find ways of getting outside the box of yourself—which is why I started writing essays. I go back and forth between fiction and essays. I hit a wall in one genre and then switch over to the other. Usually, it's switching from fiction over to essays, which allows me to go out into the world and learn about a lot of stuff through reading and observation and interviews.

But you have to find ways of getting outside the box of yourself—which is why I started writing essays.

How does the research you do for essays make its way into your fiction?

Some of the places I've visited researching essays have become story settings. I have three or four stories in a new collection that have factory settings that come from having visited those places while I was doing research for *Fabrication.*

I'm curious about a lot of things. When you ask a lot of fiction writers, maybe particularly short story writers, what they are reading, the answer will be nonfiction. Think of a writer like Iris Murdoch, who in one book had to know everything about medieval architecture and everything about wine. You have to have language and opportunity for images. In writing an essay, I've got something to focus the reading on. But then I'll think, German Expressionism. I don't know anything about that. So I go to the art library and start looking at books and that leads to websites. And more reading that comes from the original fascination that started me off on the essay and works its way into stories.

Are there stories by other writers that have been particularly instructive to you?

There's a letter that Flannery O'Connor's mentor, Caroline Gordon, wrote to her. In it, she says you've got to have three details to describe each person. If you don't have three, it's like a chair with two legs. It's going to fall. She has a whole list of "rules," and they are all right. If you go back and look at the revisions of O'Connor's stories, you can see that she did what Gordon told her to do, that she took every suggestion. One reason O'Connor's so great to study, especially in terms of learning how to write dialogue, is that she didn't come by it naturally. She had a great teacher. On drafts of "A Good Man Is Hard to Find," Gordon wrote that if a character says something momentous and the next character replies too soon, the line doesn't have time to resonate. She talks about having throwaway lines. You see this when the Misfit says something and the grandmother notices the way the sky looks before responding. O'Connor had such incredible sense of metaphor, so the lines have meaning. But the pause that the "throwaway lines" create has the effect of letting what he said sink into her head.

What do you think beginning writers least understand about the process of writing short stories?

They don't understand that don't have to know where a story is going to end. That they don't even have to know where it's going. That it is a process, a journey. They least

That it is a process, a journey. They least understand that.

understand that. And they don't know that they don't have to know the theme. They think that it's something that a writer starts with. But theme is something somebody else talks about later on. Like English teachers. They also don't know that learning to write *is* learning to see.

I was walking along a trail with my daughter and her friend one day, and we saw this man who was balancing rocks. He would take one rock and balance all these bizarre shaped rocks on it. We started talking, and he asked me what I did. When I told him I was a writer and a teacher he said, "Let me give you something. Every time you go for a walk or do anything, count up to a hundred. With each number, look at something different. Look at a hundred things. Focus your eyes on a hundred things. Don't think about what they are. Just look. One, two, three, four, five." In this room, just counting to five, I see a gold candle that's burned into a U-shape, with wax that looks like a little flame sticking up, a doll with a polka-dot dress, with pumpkin-colored hair, and reading glasses that are painted on her. If you do that everywhere you go, you've got "stuff." And without stuff, you don't have any meaning. You don't have metaphor. There's nowhere for the story to grow.

Writing Prompts

READ: "Night Train" and the interview with **Susan Neville.**

PONDER: How Neville tells the story of a historical incident "sideways" by inventing a character whose life was profoundly affected by it.

WRITE: Research a historical incident and invent a character whose life was affected by it some way. Let that character tell the story through the lens of his experience.

PRACTICE:

- Thinking of a character's life as a long line, identify various points (or moments) on it that imply the whole line and might be made into a story.
- Choose a life-changing event—a death, divorce, marriage, graduation. Make a list of scenes or moments surrounding it and discover the one with the most metaphorical resonance. Let that be the place you "stand" to tell a story that conveys the feelings you want to convey about the general event.
- Identify an illness or condition (your own or someone else's) that has had a profound effect on your life. Write a scene that evokes the raw feelings you had dealing with it. Then research that illness or condition and write a personal essay that tells the story of how it affected your life and how you came to understand and accept it.
- Identify a musical form and write a story whose structure, language, and rhythms mirror it.
- What are your "hard-wired obsessions," the personal and/or political issues you find yourself returning to again and again? Choose one and browse in a library, bookstore, or video store for materials that might deepen and complicate your understanding of it.

Consider trips you might take to add to your knowledge. Stay open to story possibilities that may arise while you are feeding your head.

- Consider what you might read, what movies you might watch, or what trips or tours you might take to give you more words and images to draw on in writing a story you want to write.
- Take a walk, counting to one hundred as you go. With each number, look at something different. Don't think about what the objects are. Just look. At the end of your walk, freewrite your impressions. You may do this same exercise sitting in one place—for example, a mall, nursing home, or school.
- Search the newspapers for one week and cut out any article that you think might provide the basis for a story.

Grace Paley

Grace Paley (b. 1922) is the author of four collections of short stories and three collections of poems. Born in New York City, she attended Hunter College and New York University. Her honors include a Guggenheim fellowship, a National Council on the Arts Grant, the National Institute of Arts and Letters Award for Short Story Writing, the Edith Wharton Award, the Rea Award for the Short Story, the Vermont Governor's Award for Excellence in the Arts, the Jewish Cultural Achievement Award for Literary Arts, the Lannan Foundation Literary Award for Fiction, and nominations for the National Book Award and the Pulitzer Prize. She was named the first official New York State Writer by Governor Mario Cuomo in 1989. Paley has taught at Columbia University, Syracuse University, and Sarah Lawrence College. She lives in New York City and Thetford Hill, Vermont.

For Further Reading:
The Little Disturbances of Man: Stories of Women and Men at Love (1959), *Enormous Changes at the Last Minute* (1974), *Leaning Forward* (1985), *Later the Same Day* (1987), *New and Collected Poems* (1992), *The Collected Stories* (1994), *Begin Again: Collected Poems* (2000).

Debts

A lady called me up today. She said she was in possession of her family archives. She had heard I was a writer. She wondered if I would help her write about her grandfather, a famous innovator and dreamer of the Yiddish theater. I said I had already used every single thing I knew about the Yiddish theater to write one story, and I didn't have time to learn any more, then write about it. There is a long time in me between knowing and telling. She offered a share of the profits, but that is something too inorganic. It would never rush her grandfather's life into any literature I could make.

The next day, my friend Lucia and I had coffee and we talked about this woman. Lucia explained to me that it was probably hard to have family archives or even only stories about outstanding grandparents or uncles when one was sixty or seventy and there was no writer in the family and the children were in the middle of their own lives. She said it was a pity to lose all this inheritance just because of one's own mortality. I said yes, I did understand. We drank more coffee. Then I went home.

I thought about our conversation. Actually, I owed nothing to the lady who'd called. It was possible that I did owe something to my own family and the families of my friends. That is, to tell their stories as simply as possible, in order, you might say, to save a few lives.

Because it was her idea, the first story is Lucia's. I tell it so that some people will remember Lucia's grandmother, also her mother, who in this story is eight or nine.

The grandmother's name was Maria. The mother's name was Anna. They lived on Mott Street in Manhattan in the early 1900s. Maria was married to a man named Michael. He had worked hard, but bad luck and awful memories had driven him to the Hospital for the Insane on Welfare Island.

Every morning Anna took the long trip by trolley and train and trolley again to bring him his hot dinner. He could not eat the meals at the hospital. When Anna rode out of the stone streets of Manhattan over the bridge to the countryside of Welfare Island, she was always surprised. She played for a long time on the green banks of the river. She picked wildflowers in the fields, and then she went up to the men's ward.

One afternoon, she arrived as usual. Michael felt very weak and asked her to lean on his back and support him while he sat at the edge of the bed eating dinner. She did so, and that is how come, when he fell back and died, it was in her thin little arms that he lay. He was very heavy. She held him so, just for a minute or two, then let him fall to the bed. She told an orderly and went home. She didn't cry because she didn't like him. She spoke first to a neighbor, and then together they told her mother.

Now this is the main part of the story:

The man Michael was not her father. Her father had died when she was little. Maria, with the other small children, had tried to live through the hard times in the best way. She moved in with different, nearly related families in the neighborhood and worked hard helping out in their houses. She worked well, and it happened that she was also known for the fine bread she baked. She would live in a good friend's house for a while baking magnificent bread. But soon, the husband of the house would say "Maria bakes wonderful bread. Why can't you learn to bake bread like that?" He would probably then seem to admire her in other ways. Wisely, the wife would ask Maria to please find another home.

One day at the spring street festival, she met a man named Michael, a relative of friends. They couldn't marry because Michael had a wife in Italy. In order to live with him, Maria explained the following truths to her reasonable head:

1. This man Michael was tall with a peculiar scar on his shoulder. Her husband had been unusually tall and had had a scar on his shoulder.
2. This man was redheaded. Her dead husband had been redheaded.
3. This man was a tailor. Her husband had been a tailor.
4. His name was Michael. Her husband had been called Michael.

In this way, persuading her own understanding, Maria was able to not live alone at an important time in her life, to have a father for the good of her children's character, a man in her bed for comfort, a husband to serve. Still and all, though he died in her arms, Anna, the child, didn't like him at all. It was a pity, because he had always called her "my little one." Every day she had visited him, she had found him in the hallway waiting, or at the edge of his white bed, and she had called out, "Hey, Zio, here's your dinner. Mama sent it. I have to go now."

A Conversation with Grace Paley

You came of age during World War II and began writing in the 1950s. Would you put that world and time in context for readers—both personally and in terms of the changes that were beginning to happen when you were a young wife and mother?

You want to know how I began to write stories. I could begin by saying that I was always a writer. I was mostly a poet as a kid, though I never thought of myself as a poet. I just thought of myself as someone writing poems. Every now and then, I would try a story, and for some reason the teacher or professor would usually say it wasn't much good. This was the historical period after the Second World War. The Second World War was an all-encompassing war for the people of our country, so that there wasn't anybody who didn't have somebody in the army. Many of us married for that reason. I was nineteen and I married this boy I was going around with, and he was in the army. My brother was a doctor in the army, and [my husband] Bob, I met him later on, he was in the army. Everybody was. So it was a very masculine period for that reason, and the work that came right after the war was very masculine, naturally. How could it not be? These guys had stories to tell and they told them.

I was mostly a poet as a kid, though I never thought of myself as a poet. I just thought of myself as someone writing poems.

When my husband came home from the army, like all the other boys and my friends, we all had some children—at that time we didn't really question the idea of what children would do to our lives. I was so dumb in a way that I probably would have had a child when I was nineteen with Jess because I like kids so much—and I've continued to have a feeling for children that is really very large. Anyway, we had kids. So I got into that world. I tend to really live where I am in whatever situation, and I was now living in a world with women. I've always had best girlfriends and, at the same time, as a kid, I always wished I could be a soldier or something. I had that cross of tomboyishness and extreme femaleness at the same time.

I got awful close to a lot of these women and their kids, and—being city people—we spent a lot of time in the park. City people have to go to the park. They have to go someplace where the children can run around, for God's sake. A lot of people didn't like it, but I liked very much being with the women and I liked the other people's children, too—and I became very involved in the politics of the park. So two things were happening. One, I was part of a community, which was Greenwich Village and, two, I was a part of a group of people called women. I became really interested in them and

I didn't see much stuff about women in the contemporary literature, so when I began to have a very strong urge to write stories, I was pressed to write about these lives, these women.

very concerned with their lives. I was writing poems then, but I wanted to write a story. I wanted to see if I could. I was a big reader, but I didn't see much stuff about women in the contemporary literature, so when I began to have a very strong urge to write stories, I was pressed to write about these lives, these women. I had the opportunity, I had some time. The kids went away to daycare—and this should be a lesson to every writer in the writer in the world! I was able to sit down and write, and I did. What I wrote were stories, mostly about women.

You had no formal training as a writer then?

No. But I read a lot. By the time I was in the upper grades in high school, I really could talk about poems when the teacher brought them up, although she was astonished because I never spoke in class otherwise. And I did write, constantly. I didn't take a course of study, but I studied. I was reading—fiction and poems—and thinking all the time I was writing. It's why I tell students, you must read, you must read, you must read!

It's why I tell students, you must read, you must read, you must read!

In "Listening," Jack asks Faith, "Why don't you tell me stories told by women about women?" and she responds, "You have your own woman stories. You know, your falling-in-love stories, your French-woman-during-the-Korean-war stories, your political-comrade-though-extremely-beautiful stories." You were one of the first to tell the kind of stories women tell to one another, set in the world they lived in. Would you talk about how you got the courage to write about home, school, and the neighborhood?

The great thing about this was that if I could have written a story with development in it, I would have. I couldn't do it. I didn't know how. I couldn't write the stories that I was reading. The one I thing I learned from, as far as short stories, was *Dubliners.* That gave me a hint of how you didn't have to write twenty-five pages and develop this character with lot of description. I wasn't good at it, so I didn't do it. I don't have a lot of courage. But if I can't do one thing, I'll do something else.

Politics—from a woman's point of view—often enters your work. Some of your stories make strong political statements, yet they never feel manipulative or didactic. How did you manage that?

The political part is part of my life, so it has to be there in one way or another. It's the way I see the world.

The political part is part of my life, so it has to be there in one way or another. It's the way I see the world.

So that's how you came to your own style. Your stories are—yours. They're autobiographical in a lot of ways. One of the things students often say when you tell them that a story doesn't work is, "But it's real." When you're writing from your own life, using real things, how do you know which factual things are going to work and which won't?

Actually, the first story I wrote was "Goodbye and Good Luck," certainly not autobiographical. On the other hand, I knew the woman the main character is based on. It was Jess's aunt, my husband's aunt. She came to visit us, and said that sentence, "I was popular in certain circles." It's her line. I took that line and—I can't say I ran with it, because it took a long time to write the story. I lumbered along with it. Very slowly.

Kids all have good imaginations. People have to learn imagination. They have to remember that they were children and they made up stories. I take a face or a line and it's resonant for me and I can go from there. Then there are other people that you've met somewhere, like the actor who comes in to "Goodbye and Good Luck." At that time my former husband was in films, so I got to know some people in the Yiddish theater. You bring all your knowledge together. I was thinking about Jess's Aunt Rose and my own aunt and I wanted to give them both a little bit of life. They should have a nice life.

People have to learn imagination. They have to remember that they were children and they made up stories.

Along those same lines, would you just talk about what truth is in fiction as opposed to fact?

First of all, between fact and truth is language. And in the telling of the facts you bring in people. If you're writing a story, you bring in people. You really don't know them, so you're going to start inventing right away. A student will say to you, "This really happened," and your answer will be, "But who did it happen to?" As soon as you think, "Who did it happen to?" you begin to invent. Also, I always like to say that the first time you tell a story, you tell a story, the second time you tell it it's fiction. No matter what. Really, no matter what.

What was the kernel of truth for "Conversation with My Father," which is probably your most anthologized story?

My father was in bed. He was eighty-six and he had lots of things attached to him. That was the fact. The thing he says, "Why can't you write a simple story?" was not fact. On the other hand, I could imagine him saying it. He really loved my first book, and he died in the early '70s, before my second book came out. I think he saw some of the stories. It wasn't that he didn't like them. He liked them. But he liked a story like Chekov. He was hoping I'd be Chekov.

Actually, the argument I had with him was really more political and historical. We had different ideas about, not only storytelling, but of what could happen to a person in life. The story that the narrator writes about the woman taking drugs with her son was common in our neighborhood at that time. I didn't know anybody it happened to like that, but it seemed like it could happen to anybody. And then the son giving it all up and leaving her behind. And her being rehabilitated. It was something that my father could not recognize. He wouldn't. He was always talking about character. If I did something wrong, he would remind me about character. When he talked about people, he'd say, "He's a good man, he has strength, he has a character." I used to get mad at that because I really had from an early age a strong feeling that people could change. That everybody could become wonderful and good—or at least that they could get a *job.* He felt sometimes people wouldn't because they didn't want to.

There are lots of things in your life that you could have written about. How do you recognize material for a story in the things that happen to you and the people around you? How do you know it's yours?

It's where certain pressures hit me. Sometimes they come from the first lines—a sentence or a couple of sentences that I may work with for two years. Writing about the park—"Faith in a Tree"—I had no idea which way it was going to go. Then I said, "Just when I most needed important conversation, a sniff of the man-wide world, at least one brainy companion who could translate my friendly language into his tongue of undying carnal love, I was forced to lounge in our neighborhood part, surrounded by children." It was a gift given to me, the gift of that subject matter. So that was important. That life, those people, the children, and the park itself.

You have great first lines, at the same time economical and loaded with information to ground the reader in the story. Are the first lines in the finished stories usually lines you got early in the process?

Yes, although I worked on that first paragraph of "Faith in a Tree" for a long time. I had to get it right. It took me time to get it right.

Many writers observe that actually writing a story takes a long time, but your story "Debts" throws a more complicated idea into the mix. In it, a woman asks the unnamed narrator, a writer, for help writing her grandfather's story. Having refused for various reasons, the narrator observes, "There is a long time in me between knowing and telling." Would you talk about how and why some stories need so much "cooking" time before they are ready to be told?

I think almost all writers are like that, really. All *people* are like that. The difference is that most people know something and they tell it right away. But writers, they know things a long time that they tell later. I have a story called "Friends," for instance, about a visit. I knew that story. I changed it. It's not that close to what happened. My friends think we all went together. We never did that. But I did write the story thinking about my friends. I knew about the main character and I knew what her life had been like. But it took me a very long time to sit down and write the story.

But writers, they know things a long time that they tell later.

The subject matter of "Debts" actually reflects that process. Would you talk about where that story came from and how the story about Lucia's family became a part of it?

That's my friend, Lucia. It actually happened just that way. Talk about something being factual and true! Lucia was my very good friend. I just loved that story about her mother that she told and retold. I was trying to figure out how I was going to tell it—and I just told it. I must say, I knew it a long time. I knew it a really long time. I'd say, "Lucia, tell me that story about your mother." She'd tell the story and she'd say, "My mother really hated him."

Lucia's mother was Anna in the story, then—the one who takes the meal to the nursing home?

She was the little girl and it was her stepfather. I was always so touched by the story. Thinking of New York at that time and thinking of her going to Welfare Island, bringing him food to the hospital. I had a terrible desire to tell the story as simply as I could.

Because the story grieved you so?

It was the fact that it was so long ago and was so important to them. It had a sense of time in it. There was a child, which I was interested in. And it was my friend's story. It would disappear if I didn't tell it. Sometimes you want to tell the actual story as best you can. There was a pressure to tell it.

It's interesting how that story, the one you wanted to tell, connected itself somehow to one you felt you couldn't tell.

Oh, that's right! I forgot that. I was wondering what finally made me tell it. This woman comes to me and asks me to tell the story about the Yiddish theater, but I say to her, "Every single fact is in 'Goodbye and Good Luck.' I don't know one more thing about the theater." And that's true. Then I thought about it. How people wanted stories told about their families. Lucia and I were talking about it. She never said to me, "Tell this story!" I thought of that—and thought, that's a story I *can* tell.

So it was in being confronted with the story you knew you couldn't tell that a way to tell Lucia's story finally presented itself.

Yeah, you're right. See, you told me this! I knew it then, but I forgot it. It's true, it's really true. Often stories come from what you can't do. It's just like what I said before, I couldn't do a certain kind of writing, but I could do this.

Often writers talk about how stories gather. You might have a face from somebody you saw on a train, a little sliver of a scene that you observed at the supermarket—and they somehow come together. Do stories gather for you in a similar way?

Well, they do. You remember different things; you imagine different things that will be in the story. Sometimes you're stuck for a long time. You have to bring in another person, another character and let them throw their two cents in. I have a story that I have a first line for right now. I know a lot, but I haven't figured out how to tell it. Once you come to the telling you begin to approach form, and once you approach form you're very often in hot water because that's the *how* to tell the story. I do a workshop at which that's talked about more than anything else. How are you going to tell the story? Tell us some stories that you haven't figured out how to tell. A lot of people have such stories.

I have a story that I have a first line for right now. I know a lot, but I haven't figured out how to tell it.

Is it partly finding a place to stand?

You could put it that way. But sometimes you have a place to stand and you can't figure out which way to turn your head to look. Very often I will start with place. Not always.

There are two "sets" of stories in your work—the stories about Faith and the stories about Ginny. Did you ever think there might be a novel in either of them? Were you interested in the novel at all?

When I published my first book, the following people published at the same time as me: Philip Roth and, within the year, Tillie Olsen. The three of us were told we had to write novels. Roth did. Tillie and I didn't. I tried. I really made an honest try. I spent two years killing myself, trying to write a novel. It was so pedantic, so bad. I could see that I was trying to teach myself to write the way other people write. I just dropped it after over a hundred pages.

You didn't like working in that form?

I didn't do it well. The short story is closer to poetry than it is to the novel. I didn't know it when I started the short story. But as I worked on it, I saw. You bring a short story in one hand, hold it in one hand, and you do that in a poem. With a novel you have to use both hands, and it may drop out at any time. So stories and poems are much closer. I decided the short story was my medium, and that's what I liked. When I wanted prose, that was my prose.

I decided the short story was my medium, and that's what I liked.

You do something in your short stories that poets do: You know exactly what can and should be left out. You never underestimate the reader. You always assume he can make the leap. How did you learn to do that?

I had the courage because I did it in poetry. I learned in the stories by having done it in the poems—and from Isaac Babel, whom I began to read. He didn't think twice about it. Writing the stories was so useful to me; they helped the poems a lot. It was useful to go back and forth.

Would you talk generally about your process, how you work your way through a story beginning to end, including revision.

First of all, I have a folder—several folders, a bunch of stuff, a lot of papers—and in it are the beginnings of many stories. Or the middles or whatever. Paragraphs written. I go through it every couple weeks. I'll add a couple sentences to something, I'll take a sentence out of something else. At some point, there's a story I want to work on, and that's what I do.

So out of all the things that could be stories, one begins to emerge.

Yeah. It begins to have body. It becomes peopled in some way. Once I have that, I begin working on it. I don't know which way it's going, usually, until I'm halfway done. I have to keep working with these people. I don't know what they're going to do. I don't know what kind of story they're going to give me.

It becomes peopled in some way. Once I have that, I begin working on it.

There's a very interesting turn in "The Long Distance Runner," when Faith goes back to her old neighborhood. Did you know when you started out that there would be that sequence of three weeks living with the family in her old apartment?

No. I had no idea. You notice, everybody jogs in that story. Bob is a long-distance runner. For some reason, that's what was halfway on my mind. I didn't use him. I used a couple of his sentences about running well. Also, I was considering taking up running myself. I thought about running in the neighborhood. Then I imagined going back to my old neighborhood.

What about revision? Is there a particular kind of revision that you usually end up doing?

I have a way of describing it: I say I go through a story for lies. I might discover the lie of trying to show off. Sometimes they're lies of character. Sometimes they're lies of writing the most beautiful sentence in the world that has nothing to do with the story. Sometimes I take out whole paragraphs. Sometimes I have the wrong person telling the story. In "Zagrowski Tells," I had Faith telling the story first. Then I realized she didn't know the first f---ing thing about that man's life. She didn't know anything. What was she going to say? I wrote that story here in this house one summer, and I was stuck. I couldn't go further. A half a year later, back in New York, I realized

I go through a story for lies.

the wrong person was telling the story. Then I came here the next summer and wrote the story from his point of view.

Students so often don't understand so much of the process is discovering the story that needs to be told.

That's a good way to put it. You begin with knowing something, but then you write about what you don't know from then on. You write because you don't know and you want to try to know and understand. You begin to take a story apart and say, in this scene, what does the writer tell you? Where's the tension? Who wants what in this story? Then students begin to sense the bones beneath the story. There's a reason the story moves this way. To teach writing, that's all one can do. You can't teach them to have an imagination.

How do you imagine dialogue? Dialogue in a good story isn't exactly how people really talk, so how can a student use his imagination to create dialogue that's realistic?

Everyone has a tune in their head of the way their families spoke when they were little. There's some music in everybody's head who wants to write. You have to be *interested* in dialogue. If students aren't interested in how other people speak, they're in trouble. You have to listen. You have to submit yourself to criticism. I had a couple of black stories. The one about the little girl, I read it to the guy who told me the story three times. If he had told me it didn't sound right, I'd have changed it.

If students aren't interested in how other people speak, they're in trouble. You have to listen.

Is there any difference in your mind between dialogue and voice?

I wouldn't know how to describe that. The voice of the story is the whole story, really. I used to say—and it's true—that I didn't know what my voice was until I had lots of other people speaking. Like Aunt Rose was speaking. By the time I got all those voices, *I* had a voice.

What do you think are the requirements for short fiction? What makes something a story?

I hate the word "*fiction.*" In the *Times* there was a discussion of Israeli writers and someone said, "We don't have a word for fiction. We just have the word *story.*" It's just the way I feel. I write what I am. I'm a storyteller.

Do you ever wish you could stand over a reader's shoulder and tell him what you think he needs to know to fully understand and appreciate your work?

I don't have that feeling at all. My general feeling is, once you write it it's gone. What's fun is that different people read it differently. I just face the fact that it's gone. That's it.

Writing Prompts

READ: "Debts" and the interview with **Grace Paley.**

PONDER: How the narrator's failure to connect with a story a stranger hoped she would tell triggers the telling of a story she had known for a long time but had not been able to find a way to tell.

WRITE: Think of a story someone told you some time ago, one you've never been able to forget. Invent a situation in the present time that would bring that story to mind and connect the two somehow.

PRACTICE:

- Write a scene in which a character receives something that seems to be something that he would want, but, in fact, turns out to be otherwise.
- Identify a group of people with whom you feel an affinity. Write a scene or story that reflects what you have in common with them without naming it.
- Identify a place you *have* to spend time in because of the nature of your day-to-day life and consider what "gifts" of subject matter might be inherent in it.
- Think about a face that is resonant to you—someone you know or someone you've only seen. Let that face be the jumping off point for a story.
- Write something that happened to you exactly as you remember it. Then look at what you've written for places you might embroider or invent to transform it to fiction.
- Identify an argument you have over and over with a family member or friend. Write a scene in which all the arguments you've ever had are distilled into one argument. Feel free to invent dialogue, but make sure the dialogue you invent is true to the spirit of the people involved.
- Write a scene in which a political belief of yours is reflected but not named.
- Describe a story you haven't figured out how to tell. Then ask for feedback from others to discover some possibility for telling it that you haven't considered before.
- Close your eyes, sit quietly, and bring up childhood memories of people talking to you to discover the "tune inside your head." Write those voices.

Joan Silber

JOAN SILBER (b. 1954) is the author of two collections of short stories and three novels. Born in Millburn, New Jersey, she was educated at Sarah Lawrence College and New York University. Her honors include the PEN/Hemingway Award for Best First Novel, a Guggenheim fellowship, an NEA fellowship, a New York Foundation for the Arts Grant, the Pushcart Prize, a Nelson Algren Award nomination, and a National Book Award nomination. Silber teaches at Sarah Lawrence College. She lives in New York City.

For Further Reading:
Household Words (1980), *In the City* (1987), *In My Other Life* (2000), *Lucky Us* (2001), *Ideas of Heaven: A Ring of Stories* (2004).

Bobby Jackson

We were sitting around at night after work. I was a busboy at the time, hanging around in my sweaty T shirt, drinking free Jack Daniel's. The bar didn't close until four in the morning, but the staff got off anywhere from eleven on and gathered at one of the booths. Nancy, my favorite of the waitresses, was braiding my ponytail and fidgeting with my sideburns and arguing with me. Nancy was waiting for her boyfriend, an English guy who was a painter. I used to torment her by singing. "England swings, like a pendulum do." She liked me well enough to flirt, and during work hours we would stand near the bus-box with our arms around each other's waists, very friendly and collegial.

"Totally wrong," Nancy said. We were arguing about the restaurant's cats. Gordon, the owner, had brought in a cat to fend off the rats in the basement. The cat was a scared, undersized adolescent who had surprised everyone by having a litter of kittens right away. Did people mind if the kittens were all over the place, climbing on tables, stepping into dinner plates? I said yes, Nancy said no. Nancy's friend Donna said, "Find one person sober enough to notice."

I got up and walked through the aisles looking. This was in 1969 and I was twenty-two, showing off. I ran into Bobby Jackson, the second cook, coming out of the men's room after his shift, and I brought him to the table as my specimen of sobriety. Bobby grouched about the cats, but he was the one who fed them shrimp scraps. Every night he whispered to them on the cellar stairs, *psst,* chow time. When he shut the door fast, he'd seen a rat.

By the time we got to the table, Nancy was off cats and on the subject of where she was saving money to travel to. Even as a busboy I was doing pretty well financially. The restaurant was a madhouse. Every night it got more packed and noisy and out of control; it was having its day as the red-hot center. My own plan was to go to India. "Step outside for free," Bobby Jackson said. "We got Bombay right here." Aziz, the porter, had taught me some words in Urdu, which I made everyone listen to. He had drilled me in dirty slang, long insults about your grandmother's private parts. "Get in trouble that way," Bobby Jackson said. "Come back as a chutney yourself."

At first we'd all thought Bobby Jackson was from the South. He spoke in a slow drawl, he walked with a stoop. Nancy used to imitate his way of looking at us sideways like Stepin Fetchit. When she showed Bobby, he did one of his low snorty chuckles. Nancy was from Virginia; I thought she understood Bobby better than I did, to know what he'd take as a joke.

Actually Bobby was from Harlem. And he was a lot younger than he looked; he was twenty-five. After his shift he had a long subway ride home. If he fell asleep on the train, he woke up going the wrong way back downtown. Sometimes he fell asleep again and wound up on the subway all night. He would talk about it the next day, shaking his head and snorting at himself.

I think we were his first downtown job. God knows we thought we were interesting. At the moment Nancy and Donna were putting Led Zeppelin on the jukebox, which Gordon the owner was famous for hating. They had a bet going about how many seconds it would take Gordon to turn it off. Bobby was into this, and he raised the bet by a quarter. I was in such a good mood I didn't even mind that much when Nancy's boyfriend showed up. I made room for him at the table, and I stayed around after they left.

I was never a great busboy. I sort of worked my tail off in fits and starts and then malingered in between. I had been like that in college too. All the same, when one of the bartenders was fired for stealing, I got promoted to working behind the bar. "Climbing that corporate ladder," Bobby Jackson said. I had to train, which meant learning to make five basic drinks and listening while Gordon told me he had one piece of advice. Actually he had several. "This is it," he said. "You can drink it, you can give it away, you can steal it, but you can't do all three."

Bobby Jackson was at the bar at the time getting himself a belt of ginger ale, and he gave me a fish-eyed, knowing look. "Huh, our Gordon," he said to me later. "Malcolm Forbes."

Bobby himself had started as the dishwasher. It was Reginald the chef's idea to train him for greater things. Bobby's cooking (cold appetizers and grilled items) was fine but he was slow—that was his one big drawback—and he was accident-prone. He cut his hand all the time opening the clams and oysters; he seemed to forget his own palm was under the shell. He'd come to the bar looking like a train wreck, and I'd put vodka on the bleeding cut. I'd pour him a shot of Dewar's—his brand, but he'd swallow it in one shudder and make a face. Usually he said, "That scotch is nasty stuff."

I was doing better with women since I'd been made a bartender. Women would hang around till my shift was over. Beautiful, hip women, some of them; I had my flings. Brief flings, but usually good-willed on both sides. Nancy went around insulting me, which I took as a sign of interest. She'd complain about my sloppy martinis when she came to pick up her drinks. Once she pelted my T-shirt with maraschino cherries, very fifth-grade.

We were all keyed up from working at full tilt. The pace of customers kept us going, and the jukebox. Nancy walked around singing lyrics to herself and being rude to people at her tables. She'd tell them the fish of the day was tadpole; she'd walk away if they took too long ordering. Bobby liked Nancy. He called her Miss Nan.

I was waiting out Nancy's romance with the Brit. I liked to watch her parading around the floor in her micro-miniskirt and her black taffeta apron, like a French maid's. As far as I could see, a good part of her life was spent dealing with men expressing their lust in various ways. Mostly it wasn't any kind of aggravation to her. She brightened, out on the floor. All this brightness helped me.

One night Nancy came down into the basement after I had been tapping a beer keg, and there was no one else there. I moved in for the clinch and there we were, finally, a kissing couple. For the rest of the night I could hardly stand it. But when we both got off work, we hung around drinking at one of the booths. I don't know why we did this, although I remember that hour at the end of the night as festive and sexy.

Bobby sat with us, and a lot of other people settled in. Nancy was talking about where her family lived in Virginia, and Bobby wanted to know if they had horses. It turned out Bobby was crazy about horses. Who would have guessed this? Nancy said her family had horses when she was little, but then her father's business slipped and he had to sell them. "Should've sold the children and kept the horses," Bobby said.

Bobby told us he'd gone riding a bunch of times from the stables near Central Park. Had I ever been there? I hadn't.

"My father keeps driving his company into the ground but he always bounces back," Nancy said.

"Probably has something to bounce on," Bobby said. "Money."

There was a discussion about what you would do if you lost everything—none of us had anything, but in any case no one could picture not being able to start over. You could sell stuff in the street, you could go back to school, you could always hustle somehow. Donna and Marcia, another waitress, talked about how much you could actually make being a hooker. Hector, one of the customers, talked about karma and dealing with the task given to you. We were a strange mix of the spoiled and the soupy and the game.

Jay the bartender went into a story about losing money at the track and by the time he finished it, Bobby Jackson was asleep with his head on the table and Nancy was giving me the eye. Jay said he would get Bobby up later and make sure he got on the subway. I certainly didn't want to be the one to do it then.

But in fact Nancy and I went off to another bar, a darker, louder one than ours. Why did we have to do this? We were aching to get into bed, but all we could think of was more parading around, more social excitement. We believed the real world was in the public life of the night, and we wanted one more dip while we were feeling good.

We did get home to my place finally, and after that night I was a man drowned in love, or at least paralytic lust. All I did in my waking hours was have erotic daydreams about Nancy, or else I really was with Nancy. I was swimming around in fulfilled wishes. I thought this was because I had attained whatever knowledge it takes to be lucky.

The whole first month we didn't get out of bed till three in the afternoon. It wasn't only the sex that kept us there, but those afternoon sleeps, the waves of waking and sliding back—the ghostly freedom and the delicious waste. Sometimes we were still in bed at twilight, when squares of blue light showed at the windows.

We had fights, of course. Nancy was a moody and demanding person, and she could turn on me when I least expected it. Also I got sidetracked myself: I forgot when I was supposed to meet her places. Mostly we didn't go anywhere much; we moved around from our bar to the other bar people went to, in a loop.

It was around this time that Bobby asked Nancy to get him some acid. He didn't like it, as it turned out. "Could forget where you parked your mind, on that," he said. He had taken it after work, in his leisure time. But what was he doing standing around in his apron at two in the morning, tripping, in the middle of a room filled with milling white strangers? He must have been as curious as anyone, as eager to see what he could in his time around us.

One night when Nancy and I both got off work early, we told Bobby to meet us at the other bar. The place had a disco upstairs, and in the crowd we forgot about Bobby when he didn't come. The next day Bobby told Nancy he'd shown up but they hadn't let him in. All full tonight, the bouncer said. They let in blacks but not blacks who looked like Bobby, with his stingy-brim hat and his banlon shirt. "Shit," Nancy said, "we should've known." "I'm a jerk," I said to Bobby. Bobby just rolled his eyes to the side. None of us wanted to talk about it.

Probably Bobby had wanted to see the other bar, which was bigger and more famous than ours, although not famous in his circles. We didn't ask too much about his circles. Jay knew more than we did. Jay went uptown with him to buy drugs.

It was from Jay that I first heard that Bobby was a junkie. Jay said, "You knew, right?" Maybe I half knew. Actually I don't think so. And once we all knew, I thought there must be thousands of people like Bobby, holding down jobs, showing up every day, doing what they had to, for years and years. Even Gordon didn't care really. Bobby was slow, but not crazy or raging or alcoholic, like half the kitchen staff.

Jay asked if I was by any chance interested in going uptown with them the next time. Jay was out to extend my education. Nancy was not pleased about my going on this buying trip. "One short ride on the subway," I said.

We went after midnight, and the subway car, with its few solemn riders, emptied out, stop by stop, until there was just us and a cluster of black and Hispanic people wondering if Jay and I knew where the hell we were going. I said something to Jay about how if we had to travel this long to get high we must be truly dedicated. "Sincere is the word," Bobby said. I said, "High-minded." Jay groaned, and Bobby did his long hissing laugh. He jabbed my shoulder, an unusual sign of giddiness from him. Three jolly guys, that was us.

125th Street was hopping when we got out—a summer night, everybody on the street, radios going full blast. Nobody acted as if we were worth noticing. We cruised along with Bobby for a few blocks and he was quiet, with the same stillness in his face he had at work. Jay and I managed to shut up, but we were nosy and tense and exhilarated. At a corner a man came up to Bobby and clapped him on the back, very chummy. "What do you know?" Bobby said. "Hey."

Upstairs in someone's apartment, Bobby was all business. No winks or nods, no horsing around, no chatty introductions. Contrary to what you hear now, nobody wanted us to shoot up right then and there to prove we weren't undercover somebodies; they wanted us to pay and get out. In the kitchen, where they took us, there was only the dealer and a very skinny girl sitting on the floor drinking a beer. We shook hands all around, and the guy made a salesman's sort of joke about our long journey to get the best. The dealer was not young, and he was loud-voiced and hearty, like somebody's uncle. I could hear men's voices in another room and a TV tuned to a program with a laugh track. "How long did it take you to grow that ponytail?" the dealer said to me. "Couple years, man" I said. "Very stylish," he said. "All my friends are stylish." Bobby said "Do tell," the dealer said.

Bobby went with us back down to the street, like a man walking his date to a cab. I was disappointed that things had happened so quickly—I felt overprotected, the way women must feel in the face of certain gallantries. Bobby, who'd made a purchase himself, must've been eager to get home, but he lingered with us on the block. He talked for a few minutes about how the night had cooled off. Not an interesting subject, and none of us were what you could call relaxed, but we made some jokes about the air conditioner at work and how cheap Gordon was, and we hovered around aimlessly as if we were high already. Bobby was in good spirits when we said good night.

As it turned out, that was my one trip up there. Bobby didn't take us again, not me anyway. Still, the next day, Bobby said, "Everything okay? Glad to hear it. Everything fine, right?" He must've been glad enough to show off for us. In our various ways, we were all three proud of our teamwork. "Hands across the waters," Jay said. Jay was especially thrilled with what we'd brought back—you'd think he'd smuggled it from the poppy fields personally—and it was in fact stronger than any heroin I'd had, not that I'd had so much. I'd had some.

Nancy was not overjoyed about any of this, although I couldn't keep from bragging to her anyway. It was a big topic between us from then on. We had a scene about it right in the middle of work, during a slow spell. For a Southern girl, Nancy had a voice that could get very shrill, and I couldn't, of course, be argued out of anything. She warned me about all the parts that didn't frighten me. I was not afraid to die, unlikely as that may sound—I had the dreamy curiosity about death that small children have, trying to see if they can hold their breath on and on. And my existence so far had been proof that old cautions didn't hold—I didn't have tracks or a habit or expenses I couldn't afford; I wasn't undernourished and no one was arresting me; I had a job, I was fine. "Look at Bobby," I said.

"Don't get yourself in an uproar," I said, which was Jay's expression. Jay and Nancy did not get along, I had to see them each separately in my off-hours. When I talk to Jay now—we still talk but not often—he seems to remember me as someone who was forever tentative, that is, who made a big show of his reluctance but who had a comically strong appetite. A zany secret glutton, that's Jay's version of me.

I don't think I can explain now how tickled I was with myself at this time. I was glad, not only for the floods of sensation I could call up at will (which I still think of fondly, to be honest), but for the part of the world I had edged into, the layer under the surface that I was now a familiar of. I had always liked walking home from supper in Chinatown at dawn while everyone else was getting ready to go work, and this seemed like that, moving through another city.

Two things happened within a few months of the time I'm talking about: I lost Nancy, and I started to steal from the bar. I might have lost Nancy anyway—she was a lively girl eager to try out her powers—but I neglected her. My days developed a different drama; Nancy seemed less important to me. And I stopped being great shakes in bed, if you want to know the truth. All that was spectacular and precious about Nancy—and is to me still—seemed distant and replaceable to me then. Nancy went back to her Brit boyfriend (she might have been seeing him all along but I prefer not to think so), and I watched him come into the restaurant at night to pick her up after work. In the end he went back to England, and soon after, Nancy took off for London to live with him.

I tried to be a good sport about it, and I even went with her—and about twenty other people from the restaurant—to say goodbye at the airport. Bobby went too. He kept saying, "Shouldn't leave us like this, Miss Nan." The flight didn't take off till three in the morning so we were pretty drunk and wasted by the time she took off—I remember Nancy waving at the gate, a blur of blondness to me—and then we all went for breakfast at one of those plastic airport coffee shops. I had pancakes. At that age I could always eat. When we lined up to pay, the cashier said Bobby had taken care of the checks for all of us. "Oh, no," Donna said. Susan said, "He can't do that. You know how much that cost?" "He wants to," I said. "Let him." And then we all thanked him, much too profusely.

The first and only postcard I sent to Nancy said, "Business downhill since your departure. Customers complain service too polite." My own life was not without variety—I had some girlfriends and I hung out with Jay, who was good at making an evening ceremonious. But I waited for Nancy to write, which she never did. (She sent a card to the whole restaurant—a portrait of Prince Charles as a young chinless nerd, looking remarkably like Alfred E. Newman—and Bobby tacked it over the clam bar.)

The restaurant was losing some of its popularity, as places do, although this took us all by surprise. My tips were not what they had been. Every night Jay and I emptied out the tip cup and made witty remarks about our futures as janitors. I didn't start stealing until I had an increase in my needs, but once I started I wondered why I hadn't done it before. It was easy, and at the end of the night I could go home without feeling mad.

Gordon didn't notice the stealing at first, but he gave me lectures about my appearance. Why did I wear the same cruddy shirt three days in a row? Were my teeth getting worse or what? See that man at table four, Gordon said. He used to be smart and prosperous, but now he's skinny and drugged out and stupid, look at him now. Look, he said.

That was when I thought about the steaks. Steaks were the most expensive things on the menu, and now only Gordon ate them. The chef had bought them fresh but these days they were all stockpiled in the freezer. Nobody knew how many were there. Suppose I could sell a few boxes of them, what would that bring? Jay would know someone to buy them. It was a dumb idea, risky for too little money. I was getting dumb and reckless.

Meanwhile Gordon went around trying to shrink his business losses. He cut back on ordering everything, he bothered all the waitresses about smiling and looking friendly (Donna almost quit over this one), and he made a nuisance of himself in the kitchen over waste control. Bobby would say, "Get that man a vacation," when Gordon left the room. And the restaurant's equipment, which had been bought secondhand, started to give out all at once. The oven got unreliable and burned the roast meats; then the dishwashing machine konked out, and for three nights the staff had to wash everything by hand. I told Bobby that the building was returning to a state of nature. "*The Dismal Swamp*," Bobby said. "*Planet of the Apes*," I said.

At closing time when I was depressed about my finances I went back to contemplate the steaks and count how many were in each box. I looked over the produce too, the butter and milk. The cats watched me, hoping for a handout. By mistake I locked one of them in the walk-in icebox overnight. Bobby said the cat walked out fine the next day, spry and crabby, swishing her tail. But everyone wanted to know who was the jerk who'd been in the refrigerator, and it made me lay low for a while.

For a while I thought about dealing. There were a lot of people close at hand who might be interested in buying; also, if you're a dealer it's good to be findable all the time, and there I was behind the bar. I did need a career advancement. When I talked to Jay about it, he was discouraging—aghast is more like it. He said I'd get caught in about five minutes, stuck in one public spot like a sitting duck.

But I couldn't stop hanging around the steaks. One night I took out a whole box to try to guess their weights—were they really full one-pound sirloins?—the cardboard by this time was thickly frosted and blood-smeared and dank. I heard a footstep near me, and in my panic I actually jumped. It was Reginald, the head cook, and he said, "No good." I thought he meant me, caught in the act, but he meant the steaks. He opened the box and sniffed one of the paper-wrapped hunks, which gave off an odor like a monthlong garbage strike. "This freezer is crap," Reginald said, and for my loitering in the area I got stuck on my break helping him clean the thing out. I smelled rotten when I got back to the bar.

I thought of finding a job at another restaurant. My other plans for my future were vague and childish, and I did not confide them to anyone. One night I went back into the kitchen to scrounge for extra lemons, and when I turned around, I almost tripped over Bobby, who was in the corner, slumped against a bag of onions, out cold. It was the middle of his shift, for Christ's sake. Donna walked in to place an order, and we both yelled. "Hey, Bobby. Yoohoo. Hey." Donna tapped his shoulder in a fast, scared way, and I shook him. "Bobby, please," I said. "Up, up. Get up."

Very slowly, Bobby raised his head—I could see he didn't know where he was—and then his eyes focused on us. His mouth was slack, his face was still gone. It was hard to watch him. I'd seen enough people like that, dimmed out and adrift in the private shell of the body, but with Bobby it was more than I wanted to see, none of our business. "Shit," he said. He stood up and pulled his apron around. "Caught me napping," he said.

When I told Jay, he went back and had a grim little conference with Bobby, although I couldn't see how Jay had anything useful to say. The rest of us stayed quiet, and it was a bleak night, with long spells of dullness. I was glad Nancy wasn't there to see me, walking up and down the duckboards, making wisecracks, looking for someone to serve. I meant to go back to check on Bobby, but I lost track of time—since Nancy was gone, he didn't stay around after work—and he went home without my knowing.

Bobby started showing up for work late, which always threw Gordon into a panic. Gordon would want to call Bobby at home, and then he'd remember there was no phone number for Bobby, and then he'd mutter about how every worker in the place was robbing him blind, and then Bobby would walk in, looking bothered, complaining about the subway.

One night a woman showed up at the restaurant looking for Bobby. "Bobby's *girlfriend* is here," Donna said. We hadn't thought about this side of his life. Why hadn't we? You could get a knowing glance from Bobby if you made a racy remark, but he didn't talk about females himself and he never flirted with the waitresses like some of the other cooks. The woman who came to visit him—she was sitting on a stool in the kitchen when I saw her—was a plainfaced, grumpy person in a cotton dress and flip flop sandals. We all said, hey, nice to meet you, and she grunted in reply. Bobby was clearly not happy about her being there.

She wasn't leaving either. She stayed through most of the night, not budging from the spot. Bobby walked around muttering. It was plain her visit was part of a longer argument between them. She was there to get money, or to spite him, or to check out this place that was supposed to be so great. When Bobby came to the bar for his scotch, he wouldn't take a drink back for her when I offered. Even Jay kept away from her.

Donna said Bobby was screwing up the food orders tonight. "Who cares?" I said. But we weren't used to seeing him like this. Usually he was patient, above the fray. Remain cool, the evening is young: he was the one who said that. When I went into the kitchen, I made some smart-aleck remarks to Bobby, so the girlfriend would see our usual friendly rhythm, but he was not exactly crackling with backtalk tonight. The woman didn't say a word—I never did hear her speak. Maybe they had lived together for years, maybe they had just met. Bobby's tenderer feelings for her were certainly not evident at this moment, but who knows what they had together? Donna reported overhearing them quarrel, but they stopped when she came into sight.

In the end Bobby did get the girlfriend to leave. She went out through the dining room, tugging her skimpy jacket around her and slapping her sandals against the floor. She still looked mad, so he may not have given her what she made the trip for. (Not that she could've been expected to wave a glassine envelope in the air and shout happily in front of us.) Bobby seemed every bit as irritated after she left. "God*damn*," he'd be saying to himself when anyone walked into the kitchen. We were fading for him, by then.

Slow as business was that night. I kept filching as much money as I could, out of sheer dissatisfaction and itchiness. On the way home from work I made a stop I shouldn't have made, and on the way home from that I must have fallen in the street. I woke up a mess. I was lying in the doorway of a store, in the thin light of early morning, and my head felt as if someone had stepped on it. My hair was stiff with dried blood in the back, and one side of my face was scraped and swollen. Probably I had just hit my head on the sidewalk when I passed out, but I found out someone had gotten my wallet, which frightened me to think of. When I got to my feet, I ran home to my apartment, picking up speed as I went.

I was okay in the morning, but in the afternoon I felt so bad I took myself to the emergency room at St. Vincent's. They told me I had a concussion and put me under observation. Why that is supposed to be such a great hospital is beyond me; the food was lousy and the nurses were mean. The word *detox* was not really popular then, and I was left to my own devices.

Donna and Jay came to visit me, and Donna flirted with me, which was nice of her, considering how I must've looked, a scabby, unshaven goon in a seersucker hospital gown. Jay asked if there was anything needed—my nose was running like rain, a recognizable sign of how strung out I was—but I'd been through the worst already and the thought of shooting up in the St. Vincent's john really chilled me to the bone. I couldn't stay there long—there was no insurance, nothing like that—but when I got home I didn't go anywhere or eat much and I just stayed inside. I didn't answer my door or my phone.

In my long days at home I would take naps. I dreamed of Nancy and other women I'd been with, and I always woke up happy, despite the absence of real life women in my house. My old longings made me happy. When my mother called from Toledo, I told her I was having a vacation in my own home. Sometimes my dreams got mixed in with the TV I was watching.

When I went back to the restaurant, Bobby was gone. There was a new second cook in his place. Donna said Bobby had been coming to work later and later, and one day he just didn't show up. No one knew where he was or had a way to find out. Gordon didn't want me back either, as a matter of fact, since my absence had only pointed out whose sticky fingers had been in the till. I was done with that job anyway. I knew that.

I was not as ready to go on to other things as I would have thought. I tried bartending in other places, and I did try dealing. My ideas were always circling the same spots. Then I tried brainless jobs—bike messenger, salesman in a T-shirt shop. I was just walking through everything and waiting. All the same, time passed, and now I have a different life.

My daughter, who is eleven and whom I see on weekends, is crazy about horses, and I take her riding from the stables near Central Park. I often think about Bobby when I'm there; I think about running into him while we're both on horseback loping along the trail, our paths crossing in some leafy junction.

I work as a real estate agent—a hard job to have these days, but I keep my head above water. I'm out and around a lot, which I like. For a long while, I used to think I saw Bobby walking toward me in the street; then I would think that by this time Bobby was probably dead. He might be, but why did I think so? What was wrong with my imagination that I couldn't picture his life looping around, getting worse and then better? He had much more experience than I did in leveling off and fucking up all over and getting cleaned up again. He may well be fine. I like to think that he is a cook somewhere, the one profitable thing he got from his time with us.

I have not been to Harlem, except to get a cab from the train station, since I made my trip to 125th Street with Bobby. And wherever Bobby is, I don't think he's downtown. That was then, this is now, as my daughter would say. Bobby, whatever he's doing, is doing it in a separate realm, invisible to me.

It is Nancy who is dead, although I can still sometimes forget this. It seems like a mistake to me, a misreporting. She drowned swimming off the coast of Ibiza. She had been drinking and drifted out too far from shore. A lot of people drink themselves silly on the beach; it still makes me angry that she couldn't afford this particular bit of stupidity. I feel she should have been allowed more than that, Nancy of all people.

I don't know how she would have liked the decade of her forties, which for me has been very good. I notice that I've become someone who takes great private pleasure in things around me. On some days my own apartment seems like a vale of peace and light. My daughter is growing into this amazing creature; she's a sharp girl, terrifically smart. She thinks I am a flake and definitely a bit much in public. I have habits left over from being a bartender. I joke with people I don't know; I get into gabby exchanges with people in stores, much to my daughter's mortification. I am a curious, sometimes clumsy person. I understand that in many ways I have been very lucky in my life.

A Conversation with Joan Silber

In a time when there's such fascination with how small and focused a story can be, your stories are really vast. Some cover whole lifetimes, taking the reader through a series of changes in the characters' lives, each one adding weight and bringing perspective. Would you talk about how you came to write this kind of story?

The first book I wrote was a novel, *Household Words,* and that covered a twenty-year time span. I just wrote that out of ignorance! I just had fun doing it. Most people start with stories and then move on to novels, but I did it backwards—just jumped into this novel. Stories seemed too small. I had this bigotry against them, which was really ridiculous. Alice Munro was very influential in the stories I finally did write. I loved the way her stories encompassed huge amounts of time. I was interested in these slow accumulations of change, and the older I get the more interested I am in conveying the sense that lives contain a lot. One of the first stories I wrote that did something like that was "Bobby Jackson." It had a jump in time that I didn't even know that I was going to make until I got to that point in the story. I liked the way the jump worked, how it brought the story together, which made me think that I wanted to do it again.

I was interested in these slow accumulations of change, and the older I get the more interested I am in conveying the sense that lives contain a lot.

Would you talk about "Bobby Jackson"?

I worked in a bar when I was in my twenties, and there was a guy who worked the salad bar, obviously new to this kind of work, named Bobby Jackson. He was really very much like the Bobby Jackson in this story. He was very bright, knew exactly what was going on around him. It emerged slowly that he was a junkie. When I realized that I wanted to write stories about the 1960s, he was a character who rose to mind. But I knew I couldn't tell a story from his point of view because I knew him only in this peripheral way. The guys were closer witnesses and had more access to him than I did, so I invented the person who narrates the story. There was some real-life buying of drugs together. I think I made up the trip to Harlem they all made together. I can't quite remember. It was the sense of their paths crossing, however briefly, that was important to me because it was an era in which there was more intermingling of class and race, with all the complications, than there had ever been before. Also, we were all working in a bar together. I wanted to talk about that and about my sense of where he is now. I used to think about us passing in the street and we wouldn't know each other after all these years.

Creating the narrator to tell Bobby Jackson's story has a kind of double effect: Telling Bobby Jackson's story, he also tells the story of his own life.

I think that happened because my original attraction to the material was the primary thing. I wanted to talk about Bobby Jackson. I really didn't want to talk about the narrator, but once I had this guy telling the story I had to make up a story that would contain him. So "Bobby Jackson" became a story that was also about how the narrator got from here to there.

What surprised you in the process of writing that story?

I knew the bar stuff was going to be in here, but I didn't know that the story was going to jump to the present. That was a surprise. And the character of Nancy—she was based on someone who was a very close friend. She and Bobby Jackson did goof around, and that was a detail that I remembered from all those years. I didn't know she was going to be the narrator's girlfriend. You invent ways to link characters. You have these elements and then you think, oh! They could have a thing, couldn't they? Tinkering brings that about. The real Nancy did die of ovarian cancer, but I didn't know her death, the sadness of her death, would figure in the story as an important note. It adds a kind of resonance, a kind of weight.

You invent ways to link characters. You have these elements and then you think, oh! They could have a thing, couldn't they? Tinkering brings that about.

The feel of the narrator's life evolving and the structure it implies—is that something you sensed when the story first started to take shape in your mind?

I knew that it wasn't going to be one scene, which is the more classic model for a story. I knew I couldn't have just one night in the bar where Bobby Jackson is revealed. I don't experience life that way. It takes me a long time to get to know a person. I don't often trust my first impressions, even now. It takes me a long time to figure stuff out, generally, and I wrote this story to express that, too.

Do you usually have a sense of what the timeline of a story will be when you start it?

I usually know in advance, but not always. I know more now that I'm more experienced with storywriting. I'm a little more in control.

When you cover a lot of time in a story, you have to decide what should be scene and what should be exposition, otherwise the story becomes unwieldy. How do you do that?

Technically, I treat habitual action as a scene. "Every day I walk down the street" becomes one walk that I describe. Also, I give summary the quality of scene. The problem with summary—as everybody knows—is that it's often the weakest part of the story because it's too vague. "I used to feel good when I walked down the street." Now that doesn't get us anywhere. In summary, you want to have as much sensory detail as you would have in a direct scene. You want to make it as immediate and particular as scene. It's easy, then, to slide into a specific scene from summary. "Every day he walked down the street. One day he was hit by an icicle." It's a fairly fluid way of doing it, and it works very effectively. Writers tend to be afraid of exposition, but it's really not any more alien to storytelling than anything else.

Writers tend to be afraid of exposition, but it's really not any more alien to storytelling than anything else.

Markers help make that slide happen in a way that keeps the reader grounded in time.

It took me a while to get transitions. You want people to know where the hell they are; you don't want a floaty kind of story. Mostly, I use a marker something like "six years later" or "two months later." Usually they come easily, but not always. Some take tinkering. I don't always know when I'll make a jump in time. It depends on the story.

How do you think about plotting these stories that cover large amounts of time?

I try to have a rise, a crucial thing that happens. Often it's a crucial moment of reflection. Peter Ho Davies, a wonderful writer and a student of mine when he was at Sarah Lawrence, said, "One of the differences between a story and a novel is that you can say, 'Well, I liked the novel but I didn't like the ending.' But with a short story, if you don't like the ending, you don't like it." A story really hangs on the ending. So I'm very aware that the ending has to figure out what the story means. Sometimes I only half know by the time I get there or I know and I don't know how I'm going to portray it dramatically. I'm feeling for that. The motivation for writing the story is one of the things I look to in trying to figure out the end.

A story really hangs on the ending.

You said it was a surprise that "Bobby Jackson" made a jump to the present in the end. Do you remember how that happened?

I knew there was going to be some music. The voice talking, the way it could kind of roam around, talking to the reader—that was important, too. I remember that I sat down and it was when I was writing on the page that the ending came out. I can't say it more specifically than that.

There's a sense of wonderment as that story moves toward the end—and in many of your other stories, too. One way or another, the characters convey the feeling that "we never knew life would be like this."

That's my "stuff," my territory. Even *Household Words,* which is about a character that I drew from my mother and told from her point of view, is about the rug being pulled out from under the character, about life turning out so differently from what she thought it would be. Even when I was too young to have had that feeling completely for myself, I had the crucial sense of that being how life worked. The truth is that no one can be prepared for everything. If you can be, there's something wrong with your life. You've circumscribed it so utterly that there are other frustrations. My fiction is about the parts of life my characters weren't prepared for.

My fiction is about the parts of life my characters weren't prepared for.

Why do you think that material plays out more frequently in stories than in novels?

I like stories better. I like the compression in stories, even though I'm asking the stories to contain a lot. I like getting it in one go, though that doesn't happen with the longer stories. The difficulty with novels is you have to get the people from here to there. Sometimes they are too plodding. There's less risk of that with a story.

How long does it usually take you to write a story, as opposed to a novel?

I think the shortest was about a month. But that's very unusual. Usually, it takes about six months to write a story. A novel takes three years, minimum.

Do you feel as involved with the characters in these long stories as you do with the characters in a novel?

More and more. But I also don't have a chance to get sick of them. It's a more contained relationship.

When you're working on one story, do others often bubble up while you're in process?

The stories in my collection *Ideas of Heaven* are linked, and that was fun. The first story, "My Shape," came out very quickly, and that was a good experience. I didn't have the idea immediately, but I decided I wanted the villain of the piece to have his own story, too. Once that happened, it was really nice. The reader knew him as a baddy, then knew him in "The High Road" as a living human being. I liked that so much that I began to think of other links. I'd been thinking of Gaspara Stampa a lot. She was like a great blues singer; she thought that suffering for love was a good thing. Some of those ideas were in the other stories, so I wanted to pattern out of this. I had thought that if I ever wrote about her it would be a monograph. I had never done a historical story before. But I had lived in Italy for a year and visited Venice a bunch of times. I'd looked at a lot of Renaissance paintings. I thought if I could ever do another era or another place, I could probably do this one. Once I had the first three stories, I wanted to do more linking.

Would you talk about the first story in that book, "My Shape"?

The core incident about the humiliation by the dance master was a story that someone told me. I totally understood how she could want a thing so desperately that she was willing to do what she did. It was a passion that had been mischanneled. But I knew I couldn't just write that one scene. Although it was very dramatic, it couldn't contain what I wanted it to contain. It would just be a rude scene; it wouldn't have much resonance.

You had to bring her to the point where the reader would believe she'd do it.

My danger as a writer is that sometimes I really get caught up in the going back and it gets tedious. I digress from the story. I've learned to cut—somewhat.

Exactly. Otherwise you think, who *is* this fool? Then I realized that I wanted to go way back. My danger as a writer is that sometimes I really get caught up in the going back and it gets tedious. I digress from the story. I've learned to cut—somewhat.

The stories in In My Other Life *are linked differently. Most hinge on the characters' coming of age in the 1960s. Would you talk about how your own coming of age then shaped you as a writer?*

Often the characters are just dodos when the stories begin, but because the stories cover such a time span they are relatively cogent and sagacious by the end of the story. That turn is interesting to me. There was a kind of willed dopiness in the '60s. It wasn't that people were less intelligent then. But probably because we were coming out of such a stodgy period, such a rigidly conventional period, we ignored other people's wisdom. We were inventing it all ourselves, figuring it out ourselves. So we were living on a more childish level. Some of the stories in that collection were confusing to people. The characters live in this chaotic world where they do transgressive things. They are not conventional citizens. But the stories themselves have this very calm tone. They are crafted stories. The wildness is not in the language of the stories. Those two things, it seems to me, can live very easily in one space. But it threw some people off.

There's an intimacy in the matter-of-factness, the feeling that it's one end of a conversation a person is having with someone he trusts. Why did you chose to write the stories in that tone?

I'm uncomfortable when people are too self-dramatizing, and I don't want to give that quality to my characters.

I like matter-of-factness. I'm uncomfortable when people are too self-dramatizing, and I don't want to give that quality to my characters. So they tend to be what we used to call phlegmatic. I prefer characters with that kind of detachment.

It works in an interesting way against the rhetorical questions your characters often ask themselves, like "What did I expect?" "What was I thinking?" "Why did I do that?"

I remember starting to do that early, in "Bobby Jackson." It worked in that story and became a habit, something that was handy to do at certain junctures. It's a way of being wry about something.

Which is really just a different kind of detachment. The detachment in the earlier stories is deepened with the new collection. Your interest in Buddhism seems to be reflected in the calm intensity of the stories, in the longing and letting go. Would you talk about the influence of Buddhism on your work and on you as a writer?

My active interest in Buddhism is relatively recent. Because New York is so amazing, I go to different meditation groups. But I'm a terrible meditator. It's the least interesting aspect of Buddhism to me. And I'm not interested in becoming part of a cultural institution. I'm an American. I don't want to become a Thai Buddhist. But my interest in Buddhism has helped my work a lot. It gave me a container for various ideas I had. It gave me a way of knowing that I wasn't a fool for not caring about certain things. Buddhism gives you a whole different model for success and failure. It says that loss is built into everything. I once went to hear a Zen Buddhist speaker who said that depending on things turning out well is a very high-risk way to live—not that I'll overcome it in the next twenty lifetimes, but it's been a very helpful guide. It made me write differently. What I wanted from my characters was different. I judged them differently.

But my interest in Buddhism has helped my work a lot. It gave me a container for various ideas I had. It gave me a way of knowing that I wasn't a fool for not caring about certain things.

That seems to be reflected in the way Noelle, the narrator of "Ragazzi," *talks about her lifelong friend's difficult teenager. Where did that story come from?*

I was living in Italy at the time, and I was very interested in other Americans who lived abroad. I knew that I wanted to write about rock-star girlfriends. I didn't know any, but I knew people who were kind of like that. The two things came together in that story. There was a dangerous street to cross near where I was living. No traffic light. Motorcycles, bicycles. Unbelievable! Every time I crossed it I would think, are these people crazy? That observation led me to the image of the boy.

Is he based on anyone you knew then?

The boy in "*Ragazzi*" is based on a student I had at Sarah Lawrence. There was an incident of kids writing racist slogans and probably anti-lesbian graffiti, but I made up the actual words that are in the story.

You create a nice play on your usual material with him. The narrator, Noelle, has that same wry tone that so many of your other '60s narrators have. The reader knows how her and Damien's mother's lives turned out, but he doesn't know how Damien will turn out. The story hinges on that. You really capture what it's like to be young, how life might turn out any way for him. It plays against Noelle's memories of being young, the mixture of longing she feels for the past and relief at having survived it.

I had a very intense youth. I don't want to be a person my age who pretends to be twenty-five, but I have a feeling for those days. I think longing is a nice word for it, better than nostalgic.

Damien's obsession with Noelle's former boyfriend, Bud, who died of an OD, intensifies the longing and also serves to link the present with the past.

Well, there's always something dead in my stories. I do realize that. I had a very early experience with death. My father died when I was five, and my mother died when I was twenty-six, so that's just embedded in me. Then I lost my best friend, who died much like the Nancy character in "Bobby Jackson." She was in her early forties. She takes various forms and bubbles up now and then. So that's always in there and also—just historically—there were a lot of rock stars who overdosed. I think I needed a contrast. Noelle's boyfriend now is just kind of an old, overweight guy, not very interesting anymore. So I needed someone who was a more romantic figure.

The story has a traditional arc, but doesn't give the reader any easy answer about Damien at the end. Noelle "wants to think he's not a bad kid, but he might be."

There was a will in writing not to sentimentalize the story. I didn't want Damian embracing his mother and saying, "I love you, after all." That's like a really bad movie. If he's all evil, there's no story either. So there's one moment where he's nice to his mother. The task was to convey that dramatically.

In a way, the story works similarly to "Bobby Jackson." Telling the story of Damien's difficult summer, Noelle tells the story of her friendship with Jennifer.

Grace Paley said that it always takes two stories to make one story. Some writers can do a single-strand story, but I always need at least two. Often the search in the story is to find the other strand. The two women came to me very naturally. I knew everything about them. But once I threw Damien in, it became a story.

Some writers can do a single-strand story, but I always need at least two. Often the search in the story is to find the other strand.

Where did the title of the story come from?

When I was in Rome, I was in a museum when there was a crowd of kids. Kids always get taken to museums there, and their interest in what's in the museum is not that much greater than our kids' would be. There was this young, pretty, quite good-humored grade school teacher yelling at the top of her lungs, "*Ragazzi!*" It means, of course, boys and girls. It can also just mean boys. That seemed to fit that story.

A lot of the characters in your stories travel. How does travel serve you as a writer, how does it make its way into your work?

Travel is very romantic to me. A lot of my notions are satisfied by traveling. But I haven't always traveled happily. I had a very interesting year in Rome, which led to some of these stories. It was very difficult the first few months. You know, you're a baby. You're the one who doesn't know what's going on.

Did you speak Italian?

If someone was talking to me fairly directly in simple language, I could follow it. But I certainly wasn't conversant. That was actually quite painful. We don't like to be the dope—at least so *visibly* the dope in front of everybody. When you're in a foreign country, anyplace strange, your experience there is defined by not knowing what's going on. When you come back and you tell your friends about it, they know much less than you do. So you are the expert. It's very pleasurable to tell travel stories in that sense. One thing I love about travel is how there's all this interesting data in things like just going to the market. I inadvertently got some of the material for "*Ragazzi*" that way.

A lot of the stories in In My Other Life *center around sexuality. The characters in* Ideas of Heaven *wrestle with that, too, but spirituality is thrown into the mix. How do those issues converge for you?*

I do think of them as fighting over the same ground—the last story in the collection is *titled* "The Same Ground." When I would tell people that I was working on stories about sex and religion, they thought I was talking about sex so good it was like religion. I have nothing against fabulous sex, but it was the sense of consolation in both and the sense of devotional capacity that I was interested in. I think I started with Rilke's notion that somebody who loves in that kind of transporting way is on the verge of the arrow that shoots the mark.

Is it a mind/body thing?

No. It's not about different kinds of concentration, rather that one is physical and one is not. I'm more interested in ecstasy that happens standing outside the body than I am in passion. There's plenty of bodily passion that happens in "The Same Ground." There's also the obsessive dedication of thought to the beloved. The power of that longing.

Writing Prompts

READ: "Bobby Jackson" and the interview with **Joan Silber.**

PONDER: How the narrator moves through time to tell the story, rereading to highlight the language and techniques Silber uses to make the movement happen.

WRITE: Imagine three scenes that fall consecutively in a story, but are not necessarily chronological. Summarize what happens in each and then write the transitions necessary to move the reader seamlessly, from one scene to the next. Make at least one transition a full paragraph long.

PRACTICE:

- Think of someone you knew peripherally through work or school and who intrigued you somehow. What do you know about the person's life outside work or school, and how do you know it? Invent a colleague or schoolmate who shares your interest in the person. Let this character invent a story about your three-way relationship that jumps beyond the time you spent together and becomes a way of telling the story of her own life. Feel free to use real details, changing them and inventing new ones to suit the needs of the story.
- Think of something you do every day, a habitual action, and summarize it with the immediacy and particularity you would use to write a scene. Slide from the summary of habitual action into the first few lines of scene in which something out of the ordinary happens.
- Choose a minor character in a story you have already written and give this character his or her own story, one completely apart from the original story.
- Write a scene in which a character must deal with something he or she was not prepared for.
- Write a monologue in which a character uses a simple, matter-of-fact tone to talk about something dramatic. Include at least one rhetorical question.
- Write a story about a conflict between a parent and an or adolescent child that moves toward a subtle, unsentimental, open-ended moment of resolution.
- Invent two characters whose history and relationship is clear to you. Write a scene in which a third character (one you're not so sure of) does something that creates tension between them and complicates their relationship somehow.
- Set a story in a place you've visited on your travels, creating plot from something that happened to you or that you observed while you were there.

Elizabeth Tallent

Elizabeth Tallent (b. 1954) is the author of three collections of short stories and one novel. Born in Washington, D.C., she was educated at Illinois State University at Normal. Her honors include an NEA fellowship, the O. Henry Prize, and the Pushcart Prize. Tallent directs the creative writing program at Stanford University. She lives in Fort Bragg, California.

For Further Reading
In Constant Flight (1983), *Museum Pieces* (1985), *Time with Children,* (1987), *Honey* (1993).

Honey

Solidity, sober commitment, a roof over each dark Dominguez head—those are the things Mercedes desires for her children, desires with the erratic detachment from them illumining this, her sixty-third year. She did not bring seven children from Nicaragua in order for them to choose the doomed American existence of nerves rubbed raw by divorce, of quarrels, mutual contempt, and lawyers' costly ministrations, but their lives unravel in spite of her, coming undone even as she grows older, more secretly watchful, and increasingly pained in her estimation of what they are wasting. In the wavy mirror with which the airline has grudgingly outfitted its ladies', Mercedes could be sixty-eight, her pinned hair harshly white, or fifty-five, her pupils as pitch-black as when her husband, long dead, found his tiny horseshoe-mustached reflection there. Mercedes observes her eyes lovingly in the mirror and discovers she can no longer summon up his face.

She was his life, he said, his heart, his dove, tendernesses that, thus recollected, sting faintly as they pass through on their way back to the cool black vault that holds her marriage, her children's childhoods, and their life in Nicaragua. For an instant, under unlocked Nicaraguan palms, a child rides her shoulders, rubbing a leaf over Mercedes's forehead; another child swings crying from her husband's hand, two more race barefoot down the darkening dirt road before them. The friction of these details against Mercedes's composure is acute; far worse is the shock of her gross, consummate infidelity in having forgotten her husband's face. Her heart thuds alertly, fearfully trying to take the measure of this event. This is the first form grief takes with her—a sudden despair in standing still—and because the dim stainless-steel wedge of a bathroom could not be more confining, she turns stiffly around and around until dizziness seats her politely on the closed lid of the toilet. Someone knocks and goes away. The ache, which belongs to her heart, abruptly descends to her stomach. Mercedes kneels to vomit. The pilot, a voice from far away, announces they are beginning the initial descent into Albuquerque, New Mexico, where the temperature on the ground is ninety-nine degrees. Mercedes scarcely has the will to wash, to repin her disheveled hair, to neaten her clothes, before finding her seat between two salesmen. On earth, she is met by someone ponderously tall, absurdly red-haired, breathing wine into her face as he bends to her, as he tastes her pitiless old cheekbone with a son-in-law's kiss.

This son-in-law, burdened by her bags, blind to her mood, finds the chip of emerald that is his old BMW in the glittering midsummer parking lot. Mercedes feels herself begin to fear it, the desert. In the car's backseat, sheltered from the sun by the almost subsonic murmur of air-conditioning, is a boy, chin on his knees, eyes closed, Sony Walkman riding his ears. The boy has achieved the otherworldly privacy of a fetus, and is not about to acknowledge their arrival. Stranger still, the son-in-law offers no apology for his son's rudeness. Mercedes remembers him distinctly as a nice boy, too tall for his age, an elusive, embarrassed presence at his father's wedding to her daughter. Swinging out into swift late-afternoon traffic, the son-in-law runs through deferential Spanish phrases. He inquires whether she recalls his son from the wedding. Yes: Mercedes from her vantage point studied the boy sharply, believing him to be the chief obstacle to her daughter's happiness, but he had not seemed troubled by the marriage. He had known just where the ring was. He had been wearing it on his own little finger. A twist, and he offered it up, smiling. Mercedes's son-in-law wonders whether her flight was comfortable, hopes that she is not overtired, and assures her that her daughter will be insanely happy now that she is here at last.

Mercedes prefers to keep her distance from her children, her two sons and five daughters. In the domino theory of daughters, each, submissively tipping into domesticity, sets the next in motion. Only Caro resisted. Rumors of her love life filtered across the U.S.A. to the Brooklyn garret where Mercedes sews for her living, though none of her children like it that she lives alone. Anything could happen to her, they threaten. Seven children have taken turns at badgering or sweet-talking her out of Brooklyn. Her own vigilance, which made her more or less successful at protecting small, straying children, is irritating to Mercedes, now that it has been instilled in those very children. What Mercedes likes is settling each morning to her old Singer before her domain of roofs, of spires, of bare trees and tire swings. Summer is best, when the wind balms the nape of her neck, exposed by the pinned-up wiry wreck of her old hair, her cat sleeps on the windowsill, and the Brooklyn light falls lovingly on the cloth.

A lunar mountain range glides by on the right, steep points of bare stone, crevasses shadowed in powerful deathly blue. Her son-in-law wonders in English whether she is feeling the altitude. "It might make you sleepy," he says. The mountain range is replaced by a vast dun horizon in which there is no hope at all. "Why did you come, Kev, if you're not going to talk?" Hart asks. No answer, only the popping and sizzling of miniaturized rock and roll.

In the strange, rambling house, Mercedes follows the boy. Like his father, he is an American giant, burdened by her bags, constrained by her frailty. Already she is tired of making tall people uncomfortable. He runs through an explanation she can't follow, either because she's exhausted or because in his embarrassed adolescent way he talks too fast. Swinging around at a doorway, he says, "Sorry," and offers with transparently faked, kind-to-a-stranger patience, "I was only saying Caro's sleeping. She's never out of bed in the afternoon anymore."

Determined to convince him she's understood perfectly, Mercedes fixes her face into a trance of shrewd attentiveness, but the expression fails to convince him, because her elderly foreignness slides between them like a glass door.

Her beautiful daughter must have been eating like a pig. Her deep-set Dominguez eyelids have fattened, her small jaw is soft, and her belly is the moon. "Oh, Mama," Caro says, pushing up in bed. "You know what I want? I want you to braid my terrible hair." They touch cheeks; they kiss; this time it is a mother-and-daughter kiss, tolerance on one side, charming pleading on the other. Caro has always wanted something from her mother; what she wants varies, but invariably she never quite gets it. Mercedes confronts her mass of hair, warm because Caro's been sleeping in it. It is Mercedes's own hair of thirty years before. Mercedes says, "A brush," is handed one, and notices, as she begins with a particularly cruel snarl, that her daughter's left ear, triply pierced and once adorned with opals and gold, is naked, and therefore touchingly child-like again.

"I went to the doctor this morning, Mama."

"You did? So?"

"Nothing, *nada,* no dilation, no softening of the cervix. No sign that I'm going into labor. Time is so long now, Mama. A day is ten years."

At her wedding, Caro acquired not only her older husband but that husband's son, complex relations with the husband's Waspy ex-wife, and this house set remotely in the Rio Grande gorge. At first it was the house—a straggle of dim adobe rooms, very old—that puzzled Mercedes most. Dirt walls, water bugs, and neighbors with goats—they had those in Nicaragua. How to keep the grandchild from falling into the river that breathes a reedy dankness right into the house when a window's left up? Caro has no idea how children are.

"She said—"

"Who said?"

"Mama, the doctor said we might try making love. Sometimes sex gets labor going."

How children are: they scald their hands, and puffs of blister as translucently unreal as jellyfish fill their palms. They get stung, and howl. They stain themselves with food, muck, blood, dust. In their bowel movements appear lost buttons and snail shells. Rashes flourish on their thin arms and disappear overnight. Storms of coughing begin at moonrise.

"But, Mama, it's been months since we made love. Months."

In swift, habitual rhythm, Mercedes braids.

"I have to tell you what's wrong with Kevin, too." Caro glances over her shoulder to stop her mother's hands. Caro says, "A girl he liked killed herself five months ago. She swallowed a bottle of her mother's prescription pills."

Mercedes touches forehead, heart, shoulder, shoulder, "Her poor mother," Mercedes says. "Her poor father."

"Her father wasn't there."

"And why not?"

"Mama, that's irrelevant. They were divorced a long time ago. Kevin didn't even know this girl long enough to love her."

"He says that?"

"He says he loves her. How would he know? Does he have to wreck his own life now, is that love?" Caro sighs. "Hart and I try, but no one can reason with him. It will take time, we say, and he shrugs as if he hates us. He seems so far away from all our little concerns. I love him, you know. I keep trying to draw him back in."

"And?"

"Nothing works. Nothing. He's making his father crazy." Caro yawns. "And, Mama, I'm selfish enough to wish they weren't all I was thinking about right now. The baby has only this little leftover piece of my attention. Look." She tosses *Your Baby and Child* at the closet, jammed with the winsome thrift-shop dresses the unpregnant Caro fancied. "I wanted to start there," Caro says. There is a crib in the corner, but it isn't made up. The exposed mattress ticking bothers Mercedes, as does the decal of a dancing bear, one of its paws torn off. "I thought I'd get the nesting instinct," Caro says, "and instead I'm the Blob." Mercedes counts dirty teacups on the dresser. She had expected Caro's house to be cleaner, and finds herself disapproving. The disapproval is a mother's, nimbly inserting itself into a welter of other, more reasonable emotions, where it will be hard to weed out.

"Lie down. Put your head in my lap," Mercedes instructs. A pregnant daughter calls on her mother for solidity, reassurance, proof that her fears are thin as air, and will vanish at the first maternal reproof. Caro sleeps. Mercedes has her work cut out for her. This room, then the rest of the house. What is needed here is not only Mercedes's brand of astringent housekeeping but a makeshift serenity. A harmony sufficient for a baby to be born into. The old sensation of being hemmed in by need sweeps over Mercedes. Today she has come three thousand miles. She arches her tired back, and doubles an elastic band around the end of Caro's braid. On the messy bed in the sad room, Mercedes begins to shake her head, slowly at first, anxiously, tiredly, then stops. Stops to wonder what she thinks she is doing here, and how she found the strength to stay away so long.

This old woman with the quaintly strained English, her dry cheeks collapsed inward below cheekbones that bleakly suggest the skull, her still-dark eyes critically aglitter, causes Hart to feel himself a lurching monster in his own house. He rests his Frankenstein forehead in his huge white-male hands and appeals for help, for something to save him from this plate of black beans, rice, and *huevos,* two doilies of fried egg slopped from the spatula onto his plate as his wife's belly bumps the back of his chair. *Consider your secretiveness,* Phil Donahue says, far back in Hart's brain. *Has he been drinking already this morning, can anyone in this audience tell?* The old woman wields her flatware with an immigrant daintiness. She's here to save her daughter, that much is unmistakable. Black beans and rice mean home to Mercedes: her daughter is dishing up Nicaragua, where they gossiped endlessly without the benefit of U.S. Sprint, where they cooked up steaming messes of beans and rejoiced in the reign of the father.

Breakfast, for Kevin, is a cup of loganberry yogurt. He is so silent Caro does not argue with him about eggs. He can stand his father, stepmother, and Doña Mercedes only as long as it takes to consume three hundred calories. He is six feet tall.

Kevin's mother, Hannah, is away now, gone to Europe with her boyfriend, Florian, a doctor who has his own house on a canal in Amsterdam. A modest house, but filled with aqueous shimmer, with goose-down duvets, mirrors, antiques, and a bathroom with bidet, heaven for Hannah, whose home has no bathroom at all. She has been poor ever since the divorce, maliciously, flauntingly penniless, with a poverty she can throw in Hart's face. She sold their big suburban place after the divorce to buy, near El Rito, a ruin needing everything: floors sanded down, roof insulation laid in, windows double-glazed against the northern New Mexico winters. In short, a fortune vanished there. The house was a black hole, but Hannah will never divorce it, and Kevin, cutting kindling, lugging a chain saw out through biting wind to the woodpile, latching the outhouse door against the vast nights, grew up fast. In that house, alone with Hannah, he had responsibilities, and they did him no harm.

Of course Kevin led another, parallel life, as children of dissolved marriages do. Hart went through a series of viewless condos and cheap apartments. Into each of these, one after the other, Kevin helped him move. Hart would boil up two of those frozen dinners that came in pouches, then tip the steaming water, with its pale plasticky smell, into cups for instant coffee. He was troubled by insomnia, the worst of his life, and he fell in love every other month, and was bewildered when an ex-lover came knocking on his door, or ranted at him over the phone. Living long weekends with Hart, Kevin learned roughly a thousand times more about him than Hart ever knew about his own father. Moreover, Kevin seemed infatuated with an existence in which he could be the ordering force. He slid Roach Motels behind the grimy stoves, he dyed the water in the toilets azure. He scoured the sinks, he read letters left lying around, he knew and forgave everything, at least until the unexpected happened: his father and his mother began going out together. Parties, galleries. Oh, they were careful with each other, and very careful to be sure that Kev's hopes were not aroused. Hart came in so very, very softly from those dates that, one night, he overheard "You love each other, you love each other" recited by Kevin, belly-down in his soiled sleeping bag, the door of his room half open. But Hart and Hannah failed again in slow motion, because sometime in the middle of this, Hart met Caro.

Kevin swigs coffee. "Not so fast," Hart says, surprised to find himself talking in Phil Donahue's paternal tone, and is countered by his son's silence, the slender, nervous gliding of bolts into place.

Kevin met Katie at a party on their lawn alongside the river last spring, when the Rio Grande had a glassy green, rising smoothness from snowmelt, and the guests were all pleasantly sweated up from working on the fence on the slope. Among the hammering, nailing grown-ups was a girl. A mare's tail of fine dark hair clung to her baby-oiled back, and when she turned to stare at somebody over her shoulder, a line of new tenpenny nails glittered in her clenched mouth. Hart has thought back to it again and again, that girl with the indifferently beautiful back turning to reveal her sea-urchin mouth.

She was looking at Kevin for the first time. At Kevin whose dark head is bent tediously over yogurt. Hart asks, "Have you gone through that blue book yet?"

"What?"

"You were supposed to check those used-car prices, so that when we went looking you'd know what was a fair offer. You said you'd take an active part in this."

"Hart." Caro intervenes so softly it stops him. Too late.

"I will. I'm going to." But Kevin's tone is defensive, and Hart guesses he can be no help to anyone on anything yet, but it would be a good thing if he had a car. They're so isolated, out here in the gorge. They're about to disappear into baby world, leaving Kevin behind, on his own. On his slender own.

"I expect you to do what you tell me you'll do," Hart says.

Kevin swears, rattling Doña Mercedes, who draws herself up, frigid Catholicism in a housedress.

Hart, who has never had much room for anyone else's disapproval of Kevin, jumps into decisiveness. "We'll go this afternoon anyway, all right? Want to, Kev?"

"Not today," Caro says. "Not now." "*Now*" rhymes with "*miaow,*" it's so plaintive.

Is it doing Caro any good, having her mother here? At night, Caro seizes Hart's shoulder or tugs at his hair; grinding his molars together to stifle his yawn, eyes slitted, he rolls over, he asks her tenderly, "What?" and she tells him. She dreamed she was about to give birth in a strange, dirty swimming pool. She was going into labor in the stall of a public restroom, graffiti spangling its walls, "FUCK YOU" and "FUCK ME" and the telephone numbers. Or the baby was born and she'd lost it. This last dream was particularly vulnerable to transmutation. She'd lost the baby in Safeway, she'd lost the baby in the hospital, or she'd left the baby sleeping on the lawn and it rolled into the river. After any of these nightmares, she is slow to be consoled. A back rub, a cup of tea, another quilt added to her heap, and she cries in his arms before sealing herself back into sleep, leaving him awake to prowl the house, studying the black, child-eating river through the living room's plate glass.

"I won't know where to find you," Caro says, "if you're wandering all over Santa Fe."

"Your mother is here," Hart says. The old woman gleams his way, dispatching her coffee. Caro travels light-footedly to the pot. Odd, for all her bulk, that she is still so prettily swift in anticipating her mama's wish. Mercedes pats the arm that pours the coffee, and Hart sees what he sometimes doubts: that they are, they clearly are, mother and daughter.

"Maybe you should go." Reversing herself, Caro grows cheerful. "Maybe your being gone will bring it on. A watched pot."

"I'll call in the middle of the afternoon," Hart promises.

The daughter bends for a hairpin and deftly drives it into the old woman's knot of white horsehair without again acknowledging her husband's existence.

One after the other, the cars they search out are junk. Blasted Chevys, battered Volkswagen Beetles well into their second or third mechanical reincarnations. All morning and well into afternoon, the only car Kevin likes is a brutalized MG with a bumper sticker reading HUG A VET. The vet is Monroe, idly tossing Oreos to his rottweiler while he explains that though he has led a long and happy life with the car, he could be persuaded to part with it now for seven hundred and fifty dollars. "What a crock," Hart says, over cheesecake at Denny's. Kevin argues hard. He's mechanical, and anyway he has a friend who works on foreign cars and owns all the wrenches. The MG is cool.

"No," Hart says, but the MG appeals to him as a car for Kevin. Its pleasingly seedy interior, so small that a girl (What girl? When will Kevin risk another girl?) would have to ride knee to knee with the driver, its quality of scraped daredeviltry so great for a first car. So infinitely desirable. "It'll cost a fortune in parts."

"I can take care of it. I will." Kevin's fingers alight on his breastbone—a vow, an unconscious one. Wow, Hart thinks, happy at this eagerness, which could not be more genuine. For once, possibly for the first time, Kevin has forgotten Katie Dubov.

"You'd have to."

"So, let me show you."

"So, let me think about it."

"I had an offer this morning," Monroe says when they swing by for a parting look. "It might still come through. I can't guarantee you this car will still be here when you get around to making up your minds."

"Let's go for it," Kevin pleads.

"That's not the way to make a major purchase, honey, under pressure," Hart says, and the magic of covetousness dies from his son's face. Hart has slipped and called Kevin "honey" in front of this earringed vet with his mean dog careening around his bare yard and his afternoon's beer cans lined up on the MG's hood, and something of the car's promise, the smallscale imported machismo it holds out to Kevin, dims.

Therefore, and probably predictably, Hart grows anxious to have the car. A subtle current of remorse, Hart's toward Kevin, runs just underneath the surface of the transaction, which Monroe senses and would exploit if he did not feel sorry for Kevin.

Kevin twists the key, and the MG startles into rattletrap authority. This is the thrill Hart has sabotaged for his son: Kevin's pleasure is partly, mostly, faked, and rings false. Hart says, "I'll follow you," and does, taking from his glove compartment a Spice Islands jar that once held—he sniffs—nutmeg. He drinks Johnnie Walker Black and tries to remember what newborns are like. They can't hold up their heads, he thinks, and when they mew, you wrap them tightly in a blanket so that only their faces show, making little Taos Indians of them. He thinks he remembers Kevin that way. How could that girl bear to kill herself? The MG's canvas roof is up. It is evidence of Kevin's tense, imperfect bliss that he did not at once wrench the roof down for this first drive. Black exhaust smokes from the MG's tailpipe on a long curve, and the father's heart goes *guilty, guilty, guilty,* all the way home.

Caro comes up the slope, her belly leading, her flip-flops clapping. The MG is exposed in all its failings. Its dented fender, its dappling of rust. Its broken headlight, crackled white quartz in chrome. Caro's disbelief, hidden by her sunglasses, finds a gesture: the flat of a hand set in the deep saddle of her back, her back arching more deeply, her belly jutting more extravagantly. "How much?"

"Seven hundred and fifty. What do you think?"

"Do I think we have seven hundred and fifty?"

"Would I have bought the car otherwise?"

"You don't agree you're sometimes impulsive?"

"No matter what it cost, you would have implied 'Too much,' Caro, wouldn't you? Anyway, it's too late now. It's done."

"He'll take it back."

"You don't know this guy."

"He'll take it back," she repeats. "The stupid, senseless greedy who sold it to you, you'll make him take it, you'll tell him it's not what you want after all. It's not safe. It's already been wrecked once, hasn't it?"

"Don't," Kevin says.

"Kevin is a good, reliable driver. You have to—"

"How can you yell?" Kevin says. "She's pregnant. How can you stand there and yell at her? If she hates the car, I don't like it either. I don't want it. I could see you thinking it would do me good."

Caro turns dark sunglass lenses his way. "Would it?" she asks. "Help?"

"Right. Would it help for me to have a car you hate? Right."

"If I stopped hating it?"

"If you stopped hating it, you'd be lying."

"If it was something you wanted, I wouldn't hate it. I'd stop."

"Because you think it would make me better."

"Because nothing else seems—"

"You think a *car* could do that?"

"Kev," his father warns.

"It's not going to be a car," Kevin says.

"I can see that," Hart says. "Then what?"

"It's not going to be you," Kevin says. "Not a swine like you." He looks at Caro. "And it's not you. I don't know you."

She protests, "You know me."

"Kevin, you stop," Hart says.

"You love my father who left my mother when she did fucking nothing to deserve it. You don't know how good she is. I don't have any idea why you married someone like him. I don't have any idea why you're having this baby."

Caro says, "Ow," her expression a delicate mix: alarm, satisfaction, wistfulness, fear. "It doesn't hurt," she says, marveling downward so that her sunglasses slide to the end of her long, upturned nose. "It feels like a little ribbon rippling around, like a drawstring getting drawn in."

"It's my fault," Kevin says.

"So what?" Caro says. "This is a fine time."

"You think everything in the world is your fault," Hart says to Kevin, and to Caro, "You're supposed to walk."

"To walk? Walk where?"

"Down the road. To encourage the contractions. Come on."

"Come too, Kev? Keep me company?"

He won't. "I don't want to be here."

Hart takes her elbow. "Another little pain's coming girdling around," she says. "Ow. It's nice. Ow. If my mother wasn't here, nothing would have been done in time, would it? The baby's bed would never have been made. Do you think she's cooking dinner?"

"Walk," Hart tells her.

Kevin runs down the slope. The screen door's single bark rides up the hot air toward them, and Caro asks, "Why did he run?"

"To boil water," Hart says.

They walk down the dirt road, Caro swatting early mosquitoes from her bare arms, her gait wary and majestic. "Nothing else," she says, and ten minutes later adds, "It's not happening." She's still wearing her sunglasses, but her mouth, when she turns her face up, is stricken.

"Hey, so we go eat Mercedes's dinner," Hart says. "It's not the end of the world."

"Don't you want this baby?" Caro asks. And clop-clops away from him through hard sunlight, full of hurt. She would run if she could.

"We won't let you go on too long after your due date, no," Dr. Mendez says.

Caro asks, sounding anxious, "You don't induce labor, do you?"

"When the baby is two weeks late, the placenta is aging, and may no longer be supporting the baby well, and, yes, we sometimes do induce labor. First we'd run some tests to determine whether the baby is under stress—"

"Then Pitocin," Hart says.

"Then Pitocin, possibly, yes," the doctor says. She smiles from Caro to Hart, who is visibly anxious too, and asks, "Did you try my suggestion?"

They both glance guiltily away.

Hannah's Dutch boyfriend, Florian, has a head of curly hair and a libertine's merry eyes. He has, in addition, a quality of possessing great personal freedom in his relations with women. He is simply very clever with women; he knows how to catch them up immediately into conversation, a kind of conversation that another man would find repellent, almost viciously competitive—Florian presenting himself and his virtues—but often enough, women respond to this approach delightedly, indulgently, coquettishly. Sexually. Women love Florian. He wandered into a bookstore in Santa Fe and captured Hannah, who had been slouching against a wall under a bad but beautifully framed print, abstractedly rubbing strands of her own hair between thumb and forefinger, estimating their loss of silkiness, the onslaught of her own middle age, the probability that she would never have another child, her positively oppressive sense that she should at last read *The Mill on the Floss,* she should devote herself to that fat paperback for a hundred nights under her electric blanket although *Great Expectations* looked like more fun. Spendthrift that she was, she could afford both, and just as she was about to throw herself into the arms of the Victorians, there was cool Florian, his sexually forthright city as far from dampened England as it was possible to get in Europe, his eyes wondering just who *she* was, evaluating and elevating her, because there had been in Hannah's recent life such a dearth of male attention of any kind, shape, or form—except for that of her son and her ex-husband, of course; how could they count?—that finding herself read as a sexual creature caused her to unslouch herself, shake her fair head, and let her eyes focus on this interested foreign face. Here was Florian, full of promise. He'd come for her. Both knew it. It wasn't long before they disappeared together.

Now, whatever has happened between the divorced husband and wife, and almost everything has, she has never before left Hart behind. Hart knows about Florian because Hannah has always confided in him. Her confiding in him is a symptom of the fact that from the world of men who approached her, Hannah had chosen Hart for herself, and remained assiduously true to her choice well after they were divorced, suffering rather lightly the inevitable desertion of one fleeting boyfriend, a carpenter she had taken on more passively than passionately. Or so it seemed to her ex-husband. Since the carpenter, who left last year, the one and only man Hannah has slept with is Hart. Their lovemaking was an act so baldly needy and spontaneous, so short, unadorned, and potentially devastating, that Hart can't bring himself to weigh its meaning. Oddly, it appeared to mean more to him than to Hannah. What right has Hannah to flaunt her new equilibrium in his face? She was once sure she could not live without him. No longer. She doesn't even like him, she told him in bed. An amazing, cold, unexpected remark. It hurt and stirred him. In bed with her he had felt the change begin, a subtle thing and small, dwarfed by the bitterness in her voice when she repeated, "I don't like you. I don't like the things you do." The change, pitted from the first against skepticism harsh as Hannah's, had nonetheless begun there, in Hannah's bed, under Hannah's quilts, with Hannah's electric heater purring away at the sole of the single lovely, high-arched foot she aimed at it, with roughly the same degree of unself-consciously sensual practicality with which she had, five minutes before, shoved her pelvis upward to receive him more deeply. More satisfactorily. She had managed that for herself, though she no longer loved him.

Worse, as he soon came to realize, she was ashamed of having slept with him. As she came and went, dropping off or retrieving their son, Hart kept getting whiffs of her shame. Caro, five months pregnant, had begun to show. Hannah's shame smelled like a child's dirty hair, a sodden diaper, a cast about to come off a broken arm—some soiled, infinitely intimate thing.

This was the situation Florian stole her from. Hart, who can't blame her for going, can't forgive Hannah, either, for causing him to feel as if he has just, freshly, lost her; as if it were not he who had brought about their divorce, but her whimsical infatuation with Florian that tore apart some old, honest, married love.

When really Hart's only honest, relatively sane love is for Caro. Until she got pregnant she was, in bed, rich felicity, his great good luck. Pregnancy made her queer and touchy; her tongue flew through astounding recriminations even as her body receded from him to the pearly white, indifferent shore of late pregnancy. The fetus defeated its father, or at least its father's desire. It was, in Hart's experience, an unprecedented thing for desire to do—simply to leave him as easily as it had come—but once it was gone, he settled himself in to play expectant husband. He could believe himself happy among the squatting and blowing couples of their natural-childbirth class. He could time a pretend contraction with the best of them, and never avert his eyes from the film when the baby's head, surfacing like the glossily dark pit of a halved avocado, crowned in the huge vagina.

He pads barefoot into the cold kitchen. Mercedes has tidied it until it reflects the stasis of—of Heaven, he supposes, or possibly of her Brooklyn garret, sanctified by widowhood. He throws open the refrigerator door. His scrotum contracts in brilliant Arctic air, his heart aches, and he smells old bologna. He makes himself a huge, comforting feast of a sandwich, like a cartoon husband comically unaware of his place in the world—his humiliatingly small niche gazed into by huge, decisive women as they pass. Well, hello, telephone. The receiver's poison-control-center sticker, skull and crossbones, glows in the dark. Hart remembers the way that, in Hannah's warm bed, he felt the brisk angel's wing of his future pass over his heart. What had he wanted, how had he judged his chances, at that instant, her heater purring, the points of her collarbone flaring in her flattish, freckled chest when she threw her head back into the pillow, when she came? There is the telephone. Her number is on a slip of paper held with a magnet to their refrigerator. Like it or not, here it is, his new life: his ex-wife's number on the refrigerator among the coupons for Pampers, the Polaroids of friends' kids, the pre-divorce, pre-distrust picture of Kevin, then smaller and more radiant, crowned by a soccer ball, crowing with triumph, sun pouring down or him, on the green field he spent his eleventh summer on. Caro's eternal unfinished shopping list that reads *Skim milk, chicken breasts, toilet paper.* As far as he knows never a day passes when his household does not need chicken breasts. Caro is ready for this baby. Is he? He examines himself with an intensity that eats away a great rust of habitual, second-nature self-deceit and finds that, no, astonishingly, no, assuredly, *no,* he's not ready for this baby. He wades through the muck of this *no,* this terrifying black *no* nothing in him rises up to refute, to the telephone, and taps out the digits that will fly his voice toward a satellite, ricochet it off spacy cold metal to Europe, to that decaying old sea city where she is. *She answers on the second ring.* His surprise is minor, given the event.

But then again, so is hers. "You don't sound good," she says. "Let me sit up so I can think. There. I'm sitting." Then she recollects the terms they parted on. "What do you want? Is it Kev?"

"Nothing's wrong with Kev. This is me."

She's silent. "Hannah," he says.

"Yes. I said, *yes,* here I am, you found me. I'm hanging up."

"No, Hannah, no, it's this baby. I don't want this baby. I'm not ready."

She laughs.

"Hannah, don't laugh. I don't want it."

"Then you *are* in trouble," she says with a lilt, her voice not as unkind as her words.

"Don't tell me that."

"Don't tell you that? When anyone can see it? I'm going now."

"Hannah. Say you won't go until I'm all right."

"I can't do that," she says.

"*Please.*"

Hart turns, hearing a sound. Behind him in the darkened kitchen, gazing at him with merciless, timeless recognition, is his mother-in-law. His mother-in-law has just heard him beg, despairingly, in the dark kitchen, "*Please.*"

He swipes a dish towel from the counter and hangs it in front of his genitals. He says very clearly, "I'm not a bad man. Not as bad as you think."

Hannah says distantly, into his ear, "Try A. A., Hart."

Mercedes says nothing at all.

He fidgets the dish towel until his genitals are completely sheltered. How long does she mean to stand there? He says, "I can change."

Hannah says distantly, into his ear, "Good-bye."

Mercedes says nothing at all.

It leaves him nothing to go on, no clue about what will happen, the silence in which Mercedes sweeps from the kitchen.

In the small bathroom, in a dimness that seems to her unnatural—no lights outside the window; sounds, but no lights—Mercedes undresses down to the nitroglycerin patch she donned two hours ago against proof of her son-in-law's infidelity. It had been, for Mercedes, a scene of great violence, the big man with the dish towel hanging before him; the woman, whoever she was, who is so shameless as to fool with the husband of a hugely pregnant woman, to quarrel with him over the telephone in his own home in the middle of the night. In the middle of the night when such things should have been long ago settled, and the husband and wife in bed together.

Of course, Mercedes reflects, her own husband sometimes left their bed at just such an hour. Of course he went catting around, dishonoring their life together and all she was. His infidelity, great secret that it was, still pains Mercedes, two decades later and thousands of miles away, as she is an old woman meticulously flossing her long, elegant yellow teeth. He was unfaithful, and it was love between him and Mercedes. Though he was unfaithful, it was love and it remained love. Once or twice when he'd left the bed, she'd been no less pregnant than her besotted daughter is now. The difference between Caro and Mercedes is that she, Mercedes, will never see her husband's face again. No one exists to come back to bed. In her garret there are pictures, of course, but none of them are precisely the face she wants. The long, gallant salt-and-pepper mustache, the wide wings of the aggressive nose, the cobble of chin, the bright lover's eyes, had not photographed well. They are inexact as memory never was. Seizing the nitroglycerin patch by its corner, Mercedes peels it away. It leaves a small chemically scorched rectangle, pink as sunburn, over her heart.

He said, "I'm not a bad man," and though that was a baffling thing for him to assert under the circumstances, there is something in it Mercedes can't dismiss. When he said "I can change," it was, and she knows it was, the truth, and so they will go on together, her daughter and this palely alien American, and their life together will baffle Mercedes, surely, whatever else she learns about it, just the way her life would baffle them—or, for that matter, any of her children—if she ever chose to tell them anything about it. But really it was none of their business, how you lived. It was their business that you took care of them, that you were there to nurse them through fevers and catch them before they fell into the river, but what, apart from love like that, did they need? The truth is that she is almost done with them.

In her robe she stares down the hallway to the opening window, and finds Kevin climbing clumsily in. To Mercedes's surprise, he is naked except for drenched cutoff jeans. This must be her night for coming across hugely tall, nearly naked Anglos. He is as astonished to see her as she is to see him. He could not have expected from her such a torrent of hair, or such self-possession.

"I'm sorry," he says, crouching over the window. "You heard something, and were frightened."

"Do I look frightened? Is this the way you come into the house?"

"I am sorry," he says, and then, as if she were not standing there, he rakes his hand down his side, his long boyish bare rib cage, and Mercedes, coming closer, sees the rising dappling of hundreds of mosquito bites. He goes for them feverishly with bitten fingernails, so harsh with himself she can hear the scratching. She says, "You'll bleed." "I can't help it." "Stop that," she commands, but his is the impotent impatience of someone whose skin is *itching,* and despite his evident wish to appear polite to her, he can't stop. She reaches forward and seizes his wrist, which has a compact, knit-together solidity that feels adult and male, as does his reluctance to yield to her, but she is a general of little emergencies. "My room," she directs, and once there daubs his spots with oil of camphor from a neat brown bottle as he sits on the edge of her bed, leaning forward, his huge elbows on his big knees, his entire attitude a fusion of miserable courtesy and real relief. Through the tonic vapor of camphor she smells cold water drying from a child's skin. "You were in the river," she accuses his back.

Embarrassment freezes him.

"I could never have gone into a river," she tells his back. At his nape, his hair is drying in a curl. "No matter what I felt, I could never have gone into a river."

"It's our river," he says, and shudders when she touches his back again.

"You mean you're used to it."

"The way you're used to the subway, and the gangs."

"I do not court death," she says.

"Because to you, it's a sin."

"To you, it's not?" she asks, her voice going provocatively rueful. "And your father, and my daughter who loves you now, and the little brother or sister who is coming? You go into the water thinking of what they'll feel?"

His resentment is intact again. It lies in the millimetric tensing of his cold white back, and in the texture of his skin, which shifts in that instant from a grateful to a guarded passivity, so that she stops her doctoring and waits until he says, "I do think of them."

"You don't think of them enough, then. Imagine a vast hurt."

She gives him a moment to imagine it.

"Imagine them feeling it."

She gives him another moment.

"You would cause them such pain."

The expanse of his bare back, with its fine muscles, its rather daintily set shoulder blades, and the long channel, deeply indented, of the spine, waits on her.

She says, "You can't do that to them."

She says, "It's simply a thing you can't do."

She says, tipping the bottle into cotton, fitting cotton to a welt, "You're through with this now?"

He says, "I just want to stop feeling what I feel."

She takes a deep breath. She inhales hugely, as against some formidable physical task. She apologizes to her dead husband's beautiful forgotten face for the calm with which she is about to tell this truth. She says, "You will."

When Hart rolls over, he is as quiet as can be, but it's no use. He dislodges Caro from sleep. Her curly long hair lies in a mess on the pillow. When she turns toward him, he tries to take his bearings from her expression. "I had a good dream," she says. "I was riding my mother's shoulders down this dirt road, and it was going dark, and I was rubbing a leaf across her forehead, I don't know why."

"Why was that a good dream?"

"I had some idea the leaf was magic. That is could keep us all safe."

"You know what I wish?" Hart says. "I wish that damn girl had listened for her mother's key in the lock before she started swallowing."

"No one could have expected there to be a traffic jam that evening," Caro says.

He tries to settle into a position that is both companionable and will still allow for the possibility of sleep, but she sits up tailor-fashion and begins caressing her belly.

"Anything?" Hart says.

"Not a thing."

"You and your body," he says. "Don't you think you're as stubborn as your mother? Let me ask you something."

"Ask."

"What is it? Why hasn't she ever liked me?"

"She likes you." He looks at her, arching his eyebrows morosely. "My mother," she says. "My mother is a mystery. All the time when we were children, living together in the tiniest house"—she fixes him with a dark, judicious, almost accusing gaze—"in intimacy you can't even begin to imagine, each of use knowing every single thing about all the others, we still knew she was a mystery. I don't think you can change her mind about you, Hart. But it doesn't matter to me, what she thinks."

What will happen now?, Hart wonders, resting his knuckles on her defiant belly, pretending to knock, saying softly, "Come out, come out, and I'll be good to you," and she laughs and falls carefully onto her side in the rumpled sheets, the quilt sliding silently from the bed, she bringing her knees up and giving him a quarter-profile glance, and he locks a long arm around her, above her belly, under her breasts, and enters her from behind, and their pleasure in each other is so acute they forget it is meant to bring on pain.

A Conversation with Elizabeth Tallent

Would you talk, generally, about how stories gather for you and finally make it to the page? How do you recognize an idea or detail as your own—something from which you might try to make a story?

You just know, like the way you know you're interested in a person. It is almost a body intuition. Sometimes I've had a more cerebral take on something, especially if it was political, and I always think it would be terrific to work with that. But unless I get something more visceral, it's not going to happen as a story. Sometimes I come at a story backwards, by trying to write an essay. I'll get an image that's more fictional. Or a character gets into an essay that I think might be somebody I like and I want to stay with a little. But it's really messy. It's hard to explain to students: You're just getting these little corner-of-the-eye glimpses, and then you're going to try and make something of it, and it's mostly a very arduous and piecemeal process—kind of leapfrogging from something you're more sure of to different things you're trying on, different ways a story could go. It feels overwhelming to them.

Those little corner-of-eye glimpses. Do you have a lot of them going on at any given time? How do you organize them in your head—or not?

It used to be all scraps of paper in my pocket, but then I did make a conscious commitment to getting it down in a notebook. I have three different notebooks right now, but what I like best is the computer. I like going right to that and having a file, because it feels even more ephemeral than ever. You can put anything there, and all you have to do is do the delete the thing and it's gone. I like that feeling as a way to take care of those little glimmers.

Is there a folder on your computer for each idea?

No.

So it's just one big, amorphous glimmer folder. Do you ever print it out and look at it? How do you use it?

I print it out to be sure that it exists. Sometimes I'm searching for something that's in there that could go in a work of fiction, but I don't know where it is. So I have to read back through the whole thing. Sometimes there's something very unexpected about a character in there, and I think, that could be *this* person. The disorganization works for me. If I were more organized, I'd lose lots of things.

If you were actually to print what's in the folder on any given day, how many pages might it be?

Not as many as you'd think. Single-spaced, probably fifteen pages. And they're the briefest annotations. They're totally cryptic. They'd be useless to anyone else. I remember them for years and years. I have one that just says, "gloves on the dashboard" that I've never used, but every time I think of that I really remember that dashboard, the snow that was falling, seeing the gloves. And I know that's a story. It's just—waiting.

I have one that just says, "gloves on the dashboard" that I've never used, but every time I think of that I really remember that dashboard, the snow that was falling, seeing the gloves.

Do you think that the ambiguity of process is what students have most difficulty with?

I have a short list of what's difficult for them and that would be on the top. They often don't understand how long it is from the mess to the story. Also, thinking of experience apart from the way they've seen it presented—originality or resistance to the narratives that they inherit—gets to be more and more difficult as we have this saturation in narrative from pop culture.

Do you mean they can't get out of their own experience? For example, you might say, "This would be a stronger story if the main character were an only child," and the student would respond, "But I have three brothers"?

No. It would be their cliché of what an only child would be. Or coming out, or suicidal friends. They don't know it, but they're seeking reassurance when they tell something in a familiar way. They feel passionate about it, and passion feels fresh. It's hard to say, okay, this *is* passionate, but it's drawn entirely along conventional lines.

Looking at a draft of a story, how do you recognize problems and then go about solving them?

What works best is just parting from it for a while, which I find difficult because there's this bond you feel, and to back away from it long enough to be able to get a clean take on it is hard. I'm really obsessive. I want to just be there with it! But that's what I do. I put it in a drawer. Then I come back and I do a reading, beginning to end, trying to be as honest as I can.

You mark on the manuscript as you go.

I do—like I would do the work of a student writer. I get distracted thinking, that could be good, that could be good—and then it's just *not.* So I have to give it my genuine response. Sometimes I write, "Could be good." But not yet!

Are there particular problems you always seem to have? Are you more likely to revise by adding or taking out of a draft?

I get really fancy, so I have to fix that. But I'm not a taker-outer. I am more interested in getting at whatever I wanted to get at. That's been a real change for me from the early work, which was a lot about taking out, refining. That dove-tailed with *The New Yorker*'s aesthetic of the time. I'm so much less interested now in refining and much more in pursuit. I think, if I got interested to begin with, I'm going to really try and see if I can find it.

I'm so much less interested now in refining and much more in pursuit.

To pin it down?

Trying to get to it. More like archaeology.

So it feels like it's there. You just have to find it.

Yes. But it took me a long time to believe that. Taking things out, you can work so fast. If you go through work with students at any workshop and say, "Let's take four pages out of this story," you make it a better, tighter story. Of course, I want them to know about cutting. But now I'm more interested in a kind of work and a kind of teaching that says, "What were you *after?*"

How do you know a story's finished?

Again, you just have a feeling. Suddenly, it's as if you're holding a perfect river pebble. Once something's published, I could probably go back and find things that I could do, but it would be a matter of *me* changing, me becoming a different reader and a more grown-up one. I have to let the story be itself and be willing to say certain flaws were probably implicit to my voice when I wrote it. The *self* is flawed, and by process you can get past that wish for perfection. Most of the narratives I love are really highly imperfect.

Most of the narratives I love are really highly imperfect.

Like raising children. They become what they become; you have to let them go.

It is. It so much is.

Would you talk about your story "No One's a Mystery" in terms of the process you just described?

Well, this is where I completely contradict myself. That story—I was *sure* it was a novel. I was sure it would include a lot about veterinary medicine. I had all these pages and pages that were about dealing with animals. I was interested in considering two different relationships to animals—the veterinarian and the girl who didn't know much about medicine and was only seeing damage and animals in fear. I was really entranced by that. But I kept going back to this one little piece of it, and finally one morning I looked at it and I thought, this *is* their relationship. It was that river pebble thing. There's a lot more about them that I could have gotten into the story, but that was really all I wanted—or all *they* wanted.

That one moment in the truck.

Yes. I was interested in confinement and uneasiness in couples. A lot of that happens for us in cars—and, in the West, pickup trucks, which are even smaller than cars because the space you occupy is smaller.

Is the finished story pretty much the same as the piece of the novel you kept looking at?

Yeah. I was so disappointed. I looked at it and I thought, you're just not going to move, are you? It was an exception to the way I usually work. I don't remember fiddling very much with it at all. I knew he had given her this diary. In the novel, of course, she was going to write in it. But I liked the idea of the book before she inscribes her own experiences. Just getting it, having it given to her.

Student readers sometimes observe that it's a "little girl" present, that he infantilizes her in giving it.

It's so interesting that they would see it that way. I think they're quite right. He gives a gift that suggests that, but also he gives her something that she can lock. I think he's saying, "Keep some things apart," which reflects adult love. She's so much younger; she's enamored. He's saying, "Love is not about giving absolutely everything." So he has it both ways. He *does* see the little girl that she also is.

There are other objects in the story—and small, specific, personal details, too—that resonate with meaning. The bleached white seam of Jack's jeans, the bottle of tequila between his legs. They work like seeds. The information they carry within them springs up in the reader's mind full-blown, like a flower.

Somebody asked me, "Is reality really like this for you?" I said, "Yes." It's the way reality arrives on my nerve endings. I come from a sort of Updikean way of thinking. "We are here to praise." I don't mean that in the religious way. I mean it in the sense that in physics they now think that without human observation we can't have a complete account of the universe. That's what writers *do*. That's what I like to try to get on the page. I'm interested in time, which I don't think any other art but writing can convey. Painting can be viewed with intense perception, but it's prized out of time. Writing, you can perceive time at work. And I'm just so in love with that.

I'm interested in time, which I don't think any other art but writing can convey.

To just, in the most literal way, create the world on the page.

Yes. To record it as it is human.

That goes a long way to explain the strong sense place plays in your work, generally—whether it's the interior of a pickup truck or the larger western landscape.

What does it *smell* like in this pickup truck? I can't imagine anyone else would be interested in that, but that's what I'm trying to get on the page. Place and particularity, part of the drive to write comes from that. There's a terrific book by a colleague of mine, Robert Harrison, who teaches here. It's *Dominion of the Dead.* He said that we are among the first generation in human evolution who didn't live where their parents were buried. He used it as an argument about what it does to our sense of ourselves as human. When I read that, I thought—we are the ones who are writing about that kind of transience, where people don't connect to place in the traditional ways.

Do your characters grow from your strong interest in a certain place?

Not really, but as soon as I'm aware of the character, I'll start trying to perceive how they fit into the place. They could have just got there. I like that we could be writing about just getting there. But *I* always want to know the place myself, as the narrator. I think a lot of what we do wrong in American culture is because we have so much presumption about how little it takes to know a place. Philip Roth says this great thing. When he married the actor Claire Bloom, he went to England. He said, "I couldn't write about England for ten years." Ten years sounds about right to me. He said he couldn't do English voices. The common assumption is, you hear one English voice, you hear them all. But it's subtle and elusive.

Jack's a middle-aged married man, cheating on his wife with a high school girl. We shouldn't like him, but we do. Why?

If I have an answer to that it would be because I think that we might like characters as far as we might discern their capacity for empathy, their capacity to like another character or to engage. But as soon as I say it I can think of all the counterexamples to that. Still, they can behave really badly, but if they can do that one thing we're drawn to them.

What's your sense of Jack? Who he is, why is he in that story?

I was very interested in the binds we get into. It's hard to live in America and not be aware that you could shrug your sadness off, you could run away. [Updike's] Rabbit runs away. It's a tremendous American narrative, lighting out for the territories. I'm interested in the people who can clearly see that as an alternative, but haven't done it. I don't think of it as

I was very interested in the binds we get into. It's hard to live in America and not be aware that you could shrug your sadness off, you could run away.

being noble. I just got interested in what could keep you right there. I don't even know if Jack could articulate his unhappiness.

What about the girl? We don't get any information at all about the way she looks, about her family or her life. We know her only through what she sees and how she responds to it. We don't even know her name. Why?

I knew more about her, I had written more about her, but when I looked at the piece it seemed not to need that. I wrote the story a long time ago. Now I would probably resist that and say more is what I want.

Still, it works perfectly as it is. So your instinct to leave a lot out must have been right. How can a writer know what needs to be in a story and what is better left out?

That is such a consuming question, and the answer changes story to story. What I tell my students about, what I try to feel in myself, is interest. As long as I'm working and I'm interested in this aspect or there's a question and I don't know the answer yet but it feels like, oh yeah, that *is* a good question about that person and to consider it might give me a way to approach the story, I keep going. Look at "Hills Like White Elephants." You are—satisfied sounds too cold, given the story, but you *get* that relationship, you understand it. You don't need to stay with them through the actual abortion.

Maybe what you're saying, really, is that the writer needs to know what the story is in order to know what can be left out. It's part of what you're puzzling out as you figure out what the story is. When it becomes that pebble, it is what it is.

Yes. It tells us a lot. As soon as you write a page, that page can talk right back to you. I think there's a transition in one's development as a writer where at first you think, you have to bring everything to this page, you have to know just how to go about this. The further along you get the more you know that, eventually, there's going to be that word, that one word, that you will recognize as interesting, and it's going to tell you what to do with the story.

Eventually, there's going to be that word, that one word, that you will recognize as interesting, and it's going to tell you what to do with the story.

So as you're trying to learn what the story is, the story is speaking back to you saying, yes, no, this, that. This is difficult for students: the idea that the great questions about writing fiction are not answerable questions, just—questions. It's all about discovering ways to think about your story, or any story.

And to let each story be different. I think that there's a tremendous impulse to get the hang of it. To get students to slow down, to go story by story so that their stories begin to be different from each other, seems to be valuable, a thing we can do as teachers.

Information comes to the reader so economically in the story, often sideways, almost an afterthought. The narrator is looking at his boots, and she says, "the same boots he'd been wearing for the two years I'd known him." It also comes by way of dialogue. In fact, except for a few little descriptive passages, that story is almost all dialogue. How do you know when to convey information in a story? How do you create dialogue that informs, but doesn't feel like it's doing that?

I am interested in information. I have a visual analog, thinking of it as like the vanishing point in a painting. You need to feel secure about that, and that security is *instantly* translated to the reader's sense of security. Here it gets sort of quasi-mystical, because I think if *you* don't know certain things—and that's the Hemingway thing—then there will be a muddle or obscurity, some kind of waffling in the text. Reworking it, if you can point to that waffling, you know what you need to clear up.

So what you're saying is that it's organic, in a sense. If the writer knows—

It will be there. But you can also pick up on the things you didn't know. If it never occurs to you in the emotional narration to figure out what they had for lunch, then you don't need to know it. If it somehow figures, then you're going to need to get it in there. I used to be really into doing it in slivers, and now I still think that's useful, but only one way to get at it.

What other techniques have you developed?

I might try to do it with objects if I thought it could get us to something good. Why those boots? How does a guy get invested in a certain pair of boots? You know those guys with the boots; it's their identity. But what do they actually go through? Do you know the first time you put the boots on that those are *the* boots? Now I might get more caught up in that than I used to.

How do you think that evolution in your own work happened? Was it a shift in what you wanted to accomplish with your work?

Yeah. I think you stay with one thing until it ceases to reward you. I wrote an awful lot of stories where I wasn't feeling very engaged by what I was doing. So I kind of had to f--- up. And it was, like, a *long* time. But I persisted because I had this sense that this was what I did well.

I think you stay with one thing until it ceases to reward you.

Staying with something familiar.

Yes, exactly. Yes! I think a good teacher could maybe have made me see that. But I didn't work with any teachers, except for Grace Paley—for one week. I have no MFA.

How did you come to writing, then?

Archaeology. When I found archaeology in college, it was what I wanted. I thought that was really how I'd spend my life. I love objects. I love old things.

And writing is archaeology, in a sense—archaeology of the heart. Finding the right detail is like finding that detail in a civilization that says, oh look, this is how they stored their grain.

Yes. What I think about with short stories—and I did southwestern archaeology—is how if someone was really good with ceramics they could take a pot shard from someplace in a pueblo ruin and tell you something about the matrilineage.

The diary in "No One's a Mystery" works exactly like that. It's an artifact that causes the reader to puzzle about the person, the relation. And the black dress in "Black Dress."

What I liked about a black dress was that there are not that many artifacts in our culture that we read in common, but we read the little black dress in certain ways.

Objects are so important in stories. One chronic problem you see in student writing is a kind of random, ineffective choice of objects. How do you approach that problem with your students?

Somebody had "Smells like a rose," in a story, so I went into the garden and got five different kinds of roses. There's one that's supposed to smell like myrrh—not that I've ever smelled myrrh. But it's extremely erotic. Then there's tea rose—that smells very clean. And all the roses from the '50s, which were about gaudiness, that don't smell at all. I brought them in, passed them around and I said, okay, "Smells like a rose." I tested them this way, too. I said, "Name ten things that bloom on this campus." And they couldn't!

"Honey" is a longer, more complicated story than "No One's a Mystery," more representative of your work. You juggle all these things—love, infidelity, divorce, children of divorce, reconfigured families, a house out in the country, babies. Lots of babies! They keep refiguring into new patterns, like bits of glass in a kaleidoscope. Would you talk about your material, what it is about these things that fascinates you?

I had some partly ignorant sense that babies and infants, toddlers had mostly been excluded from fiction, and that pregnancy, which seemed to me the most fascinating ontological condition, had mostly been excluded from fiction. When I was in labor, I remember thinking, I read all the time and I've never read this in fiction! In fact, it is pretty rare. Maybe you need to be a little willfully ignorant; I mean, there are certain things I probably kept on the periphery. But I had a sense that this was new stuff. I'm so enamored of how the body gets into fiction, especially the sexual body. I was also interested in those moments where

I'm so enamored of how the body gets into fiction, especially the sexual body. I was also interested in those moments where readers would resist it.

readers would resist it. I had amniocentesis. What is more interesting than the experience of protecting something and then having the culture say, you know, you absolutely have to stick a needle into the womb? So I wrote about that and my *New Yorker* editor said, "But we have never had amniocentesis in a story in *The New Yorker* before. We'd like you to take it out." I felt like I got to see a moment where the culture tries to say, "Don't write that. Don't go there." She said, "We made Laurie Colwin take out amniocentesis." And I thought, "You know what? You already got Laurie Colwin, you're not going to get me."

"Honey" isn't exactly about pregnancy, but it's Caro's pregnancy that brings the tensions in the story to bear. It's told, not from her point of view, however, but from the points of view of her husband and mother. Writers don't use multiple points of view much anymore. What made you decide on using both points of view in this story?

I still like the thing fiction can do in giving you the event refracted through different sensibilities. I like what it does to structure because, right from the get-go, it rules out any kind of classic arc—conflict, crisis, resolution. Because the characters are not going to perceive things the same way, sometimes they don't perceive the same conflict. Then how could they see the same thing as a crisis? Can a person in a story have a crisis that remains invisible to other people in the story? Can one person come to closure, but nobody else in the story does? It's a good way to take form apart and come at it from really different angles. I had the sense that the short story form was getting tremendously refined—I had definitely leanings that way, but that it was secretly this elastic, accommodating form, actually closer to the loose, baggy monster than anybody knew and that we could start doing all kinds of things. The great writer of the loose, baggy short story is Munro. It's so fantastic what she's done for the form. She's complicated it; she's rescued it. It was getting pretty anorexic.

I still like the thing fiction can do in giving you the event refracted through different sensibilities.

What mistakes do inexperienced writers most often make when they work in multiple points of view? What advice could you offer them?

In a way, if they're making interesting mistakes, that's something to go with. It's possible to do a beginning writer a disservice by cleaning a story up. You can reduce it to one point of view and get a story that's better, that's more likely to be published—at least wherever they want to start publishing. But I would want to listen to what they were after with the multiple points of view.

Sometimes students try to complicate a story by having two points of view rather than having two complicated points of view. They use multiple points of view because they can, not because the story demands it. How do you recognize that? How do you figure out that a story needs two points of view and not one?

Sometimes it feels like playing to me. Let's just try this over here. Does it do something that's complicated?

When you started off to write "Honey," did you know it would be two points of view?

No.

Did you think it would be from the point of view of the mother, Mercedes?

I probably thought that, yeah. I can't quite remember. I really liked her. If I thought anything, I thought it would be her story.

The beginning of the story has such grounding in her point of view. At what point in the writing process did you realize that that wasn't going to be enough?

It feels like you're crossing a stream and you go from steppingstone to steppingstone. If you're going to have different points of view, it's a question of when you have a gap. Forster, in *Aspects of the Novel,* calls it "popping." You pop the point of view. The point of view you're in has to release it. There has to be some kind of satiation with that point of view, and then you need the next one to start very fast. That's a problem I do see in students. They don't understand that going to the next point of view is like starting the story over. It cannot be down time.

They don't understand that going to the next point of view is like starting the story over.

When you get to the place where it's time to go to the next steppingstone, the next point of view, does it feel like you just don't know where to go from here, or do you see the next steppingstone?

Not knowing would keep me *in* the point of view. It's a sense of, that's finished, I *get* that piece that makes me move on. I'm saturated in that point of view, there's a feeling of enoughness. And then, ooh, what comes next that makes this first piece even more interesting? Who's looking at that that makes it even *better?*

Is it an organic kind of thing, or is it like you turn your head and there it is?

Like you turn your head. It's conscious.

So when you came to the point where you saw that we've had enough of Mercedes right now, there was Hart. You didn't think, should it be Hart?

No. If I had that question, I would think it wasn't working.

How do you know if a story should be written in first person as opposed to third?

It's like writing in English. I've always been really startled when a student comes in and says, "I've got to change this from third person into first" because I can't. I couldn't do that.

"Honey" is one of a cycle of five stories about this family. What attracts you to the idea of writing multiple stories about a group of people?

Writing story cycles is like having your cake and eating it, too. For a long time, there weren't very many story cycles. I think of Nabokov's "Cream," which was a big influence on me—not so much stylistically, but in the way it resolves things. There are concerns that connect all the stories to each other. There's this integration, but epiphany, too.

One benefit of writing story cycles is that you don't have to create a new character for every single story.

I find it hard to part with characters. A story cycle has the pleasures of the open-endedness. Nobody can tell you you need to hurry up and finish. Characters keep coming back. They have different problems, and a lot of times that's how I begin the story. I'll be thinking, this is a kind of problem that's new to this character that I already know. I had a close friend whose kid was going through some things, and I was thinking about that father and son a lot, writing this cycle. Will a son tolerate tenderness from a father when the relationship is already so charged with different levels of irresponsibility and failures of empathy?

So do you feel that this cycle is more about the father and son than about the husband and wife?

No. It's about all of them. It feels to me like a constellation, like they don't exist apart from each other. I think it's interesting to resist that in short stories. You get Chekhov saying that the essence of the short story is the two poles, male and female, and what happens between them. He doesn't do that himself. He always gives you minor characters who speaks somehow to that central tension. I like community in stories. I like little communities, little tiny communities.

What would you say "Honey" is about?

It was something about the son's beginning to get a pretty confident sense that his father needs to be seen with skepticism. He's emerging from the childhood desire to idealize and trust. He's beginning to think, to be cognizant that mistrust could have a use. And that is so painful. Then the father, in the way that you do in really tight relationships, immediately knows that the son has got a new degree of detachment that he wishes to confiscate—but not because he's a bad person. Just because it is so darn sad when your kid turns around and looks at you and you're flawed.

What were you hoping to accomplish by throwing Mercedes into the mix?

That she would have a different sense of what it is to love.

And the connection for Kevin in all that is—?

He's beginning to figure out that he's going to have to cope with a new way of doing it. But isn't that like American generations? You look at your parents and think, you know, they went about marriage and family the wrong way. *Most* cultures want to say, Look at your parents. They're doing this the right way. What you want is to come as close to that as you can. Americans have the tremendous fortune as writers to be able to see people having to make it up. But we're not so great at it. You see it in the resistance to queer marriage. No! Marriage looks like *this.* Let's keep replicating *this*—and not look at the couples who are profoundly committed to each other and say, you know what? That looks a lot like marriage, too.

How do you know a set of characters will become part of a story cycle?

I always hope they will be. A way of conning myself into parting with them is to say, you can come back. There could be another story. Mostly, they don't.

One thing that "No One's a Mystery" and "Honey" have in common is their western setting. Did you grow up in the West?

Basically, yeah. I got married really young, and we went to New Mexico. It was just wonderful for a writer—which I didn't know then that I was. It's one of those places where different cultures come together and so it appealed to the anthropologist in me. I grew up in the Midwest. I have one degree, in anthropology, from the University of Southern Illinois. I was supposed to go to graduate school and, driving there, we got to a literal fork in the road where the highway went south to Albuquerque and north to Santa Fe. One of us said something like, "You know? I can't remember the last time we took a day off." So *should* we? We used to resolve things by flipping a coin. So we got out of the car, he flipped it, and it fell right on the highway. I forget if heads or tails was Santa Fe. But anyway, we went. I didn't leave. I didn't go to graduate school.

But eventually I had a kind of breakdown because that was *my* narrative: go to grad school, become an academic. Everything I'd done was riding on that. It was a terrific clinical depression, but I had no idea what it was then. Eventually, I climbed out and got a job in a bookstore right on the plaza in Santa Fe where they had this great typewriter—the first electronic typewriter I'd ever seen. So I started writing stories. I worked as much at the store as I could, sort of stealing time from my employer. My first story was, naturally, deeply grounded in my experience. It was about—a sheepherder. From that story, I got one sentence, which was, "The whole world was bare as high as a sheep could reach." Then, I *knew.* Everything else in the story was—throw it *away!* But I'd written that one sentence, and I just wanted to do that again. I wanted a kind of stolen life. I wanted to do what I wasn't supposed to be doing.

But I'd written that one sentence, and I just wanted to do that again. I wanted a kind of stolen life. I wanted to do what I wasn't supposed to be doing.

Once you knew you wanted to write, how did you educate yourself as a writer?

I was in a great place. I had a good friend who was a poet, and I learned a lot from him. 'Til then, I'd been reading for my degree and hadn't read very much. So he was a crucial friend because he brought me books.

Did you attend writing workshops?

I just wrote. I had this game of sending one story a year to *The New Yorker.* That was the only place I knew about. I really didn't know *anything.* The first story came back. It had this really perfect Bryn Mawr-like handwriting. "No thanks." That just about killed me! I threw that story away. I just took it out of the envelope and threw it away. But the next year—it was the same editor; I knew her handwriting—she took that story out of the slush pile. At the same time, I had had some inkling that I should listen to somebody else. I somehow came across the Berkeley Writers' Conference and saw that it was going to be Grace Paley, so I sent the story *The New Yorker* took—but before they'd taken it. Somebody called and they accepted me. I was delighted, but I said, "But I don't have the money. I can't get to Berkeley." Then the next day, Leonard Michaels called and said, "You're coming!" He paid for everything for me. He was this fiery, fast-talking—he was just great. And Grace Paley was—Grace Paley! That was the extent of it. The only writing workshop I ever did. But it was one of those rare things where you suddenly go into a room and you meet three people who are very important to you. Leonard Michaels kept talking to me like I was someone. I kept wanting to assume that lower student position and finally he just looked at me and said, "You're a writer. You'd better just adapt." It was *all* I needed to hear.

Finally he just looked at me and said, "You're a writer. You'd better just adapt." It was *all* I needed to hear.

Some of the most interesting, innovative writers have come to writing sideways, as you did. Experiences they had before becoming writers, passions that consumed them—anthropology and archaeology in your case—are breathed into their work. The work of writers who spend their whole lives in academia, studying nothing but literature and writing, often lacks a kind of edge. What advice would you give to a young person who already knows he wants to be a writer?

I think it's tremendously impoverishing to just do literature the whole time. When I see someone who is eighteen and wants to go straight from a bachelor's degree in English to an MFA program, I often argue really hard against it. They're going to want to get to their own childhood and adolescence, and they are going to do it too soon. They're so—uncooked. I want to urge them to *live.*

Writing Prompts

READ: "Honey" and the interview with **Elizabeth Tallent.**

PONDER: The way Tallent uses multiple points of view as steppingstones through the story. Consider how each point of view change complicates the reader's understanding of what's happening in the story.

WRITE: Think of a specific occasion. Write the first part of it in third person from one character's point of view. Then switch to another character and tell the next important thing from that character's third-person point of view. Remember, the "hand-off" must serve the story.

PRACTICE:

- Write a dialogue between two people who are uneasy with each other and are occupying confined space. Pace the dialogue with action and description.
- Consider clichés of experience—for example, an only child, a coming out, a suicidal friend. Write a scene in which your characters behave in a way that goes against the conventional wisdom surrounding that kind of experience.
- Identify an object that resonates with meaning. Introduce it into a scene so that it reveals something about a character and/or a relationship.
- Take a walk through the woods or a public garden with a nature guide and use the photographs in it to identify and list the names of plants, trees, flowers. Write a scene that includes descriptions and names of at least one thing you observed.
- Consider something that you usually lump into one category—like roses. Discover how many different varieties there are within the category. Write a scene that requires the use of at least three separate categories.
- Make a list of visual details about someone you know well. Go beyond general details to look at particular things like the bleached seam of a pair of jeans or the way the heel of a boot is worn. Extend the list to include the visual details of this person's surroundings. Use the details to create a character sketch that evokes some aspect of this person without naming it.
- Invent a character who is in some kind of bind. Write a scene that illustrates how the character is dealing with it. Escape is not an option.
- Write a dialogue between two people discussing a problem they share. Do not name the problem.
- Read and reread Tallent's widely anthologized "No One's a Mystery," highlighting for details that convey information about character and situation. Consider what she does not tell you and how specific details work as clues to allow you to figure out what is happening between character and situation.
- Identify the central event of a story you want to write and look at it refracted through the sensibility of each character involved. Consider how their different perceptions of the conflict or crisis and different requirements for closure might allow you to tell the story without using a traditional arc. Do they all perceive the same conflict? Could one person come to closure when others don't?
- Write a scene that reflects an adolescent's dawning realization of a parent's flaws.

Luis Alberto Urrea

Luis Alberto Urrea (b. 1955) is the author of a collection of short stories, two novels, a memoir, two collections of poems, and three works of nonfiction. Born in Tijuana, Mexico, he was educated at the University of California, San Diego. His honors include the Christopher Award, the Colorado Center for the Book Award, the Western States Book Award, the American Book Award–Before Columbus Foundation, and the Lannan Literary Foundation Award. Urrea teaches at the University of Illinois at Chicago. He lives in Naperville, Illinois.

For Further Reading:
Across the Wire: Life and Hard Times on the Mexican Border (1993), *In Search of Snow* (1994), *The Fever of Being* (1994), *By the Lake of Sleeping Children: The Secret Life of the Mexican Border* (1996), *Ghost Sickness* (1997), *Nobody's Son: Notes from an American Life* (1998), *Six Kinds of Sky: A Collection of Short Fiction* (2002), *The Devil's Highway* (2004), *The Hummingbird's Daughter* (2005).

Father Returns from the Mountain

The car is red. It has a sun-baked and peeling black top. Little flakes of fake leather blow away in the wind. The roof is crushed. Windows are shattered. The front end is crumpled. The axles are split and the tires slant crookedly. Dry blood on the hood. The steering wheel is twisted. Details of violence. An American Motors Rambler 440, 1966 model. Slivers of glass are stuck in the carpets. Dust settles on the stains. A photograph of my father and me is caught under the seat, fluttering like a flag, like a bird trapped in the wind. There is a dime in the broken driver's seat. Blood where the radio should be. / This is the truth. The truth is a diamond, or at least a broken mirror. There are many reflective surfaces, and we observe the ones we choose. We see what we can. / The car is red. It stands in a dusty compound among other crushed machines. A note to my father in a flowery woman's hand blows out of the glove compartment. It whispers "Querido Alberto" a hundred times as it spins away. There is a chain-link fence that rattles in a breeze that smells of dogs and perfume. A yellow sticker is pasted to the hood because there is no glass to hold it. Children scare each other by touching the crusty patches of my father's blood. "He'll come back to eat you!" The dead man, the dead man. / A Mexican cop slides down the slope. He squints in the early morning sun. He can hardly see my father in the wreckage. He runs back up and calls for help. The blue light atop his car flashes, flashes, casting marching shadows over the rocks. Pink urine spreads across my father's clothing. The pain is a sound that hums inside his gut, that pierces his skull. Darkness. Sleep. / The telephone feels warm. I look out the window at a Monday sky. "Hello," he says. It is a family friend. "Do you remember me?" The morning sunlight reaches through the trees. "Of course I remember you. What's up?" His silence buzzes for a moment. When he speaks, he speaks carefully. "Your father. . .has had an accident." "Is he hurt?" "Yes." "Badly?" "Yes." I lean forward. I think of my father being hurt. I think of him in pain. The tiny agony of tears pinches the corners of my eyes. / We are on a balcony in Puerto Vallarta. I am in love with the most inconceivable girl in Rosario, Sinaloa. Ebony crabs have come in from the jungle, mad with the rain that hasn't stopped for two days. They climb the stairs of the hotel, wait before our doors, attack us when we come out. His hand is on my shoulder. I cannot contain the feelings as we watch lightning bombard the hilltops. Rain undermines the streets and floods the river that eats great rifts in the jungle. We spend the entire night in each other's confidence. And when the tears come, he lets me cry. / My father is severely damaged. His eyes are open, but will not function. They scrape up and down, but they cannot break the thick shell of darkness that covers them. His body will not move—he tells it to—to get the hell up, get back in the car, light a cigarette, go bowling, something. Anything. But he is frozen. His mouth is a traitor that will not function. It fills slowly with liquid. When it reaches his lips, there is a gradual, endless snail of red slipping down his cheek and hiding in his ear. I am sitting in my room listening to music. / "How bad?" I ask, a little afraid, a little unwilling, a little uncertain. "Very bad. He flew off a mountain. He fell in the desert." The sun is bright. / The car is red. The police compound is quiet. A scrawny cat licks the speedometer. / The police lift him into the ambulance. He tries to talk, he tries to see he is a slab of meat and it makes him angry. The pain makes him angry. The cuts on his face sting. And through the morning, dawn scorching the paper-sheet horizon, ravens smelling the blood and exploding off the road before them, the ambulance crew flies. To a hospital—well, a clinic. Scorpions drowsing in its shade. And there, the nurses find him almost dead, and strip him bare, and shoot a load of morphine in his fallen veins, and tie him down in case he kicks, and leave him naked eight hours alone. He knows he's naked—God, he's mad. But the poppies blooming in his arms send out their odors, their perfume already bubbles up his throat, and down, down, beyond his belly, to where the memories dwell. The blood has made his throat black. / I sit alone in the funeral home. There is little sound from without: even downtown Tijuana has to sleep. 3:00 a.m. No sleep for me. Me and the body, we're wired. / I open the coffin lid and look at him. He is broken. His chin is a black openness. He was always shaved pink and now little gray whiskers are pushing their heads up through the wounds. His shirt is stained. I put my face to the side of the box and stare and stare. I watch for a flicker, a twitch. I wait for a microscopic flare of the nostrils. The sealed eyelids seem ready to pop, to rise and lower. I want, in terror, to see him lick his lips so that I can break the Mexican sealing glass, pull him up, save him, embrace him. There is no movement. There is no sound. / I found a photograph just yesterday. In it, my father stands with the president, with generals, senators. His captain's uniform looks as crisp as a salad. At times, I shuffle through his official papers and look at his federal police badge. His smiles look like mine. We are connected by the lips. The grin is our chain. / I lie on the floor beneath the coffin. He's up on a table laid out like God's buffet. I close my eyes to sleep, my last night beside him. I am a poet at that instant. A shadow passes over my face. I jump up, thinking that someone is approaching. There is nothing. Again the shadow. Again nothing. Again and again. I imagine him waving farewell. As I slip into sleep, I have a vision of a stiff hand reaching for me over the edge. / The dreams have come in a series. They are diamonds. They are broken mirrors. In the first, I am run over by a truck. My half-brother stands on the curb and smiles down at me. I pull at people's legs from the black street. / Death is here now. I am finally aware of it. Perhaps childhood is not knowing that it is grinning at you from the corner. It has pressed its face against the windows, it has stalked in with the fog and awaits its turn. / At 8:00 p.m. he tried to open his eyes. His straining led to nothing. My father was born in Rosario, little gem at the southern end of Sinaloa. He died in San Luis Rio Colorado, a dry husk in the north of Sonora. I can imagine his gray hair against the pillow. His lips, white, rolling back almost in a smile. His abdomen searing red hot, then tingling pink as he passed through to the new side. Possibly music, a fragment of a tune wafting through the haze. I hope he heard music. / The family friend calls again. "Tell me," I say. "His condition deteriorated for several hours." "And?" "And your señor. . .rested." "Dead?" "Dead." "Just now?" "Yes." "Thank you." "Are you all right?" "Thank you." / No one comes to the funeral home to spell me. It's a wake, and I'm awake. I have watched the corpse for seven hours. I have closed the lid. I have not eaten since the day before. "I hate waiting," I say out loud. His voice: "I know, Son. I always hated it too. It's boring." I spin around, but the lid remains closed. There's nobody else in the room. "Do you hear me?" I ask. "Yes," he replies. "I love you," I say. "I know," he says. / Mexicans love the dead. They are a lovely treat with which to terrify each other. Dawn's light, and people passing in the street push open the door to peek at the coffin. "What are you looking at, you vampires?" I yell at them. "El muerto," they whisper. "El muerto." / We carry the coffin to the graveside. I have to go to the bathroom. Dogs are running on the graves. Whores and cops and ice cream men are working downtown. People are eating and laughing and sweating and making love all over the world and my father is dead. The world has not even hesitated. Nobody has noticed. / The hard part is watching the box go down. Watching it being pushed into the black mouth, knowing that his flesh is being hid from you, and if you should search for a touch of it again you will find dusty corruption. The body goes. I walk away from the weeping. White clouds on the border. I keep my back to the mourners. Tijuana looks pretty from a distance. I was born there. / I sit in my house alone, working on the third draft of a book no-one will ever read. I hear a car in the driveway. When I open the door, the car is red. My dead father is leaning on the steering wheel. His hair is in disorder, his eyes are uncertain. I go to him, take his cold hand, lead him inside. He sits on the couch, settling like a white feather. "What happened?" he asks. I look into his face. He doesn't know. He doesn't know he's dead. Maybe I can fool him. Keep him alive. But I know as I hope it is impossible. I kneel at his feet. "Papá, you were killed." "Killed! But I'm right here!" "You were killed in an accident." "But the car's in the driveway. Brand new." "No." "It can't be," he says. I am afraid of hurting him, but I must. "Papá," I say, "go away. You're dead." "I can't be dead," he insists, pain and frustration mixing on his face. / As a child, I would ride standing beside him as he drove, holding tight to his shoulder. / I take his pant-legs in my hands. "Papá, go away. You can't stay here. You're dead!" He shakes his head sadly. I weep like his little boy wept, with my head on his knees. "You're dead, you're dead, you're dead." / A stonemason gets in the grave and spreads concrete over the box. We don't have enough money for a headstone. Maybe a tree will grow here, or a stand of mustard, goldenrod. Other mourners file in to feed the hole beside my father's. / The car is red. The cold desert wind moans in it at night. There is a scar on the mountain where he crashed. His glasses bend the moonlight between the crumbled rocks. / I hear his engine again. He looks much better. "Get in," he says. I get in. He takes me through miles and miles of dreamlands. Things that do and do not exist pass by, one after one. We are free to go anywhere we choose. He wants to go home to Rosario. / "Did it hurt to die?" I finally ask. "Well," he says, "it hurt before I died." "Were you afraid?" "Of course. I listened for you, but you never came." My stomach tightens. "I wanted to be there. I couldn't get to you. Don't you think it hurt me to let you die?" He smiles. "I know," he says. We pass the ruins of a railyard. "Your grandfather is proud of you," he says. I look at him. The tears come. I try to stop them, but they force their way out anyway. "I don't want to be without you," I blurt. He looks at me for a long while, then taps me on the knee. "You've got to stop crying. You sound like a little girl." Then: "You aren't without me. Remember that." His eyes are clear. "Where are your glasses?" I ask. "Back on the side of the road," he says. "But that's all right. I won't be needing them now." "Were you cognizant at the hospital?" I ask. "Yes," he says with disgust. "I was trapped inside that damned dead body. I hated that." "I'm sorry, Papá," I tell him. He looks at me. "Don't be sorry. You waste so much time that you need for yourself." I nod. "I closed the coffin," I say. "Thank you. I didn't want to be on display." I touch his arm. "Papá, did you... did you see God?" He smiles at me and turns on the radio. / When I was fourteen, my father and I spent hours laughing in the night about nothing, nothing at all. / The car is red. The driver's seat is torn. A beehive swells inside it. Bees fly where his eyes used to be. They fly through the air that used to touch his lips. They walk on the bent wheel that cracked his ribs. They sit where he used to sit. A slow, warm cascade of honey spreads over the traces of demolition. It is gold. It catches the sunlight and reflects the clouds that move in its depths, minute and sparkling white. Droplets reflect the blue of the sky. They hint at the smile in my father's eyes.

Rosario, my earth
little town in which I learned to love
I dream of you, I miss you
thinking someday I'll return

Life took me from you,
but I never, never forgot you
my grandest illusion now
is to return to you once more
in the years of my nightfall

—ALBERTO URREA
June 2, 1915–January 10, 1977

A Conversation with Luis Alberto Urrea

Your memoir Nobody's Son *begins, "My mom said, 'I'm so tired of your Mexican bullshit,'" and what follows is this riff on English words that illustrates how pure a race we're not. Would you talk about your fascination with words and your struggle to define your half American, half Mexican self and how that made a writer of you?*

I was born on a main drag in Tijuana, in a little clinic upstairs from a drugstore. My mother lived with my dad in my grandmother's house on a dirt street up in the hills, and she was the only American and the only English speaker. She would go every day to San Diego to work. I was left every day with my grandma and my aunts and cousins, so all I heard every day was Spanish. My mother would only see me in the evenings, so the family legend was that I'd say to them in Spanish, "She's crazy," because I couldn't understand her words. It was very funny until I realized how lonely it must have been for this woman from Manhattan to be stuck in Tijuana with people who didn't like her culture, didn't like *her*—and with a language she didn't understand and a child who didn't understand her. She used to tell me the story that, as a treat on a weekend, she would walk with my stroller a couple of miles to a drug store at the bottom of the hill and get an ice cream soda and sit there and read American magazines. When we left there, I was almost five. We escaped Tijuana and moved to southeast San Diego, which over time changed from a Mexican barrio to a black ghetto. I was starting to understand that on my dad's side I was considered to be Mexican and on my mom's side I was considered to be American. My dad always called me Luis and my mom always called me Louis. My mother was from Virginia people, plantation owners who had gone up north to establish themselves in New York. I'm sure when she married Dad she thought she was going to some great Mexican hacienda with Gilbert Roland and mariachis and Pancho Villa, and she ended up on this terrible dirt street in Tijuana—which to me was exciting because it was what I knew, but to her it was appalling. When we left, the only thing we could afford was this slum dwelling, also on a dirt street, so she never escaped that chain. It became very important to her, I think, that I understand that English was of primary value. My father, on the other hand, thought Spanish was of primary value. My mother got the upper hand. She spent the most time with me because he was very macho and had girlfriends and other families. She would read to me every night and, being a very late-Victorian lady, she felt that it was especially important that I get Dickens. I could not understand a word, but I would get drunk on this language. Sometimes I would fall asleep seeing these pages of words go by. She read me Mark Twain—I was crazy for Mark Twain. *The Arabian Nights.* My father, on the other hand, he wanted me to observe Mexican culture, but he didn't necessarily have the kind of school learning to do so. He'd bring me records—

seventy-eights, of course, back then. There's a great story: He came home one day from Tijuana and he had a Spanish translation of *The Iliad* and *The Odyssey.* He put them down on the table and said, "I want you to read these in their original Spanish." Even I knew it was Greek, but I didn't say anything because you didn't do that. He was like, *"Homero!"*

The barrio turned more violent and crazy. I hate to say it about my parents, but my mom had retained the plantation owner's attitude about black people and my father, being a white, blonde Mexican, had a very racially aware sense of himself. So we were automatically better than our Filipino neighbors, better than our brown Mexican neighbors, and certainly better than our black neighbors. The black neighbors weren't that crazy about us. The Chicanos weren't that crazy about us. My glib line at readings is, "I got my ass kicked by every ethnic group in the neighborhood, so I thought, shoot, I'll stay home and read, and see what Tom Sawyer is up to." In some way that pushed me to be a writer also.

We left that neighborhood, at the end of fourth grade, after a black man tried to stab me with a knife and chased me down the street. We moved to the north part of San Diego, to a white, working class suburb. I was suddenly, for the first time in my life, ashamed. None of the people in that neighborhood recognized L-U-I-S; they called me "Louis" as my mom did. So I became "Lou." "Hey Lou." I was, like, call me what you want, I don't care. That was when I started hearing the words that I talk about in the book—you know, *wetback, greaser, taco-bender.* I had heard people using the language to punish and oppress black people. I had heard Richard Pryor say that once someone had called him the *N* word and he went home and said Mama, what is an *N*? And she tried to explain it to him. It really struck me that if my parents would use that word, I'd fight them and say, "You can't do that." So when somebody started using those kind of words back at me it really struck home. I thought, my God, other people see us that way? What's that all about? When I was in high school, too, it was the time of David Bowie and the big Gender Explosion. There were all these kids who, before and after, would have been closeted and gay, but all of them just suddenly realized, hey, Ziggy Stardust can do it, *I* can do it. And they all came out and got rooster haircuts and wild stuff. They were my pals because I was a drama guy. So I was suddenly in this world of acceptance that we wrestled for ourselves—you could be black, you could be gay, you could be Mexican. Whatever. We thought that was the way the world was going.

Do you think writers always are outsiders?

It seems inescapable to me that they are on some level. I tend to see writing on a very mystical level. I see it as a kind of shaman's pursuit. I see it as an ancient ritual that we enact, so I feel in part that it's a kind of spiritual practice. I kid my writing students that I try to practice writing fu. But it actually comes from a real thing. One of the first writing textbooks was by a guy named Lu Chi, and it caught my eye

I tend to see writing on a very mystical level. I see it as a kind of shaman's pursuit.

because my nickname in Tijuana was Louchi. I thought, ooh, that's great, Lu Chi and Louchi! He had this thing called *wen fu*—the tradition and practice of the art of writing as a spiritual discipline. *Wen* is the most ancient Chinese word they have a record for, and it means writing now, but in ancient days it meant the summoning of spirits. Speaking to ghosts.

So would you say that your childhood and adolescence taught you that it is because words can be so harmful that they have power?

What I really learned is that words are a bridge and words are healing—the exact opposite. You know as well as I do that calling somebody a *faggot* is not that far removed from actually physically hurting them—or calling someone the *N* word or calling a woman *Bitch.* Seeing that happen to people really upset me. And you know, I was a Cali youth, a California guy. I wanted to be a rock star, I wanted to be Jim Morrison or something, and I hung out with rock bands. I didn't know what was going on. I was writing poetry like a maniac and I was in love with my girlfriends. I filled book after book with these absurdly bad poems. I wasn't really thinking about this cultural stuff so much, just the words. I found out that words were powerful and magical.

And I discovered all these writers! One of my teachers said, "You need to go read Stephen Crane," and I thought, oh dude, *The Red Badge of Courage,* no way. He told me, "No. Go get his collected poems. They will change your life." I thought, Okay, I'm game and I got it and he was right. It changed my life. It was probably ninth grade, junior high. I got the collected poems of Stephen Crane, and I was just blown away—partially because they were tiny, which I thought was great, and because they were free verse. I'd never seen it. And the pithy, dark, weird, surreal nature of the stuff just killed me. So right as high school started I started using my allowance to buy books. I was in this bookstore and I found Charles Bukowski—and you can bet a tenth grader freaked out when he read Charles Bukowski. I thought, What is this! So I had gone back to look for more Bukowski and I was looking on the shelf and I saw Jim Morrison's book, *The Lords and the New Creatures.* I was totally shocked. I thought, Whoa! Morrison! And next to Morrison was Bob Dylan's *Tarantula* and next to that was John Lennon's *A Spaniard in the Works* and next to that was the collected poetry of Leonard Cohen, *Spice Box of the Earth,* and his novel *The Beautiful Losers.* I almost passed out. It was this moment when I thought, these guys are poets! Jim Morrison doesn't just put on leather pants, he's a poet! It was this absurd epiphany that only a dumb rock 'n' roll boy could have. The light broke—Oh my God, Deep Purple were poets. So I bought *The Lords and the New Creatures* and John Lennon. I was just overwhelmed at the possibilities. The other sort of magic ingredient was Richard Brautigan's *Trout Fishing in America.* Drop that in and that was it. That was me, man. That was where I wanted to go. I didn't care how I got there, but that was where I wanted to go. I read voraciously.

We were the high school that became known as Ridgemont High in *Fast Times at Ridgemont High.* The evil teacher that Ray Walston plays was actually our English teacher—Dick Curtis. But I loved him. He fed me stuff like Kurt Vonnegut, and I was flying and writing stuff. Then I went to college, and college for me was the ultimate. Three major things happened for me. I reconnected with Latin American literature and Spanish, which I had lost in high school. I discovered Asian literature. And I discovered women's writing.

I was in UCSC bookstore and in a box of used books, there was Diane Wakowski's *Motorcycle Betrayal Poems* for a dollar. I picked it up, read the dedication, "To all the men that have betrayed me in hopes that they fall off their motorcycles and break their necks." I went crazy. I thought, This woman is my god. And right about then Patti Smyth showed up. My friends, all the guys, ran like hell. But all of a sudden these powerful women came into my life. That was a real transformation. So I learned the best stuff in college, but it was outside of class. The best stuff is always outside, but college gives you the environment to do it. All these wild souls that are in this place, experiencing and discovering. All these women I was hanging out with got nice, really hairy armpits, and they would always stand so you could see them, like a Patti Smyth cover. The guys were really terrified of this feminism. But I was just so delighted because I felt like I was discovering *again.* I would take these classes like feminist lit; I'd be the only guy in class, which I thought was kind of cool.

You've worked in a lot of genres, you've done a couple of nonfiction books, a couple of novels—and, of course, your short story collection. How do you know what genre will work best for the material you want to work with?

The material dictates to me what it wants to be. Short stories are a torment; I hate them. There's no pleasure in it. Putting together *Six Kinds of Sky,* I thought, I've been writing since I was thirteen or fourteen years old and I can only come up with six short stories? That was kind of sad. I took those six because I thought they represented six kinds of approaches to the infinite, to destiny and grace and God and all those things. Novels are great fun. They take so much time, however. I have the one novel out, *In Search of Snow.* My next novel's coming out in 2005, called *The Hummingbird's Daughter,* and that's taken over twenty years' research and travel to write. It's a historical novel. That is one that I wrestled with. I didn't know if it was nonfiction or fiction. When I realized, finally, that I knew the people in the book so well in a way that I could not footnote, I realized it had to be fiction. The poetry is a special urge that comes on me. I always have my notebooks with me, so all of it goes into something. It's been a real blessing to me because I never reach a writer's block. I'm trying to learn my own style, which is fairly tidal and seasonal. Some people write every day and I think that's incredible, but I don't. I write till I don't write and then I stop for a while and listen to music and watch movies, and all a sudden the poem starts to come.

The material dictates to me what it wants to be.

Still, you've been very prolific.

I'm pretty disciplined about being a writer—I have easily two hundred notebooks completely full of writing. I could never write another word and probably publish ten more books. But I'm having to learn to be more disciplined in my scheduling as the public interest has risen. I had the weird benefit of being completely obscure for a really long time, which at the time I didn't think was a benefit. But it is because you're free to do whatever you want. Now that I'm established, they look at poetry books with some respect and say, "Well, do what you have to do."

Your story "Father Returns from the Mountain" has characteristics of fiction, poetry, and nonfiction. Would you talk about the occasion for writing the story and how you came to its very untraditional structure?

In 1977, January 10, my father was killed in a car accident. He didn't die immediately. He was left eight hours naked on a table in front of a broken window to die. I was in my senior year of college and he died bringing me a thousand dollars from his bank account, because I was the first one to get out of college. When he had his car wreck, he urinated on himself, so the money was soaked in urine and blood. So the police, who stole everything else, didn't steal it. Later on, when they brought me the body in a station wagon in a cardboard box, they made me pay bail. They said, "Even though he's dead, he's under arrest, and if you don't pay bail we'll just take him back with us." So they charged me seven hundred and fifty bucks to buy the corpse, which I paid with his wet money. They gave me the body, and I paid the rest of the money for the funeral. At one point, everybody was doing the Mexican wake and they took me to my dad at about two in the morning. Nobody came back, so I spent eighteen hours in a room with my father's corpse, just the two of us. There's a place in the story where it says I was sitting next to him, then laid down on the floor, and he started talking. Afterwards, when it was all over, I started having dreams where he was coming to me. I was, all that time, talking to people who were healer types to research this other book, and they were all saying that the dead speak to you in dreams. If they die violently, they don't know they're dead so you have to send them away. That's the first dream: He was lost and I sent him away. And at the end of them, he went away with his friends. It was very strange.

Anyway, Ursula LeGuin was coming to my college to do a workshop, and I wanted to get into this class very badly. You had to audition, so I actually typed that story out on a mimeograph master as my audition piece. She accepted me into the class, and we revised it. Then she accepted it for an anthology, so it was the first sale I ever made. She really started everything for me. It came out in this anthology in 1980 called *Edges,* which she edited. It's kicked around, and people have found it and have been really connected to it because of their experiences. When it came time to do this book, I wasn't going to put it in. Then I thought, no, I really should because it's been identified as a poem, a short story, and an essay—and it could be any of those.

In what ways do you think it works as a short story?

At the time, like many young, smart-ass males, I thought that experimental fiction was the answer to everything. I was going to be Robert Coover, Jr. I thought that sort of anti-story was really cool, so I used those techniques to tell it. I also took fictional elements that were the dream and reported them as reality. So, in that sense, I think it was a short story. There's a repetition of the red car, which I wanted to be a kind of funereal motif. The structure of it is all one long paragraph, with slashes breaking up pieces; some things are out of sequence and intermixed. I wanted it to represent the shattered glass and mirrors of the car. You're looking at broken glass and it's reflecting things, sometimes out of sequence; but, still, it's a mosaic that makes a whole. So it was fictional techniques, or at least anti-story techniques, that I used to tell the story. None of my experimentalist stories are in *Six Kinds of Sky,* except that one. I say in the afterward that it was a moment where I melded two things that worked together for my purposes.

What advice do you give to students who want to experiment with fictional technique?

I tell my students that before Picasso painted cubism, he learned how to draw and how to paint. You will find that a lot of writers in graduate school are stone cold experimentalists—mostly, I think, because they don't know how to tell a clear story. They do whatever trick they can do to avert your attention. I have met a few people who absolutely vibrate to that note. They are experimentalists all the way, and you can tell because it's their voice, their muse. I always want to make sure that people can actually communicate something first.

You will find that a lot of writers in graduate school are stone cold experimentalists—mostly, I think, because they don't know how to tell a clear story.

In what ways is the published story different from the draft you wrote for LeGuin?

Some of the language is refined. In the early draft, you can tell certain things are by a very young male. Stuff that I looked at later and thought, What are you *talking* about?

The lyricism in the story, the beautiful repetition—did that come in the revision?

That was always there. The revisions were more a technical thing, to make things clearer—just little tiny, tiny changes. I've always been interested in that kind of a voice, it's always been my voice. I wanted that sense of inevitability: You cannot escape this, *none* of us are going to escape it. We're all going to die. You're going to lose someone you love, there's no way out of it.

That's mirrored in the way that there's just no white space. There's literally no escaping the story itself. Were there other things that influenced you as a writer during that time?

I worked with a poet in college. I kept trying to write about my father's death, but I was so devastated and shocked by the horror of all that had happened I was out of control. I had never been confronted in a hard way before. I had made it my job to be better at writing than everybody else, so that I was always the cool guy in the workshop. But this guy called me in and sat me down and said, "Look, this is dreadful." I said, "What do you mean it's dreadful?" He said, "It's dreadful, it's dreadful. You're trying to hurt me. It's not my father who died, why should I care?" And I was like, "How *dare* you?" He said, "I'm sorry. But if you want me to care that your father died, get a little control of yourself and write it coldly and calmly. Don't be screaming at me, because I will just walk away from you." At the time, I was red-faced. I was twenty-one years old and I thought, my writing career is over. I learned a lesson, though, that has been good for me as a teacher. I can tell my students, "Just because you have something intense to say doesn't mean you have to write it that way." Why do you think all the hacks are writing true crime books? Because if a guy makes soup out of his grandma it's hard to go wrong with that material. But if you can have somebody kiss someone on the cheek and have your reader weep, then you're really writing."

But if you can have somebody kiss someone on the cheek and have your reader weep, then you're really writing."

You actually accomplish that in "Sanctuary," the part of Nobody's Son *that describes the family you spent so much time with as a child.*

There's a kind of interesting history of "Sanctuary." If you look at *The Fever for Being,* my first book of poetry, there are a couple of poems talking about that family. I worked my way up to my novel *In Search of Snow.* The last third of it is about that family, but it took me ten years to actually be able to sit down and write their true story. The art allowed me access those feelings and emotions that were overwhelming to me.

As it did with "Father Returns to the Mountain."

Yes. This piece allowed my father's death to become a story. I could then separate from me what had happened. Later, when it was time for me to write an actual full account of what happened, I could do it.

In the essay, "Amazing Grace," you said "Father Returns to the Mountain" was the only story in Six Kinds of Sky *that was utterly true. Would you talk about the relationship between truth and fact in fiction?*

Oh, wow. Well, I think of *On the Road.* Jack Kerouac just typed out his wild adventures, fictionalized a few names. I think fact shows up often. How could it not? You want to be careful, you don't want to be sued, you don't want to hurt people. I say in *Nobody's Son* that it's part of our job as writers to betray the dead. But you need to know how much you need to betray them to tell the story. I know secrets I will take to the grave. I know some awful things, everybody tells me everything. They don't think, oh, he's going to put it in a book—though I often do. So in my fiction things show up. For example, "First Light." I was in love with my first cousin; she loved me. Nothing that happened in that story was true. Nobody got pregnant, there were no beatings, none of that. But she would come to breakfast and put her foot on my foot, touch my foot.

That small detail shows more about the relationship than having written about them having sex together could have. In "Amazing Grace," you said you felt "responsible for the details." What did you mean by that?

The details to me are what make a piece of writing. For example, in "First Light," the cousin named Panchito, the wacky guy, he's my real cousin, Jaime. He really did the cricket chirp that I can't do. He and I really did drive around in my uncle's radio car making up announcements. We didn't do a blow-by-blow account of dogs copulating, but we did do something like that that I couldn't remember. We were always pulling pranks, and his little cricket thing to me represented the volumes of what this guy's soul was like. In all this macho posturing, there was this guy with a weirdly pure soul. All the other cousins would come to me and say, "That guy's a queer," and he was very happily sleeping with their girlfriends. He was a painter, he loved watercolors—again, he was a queer. He loved the most delicate. He was this beacon; he formed me. He really was a Beatles freak, and we would sit up all night on the roof, singing these Beatles songs— "Hey, Bungalow Beel, wat did you keel?" And then we'd have to translate them. All those details came into that story, and it's dangerous to me because they're so real to me that it makes it seem like the story is real. I have to be careful.

"Mr. Mendoza's Paintbrush" was based on the practical joke king of Mexico. He was a real guy who did these awful stunts. So there are always inspirations. I can't think of any story of mine that just came full-blown out of my mind except "In Search of Snow." It was just this wild-assed thing, this crazy story. Later, after it was published, somebody said, "Now, wait a minute. There's an Anglo guy and there's a Chicano guy, and that's about two-thirds worth of this novel. Then the last third is divided up between an Apache guy and your godparents. You don't see that those are all you, that you divided yourself in pieces and wrote a novel about yourself at war with yourself?" You always take credit for this stuff later.

It's so important for students to know how much writers work with their own lives— consciously and subconsciously—particularly in the short story.

You have to, because it's the material that's given to you. It's what you wrestle with. Like they say in AA, "The worse it is for you, the better it is for somebody else." Well, it's same for us as writers. The more difficult things we've been through, the better our stuff.

The more difficult things we've been through, the better our stuff.

Writing about the genesis of "In First Light," you described a hilarious experience with Kentucky Fried Chicken that actually triggered the story. It's not in the story, though. Another useful thing to know as a beginning writer is that what starts a story may not end up in the story! How do you know to let go of wonderful stories, wonderful writing that just doesn't end up belonging in the finished story?

That story just didn't fit in what I was doing. But you don't always know. Somebody with a really good eye will trim and change it. That's what editors are for.

Was the incident in any draft of the story?

No. But it stuck with me so strongly that it inspired the character of Garcia Garcia, the big blustery uncle. My real uncle was in the "This is the worst salsa I ever ate" scene.

He really did have a movie theater that really did have bats in the ceiling. This persona, this wild man persona, suddenly fueled that story—and also the memories of this cousin. The whole thing in the end when she makes him a shirt? All that was actually in a note that she put in my bag when we left before anyone was awake.

Rosario, the mythic Mexican village where a number of the stories in Six Kinds of Sky *take place, has as a counterpart the village where your father was born. How do the real and fictional places differ?*

Setting is of absolute importance in my writing. Landscape is always a character in Western writing, as witnessed in Kitteridge or Edward Abbey. Land is a character to me, too. So those Rosario stories are all about an imaginary place. When you actually go to the town, it's just a little smelly Mexican town on the edge of the highway. There's nothing there. But, like I said in the afterward, when I go there, I think, oh yeah, okay, so and so was over here once and this romance happened here. It's that overlay of stories that I know. All these things happened in places that are there.

Setting is of absolute importance in my writing. Landscape is always a character in Western writing, as witnessed in Kitteridge or Edward Abbey.

Not everybody has a Rosario, but everybody comes from somewhere. What advice would you give students about mining the territory they know themselves?

What we need to do is understand, first, that the place we come from is special and worthy of attention. One of the assignments I do with a lot of my writers is called "The House." I ask them to remember a place that is deeply, deeply ingrained in them. Good or bad, I don't care. It doesn't have to be a house, it can be work or business or summer camp. But start walking through that place, make a sheet for each room, title each sheet with the name of the room—or each place or tree or whatever. Have at least five of these places. Then start jotting down every detail you can remember about each one. Keep going back and forth till you get a lot of details. Now start writing about them, because each one of those rooms is a chapter: the walk to the porch or the kitchen, the entrance, the room. I say, "You are describing a house of memory." In the living room, where's the couch? Who sat there, what happened there, whose picture is over there? You start to see it again. I say, "Tell me a story about the picture—Uncle Bill, the one who hung himself. Why? Who sat over here? She's dead. Well, who is she and when did she die?" Pretty soon, if they connect, they will find out that they have, perhaps, a chapter per room. I keep pushing them until they find *the* room. Maybe it's the bathroom, nobody wants to write about the bathroom. Maybe it's the bedroom. People always get giggly. I say, "Giggle all you want, but what happened in the bedroom?"

Every time I teach a workshop, the first assignment is an even more personal one because I think our personal continent is important. I give them this assignment: What do your hands remember? I've had so many people come in and say, "I didn't write well," and it turns out to be the best thing they've ever written all semester. I tell them, "Look, it's different from what your eyes remember. It's different from what your mouth remembers. What your hands remember is very complex and you should explore it. I know you're going to act either shocked or really giggly when I say this, but your penis or your vagina remembers also. Everything about you remembers, and the things you giggle about, if you really pay attention, remember more sorrow than you think." I want to shock them into realizing: You are a nation. You're never without something to write about. I ask them, too, to have compassion. I say, "There are two sturdy saints in your feet and they've put up with a lot of hell. You should let them speak with a little compassion." They're just ways to make them understand that they have material, even if they think they don't have material.

Humor is a big part of your work. "Taped to the Sky" is laugh-out-loud-funny—and heartbreaking, as well. Would you talk about the relationship between humor and sadness in your work?

The humor is always sad. Sometimes the sadness is just straight-up sad by itself, but the humor is almost always sad. I think that may have come from Japanese literature for me. You know, Basho, the great haiku master? I keep a picture of Basho on my desk all the time. He talked about how the sense of melancholy is important because we are all going to die. And not only are you and I going to die, but this chair is going to die—and if you learn to have compassion for this poor chair, then you'll walk with a little grace. He talked about imagining a very old man putting on his armor that's just too big for him to wear anymore and volunteering to go to battle—and I thought, oh, my God, he was talking about Don Quixote two hundred years before. It was so brilliant, that feeling of comic sadness that he talks about. He says, of course, that same man putting on a very old suit to go to a party has got the same sort of tenderness to it. That touches me a lot. And I come from really funny people. I set out to write serious stuff, but—I just can't help being funny.

"Mr. Mendoza's Paintbrush" combines that comic sadness you describe with magic realism, which is often a characteristic of Hispanic literature.

Magic realism. I don't use it as any kind of a device that I'm consciously aware of, but it creeps into my work all the time. García Márquez once said he grew up seeing this stuff. He told a story about a medicine person or a shaman who cured cattle of tapeworms by speaking to them. He saw this happen and he thought, If I've seen that, then what's so weird about a virgin flying? Mr. Mendoza. I started out as a cartoonist, and one of my sketches was of a guy with a pen drawing a stairway and walking up it. It was probably my attempt to do an M. C. Escher picture, but I didn't have the chops to do it. But I always thought, well, that's a really cool picture. So when I started thinking about the story of this guy who could have been some kind of king of something in Rosario, I remembered that drawing and I thought, okay, he paints his way into the sky. But why? That image came first, his walking into the sky, but I wanted to write in words what I had drawn.

I think we often make the mistake of telling white kids they don't have a culture. I can't tell you how many of my midwestern Anglo students tell me, "Well, I don't have a culture," and I say, "Really? You don't? Because when you start talking, you tell me all this stuff I have no idea about. What's wrong with that? What's wrong with that as a culture? It's fascinating." Every culture, no matter what it is, has magic stuff in it. A lot of the tales that our old-timers tell—it's not actual flying around stuff magic, but it has strange little details that are always kind of haunting. I'm always looking for those strange details that haunt or that are just really cool ideas.

Why do you think the Hispanic culture is more apt to see the world that magical way?

There's a sort of mythic, mad Catholicism. In Chicano literature, we always joke that there's the "Jesus in the Tortilla" myth—you know, some insane miracle. But we do have it. There's this world of accepted magic. Our basic faith is of magic, our religion is based on magic. We go to Mexico City and crawl three miles on our knees to see the Virgin of Guadeloupe up on the wall, and she's magic. When they did microscopic research into the painting, they found that in her eye there's a chip of light and in it you can see the men kneeling at her feet. Now how the hell did that get in there? We in Latin America spend a lot of time watching science prove us right. I think that's all very important. I think history lives among us in ways that, walking around, we do not honor. I often think it must be the United States' Protestant approach that discourages magic. I'll tell you something about magic realism, though. García Márquez said it came from Faulkner.

There's this world of accepted magic. Our basic faith is of magic, our religion is based on magic.

Southerners do have that same kind of sense that nothing is stranger than life. The weirdest people are the people who live next door to you.

Before I came here, I taught in Louisiana for a while, and it was heaven. That culture off the bayou—I thought, these guys are just Mexicans, man! They've got accordions, hot peppers! They eat really appalling stuff with a lot of sauce on it! They have a cultural struggle very similar to what happened with the Chicano culture: The Cajun culture's been overwhelmed by white southern culture. The Klan was there, really, not to kill black people, but to kill Catholics. And just the landscape! It became my favorite activity to go to the swamp and I'd look at the gators. My wife Cindy, on our first trip there, got chased by an alligator—and I thought, this just doesn't happen in San Diego or Chicago. It was the best. My Cajun brothers were real good to me.

So, in a sense, the magic realism is coming from the way you perceive the world. The way the world is for you. It's not something you can make up.

I think so. I think magic realism lends itself to cheese, also. There's a lot of really bad writing, really tacky, kitschy writing that assumes all you have to do is have something wacky happen and it's magic.

You have to believe in it for it to work.

Magic realism that works reflects a kind of innocence in the eye and soul of the writer who sees it. For example, if you read the first, say, hundred pages of the García Márquez memoir that just came out—he's on a train trip with his mom and he's realizing *One Hundred Years of Solitude.* It's a tour de force; it's brilliant. It's an essay, but there it is. You see leaf storms, and he's telling these stories about how there was a ghost who would walk through their house as they were all trying to eat supper.

Magic realism that works reflects a kind of innocence in the eye and soul of the writer who sees it.

Do you think a writer's connection to place—his own history in a place—is crucial in whether or not magical realism works?

Absolutely. A really graphic example is the cathedral in the main square in Mexico City. The Spaniards blew up the pyramids and built the cathedral out of them, so you have this overlay of history that is just mind-boggling. Here's this Catholic place, where they have the mass, and some of those stones have the blood of people who were sacrificed to the sun on them. I had an experience there that seems magic realist, but it really and truly happened. I was with a writer friend, around midnight. They had uncovered one of the pyramids across the way from the cathedral, and the excavation was illuminated as they were digging it out. There was no one around at all, and I started to hear voices—as if a crowd of a hundred people were standing around me.

Did your friend hear the voices?

No. I could hear this tumult, like people were walking—footsteps. And voices. I thought, I'm going crazy. It was a weird moment, a personal moment that I can't really explain. I don't know if it was an illusion or not. But if you take those illusions as real, you have magic realism.

I don't know if it was an illusion or not. But if you take those illusions as real, you have magic realism.

Medicine men, shaman types—a lot of them deal in a kind of perception reversal. I was writing about Terecita, my aunt, and, as I was researching her, I started having these dreams of three old Indian men, all in white peasant clothing with straw hats. After a few nights, they started saying, "Hi." When I was dreaming of other things, if I turned around they'd be behind me, watching, and they'd nod and salute. I finally called Esperanza, my cousin, and said, "Something really weird is happening." And she said, "What's happening *mi hijo?*" I said, "I'm having these dreams. These three men, they're dark, white pants, white shirts, you know? Belts, straw hats? What are they?" She said, "Ah, that's *son joaquis.*" I said, "Okay, all right, but why am I dreaming them every night?" She said, "You're not dreaming them, they're dreaming about *you.* Somewhere, someplace—it could be now, it could be 1873—some *joaquis* found out what you're doing and they're coming to check your dreams to make sure that you're all right for the information." Those kinds of reversals happen a lot.

And that makes for good fiction—those moments where a story torques.

And it makes a really good personal approach to the world. One of the things I have always taught is that it's about seeing. It's about paying attention. Mary Oliver says that's the whole of the law, "You must pay attention." The more you learn to see, the more you see.

In "Amazing Grace," you say that what a writer must do is best expressed in the French verb ententre: *wait, listen, heed.*

It's the only journey you take by stopping. We're in a big rush, pushing and rushing. I tell my students all the time, though they don't really listen to me, "You have an old-timer in your family that keeps telling you the same damn story and you're so sick of hearing it, you blow them off and say, 'Yeah, yeah, yeah, whatever.' Well, she'll pass away, and I guarantee you'll say ten years later, 'What was that story about Uncle Bill?' She was trying to pass on this genetic nugget of story to you, and you were the only one who could have received it and you rejected it. And she's gone and it's gone." You have to, at some point, try to hear, try to see. We give each other little subtle messages that we miss. People leave story everywhere and we miss it.

There's a magazine about Chicago called *Found Magazine.* It's a magazine that is made of just junk found on the street. They have people mail it to them from all around the world—letters, notes, anything they find—and these guys publish it. That, to me, is just brilliant. I feel like we're always carrying story, and we've got to stop and honor the story. Our culture no longer honors story. We don't have *wen fu* masters. We don't gather at a fire in the morning, as some cultures do, and discuss our dreams. We don't listen. We really don't. We hear a lot, but we don't take heed.

You have to actively read. You've got to get into reading. A lot of times writers who are starting to get successful talk to me about, Why are the fans so insane? Why do they get a little wacky and do weird things? Some of them get overinvolved. But they're carrying you in their hand, against their chests. They're taking you to bed. They have your words on their tongues and on their lips. They take you naked into a bath. I mean, you are in their world, way deep. It's very intimate.

We have to learn to honor all those things. I get reamed a little bit, especially among grad students, who say, "You like everything." And I say, "No, I dislike almost everything. You are writing students and hence what you're writing is in process. It's not great writing. But I love something in everything you write." If you pay attention to how I workshop, I'm looking for the plant that I can water. I don't believe in the confrontation form. At Harvard they believe in teaching through intimidation in the writing program. This guy there had two rubber stamps in red ink. One said, "BULLSHIT" and the other said, "SPEAKING IN ENGLISH?" He would stamp it all over students' work and give it back. That's not the way I like to do it.

Speaking of Harvard's methods, in "Amazing Grace" you talked about rethinking their philosophy about the indirect means of telling a story.

Yes, right. The under-story. We used the indirect means of telling a story at Harvard, which is what appeals to me most in writing—the hidden story that drives the story more strongly than the words you see. The perfect example is that essay, "A Hanging," by George Orwell. If you analyze every single move as a strategy to get the story across, you find so many techniques. I teach it every semester because it's so brilliant. The under-story is essentially what goes on beneath the surface. Hemingway said that a story was one-eighth above and seven-eighths under water, like an iceberg, and that thing under the water is the bulk and the power of the story. I started thinking about that, and I thought, no, it's not an iceberg, it's a snapping turtle. The piece of the shell and the head are what stick out of the water, but the engine room—the gut and the heart and the beating paddles—are under the water. And that sucker really moves the story. But the *real* thing that's driving a story is the stuff it carries with it. Those little details, those motions and movements. Colors, word choice, images. I show students Eudora Welty's "A Worn Path." There's a marvelous piece of miraculous imagery in that story at the very beginning: Phoenix Jackson walking across a frozen gray and black field with dead trees in it and her cane and a broken umbrella that cheeps like a solitary little bird. I say, "Is this a happy story? Obviously not." So they learn a lot just in the first sentences of Eudora Welty. One of the old women that I interviewed for the Terecita book told me that when you write you flare up a huge fire in the spirit world. Your soul glows very brightly as you're writing, and those spirits that are lost come to the writer.

But the *real* thing that's driving a story is the stuff it carries with it. Those little details, those motions and movements. Colors, word choice, images.

You talk a lot about issues of the soul, about grace. Writing feels almost like a kind of religion as you describe it.

Well, I was a very serious little Catholic boy. Then I went through an atheist period. Then I hooked up with Baptist missionaries. So I have a pretty God-soaked, Christ-soaked past. Since then, I have proceeded on my own path, but I really do feel grace in writing, almost in a religious sense—in terms of forgiveness, absolution, and reconciliation. There was a great phrase, when Neal Cassidy told Jack Kerouac, "Grace beats Karma." I think if you try to approach your work as I do, it leads to a kind of compassion and forgiving stance towards the rest of the world. One of the hardest assignments I give writing students is, "Today you walk through that door and find yourself at seven. Help that child." It's very difficult to do because we don't love ourselves. I find that child, and I actively dislike him. I'm ashamed of him. I'm still working on that. But if I can bring grace down to that poor kid it helps me, I think, with my own children and in all my relationships with people. I think about Basho's old man and his armor a lot. John Anderson, a poet, had a booklet I bought in Harvard Square for a quarter; it was thirteen

And Rule Three, maybe, was "Remember the world of ghosts and small gestures." That has become my ultimate writing rule.

helpful hints on the writing of poetry. A stapled booklet. And Rule Three, maybe, was "Remember the world of ghosts and small gestures." That has become my ultimate writing rule. Moments in "Father Returns from the Mountain" came because it was what happened in the dream. I said, "Father, did you see God?" And he looked at me and turned on the radio and smiled. Not only was that gesture the whole story for me, but that was my dad, too. That's the kind of thing my dad would have done. Those are grace notes. But it also represents God to me, how God can come into a story.

Writing Prompts

READ: "Father Returns from the Mountain" and the interview with **Luis Alberto Urrea.**

PONDER: How Urrea uses word choice, sentence rhythms, repetitions, imagery, and structure to replicate the atmosphere of the actual experience.

WRITE: Remember an intensely emotional event in your life. Write it so that the essence of the emotion is mirrored in the language, imagery, and structure of the piece.

PRACTICE:

- Write down a dream you had in all the detail you can remember. Expand and invent to transform the dream into a story. Or create a story that makes use of the dream.
- Write a scene in which small details and gestures convey a clandestine relationship.
- Imagine a story based on a drawing or painting you made or one that holds some mystery for you.
- Identify a person you know with mythic qualities. Write a scene in which the mythic qualities are portrayed without naming or explaining them. Feel free to embroider and invent.
- Think of a place that would seem ordinary to most people but is magical to you because of your own experiences there and/or because being there evokes the stories of others. Write a paragraph of description that might serve as the beginning of the story. Heighten the visual and sensory details and invent new ones to create the magical effect that you feel.
- Remember a house that is deeply ingrained in your memory and, in your mind's eye, walk through it, noting details as you go. Make a sheet for each room, title each sheet with the name of the room, and start jotting down every detail you can remember about each one. Choose one room and freewrite about what happened or might have happened there.
- What do your hands remember? Freewrite. Choose other parts of your body and do the same thing.
- Write a scene that is both funny and sad.
- Think of a story a living family member tells all the time, one you are sick to death of hearing. Interview the person about the events surrounding the story, asking questions that might allow you to discover something new and surprising about the person and/or the story.

- Spend a week collecting interesting pieces of junk that you come upon going about your daily routine. Make a story from one or more of them.
- Walk through a door in your mind's eye and find yourself at seven years old. Write something that will help that child.
- Make a list of words that seem magical to you and/or seem to have positive or negative power. Write a story using as many of those words as you can.

Daly Walker

Daly Walker (b. 1940) is a fiction writer and practicing surgeon. Born in Winchester, Indiana, he was educated at Ohio Wesleyan University, Indiana University School of Medicine, and the University of Wisconsin School of Medicine. His work has appeared in numerous publications including The Atlantic Monthly, The Sewannee Review, The Sycamore Review, *and the* Louisville Review. *His stories have been short-listed for* The O. Henry Prize Stories, The Best American Short Stories, *and* The Best American Magazine Writing 2001. *He lives Boca Grande, Florida.*

I Am the Grass

Because I love my wife and daughter, and because I want them to believe I am a good man, I have never talked to them about my year as a grunt with the 25th infantry in Vietnam. I cannot tell my thirteen-year-old that once, drunk on Ba Muoi Ba beer, I took a girl her age into a thatched-roof hooch in Tay Ninh City and did her on a bamboo mat. I cannot tell my wife, who paints watercolors of songbirds, that on a search-and-destroy mission I emptied my M-60 machine gun into two beautiful white egrets that were wading in the muddy water of a paddy. I cannot tell them how I sang "Happy Trails" as I shoved two wounded Viet Cong out the door of a medevac chopper hovering twenty feet above the tarmac of a battalion aid station. I cannot tell them how I lay in a ditch and used my M-60 to gun down a skinny, black-haired farmer I thought was a VC, nearly blowing his head off. I cannot tell them how I completed the decapitation with a machete, and then stuck his head on a pole on top of a mountain called Nui Ba Den. All these things fester in me like the tiny fragment of shrapnel embedded in my skull, haunt me like the corpse of the slim dark man I killed. I cannot talk about these things that I wish I could forget but know that I never will.

Twenty years have passed since the summer of 1968, when I flew home from the war and my "freedom bird" landed in the night at Travis Air Force Base, near San Francisco. I knew that in the city, soldiers in uniform were taunted in the streets by flower children. So I slipped quietly into a restroom and changed from my dress khakis into jeans and a flannel shirt. Nobody was there to say "Welcome home, soldier." It was as if I were an exile in my own country. I felt deceived and confused, and most of all angry, but I wasn't sure at whom to direct my anger or where to go or what to do, so I held everything inside and went about forming a life day by day.

After I was discharged from the Army, I went home to Chicago and hung around there for a couple of years, haunted by memories and nameless faces. Devoid of hope or expectations, smoking dope and dreaming dreams of torment, I drifted from one meaningless endeavor to the next. I studied drawing at the art academy, cut grass with the grounds crew at Soldier Field, parked cars at the Four Seasons. Nothing seemed to matter; nothing changed what I was. I was still fire and smoke, a loaded gun, a dead survivor, a little girl on a bamboo mat, a headless corpse. I was still in the killing zone.

Gradually I grew weary of my hollowness, ran out of pity for my own self-pity. I wanted to take my life and shake it by the hair. I decided to use the GI Bill and give college a try.

I enrolled at the University of Wisconsin at Madison, the headquarters of the Weathermen and the SDS. I lived in a run-down rooming house on Mifflen Street, among all the long-haired war protesters and scruffy peaceniks. During the day I went to classes and worked as an orderly at a Catholic hospital, but at night, after work, I went back to my room to study alone. Through the window of my room I could see mobs of students marching through the streets, chanting "Ho, Ho, Ho Chi Minh" and "Bring home the war." What did they know about war? I watched them, and I wanted to kick their hippie asses.

It was in caring for the patients at the hospital that I seemed to find what I had been searching for. While bathing or feeding a patient I felt simply good. It was better than my best trips with Mary Jane. I decided to apply to medical school, and I was accepted.

One night when I was a senior med student, a couple of radical war protesters blew up the Army Mathematics Research Center on campus. The explosion shook my bed in the hospital call room like the rocket that blasted me out of sleep the night of the Tet Offensive. I have never been a brave man, and I lay there in the dark with my heart pounding, thinking I was back in Firebase Zulu the night we were overrun. A nurse called me to the emergency room to help resuscitate a theoretical physicist who had been pulled from under the rubble. His chest was crushed and both his lungs were collapsed. He didn't need resuscitation. He needed a body bag. The war I was trying to escape had followed me home.

Now I practice plastic surgery in Lake Forest, a North Shore Chicago suburb of stone walls, German cars, and private clubs. On my arm is a scar from the laser surgery that removed a tattoo I woke up with one morning in a Bangkok whorehouse. The tattoo was a cartoon in blue and red ink of a baby in diapers, wearing an Army helmet and a parachute with the inscription "Airborne." I feel that I am two people at once, two people fighting within myself. One is a family man and a physician who lives a comfortable external life. The other is a war criminal with an atrophied soul. Nothing I do can revive it.

Even as a surgeon I have a split personality. I sculpt women's bodies with breast augmentations, tummy tucks, face-lifts, and liposuction. I like the money, but I'm bored with these patients and their vanity, their urgent need for surgical enhancement. I am also a reconstructive plastic surgeon who loves Z-plastying a scar from a dog bite on a little girl's cheek or skin grafting a burn on the neck of a small boy who fell against a space heater. I love reconstructing a lobster-claw deformity of the hand so that a child can hold a spoon and fork. I'm no Albert Schweitzer, but every summer I spend a couple of weeks in Haiti or Kenya or Guatemala with Operation Smile, repairing cleft palates and lips. Removing the bandages and seeing the results of my skill sends a chill up my neck, makes me feel like something of a decent man, a healer.

Today, in late September, I am sitting in a window seat in a Thai Airways jet on its way from Bangkok to Ho Chi Minh City. I am headed to the Khanh Hoa Hospital, in Nha Trang, for two weeks of my own little Operation Smile, repairing the cleft palates and lips of children on whose land I once wreaked havoc, whose parents and grandparents I murdered and whom, somewhere deep inside me, I still hold in contempt.

I stare out the airplane window at tufts of white clouds that look like bursts of artillery flak, and I break into a sweat, remembering the descent of the airliner that flew me, a machine gunner, an Airborne Ranger, an eighteen-year-old pissed-off, pot-smoking warrior, cannon fodder, to Vietnam. The pilot lurched into a steep, spiraling dive to minimize the plane's exposure time to ground fire. I pitched forward in my seat, the belt cutting into my belly, my heart pounding. Until that moment I had felt immortal, but then fear came to me in an image of my own death by a bullet to the brain, and I realized how little I mattered, how quickly and simply and anonymously the end could come. I believed that I would never return home to my room with the old oak dresser and corner desk that my mother dusted and polished with lemon oil. Tears filled my eyes.

With the plane in a long, gentle glide, I gaze out the window and search for remnants of the war. I see a green patchwork of paddies and fields of grass, dirt roads whose-iron-red dust choked me, whose mud caked my jungle boots. A sampan floats down a river. Smoke curls lazily from a thatched-roof shack. An ox pulls a cart. The land seems asleep, and the war only a dream. I drop back in the seat and close my eyes. Stirring in my chest is the feeling that a dangerous demon is setting itself free inside me.

I spend the night in Saigon at the Bong Song Hotel, a mildewing walk-up not far from the Museum of American War Crimes. The toilet doesn't flush. The ceiling fan croaks so loudly that I turn it off. Oily tropical heat drenches the room, and I can hear rats skittering across the floor. I feel as I once did trying to grab a little shut-eye before going out on ambush patrol. I can't sleep. My mind is filled with the image of myself dragging the lifeless body of a kid named Dugan by the ankles through mud.

In the orange light of dawn I board an old minivan that will take me north to the hospital in Nha Trang. The tottering vehicle weaves through streets teeming with bicycles, three-wheeled cyclos, motorbikes, an occasional car. People gawk at me as if I were a zoo animal of a breed they have never seen before. The driver is Tran, a spindly man with wispy Ho Chi Minh chin whiskers. He has been assigned to be my guide and interpreter, but he is really the People's Committee watchdog. When I was here before, I would have called him a gook or a slope, a dink motherfucker, and those are the words that come to me now when I look at Tran. I picture his head on a pole.

We cross the Saigon River on Highway One, Vietnam's aorta, the artery connecting Hanoi with Saigon. The French called Highway One "*la rue sans joie.*" We called it "the street to sorrow." During the war I often traveled this road in convoys of tanks and half-tracks whose treads pulverized the pavement. I was always high on Buddha grass. Armed to the teeth. Frightened and mean. I was so young. I didn't know what I was doing here. A few miles out of Saigon, Tran slows and points to a vast empty plain overgrown with olive-drab grass and scrub brush.

"This Long Binh," he says.

"Stop," I say.

He pulls off the road and parks by a pile of rusty wire and scrap metal. I climb out of the van and stand, looking at acres of elephant grass blasted by the tropical sun. I think of Long Binh when it was an enormous military base, a sandbag city of tents barbed wire, and bunkers. We called it LBJ, for "Long Binh Jail." It was where I spent my first night "in country," sweat-soaked on a sagging cot, listening to the distant chunk of artillery, fear clawing at my chest. Now all I see is emptiness. Nothing to verify my past, nothing to commune with. How hot it is. How quiet.

Since Nam, I have spent a lot of nights with bottles of wine, reading the poetry of war—Homer and Kipling, Sandburg and Komunyakaa. Through the haze of my thoughts, words by Sandburg are moving. The words are about grass and war and soldiers in Austerlitz and Gettysburg and Waterloo, but they are about this place, too. *Shove them under and let me work—I am the grass; I cover all.* I gaze out at Long Binh's grass. It ripples in hot wind like folds of silk.

I climb back into the van, and we jostle on through paddies and rubber plantations, green groves of bamboo and banana trees. I have the strange feeling that my life has shrunk, that just around the bend an ambush will be waiting. I lean forward in my seat and ask Tran if he remembers Long Binh when the American soldiers were here.

"Vietnam believe it better not to remind of the past." He speaks looking straight ahead through aviator sunglasses. "We live in present with eye on future." The words sound rote, as if he is quoting from a propaganda paper. "Vietnam want to be thought of as country, not war, not just problem in other country's past."

On a berm old women in conical hats spread rice and palm fronds to dry in the sun. Charcoal fumes waft from cooking fires. White-shirted children with red kerchiefs tied around their necks march to school. Two men, brown and bent like cashew nuts, face each other over a big teak log and pull a crosscut saw back and forth slowly, rhythmically. For a brief moment the smell of gunpowder comes back to me, and I see little Asian men running headlong through tall grass, firing weapons and screaming. I see GIs running through smoke with green canvas stretchers.

The arrangements for my mission in the coastal city of Nha Trang were made through Dr. Lieh Viet Dinh, the director of Khanh Hoa Hospital. The morning after my arrival, Dinh sends word to my hotel that he wants to meet me for a welcoming meal at a restaurant on the South China Sea. I have been told that Dinh was once in the North Vietnamese army and now is a high official in the province's Communist Party. What does he want? For me to say I'm sorry?

I hire a cyclo driver to pedal me to the restaurant. Mopeds with their exhaust tinting the air blue and bicycles piled high with cordwood tangle the streets. The Sunday-afternoon sun is so bright it hurts my eyes. But there is a cool ocean breeze and the scent of bougainvillaea in the air. Under flame trees with brilliant-orange blossoms barbers trim hair and clean wax from ears. Street vendors hawk flowers and loaves of French bread. Everywhere I look, I see Vietnamese getting on with their lives. I marvel at their serenity. They are no different from the people that I was taught to distrust, that I once machine-gunned. This street is no different from streets that I once helped to fill with rubble and bodies. A man on a Honda raises his index finger and calls, "Hey, Joe. U.S. number one." But I look away from him.

The restaurant is a rickety tile-roofed pagoda perched on stilts over a beach of sand the color of crème brûlée. Below, in a natural aquarium, sand sharks and tropical fish dart among the rocks. In the distance a soft vapor hangs over mountain islands in the bay. The restaurant is empty except for a gnarly little man sitting alone at a table with the sun splashing off turquoise water behind him. He is a militant figure with penetrating black eyes and hollow, acne-scarred cheeks that give him a look of toughness, a look that says, You could never defeat me no matter how many bombs you dropped. I know he is Dinh. The contempt that boiled inside me during the war bubbles up. I can feel it in my chest.

He calls to me to join him. I settle into a wooden chair across from him and extend my hand for him to shake, but he ignores it and offers a stiff little bow of his head. Nervousness dries up the saliva in my mouth. A waitress in a blue *ao dai* brings us bottles of Ba Muoi Ba beer. With her lustrous black hair and slim, silk-sheathed figure, she is beautiful and exotic like a tropical bird. The shy young girl with a dimple in her cheek that I took on the bamboo mat in Tay Ninh would be about her age now. I wonder what became of her.

In English that I have to listen to closely to understand, Dinh talks for a while about the Khanh Hoa Hospital, the only hospital for the one million people of his province. He tells me that my visit has been advertised on television, and that thirty children with cleft lips to be repaired will be there. His jaw tight, his voice intimidating, he tells me that the hospital has trouble getting medicine and equipment because of the American embargo. I pick up my bottle of beer and press it to my lips and tilt it. The liquid is warm, with the slight formaldehyde taste that I remember from the war. I look at Dinh's slanty black eyes and stained teeth, thinking how easy it would be to kill him. I've been taught to do it with a gun or a knife or my hands. It would come back to me quickly, like sitting down at a piano and playing a song that you mastered a long time ago but haven't played in years. Suddenly the thought of operating on little children in all this heat and dirt, with archaic equipment, jolts me back into the present. I ask him who will give the anesthesia.

"My doctors," he says. "Vietnamese doctors as good as any in the world."

The waitress brings a plate of lightly fried rice paper, bowls of rice and noodles, and a platter of sea bass smothered in peppers, onions, and peanuts. She gives me chopsticks and Dinh a metal spoon. When we begin to eat, I see Dinh's hands for the first time. I am startled. Now I know why he didn't shake with me. His thumbs are missing. I watch him spoon rice onto his plate, clutching the utensil in his thumbless hand. He has learned a pinch grip between his second and third digits, like children I have operated on who were born with floating thumbs or congenital absence of the first metacarpal bone. Using his fingers as if they were tongs, he wraps some fish in a sheet of the rice paper and dips it in nuoc cham sauce. The sauce smells rancid, and a sourness rises up my esophagus.

"I hear you in Vietnam during war," Dinh says between bites of fish and rice.

"Yes," I say. I can't take my eyes off his hands.

"Where?" he asks.

"South of here, along the Cambodian border near Tay Ninh."

"You see Nui Ba Den," he says. "How you call it? The black virgin mountain. This fish good. Dip your fish in nuoc cham."

I picture that black-haired man's head skewered on a bamboo pole.

"Yeah, I've seen Nui Ba Den," I say, feeling as if he must somehow know what I did on top of the mountain.

"Were you Army surgeon?"

"No. That was before I went to medical school. I was with the infantry." I take a gulp of beer. "That was a long time ago."

"Not so long ago," Dinh says. His lips curl into a smile that is filled with crooked yellow teeth. "Americans always think time longer than it is. Americans very impatient. Vietnamese very patient. We believe life is circle. Everything comes and goes. Why grasp and cling? Always things will come around again if you give them time. Patience is why we win victory."

In the filthy little village across the bay I can see tin-roofed shacks, teeming streets, the haze of smoke from cooking fires—the thick stew of peasant life.

"How about you?" I ask. "Were you a doctor during the war?"

He wipes his mouth with his shirt-sleeve and says, "In war against French colonialists, I was Vietminh infantry man. Fifteen years old."

He raises a maimed hand and, with a wave motion to demonstrate high altitude, tells how he twice climbed the mountains of Laos and Cambodia on the Ho Chi Minh Trail—once to fight the French and once to fight the Americans and their Vietnamese puppets. He was wounded at Dien Bien Phu. I wonder if that was when he lost his thumbs. I'm fascinated by his thumblessness. The ability to oppose a thumb and a finger is what sets us apart from lemurs and baboons.

"We have little to fight with," Dinh says. "After we shoot our guns, we pick up empty cartridges to use again. We eat nothing but tapioca roots and half a can of rice a day. For seven years I fight hungry."

I listen to him tell of his wars, and it takes me back to mine. Cold-sweat nights peering out of a muddy bunker through concertina wire at tracers and shadows. Waiting. Listening. Grim patrols through elephant grass and jungle greased with moonlight. I can hear screams, see faces of the dead. What is memory and what is a dream? When it comes to the war, nothing seems true. It seems impossible that something that tragic, that unspeakable, was once a part of my life. Suddenly I'm overwhelmed with emotion. I wonder if Dinh ever feels like crying. In the shallows below the restaurant a sea turtle snaps at silver fish trapped in a net.

"How about in the war against America?" I ask. "Were you a doctor then?"

"I was surgeon in the war against you and your South Vietnamese puppets."

"Where did you serve?" I ask. "Were you in a hospital?"

"My hospital the forest. My operating table the soil of the jungle." He holds up both hands and rotates them for me to see. "I have thumbs then. I clever surgeon. I operate on everything from head to toes." He looks up at the ceiling as if an airplane were circling overhead. "Your B-fifty-twos drop big bombs. They make earth shake. They scare hell out of me."

Dinh flashes a smile that makes me uncomfortable. He takes a drink of beer.

"Were you wounded?" I ask.

"You mean my hands?"

"Yeah. What happened?"

He rests them on the table, displaying them as he talks. He tells me that he was captured in the central highlands, not by Americans but by South Vietnamese Special Forces in their purple berets. When they learned he was a doctor, they chose him for torture. They tied him to a stake under merciless sun and every day pulled out one of his fingernails with a pair of pliers. At night they locked him up in a tiger cage. He speaks softly. On the eleventh day they cut off his thumbs. Then they cooked them in a soup and told him to drink it. He hadn't eaten for two weeks, so he did.

"How did you survive?" I ask. "Why didn't you go crazy?"

"I pretended to be somewhere else. Somewhere at a time after our victory. I always knew we would win."

Dinh looks at my hands.

"You lucky," he says. "You have thumbs to do surgery. I can't even eat with chopsticks." He raises his hands, flexing his fingers. He glares at me with eyes as hard and black as gun bores. "This should happen to no one."

We finish our meal in silence. Under the afternoon sun the restaurant is stifling, and I feel queasy. I can get down only a little rice. But Dinh eats hungrily, shoveling in the food with his spoon as if to make up for all those years of rice and tapioca roots. When his plate is clean, he rinses his hands in a bowl of hot lime water with tea leaves floating on the surface.

He looks up at me and says, "To take the smell of fish from your skin."

In the morning I walk from my hotel through steamy air, on streets boiling with people, to the hospital. Around the entryway dozens of crippled peasants and ragged children with skin sores squat on the powdery earth. Everything is dusty. I understand why Vietnamese peasants call themselves "the dust of life." A boy with weight-lifter arms calls to me in English from a bicycle that he pedals with his hands. He wants me to fix his paralyzed legs.

Khanh Hoa's pale-yellow façade gives me an impression of cleanliness and light, but inside, the wards are dim and grungy, with no glass or screens in the windows to keep out flies and mosquitoes. Often two patients occupy a single narrow bed, with family members sleeping on the floor nearby to assist with the feeding and bathing, the emptying of bedpans. A tiny, toothless woman with skin like teakwood waves a bamboo fan over a wasted man on a mattress without sheets. She gazes at me with longing. Everywhere I go, someone with sorrowful eyes looks at me as if I were Jesus.

During my first week I don't have any more conversations with Dinh, but I see him every morning when he comes in his white lab coat to the surgery suite to watch me operate. At the door he slips off his sandals and pads barefoot into the room, where he stands at the head of the table, his black eyes peering at the children whose lips are like hook-ripped fish mouths. He rarely speaks, and when he does, it is usually to address the Vietnamese doctors and nurses in a tone that suggests sarcasm.

It is impossible to know what his silence toward me means, but I become immersed in my work, and I don't worry about him. Once the operation starts, my concentration is complete, my only concern the child's face, framed in blue towels and bathed in bright light. I have always been gifted at drawing and carving, and with a scalpel in my hand I feel like an artist, forming something beautiful out of chaos. I love mapping out flaps of skin around a child's mouth and then rotating them over the cleft to create a nice Cupid's bow of lip with a clean vermilion border. My sutures are like the brushstrokes of a portrait. Dinh must envy the collaboration of my brain and fingers.

Between cases I rest in the doctors' lounge at a wooden table. I drink a pot of pale-tan tea, eat litchi fruit, and look out into the hospital courtyard that serves as the waiting room. I often see Dinh with his hands hidden in the pockets of his lab coat, squatting in the dust, talking with the parents of the cleft-lipped children who are undergoing surgery. His face, glistening under the hot sun, looks as if it has been oiled. His chronic scowl has become a comforting smile.

At the end of my first week I call my wife and daughter to tell them that all is going well. When I report that I have repaired eighteen cleft lips without a complication, my wife seems proud of me. I am getting to like the nurses and doctors in the operating room. My feelings of guilt and ambivalence are being replaced by a sense of good will and atonement, as if Vietnam and I were two bad people who had unexpectedly done something nice for each other. But on Sunday, Dinh sends word for me to meet him in his "cabinet," as he calls his private office. I worry that I have done something wrong.

The room is the size of an armoire and sparsely furnished. A single bookcase contains the medical texts of the hospital's meager library. On the wall is a little green lizard and a yellowed photograph of Ho Chi Minh. From a cassette player on a homemade wooden table comes the music of a symphony orchestra playing Vivaldi's *The Four Seasons.* The hospital sewer system is backed up, and the air smells brackish. My stomach churns. I sit in a straight-backed chair across a metal desk from Dinh. My office in Lake Forest, with its Oriental carpet and polished cherry furniture, seems infinitely far away.

"Vivaldi," I say to break the silence.

Dinh looks up from a journal article in which he is underlining with a wooden pencil. His face, shadowed by years of hardship, is expressionless. He wears a white shirt and a clipon red rayon tie. He has a small Band-Aid on his chin where, I assume, he nicked himself shaving. I imagine him handling a razor, buttoning a shirt, tying a tie or shoestrings. Without a thumb's ability to pinch and oppose, even simple tasks must be difficult for him.

"Do you enjoy Vivaldi?" he asks.

"*The Four Seasons* is one of my favorites. When did you develop a taste for Western music?"

"When I was in medical school in Hanoi, French doctors play music in surgery room. Music only good thing about Frenchmen. Music good healing medicine. I play music to calm my patients."

He clicks off the tape and hands me the article he has been reading. It is a reprint from a French journal of hand surgery. I leaf through its pages, scanning illustrations that depict an operation in which a toe is transferred to the hand to replace a missing thumb.

"Can you make thumb?" Dinh asks.

I sit for a moment, remembering my last toe transplant, performed a couple of years ago. It was on a young farm boy who had lost his thumb in a corn picker.

"Yes," I say. "I've done this operation. Not often, but I've done it."

"I want you do this to me," Dinh says.

"Here? Now? You want me to make you a thumb?"

"Yes. I want you make me new thumb."

It is as if, fighting a losing battle, I suddenly see the enemy waving a white flag. For a moment I look at his narrow, bony hands with the red ridges of scar tissue where thumbs once protruded.

"It's a very hard operation," I say. "Quite delicate. A microvascular procedure. Even under perfect conditions it often doesn't work."

"I watch you operate." Dinh lowers his eyes and his voice.

"You very careful surgeon. I know you can do."

"Let me see your hand."

He extends his right hand toward me. I rise and move around the desk. I take his hand in mine and turn it slowly, studying skin tone and temperature. His radial pulse bounds against my fingers. His nail beds are pink with good capillary circulation. The skin of the palm is creased and thickly callused.

"Thumb reconstruction must be carefully planned," I say. "You don't just jump into it. There are several techniques to consider."

In my mind I review them: using a skin flap and a bone graft from the pelvis; politicization, in which the index finger is rotated to oppose the third finger; and my favorite technique, which uses a tube graft of abdominal skin—but it has to be staged over several weeks.

"The new thumb must be free of pain," I say, carefully palpating the bones of his hand, searching for the missing thumb's metacarpal. I find it intact. "It has to have sensation so it can recognize objects. It has to be long enough to touch the tip of opposing digits. It must be flexible."

"You don't have to teach me," Dinh says gruffly. "I know about this. I read everything in literature. Toe transplant best for me."

"I'm not so sure about that."

"Toe transplant best."

"Maybe so, but you're the patient this time. I'm the doctor. Let me decide."

I bend over and lift his dusty foot into my lap. I slip off his tire-tread sandal. His foot is the size of my daughter's, the toenails poorly cared for. My fingers find strong dorsalis pedis and posterior tibial pulses at the ankle. I would prefer to transplant the second toe, but his is very small; I decide the big toe would make a better thumb.

"What you find?" he asks anxiously.

"You have good circulation and a metacarpal bone."

"So what you think? Toe transplant?"

I look up at Dinh's face. It is pale yellow, contrasting with the density of shadowed books and wall behind him. His haughty eyes have softened into a look of hope and longing.

"I agree," I say. "A toe transplant would be best for you."

"You must do it, then," he says.

"Maybe you could come to the States and have it done."

"I no rich American. No can get visa."

"There's a good chance the graft won't take. I don't have an operating microscope or some of the instruments I use."

He flexes and unflexes the four fingers on his right hand and smiles.

"Do it here tomorrow. I want to hold chopsticks again. I tired of eating like a Frenchman."

"Look," I say, "You don't realize how many things could go wrong."

"It work. I know it work."

I think how the fortunes of the Vietnamese always seem to be in the hands of others.

"Okay," I say. "I'll do it. A local anesthetic would be safest. Would that be all right?"

"Pain no matter. You do it."

"You're on. But don't be surprised if it doesn't work."

That night I lie awake under the mosquito net on my bed, reviewing the technique of toe transplantation, suturing in my mind tendons and tiny digital nerves, minute veins and arteries. Tropical heat drenches me. The bark of dogs comes in from the street. When I finally fall asleep, I dream again of the man whose head I severed and stuck on the end of a pole. We meet in the Cao Dia temple in Tay Ninh, a vast, gaudy cathedral with a vaulted ceiling, pillars wound with gilded dragons and pink serpents, and a giant eye over the altar. He stands naked in front of me, holding his head with its sheen of black hair in the crook of his elbow.

The surgery suite is high ceilinged, with dirty windows and yellow tile walls, like the restroom in an old train station. The air is drowsy with the odor of ether that leaks from U.S. Army surplus anesthesia machines. Outside the operating room I attach magnifying loupes to a pair of glasses. I focus the lenses on the lines of my fingertips and begin scrubbing my hands in cold water at an old porcelain sink. Through the door I see Dinh sedated and strapped to the operating table. Bathed in fierce white light, with his arms extended on boards at right angles to his body, he looks as if he has been crucified. I have sent an orderly to his office for his cassette player, and *The Four Seasons* plays softly at the head of the table.

For a moment I rinse my hands, designing in my mind skin incisions and tendon transfers. In the past, to decrease operating time and diminish my fatigue, I used a second surgical team to prepare the recipient site in the hand while I removed the donor tissue from the foot, but here I am alone.

With water dripping from my elbows, I step into the room. Suddenly I feel a surge of force, a sense of power that has been mine in no other place but surgery, except when my finger was on the trigger of an M-60.

The instruments I have brought with me lie on trays and tables. My weapons are tenotomy scissors and mosquito hemostats, atraumatic forceps and spring-loaded needle holders. A scrub technician, who worked as an interpreter in a MASH unit during the war, hands me a towel. Two masked nurses prep Dinh's foot and hand with a soap solution. The surgery team's spirits are high. Listening to them talk is like hearing finches chirp.

Gowned and gloved, I sit on a stool beside Dinh's right hand. I adjust the light and begin the numbing with an injection of Xylocaine. The prick of the needle rouses him from his narcotized slumber, and he groans.

"Everyone ready? Let's go. Knife."

The nurse pops the handle of the scalpel into my palm. A stillness settles over me and passes into my hand.

Dissecting out the filamentous vessels and nerves that once brought blood and sensation to Dinh's thumb is tedious and takes more than an hour. While I work, a nurse sits at Dinh's head, murmuring to him and wiping his forehead with a wet cloth. I wonder what Dinh is thinking. Is he remembering the men who cut off his thumbs? Is he dreaming of what he might do if he met them again? When all the digital nerves and vessels and tendons are isolated and tagged with black-silk sutures, I cover the hand with a sterile towel. Before I move to Dinh's foot to harvest his spare part, I step to the head of the table.

"It's going well," I say. "You all right?"

"Don't worry about Dinh," he replies. "Worry about operation."

I make a circular incision around the base of the phalanx, taking care to preserve skin in the web space so that the defect can be closed without a skin graft. When the toe is finally transected, with its trailing tentacles of tendons, nerves, and vessels, it looks like a baby squid. I wrap it in saline-soaked gauze and carry it to the hand. I'm tired and sweating. My back hurts. My eyes ache. I feel as if I were on a long forced march.

First I join the bones, using wires to fuse the toe's bone to the hand's metacarpal in a position of flexion and pronation, to provide Dinh with a good pinch. Next I unite the tendons with strong nylon sutures—extensor hallucis longus to extensor pollicis longus, flexor hallucis longus to flexor pollicis longus.

Fighting off fatigue, I begin the most critical and tedious part of the procedure—the anastomosis of filamentous nerves and vessels. It is like sewing strands of hair together. Under the magnification of the lenses the delicate instruments seem big and blunt; the slightest tremor of my fingers appears to be an awkward jerk. Blood oozes into the wound and obscures my vision. A few drops seem like a crimson flood.

"Suck. Will someone please suck."

I take a stitch in the digital artery, and Dinh's hand rises from the drapes. I push it down, pinning it to the table.

"Goddamn it," I say. "Hold still, Dinh."

"*Dau,*" Dinh moans in pain. "*Dau. Dau.*"

"He feel it," the nurse says.

"More Xylocaine," I say. His hand jerks again. "Hurry up, Goddamn it. Xylocaine."

After four hours Dinh has a new thumb, pinned in place by Kirschner wires through the bones and a neat ring of black-nylon skin sutures. Exhausted, I sit for a moment cradling his hand in mine and staring at my work. The graft is cool and cadaveric, as pale as plaster, but it twitches slightly with his pulse. I haven't prayed in years, and doubt that it does any good, but I silently ask the Lord to give the transplant life. The nurse hands me a sterile dressing, and I wrap Dinh's fingers in loose layers of fluffy gauze followed by a light cast of plaster of paris. I strip off my gloves and step to the head of the table. I look down at Dinh's face, resting my hand on his shoulder. His pitted cheeks puff with each breath, and his half-closed eyelids flutter.

"All done, Dinh," I say.

"How does it look?" he asks groggily.

"Like a thumb."

Dinh believes that our lives move in circles, repeating themselves endlessly like the four seasons, like the cycle of his country's rice crop. Planting. Weeding and waiting.

Harvesting. Fallowness. Planting again. If things don't work out, so what? Another chance will come around, the way winter always gives in to spring. But I believe that my life is somehow outside these circles, that I am on a straight march toward something final, and on that journey to the end of existence, the journey itself is all there is. When I fail along the way, when something I need eludes me because of a mistake I have made, the mistake itself becomes a defeat, and I am left with only loss, with emptiness, uncertainty, and regret.

Because that is my nature, the fate of Dinh's transplanted toe takes on a monumental importance. I lie awake at night in unbearable heat, sweating and worrying about infection and thrombosis. Each morning, before I start my surgery schedule, I visit Dinh in his stark hospital room, with its metal cot and the clay pot that serves as a bedside commode. Peering up at me from his pillow through circular Uncle Ho wire-rims, he seems calm and confident, talking of all the things that will be easier for him to do with his new thumb—holding a pen when he writes haiku, picking hibiscus blooms for his wife's table, playing his bamboo flute, and, of course, eating with chopsticks. He says he may even do a little minor surgery. The thought of him trying to operate makes me cringe.

One day I show him a few snapshots of my daughter. He leafs through the pictures and nods politely. Then he talks about all the children I operated on who can now smile and suck their bottles. The children, tender and pliant, are what is important, he tells me, not old people like him, who have become dry and rigid and whose lives are behind them.

When I examine him, I am relieved to find that he is free of fever. His pain is minimal. The dressing smells clean, and a little blood stains the cast, which is a good sign. The graft has to be taking. I begin to look forward to removing the dressing and seeing a nice new pink thumb. It will be a kind of miracle.

The day before I am to leave Vietnam is the day of atonement, the time of truth, the moment to unwrap Dinh's hand and see if his thumb is viable. It is also the end of the rice harvest, and the farmers are burning off the fields to the west of the city. As I walk to the hospital, I can see a gray haze of smoke hanging over a horizon curtained with flames. It is a scorched-earth image, reminiscent of napalm and war.

In the surgery clinic I meet Dinh, sitting in a wheelchair with his bandaged hand in a sling and a confident smile on his face. Hoa, a petite nurse with a pretty smile and pearl earrings, places his hand on a white towel. A hush hangs over the room. My heart gallops. I cut the cast with heavy scissors and begin carefully unwinding the dressing. The gauze is stuck with dried blood, so I moisten it with saline and let it soak for a few minutes while I re-dress his foot. I am pleased to find the donor-site incision clean and healing well, but when I peel the last layer of gauze from his hand, I smell the faint odor of necrosis. Dinh's new thumb is the cold clay color of mildewed meat. I feel his eyes on me. I want to leave now, get on an airplane and fly home, let someone else amputate the dead thumb, let someone else clean up my mess. I glance up at his face. He is staring at the dead toe. God damn this dirty little Job of a country. Nothing turns out right here. I look out the window. The monsoon season is only a few days away, and already it is raining. Big drops kick up dust like rifle fire.

"It doesn't look good," I say. "Maybe I should re-dress it and give it a little more time."

"Gangrene," he says. "It dead. Take it off."

In the operating room everyone works in silence. On the table Dinh looks small and fragile, exhausted, as if he had just climbed one of those mountains on the Ho Chi Minh Trail. I pull the Kirschner wires from his hand with a hemostat and snip the nylon sutures. It is a bloodless operation. The necrotic transplant falls off onto blue drapes, stiff and cold, no longer a thumb or a toe. Looking at it, I can scarcely believe my childish hope that it would survive. I pick it up with sterile forceps and drop it into a stainless-steel pan. I think of Dinh's torturers in their purple berets chopping off his thumbs with a big knife. I see him drinking soup made with his own flesh and bone.

The day of my departure Dinh sends a driver in an old Toyota to take me to the airport. I am disappointed that he isn't riding with me, but something tells me he will be waiting for me in the terminal. I want to apologize to him because the transplant didn't work, and then have him laugh and say no problem, that in his next life he will have thumbs.

I check my bags at the ticket counter and hurry to the lounge, hoping that Dinh will be waiting there in a rattan chair with his bandaged foot propped up while he drinks a cup of green tea. Over the door to the sunny room a sign announces, NHA TRANG A GOOD PLACE FOR RESORT. With my heart hammering high in my chest, I step inside. No Dinh. The lounge is empty and silent except for the groan of a ceiling fan that churns warm, viscous air.

I move heavily between tables and out glass doors onto the tarmac. Silence surrounds me. The sun. The quiet blue sky. I stand for a while, gazing at tall brown grass and prickly pears that sprout through cracks in the airstrip. Concrete revetments built during the war to shelter American F-4 fighter jets from rocket attacks are empty and crumbling, like mausoleums of an earlier civilization. Beside the runway rests the rusty carcass of a US C141 Starlifter. I watch an old F-4, now a Vietnamese fighter jet with rocket launchers riveted to its wings, practice a touchdown. The plane bounces on the concrete, its tires screeching like the cry of some fierce predator. The gray gunship rises into sparkling blue sky. My eyes follow its flight until it disappears into the glare of the sun.

Soon an Air Vietnam passenger plane lands on the runway and taxies to the tarmac, where it shimmies to a stop. It is an old Russian turboprop with a dented skin and chipped blue-and-white paint. I have heard that Air Vietnam's planes are in poor repair because the airline has trouble getting parts, and that Japanese businessmen refuse to use it.

I mount the steps into the aircraft. Inside the fuselage, heat and the oily odor of fuel squeeze the breath out of me. Only two other travelers are on board, a mamasan in a conical hat and the baby she carries in a broad sling around her waist. She stands in the aisle, swaying back and forth to rock the infant. I choose a window seat with tattered upholstery. Soon the engines on the wings cough and sputter to life. I try to buckle my seat belt, but the clasp doesn't work. I shake my head and smile. In Vietnam danger has always been ubiquitous, life tenuous. For some reason I welcome the risky ride. It makes me feel a part of the land.

A Conversation with Daly Walker

Having come to writing fiction as a surgeon, naturally your work reflects that world. Your fictional doctors are often ambivalent about their success. They feel trapped in their lives, at the same time they enjoy the personal and financial rewards that come with the profession. Looking at death on a daily basis as they do, they wrestle with unanswerable questions and suffer the consequences of irrevocable, unfixable acts. What is it about medicine that makes it so rich for fiction for you?

First of all, it was my little niche of the world, something I know about. Also, an awareness of the human condition is paramount to being a decent writer and a decent doctor. A physician is privy to the very things about people that nobody else is, even counselors and ministers. Patients come to you when they are the most vulnerable, when they are hurting. They want to trust you and open up to you. That is great material to write about. You just have to protect their confidentiality.

Because you're holding a person's life in your hands, or that person feels that you are?

Yes, that is certainly part of it. They often expect more from the physician than he or she can give. In "Pulsus Paradoxis," for example, the daughter says, "Why didn't you save him? You save everyone." My own daughters look at me like that. They think I can fix all their problems. But of course I can't, and it disappoints them.

The kind of helplessness that doctors sometimes feel in the face of that is complicated in a number of the stories whose main characters served in Vietnam. Strangely, though, war and medicine seem to have something in common in the passion and intensity surrounding them, a heightened sense of being alive. This is especially true in "I Am the Grass," in which the narrator observes, "I feel a surge of force, a sense of power that has been mine in no other place but surgery, except when my finger was on the trigger of an M-60."

Both a soldier and a doctor have that power over people's lives that we have been talking about. Are you going to pull that trigger or not? Are you going to operate? Power is part of being a writer, too. You decide what's said and how it's said, how people behave. It's godlike. I hate to admit it, but I suppose it's one reason I like to write.

Power is part of being a writer, too. You decide what's said and how it's said, how people behave. It's godlike.

When did you begin to write stories—and why?

I started when I was about forty, twenty-some years ago. A friend talked me into taking an undergraduate course at Indiana University. Sena Jeter Naslund was teaching at IU then, and I was lucky enough to get into one of her classes in the MFA program. She is a master teacher and got me pointed in the right direction. When she returned to teach at the University of Louisville, she formed a group of five writers including herself who met monthly and read each other's work. We did that for years.

Throughout your untraditional training as a writer, were there particular stories that you found instructive?

James Salter, in both his stories, like "Dusk," and his great novel *Light Years.* I love finding surprises in a story, and almost every sentence in Salter's stories surprises me. His selection of detail is quirky, but impeccable. He seems to look at things differently than anyone else. Raymond Carver, too. His minimalism was very important to observe and understand. I don't consider myself a minimalist, but I think he helped me learn how to distill things, get rid of the impurities. Tim O'Brien's masterful *The Things They Carried* and *Going After Cacciato* helped me in writing about war, as did Tobias Wolff. O'Brien's stories taught me about conflict, how there should be a central tension that you never let go of in the story. Of course, there is Chekhov. Everybody seems to go back to him. That he was a doctor inspired me. I keep rereading him and rereading him.

What were your first stories like?

Not very good. You know how it always comes up, write what you know? My first story was a fine example of why that's important. I've always been intrigued by mountain climbers, but I had never climbed a mountain and knew nothing about it. In fact, I am afraid of heights. Anyway, I wrote about two climbers who fall into a crevasse and the choices they have to make in trying to get out. When I told the creative writing instructor it wasn't working and that I had an aversion to heights, he said, "Write the story about someone trying to climb the mountain who's afraid of heights." I did that, and the story still wasn't good. There was no real emotion in it. It was, in a way, a lie. But at least I learned something in the writing.

So it took you a while to get to the "hot wire."

Yes. Eventually I started writing about medicine and my own life. In doing so, I was coming to terms with my life and understanding the significance of my personal experiences. I think my best stories hit close to home.

Eventually I started writing about medicine and my own life. In doing so, I was coming to terms with my life and understanding the significance of my personal experiences.

Terrific authority comes from writing the world you know so well. The medical procedures you describe are technologically precise, yet the language is completely accessible to a layperson. How do you manage that?

It's almost like introducing foreign language into a story. Notice how much Spanish there is in Cormac McCarthy's novels—the way he's woven it into everything, in context with language that's familiar. I try to do that with the medical terminology. I want it to lend authenticity to the story. I don't think it's important that the reader really understand everything I'm saying, but he has to trust that what *is* there is accurate.

I first heard about the importance of trust when I read John Gardner's *On Becoming a Novelist.* He talks about the fictional dream and keeping that dream alive, avoiding anything that makes the reader question and break through to the surface of the story. He expressed it better than anyone else. Michael Curtis at *The Atlantic Monthly* is obsessed with truth and accuracy in the stories he publishes. For instance, his editors checked out the hand surgery's validity in "I Am the Grass" at the Harvard Medical School.

The reader has to be able to trust all the language in a story, really—and the quality of language is one of your strongest suits as a writer. A metaphor from another story, "Phantom Pain," comes to mind—a surgeon compares snow falling to bone dust coming off of a surgical saw.

It is in the language of a surgeon. I think only a surgeon would see snow that way. Inexperienced writers often want to use language in a beautiful but showy way, trying to be lyrical or poetic, but in doing so it draws attention to the writer rather than the story. That fictional dream we were talking about is interrupted.

Inexperienced writers often want to use language in a beautiful but showy way, trying to be lyrical or poetic, but in doing so it draws attention to the writer rather than the story.

As I do each year, I recently addressed an advanced high school English class. The teacher has the students and their parents read "I Am the Grass." They spend two days on the story. First they talk about it in class. Then the next day I come to the class to participate in their dialogue. Anyway, they had picked up on the grass metaphor, so we talked about that. I remember warning them that metaphors are really dangerous to use. They can be dreadful and obvious. But when they're right—! And in that story, I kept after those metaphors more than I ever had before. Just little things, like the guy comes back and cuts the grass at Soldiers Field. He worked at Four Seasons. It's fun trying to get them right.

I remember warning them that metaphors are really dangerous to use. They can be dreadful and obvious. But when they're right—!

The title itself is rich with possibilities for metaphor. Did you have it from the beginning?

No. I didn't. I was reading some poetry in the midst of writing this and I read the poem by Carl Sandburg. I thought, man, this is it. This is my whole story in just a few lines. I can't believe how lucky I was to run across it. But discoveries like that are one of the recurring joys of writing.

There's some very strong language in the story. At one point, the narrator looks at a Vietnamese man and observes, "When I was here before, I would have called him a gook or a slope, a dink motherfucker." When is it appropriate to use language that you know others will find offensive?

The language must fit the character. If the character is a soldier likely to speak profanity and harbor prejudice, he must speak and think that way on the page. The reader must understand the author is not condoning profanity or prejudice; he's just trying to bring out the truth in his characters.

The language must fit the character. If the character is a soldier likely to speak profanity and harbor prejudice, he must speak and think that way on the page.

Given the influence of political correctness on language these days, did using those words in the story make you anxious?

Only because I knew that my mother was going to read it someday, and I'd hear from her! This brings up something interesting that happened when the story was being edited for *The Atlantic Monthly.* In the opening the narrator says, "I cannot tell my thirteen-year-old that once, drunk on Ba Muoi Ba beer, I took a girl her age into a thatched-roof hooch in Tay Ninh City and did her on a bamboo mat." In the earlier version, I used "fuck" instead of the less profane "did her." Michael Curtis called me and said, "I'm not going to make you change this, but would you, please?" Another story he'd recently published had used some opening vulgarity and he said, "We just got bombarded." So I agreed to the change.

How did you feel about changing it?

I didn't mind changing the word in the opening, but I told him I wanted to keep it later in the story. As I mentioned earlier, it's a soldier's story, and soldiers use the *F* word. That's the way they talk. It's part of the truth.

In fact, omitting it at the beginning makes the word stronger when we finally hear it—and also mirrors what's happening as he goes back into himself as he was then. Now he says "did," then he said "fuck." He can't keep it under anymore. It's interesting that an editorial issue actually strengthened the story in an unexpected way, rather than being only a compromise.

I agree that it made the word stronger, and I imagine, at some level, Michael Curtis knew that, too. He's a very astute editor.

All of this relates to voice.

Voice is difficult to talk about, because I'm never exactly sure what voice is being discussed. There's the writer's voice, like Eudora Welty talks about in "finding your voice," that's not related to any one story. Then there's the voice of the characters in the story, and the voice of the story itself, which has to do with how it sounds. I think what we were talking about was the voice of the character, which must be authentic.

There's the voice of the characters in the story, and the voice of the story itself, which has to do with how it sounds.

Was "I Am the Grass" the first story you wrote about your experience in Vietnam?

Yes. I had buried that time in my life. My daughters and wife had never heard anything about my war experience. They didn't know what I did in Vietnam or how it affected me because I never talked about it—and I guess I didn't know it either.

So the narrator's experience mirrors your own in that he, too, suppressed what had happened to him in Vietnam; in fact, that's where the true tension in the story lies. Did it scare you to write the story?

It did. It was like looking into your own grave. What made the story better than the mountain climber story was that it was based on real emotion. There was truth in it. I keep looking for something else to write about that's going to scare me as much as looking back at Vietnam. I think anybody that has the craft down can come up with a story about almost anything that looks pretty on paper, but for it to really be good the author must have a deep emotional investment in what's at stake in the story.

I keep looking for something else to write about that's going to scare me as much as looking back at Vietnam.

Did you come out on the other side of "I Am the Grass" a different person?

Clearly, I did. I discovered a lot about myself, my feelings about war, how important peace is to me. It changed me politically, while at the same time parting the Vietnam clouds for me. Writing the story brought the emotional healing that comes with catharsis. I became involved in trying to help other Vietnam veterans, particularly some of the really damaged guys who were struggling with drugs and psychosis. More than anything, I think I was able to forgive myself for being part of an atrocity.

How does writing about a character whose experience is in some ways like your own offer a way of dealing with personal secrets and helping to resolve them?

The beauty of writing fiction rather than memoir is that it allows you to say things that you would otherwise be reluctant to reveal about yourself and others. Distancing yourself from fact really frees you up to get at the truth. As to resolution, there is the cathartic effect I mentioned previously. Also, by spending so much time exploring my own experience I came to understand myself in a way I never did before.

How did you end up in Vietnam, and what was your actual experience there?

When I went to Vietnam, I was a real '50s guy, a fraternity boy, flying around Indianapolis in a convertible. I didn't care anything about politics. I had this bad relationship with a girl, and I thought *I want out of here*—and this looked pretty exciting. I was drafted out of a surgical internship and had not completed my surgery training. They assigned me to an infantry division where I was a "field doctor" with a battalion. Then reality came in. The injuries we dealt with were horrendous. It is unbelievable what humans do to each other in the name of war. I can remember they'd bring these VC in by helicopter and I'd be waiting for them to come in. They'd be up there fifteen or twenty feet and they'd throw them out of the helicopter. Then I'd get these guys in surgery and I'd be trying to work on them and the intelligence people would come in and say, "Doctor, step out a minute." I could hear them in there torturing these guys. Also, I spent a good deal of time going out into the villages and treating Vietnamese civilians in the "MEDCAP" program. It was through that experience that I got to know and appreciate the Vietnamese. They are truly remarkable people—resilient and resourceful, tough and kind at the same time.

When were you there?

Sixty-seven, sixty-eight. It was during a bad time to be there, but I guess there was no good time to be in Vietnam. It was at the time of the Tet Offensive. Everything changed after Tet. Before Tet, things were pretty relaxed. We were cocky, traveling the roads, enjoying Saigon nightlife. Tet sobered us up. After that, no place was safe, and the Vietnamese were an enemy to be taken seriously.

The narrator of "I Am the Grass" was a "grunt" in the army, not a surgeon. Why?

I wanted the protagonist to be directly involved in the atrocities—a perpetrator, not just an observer. A doctor, even though he is part of the invading army, has a compassionate role. He's caring for people rather than killing them. A noncombatant just wouldn't fit with what I wanted to show about Vietnam. It would have lacked intensity.

Do any of the incidents in "I Am the Grass" come directly from personal experiences?

They do. If not my own experience, things that I observed. For example, the heads on a pole. When I was with the Ninth Infantry Division in the Mekong Delta, two VC were decapitated and their heads impaled on poles—not by U.S. troops, however. There were other powerful images that were part of my own experience that appear in the story. Like the big eye over the altar in the Cao Dia temple in Tay Ninh City. It reminded you that God was watching what we were doing to these people. Another powerful image was Nui Ba Den, the "black virgin" mountain. I had an aid station there on top of the mountain that was overrun, and six or seven of the men in my battalion were killed. Fortunately, I wasn't there that night.

When you were there and seeing those things, were you conscious of absorbing images? Did you ever have the impulse to write things down?

I don't think I was conscious of absorbing those images. Although I was interested in literature, I wasn't a writer then. I did chronicle some of them in letters I wrote to my mother. Part of my research for the story was to read those letters I sent home. They were poorly written, but they were filled with description and emotion that I was able to weave into the story. I did write an essay about going back to Vietnam in 1992 and working in a hospital. After that, the past began to bubble up to the surface. I began to confront my Vietnam demons. I knew I had to write about the war.

Part of my research for the story was to read those letters I sent home. They were poorly written, but they were filled with description and emotion that I was able to weave into the story.

Was the character, Dinh, based on someone you met when you went back?

My characters are often a conglomeration of several people I know. Dinh is a combination of two people that I met when I returned to Vietnam. The head of the hospital where I worked contributed a lot to the Dinh character. He was a big man in the provincial Communist Party, a regional vice chairman. Like Dinh, he fought the French as an infantryman when he was fifteen, then later was a surgeon on the Ho Chi Minh Trail, fighting the South Vietnamese. So he was my counterpart. He was very leery of me at first and not particularly friendly, but we got to know one another and were able to discuss the war in a cordial way. The other person who contributed to Dinh's character was the head of surgery at the hospital. He was not a Communist. He was an extremely talented surgeon. We became quite good friends, and we still stay in touch.

Were either of them injured in the way your character was?

No. I experimented with several different maladies before I arrived at the amputated thumbs. They seemed a perfect metaphor for the war. The war was so dehumanizing. Opposable thumbs do set us apart from other primates, and so to lose them is dehumanizing. So I thought it was the perfect thing.

That bizarre detail about cooking it and eating it. Did you make that up?

Yes. I agree it is bizarre, but then much of what happened there was bizarre.

The reader's first view of Dinh pretty much tells all he needs to know about the man. How did you accomplish that? Why those particular details?

I did it by pondering it endlessly and by rewriting and rewriting. Finding just the right details is one of the most important elements of good writing. When you look at a person, there are a thousand things you could choose to mention in the description of that individual. Choosing the few right details is the key, the things that will be most effective in the story.

There are a thousand things you could choose to mention in the description of that individual. Choosing the few right details is the key, the things that will be most effective in the story.

And then let them stand.

Exactly. You have to guard against overwriting and overexplaining. Sometimes I'll show what I want to about a character, then I'll add an unnecessary sentence or two to explain it instead of trusting the reader to draw the right conclusions on his own. That's where self-editing comes in. You need to go back and pull out the superfluous words.

The first line of "I Am the Grass" does double duty, at the same time telling the reader exactly what he needs to know about the narrator and pulling him into the story that's about to unfold. The writer and editor Gordon Lish once said that the beginning of a good story should feel like the writer taking the reader by the lapels and saying, "I have to tell this story or I will die." "I Am the Grass" certainly accomplishes that!

I would certainly agree with Lish. Tim O'Brien influenced my beginnings when I was in his workshops years ago. He emphasized that you have to open up with the conflict and never let go of it. Keep blasting away at it the whole time. He talked about the unity of the short story and how everything has to relate to the central tension that you introduce at the beginning. In a novel, the author can stray a bit, but not in a short story.

That litany of secrets that follows the first line, was it always part of the beginning?

It was. I added one or two along the way, but the secret atrocities were always in the beginning. They are part of that central tension we just talked about. The story builds from there.

After the litany of secrets, the story falls backwards to "Twenty years have passed . . ." and it moves chronologically, eventually working its way to his arrival in Vietnam in the present and his experience with Dinh. There are no long flashbacks, just moments that take him backward from time to time. Yet the reader always knows exactly what he needs to know.

Sometimes it's difficult for me to get time sequence right. When does a flashback work? Or a flash-forward? I tend to first write in a linear way, using a straight time sequence. Then I go back to it and try and see when the story really starts, when

I tend to first write in a linear way, using a straight time sequence. Then I go back to it and try and see when the story really starts.

the reader knows there is something at stake—and I begin the story there. Then I start moving paragraphs around. Part of the process is adding details that need to be known early. Getting transitions right often comes pretty late in the writing process. I'm often helped in this by the one or two people I trust to read my stuff. In that regard, you must guard against getting too many opinions about your work. When you're learning how to write, seeking advice is fine, but you eventually have to stand alone with your work. You can't work by committee.

Good transitions are crucial in a story that moves in and out of several levels of time as this one does. It's interesting to note that they are, for the most part, simple and purposeful. "After I was discharged from the Army . . ." Often they incorporate a bit of flavor somehow. "In the morning I walk from my hotel through steamy air, on streets boiling with people, to the hospital."

Doing things simply takes confidence. Early on, I was afraid what I was writing was somehow too simplistic. Maybe I was worried about not looking literary or smart or something, but now I don't worry about it. I think it goes along with finding your voice.

The plot of the story hinges on the thumb surgery. Did you always know it wouldn't work?

I discarded the possibility that it would be successful very early in the writing process.

Why did it have to fail?

Because all wars and Vietnam particularly are failures of mankind. No one really wins. In Vietnam, thousands of people were left dead or maimed. Vietnam isn't a free society now. The United States was ripped apart by the war, and it still hasn't gotten over it. And now there's Iraq that looks a lot like Vietnam to me and makes me realize we didn't learn much in Vietnam. How could there be a happy ending to a story about the Vietnam War?

How did you find your way to the end of the story?

I let my characters lead me there. I always knew that these two men could never end up bosom buddies. In one version, I had them meeting at the end in a cool, unemotional encounter; but finally I realized that having them meet would be trying to wrap things up in a nice package. I did want the ending to reflect the movement of the narrator's character. In the end, he wants to accept the same risks as the Vietnamese baby and mother, and he wants to be part of their land. I'm not sure exactly how I got to the ending I have, but I do remember that when I got there I knew it was right.

I'm not sure exactly how I got to the ending I have, but I do remember that when I got there I knew it was right.

Early in the story, the narrator begins several flashbacks with, "When I was here before, I would have done. . .," or "When I was here before, I would have thought. . . ." Then, talk-

ing with Dinh about how unlikely it is that the surgery will be successful, he thinks about "how the fortunes of the Vietnamese always seem to be in the hands of others." Something shifts in him. He's never thought of the fortunes of the Vietnamese before, never allowed himself that vulnerability before. How did you know to underpin the larger moment, the failure of the surgery, with this smaller, more subtle emotional fulcrum?

I didn't actually know I was doing that. It just happened. It think that's true with much in literary fiction. The author doesn't consciously manipulate things. Rather, they just come by osmosis.

When all is said and done, what would you say that "I Am the Grass" is about?

I'm looking for one word, but not coming up with it. It's a story about coming to grips with demons. Maybe *atonement* is the word I'm searching for.

What do you think is the most important thing for an aspiring writer to know about this story? What do you think it could teach someone who's learning how to write?

Most importantly, the story is really a heartfelt story. The Vietnam experience was something that was very important to me and had an emotional grip on me. I was willing to put a lot of time and effort into making it a good story because of that. It was important to me to do it right and to say what I needed to say about Vietnam. My advice is to write about something that matters a great deal to you.

Did you feel that something was over for you when you finished "I Am the Grass"?

Yes. I'm often asked, "Are you writing other things about war and Vietnam?" The answer is, I'm not. The question makes me think, well, this has been pretty successful, maybe I should expand it into a novel. But I don't feel the need to. "I Am the Grass" seems to have said everything I need to say about the war, at least for the time being. Maybe the war is over for me, but I'm not sure about that. I think Vietnam will always haunt me.

Writing Prompts

READ: "I Am the Grass" and the interview with **Daly Walker.**

PONDER: How the litany that begins the story sets up the story's theme of atonement.

WRITE: Imitate the litany in "I Am the Grass" to create an opening paragraph that prepares the reader for what the story will be about.

PRACTICE:

- Think of a world or niche in which you are an expert. Invent a character with the same expertise and set her in motion in a setting where a conflict with another person involves your character's specialized knowledge somehow.

- Create a series of similes and/or metaphors that reflect the essence of a specialized profession or pastime.
- Remember an event or a time in your life in which you did something for which you are ashamed. Invent a situation in which you (or a character based on you) might achieve atonement.
- Remember an event that scared you so much that, to this day, you avoid thinking about it. Think about it. Hard. Write the event in scene. Tell everything. Don't be melodramatic. Don't explain anything. Don't flinch.
- Reread journal entries or letters you wrote to someone long ago about a significant event or time in your life. Write a story about a character who is like you were then.
- Write three different endings for a story you are writing. Which one works best? Why?
- List the scenes or moments of your story in chronological order and, next to each one, name the emotion the character is feeling to discover the emotional plot of your story.
- Write the first paragraph of a story that establishes a conflict. Then write the story, making sure that the conflict appears and is deepened in some way in every scene.
- Think of an occasion that's rich with personal history (positive or negative)—like trimming the Christmas tree or celebrating a wedding anniversary. Write a scene that contains at least one flashback that is triggered by something that happens as the action plays out.

Tobias Wolff

Tobias Wolff (b. 1945) is the author of five collections of short stories, two memoirs, and a novel. Born in Birmingham, Alabama, he was educated at Oxford University and Stanford University. His honors include the Los Angeles Times *Book Prize for Biography, the Ambassador Book Award of the English-Speaking Union, a Whiting Foundation Award, the Lila Wallace-*Reader's Digest *Award, the Lyndhurst Foundation Award, the* Esquire-*Volvo-Waterstone's Prize for Nonfiction, and nominations for the National Book Critics Circle Award, the PEN/Faulkner Award for Fiction, and the* Los Angeles Times *Book Prize. Wolff teaches at Stanford University. He lives in Stanford, California.*

For Further Reading:
In the Garden of the North American Martyrs (1981), *The Barracks Thief and Other Stories* (1984), *Back in the World* (1985), *The Stories of Tobias Wolff* (1988), *This Boy's Life: A Memoir* (1989), *In Pharaoh's Army: Memories of the Lost War* (1994), *The Night in Question: Stories* (1996), *Old School* (2003).

The Other Miller

For two days now Miller has been standing in the rain with the rest of Bravo Company, waiting for some men from another company to blunder down the logging road where Bravo waits in ambush. When this happens, if this happens, Miller will stick his head out of the hole he's hiding in and shoot off all his blank ammunition in the direction of the road. So will everyone else in Bravo Company. Then they will climb out of their holes and get on some trucks and go home, back to the base.

This is the plan.

Miller has no faith in it. He has never yet seen a plan that worked, and this one won't either. His foxhole has about a foot of water in it. He has to stand on little shelves he's been digging out of the walls, but the soil is sandy and the shelves keep collapsing. That means his boots are wet. Plus his cigarettes are wet. Plus he broke the bridge on his molars the first night out while chewing up one of the lollipops he'd brought along for energy. It drives him crazy, the way the broken bridge lifts and grates when he pushes it with his tongue, but last night he lost his will power and now he can't keep his tongue away from it.

When he thinks of the other company, the one they're supposed to ambush, Miller sees a column of dry well-fed men marching farther and farther away from the hole where he stands waiting for them. He sees them moving easily under light packs. He sees them stopping for a smoke break, stretching out on fragrant beds of pine needles under the trees, the murmur of their voices growing more and more faint as one by one they drift into sleep.

It's the truth, by God. Miller knows it like he knows he's going to catch a cold, because that's his luck. If he was in the other company they'd be the ones standing in holes.

Miller's tongue does something to the bridge and a thrill of pain shoots through him. He snaps up straight, eyes burning, teeth clenched against the yell in his throat. He fights it back and glares around him at the other men. The few he can see look stunned and ashen-faced. Of the rest he can make out only their poncho hoods, sticking out of the ground like bullet-shaped rocks.

At this moment, his mind swept clean by pain, Miller can hear the tapping of raindrops on his own poncho. Then he hears the pitchy whine of an engine. A jeep is splashing along the road, slipping from side to side and throwing up thick gouts of mud behind it. The jeep itself is caked with mud. It skids to a stop in front of Bravo Company's position, and the horn beeps twice.

Miller glances around to see what the others are doing. Nobody has moved. They're all just standing in their holes.

The horn beeps again.

A short figure in a poncho emerges from a clump of trees farther up the road. Miller can tell it's the first sergeant by how little he is, so little the poncho hangs almost to his ankles. The first sergeant walks slowly toward the jeep, big blobs of mud all around his boots. When he gets to the jeep he leans his head inside; a moment later he pulls it out. He looks down at the road. He kicks at one of the tires in a thoughtful way. Then he looks up and shouts Miller's name.

Miller keeps watching him. Not until the first sergeant shouts his name again does Miller begin the hard work of hoisting himself out of the foxhole. The other men turn their gray faces up at him as he trudges past their holes.

"Come here, boy," the first sergeant says. He walks a little distance from the jeep and waves Miller over.

Miller follows him. Something is wrong. Miller can tell because the first sergeant called him "boy" instead of "shit-bird." Already he feels a burning in his left side, where his ulcer is.

The first sergeant stares down the road. "Here's the thing," he begins. He stops and turns to Miller. "Goddamn it, anyway. Did you know your mother was sick?"

Miller doesn't say anything, just pushes his lips tight together.

"She must have been sick, right?" Miller remains silent, and the first sergeant says, "She passed away last night. I'm real sorry." He looks sadly up at Miller, and Miller watches his right arm beginning to rise under the poncho; then it falls to his side again. Miller can see that the first sergeant wants to give his shoulder a man-to-man kind of squeeze, but it just wouldn't work. You can only do that if you're taller than the other fellow or at least the same size.

"These boys here will drive you back to base," the first sergeant says, nodding toward the jeep. "You give the Red Cross a call and they'll take it from there. Get yourself some rest," he adds, then walks off toward the trees.

Miller retrieves his gear. One of the men he passes on his way back to the jeep says, "Hey, Miller, what's the story?"

Miller doesn't answer. He's afraid if he opens his mouth he'll start laughing and ruin everything. He keeps his head down and his lips tight as he climbs into the backseat of the jeep, and he doesn't look up until they've left the company a mile or so behind. The fat PFC sitting beside the driver is watching him. He says, "I'm sorry about your mother. That's a bummer."

"Maximum bummer," says the driver, another PFC. He shoots a lock over his shoulder. Miller sees his own face reflected for an instant in the driver's sunglasses.

"Had to happen someday," he mumbles, and looks down again.

Miller's hands are shaking. He puts them between his knees and stares through the snapping plastic window at the trees going past. Raindrops rattle on the canvas overhead. He is inside, and everyone else is still outside. Miller can't stop thinking about the others standing around getting rained on, and the thought makes him want to laugh and slap his leg. This is the luckiest he has ever been.

"My grandmother died last year," the driver says. "But that's not the same thing as losing your mother. I feel for you, Miller."

"Don't worry about me," Miller tells him. "I'll get along."

The fat PFC beside the driver says, "Look, don't feel like you have to repress just because we're here. If you want to cry or anything, just go ahead. Right, Leb?"

The driver nods. "Just let it out."

"No problem," Miller says. He wishes he could set these fellows straight so they won't feel like they have to act mournful all the way to Fort Ord. But if he tells them what happened, they'll turn right around and drive him back to his foxhole.

Miller knows what happened. There's another Miller in the battalion with the same initials he's got, W.P., and this Miller is the one whose mother has died. The Army screws up their mail all the time, and now they've screwed this up. Miller got the whole picture as soon as the first sergeant started asking about his mother.

For once, everybody else is on the outside and Miller is on the inside. Inside, on his way to a hot shower, dry clothes, a pizza, and a warm bunk. He didn't even have to do anything wrong to get here; he just did as he was told. It was their own mistake. Tomorrow he'll rest up like the first sergeant ordered him to, go on sick call about his bridge, maybe downtown to a movie after that. Then he'll call the Red Cross. By the time they get everything straightened out it will be too late to send him back to the field. And the best thing is, the other Miller won't know. The other Miller will have a whole other day of thinking his mother is still alive. You could even say that Miller is keeping her alive for him.

The man beside the driver turns around again and studies Miller. He has small dark eyes in a big white face covered with beads of sweat. His name tag reads KAISER. Showing little square teeth like a baby's, he says, "You're really coping, Miller. Most guys pretty much lose it when they get the word."

"I would too," the driver says. "Anybody would. It's *human*, Kaiser."

"For sure," Kaiser says. "I'm not saying I'm any different. That's going to be my worst day, the day my mom dies." He blinks rapidly, but not before Miller sees his little eyes mist up.

"Everybody has to go sometime," Miller says, "sooner or later. That's my philosophy."

"Heavy," the driver says. "Really deep."

Kaiser gives him a sharp look and says, "At ease, Lebowitz."

Miller leans forward. Lebowitz is a Jewish name. That means Lebowitz must be a Jew. Miller wants to ask him why he's in the Army, but he's afraid Lebowitz might take it wrong. Instead he says conversationally, "You don't see too many Jewish people in the Army nowadays."

Lebowitz looks into the rearview. His thick eyebrows arch over his sunglasses, then he shakes his head and says something Miller can't make out.

"At ease, Leb," Kaiser says again. He turns to Miller and asks him where the funeral is going to be held.

"What funeral?" Miller says.

Lebowitz laughs.

"Fuckhead," Kaiser says. "Haven't you ever heard of shock?"

Lebowitz is quiet for a moment. Then he looks into the rearview again and says, "Sorry, Miller. I was out of line."

Miller shrugs. His probing tongue pushes the bridge too hard and he stiffens suddenly.

"Where did your mom live?" Kaiser asks.

"Redding," Miller says.

Kaiser nods. "Redding," he repeats. He keeps watching Miller. So does Lebowitz, glancing back and forth between the mirror and the road. Miller understands that they expected a different kind of performance than the one he's giving them, more emotional and all. They've seen other personnel whose mothers died and now they have certain standards he has failed to live up to. He looks out the window. They're driving along a ridgeline. Slices of blue flicker between the trees on the left-hand side of the road; then they hit a space without trees and Miller can see the ocean below them, clear to the horizon under a bright cloudless sky. Except for a few hazy wisps in the treetops they've left the clouds behind, back in the mountains, hanging over the soldiers there.

"Don't get me wrong," Miller says. "I'm sorry she's dead."

Kaiser says, "That's the way. Talk it out."

"It's just that I didn't know her all that well," Miller says, and after this monstrous lie a feeling of weightlessness comes over him. At first it makes him uncomfortable, but almost immediately he begins to enjoy it. From now on he can say anything.

He makes a sad face. "I guess I'd be more broken up and so on if she hadn't taken off on us the way she did. Right in the middle of harvest season. Just leaving us flat like that."

"I'm hearing a lot of anger," Kaiser tells him. "Ventilate. Own it."

Miller got that stuff from a song, but he can't remember any more. He lowers his head and looks at his boots. "Killed my dad," he says after a time. "Died of a broken heart. Left me with five kids to raise, not to mention the farm." Miller closes his eyes. He sees a field all ploughed up and the sun setting behind it, a bunch of kids coming in from the field with rakes and hoes on their shoulders. While the jeep winds down through the switchbacks he describes his hardships as the oldest child in this family. He is at the end of his story when they reach the coast highway and turn north. All at once the jeep stops rattling and swaying. They pick up speed. The tires hum on the smooth road. The rushing air whistles a single note around the radio antenna. "Anyway," Miller says, "it's been two years since I even had a letter from her."

"You should make a movie," Lebowitz says.

Miller isn't sure how to take this. He waits to hear what else Lebowitz has to say, but Lebowitz is silent. So is Kaiser, who's had his back turned to Miller for several minutes now. Both men stare at the road ahead of them. Miller can see that they've lost interest. He feels disappointed, because he was having a fine time pulling their leg.

One thing Miller told them was true: he hasn't had a letter from his mother in two years. She wrote him a lot when he first joined the Army, at least once a week, sometimes twice, but Miller sent all her letters back unopened and after a year of this she finally gave up. She tried calling a few times but Miller wouldn't go to the telephone, so she gave that up too. Miller wants her to understand that her son is not a man to turn the other cheek. He is a serious man. Once you've crossed him, you've lost him.

Miller's mother crossed him by marrying a man she shouldn't have married. Phil Dove. Dove was a biology teacher in the high school. Miller was having trouble in the course, so his mother went to talk to Dove about it and ended up getting engaged to him. When Miller tried to reason with her, she wouldn't hear a word. You would think from the way she acted that she'd landed herself a real catch instead of someone who talked with a stammer and spent his life taking crayfish apart.

Miller did everything he could to stop the marriage, but his mother had blinded herself. She couldn't see what she already had, how good it was with just the two of them. How he was always there when she got home from work, with a pot of coffee all brewed up. The two of them drinking their coffee together and talking about different things, or maybe not talking at all—maybe just sitting in the kitchen while the room got dark around them, until the telephone rang or the dog started whining to get out. Walking the dog around the reservoir. Coming back and eating whatever they wanted to eat, sometimes nothing, sometimes the same dish three or four nights in a row, watching the programs they wanted to watch and going to bed when they wanted to and not because some other person wanted them to. Just being together in their own place.

Phil Dove got Miller's mother so mixed up she forgot how good their life was. She refused to see what she was ruining. "You'll be leaving anyway," she told him. "You'll be moving on, next year or the year after"—which showed how wrong she was about Miller, because he would never have left her, not ever, not for anything. But when he said this she laughed as if she knew better, as if he wasn't serious. He was serious, though. He was serious when he promised he'd stay, and he was serious when he promised he'd never speak to her again if she married Phil Dove.

She married him. Miller stayed at a motel that night and two nights more, until he ran out of money. Then he joined the Army. He knew that would get to her, because he was still a month shy of finishing high school, and because his father had been killed while serving in the Army. Not in Vietnam but in Georgia, in an accident. He and another man were dipping mess kits in a garbage can full of boiling water and somehow the can fell over on him. Miller was six at the time. Miller's mother hated the Army after that, not because her husband was dead—she knew about the war he was going to, she knew about ambushes and mines—but because of the way it happened. She said the Army couldn't even get a man killed in a decent fashion.

She was right, too. The Army was just as bad as she thought, and worse. You spent all your time waiting around. You lived a completely stupid existence. Miller hated every minute of it, but there was pleasure in his hatred because he believed that his mother must know how unhappy he was. That knowledge would be a grief to her. It would not be as bad as the grief she had given him, which was spreading from his heart into his stomach and teeth and everywhere else, but it was the worst grief he had power to cause, and it would serve to keep her in mind of him.

Kaiser and Lebowitz are describing hamburgers to each other. Their idea of the perfect hamburger. Miller tries not to listen but their voices go on, and after a while he can't think of anything but beefsteak tomatoes and Gulden's mustard and steaming, onion-stuffed meat crisscrossed with black marks from the grill. He is at the point of asking them to change the subject when Kaiser turns and says, "Think you can handle some chow?"

"I don't know," Miller says. "I guess I could get something down."

"We were talking about a pit stop. But if you want to keep going, just say the word. It's your ball game. I mean, technically we're supposed to take you straight back to base."

"I could eat," Miller says.

"That's the spirit. At a time like this you've got to keep your strength up."

"I could eat," Miller says again.

Lebowitz looks up into the rearview mirror, shakes his head, and looks away again.

They take the next turn-off and drive inland to a cross-roads where two gas stations face two restaurants. One of the restaurants is boarded up, so Lebowitz pulls into the parking lot of the Dairy Queen across the road. He turns the engine off, and the three men sit motionless in the sudden silence. Then Miller hears the distant clang of metal on metal, the caw of a crow, the creak of Kaiser shifting in his seat. A dog barks in front of a rust-streaked trailer next door. A skinny white dog with yellow eyes. As it barks the dog rubs itself, one leg raised and twitching, against a sign that shows an outspread hand below the words "KNOW YOUR FUTURE."

They get out of the jeep and Miller follows Kaiser and Lebowitz across the parking lot. The air is warm and smells of oil. In the gas station across the road a pink-skinned man in a swimming suit is trying to put air in the tires of his bicycle, jerking at the hose and swearing loudly. Miller pushes his tongue against the broken bridge, lifting it gently. He wonders if he should try eating a hamburger, and decides it can't hurt as long as he's careful to chew on the other side of his mouth.

But it does hurt. After the first couple of bites Miller shoves his plate away. He rests his chin on one hand and listens to Lebowitz and Kaiser argue about whether people can actually tell the future. Lebowitz is talking about a girl he used to know who had ESP. "We'd be driving along," he says," and out of the blue she would tell me exactly what I was thinking about. It was unbelievable."

Kaiser finishes his hamburger and takes a drink of milk. "No big deal," he says. "I could do that." He pulls Miller's hamburger over to his side of the table and takes a bite out of it.

"Go ahead," Lebowitz says. "Try it. I'm not thinking about what you think I'm thinking about."

"Yes you are."

"All right, now I am," Lebowitz says, "but I wasn't before."

"I wouldn't let a fortune-teller get near me," Miller says. "The way I see it, the less you know the better off you are."

"More vintage philosophy from the private stock of W. P. Miller," Lebowitz says. He looks at Kaiser, who is eating the last of Miller's hamburger. "Well, how about it? I'm up for it if you are."

Kaiser chews ruminatively. He swallows and licks his lips. "Sure," he says. "Why not? As long as Miller here doesn't mind."

"Mind what?" Miller asks.

Lebowitz stands and puts his sunglasses back on. "Don't worry about Miller. Miller's cool. Miller keeps his head when men all around him are losing theirs."

Kaiser and Miller get up from the table and follow Lebowitz outside. Lebowitz is bending down in the shade of a dumpster, wiping off his boots with a handkerchief. Shiny blue flies buzz around him. "Mind what?" Miller repeats.

"We thought we'd check out the prophet," Kaiser tells him.

Lebowitz straightens up and the three of them start across the parking lot.

"I'd actually kind of like to get going," Miller says. When they reach the jeep he stops, but Lebowitz and Kaiser walk on. "Now listen," Miller says, and skips a little to catch up. "I have a lot to do," he says to their backs. "I have to get home."

"We know how broken up you are," Lebowitz tells him. He keeps walking.

"This won't take too long," Kaiser says.

The dog barks once and then, when it sees that they really intend to come within range of his teeth, runs around the trailer. Lebowitz knocks on the door. It swings open, and there stands a round-faced woman with dark, sunken eyes and heavy lips. One of her eyes has a cast; it seems to be watching something beside her while the other looks down at the three soldiers at her door. Her hands are covered with flour. She is a gypsy, an actual gypsy. Miller has never seen a gypsy before, but he recognizes her as surely as he would recognize a wolf if he saw one. Her presence makes his blood pound in his veins. If he lived in this place he would come back at night with other men, all of them yelling and waving torches, and drive her out.

"You on duty?" Lebowitz asks.

She nods, wiping her hands on her skirt. They leave chalky streaks on the bright patchwork. "All of you?" she asks.

"You bet," Kaiser says. His voice is unnaturally loud.

She nods again and turns her good eye from Lebowitz to Kaiser, then to Miller. Gazing at Miller, she smiles and rattles off a string of strange sounds, words from another language or maybe a spell, as if she expects him to understand. One of her front teeth is black.

"No," Miller says. "No, ma'am. Not me." He shakes his head.

"Come," she says, and stands aside.

Lebowitz and Kaiser mount the steps and disappear into the trailer. "Come," the woman repeats. She beckons with her white hands.

Miller backs away, still shaking his head. "Leave me alone," he tells her, and before she can answer he turns and walks away. He goes back to the jeep and sits in the driver's seat, leaving both doors open to catch the breeze. Miller feels the heat drawing the dampness out of his fatigues. He can smell the musty wet canvas overhead and the sourness of his own body. Through the windshield, covered with mud except for a pair of grimy half-circles, he watches three boys solemnly urinating against the wall of the gas station across the road.

Miller bends down to loosen his boots. Blood rushes to his face as he fights the wet laces, and his breath comes faster and faster. "Goddamn laces," he says. "Goddamn rain." He gets the laces untied and sits up, panting. He stares at the trailer. Goddamn gypsy.

He can't believe those two fools actually went inside there. Yukking it up. Playing around. That shows how stupid they are, because anybody knows that you don't play around with fortune-tellers. There's no predicting what a fortune-teller might say, and once it's said, no way of keeping it from happening. Once you hear what's out there it isn't out there anymore, it's here. You might as well open your door to a murderer as to the future.

The future. Didn't everybody know enough about the future already, without rooting around for the details? There is only one thing you have to know about the future: everything gets worse. Once you have that, you have it all. The specifics don't bear thinking about.

Miller certainly has no intention of thinking about the specifics. He peels off his damp socks and massages his crinkled white feet. Now and then he glances up toward the trailer, where the gypsy is pronouncing fate on Kaiser and Lebowitz. Miller makes humming noises. He will not think about the future.

Because it's true—everything gets worse. One day you're sitting in front of your house poking sticks into an anthill, hearing the chink of silverware and the voices of your mother and father in the kitchen; then, at some moment you can't even remember, one of those voices is gone. And you never hear it again. When you go from today to tomorrow you're walking into an ambush.

What lies ahead doesn't bear thinking about. Already Miller has an ulcer, and his teeth are full of holes. His body is giving out on him. What will it be like when he's sixty? Or even five years from now? Miller was in a restaurant the other day and saw a fellow about his own age in a wheelchair, getting fed soup by a woman who was talking to some other people at the table. This boy's hands lay twisted in his lap like gloves somebody dropped there. His pants had crawled up halfway to his knees, showing pale wasted legs no thicker than bones. He could barely move his head. The woman feeding him did a lousy job because she was too busy blabbing to her friends. Half the soup went onto the boy's shirt. Yet his eyes were bright and attentive. Miller thought: That could happen to me.

You could be going along just fine and then one day, through no fault of your own, something could get loose in your bloodstream and knock out part of your brain. Leave you like that. And if it didn't happen now, all at once, it was sure to happen slowly later on. That was the end you were bound for.

Someday Miller is going to die. He knows that, and he prides himself on knowing it when everyone else only pretends to, secretly believing that they will live forever. But this is not the reason the future is unthinkable to him. There is something else worse than that, something not to be considered, and he will not consider it.

He will not consider it. Miller leans back against the seat and closes his eyes, but his effort to trick himself into somnolence fails; behind his eyelids he is wide awake and fidgety with gloom, probing against his will for what he is afraid to find, until, with no surprise at all, he finds it. A simple truth. His mother is also going to die. Just like him. And there is no telling when. Miller cannot count on her to be there to come home to, and receive his pardon, when he finally decides that she has suffered enough.

Miller opens his eyes and looks at the raw shapes of the buildings across the road, their outlines lost through the grime on the windshield. He closes his eyes again. He listens to himself breathe and feels the familiar, almost muscular ache of knowing that he is beyond his mother's reach. That he has put himself where she cannot see him or speak to him or touch him in that thoughtless way of hers, resting her hands on his shoulders as she stops behind his chair to ask him a question or just rest for a moment, her mind somewhere else. This was supposed to be her punishment, but somehow it has become his own. He understands that it has to stop. It is killing him.

It has to stop now, and as if he has been planning for this day all along Miller knows exactly what he will do. Instead of reporting to the Red Cross when he gets back to base, he will pack his bag and catch the first bus home. No one will blame him for this. Even when they discover the mistake they've made they still won't blame him, because it would be the natural thing for a grieving son to do. Instead of punishing him they will probably apologize for giving him a scare.

He will take the first bus home, express or not. It will be full of Mexicans and soldiers. Miller will sit by a window and drowse. Now and then he will come up from his dreams to stare out at the passing green hills and loamy ploughland and the stations where the bus puts in, stations cloudy with exhaust and loud with engine roar, where the people he regards through his window will look groggily back at him as if they too have just come up from sleep. Salinas. Vacaville. Red Bluff. When he gets to Redding Miller will hire a cab. He will ask the driver to stop at Schwartz's for a few minutes while he buys some flowers, and then he will ride on home, down Sutter and over to Serra, past the ball park, past the grade school, past the Mormon church. Right on Belmont. Left on Park. Leaning over the seat, saying Farther, farther, a little farther, that's it, that one, there.

The sound of voices behind the door as he rings the bell. Door swings open, voices hush. Who are these people? Men in suits, women wearing white gloves. Someone stammers his name, strange to him now, almost forgotten. W-W-Wesley. A man's voice. Miller stands just inside the door, breathing perfume. Then the flowers are taken from his hand and laid with other flowers on the coffee table. He hears his name again. It is Phil Dove, moving toward him from across the room. He walks slowly, with his arms raised, like a blind man.

Wesley, he says. Thank God you're home.

A Conversation with Tobias Wolff

Your introduction to the anthology Matters of Life and Death *is, in the true sense of the word, an apology for the fact that fiction matters—that telling the truth in a fictional way is an important enterprise and a noble thing to do. You wrote that book a long time ago, but based on work you've done since then, it seems an idea that probably still rings true for you.*

Oh, I think it is! It would be hard to sustain a life of writing fiction if you didn't think it had some value in the world. One of the things that I love about fiction, both reading it and what I hope to do writing it, is the way it forces you to enter deeply into the spirit of others. You break out of the shelter you're in most of the time, you are forced to enter other ways of seeing, other ways of living, other ways of being, the particular realities that other people inhabit. One of the banes of this world is how easily we reduce others to Them. The minute you get one of Them up close, suddenly your ideas don't hold up.

One of the things that I love about fiction, both reading it and what I hope to do writing it, is the way it forces you to enter deeply into the spirit of others.

There are several "zones" that can be identified in your work. You write about military service, school, marriage, family—and often with emotional overlays that have to do with things we choose and the way those choices so often escalate as they play out, wreaking havoc in our lives. "The Other Miller" falls into the army "zone." Would you talk about that "zone" in your work and why it's provided such rich material for fiction?

I spent four years of my life in the army, so it would be natural for me to write about it. I went in when I was eighteen. The rap is that everybody gets put in the blender and comes out the same, but the odd thing is that—being forced to wear uniforms, to look the same, to live the same life and keep the same hours, walk in step, sing the same songs—the eccentricities and peculiarities of people become much more pronounced, much more vivid. I have colorful memories of people I knew in the army and the oddities of life in the army. And it replicated the experience I had growing up, moving all over the country with my mother. We lived in the South, we lived in the West, we lived in the East, we lived in the Northwest. We lived just about everywhere. The army contains the whole country; it's the country in miniature.

Of course, that leaves the women out. Men act very differently in the absence of women, there's no question about it, and that's something, too, that's interesting. As I recall, the young men I knew in the army were very much in the process of being formed. School, the army—writing about young people, I find myself doing that quite a bit. I'm interested in people who are in the process of becoming who they are. Maybe we're never really there, but it's more dramatic when you're young.

I'm interested in people who are in the process of becoming who they are.

The main character in "The Other Miller" reflects your fascination with this time in life. Would you talk about the genesis of that story and how it evolved? What did you know at the outset, and what surprised you along the way?

This is a guy not unlike others I knew in the army. Very raw, in the army for a stupid reason. Almost everybody enlists for a stupid reason. It can be anger—signing up for three years because you're mad at your dad or mad at your mom. So here I have an image of this guy and of all the afternoons I spent out in piney woods somewhere digging holes in the ground, rain soaking my poncho, and these people around me with their heads sticking out of holes. Just one stupid thing after another. I don't remember in what order all these things occurred to me, but I had this idea about somebody taking advantage of a situation where he thought that someone else's mother had died. A character who lacked the imagination to understand that, though he had been mistaken for that other person in the past, it might *be* his own mother! And in the course of the afternoon to begin to taste maturity to the extent he could begin to imagine the mortality of his own mother, as he does as the story progresses, and to consider the future, his terror of the future. It's a little step that he makes, but the story shows a change in his thinking that will probably change the course of his life. Characters face a certain direction, move in a certain direction at the beginning of a story—if you alter just by a few degrees the angle of their vision, they'll end up very far away at the very end of their lives.

It's those little things that are so crucial. The short story allows you to work in that psychological territory best, the subtle shift of the character. It was a psychological atmosphere that I wanted to create from what I remembered of my own immaturity. It's really about growing up and the admission of one's own mortality and the mortality of those you love. The condition of immaturity is that you allow yourself to be angry and to nurse grudges and to hold other people apart from you. That precludes a sense of reality of the other person and the other person's frailty. You're presupposing that they're always going to be there when you hold them in that relationship, and you're in another world once you realize that that's not the case.

Do you remember if anything surprised you in the writing of the story?

The very ending did, when he enters into the death of his own mother so thoroughly. I had meant it to be more of a glimpse, or intuition, rather than for him to surrender so wholly to the knowledge of his mother's death.

But the reader never learns whether or not she's actually dead. The ending is constructed so that you could go either way.

Someone once told me that it reminded them of "The Lady and the Tiger." She might be or she might not be. The important thing is whether or not he's willing to take that in as a possibility, as he finally does. That was something that I wasn't prepared for. I'm not sure that I had thought of having a fortuneteller in the story. I think that image occurred to me in one of the successive drafts.

Interesting that it was a surprise for you. It surprises the reader, as well. At the same time, it's absolutely believable.

Well, he needs to be cajoled. He's not going to just come to it on his own.

Yes. The fortuneteller triggers the memory of the boy in the wheelchair, how his mother treated him so carelessly, and it makes him remember his own mother's touch and to think she'd never treat him that way. And, boom! You come to that moment of understanding. That was an "accident" of process for you. The first line of the story is, "For two days now Miller has been standing in the rain with the rest of Bravo Company, waiting for some men from another company to blunder down the logging road where Bravo waits in ambush." The use of the word blunder, *which is such a telling, visual word, and also the way the idea of an ambush mirrors the kind of emotional ambush the story is about—were those accidents, too, or an example of craft? Is that the first first line you wrote for the story?*

I don't remember. The truth is that by the time I get to the end of a story, I've rewritten every sentence. Very little goes untouched. I rewrite every day; I rewrite when I finish the story. My guess is that I probably didn't get the wording just like that until the last draft.

What about characters? How do they evolve for you?

Characters generally rise up out of the work of the writing. I have a certain conception of who I'm writing about and couldn't begin to write without that, but in the course of the writing that often gets left behind. As I write, the character begins to coalesce and take on particularity. I usually can't start with all that in mind. I know that some writers probably do, and everybody works differently, but that's the beauty in doing most of your work in revision as I do. You know you're going to be rewriting and you know you're going to be adding and changing things to allow your conception of the character to grow and change. I've even changed the gender of my characters halfway through a story. I realize that the character I'm writing about is not a young man but a young woman. I am not able to write a story straight down from the head to the paper and have it all there. It has to be done in the work itself, and the imagination or trance that I enter into when I'm writing and the language gives me things I wasn't expecting.

I have a certain conception of who I'm writing about and couldn't begin to write without that, but in the course of the writing that often gets left behind.

About three pages into "The Other Miller," Miller "feels a burning in his left side, where his ulcer is." It's a piece of information about him, an important one—the reader suddenly knows, not only does this kid hate the army, but it (or something) is giving him an ulcer. The information cranks the tension, yet feels absolutely organic. What advice could you give to writers when and how to tell the reader what he needs to know about the character and situation of a story?

Information is one of the hardest things to impart in a story. Stories are not good conveyors of information. So the test for information is what I would call dramatic occasion. What is the dramatic occasion in the story for knowing something? Then it can be said naturally. Where information occurs naturally, you don't notice you're being told things. That's when it's working best. At the same time, I tend not to have—though I sometimes will have—an opening of the kind like, "Ivan Illych's life was most simple and most ordinary and therefore most terrible," and go on and talk about the character and where he comes from and his background and all that, as Tolstoy does. Chekhov writes his stories very differently. He will just start with three people walking down a road, and you gradually find out who they are. I have written stories where I used a more Tolstoyan method of storytelling. "There were two brothers." In fact, "Ali Baba and the Forty Thieves" begins with that line. Probably Cain and Abel could be told that way. It doesn't actually begin with those lines, but it could. It depends on the kind of story I'm telling, but usually I would prefer to have the information come out as it does in ["The Other Miller"], as the story seems to call for it to be there.

So the test for information is what I would call dramatic occasion. What is the dramatic occasion in the story for knowing something? Then it can be said naturally.

Actually, there are two kinds of information in the story. The reader sees the sergeant, he sees the Jeep, he sees and feels the rain and mud; he gets all the information about the locus of the story, the situation, in a pretty straightforward way. It's the emotional information that comes sideways. Are you conscious of this as you work, or is it just the way the story unfolded?

Much of what I do as a writer is so internalized now that I don't deal in precept and theories of writing. Every story, indeed, seems to have its own theory. How do you tell *this* story? It doesn't seem to work for any other story. So when I teach undergraduates creative writing, I never use manuals. I hate writing jargon like "backstory" and "begin in scene." I don't want them to talk like that. I want them to ask, "What is the particular story being told here?"

Every story, indeed, seems to have its own theory. How do you tell *this* story?

My vision of this story was, first of all, a dramatic vision. I wanted this person to be caught up in a world where things are happening, things he doesn't understand, because he's uncomprehending in general. So the opening places him in a world where he's at the mercy of things. He's put himself there and doesn't really understand what's going on, but thinks he does. He thinks he's master of the situation. Anybody could figure out, well, yeah, it *might* be the other guy's mother, but why are you so damn sure it's not yours? Any reader can think that, but *he* can't.

The great pleasure reading the story is thinking, "Hello? How can he not know this?" One of the pitfalls of too much information is that the reader doesn't get the experience of puzzling things out or knowing things that the character doesn't know.

Exactly. But you can't place the reader in too superior a position to the character because you have to be able to see that we all have grudges. There's that great line about holding a grudge, that it's like poisoning a dish for someone else and then eating it yourself.

I couldn't have written the story if I thought [Miller] was just a freak. I see the potential for that kind of behavior in my life and in things that friends of mine have done. We sometimes talk about the idiotic things we've done in just that kind of emotion.

Why is it a present-tense story?

I haven't written a lot in the present tense. But this guy, that's where he lives. There's something reflective about past tense, something implied about knowledge that one's attained looking back on the story that's being told. I wanted him to be very much caught up in this and I didn't want there to be any sense of the backward view, of the informed vision. He lives in the present, almost like an animal. So that was, it seemed to me, the natural tense for the story.

There's something reflective about past tense, something implied about knowledge that one's attained looking back on the story that's being told.

Early in the story, the reader learns that Miller broke the bridge over his molars the first night out. Strangely, that situation mirrors the structure of the story. Once he loses his power to ignore the broken bridge, he can't stop worrying it. He feels the pain. When did that work its way into the story?

I don't remember, but I believe that the bridge shows up in later drafts of the story. It prepares for the way he worries the idea of his mother and starts probing that. It's a kind of dogged quality that can be stupid, but also lead to something productive, too.

It works, then, as a kind of symbol—and symbols are problematic for student readers and writers. One young writer actually said, "I'm almost finished with this story, but I still have to put the symbols in." Would you talk about the importance of symbols and how they make their way into stories?

Well, I have never in my life thought, "This is going to be a symbol of something." But certain things become important in stories. You can see larger elements of life reflected in smaller things. When we try to understand ourselves, we try to see a pattern in our behavior and how it writes itself large in our lives. Maybe you're polite most of the time, but you yell at people in traffic and you give them the finger. You give yourself permission to be someone in that car that you don't like to think you would be otherwise. So what does that say about you—or about *me?* I was taking a student home once, one of my graduate students from Syracuse. It was in the winter and somebody cut me off—and in a way that really ticked me off. So here I am with this poor student sitting beside me and I start getting into this thing with this guy. I mean I'm a *professor* and I've got a student in the car with me and I'm shouting! I got to the light before guy did, he was behind me. It was a brilliant beautiful day. I had a sunroof on my car, so we stop at the light and I think, okay. I hit the button to put the sunroof back. Well, it had snowed the night before. There was about eighteen inches of snow, hardened snow, and it all fell on my head. And the guy behind me could see it happen. I could see him just howling with laughter in the mirror. "That asshole got his," you know? And my poor student is just thinking *I have to go back into class with this guy.*

I have never in my life thought, "This is going to be a symbol of something."

But surely that was a symbol for something.

I sure took it as one.

So they come organically.

You don't just stick symbols in a story. Like Freud said, "Sometimes a cigar is just a cigar." But in, say, *Huckleberry Finn,* the river is the river, yeah. It's not milking the story too much to say that there are more things in that river besides water. But it's also a river, a real river. Nothing should be detachable from the story like a badge that's been hooked into it and can be taken off. It should be so much a part of the story that it can't be spoken of apart from the story.

Back to the issue of tense. There's a daring flip to the future tense near the end of the story. Would you talk about that?

It's important that he break through to some consciousness of futurity, of what *can* happen and where things are going. It's exactly where he would not go, into the future.

Choosing to end the story with an image of Phil Dove, the man to whom Miller has had such a visceral response, feels like the ambush that first sentence promises. The story comes full circle in that way. Is that how you knew the story was finished?

Yes. I knew the story was finished. And he's not just awakened to the mortality of someone he loves, but it's also an awakening of compassion in him, the understanding that others love, too, and can experience loss. That is a kind of homecoming, that awakening. That's the home we're supposed to arrive at eventually. It's evocative of the prodigal son. He's a son at the end, which he has refused to be before.

Would you talk generally about how stories gather and evolve for you?

Stories tend to grow in the writing of them, and to begin to define themselves as I work on them. Characters become clearer, the outlines of the story emerge in greater clarity. They undergo change. Things I thought I was interested in I'm no longer interested in by the end of the writing, and things that hadn't been in the story at all are very important in the story by the end. It's not like drawing a blueprint and then following it. I couldn't write a good story that way. It really has to happen in the process of the writing for me.

Stories tend to grow in the writing of them, and to begin to define themselves as I work on them. Characters become clearer, the outlines of the story emerge in greater clarity.

How do you keep track of incubating stories?

I have notebooks full of notions. Stories start in all sorts of ways. They can start with me remembering something. A piece of music that I've heard could take me back years; something that someone says starts off a little line of thought in me. I remember Ray Carver telling me that his wife, in the middle of an argument at Christmas, once said to him, "This is the last Christmas you're going to ruin for us," and—even as she said it in the middle of this awful situation—he knew he was going to use that line in a story. And indeed he did.

How do you know when the moment is right to start a story that's been percolating in your head?

I try to write every day. Sometimes I don't, but I generally try to. You just feel the pressure of the story. I've always got some ideas that I'm interested in exploring, but they don't need to be fully formed for me to sit down and start working on them. It isn't a question of waiting for something to completely jell before I sit down to write it. Other writers I know do work that way, though writers are generally not to be completely trusted with what they say about writing. Hemingway used to say that every day he reread everything he had written in the book he was working on up to that point, and rewrote everything up to that point. Do I really believe that? I don't think I do. He also said he always left off each day in the middle of a really good sentence so that he'd have something to push off from the next day. I don't believe that either. I don't know any writer who could really leave a good sentence in the middle and not be afraid of forgetting it.

Speaking of truth and deception, your popular story "Say Yes" reflects your fascination with this aspect of humanity. A lot of your characters lie, but this character can't lie—and the story is really about how not being able to lie can do as much damage as lying does in some situations. Why is it that truth and lies so often show up in your fiction?

I can't explain it. I don't start off to write about truth and lies or of fraudulence and deceit in the abstract. I set out to write about human beings, and that seems again and again to plunge me into questions of, among other things, truth and lies and the appetite for truth in people who are fraudulent.

Would you just talk about where that story came from?

That story came from an argument I had with my wife! It was, indeed, an argument that brought us to a pretty rough spot one night.

Was it the same argument as the one in the story?

It had a lot of the same elements, but the story is different. I changed the story. It wasn't an assertion of racism so much as I thought that there something ontologically important about the fact that if she were black she would not be who she was. And she would not get off the dime about but if she *was* who she was and black. And I said no, that's impossible. I shifted the ground a little bit in the story, but we had quite a set-to over that question one night, and I very soon afterwards wrote the story, which she likes a lot. So we got something good out of it. It's a kind of an interesting question. Really, the story is about love and whether love is, at bottom, conditional. I think what the wife in the story is hearing is that her husband's love is conditional on his "knowing her," when, in fact, our knowledge of each other really is limited. Even for those of us who are married, there is always this distance beyond our knowledge of the other person. She's insulted to think that she's so fully comprehended and that, in fact, her husband's love *depends* on his fully comprehending her and accepting everything he comprehends. So there's a shift in things that night, and he has to venture into new territory here.

Which is to lie. At any given moment, he could have stepped in and said, "Yes, I'd love you no matter what." But he can't do that. He can't lie. The dialogue in the story reflects this aspect of his character—and also how people are so often at cross-purposes in conversation because they're not really talking about the same thing. She was talking about love, and the male character was not talking about love at all. There's a tremendous amount of tension that occurs in the story because of the way that the dialogue works. Would you talk about that and about dialogue, generally?

Well, writers use dialogue in different ways. Elizabeth Bowen said once that dialogue is what characters do to each other. It is not a passive element in the story. Dialogue should be revealing of character as it progresses. It shouldn't be used to give information and it shouldn't be used for characters to tell each other things that the writer wants the reader to know. It

Dialogue should be revealing of character as it progresses. It shouldn't be used to give information and it shouldn't be used for characters to tell each other things that the writer wants the reader to know.

really has to do with what goes on between them, and it should contain unspoken understandings.

A great example of that in "Say Yes" is when she's talking about interracial marriages. He says most of those marriages break up and she says, "Statistics." The reader knows exactly how she says that and that what she's really saying is "Statistics, again." How do you do that? How do you create dialogue so that what the reader doesn't know adds to the tension rather than creating confusion?

I think it has to do with your knowing your characters really well.

The husband in the story is a bit smug and self-righteous throughout a lot of the argument. He gets comeuppance in the end, but the reader isn't exactly glad. Would you talk about how you made the reader sympathetic toward him despite the fact that he was being such a jerk?

He was being a jerk, but in a way that most of us are jerks. When we get into an argument, we can watch ourselves keep going when we know we shouldn't. The desire to come out on the right side of an argument is a stupid, childish desire, but we all get into it. We've all taken an argument where we shouldn't. I think married people stop doing it after a while. I don't think *we* do it anymore. Now we look at each other and we say, "This is one of those conversations." We'll laugh and just let it go.

Near the end, she's in the bathroom and he apologizes. He says, "I'll make it up to you I promise." She asks, "How?" and he whispers, "I'll marry you." She says, "We'll see," and sends him off to bed. Lying there alone, "His heart pounded the way it had on their first night together, the way it still did when he woke at a noise in the darkness and waited to hear it again—the sound of someone moving through the house, a stranger." And the reader knows that they're not the they *that opened the story, doing the dishes together.*

They're not *they* anymore, but maybe they can be another *they.* But it's not going to be that smug corporate *they* that he thought they were.

Right, and that's the stranger that's entered. That's just masterful. The last sentence brings to mind Poe's observation that a story should be written for the sake of the last line.

I sometimes read stories in which I feel that the story has been written for the last line and I don't like it.

That's a danger, too, though. I sometimes read stories in which I feel that the story has been written for the last line and I don't like it. If I feel it's "waiting in ambush," so to speak.

The tension in "Say Yes" ratchets up constantly as the argument escalates. How do you create tension on the page?

When we tell stories, we naturally want to make the temperature rise. And then and then and then. That's so naturally built in to the storytelling enterprise that I don't know how to detach it.

"Say Yes" is part of the anthology called Sudden Fiction: American Short-Short Stories. *Would you say something about sudden fiction?*

I found it interesting to read those stories. I can't read a whole lot of them at a time, but it's always interesting to see what people can accomplish in a short span. Some of my favorite stories are very, very short. Chekhov's story, "At Sea," which is about three and a half pages long—a brilliant story in which a whole world is revealed. His story, "Oysters," which is about three pages. Cheever has some really short pieces, too. There's one about a young boy who meets his father for lunch now and then, and his father always screws it up by insulting the waiters. It's funny, but sad, sad, because what you know that the boy doesn't know is that the father is grief-stricken at the separation from his son and he doesn't know how to talk to him and this is how it comes out. They get thrown out of every restaurant. It's a three-page story and it tells a whole life, and I love that.

Students will often ask, "How long does a story need to be?" How do you answer that question?

As long as it needs to be.

Generally, what is your best advice to writers just starting out?

My advice is to be patient yourself when writing a story—very few people are going to write a great story the first time out. I sure didn't. And not to be afraid to imitate writers at the beginning. We all learn by imitation. We learn to walk, talk, sing—everything we do we learn by imitation. If you love Hemingway, try writing a Hemingway short story. It will make you aware of how he puts his stories together. If you like Eudora Welty, try writing a story in her manner. The big thing is not to be too hard on yourself and realize that it's a process that takes time. Write a draft and then write another draft when you finish that.

The big thing is not to be too hard on yourself and realize that it's a process that takes time.

The truth is that most people aren't going to be writers. Nobody should ever be embarrassed about not being a writer. It frees you up to do some other wonderful thing with your life—and there are a million other great things to do in this life than be a writer. But you can learn to be a much better reader by trying to write. It awakens your appreciation for the things you read. You appreciate what went into it—not just the difficulty, but the joy.

Writing Prompts

READ: "The Other Miller" and the interview with **Tobias Wolff.**

PONDER: How Wolff moves the character toward a shift in thinking about himself and his relationship with his mother and creates an ending that leaves the reader uncertain about what the effect of the shift will be on his life.

WRITE: Create a character who has taken a strong stand about something. Then put the character in a scene that will slightly shift his angle of vision so that he makes a small beginning toward changing his mind.

PRACTICE:

- Create a character who holds a grudge toward someone. Write a scene in which she begins to soften.
- Think of something you know about a character and then create a dramatic occasion that will make it necessary to convey that piece of information and also provide the means to convey it naturally.
- Break the rules! Write a sentence that makes a general statement about a character as Tolstoy did: "Ivan Illych's life was most simple and most ordinary and therefore most terrible." Use the sentence as the first line and write three to five paragraphs that could serve as the beginning of a story.
- Write a scene in past tense and then write it again in present tense and observe the difference in effect.
- Build a three-page story around an argument that creates a small shift between two people who have known each other for a long time. The dialogue should include unspoken understandings between them and subtle references to past conflicts.
- Write a scene that imitates the style of a writer you admire.
- Write a scene that involves a character being a jerk in a way that readers are likely to have been jerks themselves.

appendix a

Stories Loved by the Writers in This Book

By no means a conclusive list of great short fiction, the following are stories that the writers interviewed for *Story Matters* especially admire.

Alexie, Sherman, "The Lone Ranger and Tonto Fistfight in Heaven," "What You Pawn I Will Redeem"

Al-Saadawi, Nawal, "The Thirst"

Anderson, Sherwood, "Death in the Woods"

Babel, Isaac, "Odessa Tales," "Red Calvary"

Baldwin, James, "Sonny's Blues"

Barth, John, *Lost in the Funhouse*

Barthelme, Donald, "Rebecca," "The School"

Beattie, Ann, "Janus"

Benedict, Pinckney, "Town Smokes"

Borges, Jorge Luis, "The Hero," "The Theme of the Traitor"

Capote, Truman, "A Christmas Memory," "Miriam"

Carver, Raymond, "Cathedral," "What We Talk About When We Talk About Love"

Chappel, Fred, "Children of Strikers"

Cheever, John, "A Country Husband," "The Enormous Radio," "Swimmer," "Torch Song"

Chekov, Anton, "The Darling," "Gusev," "The Kiss," "The Lady with the Dog"

Chopin, Kate, "The Story of an Hour"

Cisneros, Sandra, "The House on Mango Street"

Cunningham, Michael, "White Angel"

Dark, Alice Elliott, "Watch the Animals"

Davis, Lydia, "City Employment"

Dybek, Stuart, "Paper Lantern," "Pet Milk"

Earley, Tony, "A Prophet of Jupiter"

Erdrich, Louise, "Fleur," "The Red Convertible"

Faulkner, William, "Dry September," "A Rose for Emily," "Two Soldiers"

Fitzgerald, F. Scott, "Babylon Revisited"

Flaubert, Gustave, "A Simple Heart"

Forché, Carolyn, "The Colonel"

Gass, William H., "In the Heart of the Heart of the Country"

Gustafson, Lars, "Greatness Strikes Where It Pleases"

Hemingway, Ernest, "A Clean Well-Lighted Place," "Hills Like White Elephants," "Indian Camp"

Heman, Aleksandar, "Islands"

Hempel, Amy, "In the Cemetery Where Al Jolson Is Buried"

Holladay, Cary, "Merry-Go-Sorry"

Jin, Ha, "The Bridegroom," "Sabateur"

Johnson, Denis, "Emergency"

Joyce, James, *Dubliners*

Kafka, Franz, "A Hunger Artist"

Kauffman, Janet, "Patriotic"

Kesey, Anna, "Bright Winter"

Lawrence, D. H., "The Sick Collier"

Leavitt, David, "Gravity"

Link, Kelly, "The Specialist's Hat"

Lyons, Daniel, "The First Snow"

Martone, Michael, "Everybody Watching and Time Passing Like That"

Mason, Bobbie Ann, "Shiloh"

Maupassant, Guy de, "The Necklace"

Mazza, Cris, "Is It Sexual Harrassment Yet?"

Minot, Susan, "Lust"

Moore, Lorrie, "How to Be a Writer," "People Like That Are the Only People Here"

Mukharjee, Bharati, "The Management of Grief"

Munro, Alice, "The Albanian Virgin," "Circle of Prayer"

Oates, Joyce Carol, "Heat," "Where Are You Going, Where Have You Been?"

O'Brien, Tim, *The Things They Carried*

O'Connor, Flannery, "A Good Man Is Hard to Find," "Parker's Back"

Olsen, Tillie, "I Stand Here Ironing"

Ozick, Cynthia, "The Shawl"

Packer, Z. Z., "The Ant of the Self," "Brownies"

Richard, Mark, "Strays"

Robison, Mary, "Widower"

Rodoreda, Mercé, "The Salamander"

Schell, Alice, "Slamming on Pig's Misery"

Schoemperlin, Diane, *Forms of Devotion*

Smiley, Jane, "Age of Grief," "Good Will"

Spence, June, "Missing Women"

Tallent, Elizabeth, "No One's a Mystery"

Tan, Amy, "Two Kinds"

Updike, John, "A & P," "Flight"

Vaughn, Stephanie, "Dog Heaven"

Walker, Alice, "Everyday Use"

Welty, Eudora, "The Petrified Man," "Why I Live at the P.O.," "A Worn Path"

Wharton, Edith, "Roman Fever"

Wideman, John Edgar, "Fever"

Williams, Joy, "The Wedding"

Williams, Lynna, "Personal Testimony"

Wolff, Tobias, "Bullet in the Brain," "Say Yes"

appendix b

Fiction Writing, the Writing Life, and the Creative Process

Beyond this book lie hundreds of works by writers about writing. The following list is just a small sampling of books with further insight into writing in general, the lives of writers, and how those writers describe their own work.

Allison, Dorothy, *Two or Three Things I Know for Sure*

Baxter, Charles, *Burning Down the House: Essays on Fiction*

Baxter, Charles, and Turchi, Peter, eds., *Bringing the Devil to His Knees: The Craft of Fiction and the Writing Life*

Bernays, Anne, and Painter, Pamela, *What If? Writing Exercises for Fiction Writers*

Bradbury, Ray, *Zen and the Art of Writing*

Brande, Dorothea, *Becoming a Writer*

Briggs, John, *Fire in the Crucible: The Self-creation of Creativity and Genius*

Burroway, Janet, *Imaginative Writing: The Elements of Craft*

———, *Writing Fiction: A Guide to Narrative Craft*

Cameron, Julia, *The Artist's Way*

Davies, Robertson, *The Merry Heart*

Dillard, Annie, *The Writer's Life*

Elbow, Peter, *Writing Without Teachers*

Epel, Naomi, *Writers Dreaming*

Fitzgerald, Sally, ed., *The Habit of Being: Letters of Flannery O'Connor*

Friedman, Bonnie, *Writing Past Dark: Envy, Fear, Distraction, and Other Dilemmas in the Writer's Life*

Gardner, John, *The Craft of Fiction*

———, *On Becoming a Novelist*

Gilchrest, Ellen, *Falling Through Space*

Goldberg, Natalie, *Writing Down the Bones*

Hemingway, Ernest, *A Moveable Feast*

Keyes, Ralph, *The Courage to Write: How Writers Transcend Fear*

King, Stephen, *Misery*

———, *On Writing: A Memoir of the Craft*

Lamott, Anne, *Bird by Bird*

Maisell, Eric, *Staying Sane in the Arts*

May, Rollo, *The Courage to Create*

Nelson, Victoria, *On Writers' Block*

Plimpton, George, ed., Writers at Work series

Price, Reynolds, *Clear Pictures*

Reeves, Judy, *Writing Alone, Writing Together: A Guide for Writers and Writing Groups*

Rico, Gabrielle Lusser, *Writing the Natural Way*

Rule, Rebecca, and Wheeler, Sue, *Creating the Story*

Shoup, Barbara, and Denman, Margaret-Love: *Novel Ideas: Contemporary Authors Share the Creative Process*

Storr, Anthony, *Solitude: A Return to Self*

Strunk, William, Jr., and White, E. B., *Elements of Style*

Uleland, Brenda, *If You Want to Write*

Vonnegut, Kurt, *Palm Sunday*

Welty, Eudora, *One Writer's Beginning*

Wharton, Edith, *The Writing of Fiction*

Woolf, Virginia, Diaries (many volumes)

———, *A Room of One's Own*

Zinsser, William, *On Writing Well*

acknowledgments

Text Credits

ALLISON, DOROTHY: "River of Names" from *Trash: Stories*, 2002. Reprinted by permission of Frances Goldin Literary Agency, Inc.

BANKS, RUSSELL: "With Ché in New Hampshire" from *The Angel on the Roof: Stories by Russell Banks*. Copyright © 2000 by Russell Banks. Reprinted by permission of HarperCollins Publishers Inc.

BAXTER, CHARLES: "The Cures for Love" from *Believers: A Novella and Stories*. Copyright © 1997 by Charles Baxter. Used by permission of Pantheon Books, a division of Random House, Inc.

CHAON, DAN: "Big Me" from *Among the Missing* by Dan Chaon, copyright © 2001 by Dan Chaon. Used by permission of Ballantine Books, a division of Random House, Inc.

DYBEK, STUART: "We Didn't" from *I Sailed with Magellan*. Copyright © 2003 by Stuart Dybek. Reprinted by permission of Farrar, Straus and Giroux, LLC.

EGGERS, DAVE: "After I Was Thrown into the River and Before I Drowned" from *How We Are Hungry*, 2004. Reprinted by permission of the author.

FERRELL, CAROLYN: "Can You Say My Name?" from *Please Don't Erase Me* by Carolyn Ferrell. Copyright © 1997 by Carolyn Ferrell. Reprinted by permission of Houghton Mifflin Company. All rights reserved.

HEMPEL, AMY: "Going" from *Reasons to Live*, 1985, p. 69. Reprinted courtesy of Darhansoff, Verrill, Feldman Literary Agents.

HOLLADAY, RUTH: "Prison Sentences Won't Stop Activists' Fight for Democracy" by Ruth Holladay, Indianapolis Star, 2003. Reprinted by permission of the Indianapolis Star.

HOUSTON, PAM: "How to Talk to a Hunter" from *Cowboys Are My Weakness* by Pam Houston. Copyright © 1992 by Pam Houston. Used by permission of W. W. Norton & Company, Inc.

JIN, HA: "Love in the Air" from *Ocean of Words* by Ha Jin. Published by Zoland Books, an imprint of Steerforth Press of Hanover, New Hampshire. Copyright © 1996 by Ha Jin.

KINCAID, JAMAICA: "Poor Visitor" from *Lucy* by Jamaica Kincaid. Copyright © 1990 by Jamaica Kincaid. Reprinted by permission of Farrar, Straus and Giroux, LLC.

LAHIRI, JHUMPA: "A Temporary Matter," from *The Interpreter of Maladies* by Jhumpa Lahiri. Copyright © 1999 by Jhumpa Lahiri. Reprinted by permission of Houghton Mifflin Company. All rights reserved.

MARTONE, MICHAEL: "Watch Out" from *Safety Patrol*. pp. 58-69. © 1988 by The Johns Hopkins University Press. Reprinted with permission of The Johns Hopkins University Press.

MCCORKLE, JILL: "Hominids" from *Creatures of Habit* by Jill McCorkle. © 2001 by Jill McCorkle. Reprinted by permission of Algonquin Books of Chapel Hill.

NEVILLE, SUSAN: "Night Train" from *In the House of Blue Lights*. Copyright 1998 by University of Notre Dame Press, Notre Dame IN 46556. Reprinted by permission of the publisher.

PALEY, GRACE: "Debts" from *The Collected Stories* by Grace Paley. Copyright © 1994 by Grace Paley. Reprinted by permission of Farrar, Straus and Giroux, LLC.

SILBER, JOAN: "Bobby Jackson" from *In My Other Life* by Joan Silber, published by Sarabande Books, Inc. © 2000 by Joan Silber. Reprinted by permission of Sarabande Books and the author.

TALLENT, ELIZABETH: "Honey" from *Honey* by Elizabeth Tallent, copyright © 1993 by Elizabeth Tallent. Used by permission of Alfred A. Knopf, a division of Random House, Inc.

URREA, LUIS: "Father Returns from the Mountains" by Luis Urrea from *Six Kinds of Sky*, published by Cinco Puntos Press, www.cincopuntos.com. Copyright © 2002. Reprinted by permission of Cinco Puntos Press.

WALKER, DALY: "I Am the Grass" from *Atlantic Monthly*, June 2000, Volume 285, No. 6. Reprinted by permission of the author.

WOLFF, TOBIAS: "The Other Miller" from *The Night in Question* by Tobias Wolff, copyright © 1996 by Tobias Wolff. Used by permission of Alfred A. Knopf, a division of Random House, Inc.

Photo Credits

Page 71: © John Foley; **page 94:** © Marion Ettlinger; **page 120:** © Bettina Strauss; **page 144:** © Betsy Molnar; **page 164:** © David Kamm; **page 185:** © Meiko; **page 206:** © Lorin Klaris; **page 222:** Rake Blaze; **page 238:** © John Gary Brown; **page 261:** © Tracy Powell; **page 275:** © Kenneth Noland; **page 299:** © Marion Ettlinger; **page 315:** © Theresa Pappas; **page 333:** © Debi Milligan; **page 350:** © Cheryl Soden Moreland; **page 365:** Gentl & Hyers/Arts Counsel, Inc. © 1994; **page 384:** © Barry Goldstein; **page 407:** © Deirdre Lamb; **page 425:** © Nina Subin; **page 454:** Ronny McAulay; **page 474:** Marion Ettlinger.

index